ACKNOWLEDGEMENTS

We gratefully acknowledge the help of our representatives for their efficient and perceptive inspections of the lodging and dining establishments listed and the establishments' proprietors for their cooperation in showing their facilities and providing information.

We also extend our thanks to NASCAR and the individual track owners who assisted with this project.

Mobil, Exxon, and Mobil Travel Guide are trademarks of Exxon Mobil Corporation or one of its subsidiaries. All rights reserved. Reproduction by any means, including, but not limited to, photography, electrostatic copying devices, or electronic data processing, is prohibited. Use of information contained herein for solicitation of advertising or listing in any other publication is expressly prohibited without written permission from Exxon Mobil Corporation. Violations of reserved rights are subject to prosecution.

Copyright © 2005 EMTG, LLC. All rights reserved. Except for copies made by individuals for personal use, this publication may not be reproduced in whole or in part by any means whatsoever without written permission from Mobil Travel Guide, 1460 Renaissance Drive, Suite 401, Park Ridge, IL 60068; phone 847/795-6700; info@mobiltravelguide.com.

Vice President, Publications: Kevin Bristow
Publisher and Executive Editor: Margaret Littman
Project Manager: Barbara A. Bohn
Project Assistant: Jeff Borden
Editors: Deborah Douglas, Elisa Kronish, Brenda McLean, Kathy Rose, Nancy Swope
Writers: Paula Andruss, Karen Baxter, Sheri Bell-Rehwoldt, Cynthia BeMent, Jeff Beneke, Kris Bordessa, Deborah Brauser, Dara Chadwick, Karen Dean, Steve Friess, John Hawks, John Holmes, Elizabeth Blish Hughes, Jennifer Lawler, Carrie Levine, Melanie Radzicki McManus, Matt McClure, Carole Moore, Jim Morrison, Jane Optie, Jennie Phipps, Ari Tye Radetsky, Trish Riley, Paul Rogers, Theresa Russell, Kathy Summers, Apryl Chapman Thomas
Illustrator: DG Strong
Fact Checkers: Priya Khatkhate, Jason Rothstein, Erin Verkler
Editorial Intern: Jeanelle Hayner
Director of Publishing Production Services: Ellen Tobler

Publishing Coordinator: Shawn McNichols
Concept and Cover Design: idesign and associates inc.
Director of e-Publishing: Diane Connolly
Director, Sales Operations: Bobbi Alderks
Sales and Marketing Support Manager: Kellie Bottrell

NASCAR Publishing:
Senior Manager of Publishing: Jennifer White
Communications Manager: Herb Branham
Publishing Coordinator: Catherine McNeill
Coordinator of Communications: Buz McKim

Maps © MapQuest.com, Inc. Unauthorized use, including copying, of this product is expressly prohibited.

 For year-round updated information, enter MTGRACES at www.mobiltravelguide.com

The information contained herein is derived from a variety of third-party sources. Although every effort has been made to verify the information obtained from such sources, the publisher assumes no responsibility for inconsistencies or inaccuracies in the data or liability for any damages of any type arising from errors or omissions.

Neither the editors nor the publisher assumes responsibility for the services provided by any business listed in this guide or for any loss, damage, or disruption in your travel for any reason.

ISBN: 0-7627-3838-3

Manufactured in the United States of America.

10 9 8 7 6 5 4 3 2 1

NASCAR® and the NASCAR® Library Collection are registered trademarks of the National Association for Stock Car Auto Racing, Inc.

TABLE OF CONTENTS

Welcome from NASCAR 4
Welcome from Mobil Travel Guide 5
A Word to Our Readers 9
How to Use This Book 11
Making the Most of Your Trip 15
Racing Flags 19
First-Time Racegoer Tips 20
2005 NASCAR Busch Series Schedule 21
2005 NASCAR Craftsman Truck Series Schedule 21
2005 NASCAR NEXTEL Cup Schedule 23

NASCAR-Sanctioned Tracks

1. Atlanta Motor Speedway, **GA** 24
2. Bristol Motor Speedway, **TN** 42
3. California Speedway, **CA** 56
4. Chicagoland Speedway, **IL** 74
5. Darlington Raceway, **SC** 92
6. Daytona International Speedway, **FL** 106
7. Dover International Speedway, **DE** 124
8. Gateway International Raceway, **IL** 138
9. Homestead-Miami Speedway, **FL** 152
10. Indianapolis Motor Speedway and Indianapolis Raceway Park, **IN** 170
11. Infineon Raceway, **CA** 190
12. Kansas Speedway, **KS** 208
13. Kentucky Speedway, **KY** 222
14. Las Vegas Motor Speedway, **NV** 236
15. Lowe's Motor Speedway, **NC** 252
16. Mansfield Motorsports Speedway, **OH** 270
17. Martinsville Speedway, **VA** 284
18. Memphis Motorsports Park, **TN** 298
19. Michigan International Speedway, **MI** 314
20. The Milwaukee Mile, **WI** 330
21. Nashville Superspeedway, **TN** 346
22. New Hampshire International Speedway, **NH** 362
23. Phoenix International Raceway, **AZ** 378
24. Pikes Peak International Raceway, **CO** 396
25. Pocono Raceway, **PA** 410
26. Richmond International Raceway, **VA** 424
27. Talladega Superspeedway, **AL** 440
28. Texas Motor Speedway, **TX** 454
29. Watkins Glen International, **NY** 470
30. Autodromo Hermanos Rodriguez, **MX** 486

Writers' Credits 492
Photo Credits 496
Useful Toll-Free Numbers 497
Index 498
Map Index 512

WELCOME FROM NASCAR

Dear Traveler,

NASCAR is all about traveling, on and off the racetrack.

Our three national series—NASCAR NEXTEL Cup Series, NASCAR Busch Series, and NASCAR Craftsman Truck Series—consist of 98 races each year, visiting a total of 31 NASCAR-sanctioned tracks. Obviously, everyone involved in our sport can relate to travelers—especially those fans traveling to and from our events.

In the pages of the *Mobil Travel Guide: NASCAR Travel Planner,* you'll find a wealth of information that should help you enjoy your visits to the communities that host NASCAR races. The book's writers have spotlighted some of the best lodging accommodations, restaurants, and attractions in those communities.

The *Mobil Travel Guide: NASCAR Travel Planner* is a great book for NASCAR fans. It's a reliable guide to enjoyment during a race weekend.

That said, enjoy.

Best regards,

Brian France

NASCAR Chairman/CEO

WELCOME FROM MOBIL TRAVEL GUIDE

OUR TEAM

Some of the Mobil Travel Guide "pit crew": Bobbi Alderks, Barbara A. Bohn, Jeff Borden, Kellie Bottrell, Kevin Bristow, Diane Connolly, Jeanelle Hayner, Jacinda Johnson, Elisa Kronish, Priya Khatkhate, Margaret Littman, Brenda McLean, Shawn McNichols, Shane O'Flaherty, Jane Optie, Nancy Swope, Ellen Tobler, Erin Verkler, Paul Xumsai

Dear Readers,

Whether it is a cross-country family vacation planned around the Daytona 500, or just a quick weekend road trip to the Pop Secret 500, no one loves hitting the road more than NASCAR fans. The lure of the open highway and the smell of burning rubber are impossible to resist.

No one, that is, than Mobil Travel Guide. Since 1958, we've been in the car, looking for the best places to eat and sleep and rating them using our proprietary Mobil One- to Five-Star system. So, we are pleased to present to you the *Mobil Travel Guide: NASCAR Travel Planner,* the comprehensive resource for the NASCAR fan on the road. In these pages you'll find hundreds of things to do and places to go before, after, and on the way to your favorite races. You'll also find the detailed traveler necessities—like where to buy ice for your (soft-sided) cooler and gas for your RV—that you need to know in an unfamiliar city on race day.

While there are many magazines and books filled with driver and team stats, the *Mobil Travel Guide: NASCAR Travel Planner* is the real guidebook for fans visiting 31 tracks in the United States and Mexico. Only we show you the way to Bobby Allison's favorite Greek eatery in Talladega (page 451), not to mention tips for avoiding Interstate 95 congestion in Daytona (page 111).

Our writers are road travelers just like you, navigating the same interstates you drive, in order to make your trip more fun and hassle-free. Along the way, they've uncovered the secrets that bring the comforts of home to traveling. For me, that would be free Krispy Kreme doughnuts delivered to my campsite in Joliet (page 88). For you, perhaps it is the chance to drink margaritas and play sand volleyball above Turn 8 at Infineon (page 192). And our team of Mobil Travel Guide inspectors have made sure that Star-rated lodgings and restaurants meet our high quality standards, so that you and your family can plan your trip with confidence.

So, start your engines and hit the road. When you get back, drop us a note at **info@mobiltravelguide.com.** Tell us about the new shortcut—or short ribs—you discovered at the Sylvania 300. If we include your tip in next year's *Mobil Travel Guide: NASCAR Travel Planner,* we'll send you a free copy of the 2006 edition.

Your trusted travel advisor,

Margaret Littman,
Publisher and Executive Editor
Mobil Travel Guide

NASCAR-SANCTIONED TRACKS IN THE

DRIVE, EXPLORE & DINE
with someone you trust.

Mobil Travel Guide

Mobil Travel Guide publishes more than 40 guidebooks and atlases covering the US and Canada including our Regional Travel Planners with 17 titles; On the Road with Your Pet; the Where to Eat series – covering Boston/Cape Cod, Chicago, Los Angeles, and New York City; the America's Byways™ series with four titles; the Mobil Travel Guide RV & Campground atlas; and the Mobil Travel Guide standard and midsize atlases.

When it comes to travel, Mobil Travel Guide provides consumers with recommendations they can trust and the tools to get them there.

Visit www.mobiltravelguide.com or call 1-866-MOBILTG to order today.

A WORD TO OUR READERS

We recognize that your time is precious, especially the time you spend on vacation. We also know that the travel industry is ever-changing, and having accurate, reliable travel information at your fingertips is critical. Mobil Travel Guide has provided invaluable insight to travelers for 47 years, and we are committed to continuing this service well into the future. We strive to give you the best information possible, so you don't waste a second of your travel experience.

The Mobil Corporation (known as Exxon Mobil Corporation since a 1999 merger) began producing the Mobil Travel Guide books in 1958, following the introduction of the US highway system in 1956. The first edition covered only five southwestern states. Since then, our books have become the premier travel guides in North America, covering all 50 states and Canada. With this volume, we introduce our first coverage of Mexico.

Since its founding, Mobil Travel Guide has served as an advocate for travelers seeking knowledge about hotels, restaurants, and places to visit. Based on an objective process, we make recommendations that we believe enhance the quality and value of your travel experiences. Our trusted Mobil One- to Five-Star rating system is the oldest and most respected lodging and restaurant inspection and rating program in North America. Hoteliers, restaurateurs, and industry observers favorably regard the rigor of our inspection program and understand the prestige and benefits that come with receiving a Mobil Travel Guide Star rating.

The Mobil Travel Guide process of rating each establishment includes:
- Unannounced facility inspections
- Incognito service evaluations for Mobil Four-Star and Mobil Five-Star properties
- A review of unsolicited comments from the general public
- Senior management oversight

For each property, more than 450 attributes, including cleanliness, physical facilities, and employee attitude and courtesy, are measured and evaluated to produce a mathematically derived score, which is then blended with the other elements to form an overall score. These quantifiable scores allow comparative analysis among properties and form the basis for our Mobil One- to Five-Star ratings.

The process focuses largely on guest expectations and experiences, and consistency of service, not just physical facilities and amenities. It is fundamentally a relative rating system that rewards those properties that continually strive for and achieve excellence each year. Indeed, the very best properties are consistently raising the bar for those that wish to compete with them. These properties proactively respond to consumers' needs even in today's uncertain times.

Only facilities that meet Mobil Travel Guide's high standards earn the privilege of being rated in the guide. Deteriorating, poorly managed establishments are deleted. A Mobil Travel Guide listing, no matter the star rating, constitutes a positive quality recommendation; every listing is an accolade, a recognition of achievement. We conduct extensive in-house research to determine additions and deletions to our listings. Refer to the next section of the guide, "How to Use This Book," to learn how we distinguish the Mobil One- to Five-Star listings.

This book also contains recommendations from NASCAR experts (drivers, team owners, track owners, and fans). These properties are not rated, and have not undergone our extensive inspection process, but information on them has been verified.

We do not charge establishments for inclusion in our guides and have no relationship with any of the businesses and attractions we list. We act only as your advocate. In essence, we do the investigative legwork so that you won't have to.

Keep in mind that the hospitality business is ever-changing. Restaurants and lodgings—particularly small chains and stand-alone establishments—change management or even go out of business with surprising quickness. Although we make every effort to double-check information regularly, we nevertheless recommend that you call ahead to make sure the place you've selected is still open and offers all the amenities you're looking for. We've provided phone numbers and, when available, Web site addresses, to make it easier.

We hope that you have an enjoyable trip and that our books help you get the most out of your time and budget. If any aspect of your accommodation, dining, or sightseeing experience motivates you to comment, please drop us a line. We value our readers' remarks, so you can be assured that we will read your comments and assimilate them into our research. General comments about our books are also welcome. You can write to us at Mobil Travel Guide, 1460 Renaissance Drive, Suite 401, Park Ridge, IL 60068, or send an e-mail to **info@mobiltravelguide.com.**

 For year-round updated information, enter MTGRACES at www.mobiltravelguide.com

Take your Mobil Travel Guide books along on every trip you take. We're confident that you'll be pleased with their convenience, ease of use, and breadth of dependable coverage.

Happy travels!

ABOUT OUR BOOKS

In addition to *Mobil Travel Guide: NASCAR Travel Planner*, Mobil Travel Guide publishes more than 40 annual guidebooks and atlases covering the United States and Canada. Look for these helpful travel companions at your local book store, drug store, or online at **www.mobiltravelguide.com**.

Where to Eat Boston/Cape Cod, Chicago,
   Los Angeles, New York
On the Road with Your Pet
America's Best Hotel & Resort Spas
America's Byways™ Series
America's Best Hotels & Restaurants
City Guides Boston, Chicago, Las Vegas,
   Los Angeles, Miami and Miami Beach,
   New York City, New Orleans, Orlando,
   San Francisco, Washington, DC
Regional Travel Planners

HOW TO:
USE THIS BOOK

The *Mobil Travel Guide: NASCAR Travel Planner* is designed for ease-of-use, whether you're reading from your living room as you plan a trip, or from the passenger seat as you ride into town.

Twenty-nine NASCAR-sanctioned tracks in the United States and one in Mexico have their own chapters. Indianapolis Motor Speedway and Indianapolis Raceway Park are combined in Chapter 10. Each chapter includes essential information on the NASCAR track and its surrounding neighborhoods, as well as details on the attractions and geography around each track. An area of approximately a one-hour drive from each track has been included. The chapters are arranged alphabetically by track name, with the exception of NASCAR's newest addition, Autodromo Hermanos Rodriguez in Mexico City, which is Chapter 30. The Mexico City chapter is Mobil Travel Guide's first foray into Mexico, and, therefore, is abbreviated, but still provides plenty of details on the track and its environs. In each chapter, you'll find practical details like how to avoid race-day traffic, as well as locals' suggestions on how to plan your vacation before and after race weekend. Our calendars include NASCAR-sanctioned and other local events. We've also included space for collecting autographs on the opening page of each chapter.

One thing Mobil Travel Guide can't do is predict the weather, so it is important to heed hurricane and other weather warnings before heading out on the road.

The following sections explain the wealth of information you'll find in each chapter.

SEE

Mobil Travel Guide: NASCAR Travel Planner offers information about more than 500 museums, amusement parks, bowling alleys, historic sites, national and state parks, ski areas, and other attractions on the way to and near 30 NASCAR-sanctioned tracks in the United States, as well as the track in Mexico City.

Following an attraction's description, you'll find the months, days, and, in some cases, hours of operation; the address/directions, telephone number, and Web site (if there is one); and the admission price category. The following are the ranges we use for admission fees:
- **FREE**
- **$** = Up to $5
- **$$** = $5.01-$10
- **$$$** = $10.01-$15
- **$$$$** = Over $15

STAY

Lodgings are listed alphabetically under the city or town in which they're located. Both Lodgings and Restaurants are divided into two categories: Mobil-Star Rated and Local Recommendations. You'll notice many Best Western lodging options listed first in each city, as Best Western is the official hotel of NASCAR.

Mobil Star Rating Definitions for Lodgings
- ★★★★★: A Mobil Five-Star lodging provides consistently superlative service in an exceptionally distinctive luxury environment, with expanded services. Attention to detail is evident throughout

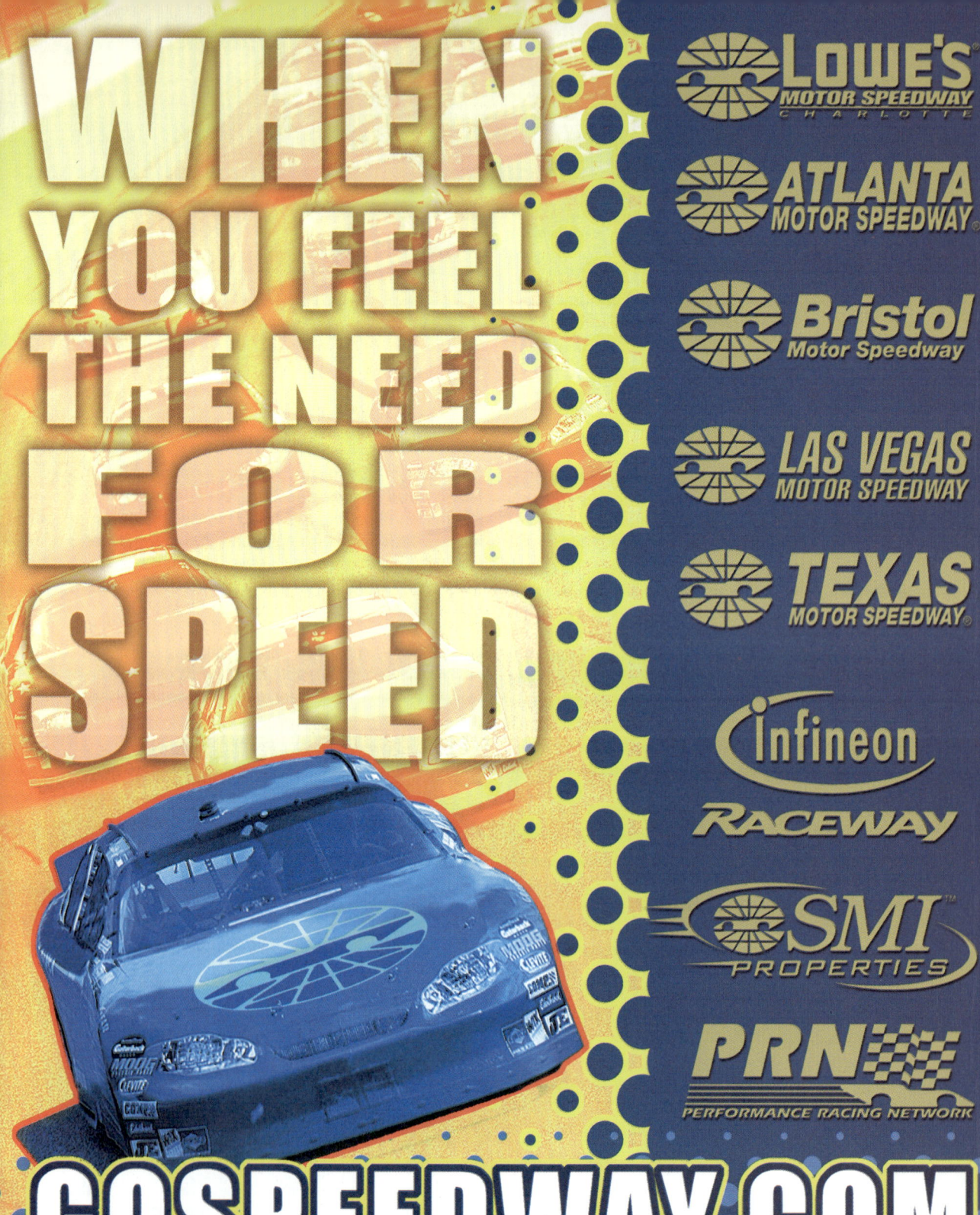

the hotel, resort, or inn, from bed linens to staff uniforms.
- ★★★★: A Mobil Four-Star lodging provides a luxury experience with expanded amenities in a distinctive environment. Services may include, but are not limited to, automatic turndown service, 24-hour room service, and valet parking.
- ★★★: A Mobil Three-Star lodging is well appointed, with a full-service restaurant and expanded amenities, such as a fitness center, golf course, tennis courts, 24-hour room service, and optional turndown service.
- ★★: A Mobil Two-Star lodging is considered a clean, comfortable, and reliable establishment that has expanded amenities, such as a full-service restaurant on the premises.
- ★: A Mobil One-Star lodging is a limited-service hotel, motel, or inn that is considered a clean, comfortable, and reliable establishment.

Information Found in the Lodging Listings
Each listing gives the lodging name, address/location (when no street address is available), neighborhood and/or directions from downtown (in major cities), phone number(s), total number of guest rooms, and seasons open (if not year-round). Symbols used in this section include:
- Business Center
- Fitness room
- Golf on premises
- Major commercial airport within 5 miles
- Pets allowed
- Facilities for people with disabilities not available
- Indoor or outdoor pool
- Tennis court(s) on premises
- Ski in/ski out access

For every property, we also provide pricing information. Because lodging rates change frequently, we list a pricing category rather than specific prices. All prices quoted by the Mobil Travel Guide are in effect at the time of publication; however, prices cannot be guaranteed. The pricing categories break down as follows:
- $ = Up to $150
- $$ = $151-$250
- $$$ = $251-$350
- $$$$ = $351 and up

Local Recommendations
These accommodations have been recommended by those who frequent the NASCAR races. They may be campgrounds and/or bed-and-breakfasts that don't meet Mobil Travel Guide's stringent criteria for inclusion as a Mobil Star-rated property. However, they may hold other distinctions or local lore that may interest NASCAR fans and their families.

RESTAURANTS

All Mobil Star-rated dining establishments listed in this book have a full kitchen and offer seating at tables; most offer table service.

Mobil Star Rating Definitions for Restaurants
- ★★★★★: A Mobil Five-Star restaurant offers one of few flawless dining experiences in the country. These establishments consistently provide their guests with exceptional food, superlative service, elegant décor, and exquisite presentations of each detail surrounding a meal.

- ★★★★: A Mobil Four-Star restaurant provides professional service, distinctive presentations, and wonderful food.
- ★★★: A Mobil Three-Star restaurant has good food, warm and skillful service, and enjoyable décor.
- ★★: A Mobil Two-Star restaurant serves fresh food in a clean setting with efficient service. Value is considered in this category, as is family friendliness.
- ★: A Mobil One-Star restaurant provides a distinctive experience through culinary specialty, local flair, or individual atmosphere.

Information Found in the Restaurant Listings
Each restaurant listing gives the cuisine type, street address (or directions if no address is available), phone numbers, Web site (if available), meals served, days of operation (if not open daily year-round), and pricing category.

Because menu prices can fluctuate, we list a pricing category rather than specific prices. Again, all prices quoted are in effect at the time of publication, but prices cannot be guaranteed.

The pricing categories are defined as follows, per diner, and assume that you order an appetizer or dessert, an entrée, and one drink:
- **$** = $15 and under
- **$$** = $16-$35
- **$$$** = $36-$85
- **$$$$** = $86 and up

Local Recommendations
As with lodging, Local Recommendations are restaurants that may not be inspected by Mobil Travel Guide's team, but are otherwise recommended for NASCAR fans. These may include quick road-food stops and diners that are good for kids but don't offer sit-down table service. Restaurants that have historical significance for NASCAR or are popular with drivers and teams are also included in this section.

We include very few chain or fast-food restaurants in our listings, because we realize you're familiar with most of them already and know that they offer consistent food and service across the country. Thanks to billboards along the highway, you also know where to find them. Instead, Mobil Travel Guide points you toward local favorites that you might not have discovered on your own.

SIDE TRIPS

We recognize that your travels don't always end at the edge of a map. While on the road to or from a NASCAR race, you may want to stop and see some of the country's great sights. For each chapter, we've selected a worthwhile side trip destination that falls outside the one-hour area around the closest NASCAR-sanctioned track. Nearby national parks, major cities, and other prime tourist draws fall into this category.

While we make great effort to verify every listing in our books, businesses do change their hours, their menus, and close their doors without notice. In addition, at press time, some hotels and restaurants were closed due to 2004 season hurricane damage. Smart travelers will call ahead to check availability.

Throughout the year, we keep up to date with restaurant openings and closings, road construction, race schedule changes, and other information that may impact your trip. With this special Web site password `MTGRACES` from *Mobil Travel Guide: NASCAR Travel Planner*, you can access this information at **www.mobiltravelguide.com** all year long. Please check back regularly for updates.

Special Information for Travelers with Disabilities
The Mobil Travel Guide D symbol indicates that an establishment is not at least partially accessible to people with mobility problems. When the D symbol follows a listing, the establishment is not equipped with facilities to accommodate people using wheelchairs or crutches or otherwise needing easy access to doorways and restrooms. Travelers with severe mobility problems or with hearing or visual impairments may or may not find the facilities they need. Always phone ahead to make sure that an establishment can meet your needs.

MAKING THE MOST OF YOUR TRIP

You may look back and laugh about that road trip when the car broke down, leaving you stranded for three days, or the time your extravagant vacation nearly left you broke. For most travelers, though, the best memories are of trips that are safe, smooth, and within budget. Here are a few tips and resources to help create a trip that's memorable only in the best ways.

SAVING MONEY

ON LODGING
Many hotels and motels offer discounts—for senior citizens, business travelers, families, you name it. It never hurts to ask—politely, that is. Sometimes, especially in the late afternoon, desk clerks are instructed to fill beds, and you might be offered a lower rate or a nicer room to entice you to stay. Also, make sure to try both the toll-free number and the local number. One may have a lower rate than the other.

State and city taxes, as well as special room taxes, can increase your room rate by as much as 25 percent per day. We are unable to include information about taxes in our listings, but we strongly urge you to ask about taxes when making reservations so that you understand the total cost of your lodgings before you get the bill.

Watch out for telephone-usage charges that hotels frequently impose on long-distance, credit-card, and other calls. Before phoning from your room, read the information given to you at check-in, and then be sure to review your bill carefully when checking out. You won't be expected to pay for charges that the hotel didn't spell out. If public telephones are available in the hotel lobby, your cost savings may outweigh the inconvenience of using them.

Here are some additional ways to save on lodgings:
- If you're traveling with children, choose lodgings where kids stay free.
- When visiting a major city, stay just outside the city limits; these rooms are usually less expensive than those in downtown locations.
- When calling a hotel, ask whether it is running any special promotions or if any discounts are available; many times reservationists are told not to volunteer these deals until asked.

- Check for hotel packages; some offer nightly rates that include a rental car or discounts on major attractions.
- Book rooms through **www.mobiltravelguide.com** where competitive rates are easy to find.

ON DINING
There are several ways to get a less expensive meal at an expensive restaurant. Early-bird dinners are popular in many parts of the country and offer considerable savings. Because tailgating is a popular NASCAR pastime, we've included many to-go options for eating. This is usually a budget-booster.

ON ENTERTAINMENT
A money-saving incentive in several large cities is the CityPass. If you plan to visit several museums and other major attractions, CityPass is a terrific option because it gets you into several sites for one substantially reduced price. Currently, CityPass is available in Chicago, Hollywood, New York, Philadelphia, San Francisco, and Southern California (which includes Disneyland, SeaWorld, and the San Diego Zoo). For more information or to buy a CityPass, phone toll-free 888/330-5008 or visit www.citypass.net. You can also purchase one from any participating CityPass attraction.

Here are some additional ways to save on entertainment and shopping:
- Check with your hotel's concierge for various coupons and special offers; they often have two-for-one tickets for area attractions and coupons for discounts at area stores and restaurants.

- Purchase same-day concert or theater tickets for half-price through the local cheap-tickets outlet, such as TKTS in New York or Hot Tix in Chicago.
- Visit museums on their free or "by donation" days, when you can pay what you wish rather than a specific admission fee.

STAYING SAFE

The best way to deal with emergencies is to avoid them in the first place. However, unforeseen situations do happen, so here are some ways to prepare.

IN YOUR CAR

Before you head out on a road trip, make sure that your car has been serviced and is in good working order. Change the oil, check the battery and belts, make sure that your windshield washer fluid is full and your tires are properly inflated (which can also improve your gas mileage).

Next, equip your car with tools and equipment needed to deal with a routine breakdown:
- Jack
- Spare tire

- Lug wrench
- Repair kit
- Emergency tools
- Jumper cables
- Spare fan belt
- Fuses
- Flares and/or reflectors
- Flashlight
- First aid kit
- In winter, a windshield scraper and snow shovel

Also, bring all appropriate and up-to-date documentation—licenses, registration, and insurance cards—and know what your insurance covers. Bring an extra set of keys, too, just in case.

En route, always buckle up. In most states, wearing a seatbelt is required by law.

If your car does break down, do the following:
- Get out of traffic as soon as possible—pull well off the road.
- Raise the hood and turn on your emergency flashers or tie a white cloth to the roadside door handle or antenna.
- Stay in your car.
- Use flares or reflectors to keep your vehicle from being hit.

PROTECTING AGAINST THEFT

To guard against theft wherever you go:
- Don't bring anything of more value than you need.
- If you do bring valuables, leave them at your hotel rather than in your car.
- If you bring something very expensive, lock it in a safe. Many hotels put one in each room; others will store your valuables in the hotel's safe.
- Don't carry more money than you need. Use traveler's checks and credit cards or visit cash machines to withdraw more cash when you run out.

Now that you're prepped and ready to go, get out on the road and start making some memories.

PACK YOUR BAGS

WE'LL DO THE REST!

Travel Packages including great race tickets, hotel accommodations, motorcoach transportation and much more!

*Fla. Seller of Travel Ref. No. ST35638

FOR TRAVEL PACKAGES CALL OR CLICK
1-800-PITSHOP.COM

YOUR SOURCES FOR ALL THE NASCAR NEWS

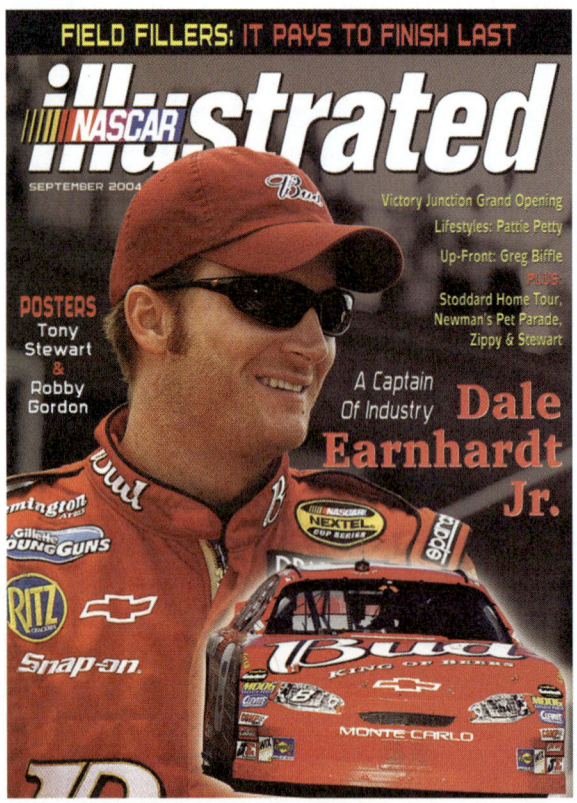

NASCAR Illustrated is your ticket inside the lives of the people of NASCAR. You'll see what they do at the track and how they live away from it. Plus, our award-winning photo gallery, gatefold posters, shop and home tours and special features.

1 Year - 12 Issues
$29.00

NASCAR Scene gives readers weekly, behind-the-scenes coverage of NASCAR racing. You get in-depth, timely coverage of each NEXTEL Cup, Busch Series, and Craftsman Truck event plus all the stock car news, driver profiles, and ALL the statistics.

1 Year - 50 Issues
$49.50

ORDER NOW AND GET A NASCAR 2005 POCKET GUIDE FREE

For subscription information, call 1-800-883-7323
International Rates Available Upon Request: Call 704-973-1300

Code 1040

RACING FLAGS

NASCAR NEXTEL Cup Series officials help signal messages to drivers during races by waving an assortment of colored flags. The flagman, who is always located on a stand high above the start/finish line, plays an important role during the event.

Green Flag: Displayed at the start of the race and also for restarts during the race. At the start of the race, cars must maintain position until they have crossed the start/finish line. The polesitter at the race start—and race leader on restarts—controls the pace and cannot be passed prior to the green waving.

Yellow Flag: Signifies caution and will be given to the first car passing the starter immediately following the incident that caused the display of the flag. All cars must slow down immediately to a predetermined pace, hold their position, and form a single line behind the pace car.

Red Flag: Signifies the race must be stopped immediately, regardless of the position of the cars on the track. The red flag shall be used if NASCAR officials decide the race should be stopped, usually for safety and/or competition-related reasons. Cars will be brought to a stop in an area designated by NASCAR officials. Repairs or service of any nature or refueling, whether on pit road or the garage, will not be permitted when the race is halted due to a red flag, unless the car has withdrawn from the event.

Blue with Diagonal Yellow Stripe: Although this flag is displayed regularly during most races, it is probably the least recognized. This flag is displayed to drivers, who are a lap down or significantly slower, that are about to be passed by the lead-lap cars. Drivers who are shown this flag must yield to the faster lead-lap cars.

Black Flag: Display of this flag requests that the car go immediately to the pits and report to the NASCAR official at the car's pit area. The car can receive a black flag for a variety of reasons, including driver/team infraction or a potential problem with the car reported by NASCAR officials, which warrants a closer inspection in the pits. It does not mean automatic disqualification. At the discretion of NASCAR officials, if the driver does not obey the black-flag directive, the driver may then be given the **Black Flag with a White Cross** at the start/finish line to inform the driver that any additional scoring of his or her car will be discontinued until furth

White Flag: Waves when the driver his final lap of the race.

Checkered Flag: The most fam black-and-white checkered flag i winner has crossed the finish lin will take the checkered flag on

FIRST-TIME RACEGOER TIPS

NASCAR has the reputation of being the fan-friendliest sport. No argument there. But even the world's most welcoming races require a little information in order to make a first-time race a happy memory, rather than one best forgotten. Consider these nine tips from the real experts, the veteran fans:

Scout seats. Unlike a concert, where seats closest to the stage are the most prized, at a race you want to get seats farther back. Also, the bigger the track, the higher up you want to be to take in all the action.

Practice patience. On race days it can take hours to enter the track. It will take just as long to leave. So, make the best of it. Have plenty of food, nonalcoholic drinks, and supplies in the car and tailgate after the race until traffic thins out.

Prepare for the elements. Sitting in the sun for hours requires sunscreen, lip balm, a hat, water, a cooling scarf, and sunglasses, which are also good for keeping track debris out of your eyes, even at night. Be prepared for weather changes. Bring a poncho—umbrellas are often not permitted inside the tracks. Don't wear white—this is a race, not a wedding—but do wear good walking shoes and dress in layers. If you get a pit pass, follow the clothing restrictions.

Prepare for noise. No matter how loud you think the track will be, it'll be louder. Bring earplugs, or, if you plan to listen to radio coverage of the race, use noise-reducing headphones. Longtime fans swear by the two-way radio sets worn by motorcyclists for communicating with their passengers in case you and your family get separated waiting in the long lines for the john.

Listen in. Many veteran racegoers enjoy eavesdropping on the conversations between drivers and crew via scanners. Buy your own—make sure the device has at least 200 channels and frequencies in the 800 to 900 MHz range—at electronics stores such as Radio Shack, where they start at about $100. Consider buying one with two earphone jacks so others can listen in. A leg strap is a nice option and keeps the scanner from taking a tumble if you rise to cheer. Bring a battery charger or extra batteries. If you don't want to invest in a scanner, check at your track to see if they're available for rent.

Read up. If your tickets came with a track guest information guide, read it. This is where you'll find track-specific rules, regulations, and information, such as the size of coolers allowed. (Also see the Track Facts section on the third page of each chapter of the *Mobil Travel Guide: NASCAR Travel Planner* for individual track specifics.)

Pack right. A felt-tipped pen for autographs, camera, binoculars, wipes or hand cleaner, pain relievers, allergy medicines, and toilet paper will come in handy for your family and make you fast friends with less prepared fans. A seat cushion is a butt-saver since most tracks have hard benches.

Shop early. Do your souvenir shopping on the days before the big race when the crowds are thinner.

Plan ahead. Tell your boss you need the Monday after the race off from work, in case the race gets rained out on Sunday. It'll be postponed until Monday, and there's no point in taking a vacation to see a race if you miss the action!

2005 NASCAR BUSCH SERIES SCHEDULE

Date	Track
February 19	Daytona International Speedway
February 26	California Speedway
March 6	Autodromo Hermanos Rodriguez
March 12	Las Vegas Motor Speedway
March 19	Atlanta Motor Speedway
March 26	Nashville Superspeedway
April 2	Bristol Motor Speedway
April 16	Texas Motor Speedway
April 22	Phoenix International Raceway
April 30	Talladega Superspeedway
May 6	Darlington Raceway
May 13	Richmond International Raceway
May 28	Lowe's Motor Speedway
June 4	Dover International Speedway
June 11	Nashville Superspeedway
June 18	Kentucky Speedway
June 25	The Milwaukee Mile
July 1	Daytona International Speedway
July 9	Chicagoland Speedway
July 16	New Hampshire International Speedway
July 23	Pikes Peak International Raceway
July 30	Gateway International Raceway
August 6	Indianapolis Raceway Park
August 13	Watkins Glen International
August 20	Michigan International Speedway
August 26	Bristol Motor Speedway
September 3	California Speedway
September 9	Richmond International Raceway
September 24	Dover International Speedway
October 8	Kansas Speedway
October 14	Lowe's Motor Speedway
October 22	Memphis Motorsports Park
November 5	Texas Motor Speedway
November 12	Phoenix International Raceway
November 19	Homestead-Miami Speedway

2005 NASCAR CRAFTSMAN TRUCK SERIES SCHEDULE

Date	Track
February 18	Daytona International Speedway
February 25	California Speedway
March 18	Atlanta Motor Speedway
April 9	Martinsville Speedway
April 30	Gateway International Raceway
May 15	Mansfield Motorsports Speedway
May 20	Lowe's Motor Speedway
	Dover International Speedway
June 10	Texas Motor Speedway
June 18	Michigan International Speedway
June 24	The Milwaukee Mile
July 2	Kansas Speedway
July 9	Kentucky Speedway
July 23	Memphis Motorsports Park
August 5	Indianapolis Raceway Park
August 13	Nashville Superspeedway
August 24	Bristol Motor Speedway
September 8	Richmond International Raceway
September 17	New Hampshire International Speedway
September 24	Las Vegas Motor Speedway
October 22	Martinsville Speedway
October 29	Atlanta Motor Speedway
November 4	Texas Motor Speedway
November 11	Phoenix International Raceway
November 18	Homestead-Miami Speedway

At press time, race titles were not yet confirmed. Dates are tentative and subject to change.

Plan your next trip *by the seat of your pants.*

With our user-friendly, comprehensive travel Web site, you can do everything from searching thousands of quality-inspected and rated establishments to making online reservations. To experience easy and trustworthy travel planning, log on to

www.mobiltravelguide.com

2005 NASCAR NEXTEL CUP SCHEDULE

Date	Track
February 12	Daytona International Speedway
February 20	Daytona International Speedway
February 27	California Speedway
March 13	Las Vegas Motor Speedway
March 20	Atlanta Motor Speedway
April 3	Bristol Motor Speedway
April 10	Martinsville Speedway
April 17	Texas Motor Speedway
April 23	Phoenix International Raceway
May 1	Talladega Superspeedway
May 7	Darlington Raceway
May 14	Richmond International Raceway
May 21	Lowe's Motor Speedway
May 29	Lowe's Motor Speedway
June 5	Dover International Speedway
June 12	Pocono Raceway
June 19	Michigan International Speedway
June 26	Infineon Raceway
July 2	Daytona International Speedway
July 10	Chicagoland Speedway
July 17	New Hampshire International Speedway
July 24	Pocono Raceway
August 7	Indianapolis Motor Speedway
August 14	Watkins Glen International
August 21	Michigan International Speedway
August 27	Bristol Motor Speedway
September 4	California Speedway
September 10	Richmond International Raceway
September 18	New Hampshire International Speedway
September 25	Dover International Speedway
October 2	Talladega Superspeedway
October 9	Kansas Speedway
October 15	Lowe's Motor Speedway
October 23	Martinsville Speedway
October 30	Atlanta Motor Speedway
November 6	Texas Motor Speedway
November 13	Phoenix International Raceway
November 20	Homestead-Miami Speedway

At press time, race titles were not yet confirmed. Dates are tentative and subject to change.

24

Powerful pickups rumble along the wall at the start of the NASCAR Craftsman Truck EasyCare Vehicle Service Contracts 200.

Atlanta Motor Speedway

Hampton, GA

1

Young fans don headphones to listen in on all the NASCAR NEXTEL Cup racing action.

TRACK FACTS

ATLANTA MOTOR SPEEDWAY. 1500 N Hwy 41, Hampton (30228). Phone 770/946-4211. www.atlantamotorspeedway.com.

SECURITY. Coolers 14 x 14 x 14 inches or smaller are allowed; alcohol is allowed except in no-alcohol grandstand. No glass containers, umbrellas, strollers, bicycles, or portable toilets. No pets except on leashes in camping/RV section.

PARKING. Park in handicapped spaces only with state-issued tag or license. For assistance, look for golf cart shuttles with blue awnings cruising the parking lots. Reserved parking spots are available on weekends for $75 per event. Unreserved parking on all 870 acres is free. Call the speedway (phone 770/946-4211) to reserve. RVs and trailers park in two infield sections; spots are sold on a yearly basis.

FIRST AID. Find first aid stations in the concourse area of each grandstand; Earnhardt, Petty, and Weaver grandstands have ambulances nearby. Infield aid centers are located near the main tunnel and service tunnel entrances. Henry County Medical Center (Eagles Landing Pkwy, exit 224 off Interstate 75) is less than 20 minutes away.

CONCESSIONS. Each grandstand has concession stands in the concourse area; other stands are scattered throughout the track. The speedway gift shop is located near the East Turn; find other souvenirs behind the Earnhardt Grandstand.

ATLANTA MOTOR SPEEDWAY, GA 27

Racers line up behind the pace car before the start of the NASCAR NEXTEL Cup Golden Corral 500.

SOUTHERN STYLE AT A CITY PACE

The city of Atlanta shimmers as the diamond of the South. And like a diamond, many unique facets comprise the gleaming surface. It's a city that embraces the history amid towering skyscrapers, where natural beauty is background for a wealth of technological advances, and where old-fashioned Southern hospitality mixes with an urban fast-lane pace.

Historians love to recount the tale of how General Sherman's troops used Atlanta as kindling wood on the famous March to the Sea. In the century since, the city has become a progressive, cosmopolitan mix of nationalities.

Some visitors still expect mint juleps, mansions, and magnolias, which are increasingly harder to find. One vestige of past times can be found at the **Fox Theatre** (660 Peachtree St, www.foxtheatre.org), where the ceiling simulates an Arabian night sky. The easygoing Southern style is still very much in evidence, despite the busy international airport, Hartsfield-Jackson, a major transportation hub—frequent fliers swear you can't get anywhere without going through the city of Atlanta.

Atlanta serves as the business and cultural capital of the New South. Fortune 500 companies such as Coca-Cola, CNN, United Parcel Service, and Georgia-Pacific make their home here (reserve a space on the **CNN Center** tour by calling toll-free 877/4-CNNTOUR). A big nod to Atlanta's contribution to the US economy can be found at **World of Coca-Cola** (55 Martin Luther King Jr. Dr SW, phone 404/676-5151, www.woccatlanta.com)—the drink's original mixture was developed by an Atlanta pharmacist in 1889; today, you can view the world's largest collection of Coke memorabilia.

More cultural options abound, as well: the **Fernbank Museum of Natural History** (767 Clifton Rd, www.fernbank.edu) offers fascinating dinosaur exhibits for the kids; the **Fernbank Science Center** (156 Heaton Park Dr, www.fernbank.edu), around the corner from the museum, offers space-related exhibits including an original *Apollo* space capsule.

The city encompasses 131 square miles, but most people include the sprawling metropolitan areas when discussing Atlanta. The ten-county metropolitan area occupies almost 3,000 square miles and is home to nearly 4 million residents.

When locals get together, they define themselves with one simple question: "Do you live inside or outside the Perimeter?"

The Perimeter refers to Interstate 285, which encircles the city. Much of the area inside the Perimeter is still technically outside city limits, but locals consider it a part of Atlanta. Areas outside the Perimeter are the suburbs of Metro Atlanta.

It's no surprise that in a city this size, traffic has become a maelstrom of discontent. In fact, Atlanta's traffic congestion is ranked one of the worst in the United States, along with Los Angeles and San Francisco. On a bad traffic day, drivers could probably get to Chattanooga quicker than they could drive across the metro area alone.

Find some time to sit out on the pier or take a dip in Lake Dow.

The ornate brick detail of this train depot, which was built in the 1880s, helped it become listed on the National Register of Historic Places.

ATLANTA MOTOR SPEEDWAY, GA   29

Making it around the city's highway system is relatively simple.

While Interstate 285 makes a full circle around the city, Interstates 20, 75, and 85 pass through town. Travelers can avoid driving through town by taking Interstate 285 and then reconnecting to their interstate on the other side of town. However, that's not always the fastest route. Rush-hour traffic can slow Interstate 285 traffic to a drunken snail's pace, particularly near Interstate 75 north, so a direct route through town may be a better option. Current traffic information from the Georgia Department of Transportation is available by calling toll-free 888/635-8287. Radio stations such as Eagle 106.7 FM or WSB 750 AM also carry continually updated traffic conditions.

Atlanta is definitely a city that requires a car to get around. The city has a mass transit system, but it pales in comparison to those of its northern neighbors. The Metropolitan Atlanta Rapid Transit Authority (MARTA) operates a bus and rail system throughout the city. MARTA rail travels both a north/south and east/west line. Service into the suburban areas is very limited, however, which reduces its usefulness.

When was the last time you went to the zoo? You can check out the tigers and much more at Zoo Atlanta.

GETTING AROUND

Approaching the track via I-75 north, you have several options: take Exit 205 (GA Hwy 16) west into Griffin; take Hwy 19/41 north to the speedway (Georgia State Patrol recommends this route). Or take Exit 212, Hampton-Locust Grove Rd, west to GA Hwy 20 to the speedway. Or take Exit 218, GA Hwy 20, to the speedway.

Traveling south, take Exit 235 (Hwy 19/41 Tara Blvd) to the speedway, about 15 miles. Expect heavy traffic. Or pass Exit 235 and continue south on I-75 to Exit 218. Take GA Hwy 20 west and follow signs to the speedway.

Enter the Petty, Earnhardt, and Champions grandstands at Gates 1, 12, 13, 14, or 15; for East Turn, use Gates 2 and 3; and for Weaver grandstand, Gates 6, 7, 8, 9, and 10.

How you exit the track depends on how you entered the parking lot: if you've entered the track from the north, you'll be directed to leave to the north; enter from the south, leave to the south. Either way, you will be directed to the interstate.

GETTING TICKETS

Call the speedway ticket office, phone 770/946-4211, or pay a service fee at www.ticketmaster.com or a Ticketmaster outlet. Adult prices range from $30 to $110.

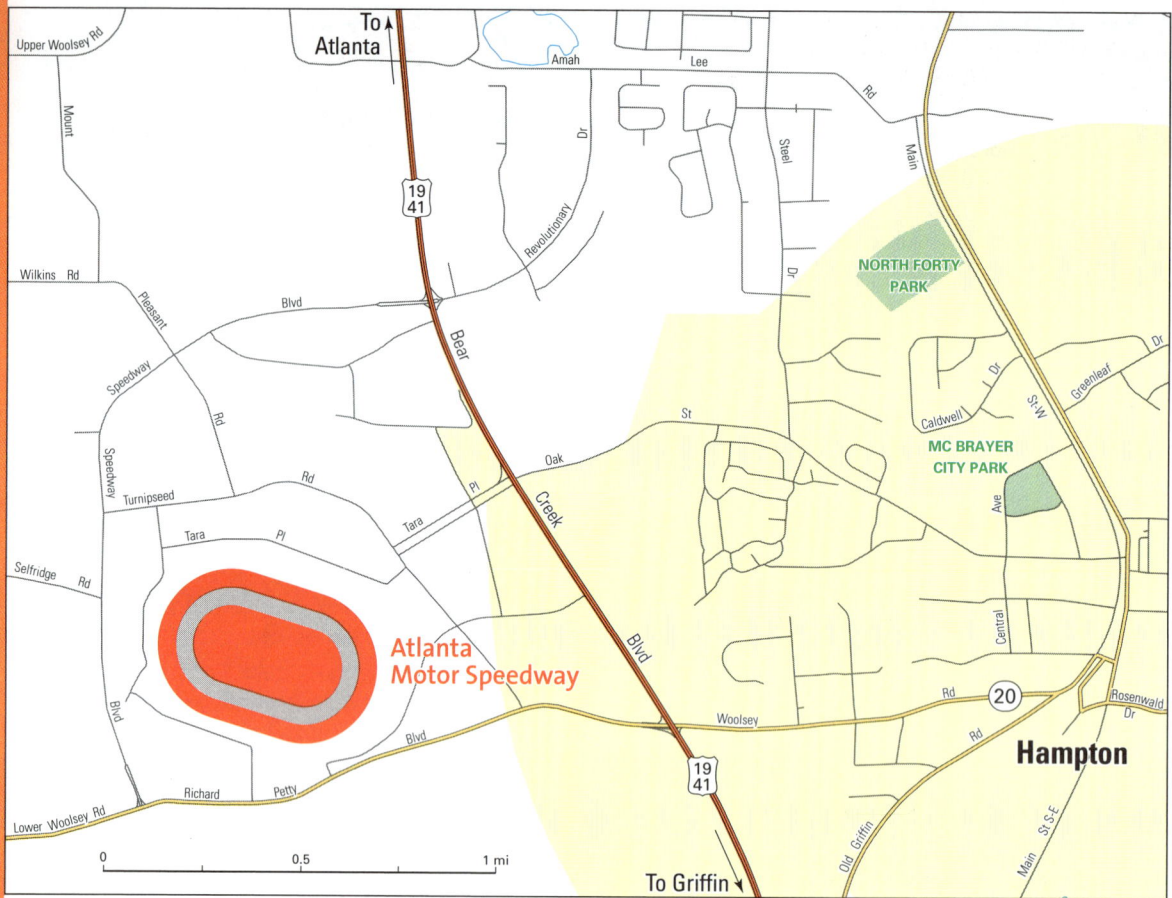

HAMPTON POLE POSITION:
The 10 miles surrounding Atlanta Motor Speedway.

The city has a strong skyline, but skyscrapers are not the only adornment on the horizon. Atlanta blossoms throughout its mild spring with dazzling white and pink dogwood trees and cool pastel shades of azaleas, while summer, which can send average temperatures into the 100s, brings vibrant crepe myrtle blossoms.

If you want to see what it's like below sidewalk level, though, visit **Underground Atlanta** (50 Upper Alabama St, www.underground-atlanta.com), a 1920s-era system of downtown viaducts that now holds restaurants and specialty shops.

Visitors will also note a fondness for Peachtrees—but we're talking asphalt, not green leafy things. There are more than 50 streets named Peachtree in town, making it somewhat difficult to differentiate Peachtree Street, Peachtree Way, Peachtree Walk, and Peachtree Road. Make sure to get specific directions.

Whether it's symphony, blues, or rap music, hip coffeehouses or gracious tea rooms, the vibrant city of Atlanta has samples of whatever your taste might be. And it's a city that will call you back again and again.

ATLANTA MOTOR SPEEDWAY, GA 31

OWNER'S PICK

Legendary NASCAR car builder, team owner, and NASCAR inspector **Ray Fox** knows a good time when he sees one. When in Atlanta, he knows how to search out other good times. "I really like the **Dawsonville Pool Hall. Gordon Pirkle** and his gang really do a good job. The burgers and steaks are great, and you can't beat it for atmosphere. He's got a lot of racing memorabilia there. It's a little bit of a drive from the speedway, but it's worth it." *E First St, Dawsonville. Phone 706/265-2792.*

HAMPTON CALENDAR

MARCH 18–20, 2005
Race weekend: Georgia Power Qualifying Night and NASCAR Craftsman Truck series; NASCAR Busch Series Aaron's 312; NASCAR NEXTEL Cup Series Golden Corral 500

MARCH 18–27, 2005
Macon, Georgia's International Cherry Blossom Festival. Macon (31201). Phone 478/751-7429; toll-free 800/768-3401. www.cherryblossom.com. Family entertainment, air shows, parades, fireworks, concerts, and dances.

MARCH 30–APRIL 3, 2005
Savannah Tour of Homes & Gardens. Savannah (31410). Phone 912/234-8054. www.savannahtourofhomes.org. Stroll through historic private homes and gardens.

OCTOBER, 2005
Georgia Mountain Fall Festival. Georgia Mountain Fairgrounds, Hiawassee (30546). Phone 706/896-4191. www.georgia-mountain-fair.com. Watch demonstrations of quilting and blacksmithing, and the state fiddling championship. Mid-October.

OCTOBER, 2005
Oktoberfest. White County, Helen (30545). Phone toll-free 800/858-8027. www.helenga.org. Bavarian food, German beer, and polka dancing.

OCTOBER 29–30, 2005
Race weekend: Georgia-Pacific Qualifying Night; EasyCare Vehicle Services Contracts 200 NASCAR Craftsman Truck Series; Bass Pro Shops MBNA 500 NASCAR NEXTEL Cup Series

Who are these fans rooting for during the NASCAR NEXTEL Cup Series Golden Corral 500? Check out their caps and shirts.

HAMPTON OUTFIELD:
The 50 miles surrounding Atlanta Motor Speedway.

SEE

ATTRACTIONS

Atlanta

CNN CENTER.
One CNN Ctr, Techwood Dr at Marietta St, Atlanta (30348). Phone 404/827-2300; toll-free tour reservations 877/4-CNNTOUR. Tour the studio, view a re-creation of the main control room, visit an interactive exhibit of top news stories, or learn the secrets of map-pointing only TV weather forecasters know. Parents: children younger than 4 not allowed on studio tour. Reservations are recommended. (Tours depart daily every 10 minutes 9 am-5 pm; closed Easter, Thanksgiving, Dec 25) **$$**

FERNBANK MUSEUM OF NATURAL HISTORY.
767 Clifton Rd NE, Atlanta (30307). Phone 404/929-6300. www.fernbank.edu. Parents of dinosaur-loving children should put this at the top of their "must-see" list. Life-size skeletal replicas are amazing; other exhibits use fossils to detail development of the many plants and animals on earth. An IMAX theater is located at the museum as well. (Mon-Sat 10 am-5 pm, Sun noon-5 pm) **$$$**

FERNBANK SCIENCE CENTER.
156 Heaton Park Dr NE, Atlanta (30307). Phone 678/874-7102. www.fernbank.edu. Stargazers, nature lovers, and the curious can enjoy activities and space-related exhibits including a moon rock and original *Apollo* space capsule. The observatory opens during clear weather Thursday and Friday nights to let visitors peek through the 36-inch reflecting telescope. The 65-acre Fernbank Forest has more than a mile of peaceful trails. Programs offered year-round. (Mon-Wed 8:30 am-5 pm, Thurs-Fri 8:30 am-10 pm, Sat 10 am-5 pm, Sun 1-5 pm) Science Center **FREE**, Planetarium **$**

THE FOX THEATRE.
660 Peachtree St, Atlanta (30308). Phone 404/881-2100. www.foxtheatre.org. The Fox Theatre is one of a few architectural gems saved by preservationists. Guests in the more than 4,000-seat theater sit in an Arabian courtyard under an azure-painted sky with hundreds of 11-watt bulbs fixed in crystals, twinkling like stars. The colossal pipe organ is the second-largest theater organ in the United States, with 3,622 pipes. Tours (Mon, Wed-Thurs 10 am; Sat 10 am, 11 am). **$$**

UNDERGROUND ATLANTA.
50 Upper Alabama St, Atlanta (30303). Phone 404/523-2311. www.underground-atlanta.com. In the 1920s, Atlanta built a system of viaducts in the downtown area, elevating and leveling out the road system in an effort to solve traffic problems. Merchants moved to the top level, leaving their old stores below. Those old shops and stores make up what would eventually be called Underground Atlanta. The old stores have been renovated and much of the original architecture restored. New restaurants, retail stores, specialty shops, and galleries now line the brick pathways. Two adjacent parking decks are available. (Mon-Sat 10 am-9:30 pm, Sun 11 am-7 pm; restaurants and nightclubs open longer)

WORLD OF COCA-COLA.
55 Martin Luther King Jr. Dr SW, Atlanta (30303). Phone 404/676-5151. www.woccatlanta.com. The drink's original mixture was developed by an Atlanta pharmacist in 1886. Today, Coca-Cola's world headquarters are here, along with the world's largest collection of Coke memorabilia. A favorite spot is the viewing room, where you can watch Coke commercials from over the years. In the International Video Lounge, taste samples of many Coke products around the world, with names like Krest, sold in Africa; Beverly from Italy; or Kuat from Latin America. (Sept-May: Mon-Sat 9 am-5 pm, Sun 11 am-5 pm; June-Aug: Mon-Sat 9 am-6 pm, Sun 11 am-5 pm; closed holidays) **$$**

ZOO ATLANTA.
800 Cherokee Ave SE, Atlanta (30315). Phone 404/624-5600. www.zooatlanta.org. More than 1,000 species of animals reside here, each enjoying a replica of their natural habitat. Visitors can view gorillas and monkeys roaming through the Ford African Rain Forest or watch giant pandas tumble in play. Lions, rhino, giraffes, and ostriches wander freely through the African Plains. There's also a petting zoo, train rides, and carousel for the younger set. (Mon-Sun 9:30 am-4:30 pm; closed Jan 1, Thanksgiving, Dec 25) **$$$$**

SEE ATTRACTIONS

Austell

SIX FLAGS OVER GEORGIA.
275 Riverside Pkwy, Austell (30168). Phone 770/948-9290. www.sixflags.com. Ten roller coasters, water rides, shows, food, and fun from wild rides to Bugs Bunny World. Guests of all ages should ride the Riverview Carousel, a carefully restored carousel on the National Register of Historic Places. (Hours vary with season; closed Nov-Mar) $$$$

Hampton

ATLANTA MOTOR SPEEDWAY TRACK TOURS.
Atlanta Motor Speedway, 1500 N Hwy 41, Hampton (30228). Phone 770/707-7970. www.atlantamotorspeedway.com. Official track tours take groups to the Petty Garden, a luxury suite, the garages, Victory Lane, and two laps in the Speedway Van. (Mon-Sat 9 am-4:30 pm; Sun 1-4:30 pm; not offered during race weeks) $

Stone Mountain

STONE MOUNTAIN PARK.
Hwy 78, Stone Mountain (30086). Phone 770/448-5700. www.stonemountainpark.com. Stone Mountain is a granite mass rising from the ground, covering 583 acres, or more than 25 million square feet, and rising 1,683 feet above sea level. Camping, boating, fishing, and hiking are available, along with a water slide complex and the Great Barn, a four-story complex with rope nets, slides, mazes, computer games, and other fun. Climb the mountain or take the skylift, ride a paddlewheel riverboat or the scenic railroad. The popular laser show projected onto the mountain runs every evening from mid-May to Labor Day, then on Friday and Saturday from Labor Day to October. A hotel and several restaurants are in the park. (Daily 6 am-midnight; attractions open at 10 am; closed Dec 25) $$$$

For more attractions, go to www.mobiltravelguide.com

STAY

MOBIL STAR-RATED LODGINGS

Atlanta

ATLANTA MARRIOTT MARQUIS. ★★★
265 NE Peachtree Center Ave, Atlanta (30303). Phone 770/521-0000; toll-free 800/932-2198. www.marriott.com. This polished convention hotel awes guests with its 50-story atrium and unlimited view of the city. Guests will delight in the elegantly appointed guest rooms and first-class comforts. 1,675 rooms, 47 story. Check-in 3 pm, check-out 11 am. Restaurant, bar. Fitness room. Indoor pool, outdoor pool, whirlpool. Business center. $$

EMBASSY SUITES HOTEL ATLANTA AT CENTENNIAL OLYMPIC PARK. ★★
267 Marietta St, Atlanta (30313). Phone 404/223-2300; toll-free 800/362-2779. www.embassysuites.com. One of Atlanta's newest, the hotel occupies a prime spot across from Centennial Olympic Park. At

FAN FAVORITE

If you're making travel arrangements, visit www.vroomz.com. Vroomz offers reservation packages for sports fans to many major venues. For race fans, Atlanta Motor Speedway has contracted with the service to offer fans discount packages. There's no service charge, and air, hotel, and shuttle service can all be arranged. If you are making reservations on your own, be aware that the rates of some hotels close to the speedway can increase dramatically on race weekends. Always get the room rate specified at the time of reservation, and don't hesitate to call around for better prices.

night, sit on the balcony and watch the dazzling light display at the Olympic Rings Fountain. Suites offer large bedrooms and living rooms with comfortable couches. 321 rooms, all suites. Complimentary full breakfast. Check-in 3 pm, check-out noon. High-speed Internet access. Restaurant, bar. Fitness room. Outdoor pool, whirlpool. Business center. $$

FAIRFIELD INN AND SUITES ATLANTA MIDTOWN. ★

1470 Spring St NW, Atlanta (30309). Phone 404/872-5821; toll-free 800/228-2800. www.fairfieldinn.com. This Fairfield Inn's ample meeting space, separate lounge with comfy chairs and Internet access, and breakfast area make it stand out from the others in the chain. It's located within three blocks of public transportation. 149 rooms, 4 story. Complimentary continental breakfast. Check-in 3 pm, check-out noon. Fitness room. Outdoor pool. $

HILTON ATLANTA AND TOWERS. ★★★

255 Courtland St NE, Atlanta (30303). Phone 404/659-2000; toll-free 800/445-8667. www.hilton.com. From the fitness center, jogging track, and basketball and tennis courts, to the pool and billiard room, this hotel is guaranteed to restore the senses. 1,224 rooms, 30 story. Check-in 3 pm, check-out 11 am. Restaurant, bar. Fitness room. Outdoor pool. Tennis. Business center. $

HYATT REGENCY. ★★★

265 Peachtree St NE, Atlanta (30303). Phone 404/577-1234; toll-free 800/233-1234. www.hyatt.com. Located in the hustle and bustle of downtown, this 23-story atrium hotel successfully combines the convenience of a downtown hotel with superb accommodations and first-class amenities. Atlanta Market Center, Georgia Dome, Underground Atlanta, and Centennial Olympic Park are minutes away. 1,260 rooms, 23 story. Check-in 3 pm, check-out noon. Restaurant, bar. Fitness room. Outdoor pool. Business center. $$

OMNI HOTEL AT CNN CENTER. ★★★

100 CNN Center, Atlanta (30335). Phone 404/659-0000; toll-free 800/843-6664. www.omnihotels.com. Offering some of the best skyline views in Atlanta, guest rooms combine sophistication and elegance with all the comforts of home. Guests are pampered with triple sheeting on beds, evening turndown service,

and cozy terrycloth bathrobes. In addition to the sixth-floor health club, a "Get Fit Kit" with small weights and bands is available for those wishing to exercise privately in their rooms. 1,067 rooms, 15 story. Pets accepted, some restrictions; fee. Check-in 3 pm, check-out noon. Restaurant, bar. Fitness room. Airport transportation available. Business center. $$

SHERATON ATLANTA HOTEL. ★★★

165 Courtland St, Atlanta (30303). Phone 404/659-6500; toll-free 888/625-5144. www.sheraton.com. Offering three restaurants, a health club, indoor and outdoor pools, and a business center, this hotel is a home-away-from-home for business and leisure travelers alike. 765 rooms, 12 story. Check-in 3 pm, check-out noon. Three restaurants, bar. Fitness room. Indoor pool, outdoor pool, whirlpool. Business center. $

WESTIN PEACHTREE PLAZA. ★★★

210 Peachtree St NW, Atlanta (30303). Phone 404/659-1400; toll-free 800/937-8461. www.westin.com. As if the superb service, relaxing ambience, and spacious guest rooms with views of downtown weren't enough, this hotel surpasses others by offering special touches such as the "heavenly bed." Guests can dine at any of the three delectable restaurants, enjoy a workout in the fitness center, or just relax at the indoor or outdoor pool. 1,068 rooms, 73 story. Check-in 3 pm, check-out 11 am. Three restaurants, bar. Fitness room, spa. Indoor pool, outdoor pool. Business center. $$

WYNDHAM ATLANTA DOWNTOWN HOTEL. ★★★

160 Spring St SW, Atlanta (30303). Phone 404/688-8600; toll-free 877/999-3223. www.wyndham.com. This contemporary hotel with intimate yet open spaces offers a friendly staff and a location that affords guests the opportunity to savor all that Atlanta has to see and do. 312 rooms, 9 story. Check-in 3 pm, check-out noon. Restaurant, bar. Fitness room. Outdoor pool. Airport transportation available. Business center. $

Augusta

AZALEA INN. ★★

312 Greene St, Augusta (30901). Phone 706/724-3454; toll-free 877/292-5324. www.theazaleainn.com. This enchanting bed-and-breakfast is perfect for a romantic getaway. Located near Augusta's Riverwalk, antiques shops, and brick-lined plazas. 21 rooms, 3 story. Complimentary continental breakfast. Check-in 3-6 pm, check-out 11 am. $

COURTYARD BY MARRIOTT AUGUSTA. ★★

1045 Stevens Creek Rd, Augusta (30901). Phone 706/737-3737; toll-free 800/321-2211. www.courtyard.com. Located on Augusta's north side, this hotel features a business center, large desks, and high-speed Internet access in each room. After a busy day, head to the distinguished Augusta National Golf Club nearby, or relax in the outdoor pool or whirlpool. 130 rooms, 2 story. Check-in 3 pm, check-out noon. High-speed Internet access. Fitness room. Outdoor pool, whirlpool. Business center. $

LOCAL RECOMMENDATIONS

Atlanta

BEST WESTERN GRANADA SUITE HOTEL DOWNTOWN.

1302 W Peachtree St NW, Atlanta (30309). Phone 404/876-6100; toll-free 800/937-8376. www.bestwestern.com. This quaint hotel, in Midtown Atlanta with a European flair, provides a courtesy shuttle to attractions within 5 miles. It is convenient to the High Museum of Art and is easily accessible to city rail (MARTA) service. 104 rooms, 4 story. Complimentary continental breakfast. Check-in 3 pm, check-out noon. Business center. $

BEST WESTERN INN AT THE PEACHTREE.

330 W Peachtree St NW, Atlanta (30308). Phone 404/577-6970; toll-free 800/937-8376. www.bestwestern.com. This hotel is located near Centennial Olympic Park, World Congress Center, and CNN Center. 112 rooms, 4 story. Pets accepted, some restrictions; fee. Check-in 3 pm, check-out noon. Fitness room. $

RENAISSANCE CONCOURSE HOTEL.

One Hartsfield Centre Pkwy, Atlanta (30354). Phone 404/209-9999; toll-free 888/236-2427. www.renaissancehotels.com. Official Hotel of Atlanta Motor Speedway. Recently renovated rooms open to a sparkling 11-story indoor atrium, and large windows offer impressive outside views. With Hartsfield-Jackson Atlanta International Airport just five minutes away, the hotel features special acoustics that keep airport noise levels minimal. 387 rooms, 11 story. Check-in 3 pm, check-out 1 pm. Restaurant. Fitness room. Indoor pool, outdoor pool, whirlpool. Business Center. $$

Augusta

AUGUSTA TOWERS HOTEL AND CONVENTION CENTER.

2651 Perimeter Pkwy, Augusta (30909). Phone 706/855-8100. The serene and airy atrium lobby is filled with towering palm trees and beautifully lush plants. Relax in the elegantly appointed guest rooms. Enjoy extra amenities like the indoor and outdoor pools, sauna, whirlpool, and fitness center. 179 rooms. Pets accepted; fee. Check-in 3 pm, check-out noon. Restaurant, bar. Fitness room. Indoor pool, outdoor pool, whirlpool. Airport transportation available. $

Griffin

BEST WESTERN NORTH PLAZA INN.

1616 N Expressway, Griffin (30223). Phone 770/227-8400; toll-free 800/937-8376. www.bestwestern.com. 49 rooms, 2 story. Complimentary continental breakfast. Check-in 2 pm, check-out 11 am. High-speed Internet access. Outdoor pool. $

PIT PASS

For inhaling exhaust fumes up close and personal, a pit pass is a must. Passes for Friday-Sunday cost $125, but the best pit action for less money can be had with the Friday-only pit pass for $75: Between qualifying, and NASCAR Busch cars revving up for the next day's race, Friday is one of the busiest days in the pits. The pits are open until 45 minutes before race time. NASCAR rules require pit area visitors to be age 14 or older. No shorts, open-toed shoes, or sleeveless shirts. And remember: the pit pass only gets you into the pit. Ticket price is separate.

Hapeville

BEST WESTERN ATLANTA AIRPORT EAST.
301 N Central Ave, Hapeville (30354). Phone 404/763-8777; toll-free 800/937-8376. www.bestwestern.com. 188 rooms, 10 story. Complimentary continental breakfast. Check-in 2 pm, check-out 11 am. Fitness room. Outdoor pool. **$**

McDonough

BEST WESTERN MCDONOUGH INN AND SUITES.
805 Industrial Blvd, McDonough (30253). Phone 770/898-1006; toll-free 800/937-8376. www.bestwestern.com. 64 rooms, 3 story. Complimentary continental breakfast. Check-in 3 pm, check-out 11 am. High-speed Internet access. Fitness room. Indoor pool. **$**

Morrow

BEST WESTERN SOUTHLAKE INN.
6437 Jonesboro Rd, Morrow (30281). Phone 770/961-6300; toll-free 800/937-8376. www.bestwestern.com. 113 rooms, 2 story. Pets accepted, some restrictions; fee. Complimentary continental breakfast. Check-in 2 pm, check-out 11 am. Outdoor pool. **$**

Peachtree City

BEST WESTERN PEACHTREE CITY INN/SUITES.
976 Crosstown Rd, Peachtree City (30269). Phone 770/632-9700; toll-free 800/937-8376. www.bestwestern.com. 50 rooms, 2 story. Complimentary continental breakfast. Check-in 3 pm, check-out 11 am. Outdoor pool. Fitness Room. **$**

Stockbridge

BEST WESTERN ATLANTA SOUTH.
619 Hwy 138 W, Stockbridge (30281). Phone 770/474-8771; toll-free 800/937-8376. www.bestwestern.com. 114 rooms. 2 story. Pets accepted, some restrictions; fee. Check-in 3 pm, check-out 11 am. Outdoor pool. **$**

COMFORT INN.
7325 Davidson Pkwy N, Stockbridge (30281). Phone 770/507-7911; toll-free 877/424-6423. www.comfortinn.com. 51 rooms, 2 story. Complimentary continental breakfast. Check-in 1 pm, check-out 11 am. Outdoor pool. **$**

RV AND CAMPING

The best place to camp is the track itself. Unreserved camping spots for tents and RVs are available for $40, payable on-site. No hook-ups are available for these sites. Camping spaces in the general RV area measure 20 feet by 40 feet. The spaces in the tent/pop-up area near the lake are 15 feet by 30 feet.

Reserved spaces are available in three locations around the speedway. A 20-foot-by-40-foot space for tents and pop-ups costs $100. A 25-foot-by-45-foot RV space costs $125. RVs must be self-contained; there are no hook-ups. Call the speedway ticket office (phone 770/946-4211) well in advance of race days for reservations.

Campers can stake out more than one space as long as all sites are paid for. Grills and contained fires are allowed. If a barrel fire is used, the barrel must be removed from the property after the event. Dumpsters and barrels are in the area for trash deposit. Several bathroom/shower facilities are available in the camping areas.

For more lodging recommendations, go to www.mobiltravelguide.com

EAT

MOBIL STAR-RATED RESTAURANTS

Athens

HARRY BISSETT'S NEW ORLEANS CAFÉ. ★★
279 E Broad St, Athens (30601). Phone 706/353-7065. www.harrybissetts.com. A popular hangout for local University of Georgia students, this old bank building on the main street of downtown Athens has retained the tin ceilings and brickwork of its original 1860s structure. Fresh seafood is flown in every day, and the barbecued shrimp is a favorite on the Cajun/Creole menu. Lunch, dinner. Closed Dec 25. Bar. Casual attire. Outdoor seating. **$$**

Atlanta

THE CABIN. ★★
2678 Buford Hwy NE, Atlanta (30324). Phone 404/315-7676. A private cabin until the 1980s, the owners converted and expanded the space to accommodate both an upstairs and a downstairs kitchen. The atmosphere and the menu of the restaurant reflect an interesting mix of Southern country charm and

contemporary influences. American menu. Lunch, dinner. Closed Sun; holidays. Bar. Casual attire. Valet parking. $$

CHOPS. ★★★
70 W Paces Ferry Rd, Atlanta (30305). Phone 404/262-2675. www.buckheadrestaurants.com. Two restaurants in one: upstairs is a clubby steakhouse where power diners chomp on delicious prime aged beef; downstairs is the Lobster Bar, where romantic diners sit in white stucco grottos and savor delicate seafood creations. Steak menu. Lunch, dinner. Closed holidays. Bar. Casual attire. Valet parking. $$$

COWTIPPERS. ★
1600 Piedmont Ave, Atlanta (30324). Phone 404/874-3751. www.cowtippersatlanta.com. With a rustic cowboy theme, this steakhouse features an expansive menu of beef and fish specialties. Imaginative details are found throughout the restaurant, including tables painted in cowhide patterns, tin ceilings above the bar, and open-beam ceilings in the dining area. Steak menu. Lunch, dinner. Bar. Children's menu. Casual attire. Outdoor seating. $$

DANTE'S DOWN THE HATCH. ★★
3380 Peachtree Rd NE, Atlanta (30326). Phone 404/266-1600. www.dantesdownthehatch.com. Surrounding diners with an eclectic mix of nautical décor, this fondue restaurant houses antiques and a ship built inside the dining room. Cabin-style booths and a pond with turtles and alligators add to the experience. Swiss menu. Dinner. Closed Jan 1, Dec 25. Bar. Casual attire. $$$

DUSTY'S BARBECUE. ★
1815 Briarcliff Rd NE, Atlanta (30329). Phone 404/320-6264. www.dustys.com. Located near Emory University, this popular spot is decorated with all manner of pig paraphernalia, but the draw is the tangy barbecue. Ask for the "sizzling sauce" if you want a more fiery experience. Locals rave about the blackberry cobbler. Barbecue menu. Lunch, dinner. Children's menu. Casual attire. Outdoor seating. $

FIRE OF BRAZIL CHURRASCARIA. ★★
118 Perimeter Center W, Atlanta (30346). Phone 770/551-4367. www.fireofbrazil.com. This unique Brazilian steakhouse is perfect for diners looking for a totally new experience. The focus here is grilled meats—beef, pork, lamb, chicken, and sausage—brought to each table and carved to the guest's liking, and accompanied by a huge 150-item buffet. Brazilian menu. Lunch, dinner. Bar. Children's menu. Casual attire. $$$

GEORGIA GRILLE. ★
2290 Peachtree Rd, Atlanta (30309). Phone 404/352-3517. www.georgiagrille.com. Serving Southwestern fare in a friendly environment since 1990, this restaurant was named for and inspired by the art of Georgia O'Keeffe. Small oil paintings are featured throughout the dining room, as are hand-painted tables and an antique cake cooler. Southwestern menu. Dinner. Closed Mon; Thanksgiving, Dec 25. Bar. Casual attire. $$

IMPERIAL FEZ. ★★
2285 Peachtree Rd NE, Atlanta (30309). Phone 404/351-0870. www.imperialfez.com. Belly dancers move to Moroccan music while customers sit at low tables with silk-cushioned seating and enjoy the exotic but traditional food under tented ceilings. Moroccan menu. Dinner. Bar. Children's menu. Casual attire. Valet parking. $$$

INDIGO COASTAL GRILL. ★★
1397 N Highland Ave, Atlanta (30306). Phone 404/876-0676. With hardwood floors, crisp white tablecloths, and an open-beam ceiling, this seafood restaurant is a quiet oasis in the middle of the bustle of the Virginia-Highland neighborhood. Specializing in fresh seafood, the kitchen also prides itself on organic vegetables and fabulous Key lime pie. Seafood menu. Dinner. Closed Tues; July 4, Thanksgiving, Dec 25. Bar. Casual attire. Outdoor seating. $$

KYMA. ★★★
3085 Piedmont Rd, Atlanta (30305). Phone 404/262-0702. www.buckheadrestaurants.com. Meaning "wave" in Greek, Kyma serves wine and appetizers on the year-round patio. Inside, sit under the unique painted constellations that adorn the ceilings. The restaurant specializes in classic Greek dishes, especially fresh seafood. In the entry is a unique piece of traditional Greek art made from bits of broken plates. Greek menu. Dinner. Closed Sun. Bar. Casual attire. Outdoor seating. $$

MARY MAC'S TEA ROOM. ★
224 Ponce de Leon Ave NE, Atlanta (30308). Phone 404/876-1800. An informal neighborhood café for more than 50 years, Mary Mac's offers traditional "meat and three" meals and super-sweet iced tea. Southern/Soul menu. Breakfast, lunch, dinner. Closed

Dec 25-Jan 1. Bar. Children's menu. Casual attire. **$**

MCKINNON'S LOUISIANE. ★

3209 Maple Dr, Atlanta (30305). Phone 404/237-1313. www.mckinnons.com. Fresh seafood is the big draw at this Buckhead location, where meals are served in the casual Grill Room or a more formal dining room. Cajun/Creole menu. Dinner. Closed Sun; holidays. Bar. Children's menu. Business casual attire. Reservations recommended. **$$**

PHILIPPE'S BISTRO. ★★

10 Kings Cir, Atlanta (30305). Phone 404/231-4113. www.philippesbistro.com. Award-winning Belgian chef-owner Philippe Haddad has made this restaurant one of the Buckhead neighborhood's most popular dinner destinations. The menu offers specialties from Haddad's native country alongside more familiar, yet innovative, upscale fare. Brunch is also a special treat here, offering, of course, authentic Belgian waffles, as well as other tantalizing dishes. Belgian menu. Dinner. Children's menu. Casual attire. Outdoor seating. **$$$**

PLEASANT PEASANT. ★★

555 Peachtree St, Atlanta (30308). Phone 404/874-3223. www.thepeasantrestaurants.com. In an old building, slightly off the beaten path of Peachtree Street, this restaurant is a local favorite for relaxed dining. It specializes in unique dishes such as lobster sliders and pecan-crusted salmon. American menu. Lunch, dinner, brunch. Closed Thanksgiving, Dec 25. Bar. Children's menu. Casual attire. Outdoor seating. **$$**

RAY'S ON THE RIVER. ★★

6700 Powers Ferry Rd, Atlanta (30339). Phone 880/955-1187. Just from looking at the menu of this river-view restaurant, it's clear that this place is serious about seafood. Selections of steak, chicken, and pork are also available. Seafood menu. Lunch, dinner. Closed Dec 25. Bar. Children's menu. Casual attire. Outdoor seating. **$$**

SOUTH CITY KITCHEN. ★★

1144 Crescent Ave, Atlanta (30309). Phone 404/873-7358. www.southcitykitchen.com. A popular, upscale restaurant featuring variations on traditional Southern cuisine. Southern menu. Lunch, dinner, brunch. Bar. Business casual attire. Reservations recommended. Outdoor seating. **$$**

THE VARSITY. ★

61 North Ave NW, Atlanta (30308). Phone 404/881-1706. The Varsity has been serving Atlanta its famous chilidogs, onion rings, and fried apple pies since 1928. Servers shout orders like Naked Dog, Walk the Dog, Jo-Ree, and Bag of Rags while avoiding collisions with each other in almost choreographed confusion. It's a show all to itself. American menu. Lunch, dinner. Outdoor seating. **$**

THE VININGS INN. ★★

3011 Paces Mill Rd, Atlanta (30339). Phone 770/438-2282. www.viningsinn.com. Featuring a range of dining areas, including the Sunroom, Bear Room, and the Attic Bar, this restaurant is great for anything from drinks and appetizers, to a romantic dinner for two, to a large family gathering. Originally a residence from the 1850s, the restaurant has become a destination for an upscale yet relaxed dining experience. American menu. Lunch, dinner. Closed Sun. Bar. Casual attire. Outdoor seating. **$$$**

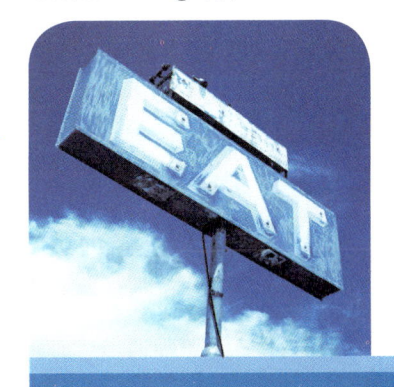

ROAD FOOD

For classic Southern food with a modern twist, Atlanta's oldest continuously operating restaurant has kept locals coming back again and again for years. Originally a country inn, **Horseradish Grill** ★★ gets herbs fresh from an outdoor patch and specializes in variations on old favorites: try the rosemary-grilled lamb chop with Dijon-mint jelly glaze, and fried green tomatoes with melted goat cheese and spicy pecans. Southern/Soul menu. Lunch, dinner. Closed Jan 1, Dec 25. Bar. Children's menu. Casual attire. Outdoor seating. **$$** *14320 Powers Ferry Rd. Phone 404/255-7277. www.horseradishgrill.com.*

ZOCALO. ★
187 10th St, Atlanta (30309). Phone 404/249-7576. www.zo-ca-lo.com. Famous for its margaritas and selection of more than 100 types of tequila, this Mexican hot spot is located just a block from Peachtree. Colorful painted tables and chairs, antique signs and pictures, and old-fashioned chandeliers give the dining area a desert saloon feel, while roll-down windows let in refreshing breezes. Mexican menu. Lunch, dinner, Sun brunch. Closed Mon; holidays. Children's menu. Casual attire. Outdoor seating. $$

Carrollton

MAPLE STREET MANSION. ★
401 Maple St, Carrollton (30117). Phone 770/834-2657. This turn-of-the-century mansion has been turned into a charming restaurant and banquet site. Some Carrollton residents insist the house is haunted by several spirits. American menu. Lunch, dinner. Closed Sun; Jan 1, Dec 24-25. Bar. $$

Norcross

ZAPATA. ★
5975 Peachtree Pkwy, Norcross (30092). Phone 770/248-0052. Serving traditional Mexican food and featuring live music on Fridays and Saturdays, this colorfully decorated restaurant offers friendly service and more moderate portions—perfect for diners who want to try a few new things. Mexican menu. Lunch, dinner. Bar. Casual attire. $

LOCAL RECOMMENDATIONS

Atlanta

BONES.
3130 Piedmont Rd, Atlanta (30305). Phone 404/237-2663. www.bonesrestaurant.com. Thick steaks, kicking drinks, and a varied wine list has kept Bones thriving amidst the intense competition. Steakhouse menu. Lunch, dinner. Closed Jan 1. $$$

FLYING BISCUIT CAFÉ.
1655 McLendon Ave, Atlanta (30307). Phone 404/687-8888. www.flyingbiscuit.com. Dependably filling breakfast entrées are served all day. The café also has a variety of vegetarian offerings. American menu. Breakfast, lunch, dinner. Casual attire. $

FRATELLI DI NAPOLI.
2101 Tula St NW, Atlanta (30309). Phone 404/351-1533. www.fratelli.net. The family-style approach at this restaurant is great for large groups and, of course, families. Classic Italian favorites are available from chicken marsala to eggplant parmigiana to fusilli with broccoli. Italian menu. Dinner. Closed Thanksgiving, Dec 25. Bar. Children's menu. Casual attire. Valet parking. $$

Hampton

M & M BISCUITS, INC.
229 Hwy 19/41, Hampton (30228). Phone 770/897-9992. This spot is popular with fans at 4 am on race day. Housed in a nondescript wooden building on the side of Highway 19/41, the owners crank out hot biscuits laden with ham, steak, sausage, or cheese. Get them while you can—the restaurant is only open from 4 am to 2 pm. American menu. Breakfast, lunch. Closed Sat. $

Lovejoy

COUNTRY BUMPKIN CAFÉ.
11714 Hwy 3, Lovejoy (30250). Phone 770/478-0240. Home-style meals at a low price are what you'll find here. Each day choose from several meat entrées, vegetables, and bread. American menu. Lunch, dinner. Closed Sun. $

McDonough

OB'S BBQ.
725 Industrial Blvd, McDonough (30253). Phone 678/432-6002. Plop down on a bench at the wooden table and get ready to feast on tasty barbecue, Brunswick stew, ribs, french fries, and the usual much-loved Southern fare. Also, try some deep-fried pickles. American menu. Lunch, dinner. $

Stockbridge

RON'S SOUTHERN SKILLET.
1704 Hudson Bridge Rd, Stockbridge (30261). Phone 678/565-5858. With dishes like pot roast, collard greens, black-eyed peas, and sweet potatoes, you'd swear you were having Sunday dinner at Grandma's. Choices vary daily. Southern/Soul menu. Lunch, dinner. $

For more dining recommendations, go to www.mobiltravelguide.com

SIDETRIP

Stately Southern style
Savannah, GA

If Atlanta is the child who succeeded in the business world, Savannah is the prettier cousin. Tucked away in the southeastern part of the state, Savannah has a captivating independence and haughtiness that only add to its allure. It may be a long drive, but one you'll be very glad you made.

With its stately mansions and gnarled branches of massive oaks draped with Spanish moss, the city oozes history. Dating to 1733, Savannah was an intricately planned city. The founders laid out a series of neighborhood grids, 1 acre each, with its own town square, family homes, and lush garden areas. The shop merchant area was separate. Historic Savannah maintains that same pattern, and is the largest urban National Historic Landmark District in the country.

The city's commitment to preserving its historic past was sparked in the 1950s by seven women who grew tired of historic mansions being torn down in the name of progress. They purchased a mansion slated for the wrecking ball. Thereafter, as the Historic Savannah Foundation, they began buying historic properties and selling them only to individuals who pledged to restore them. To the benefit of millions who visit Savannah each year, more than 2,000 buildings have been saved.

Most of the historic district can be explored on foot, but tour bus and shuttles are available. Any time is a good time to visit, but springtime in Savannah is particularly stunning.

Savannah, located in southeastern Georgia, is rich with beautiful and historic homes; they are a must-see during your stay. For more information on a visit, go to www.savannahvisit.com or www.savannahgeorgia.com.

The Riverfront, a strip of buildings along the Savannah River waterfront, houses more than 80 shops, bars, restaurants, and artist studios. Clothing boutiques, fine galleries, and many stores selling local arts and crafts dot the nine-block area.

For more Savannah recommendations, go to www.mobiltravelguide.com

With crowds topping the 130,000 mark, even the NASCAR Busch Series races are must-see events at Bristol.

www.mobiltravelguide.com 43

Bristol Motor Speedway

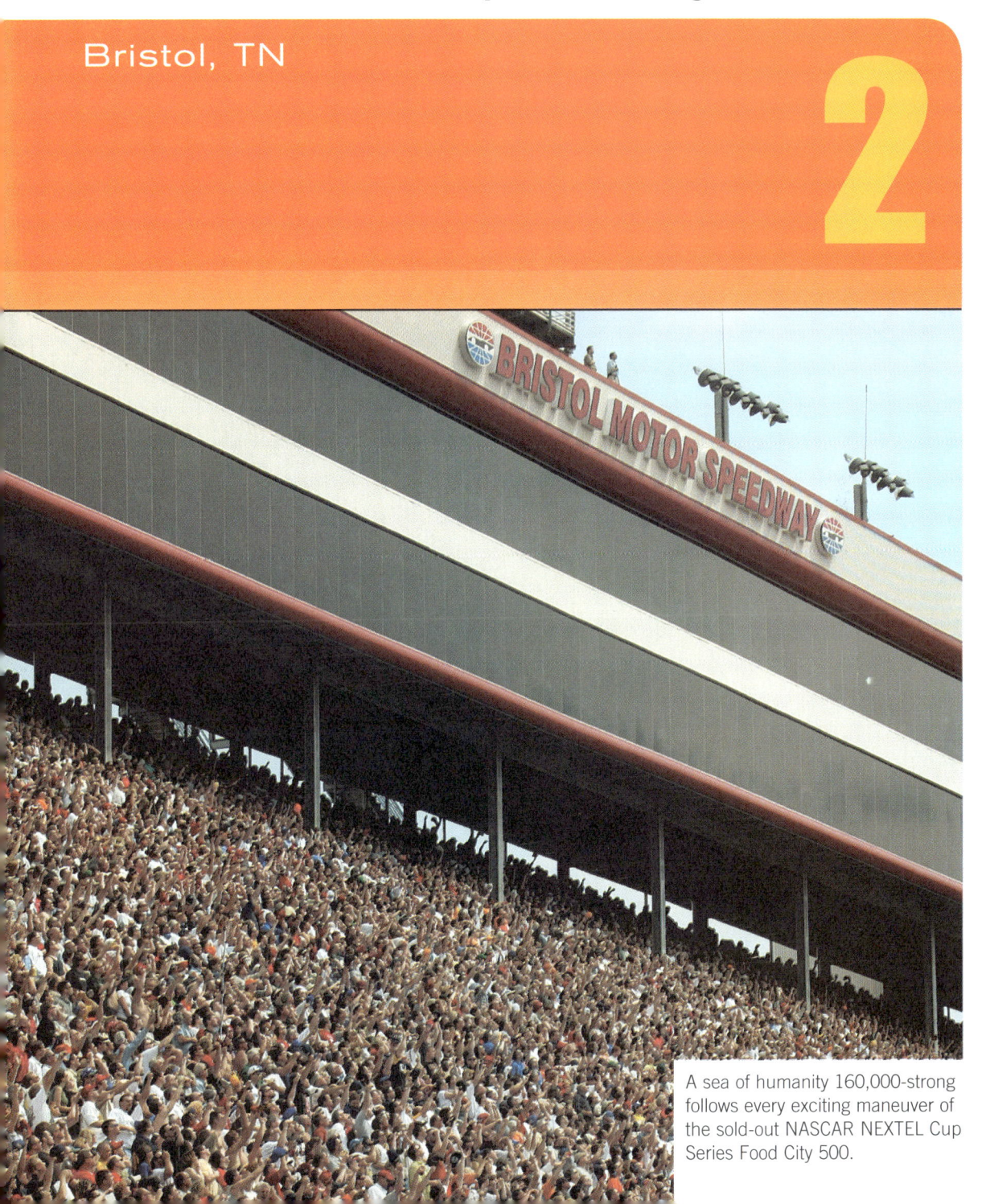

Bristol, TN

2

A sea of humanity 160,000-strong follows every exciting maneuver of the sold-out NASCAR NEXTEL Cup Series Food City 500.

TRACK FACTS

BRISTOL MOTOR SPEEDWAY. 151 Speedway Blvd, Bristol (37620). Phone 423/764-6555. www.bristolmotorspeedway.com.

SECURITY. Coolers are allowed, but they can't be larger than 14 inches long. Each fan can carry in one bag, but it must fit under a seat. The track prohibits umbrellas, folding chairs, glass containers, beer balls, noise makers, balloons, and beach balls. All bags are subject to a search, so fans should enter at least 90 minutes before the start of a race.

FIRST AID. Fully staffed first aid stations are located outside the track between Gates 7 and 8 and inside the track in the north grandstands, the east grandstands, and west grandstands. Ask a track employee which station is closest to your seats.

CONCESSIONS. Local merchants set up temporary markets near the track on race days where basic necessities can be purchased.

PARKING. Parking on the racetrack grounds is limited to those with permits. Those who need handicapped accessible parking must contact Becky Fulwider at 423/989-6931 for a space. The track operates two free parking areas on State Route 394, which offer free shuttles to and from the track. Private lots near the track charge $10-$20 for all-day parking. A parking map can be downloaded from the track's Web site.

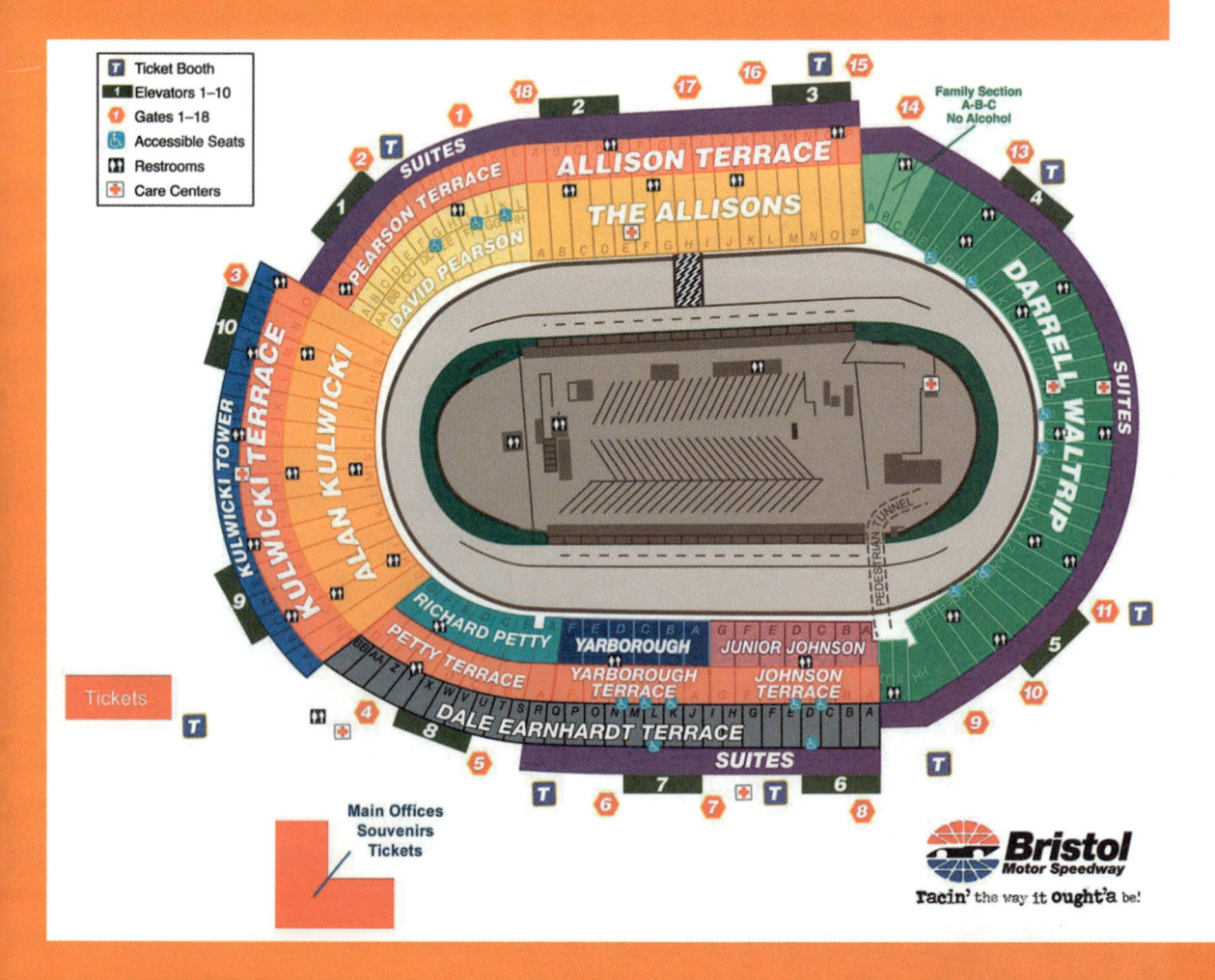

Bristol Motor Speedway
Racin' the way it ought'a be!

GETTING TICKETS

Tickets are always hard to come by for NASCAR NEXTEL Cup events. When current ticketholders give up their seats, the track holds drawings for fans seeking season ticket packages, which range from $280 to $400 per seat. The track has *very* specific instructions on how to apply. Information is available on the track's Web site.

While traveling through Bristol, racegoers might notice ticket scalpers on the Virginia side of the street, because it's illegal to sell tickets for more than face value in Sullivan County, Tennessee.

HOME SWEET (TEMPORARY) HOME

Many local residents open their homes to fans, renting either rooms or the whole house. Expect to pay $100-$200 per bedroom per night with a two-night minimum. Several agencies broker these arrangements, including: Guest Housing Inc. (phone 423/652-0292, www.guesthousing.com); Custom Accommodations (phone 423/418-3330, www.customaccommodations.com); Bristol Race Rentals (phone 423/764-3042); and Abingdon Rentals (www.abingdonrentals.com/racefans.html), which specializes in Virginia properties.

BRISTOL FAN EXPERIENCE

Housed in the administration building alongside the track, this attraction offers visitors the chance to learn more about the speedway and racing in general. It features touch-screen video and audio presentations, a motorsports art gallery, show cars, and driving simulators.

GETTING AROUND

The track is located on Volunteer Pkwy, Tennessee Hwy 11E, on the south side of Bristol. No matter where you're coming from, there's a good chance you'll be arriving via I-81. If you come down I-81 from the north through Virginia, Exit 3 is the shortest route. It leads you through the city, which means congestion on race day, but expert traffic control keeps it from being too onerous. You'll quickly cross State St, the main drag that divides Bristol, Virginia, from Bristol, Tennessee. Look to the right for the big welcome sign with one leg in each state. From the south, take Exit 69 off I-81, then turn right onto Rte 394. The track will be on the left.

The field for the NASCAR NEXTEL Cup Series Food City 500 race awaits the green flag.

Driver Kurt Busch roars across the finish line to win his third race in a row at the half-mile track.

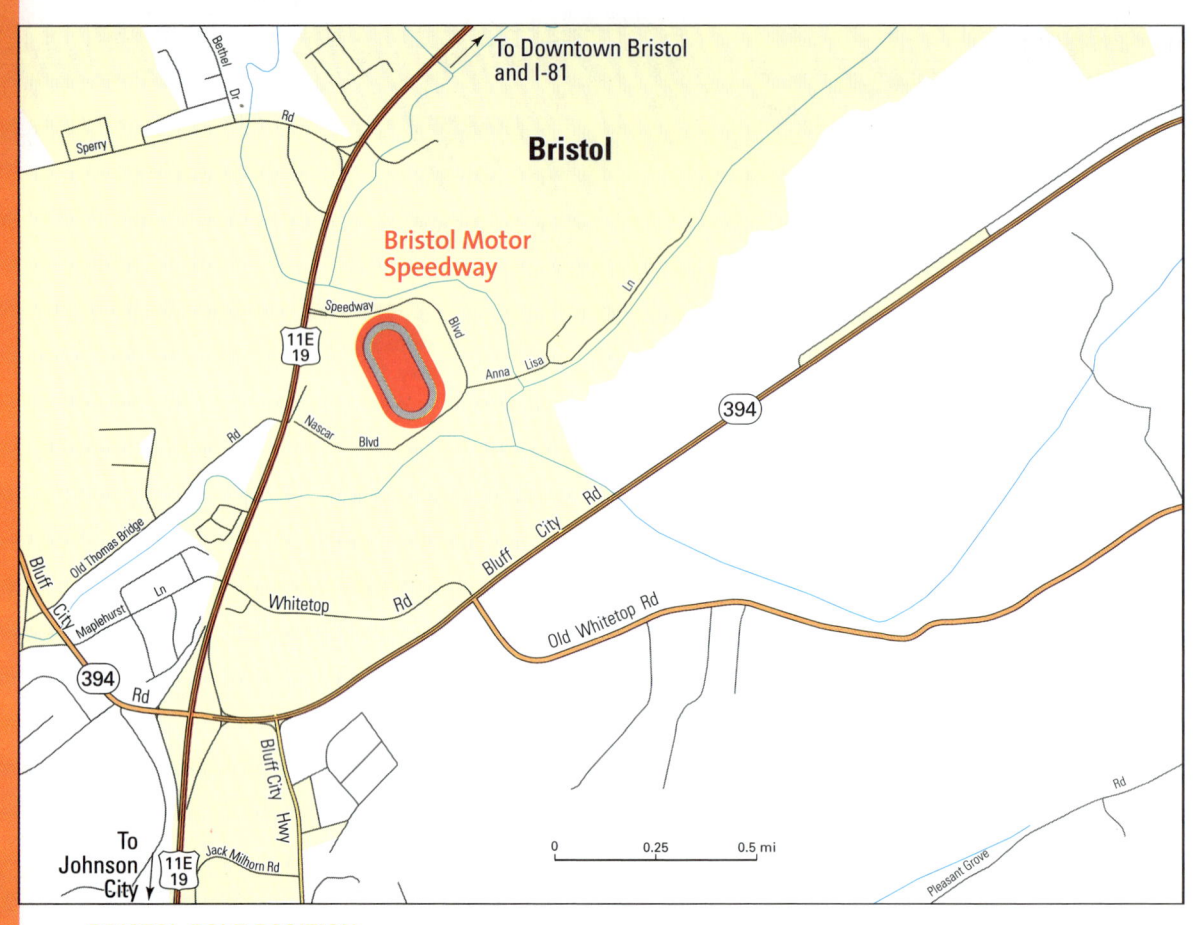

BRISTOL POLE POSITION:
The 10 miles surrounding Bristol Motor Speedway.

HOT TIMES ON THE STATE LINE

Bristol Motor Speedway is the best.

Just ask any driver. As Rusty Wallace, who has won there nine times says, "The track is small, compact, and full of drama. There are a lot of exciting [tracks] around, but nothing like this place."

Or ask a fan. "If you can only go to one NASCAR race in your life, make it the Bristol night race," says James Thomas, a Detroit diehard.

It's entirely fitting that one of the best races in NASCAR is run on a track in the hills of eastern Tennessee, where every local driver learns how to lean into the curves. The rolling back roads in the verdant area follow the path of least resistance around pine-covered shale cliffs towering hundreds of feet above farmland, winding rivers, and streams. This is banked territory—at 36 degrees, the corners on the track are the steepest in NASCAR—and the roads surrounding it are just as challenging. Leave your fuel-efficient compact at home and bring your honkin' 8-cylinder pickup when you visit Bristol.

And come prepared to have a good time. Bristol knows how to party. It's hot in Bristol, even for the August night race, so dress accordingly, and don't forget the sun block. A hat helps, too.

There's not a bad seat at Bristol, and there's plenty to watch. There's rarely a lap without some bumping, nudging, and serious fender-banging. Track owner O. Bruton Smith takes it in from his box above the start/finish line, but the next best thing are the seats beneath his window in Section H of the Allison Terrace. Why, you can even catch a cool breeze from behind, and there's a roof over your head if it ever rains.

BRISTOL CALENDAR

APRIL 1–3, 2005
Charter Communications Pole Day. NASCAR Busch Series Sharpie Professional 250, and NASCAR NEXTEL Cup Series Food City 500

JULY 30–AUGUST 14, 2005
Virginia Highlands Festival. Abingdon, VA (24210). Phone toll-free 800/435-3440. www.vahighlandsfestival.org. Celebrate the cultural arts with antiques, art, photography, music, home and garden tours, and more.

AUGUST 24, 2005
NASCAR Craftsman Truck Series O'Reilly 200 presented by Valvoline MaxLife

AUGUST 25, 2005
Food City Family Race Night. State Street, downtown Bristol. www.foodcity.com. This event includes driver appearances and autograph sessions, as well as driving simulators and racing souvenirs. Followed by the Blue Lizard NASCAR NEXTEL Cup Series Transporter Parade.

AUGUST 26, 2005
NASCAR Busch Series Food City 500

AUGUST 27, 2005
NASCAR NEXTEL Cup Series Sharpie 500

SEPTEMBER, 2005
Rhythm & Roots Reunion. Downtown Bristol (24201). Phone 423/764-1929. www.bristolrhythm.com. Music festival featuring Celtic, gospel, country, bluegrass, Americana, Piedmont blues, and old-time music.

The Bristol area has plenty of outdoor activities for nature lovers.

DRIVER'S PICK

Jerry Cook, Hall of Fame NASCAR Modified Series star and NASCAR Competition Administrator, gets great steaks and a little American history at his favorite Bristol-area restaurant. Built in 1779 as a tavern and stagecoach stop, it has also been used as a barber shop, post office, and hospital for wounded Civil War soliders. "My wife and I like to go to Abingdon (VA) to a place called **The Tavern Restaurant.** It's a very old place still in the original building. It's really a unique experience. They serve a kind of filet there that is terrific." *222 E Main St, Abingdon (24210). Phone 276/628-1118. www.abingdontavern.com.*

BRISTOL OUTFIELD:
The 60 miles surrounding Bristol Motor Speedway.

SEE

ATTRACTIONS

Abington, VA

VIRGINIA CREEPER NATIONAL RECREATION TRAIL.
Phone 276/676-2282; toll-free 800/435-3440. Hikers, bicyclists, equestrians, and anyone who wants to enjoy a good hike will find one on this 34-mile scenic railroad bed converted into a recreational facility. There are numerous shuttle and bike rental facilities nearby.

Blountville, TN

APPALACHIAN CAVERNS.
420 Cave Hill Rd, Blountville (37617). Phone 423/323-2337. www.appalachiancaverns.net. When it's hot, caving will cool you right off. These giant underground chambers, made colorful by deposits of manganese, copper, calcium, and other elements, served Native Americans in need of shelter, hid soldiers during the Civil War, and protected moonshiners during Prohibition. Guided tours (daily).

Bristol, TN/VA

ANTIQUING ON STATE STREET AND COMMONWEALTH AVENUE.
More than 20 large antiques shops are within a half-mile of these two perpendicular streets in downtown Bristol. Those searching for eclectic collectibles and furniture rave about the selection. Check out the Bristol Chamber of Commerce Web site at www.bristolchamber.org for more information.

Bristol, TN

BRISTOL CAVERNS.
1157 Bristol Caverns Hwy, Bristol (37620). Phone 423/878-2011. www.bristolcaverns.com. Another cool choice on a hot day. Native Americans used these elaborate caves for both attacks on and escapes from enemies. **$$**

Bristol, VA

THE BIRTHPLACE OF COUNTRY MUSIC ALLIANCE MUSEUM.
Bristol Mall, I-81, exit 1, Bristol (24201). Phone 276/645-0035; www.birthplaceofcountrymusic.org. Country music pioneers like Jimmie Rodgers, the Carter Family, Jim and Jesse, and Tennessee Ernie Ford all got their starts in Bristol. Every Thursday night, local pickers and singers gather to perform and produce a live radio show from the mall. **FREE**

BRISTOL WHITE SOX.
Devault Memorial Stadium, 1501 Euclid Ave, Bristol (24203). Phone 276/669-6859. www.bristolsox.com. This minor league team is affiliated with the Chicago White Sox. It's a great place to take the kids. (June-Aug) **$**

Erwin, TN

NOLICHUCKY RIVER.
This fast river offers whitewater rafting through some of the deepest gorges east of the Mississippi River. Available only to teens and adults. Tours are operated by Cherokee Adventures (2000 Jonesborough Rd, Erwin; phone 423/743-7733) and USA Raft (Jones Branch Rd, Erwin; phone toll-free 800/872-7238).

KIDS' PICK

Pry your kids away from their Xbox and introduce them to a real slice of Americana. **White's Mill** is a still-functioning grist and flour mill built in 1790. Just 4 1/2 miles from Abingdon, this Virginia Historic Landmark is one of the only water-powered mills in existence in southwestern Virginia. Watch as corn becomes cornmeal and don't forget to take home a sample. Nearby is the working Blacksmith Shop. Closed Monday and Tuesday. *12291 White's Mill Rd, Abingdon (24210). Phone 276/628-2960.*

SEE ATTRACTIONS

Hampton, TN

WATAUGA LAKE.
Hampton (37658). About 20 minutes east of Johnson City off Rte 321. Surrounded by the Cherokee National Forest and flanked by the Appalachian Mountains, Watauga Reservoir is arguably one of the most beautiful in the world and boasts excellent fishing. Below Watauga Dam is a wildlife observation area, where visitors can view waterfowl. The Appalachian Trail passes nearby. Phone 423/587-7037 to purchase fishing licenses.

Hiltons, VA

THE CARTER FOLD.
Poor Valley, at the foot of Clinch Mountain in Hiltons, Virginia, about 20 miles from Bristol. Phone 276/386-9480. www.carterfamilyfold.org. The Carter Family homestead offers an old-time country music and blue grass concert often by top country music performers every Saturday at 7:30 pm. The Fold was established by the children of A. P. and Sara Carter to carry on the musical and performing traditions established by their parents. In keeping with the traditional music style, no electrified instruments are used. There's lots of dancing and fun for the entire family; no alcohol permitted. **DONATION**

For more attractions, go to www.mobiltravelguide.com

STAY

NOTE: Bristol Hotel reservations are extremely hard to find on racing days. First Class Hotel Hotline tracks hotel cancellations. Fans should phone 276/466-5411 to see if any rooms are available.

MOBIL STAR-RATED LODGINGS

Abingdon, VA

COMFORT INN ABINGDON. ★
170 Old Jonesboro Rd, Abingdon (24210). Phone 276/676-2222; toll-free 877/424-6423. www.choicehotels.com. 80 rooms, 2 story. Complimentary continental breakfast. Check-in 3 pm, check-out noon. Outdoor pool. **$**

DAYS INN. ★
887 Empire Dr SW, Abingdon (24210). Phone 276/628-7131; toll-free 800/329-7466. www.daysinn.com. 105 rooms, 2 story. Check-in 3 pm, check-out 11 am. **$**

THE MARTHA WASHINGTON INN. ★★★
150 W Main St, Abingdon (24210). Phone 276/628-3161; toll-free 888/888-5252. www.marthawashingtoninn.com. Experience Southern hospitality at its finest in this historic inn, built as a private residence for a Virginia general in 1832. The original architecture has been painstakingly maintained, with wood floors, crystal chandeliers, and plaster detailing. Meals served in The Dining Room are innovative and well prepared. 62 rooms. Check-in 3 pm, check-out 11 am. Three restaurants, bar. **$$$**

Bristol, VA

COMFORT INN BRISTOL. ★
2368 Lee Hwy, Bristol (24201). Phone 276/466-3881; toll-free 877/424-6423. www.choicehotels.com. 60 rooms, 2 story. Complimentary continental breakfast. Check-in 3 pm, check-out 11 am. Fitness room. Outdoor pool. Business center. **$**

LA QUINTA INN BRISTOL. ★
1014 Old Airport Rd, Bristol (24201). Phone 276/669-9353; toll-free 866/725-1661. www.laquinta.com. A favorite with sports fans and not just those visiting for NASCAR races. The proximity to the Bristol Multi-Purpose Sports Complex is a big draw. 123 rooms, 4 story. Pets accepted. Complimentary continental breakfast. Check-in 1 pm, check-out noon. Outdoor pool. **$**

RAMADA INN BRISTOL. ★
2221 Euclid Ave, Bristol (24201). Phone 276/669-7171; toll-free 800/272-6232. www.ramada.com. This hotel has all the modern conveniences, but the real draw is its close proximity to the Bristol Motor Speedway. 123 rooms, 2 story. Check-in 2 pm, check-out noon. Restaurant, bar. Outdoor pool. **$**

Johnson City, TN

DOUBLETREE HOTEL JOHNSON CITY. ★★
211 Mockingbird Ln, Johnson City (37604). Phone 423/929-2000; toll-free 800/222-8733. www.doubletree.com. Near Interstate 81 and other major highways and within walking distance of shopping at the Roan Centre and multiscreen movie theater. 184 rooms,

Pets accepted. Check-in 3 pm, check-out noon. High-speed Internet access. Restaurant, bar. Fitness room. Indoor pool, outdoor pool. Airport transportation available. Business center. $

LOCAL RECOMMENDATIONS

Abingdon, VA

QUALITY INN & SUITES.
930 E Main St, Abingdon (24210). Phone 276/676-9090; toll-free 877/424-6423. www.qualityinn.com. 75 rooms, 4 story. Check-in 3 pm, check-out 11 am. Fitness room. Outdoor pool. Business center. $

Boone, NC

BEST WESTERN BLUE RIDGE PLAZA.
840 E King St, Boone (28607). Phone 828/266-1100; toll-free 800/780-7234. www.bestwestern.com. This hotel is located on a hillside with sweeping views of the Blue Ridge Mountains and close to a number of tourist attractions, as well as Appalachian State University. 73 rooms, 3 story. Check-in 3 pm, check-out 11 am. High-speed Internet access. Indoor pool. $

Bristol, TN

HAMPTON INN BRISTOL.
3299 W State St, Bristol (37620). Phone 423/764-3600; toll-free 800/426-7866. www.hamptoninn.com. This hotel is adjacent to the Bristol Regional Medical Center and 2 miles from the downtown area. 90 rooms, 4 story. Check-in 2 pm, check-out 11 am. Outdoor pool. $

REGENCY INN.
975 Volunteer Pkwy, Bristol (37620). Phone 423/968-9474. This comfortable facility is in the heart of Tennessee Valley Authority lake country. 39 rooms, 2 story. Check-in 2 pm, check-out noon. Outdoor pool. $

Bristol, VA

HOLIDAY INN & SUITES BRISTOL CONFERENCE CENTER.
3005 Linden Dr, Bristol (24201). Phone 276/466-4100; toll-free 866/655-4669. www.holiday-inn.com. 226 rooms, 10 story. Check-in 3 pm, check-out noon. High-speed Internet access. Restaurant, bar. Fitness room. Outdoor pool, whirlpool. $

Johnson City, TN

BEST WESTERN JOHNSON CITY HOTEL & CONFERENCE CENTER.
2406 N Roan St, Johnson City (37601). Phone 423/282-2161; toll-free 877/504-1007. www.bwjohnsoncity.com. Visitors to the Johnson City area, as well as business travelers, will appreciate everything this extensive hotel has to offer. Enjoy a great meal at the Rocky River Grill, laze around in the huge outdoor pool (the largest one in town), and check out the jukebox in the hotel lounge area. 180 rooms, 4 story. Pets accepted; fee. Complimentary continental breakfast. Check-in 3 pm, check-out 11 am. High-speed Internet access. Restaurant, bar. Fitness room. Outdoor pool. Airport transportation available. $

PIT PASS

Raring for some track time of your own? Take a ride to Sevierville, about two hours from Bristol, where you can get into the action—and into the cars—at **NASCAR SpeedPark.** Eight tracks offer levels ranging from the quarter-mile Smoky Mountain Speedway for drivers 16 and older, down to the Baby Bristol, a 200-foot starter track for kids. Or climb into a mock stock car and experience centrifugal forces, turns, and crash impacts as you "drive" a full-motion **NASCAR Silicon Motor Speedway** simulator. Other attractions include a state-of-the-art arcade, kiddie rides, an indoor climbing wall, miniature golf, and bumper boats. $$$$ *1545 Pkwy, Sevierville (37862). Phone 865/908-5500. www.nascarspeedpark.com.*

STAY RV AND CAMPING

RV AND CAMPING

The Bristol Chamber of Commerce estimates that more than half of the 160,000 racegoers camp in the immediate area. Before you rent a camping spot sight unseen, there are three important questions to ask:

1) How level is the site? Temporary campgrounds with rugged terrain can be very uncomfortable. 2) Is it in the flood plain? When it rains, low-lying campgrounds located near water will flood. 3) How long after the race is over before I can leave the track? Traffic control prevents some campgrounds from opening their gates for at least an hour, sometimes longer, after the race is over.

Abingdon, VA

RIVERSIDE CAMPGROUND.
18496 N Fork River Rd, Abingdon (24210). Exit 14, off I-81, 31 miles from the track. Phone 276/628-5333. 96 sites with full hook-ups, 68 with water/electric. Swimming pool, bingo hall, live music.

WOLF LAIR VILLAGE & CAMPGROUND.
19091 County Park Rd, Abingdon (24211). Exit 17 off I-81, 16 miles from the track. Phone 276/628-3680. 48 sites, most with full hook-ups. Half-mile from South Holston Lake. Miniature golf, swimming pool equipped with diving board and slide.

Bluff City, TN

ALL AMERICAN CAMPGROUND.
251 White Top Rd, Bluff City (37618). Behind the Darrell Waltrip Tower. Phone 423/279-0031, www.allamericancampgrounds.com. As steep as a ski slope and terraced—this isn't the place for a camper pulled by an underpowered vehicle. 1,000 reserved and 1,000 unreserved sites. Use of water, waste-dump stations, shower house, and a shuttle to the Bristol Mall included in the fee.

FARMER BOB'S CAMPGROUND.
583 White Top Rd, Bluff City (37618). Across from the Dragway on Hwy 394, Bristol Beltway. Phone 423/538-8670. www.farmerbobcampground.com. More than 100 flat acres. Showers and port-a-potties. Shuttles provided, but the walk to the track is less than a half-mile. Reservations accepted.

GENTRY'S PARKING & CAMPING.
190 White Top Rd, Bluff City (37618). Phone 423/538-6124 or 423/538-5975. Outside of Turn 3 to the left of the entrance to the All American Campground. Flat, very close to the track, but not much in the way of amenities besides port-a-potties, water, and golf carts to shuttle you to the track. No reservations.

Bristol, TN

BLUE OX CAMPGROUND AT BRISTOL DRAGWAY.
151 Speedway Blvd, Bristol (37620). Phone 423/764-1161. The track property has 1,300 campsites. RV sites are only 16 x 40 feet, which doesn't leave much tailgating space. No hook-ups, but dump stations, water spigots, and a 44-stall shower house and toilets are included in the $120 per race-week fee. These sites fill up quickly with renewing ticketholders getting the first shot. If you're a new ticket purchaser and think you might want to camp here, pay the fee. You can always resell the spot later. New $400 premium spots are being added.

EARHART STATION.
Just north of the track. Phone 423/764-4406. www.earhartcampground.com. Generally considered the most attractive off-site campground with big, flat spots, although if it rains, it floods. No hook-ups. Extra charge for using the shower house. Campground opens Sunday before the race; get there no later than Tuesday for the best locations. Reservations accepted for Earhart Ridges only.

SHADRACK CAMPGROUND.
2537 Volunteer Pkwy, Bristol (37620). About a mile from the track. Phone 423/652-0120. www.shadrack.com/camp. RV dealer offering level sites with shade. Some electric/water hook-ups, shower house, and an RV service technician available. Dealer also rents fully equipped RVs. Reservations required.

Kingsport, TN

WARRIORS' PATH STATE PARK.
490 Hemlock Rd, Kingsport (37663). Exit 59 off I-81, about 25 miles south of the track. Phone 423/239-8531. www.state.tn.us/environment/parks. 135 wooded sites with tables and grills with access to water and 94 equipped hook-ups. Air-conditioned restrooms with hot showers. On the shores of Patrick Henry Reservoir on the Holston River. Boat rental available at the marina, horseback riding, swimming pool. No reservations. Campground usually full by Tuesday of race week.

For other camping options, check the Bristol Motor Speedway Web site at **www.bristolmotorspeedway.com/fan_guide/camping**.

For more lodging recommendations, go to www.mobiltravelguide.com

EAT

MOBIL STAR-RATED RESTAURANTS

Johnson City, TN

FIREHOUSE. ★
627 W Walnut St, Johnson City (37604). Phone 423/929-7377. Set in an old firehouse in downtown Johnson City, this family restaurant prides itself on friendly service and hickory-smoked specialties. Kids will be fascinated by the old fire engine and fireman memorabilia. American menu. Lunch, dinner. Closed Sun; Thanksgiving, Dec 25. **$**

PEERLESS. ★ ★
2531 N Roan St, Johnson City (27601). Phone 423/282-2351. This award-winning restaurant is often recognized as Johnson City's best. It specializes in banquets and large groups. American menu. Dinner. Closed Sun; holidays. Reservations recommended. **$$**

Knoxville, TN

APPLE CAKE TEA ROOM. ★
11312 Station W Dr, Knoxville (37922). Phone 865/966-7848. Pop into this unbelievably quaint café for a quick lunch or snack, located among boutique shops and the Tennessee countryside. American menu. Lunch. Closed Sun; holidays. Reservations recommended. **$**

CALHOUNS. ★ ★
10020 Kingston Pike, Knoxville (37922). Phone 865/673-3444. Featuring its own microbrew, this popular American restaurant also serves a huge array of Southern pub and barbecue favorites, including prime rib, fried catfish, and, yes, fried green tomatoes. American, barbecue menu. Lunch, dinner. Closed Dec 25. Bar. **$$**

CHESAPEAKE'S. ★ ★
500 N Henley St, Knoxville (37922). Phone 865/673-3433. The seafood in this nautically themed spot is just about as fresh as you can get in a landlocked state—hence, why the restaurant is named after a known seafood mecca. Seafood menu. Lunch, dinner. Bar. Reservations recommended. Outdoor seating. **$$$**

COPPER CELLAR. ★ ★
1807 Cumberland Ave, Knoxville (37916). Phone 856/673-3411. Owned by the same company that runs both Chesapeake's and Calhoun's (see), this special-occasion restaurant boasts great American fare teamed with amazingly fresh seafood dishes like baked stuffed shrimp. Also serving Calhoun's specialty microbrew. American menu. Lunch, dinner. Closed Sun; Jan 1, Thanksgiving, Dec 25. Bar. Reservations recommended. **$$**

LOCAL RECOMMENDATIONS

Abingdon, VA

ALISON'S RESTAURANT.
1220 W Main St, Abingdon (24210). Phone 276/628-8002. Alison's used to be a drive-in and isn't much to look at with old Formica counters and plastic chairs scavenged from K-Mart's bankruptcy sale. The food, however, is great. American menu. Lunch, dinner. **$$**

ROAD FOOD

You smell the barbecue long before you round a curve to see the yellow sign and green awning of the longtime local favorite, **Ridgewood Barbecue.** The Ridgewood has been cooking barbecue the same way since 1948, from a pit dug at the side of the parking lot. As you walk in, admire the roasting pork and beef—both are good but food fanatics say go for the pork. Expect long waits for a seat in one of three dining rooms, assuming you can find this well-hidden gem. Pssssst...get directions from a local. Barbecue menu. *900 Elizabethton Hwy, Bluff City (37618). Phone 423/538-7543.*

EAT LOCAL RECOMMENDATIONS

Bristol, TN

MAD GREEK RESTAURANT.
2419 Volunteer Pkwy, Bristol (37620). Phone 423/968-4848. Besides a Greek menu, there's pizza, calzones, and stromboli. Prices are reasonable; a large pizza is the same price whether you choose one topping or ten. Greek, Italian menu. Lunch, dinner. **$$**

SIMPLY DELICIOUS MARKET PLACE.
2600 Volunteer Pkwy, Bristol (37620). Phone 423/764-3354. Also known as the Bruton Speedway Club, this New York-style deli is just a half-mile north of the speedway. The deli gives a nod to Bristol Speedway's president and general manager with the Jeff Byrd Platter of chicken and tuna salads on a bed of lettuce. Deli menu. Lunch, dinner. **$**

STATE LINE BAR AND GRILLE.
644 State St, Bristol (37620). Phone 423/652-0792. This bar rocks. On Food City Family Race Night, it's definitely the place to be. It is located in a nicely restored old building with high ceilings and lots of space, and even on a busy night, it doesn't feel overly crowded. American menu Lunch, dinner. **$$**

TROUTDALE DINING ROOM.
412 6th St, Bristol (37620). Phone 423/968-9099. This stately Victorian home-turned-restaurant has a 600-gallon trout tank and serves seven different preparations of that favored fish. A variety of steak, chicken, duck, lamb, and veal will satisfy land lubbers. Seafood, American menu. Dinner. **$$$**

Bristol, VA

BURGER BAR.
8 Piedmont Ave, Bristol (24201). Phone 276/466-6200. Hank Williams supposedly ate his last meal here in 1952. Seven of the burgers are named after Hank's songs, including "Move it on Over" with barbecue sauce, bacon, onions, and cheese. At noon, the line snakes out the door. American menu. Breakfast, lunch, dinner. Closed Sun. **$**

FISHTALES & PIGTALES.
Volunteer Pkwy, Bristol (37620). Phone 276/466-3770. Fishtales & Pigtales is located in the back of a strip shopping center. Mostly, fish comes fried. Chicken and barbecue are also on the menu as well. This is a good place for kids—spacious and very informal. Seafood menu. Lunch, dinner. **$$**

GOLDEN DRAGON.
2112 Euclid Ave, Bristol (24201). Phone 276/466-8653. The Golden Dragon looks shabby, but the food isn't. If you're starving after a long day at the track, the buffet will fill you up. Otherwise, order Cantonese and Szechuan off the menu. Chinese menu. Lunch, dinner. Closed Sun. **$**

Johnson City, TN

NASCAR CAFE.
2004 N Roan St, Johnson City (37601). Phone 423/282-9223. Open until midnight Friday and Saturday. Steaks, fish, fried chicken, salads, and lots of NASCAR memorabilia. American menu. Lunch, dinner, late-night. **$$**

COOTIE BROWN'S.
2715 N Roan St, Johnson City (37601). Phone 423/283-4723. American menu. Lunch, dinner. **$$**

DIXIE BARBECUE CO.
3301 N Roan St, Johnson City (37601). Phone 423/283-7447. Fans declare the Dixie has barbecue that's tops. Old license plates and pieces of old stock cars decorate walls. There's pulled pork, smoked chicken, and barbecue beef ribs with your choice of sauce: vinegary North Carolina style, Memphis dry rub, or the local tomato-based favorite. Barbecue menu. Lunch, dinner. Closed Sun. **$**

MID CITY GRILL.
110 Tipton St, Johnson City (37604). Phone 423/434-2741. About half the menu is vegetarian. The late-night menu includes everything from grilled tofu to Da Big Daddy Burger with all the trimmings. American menu. Lunch, dinner, late-night. Closed Sun. **$$**

SOPHISTICATED OTTER RESTAURANT & BREWERY.
400 Ashe St, Johnson City (37604). Phone 423/928-1705. The food is good, but don't go for that alone. There's also a great beer selection and plenty of TVs. American menu. Lunch, dinner. **$$**

Sevierville, TN

NASCAR CAFE.
425 Hurley Dr, Sevierville (37862). Phone 865/428-7223. Steaks, fish, fried chicken, salads, and lots of NASCAR memorabilia. American menu. Lunch, dinner. **$$**

For more dining recommendations, go to www.mobiltravelguide.com

SIDETRIP

Gateway to the Smokies
Pigeon Forge, TN

When the last lap is completed, consider taking the family to Pigeon Forge, gateway to the Smokies and home to singer Dolly Parton's amusement extravaganza, **Dollywood**.

Arrive early and immediately go to the top of Craftsmans Valley, so you'll be among the first of the day to ride the Tennessee Tornado roller coaster. Then try the Blazing Fury indoor coaster. Follow those thrills with your choice among 125 acres of rides, musical shows, and crafts. When you're hot and tired, make the Daredevil Falls splashdown ride your last hurrah.

Admission runs about $40 for a one-day pass. (phone 865/428-9488, www.dollywood.com).

Beyond Dollywood, there are plenty of other attractions, natural and man-made.

At **Cades Cove** in the **Great Smoky Mountains National Park**, you can hop aboard a hay wagon ride that departs from a reconstructed pioneer community and winds its way through the gorgeous scenery. The rides costs $8 per person. Reservations are required (phone 865/448-6286, www.nps.gov/grsm/gsmsite/home/index.html).

The **Veterans Memorial Museum** displays wartime exhibits from the Revolutionary War to present time. Among its more unusual offerings are the death masks of Abraham Lincoln and Robert E. Lee and a collection of gruesome Civil War-era medical equipment. Admission is $11, but veterans get a discount (phone 865/908-6003, www.veteransmemorialpf.com).

If you visit Pigeon Forge in 2005, you'll be among the first fans to enjoy three-time NASCAR Winston Cup Champion **Darrell Waltrip's "Racing Experience,"** a $5 million, 30,000-square-foot attraction set to open in the spring in the Belle Island Village development. Besides simulators, there'll be an interactive theater, competition radio-controlled cars, a pit crew area, an arcade, and both permanent and rotating exhibits including 15-25 actual stock cars.

While in the Great Smoky Mountains, you might meet up with an American black bear. Caution: admire only from a distance. For more information on Pigeon Forge, visit www.mypigeonforge.com, www.pigeonforge.com, or www.pigeonforgechamber.com.

For more Pigeon Forge recommendations, go to www.mobiltravelguide.com

56

The pit crew races to complete work on Kasey Kahne's car during a NASCAR NEXTEL Series race.

California Speedway®

Fontana, CA

3

A field of NASCAR NEXTEL Cup cars rumbles past the front stretch grandstand.

TRACK FACTS

CALIFORNIA SPEEDWAY. 9330 Cherry Ave, Fontana (92335). Phone 909/429-5000. www.california speedway.com.

SECURITY. Hard-sided coolers or containers, backpacks, alcohol, ice, aluminum cans, glass, and pets are prohibited. Soft-sided containers are permitted, with a size limit of 6 x 6 x 12 inches. You're also allowed one clear plastic bag for souvenirs. Alcoholic beverages are not allowed in the grandstands.

PARKING. There are 32,000 free spots, and shuttles run to and from outlying areas where parking is also available. Arrive early to beat the traffic. Call the speedway at 909/429-5000 and ask for guest services to arrange for handicapped transport and grandstand access.

FIRST AID. First aid centers are located at Gates 10, 12, and 14; there are also two centers located underneath the grandstand—one in the east and one in the west. A full-service care center, staffed with doctors, is located in the infield.

CONCESSIONS. Concession stands are scattered throughout the facility: four are at ground level, at the entrance of the grandstands; the terrace area has six. The infield has smaller "portable" stands, and the Pit Row Café is at the infield in the RV area. There are plenty of bathroom options throughout the speedway, but take advantage of shorter lines at restrooms next to Gates 10, 12, 14, and 16.

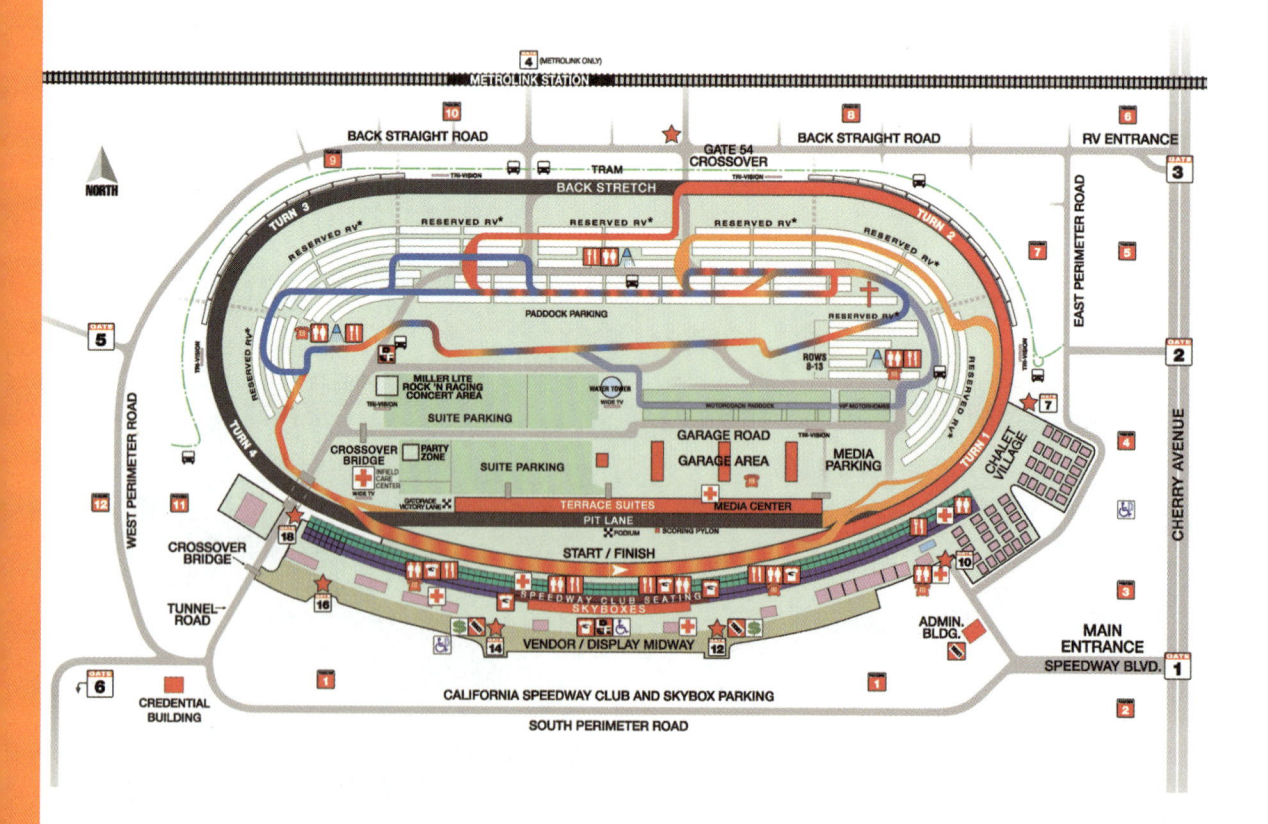

CALIFORNIA SPEEDWAY, CA

COOL CARS, HOT FANS

Established in 1913 by A. B. Miller, Fontana grew from humble beginnings as an agricultural area growing citrus, grain, and grapes, and raising poultry and swine. It was later known for its heavy industry, warehousing, and distribution operations. During World War II, the Kaiser Steel Mill produced the material used in fabricating Liberty ships—it was located in Fontana because, the thinking went, the operations would be well inland and out of range of Japanese bombs.

After the war, the city became Southern California's leading producer of steel and related products, providing the steel that built skyscrapers in Los Angeles, San Diego, and San Francisco. But by the 1970s, steel production had dwindled, and in 1984, Kaiser was forced to close the enormous mill. Although it left many people out of work, it also left an open space ideally suited for laying a track and racing stock cars. The California Speedway, with a 2-mile D-shaped oval track, opened in 1997, and the

Jamie McMurray (No. 42) and Jeff Gordon (No. 24) battle it out on the track.

The glitz, glamour, and magic of Hollywood all come alive at a movie premiere.

A Southern California landmark since 1935, Griffith Observatory sits high up on Mount Hollywood and offers visitors amazing views of Los Angeles.

former farming center has reaped the benefits of the 568-acre facility.

Today, Fontana is a busy community of about 140,000 people with a glorious mountain backdrop. About 48,000 vehicles travel daily on Sierra Avenue, a main thoroughfare between San Bernardino Avenue and the Interstate 10 entrance. (To avoid traffic, NASCAR drivers often stay in Los Angeles or Beverly Hills and take a helicopter to the speedway, which has two helipads.) Although you won't see much evidence of its agricultural or industrial past today, the city seal pays homage to the sources of its growth with images of steel mills, chicken ranches, and citrus groves.

The track itself has continued to evolve along with the city. In 2004, the superspeedway hosted two NASCAR races for the first time (the speedway's hosted a single event annually since 1997), with the second race taking place on Labor Day weekend when it "Finished Under the Lights," which were installed specifically for the new race.

The area around the speedway offers many lodging options, but, not surprisingly, they sell out quickly for race weekends. If you want to stay in the vicinity of like-minded racegoers, surf online for fan sites that often list popular accommodations for congregating. You

also might want to hit the **Ontario Mills Mall,** where many NASCAR pros hang out. The drivers like it, and locals boast about its worthwhile attractions.

Fontana itself straddles the intersection of two major freeways, the 10 and the 15, as they're called in the parlance of the "Inland Empire," the area around San Bernardino and Riverside counties. Metrolink rail service to the Los Angeles area runs through town, and there's even a stop for the speedway. Attractions such as **Disneyland, Hollywood,** and beaches are all within 50 miles.

Sun, surf, sand—what could be better?

Those 50 miles are packed with a fascinating combination of lakes and forests, urban centers, and rural wilderness. The Inland Empire is tucked between powerful Los Angeles to the west and imposing deserts to the east, and includes the cities of Riverside and San Bernardino. Everything is within reach, but you must brave some of the most intense traffic in the country to get there.

A word about driving: locals can nip across six lanes of 70-mile-an-hour traffic within a quarter-mile of their highway exit. Visitors, however, shouldn't attempt this kind of maneuver. Street signs are not always helpful or in the same place. You'll find them overhead, alongside traffic lights, posted at roadsides, or just plain missing.

In this area, if you miss your freeway exit and take the next one, there might not be a nearby entrance to quickly backtrack, so pay close attention to directions. The single most important way to stay safe and sane is to know where you're going and how to get there. Locals recommend the expensive but highly detailed, bound maps from Thomas Bros. (available at stores or www.thomas.com). If you opt for folding maps, choose one with plenty of detail, even if it means purchasing maps that cover overlapping areas. You can also pick up a *NASCAR Road Atlas* to help with directions closer to the track.

The sun may be setting on Los Angeles, but it isn't time to go to bed—there are many nightclubs and restaurants to check out.

GETTING AROUND

The speedway is accessible off I-10 from Los Angeles and I-15 or I-215 from San Diego. Before heading out, double-check your tickets for your seat assignment—which will help you determine which entrance to use at the track.

Exiting the speedway is also carefully choreographed. From Gate 1, all lanes turn right onto Cherry Ave and take you to I-10 east and west or to the 60 freeway.

From Gate 2, the right lane will turn onto Cherry Ave; then follow Gate 1 instructions. From Gate 3, turn left on Cherry. Turn left on Baseline to the I-15 interchange and follow Cherry to I-210 west. From the Napa St gate, four lanes of traffic exit to Etiwanda. Three lanes go south on Etiwanda to Fourth, where two lanes go west on Fourth to I-15. One lane of traffic follows Etiwanda to the 60 freeway west on Jurupa to I-15. The fourth lane goes north on Etiwanda. Turn left on Arrow, turn right on Rochester, take Foothill East left to I-15 south interchange. If entering or exiting leaves you confused, speedway assistants can help you out.

GETTING TICKETS

The ticket office is open Monday-Friday 8:30 am-4:30 pm. Check for updates on the official speedway Web site, www.californiaspeedway.com, or call the track toll-free at 800/944-7223.

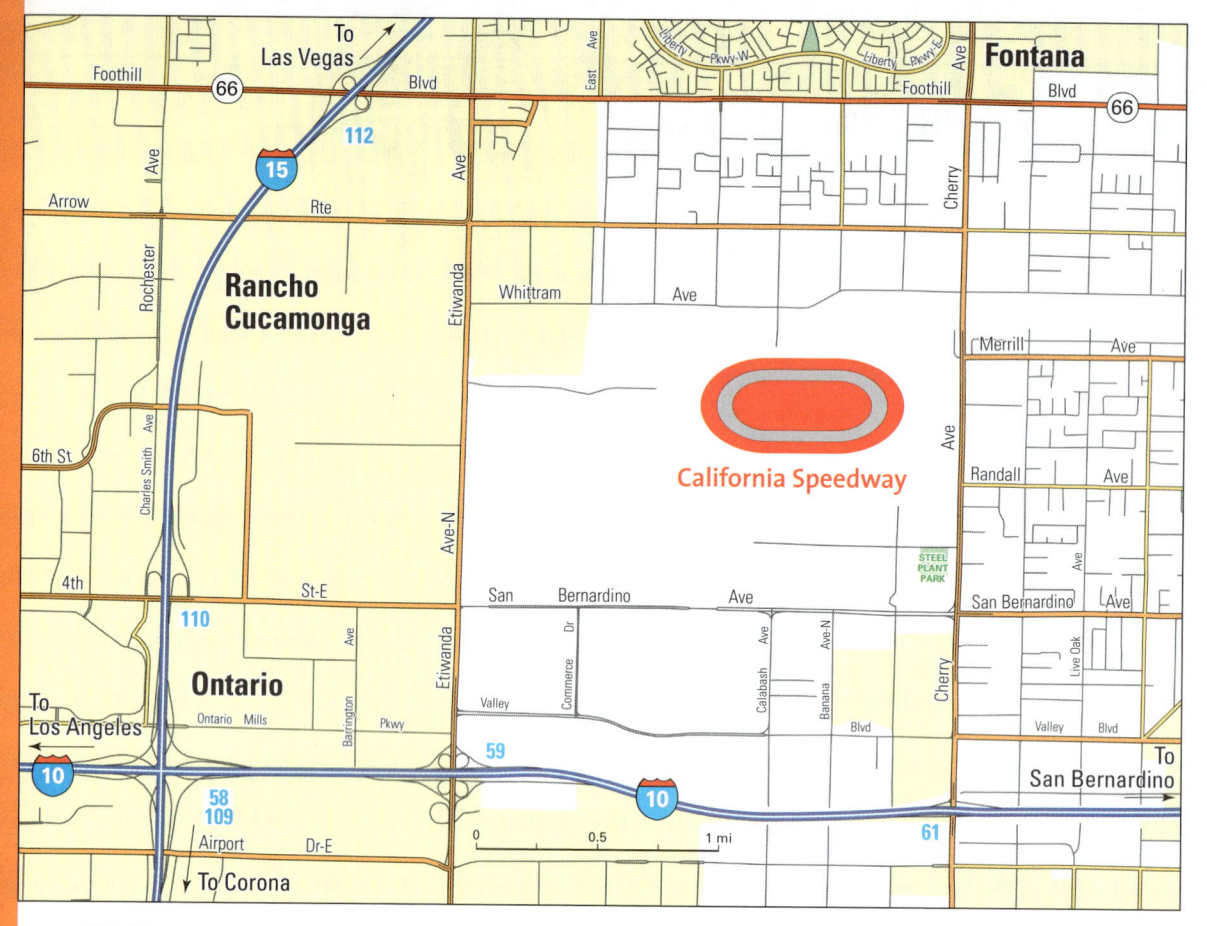

FONTANA POLE POSITION:
The 10 miles surrounding California Speedway.

If you get lost, do not pull over onto the shoulder to read a map (unless your vehicle is broken down, you are liable to be cited and fined by the California Highway Patrol). Get off at the next exit, pull into a safe place, and then figure out how to get back on track.

Other tips: buckle up (it's a state law); don't tailgate as traffic is typically stop-and-go; use turn signals; and stay out of the fast lane. Most importantly, avoid confrontations with other drivers. If your vehicle breaks down, pull over to the shoulder and stay inside with the seatbelts buckled. The California Highway Patrol scans the freeways regularly and officers will find you. Be sure they identify themselves before you unlock your doors.

Tune in to KNX 1070 AM or KFWB 980 AM for frequent traffic reports before you leave on a day trip, or tune in to NASCAR Radio on XM.

Anywhere you wind up in Southern California, the weather is always mild and cooler at night than during the day, so it's a good idea to bring a sweater. Winter weather is typically in the 60s, and the hottest months are July, August, and September, when many days can reach the 90s (close to triple digits at the speedway).

CALIFORNIA SPEEDWAY, CA   63

FONTANA CALENDAR

FEBRUARY 25, 2005
NASCAR Craftsman Truck Series

FEBRUARY 26, 2005
NASCAR Busch Series

FEBRUARY 27, 1005
NASCAR NEXTEL Cup Series

SEPTEMBER 2, 2005
NASCAR Grand National Division

SEPTEMBER 3, 2005
NASCAR Busch Series

SEPTEMBER 4, 2005
NASCAR NEXTEL Cup Series

SEPTEMBER, 2005
Legends of NASCAR Benefit Golf Tournament. Sierra Lakes Golf and Country Club, 1600 Clubhouse Dr, Sierra Lakes (92336). Phone 909/350-7620. www.fontana.org. Race weekend.

SEPTEMBER, 2005
Block Party. Downtown Civic Center Campus, Sierra and Seville aves, Fontana (92335). Phone 909/350-7620. www.fontana.org. Race weekend.

SEPTEMBER, 2005
Los Angeles County Fair. 1101 W McKinley, Pomona (91769). Phone 909/623-3111. www.fairplex.com. This county fair claims to be the largest in North America.

Casey Mears signs an autograph for an admiring fan.

DRIVER'S PICK

1973 Winston Cup Champion and popular race broadcaster **Benny Parsons** offers fans more than the inside track on where to eat when watching the races in Fontana: he offers the possibility of driver sighting—but don't interrupt a hungry driver while he's eating. "Rosa's ★ ★ ★ in Ontario is where I go when I'm out there. Rosa's is an Italian place and everything is good. If you stick around from 6 to 9 pm during race time, you'll probably see some drivers there." $$ *425 N Vineyard Ave, Ontario (91764). Phone 909/937-1220.*

FONTANA OUTFIELD:
The 60 miles surrounding California Speedway.

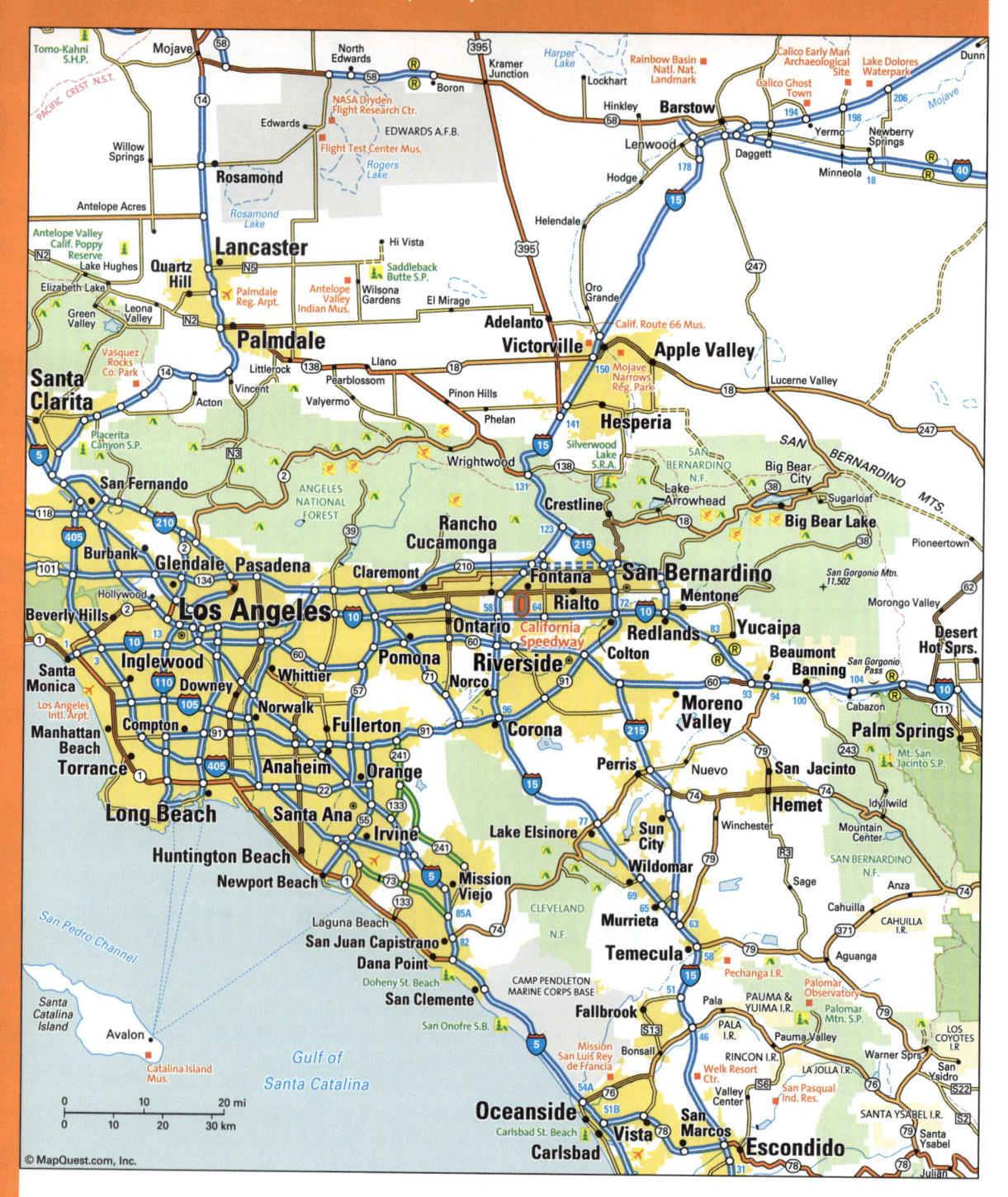

SEE

ATTRACTIONS

Anaheim

DISNEYLAND.
1313 S Harbor Blvd, Anaheim (92803). Phone 714/781-4565. www.disneyland.com. You can't visit Southern California and not go to **Disneyland,** at least the first time. Even otherwise jaded locals admit that no matter how many times they see the Magic Castle from the freeway, they still get a thrill. The "happiest place on Earth" opened in 1955 with 18 major attractions. Now, it has more than 60 attractions on 85 acres. Map out what you want to do and wear comfortable shoes, because there's a whole lotta walkin' going on even with Mouseland's shuttle tram network and monorail. **Disney's California Adventure,** like adjacent Disneyland, offers lots of bang for the buck. The Adventure celebrates the history, culture, landscape, and industry (entertainment, not biotech) of California, using educational aids such as rock climbing and wine tasting. The daily parade and light shows are worthwhile.

Downtown Disney gives you a taste of city life. The jazz is hot, the restaurants varied, and the 12-screen theater shows the latest movies. Sports fans shouldn't miss the **ESPN Zone,** complete with 175 TV screens, interactive games, and live events. If that's not enough, find the Lost Bar in the Disneyland Hotel for more televised sports.

The traditional attractions remain crowd-pleasers and must-dos for newbies. In Adventureland, the Jungle Cruise carries you along tropic rivers to view lifelike alligators, hippos, gorillas, monkeys, water buffalo, and Indian elephants on the banks.

Other lures include the Tarzan Treehouse, the Enchanted Tiki Room, and the Indiana Jones Adventure. The Davy Crockett's Explorer Canoes in Critter Country are also a fun stop. Tomorrowland boosts your faith in the possible with rides exploring inner and outer space. "Honey, I Shrunk the Audience" and Space Mountain never fail to deliver. And Fantasyland may be what most people think of when they think of Disneyland, populated as it is by Pinocchio, Snow White, Dumbo, Peter Pan, and Alice in Wonderland.

Accommodations are available in and around Disneyland, as are guided tours and ATMs. Facilities for the disabled include wheelchair rentals, ramps, and audiocassettes for visually impaired visitors.

Disneyland is open daily, with extended hours during holidays. Downtown Disney admission is free; so are the first three hours of parking. Call 714/781-7290 for a schedule of daily events and a list of attraction closures throughout the land.

Fontana

FONTANA SKATE PARK.
In Juniper Park at Juniper Ave and Filbert St, Fontana (92335). Phone 909/428-8360. www.fontana.org/main/public_serv/skate_park.htm. Rated among the top ten skate parks at www.socalskateparks.com, this facility has street action, intermediate bowl/banks, and a three-bowl clover with an 8- to 9-foot vertical. Protective gear must be worn at all times. (Mon-Wed 9 am-9:30 pm, Thurs noon-9:30 pm, Fri-Sun 9 am-9:30 pm) **FREE**

Hollywood

For many people, Hollywood is the glitzy side of Los Angeles where movie-industry icons hang out on street corners, but it is actually a real neighborhood with much more than a see-and-be-seen, celebrity atmosphere. However, don't let that discourage you from looking for movie stars, because, every so often, you will see someone famous hanging out on a street corner.

Famed **Hollywood Boulevard** is the ultimate tourist destination. It is accepted behavior to snap photos of other tourists as they take pictures of the glittering stars embedded in the sidewalk and gawk at the outlandish **Grauman's Chinese Theatre** (6925 Hollywood Blvd, phone 323/461-3331). The theater is a piece of Hollywood history: its first premiere was in 1927 (Cecil B. DeMille's silent *The King of Kings*), and it hosted Academy Awards ceremonies during the 1940s.

The **Hollywood Walk of Fame** sidewalk runs from La Brea Avenue to Gower Street, and south from Yucca Street to Sunset Boulevard. More than 2,000 celebrities from film, television, theater, and music are honored, with one or two additions a month. (If you want to glimpse a celebrity getting a star, check www.hollywoodchamber.net.)

If you're looking for a great people-watching spot, try the two-block span of Sunset Boulevard between La Cienega and San Vicente. Or you might spot a celebrity shopping at **Sunset Plaza,** a collection of cafés and high-end shops.

SEE ATTRACTIONS

The famed **Hollywood sign,** built in 1923, is in the Hollywood Hills. It started as an advertisement for the Hollywoodland housing development. Although those final four letters disappeared, the hills became a development of sorts—homes of movie stars, producers, and other industry heavy hitters are nestled among winding streets and hidden canyons. Despite LA's notorious pollution, there are some great outdoors here. Take a stroll along **Mulholland Drive,** where you'll get fresh-air vistas above the bustling city. There are also hiking trails—**Griffith Park** is a favorite local destination only 8 miles from downtown Los Angeles. With more than 4,100 acres, it is one of the nation's largest urban park and wilderness areas (www.ci.la.ca.us/RAP/grifmet/griffith.htm).

For more information on Hollywood, contact the Hollywood Chamber of Commerce (7018 Hollywood Blvd, Los Angeles, phone 323/469-8311. www.hollywoodchamber.net). Or contact the Los Angeles Convention and Visitors Information Bureau, 685 S Figueroa St, Los Angeles (90017), phone 213/689-8822.

Irwindale

IRWINDALE SPEEDWAY.
500 Speedway Dr, Irwindale (91706). Phone 626/358-1100. www.irwindalespeedway.com. Located in California's San Gabriel Valley, less than 25 minutes from downtown Los Angeles and about 35 miles from California Speedway, Irwindale's banked 1/2-mile oval hosts NASCAR events mid-March through November. The award-winning NASCAR Toyota All-Star Showdown, which the track ran in 2003 and 2004, brings together the top regional touring drivers from across the country in a one-of-a-kind, head-to-head event. The stands seat about 6,500. Ticket prices vary.

Los Angeles

PETERSEN AUTOMOTIVE MUSEUM.
6060 Wilshire Blvd, Los Angeles (90036). Phone 323/930-CARS (2277). www.petersen.org. This museum features a permanent exhibit of classic hot rods, an interactive area where kids can learn how a police radar gun works, and curated exhibitions. (Tues-Sun 10 am-6 pm; closed Jan 1, Thanksgiving, Dec 25) **$$**

Ontario

ONTARIO MILLS MALL.
1 Mills Cir, Ontario (91764). Phone 909/484-8300. www.ontariomills.com. This is California's largest entertainment and outlet mall—1.7 million square feet (that's 38 football fields) of retail entertainment under one roof. It's the kind of place where busloads of foreign tourists troop in to make mass souvenir purchases. Retail outlets include Nordstrom Rack, Off Fifth, JCPenney, and the small, but comfortable, Love Sac shop. Attractions include an enormous Dave & Buster's with a Million Dollar Midway, billiards, golf simulator, and dining room. (Mon-Sat 10 am-9:30 pm, Sun 10 am-8 pm)

Pasadena

KIDSPACE CHILDREN'S MUSEUM.
480 N Arroyo Blvd, Pasadena (91103). Phone 626/449-9144. www.kidspacemuseum.org. Scheduled to open by the end of 2004 at this new location, the museum features lots of indoor and outdoor exhibits. Kids can climb aboard raindrops as they travel through the precipitation cycle, or they can dig up fossils and dinosaur eggs. (Daily 9:30 am-5 pm) **$$**

PIT PASS

Unless you're a season site holder, renting one of 59 spots from **El Monte RV** is the best infield RV option. The company, which operates at other NASCAR tracks, also rents motor homes. Packages run Wednesday to Monday and include parking for your own vehicle; up to four infield passes; motor home delivery, pickup, and post-race cleaning; and housekeeping kits. The vehicles sleep from four to at least six people and come with a generator to run appliances. California Speedway provides showers (bring flip-flops). Purchase grandstand tickets separately. Prices for RV packages range from $2,300 to $3,500. Phone toll-free 888/337-2214 or visit www.elmonterv.com.

Riverside

MARCH FIELD AIR MUSEUM

22550 Van Buren, Riverside (92518). Phone 951/697-6602. www.marchfield.org. Located just off the Van Buren Boulevard exit of Interstate 215, this museum houses more than 60 historic aircraft, including the first operational jet used by the US Air Force and the speed record-breaking SR-71 Blackbird. Take a spin in the g-force flight simulator or explore the collection of 2,000 artifacts dating back to 1918. (Daily 9 am-4 pm; closed holidays) **$**

Santa Monica

SANTA MONICA PIER.

At the corner of Ocean and Colorado aves, Santa Monica (90401). Phone 310/458-8900. www.santamonicapier.org. Opened in 1909, Santa Monica Pier is a landmark, attracting throngs with its Ferris wheel, roller coaster, and antique carousel. Stroll out to the pier's end for expansive views of Santa Monica Bay. Restaurants range from food court-style snacks to sit-down fare. Tickets are required for all the rides.

SANTA MONICA PIER AQUARIUM.

1600 Ocean Front Walk, Santa Monica (90401). Phone 310/393-6149. www.healthebay.org/smpa. An innovative, interactive aquarium that's popular with local families. (Hours vary seasonally, so check before you visit.) **DONATION**

THIRD STREET PROMENADE.

Downtown, Third St between Broadway and Wilshire Blvd, Santa Monica (90401). Phone 310/393-8355. www.thirdstreetpromenade.com. Get into the local sensibility at the promenade, a pedestrian-only street offering theaters, boutiques, restaurants, curbside vendors, and street performers. After the obligatory beach stop, this is often the first place locals bring out-of-towners for shopping, strolling, watching a movie, or grabbing a bite to eat. If you're visiting on a Wednesday or Saturday, check out the huge farmers' market, one of California's largest, on Arizona between Second and Fourth streets. (Wed 9 am-2 pm, Sat 8:30 am-1 pm).

Universal City

NASCAR SILICON MOTOR SPEEDWAY.

Universal City Walk, 1000 Universal Studios Dr, Universal City (91608). Phone 818/763-7959. www.smsonline.com. Experience centrifugal forces, turns, and crash impacts as you "drive" a full-motion NASCAR Silicon Motor Speedway simulator. **$$**

For more attractions, go to www.mobiltravelguide.com

STAY

MOBIL STAR-RATED LODGINGS

Anaheim

DISNEYLAND HOTEL. ★★

1150 W Magic Way, Anaheim (92802). Phone 714/778-6600. www.disneyland.com. A Disneyland tradition since 1955, this family lodge remains as bright and fresh as the classic Disney-costumed characters who welcome guests in the lobby. The lagoon-style pool area and no-charge policy for parent-accompanied guests 18 and under warrant Mouseketeer cheers. 990 rooms, 14 story. Check-in 3 pm, check-out 11 am. Three restaurants, bar. Children's activity center. Fitness room. Two outdoor pools, whirlpool. Business center. **$$**

DISNEY'S PARADISE PIER HOTEL. ★★

1717 Disneyland Dr, Anaheim (92802). Phone 714/999-0990. www.disneyland.com. This family-friendly Disney hotel gets its name from Paradise Pier in Disney's California Adventure park, which is just across the street. When you stay here, you get exclusive park access. The hotel has a rooftop pool and spa, a workout room for adults, a game room, and Paradise Theater, where kids come to be transfixed by Disney movies. At Disney's PCH Grill, you can have breakfast with Mickey and Minnie, and in the afternoons and evenings, kids enjoy designing their own pizzas or noshing on burgers and fries. 489 rooms, 15 story. Check-in 3 pm, check-out 11 am. Two restaurants, bar. Children's activity center. Fitness room. Outdoor pool, whirlpool. Business center. **$$**

STAY MOBIL STAR-RATED LODGINGS

FAIRFIELD INN BY MARRIOTT ANAHEIM DISNEYLAND. ★

1460 S Harbor Blvd, Anaheim (92802). Phone 714/772-6777; toll-free 800/228-2800. www.fairfield inn.com. This hotel is a perfect base from which to explore the park. Kid-friendly features include an impressive children's arcade and pull-out sofa beds in the guest rooms, which were recently renovated. 467 rooms, 9 story. Check-in 4 pm, check-out noon. Outdoor pool, whirlpool. $$

Ontario

DOUBLETREE HOTEL ONTARIO AIRPORT. ★★

222 N Vineyard Ave, Ontario (91764). Phone 909/937-0900; toll-free 800/222-8733. www.doubletree .com. This full-service hotel is located 2 miles from Ontario International Airport and next to the city's convention center, in the heart of the "Inland Empire." 484 rooms, 4 story. Pets accepted, some restrictions; fee. Check-in 3 pm, check-out noon. Restaurant, bar. Fitness room. Pool, whirlpool. Airport transportation available. $$

MARRIOTT ONTARIO AIRPORT. ★★★

2200 E Holt Blvd, Ontario (91761). Phone 909/986-8811; toll-free 800/284-8811. www.marriott.com. This hotel is convenient to the speedway and is an hour drive away from local beaches, Palm Springs, and snow skiing. 299 rooms, 3 story. Pets accepted; fee. Check-in 3 pm, check-out noon. High-speed Internet access, wireless Internet access. Restaurant, bar. Fitness room. Outdoor pool, whirlpool. Tennis. Airport transportation available. $$

Pasadena

HILTON PASADENA. ★★★

168 S Los Robles Ave, Pasadena (91101). Phone 626/577-1000; toll-free 800/445-8667. www.hilton .com. The polished-marble lobby of this hotel welcomes dignitaries and professional athletes as well as vacationers. The Pasadena Convention Center and Old Town Pasadena—with its hundreds of dining, shopping, and entertainment options—are steps away. 296 rooms, 14 story. Check-in 3 pm, check-out noon. High-speed Internet access. Restaurant, bar. Fitness room. Outdoor pool, whirlpool. Business center. $$

SHERATON PASADENA HOTEL. ★★★

303 E Cordova St, Pasadena (91101). Phone 626/449-4000; toll-free 800/325-3535. www.sheraton.com. Customary Sheraton comfort and efficiency combined with walking-distance proximity to many of the city's attractions make this hotel ideal for business and leisure travelers. In addition to plush-top mattresses and large desks, guest rooms feature two-line phones, dataports, voice mail, and complimentary newspapers. 317 rooms, 5 story. Check-in 3 pm, check-out noon. Restaurant, bar. Fitness room. Outdoor pool. Tennis. Business center. $$

Riverside

COMFORT INN. ★

1590 University Ave, Riverside (92507). Phone 951/683-6000; toll-free 877/424-6423. www.comfort inn.com. Newly renovated and near the University of California-Riverside, this clean, comfortable hotel features easy access to the highway. 115 rooms, 2 story. Complimentary continental breakfast. Check-in 3 pm, check-out noon. Outdoor pool. $

FAN FAVORITE

The speedway's **Party Zone** opens when the gates open and features a buffet prior to race time, closed-circuit television, music, and more in the infield. The zone is close to the pits, and drivers are encouraged to stop by. The best grandstand seats for zone access are in the west, even-numbered sections at Turn 4. Saturday: $85 per person, Sunday: $125, Saturday and Sunday: $175. Prices include single day pit passes. For tickets, phone toll-free 800/944-7223.

COURTYARD BY MARRIOTT. ★★
1510 University Ave, Riverside (92507). Phone 951/276-1200; toll-free 800/321-2211. www.courtyard.com.
Convenient to area shopping, dining, and the University of California-Riverside campus, visitors will appreciate this hotel's location and amenities. 163 rooms, 6 story. Check-in 3 pm, check-out noon. High-speed Internet access. Restaurant, bar. Fitness room. Outdoor pool, whirlpool. $

DYNASTY SUITES RIVERSIDE. ★
3735 Iowa Ave, Riverside (92507). Phone 909/369-8200; toll-free 800/842-7899. www.dynastysuites.com.
Featuring a surprising array of amenities and thoughtful touches like freshly baked cookies and fresh fruit upon arrival, this budget-friendly hotel is close to area shopping and dining. 34 rooms, 2 story. Complimentary continental breakfast. Check-in 2 pm, check-out noon. High-speed Internet access. Outdoor pool. $

MARRIOTT RIVERSIDE. ★★★
3400 Market St, Riverside (92501). Phone 951/784-8000; toll-free 888/236-2427. www.marriott.com.
This hotel recently completed a multimillion-dollar expansion and renovation. Antiques stores, museums, shops, and other attractions are within walking distance. 292 rooms, 12 story. Check-in 3 pm, check-out noon. High-speed Internet access, wireless Internet access. Two restaurants, bar. Fitness room. Outdoor pool, whirlpool. Airport transportation available. Business center. $$

MISSION INN. ★★★
3649 Mission Inn Ave, Riverside (92501). Phone 951/784-0300; toll-free 800/678-8945. www.missioninn.com. A National Historic Landmark, the Mission Inn had its beginnings in the late 19th century and hosted such guests as Theodore Roosevelt and Andrew Carnegie in the early 20th century. Today, the hotel impresses from the moment you step into the expansive, ornate lobby. None of the hotel rooms is exactly like the others, but all are elegantly appointed. 239 rooms, 5 story. Check-in 3 pm, check-out noon. Three restaurants, three bars. Fitness room. Outdoor pool, whirlpool. Airport transportation available. $$

LOCAL RECOMMENDATIONS

Chino

BEST WESTERN PINE TREE MOTEL.
12018 Central Ave, Chino (91710). Phone 909/628-6021; toll-free 800/780-7234. www.bestwestern.com.
41 rooms, 2 story. Complimentary continental breakfast. Check-in 11 am, check-out 11 am. Outdoor pool. $

Corona

BEST WESTERN KINGS INN.
1084 Pomona Rd, Corona (92882). Phone 951/734-4241; toll-free 800/892-5464. www.bestwestern.com.
86 rooms, 2 story. Complimentary continental breakfast. Check-in 3 pm, check-out noon. Outdoor pool, whirlpool. $

Moreno Valley

BEST WESTERN IMAGE INN & SUITES.
24840 Elder Ave, Moreno Valley (92557). Phone 951/924-4546; toll-free 800/780-7234. www.bestwestern.com. 120 rooms, 3 story. Check-in 2 pm, check-out 11 am. Outdoor pool, whirlpool. $

Ontario

BEST WESTERN COUNTRY INN.
2359 S Grove Ave, Ontario (91761). Phone 909/923-1887; toll-free 800/770-1889. www.bestwestern.com.
72 rooms, 2 story. Complimentary continental breakfast. Check-in 2 pm, check-out 11 am. Outdoor pool, whirlpool. Airport transportation available. $

BEST WESTERN ONTARIO AIRPORT.
209 N Vineyard Ave, Ontario (91764). Phone 909/937-6800; toll-free 800/780-7234. www.bestwestern.com.
150 rooms, 2 story. Pets accepted; fee. Complimentary continental breakfast. Check-in 3 pm, check-out noon. Fitness room. Outdoor pool, whirlpool. Airport transportation available. $

Pomona

SHERATON SUITES FAIRPLEX.
601 W McKinley Ave, Pomona (91768). Phone 909/622-2220; toll-free 800/325-3535. www.sheraton.com. This is an all-suite hotel located just 10 miles west of the Ontario International Airport. 247 rooms, all suites. Fitness Room. Outdoor pool. Restaurant, bar. $

STAY LOCAL RECOMMENDATIONS

SHILO INN HOTEL POMONA.
3200 Temple Ave, Pomona (91768). Phone 909/598-0073; toll-free 800/222-2244. www.shiloinns.com. 161 rooms, 4 story. Complimentary full breakfast. Check-in 4 pm, check-out noon. Outdoor pool, whirlpool. Airport transportation available. $

Rancho Cucamonga
BEST WESTERN HERITAGE INN.
8179 Spruce Ave, Rancho Cucamonga (91730). Phone 909/466-1111; toll-free 800/682-7829. www.bestwestern.com. This is considered to be one of the closest hotels to the California Speedway. 115 rooms, 6 story. Complimentary continental breakfast. Check-in 3 pm, check-out noon. Fitness room. Outdoor pool, whirlpool. $

Redlands
BEST WESTERN SANDMAN MOTEL.
1120 W Colton Ave, Redlands (92374). Phone 909/793-2001; toll-free 800/682-7829. www.bestwestern.com. 65 rooms, 2 story. Complimentary continental breakfast. Check-in 2 pm, check-out 11 am. Outdoor pool, whirlpool. $

Rialto
BEST WESTERN EMPIRE INN.
475 W Valley Blvd, Rialto (92376). Phone 909/877-0690; toll-free 800/682-7829. www.bestwestern.com. Located just minutes from the California Speedway, this hotel is also located just 2 miles south of Historic Route 66. 98 rooms, 3 story. Check-in 3 pm, check-out noon. Outdoor pool, whirlpool. $

Riverside
BEST WESTERN OF RIVERSIDE.
10518 Magnolia Ave, Riverside (92505). Phone 909/359-0770; toll-free 800/682-7829. www.bestwestern.com. 57 rooms, 2 story. Pets accepted, some restrictions; fee. Complimentary continental breakfast. Check-in 11 am, check-out 11 am. High-speed Internet access. Outdoor pool, whirlpool. Tennis. $

San Bernardino
BEST WESTERN HOSPITALITY LANE.
294 E Hospitality Ln, San Bernardino (92408). Phone 909/381-1681; toll-free 800/682-7829. www.bestwestern.com. 83 rooms, 2 story. Pets accepted, some restrictions; fee. Complimentary continental breakfast. Check-in 3 pm, check-out 10 am. Outdoor pool, whirlpool. $

Upland
BEST WESTERN MOUNTAIN VIEW INN & SUITES.
1191 E Foothill Blvd, Upland (91786). Phone 909/949-4800; toll-free 800/682-7829. www.bestwestern.com. Located in the foothills of the San Bernardino Mountain Range, this hotel is located approximately 11 miles from the California Speedway. 114 rooms, 2 story. Pets accepted, some restrictions; fee. Complimentary continental breakfast. Check-in 3 pm, check-out noon. Outdoor pool, whirlpool. $

For more lodging recommendations, go to www.mobiltravelguide.com

EAT

MOBIL STAR-RATED RESTAURANTS

Anaheim

MR. STOX. ★★
1105 E Katella Ave, Anaheim (92805). Phone 714/634-2994. www.mrstox.com. Don't miss the fresh-baked gourmet breads at this family-run restaurant, which specializes in fresh seafood, top-quality meats, and pasta dishes. Many of the herbs used in the kitchen, which turns out contemporary California fare, are grown on the premises. The wine list offers more than 20,000 bottles from 12 countries and ten US states on offer. American menu. Lunch, dinner. Closed holidays. Bar. Business casual attire. Reservations recommended. Valet parking. Outdoor seating. $$$

YAMABUKI. ★★
1717 S Disneyland Dr, Anaheim (92802). Phone 714/956-6755. www.disneyland.com. Sushi and Disney may not seem to go hand in hand, but they pair nicely at this restaurant in Disney's Paradise Pier Hotel (see), an appealing option for parents who are tired of kid food but still need to find a family-friendly place to eat. The restaurant features a full sushi bar, teriyaki and tempura entrées, and Japanese beers and sake. Japanese menu. Lunch, dinner. Bar. Children's menu. Casual attire. Reservations recommended. Valet parking. $$

Pasadena

CROCODILE CAFÉ. ★
140 S Lake Ave, Pasadena (91101). Phone 626/449-9900. www.crocodilecafe.com. Fast, friendly service and a huge menu are hallmarks of Los Angeles's Crocodile mini-chain (another Pasadena location is at 140 S Lake Ave). From the three-section pizza—incorporating barbecued chicken, sausage, and pepperoni—to tortilla soup and grilled salmon in guajillo chile pepper sauce, virtually all of the fare is prepared with flair. Add trendy décor, and you've got a reliably fun, relaxing family food spot. California menu. Lunch, dinner. Closed Thanksgiving, Dec 25. Bar. Children's menu. Casual attire. Outdoor seating. **$$**

MI PIACE. ★★
25 E Colorado Blvd, Pasadena (91105). Phone 626/795-3131. www.mipiaceitaliankitchen.com. This Italian restaurant and bakery, whose name means, "I like it," is the place to see and be seen in Old Town Pasadena. From the kitchen come generous portions of standard Italian fare, along with some more interesting twists, like pumpkin ravioli in brown butter with sage and Parmesan. Italian menu. Breakfast, lunch, dinner. Closed holidays. Bar. Children's menu. Casual attire. Valet parking. Outdoor seating. **$$**

SHIRO. ★★★
1505 Mission St, South Pasadena (91030). Phone 626/799-4774. An imaginative fusion of French and Asian culinary influences makes a colorful splash in this virtually ambience-free dining space. Shiro's palate-pleasing pièce de résistance, sizzling catfish—stuffed with ginger, fried whole, and then garnished with cilantro and steeped in ponzu sauce—easily distracts customers from the lacking décor; it's the only constant on a menu that rotates chicken, duck, and lamb entrées. Pan-Asian menu. Dinner. Closed Mon; holidays. **$$**

TWIN PALMS. ★★
101 W Green St, Pasadena (91105). Phone 626/577-2567. www.twin-palms.com. By day, canvas sails form a ceiling over the space; at night, the sails are removed to reveal the stars and allow guests to dine in the open air. The kitchen focuses on light and flavorful preparations of locally produced ingredients, with pizzas, rotisserie meats, and seafood selections dominating the menu. Live jazz and other types of music create a festive atmosphere. Extensive salad selection. California menu. Lunch, dinner, Sun brunch. Closed Dec 25. Bar. Children's menu. Business casual attire. Reservations recommended. Valet parking. Outdoor seating. **$$$**

XIOMARA. ★★
69 N Raymond Ave, Pasadena (91103). Phone 626/796-2520. The Pasadena outpost of Xiomara glitters with modish white walls and black leather seating. (A second location is at 6101 Melrose Ave in Hollywood). At both locations, the bar specializes in mojitos with freshly juiced sugar canes from a nifty machine. The sweet, cool drinks pair well with the bold menu choices, like steamed mussels in orange juice, spicy swordfish with fried plantains and yucca, and Nicaraguan skirt steak with blue cheese mashed potatoes. French, Latin menu. Lunch, dinner. Closed Easter. Bar. Casual attire. Reservations recommended. Valet parking. Outdoor seating. **$$**

ROAD FOOD

Most folks on the NASCAR circuit rave about two local institutions: **King Taco** and **In-n-Out** (pronounced "InnNout"), both chains that have developed their own mystiques. Breakfast burritos from the King Taco stand in the speedway infield are a must for team members and track workers (try the chorizo). Locals introduce In-n-Out Double-Double burgers and fries to newbies with a breathless excitement usually observed in wine aficionados. Try the In-n-Out at 9855 Sierra Ave, Fontana (92335).

Riverside

CIAO BELLA. ★★

1630 Spruce St, Riverside (92507). Phone 909/781-8840. With understated décor and warm, mellow colors, this airy restaurant serves a variety of unique Italian dishes. Diners spend quiet afternoons and evenings amid aromas from the open kitchen and lots of natural light from the multipaned windows. Italian menu. Lunch, dinner. Closed Sun. Bar. Casual attire. Reservations recommended. Outdoor seating. **$$**

MARKET BROILER. ★

3525 Merrill Ave, Riverside (92506). Phone 909/276-9007. www.marketbroiler.com. For fresh fish, a fun atmosphere, and friendly service, locals come to this California mini-chain to choose from 18 varieties of fish and shellfish. All of the fish is mesquite-broiled and is served in pretty much any form and flavoring you could imagine. However, the menu also includes wood-fired pizzas and a "dishes without fishes" section, featuring chicken, pasta, and steak entrées. Seafood menu. Lunch, dinner. Bar. Casual attire. **$$**

LOCAL RECOMMENDATIONS

Corona

MAIN STREET BREWERY.

300 N Main St, Corona (92880). Phone 909/371-1471. www.lamppostpizzacorona.com. At least eight hand-crafted brews are offered on tap here. The menu includes individual to extra-large pizzas, salads, sandwiches, and pasta. Pizza menu. Lunch, dinner. Casual attire. **$**

Ontario

BOMBAY RESTAURANT.

405 N Vineyard Ave, Suite A, Ontario (91764). Phone 909/937-1282. Tandoori dishes are part of the Indian menu here. A daily luncheon buffet and Sunday brunches are offered. Indian menu. Lunch, dinner, Sun brunch. Casual attire. **$$**

CASA SANCHEZ.

2264 S Mountain Ave, Ontario (91762). Phone 909/983-2826. This Mexican restaurant is tucked away in a local shopping center, but it's worth seeking out. Mexican menu. Lunch, dinner. Casual attire. **$**

COCO'S BAKERY RESTAURANT.

4360 Mills Circle Rd, Ontario (91764). Phone 909/481-8644. www.cocosbakery.com. Freshly baked pies, muffins, cookies, breads, and cakes are available all day—try the cinnamon roll French toast. Besides breakfast, full lunch and dinner menus are available of salads, pasta, fish, and burgers. Bring an appetite—the chain is known for its large portions. American menu. Breakfast, lunch, dinner. Casual attire. **$**

TOKYO TOKYO.

990 Ontario Mills Dr, Ontario (91764). Phone 909/987-7999. www.tokyotokyo.com. This Japanese restaurant features a sushi bar and French-influenced Japanese entrées. There's also a koi pond, traditional tatami rooms, outdoor dining, and a full bar. Japanese menu. Lunch, dinner. Bar. Casual attire. Reservations recommended. Outdoor seating. **$$$**

Rancho Cucamonga

CASK 'N' CLEAVER.

8689 Ninth St, Rancho Cucamonga (91730). Phone 909/982-7108. This local steakhouse also serves prime rib, chicken, seafood, and fresh fish. Steak menu. Lunch, dinner. Casual attire. **$$$**

DRAGON INN.

8031 Archibald Ave, Rancho Cucamonga (91730). Phone 909/466-5680. This Chinese restaurant makes its noodles the traditional way, by hand. Chinese menu. Lunch, dinner. Casual attire. **$$**

WOODY'S BAR-B-QUE.

11871 Foothill Blvd, Rancho Cucamonga (91730). Phone 909/291-8124. Woody's uses red oak for smoking the ribs, chicken, and meats featured on its menu. Barbecue menu. Lunch, dinner. Casual attire. **$**

For more dining recommendations, go to www.mobiltravelguide.com

SIDETRIP
The Best of All Worlds
San Diego, CA

"Today will be 70 and sunny."

In San Diego, that's the weather report pretty much year-round, and just one reason why it is a popular destination, especially for tourists who can't decide between the city and the beach.

There is world-class theater, great shopping, quirky museums, and an oceanfront, where sea lions crawl onto shore to sun themselves. Kids will love **SeaWorld** (phone toll-free 800/257-4268, www.seaworld.com) and the terrific **San Diego Zoo** (phone 619/231-1515, www.sandiegozoo.org) and wildlife park; parents will appreciate the wonderful restaurants—and all will enjoy great snorkeling, surfing, fishing, biking, and hiking.

San Diego is where California began. In 1542, explorer Juan Rodriguez Cabrillo was commissioned by the governor of Guatemala to travel up the California coast. Cabrillo's statue stands at the edge of **Cabrillo Park** (phone 619/557-5450) near the spot where he is believed to have anchored his boat. In the mid-18th century, Spanish missionaries came to California, and Father Junipera Serra built the first of 21 famous missions in California. All around the city are tributes to its rich past.

There's a strong military component to San Diego because of the presence of several US Navy bases in the region and old-timers still refer to the city as a "Navy town." Still, San Diego is hardly a one-industry town.

It is the seventh-largest city in the United States, where business and the arts flourish. The city's downtown is abuzz with shops and restaurants and boasts a scenic waterfront—all best appreciated on foot. Don't miss the **Gaslamp Quarter** (www.gaslamp.org), the **Seaport Village** (phone 619/235-4014) or

See Shamu at SeaWorld, one of many kid-friendly attractions in the San Diego area. For more information, visit the San Diego Convention and Visitors Bureau's International Visitor Information Center (1040 1/3 W Broadway, San Diego 92101, phone 619/236-1212).

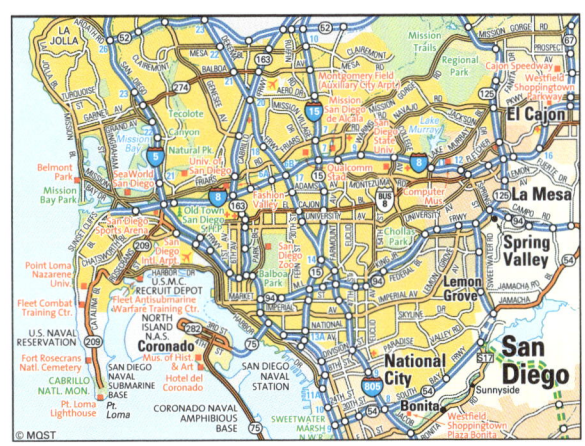

Old Town San Diego (phone 619/220-5422), which pays homage to its first settlers. Worthwhile is the **Bazaar del Mundo** (phone 619/296-3161), a colorful collection of Mexican-flavored shops and open-air restaurants, including the festive Casa de Pico.

And don't forget **Petco Park** (phone 619/795-5000), the new home of baseball's Padres, where the creative concession offerings include Rubio's Fish Tacos. This is, after all, a coastal town bordering Mexico, right?

For more San Diego recommendations, go to www.mobiltravelguide.com

74

Driver Bobby Labonte (No. 18) signs autographs for fans at the 2004 NASCAR NEXTEL Cup Series Tropicana 400.

Chicagoland Speedway®

Joliet, IL

4

Fans at the 2004 NASCAR NEXTEL Cup Series Tropicana 400 watch drivers on the front stretch coming out of Turn 4.

TRACK FACTS

CHICAGOLAND SPEEDWAY. 500 Speedway Blvd, Joliet (60433). Phone 815/727-RACE (7223). www.chicagolandspeedway.com.

SECURITY. Coolers of any kind or any food or beverages are prohibited. The only exception: ticket holders may bring a single, plastic, sealed bottle of water. You can also carry in purses, backpacks, camera bags, and other bags smaller than 18 x 18 x 4 inches, subject to security search. Other prohibited items: glass containers, strollers, folding chairs, flag poles, signs of any kind, umbrellas, and any items deemed to be an obstruction to other spectators.

PARKING. The track sits in the middle of farmland surrounded by 700 acres of free parking. If someone asks you for money to park, you are not on Chicagoland Speedway property. The lots, with space for 50,000 vehicles, open at 7 am, and tailgating is welcome. Overnight parking is not allowed except in designated camping areas. Spectators who park in Lot G in back of the backstretch can catch a tram to Turn 1 near the south turnstile gate entrance, otherwise, expect to walk.

FIRST AID. First aid stations are located under the grandstands on the main level at Sections 111 and 411. A fully staffed Infield Care Center is located in the infield between Turns 3 and 4. Heat getting to you? Misting stations are located under the grandstands. Windy City Raceway Ministries provides first aid for the soul with Sunday services on the infield and outside the raceway.

CONCESSIONS. Carnivores will drool at the choices: turkey legs, blackened chicken quesadillas, grilled pork chops, Italian beef and sausage, chicken wings with blue cheese and celery, and the old standbys—burgers, brats, and hot dogs—to name a few. On the beverage side: Pepsi products, water, beer, margaritas, and frozen daiquiris.

The grandstands and pressbox are packed during another fast-paced race.

GETTING TICKETS

Chicagoland Speedway's grandstands hold 75,000 people; the infield and suite seating pushes that number to nearly 85,000. It has hosted a sold-out NASCAR weekend all four years since its 2001 opening.

The speedway contacts existing "Track Pack" ticket holders (who have first right of refusal) beginning in September. Remaining tickets go on sale to the general public in February, the Monday after the Daytona 500. Call Chicagoland Speedway's ticket office (phone 815/727-7223, Mon-Fri 8:30 am-5 pm, or visit www.chicagolandspeedway.com) to put your name on a waiting list and ensure that you receive a chance to purchase nonrenewed seats.

Track Packs include admission for the July NASCAR Busch Series 300 and NASCAR NEXTEL Cup Series 400 races. Prices range from $195 to $260 each.

All sales are on a first-come, first-served basis, except for Founders PASS members—fans who, for a one-time fee ranging from $500 to $1,500, earn the right to buy the same seats every year. Three sections in the grandstand—the Tower, Sky Tower, and Club—are reserved for Founders PASS members and feature stadium seating, in contrast to the bench seating (with backs) in other grandstand areas.

Chicagoland was designed to give even the fans in the front rows a clear view of the entire track. Front row seats are built more than 7 feet above the outside wall. No infield structure, with the exception of the scoring tower, rises higher than 14 feet.

For RVs, Chicagoland Speedway offers 616 sites on the infield and another 80 on "Speedway Ridge," the grassy hill that runs along the backstretch wall just outside the track. RV packages in 2004 ranged from $500 to $850 (two adults, two children under 12) on the infield and $2,150 (four adults, four children under 12) on Speedway Ridge.

JOLIET JOYRIDES

With roots in freight movement and steel and limestone production, Joliet is not exactly thought of as a vacation destination, but for one extended weekend per year, the place becomes a tourist haven as NASCAR rolls into town.

The track itself sits a couple miles south of Joliet proper. If you're camping at one of several makeshift campgrounds around the speedway, the only places within walking distance are a Gas City convenience store and Subway restaurant (Laraway Rd and Rte 52, phone 815/724-0240) and the Sugar Creek Preserve (17540 W Laraway Rd, phone 815/727-8700), the main entrance to the **Wauponsee Glacial Trail.**

Finding entertainment, restaurants, and civilization (apart from the team merchandise trailers, the "Expo Village," and other festivities at the track) requires getting into the car and driving. Fortunately, you won't have to drive far. Over the past three years, Joliet has built a large-scale water park, acquired a brand new minor league baseball stadium, as well as other attractions aimed at wooing tourists.

The main NASCAR-related event is the city-sponsored downtown **Joliet FanFest,** which takes place on the Thursday before the race. The FanFest features appearances by NASCAR drivers, a classic car show, concerts on an outdoor stage, as well as at the historic **Rialto Square Theatre.** The **Racin' the Bases**

The Rialto Theatre combines French Renaissance, neoclassical, and rococo styles to create a truly gorgeous structure.

While in Joliet, spend an hour or two touring the historic homes, the architecture won't disappoint.

Millennium Park, one of the newest attractions in downtown Chicago, is a must-see.

Celebrity Softball Challenge is also a must in Joliet. In 2004, the challenge featured drivers Greg Biffle, Kurt Busch, Kyle Petty, and other media and sports personalities. For more information, visit www.jolietdowntown.com or www.chicagolandspeedway.com as the date approaches.

SUMMER IN THE WINDY CITY

It may be 30 miles away, but on a clear day, from the upper grandstands of Chicagoland Speedway, you can see the downtown Chicago skyline. Between summer festivals, museums, the lakefront, two baseball teams, and more shopping options than Jeff Gordon has wins, Chicago offers enough to entertain even the shortest attention spans.

Once downtown, practically everything can be reached by a short cab or subway ride, or even walked if you're seeking exercise. Downtown sights and activities fall roughly into two distinct areas: Michigan Avenue and the Loop (the area defined by the "L" tracks that circle the traditional heart of the city). Each has thousands of hotel rooms, many at prices equal to or less expensive than those in Joliet and the surrounding towns.

The latest addition to Chicago's downtown and a must-see attraction is **Millennium Park** (Randolph St and Michigan Ave). Don't miss the 50-foot-high water-spewing towers of the Crown Fountain, with their constantly changing human faces, or the Frank Gehry-designed band shell and bridge. The giant silver reflective *Cloud Gate* sculpture, known in common parlance as "the bean," is also a sight to check out.

Be sure to ride the Ferris wheel at Navy Pier or take a cruise along Lake Michigan for some of the best views of Chicago's famous skyline.

GETTING AROUND

The fastest route to Chicagoland Speedway is not necessarily the shortest. Four major traffic "corridors" lead to the track: northeast, northwest, southeast, and southwest. The heaviest traffic comes from the northern corridors (especially the northwest), which channels fans from metropolitan Chicago, Wisconsin, and Iowa. The least congested approaches are the two on the south side of the speedway. You may want to bypass the northwest corridor for the northeast, or loop around and approach from the south. Tune in to 1340-AM WJOL for traffic updates from 8 am to 90 minutes after the races on Saturday and Sunday. Complete descriptions of the four corridors (with color-coded maps) can be found on the Chicagoland Speedway Web site (www.chicagolandspeedway.com).

The best way to avoid traffic is simply to arrive early. Parking is free and the lot opens at 7 am.

Better yet, let someone else do the driving. Metra, the regional rail service, runs trains between Chicago and Joliet before and after the race. Check the Metra Rock Island District Line schedule at www.metrarail.com/Sched/ri/ri.shtml for a complete list of times. Tickets cost $5 each way. Chicagoland Speedway operates free air-conditioned shuttles from the station to near the front gate of the track.

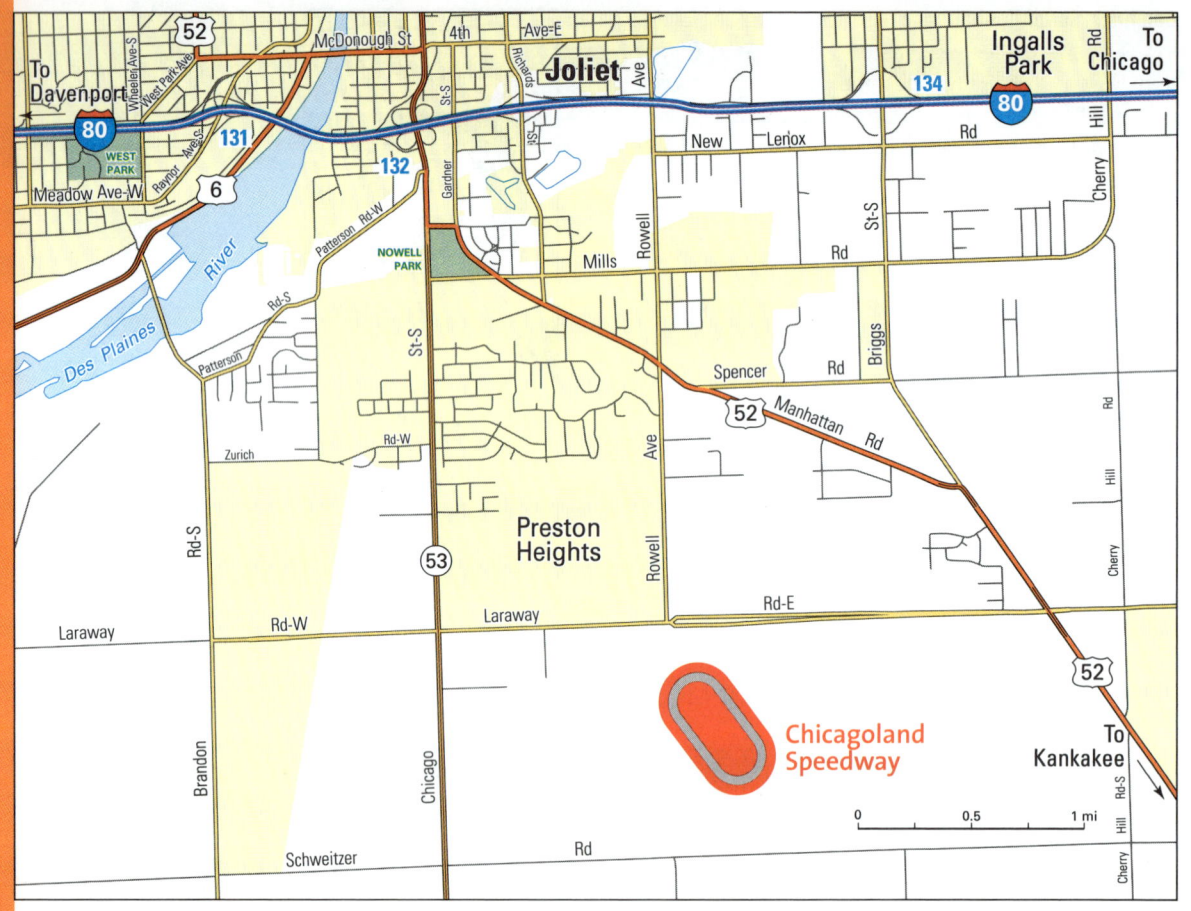

JOLIET POLE POSITION:
The 10 miles surrounding Chicagoland Speedway.

Farther north on Michigan Avenue is the **Magnificent Mile** (Michigan Ave between Oak St and the Chicago River, www.themagnificentmile.com), a 1-mile, flower-lined shopping mecca, boasting 3.1 million square feet of retail space, 460 stores, 275 restaurants, 51 hotels, numerous art galleries, the **Museum of Contemporary Art,** the **Lookingglass Theatre Company,** and the **John Hancock Center.** Shop 'til you drop at four vertical malls, including the granddaddy of them all, the newly renovated **Water Tower Place;** specialty stores like **Niketown,** the **Apple Store,** and **Crate & Barrel;** high-end department stores like **Neiman Marcus, Saks Fifth Avenue,** and **Nordstrom;** and international retailers like **Cartier, Armani,** and **Burberry.**

The Loop, two blocks west of **Millennium Park,** exudes a very different feel from Michigan Avenue: mature, classic, and businesslike. The Loop is home to the **Picasso sculpture,** the stunning **State of Illinois Building,** the **theater district,** and its own famous shopping area: **State Street** (between Lake St and Jackson Blvd). The flagship stores of Chicago's two most famous retailers—**Marshall Field's** and **Carson Pirie Scott**—anchor the street.

Come down the weekend prior to the race and you get to indulge in one of the city's most popular summertime events: **Taste of Chicago** (Chicago Office of Tourism, phone 312/774-2400). What started out more than 20 years ago in Grant Park as a way to sample cuisines from some of the city's best-known restaurants has become an all-out food fest and Fourth of July celebration that attracts more than 3 1/2 million visitors a year.

JOLIET CALENDAR

JUNE 24–JULY 4, 2005
Taste of Chicago. Grant Park, Chicago (60601). Phone 312/744-3370. www.cityofchicago.org. Millions of people chow down at dozens of food booths. Live music, including a country music festival, caps off most nights.

JULY 7, 2005
Racin' the Bases Celebrity Softball Challenge. Silver Cross Field, One Mayor Art Schultz Dr, Joliet (60432). Phone 815/726-2255. Part of the Downtown Joliet FanFest.

JULY 8, 2005
Expo Village Events. In front of Chicagoland Speedway. Features Miller Lite Rock 'n' Racing Concert, show cars, simulator rides, entertainment stages, product giveaways, food, a beer garden, and other booths by NASCAR marketing partners.

JULY 8, 2005
NASCAR Busch Series 300 practice; **NASCAR NEXTEL Cup Series 400** practice; **NASCAR Busch Series 300** qualifying; **NASCAR NEXTEL Cup Series 400** qualifying

JULY 9, 2005
NASCAR NEXTEL Cup Series 400 practice; **NASCAR Busch Series 300** driver introductions; **NASCAR Busch Series 300**

JULY 10, 2005
Pre-race concert; **NASCAR NEXTEL Cup Series 400** driver introductions; **NASCAR NEXTEL Cup Series 400**

JULY 16–17, 2005
Mayor's Cup Soccer Tournament. Montrose Harbor, Montrose Ave and Lake Shore Dr, Chicago (60601). Phone 312/744-3370. www.cityofchicago.org. Kids get their kicks for free at this annual, two-day soccer get-together.

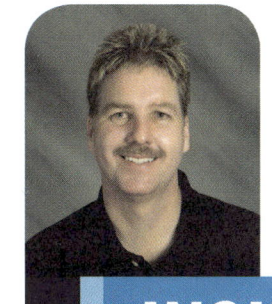

INSIDER'S PICK

Len Wood, member of the legendary Wood Brothers NASCAR NEXTEL Cup team No. 21 Ford driven by Ricky Rudd, has one entrée on his mind when he drives into the city once known for its stockyards. "If there is a **Ruth's Chris Steak House** near where we're racing, there will be at least one trip there. And otherwise, **Steak 'n Shake.**" Ruth's Chris Steak House. *431 N Dearborn St, Chicago (60610). Phone 312/321-2725. www.ruthschris.com.* Steak 'n Shake, *2675 N Plainfield Rd, Joliet (60435). Phone 815/439-9145.*

Drivers make a stop on pit road during the 2004 NASCAR NEXTEL Cup Series Tropicana 400.

JOLIET OUTFIELD:
The 40 miles surrounding Chicagoland Speedway.

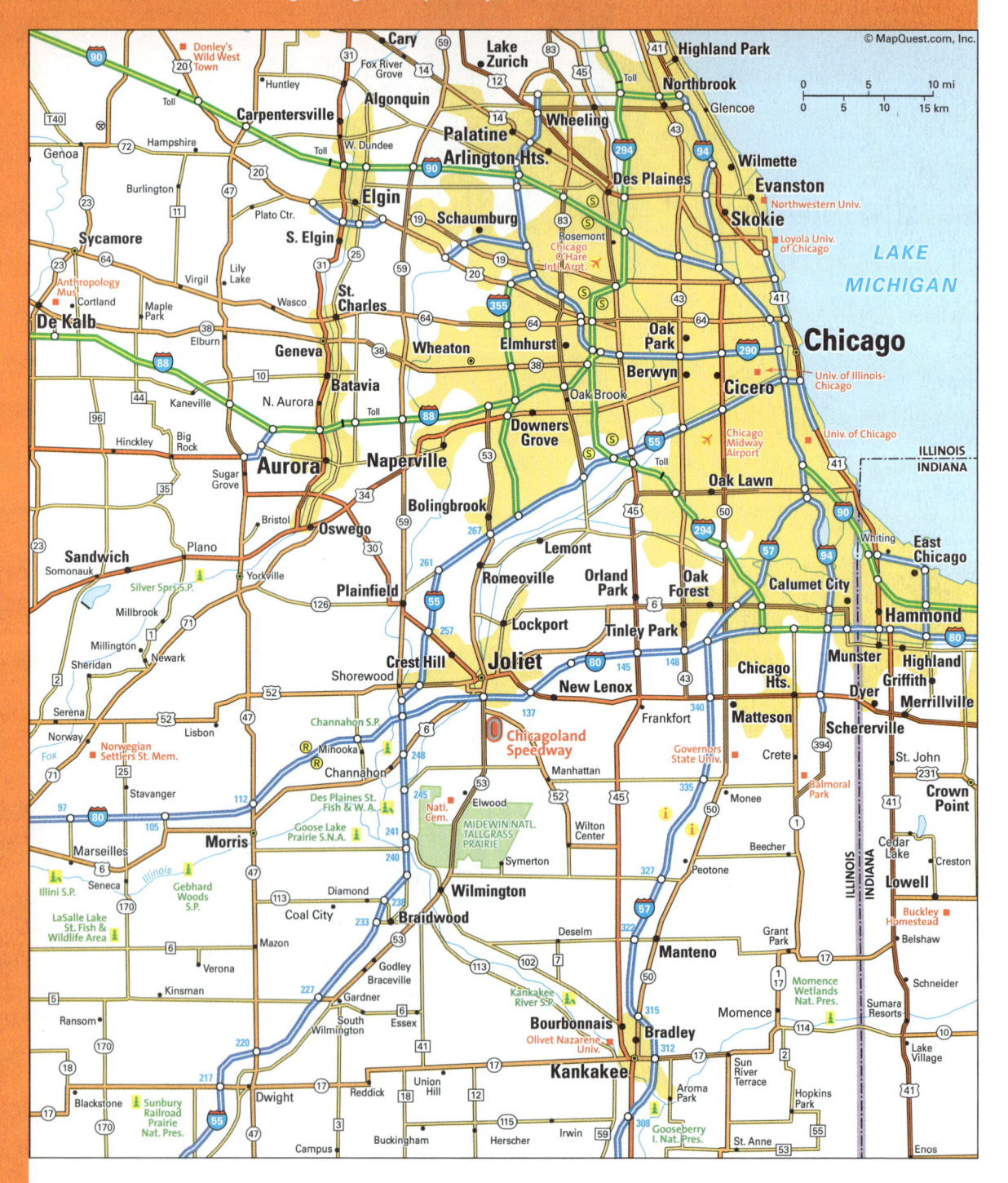

SEE

ATTRACTIONS

Brookfield

BROOKFIELD ZOO.
8400 W 31st St, Brookfield (60513). 31st St and 1st Ave. Phone 708/485-0263; toll-free 800/201-0784. www.brookfieldzoo.org. Brookfield Zoo is a world-class, 216-acre facility that houses more than 2,800 animals. Long known for its progressive approach to wildlife, the zoo was the first in the country to go "barless," installing animals in near-natural habitats instead of in cages. A favorite is Tropic World, with its rain forest exhibit, complete with waterfalls and thunderstorms. A 2-acre, 300-animal Hamill Family Play Zoo enables kids and their families to interact with the animals, and a separate Children's Zoo includes the Walk-In Farmyard and the "Pet and Learn Circle." (Daily 10 am-5 pm, extended summer hours) **$$**

Chicago

THE FIELD MUSEUM OF NATURAL HISTORY.
1400 S Lake Shore Dr, Chicago (60605). Phone 312/922-9410. www.fmnh.org. Dinosaur fans will delight at Sue, the largest and most complete Tyrannosaurus rex skeleton ever unearthed. Sue adds to an ever-growing collection of anthropological and biological displays, including artifacts from bygone civilizations like those in Egypt and Mesopotamia. Discounted admission Jan-Feb, mid-Sept-late Dec Mon-Tues. (Daily 9 am-5 pm; closed Dec 25) **$$**

JOHN HANCOCK CENTER.
875 N Michigan Ave, Chicago (60611). Phone 312/751-3681; toll-free 888/875-8439 (observatory). www.hancock-observatory.com. At 1,127 feet, the John Hancock Center is the world's 13th-tallest building. Since completion in 1969, this innovative office/residential building with its distinctive exterior X bracing—which eliminated the need for inner support beams, thus increasing usable space—has won numerous architectural awards. It also claims many notables, including the world's highest residence and the world's highest indoor swimming pool. The 94th-floor observatory features an open-air skywalk, a history wall chronicling Chicago's growth, multilingual "sky tours," and a 360-degree view that spans 80 miles and four states (Michigan, Indiana, Wisconsin, and Illinois). Visitors who want to extend the experience can dine at the Signature Room, an upscale restaurant located on the building's 95th floor. (Daily 9 am-11 pm) **$$**

LINCOLN PARK ZOO.
2200 Cannon Dr, Chicago (60614). W entrance, Webster Ave and Stockton Dr; E entrance, Cannon Dr off Fullerton Pkwy. Phone 312/742-2000. www.lpzoo.com. The Lincoln Park Zoo may be small (just 35 acres), but it has a lot going for it—it's free, it's open 365 days a year, it's located in the heart of Chicago's Lincoln Park, and it's a leader in education and conservation. The zoo added a new gorilla habitat in 2004. At the Farm in the Zoo, children can milk cows, churn butter, and groom goats. Grab lunch at Café Brauer just outside the gates at the Lincoln Park Lagoon and rent swan-shaped paddleboats for a ride on the water. (Daily; hours vary by season) **FREE**

MUSEUM OF SCIENCE AND INDUSTRY.
5700 S Lake Shore Dr, Chicago (60637). 57th St and Lake Shore Dr. Phone 773/684-1414; toll-free 800/468-6674. www.msichicago.org. Chicago's Museum of Science and Industry is sometimes called "the touchy, feely museum." Not because it evokes strong emotions in its visitors, but because it's filled with hands-on, interactive exhibits that interest adults and children alike. Tour a German U-Boat captured during World War II, venture into a re-created coal mine, walk through a giant human heart, and view a 3,500-square-foot model train layout that simulates a trip from Chicago to Seattle. If you visit one museum in Chicago, visit this one. Free admission varies by season; see Web site for details. (Daily; hours vary by season; closed Dec 25) **$$**

NAVY PIER.
600 E Grand Ave, Chicago (60611). Phone 312/595-7437. www.navypier.com. Known as one of the city's top venues for families, Navy Pier—an old naval station renovated during the 1990s and converted into an urban playground—seems to offer something for everyone. Its most visible attraction, the 150-foot-high Ferris wheel, offers spectacular views of the lake and

skyline and is modeled after the world's first, built in Chicago in 1893. During the summer, families flock to the pier for boat cruises, outdoor concerts, and fireworks. Year-round, visitors can enjoy an IMAX theater, the Smith Museum of Stained Glass Windows, Amazing Chicago's Funhouse Maze, the Chicago Shakespeare Theater, shops and kiosks, a food court, and six restaurants. Parking can be expensive, but the city offers a free trolley service from downtown hotels and other locations. (Daily)

Also here is the Chicago Children's Museum. 700 E Grand Ave, Chicago (60611). Phone 312/527-1000. www.chichildrensmuseum.org. Chock-full of interesting and interactive activities, the Chicago Children's Museum strikes a near-perfect balance between fun and learning. Overall, the exhibits encourage imagination, exploration, curiosity, and learning through experience; there's a play maze, an inventing lab where kids can perform experiments, and Treehouse Trails for children under 5 to explore the great outdoors. The programming is stellar, and, in any given week, the museum may have programs such as trilingual storytelling (English, Spanish, and American Sign Language), sing-alongs, ethnic festivals, theater shows, art classes, and even a clown college for kids. (Tues-Wed 10 am-5 pm, Thurs 2-8 pm, Fri-Sat 10 am-5 pm) $$

PEGGY NOTEBAERT NATURE MUSEUM.

2430 N Cannon Dr, Chicago (60614). At Cannon Dr and Fullerton Pkwy. Phone 773/755-5100. www.naturemuseum.org. Hands-on exploration of nature is the mission of the Peggy Notebaert Nature Museum. Permanent exhibits include a 28-foot-high butterfly haven, a city science interactive display, a family water lab, a wilderness walk, and a children's gallery designed for kids ages 3 to 8. Special exhibits are real kiddie-pleasers, judging by two recent presentations: "Grossology: The Impolite Science of the Human Body" and "Monster Creepy Crawlies." Free admission Thurs. (Mon-Fri 9 am-4:30 pm, Sat-Sun 10 am-5 pm) $$

SHEDD AQUARIUM.

1200 S Lake Shore Dr, Chicago (60605). At Roosevelt Rd. Phone 312/939-2438. www.sheddnet.org. Shedd, the world's largest indoor aquarium, features more than 8,000 freshwater and marine animals displayed in 200 naturalistic habitats. Divers hand-feed fish, sharks, eels, and turtles several times daily in the 90,000-gallon Caribbean Reef exhibit. The Oceanarium re-creates a Pacific Northwest ecosystem with whales, dolphins, sea otters, and seals. Free admission Mon-Tues (Sept-Feb only). (Daily 9 am-5 pm; closed Jan 1, Dec 25) $$$$

Joliet

CHALLENGE PARK XTREME.

2903 Schweitzer Rd, Joliet (60436). Phone 815/726-2800. www.challengepark.com. This 150-acre complex contains a skate park, miles of mountain biking trails, and 25 paintball fields, including five elaborate theme fields like Fort Courage (an Old West cavalry fort) and The Town of Bedlam (a $1 million, ten-block intricate re-creation of a small town). (Wed-Thurs 10 am-6 pm, Fri 10 am-8 pm, Sat 9 am-8 pm, Sun 9 am-6 pm)

HAUNTED TRAILS AMUSEMENT PARK & ENTERTAINMENT CENTER.

1423 N Broadway, Joliet (60435). Phone 815/722-7800. The haunted theme comes through loud and clear on the Haunted Trails mini-golf course, with scary accoutrements like creepy castles and a blood fountain. In all, the attraction offers two miniature golf courses, go-karts, "Naskarts" (a larger version of go-karts), video games, kids' rides, batting cages, a restaurant, and a picnic grove. (Mon-Thurs 3-10 pm, Fri 3-11 pm, Sat 10 am-11 pm, Sun 10 am-10 pm; closed Thanksgiving, Dec 24-25)

JOLIET JACKHAMMERS.

Silver Cross Field, One Mayor Art Schultz Dr, Joliet (60432). Phone 815/726-2255. www.jackhammerbaseball.com. Brand new Silver Cross Field is home to the Joliet Jackhammers (themselves only four years in existence), and with a capacity of 4,200, there's not a bad seat in the house, including the hot tub patio in right field. The Joliet Jackhammers play in the Northern League with nine other independent teams, meaning they are not affiliated with any Major League Baseball franchise. As is the tradition in minor league baseball, the Jackhammers' season is peppered with unusual promotions, including a hospital scrubs giveaway (sponsored by Silver Cross Hospital) and a Christmas in July Ornament Giveaway. (Season runs May-Aug; visit the Jackhammers' Web site for home dates)

SPLASH STATION WATERPARK.

2780 Rte 6, Joliet (60436). Phone 815/741-7250. www.jolietsplashstation.com. Do your own racing (in the water) at Miner's Mountain, the Midwest's only six-person racing slide. The 200-foot-high slide is one of five water features at Splash Station, a joint development between the Joliet Park District and the City of Joliet. Little ones can frolic in the Pelican Pond Zero Depth Pool, while older brothers, sisters, and parents fly down The Tunnel, The Gauntlet, Rattler, and Hot Shot body slides. (Memorial Day weekend-Labor Day weekend; closed the week prior to Labor Day)

WESTFIELD SHOPPINGTOWN LOUIS JOLIET.
3340 Mall Loop Dr, Joliet (60431). Phone 815/439-1000. www.westfield.com. Marshall Field's, Carson's, JCPenney, and Sears anchor Westfield Shoppingtown (formerly Louis Joliet Mall), but the complex features more than 100 specialty stores—from hip Aeropostale and Zumiez young adult fashions to traditional KB Toys and LensCrafters. (Mon-Sat 10 am-9 pm, Sun 11 am-6 pm; closed Thanksgiving, Dec 25)

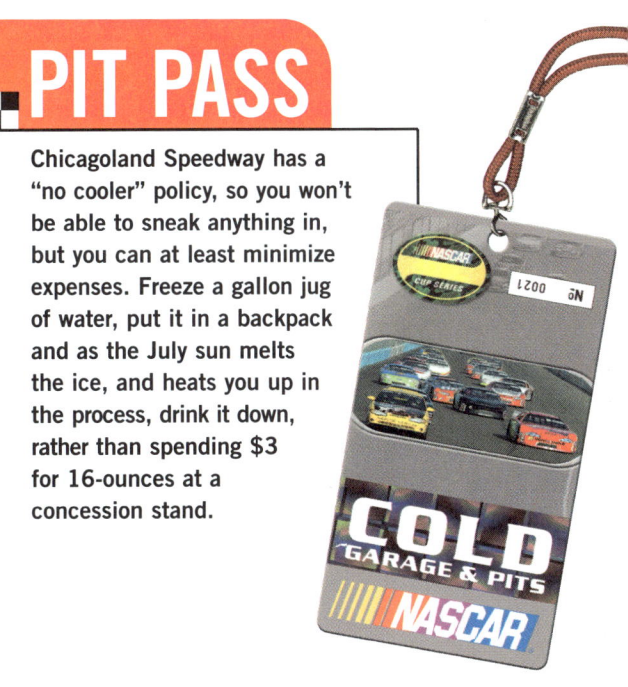

For more attractions, go to www.mobiltravelguide.com

PIT PASS

Chicagoland Speedway has a "no cooler" policy, so you won't be able to sneak anything in, but you can at least minimize expenses. Freeze a gallon jug of water, put it in a backpack and as the July sun melts the ice, and heats you up in the process, drink it down, rather than spending $3 for 16-ounces at a concession stand.

STAY

MOBIL STAR-RATED LODGINGS

Chicago

ALLERTON CROWNE PLAZA HOTEL. ★★★
701 N Michigan Ave, Chicago (60611). Phone 312/440-1500; toll-free 800/621-8311. www.crowneplaza.com. The Gold Coast's long-standing Allerton Crowne Plaza boasts both Historic Landmark Hotel status, designated by the city of Chicago, and a $60 million renovation that brought the hotel up to today's standards. Today, business and leisure travelers are attracted to its ideal location on Chicago's Magnificent Mile, as well as to all-day dining at Taps on Two restaurant. 443 rooms, 25 story. Pets accepted, some restrictions; fee. Check-in 3 pm, check-out noon. Restaurant, bar. Fitness room. Airport transportation available. Business center. **$$**

FAIRFIELD INN & SUITES. ★
216 E Ontario St, Chicago (60611). Phone 312/787-3777; toll-free 800/228-2800. www.fairfieldinn.com. Just a block off the Magnificent Mile and three blocks from the lake, this new, clean, and well-maintained hotel is a great choice for budget-minded travelers who don't want to give up location to save money. If you'd prefer to spend the bulk of your vacation dollars on shopping and fine dining rather than on accommodations, this is *the* choice in downtown Chicago. 185 rooms. Complimentary continental breakfast. Check-in 3 pm, check-out noon. Fitness room. **$**

HAMPTON INN & SUITES. ★
33 W Illinois St, Chicago (60610). Phone 312/832-0330; toll-free 800/426-7866. www.hamptoninn.com. With a convenient location, reasonable rates, a large number of suites, and ample meeting space, this hotel welcomes families and business travelers. Ruth's Chris Steak House is connected to the hotel by a second-floor skywalk. 230 rooms. Complimentary continental breakfast. Check-in 3 pm, check-out noon. Fitness room. Indoor pool, whirlpool. Business center. **$**

STAY MOBIL STAR-RATED LODGINGS

HARD ROCK HOTEL CHICAGO. ★★★
230 N Michigan Ave, Chicago (60601). Phone 312/345-1000; toll-free 877/762-5468. www.hardrock.com. This hip hotel is located in Chicago's historic Carbon and Carbide Building, an Art Deco skyscraper on the Chicago River. Inside, the lobby gives you a taste of what's to come with its piped-in music and rock-and-roll memorabilia. The theme extends through the hallways up to your room, where zebra-wood furnishings are accented by artwork like a Beatles mural in the bathroom, a Kiss mirror above the desk, and a David Bowie print above the bed. But there's plenty of comfort, too. The beds have down comforters and pillows, and each room boasts a laptop safe and an entertainment center with a 27-inch flat-screen TV and DVD/CD player. And when you come back hungry at 3 am after having spent an evening at one of Chicago's famed jazz or blues clubs, no worries: the Hard Rock offers 24-hour room service. 381 rooms. Check-in 3 pm, check-out noon. Restaurant, bar. Fitness room. Business center. **$$**

HOUSE OF BLUES, A LOEWS HOTEL. ★★★
333 N Dearborn, Chicago (60610). Phone 312/245-0333; toll-free 800/235-6397. www.loewshotels.com. With its exotic Gothic-Moroccan-East Indian décor, eye-popping art collection, and adjacent live concert venue, the hip House of Blues hotel appeals to a new generation of travelers. Guest rooms are spacious and well appointed. The namesake restaurant serves Southern American fare and hosts a popular Sunday gospel brunch. In the same complex are the chic, wine-themed bistro Bin 36 and Smith & Wollensky Steak House. The location puts guests in the heart of the River North gallery, dining, and entertainment district and close to the Loop and Michigan Avenue.

367 rooms, 15 story. Pets accepted. Check-in 3 pm, check-out noon. Restaurant, bar. Fitness room, spa. Business center. **$$**

SOFITEL CHICAGO WATER TOWER. ★★★
20 E Chestnut St, Chicago (60611). Phone 312/324-4000; toll-free 800/763-4835. www.sofitel.com. A stunning design created by French architect Jean-Paul Viguier gives this hotel an unmistakable presence in the Gold Coast, just off the Magnificent Mile. Le Bar is a popular after-work place to meet and mingle, while Café des Architectes serves up French cuisine in a contemporary setting. 415 rooms, 32 story. Pets accepted, some restrictions. Check-in 3 pm, check-out noon. Restaurant, bar. Fitness room. **$$**

Morris

HOLIDAY INN. ★★
200 Gore Rd, Morris (60450). Phone 815/942-6600; toll-free 800/465-4329. www.holiday-inn.com. 120 rooms, 2 story. Pets accepted, some restrictions. Check-in 2 pm, check-out noon. Restaurant, bar. Fitness room. Indoor pool, whirlpool. **$**

LOCAL RECOMMENDATIONS

Burbank

BEST WESTERN INN & SUITES-MIDWAY AIRPORT.
8220 S Cicero Ave, Burbank (60459). Phone 708/497-3000; toll-free 877/891-7666. www.bestwestern.com. 86 rooms, 4 story. Complimentary continental breakfast. Check-in noon, check-out 11 am. Fitness room. Indoor pool, whirlpool. Business center. **$**

FAN FAVORITE

Its log cabin exterior and décor (a deer antler chandelier, American Indian mural) doesn't really match the Polish-American cuisine, but who cares. **Taste of Polonia** offers all-you-can-eat lunch and dinner buffets in two dining rooms, featuring Polish sausage, pierogi, stuffed cabbage, homemade sauerkraut, baked ham, chicken Kiev, turkey breast with gravy, potato pancakes, beet salad, and more than a dozen other entrées and sides. Big appetites will love it. Polish menu. Lunch, dinner. Closed Sun. Casual attire. **$**
221 Ruby St, Joliet (60435). Phone 815/722-3110.

Chicago

BEST WESTERN GRANT PARK HOTEL.
1100 S Michigan Ave, Chicago (60605). Phone 312/922-2900; toll-free 800/472-6875. www.bestwestern.com. You'll be within walking distance of many of downtown Chicago's finest attractions. 172 rooms, 9 story. Check-in 3 pm, check-out noon. Restaurant. Fitness room. Outdoor pool. $

BEST WESTERN INN OF CHICAGO.
162 E Ohio St, Chicago (60611). Phone 312/787-3100; toll-free 800/780-7234. www.bestwestern.com. Located a half-block east of the Magnificent Mile, this Best Western is close to nightlife, art museums, galleries, and fine shopping. The Rooftop Terrace provides photo-worthy views of downtown Chicago and Lake Michigan. The rooms are newly renovated. 357 rooms, 22 story. Check-in 3 pm, check-out noon. Restaurant, bar. Fitness room. Business center. $

Joliet

BEST WESTERN JOLIET INN & SUITES.
4380 Enterprise Dr, Joliet (60431). Phone 815/730-7500; toll-free 800/780-7234. www.bestwestern.com. 62 rooms, 3 story. Check-in 3 pm, check-out noon. Laundry services. Fitness room. Indoor pool, whirlpool. $

FAIRFIELD INN BY MARRIOTT JOLIET NORTH.
3239 Norman Ave, Joliet (60435). Phone 815/436-6577; toll-free 800/228-2800. www.fairfieldinn.com. 63 rooms, 3 story. Complimentary continental breakfast. Check-in 3 pm, check-out noon. Indoor pool, whirlpool. $

FAIRFIELD INN BY MARRIOTT JOLIET SOUTH.
1501 Riverboat Center, Joliet (60436). Phone 815/741-3499; toll-free 800/228-2800. www.fairfieldinn.com. 64 rooms, 3 story. Complimentary continental breakfast. Check-in 3 pm, check-out noon. Indoor pool, whirlpool. $

HAMPTON INN JOLIET/I-55.
3555 Mall Loop Dr, Joliet (60431). Phone 815/439-9500; toll-free 800/426-7866. www.hamptoninn.com. 106 rooms, 3 story. Complimentry continental breakfast. Check-in 3 pm, check-out noon. Wireless Internet access. Fitness room. Indoor pool, whirlpool. $

HAMPTON INN JOLIET/I-80.
1521 Riverboat Center Dr, Joliet (60436). Phone 815/725-2424; toll-free 800/426-7866. www.hamptoninn.com. 89 rooms, 3 story. Complimentary continental breakfast. Check-in 3 pm, check-out noon. Wireless Internet access. Indoor pool, whirlpool. $

HOLIDAY INN EXPRESS JOLIET.
411 S Larkin Ave, Joliet (60436). Phone 815/729-2000; toll-free 800/377-8660. www.hiexpress.com. 200 rooms, 4 story. Pets accepted. Complimentary continental breakfast. Check-in 3 pm, check-out noon. Fitness room. Outdoor pool. $

WINGATE INN.
101 McDonald Ave, Joliet (60431). Phone 815/741-2100; toll-free 800/228-1000. www.wingateinns.com. 81 rooms, 3 story. Check-in 2 pm, check-out noon. Fitness room. Indoor pool, whirlpool. Business center. $

Monee

BEST WESTERN MONEE INN.
5815 W Monee-Manhattan Rd, Monee (60449). Phone 708/534-3500; toll-free 800/780-7234. www.bestwestern.com. 44 rooms, 2 story. Pets accepted, some restrictions; fee. Check-in 2 pm, check-out 11 am. Laundry services. Indoor pool, whirlpool. $

Naperville

BEST WESTERN NAPERVILLE INN.
1617 Naperville Wheaton Rd, Naperville (60563). Phone 630/505-0200; toll-free 800/780-7234. www.bestwestern.com. 104 rooms, 3 story. Check-in 2 pm, check-out 11 am. Laundry services. Bar. Fitness room. Whirlpool. Business center. $

Romeoville

BEST WESTERN ROMEOVILLE INN.
1280 W Normantown, Romeoville (60446). Phone 815/372-1000; toll-free 800/780-7234. www.bestwestern.com. 50 rooms, 3 story. Complimentary continental breakfast. Check-in 3 pm, check-out 11 am. Laundry services. Fitness room. Indoor pool. $

RV AND CAMPING

A number of "campgrounds" open just for NASCAR weekend around Chicagoland Speedway. These are primarily open fields that farmers stopped cultivating because they could make more money by renting space for campers. As former corn fields, they are flat and open and generally treeless. Most are less than 2 miles from the track, so walking is possible on race

Elwood

GREEN FIELDS CAMPGROUND INC.
17120 W Schweitzer Rd, Elwood (60421). Phone 815/722-0342 or 815/722-2080. www.greenfieldscampground.com. 250 sites (RV 30 by 50 feet, tent 20 by 40 feet). Located about 1 1/2 miles east of the track. Portable showers and porta-potties with sinks; pets allowed; free shuttle on NASCAR weekend (Fri-Sun). A local bakery sells doughnuts, pastries, and bagels every morning.

PRAIRIE VIEW RV PARK LLC.
17750 W Schweitzer Rd, Elwood (60421). Phone 815/861-5115 or 815/726-7060. www.prairieviewrv.com. 80 sites (RV 25 by 50 feet, tent 20 by 20 feet). Located just east of the track, which still means about a mile walk to the main gate. Pets allowed. You receive one free Prairie View RV hat per site.

Joliet

TOM RAPER RVS/CHICAGOLAND SPEEDWAY CAMPGROUND.
Rte 53 and Schweitzer Rd, Joliet (60433). Phone toll-free 800/727-3778. The campground is located on Route 66 Raceway property, just across the street from Chicagoland Speedway. 500 sites (RV 20 by 40 feet, no tent camping); limited electrical hook-ups; no pets.

Manhattan

PAUL & MARY'S RACEWAY CAMPING LLC.
23263 S Cherry Hill Rd, Manhattan (60442). Phone 815/478-5774. www.racetrackcamping.com. 150 sites (25 by 40 feet). Located about 2 miles from the track. Portable showers and porta-potties with sinks; pets allowed; free shuttle on NASCAR weekend (Sat-Sun). Each site receives a dozen Krispy Kreme doughnuts Saturday morning courtesy of owners Paul and Mary Bernhard. Kirby's Bakery sells doughnuts, pastries, and bagels every morning. Musical entertainment Friday and Saturday nights.

For more lodging recommendations, go to www.mobiltravelguide.com

EAT

MOBIL STAR-RATED RESTAURANTS

Chicago

THE BERGHOFF. ★
17 W Adams St, Chicago (60603). Phone 312/427-3170. www.berghoff.com. The Loop's beloved Berghoff, a landmark of 100-plus years, mingles tourists and locals alike. Out-of-towners line up for the German restaurant's lavishly trimmed dining room, where warm potato salad accompanies oversized weiner schnitzel and smoky sausages. Office workers pack the long, wood-paneled barroom slugging mugs of the house beer and munching carved roast beef sandwiches. The bar proudly displays the city's first post-Prohibition liquor license. German menu. Lunch, dinner. Closed Sun. Casual attire. **$$**

ED DEBEVIC'S. ★
640 N Wells St, Chicago (60610). Phone 312/664-1707. www.eddebevics.com. Treat your tweens and teens to Ed Debevic's, a retro 1950s diner where sassy, gum-snapping servers in period uniforms delight in giving diners a hard time. It's all in good fun, as is the lighthearted menu of burgers, hot dogs, and shakes, plus hearty Middle American staples like meat loaf and pot roast. American menu. Lunch, dinner. Closed Thanksgiving, Dec 24-25. Children's menu. Casual attire. Valet parking. **$**

FOGO DE CHÃO. ★★
661 N LaSalle St, Chicago (60610). Phone 312/932-9330. www.fogodechao.com. If you're in a carnivorous mood, this upscale, aromatic Brazilian churrascaria is the place to indulge. Fifteen all-you-can-eat grilled and roasted meats waft through the room on spits, borne by efficient "gauchos" who descend upon you at your whim. The massive salad bar and side dishes represent the other food groups—but at this price, save room for plenty of meat. Brazilian menu. Lunch, dinner. Casual attire. Reservations recommended. Valet parking. **$$$**

CHICAGOLAND SPEEDWAY, IL

HARRY CARAY'S. ★★
33 W Kinzie St, Chicago (60610). Phone 312/828-0966. www.hcrestaurantgroup.com. Although the legendary Cubs announcer died in 1998, his boisterous spirit thrives at this restaurant in River North, a vintage brick building emblazoned with Caray's signature expression, "Holy cow!" Inside, choose from the casual saloon with numerous sports-tuned TVs or the white-tablecloth dining room specializing in Harry's favorite food, Italian. Wherever you sit, you'll find a casual vibe and walls plastered with baseball memorabilia. Italian menu. Lunch, dinner. Casual attire. Valet parking. $$

MAGGIANO'S LITTLE ITALY. ★
516 N Clark St, Chicago (60610). Phone 312/644-7700. www.maggianos.com. From this River North location, Maggiano's ode to classic Italian-American neighborhoods has spawned spin-offs around the country. Fans love it for its big-hearted spirit as expressed in huge portions of familiar red-sauced pastas and the genuine warmth of servers and staff. But be forewarned: it's loud and crowded, better suited to convivial groups than to intimacy-seeking couples. Italian menu. Lunch, dinner. Closed Dec 25. Casual attire. Valet parking. Outdoor seating. $$

TWIN ANCHORS RESTAURANT AND TAVERN. ★
1655 N Sedgwick St, Chicago (60614). Phone 312/266-1616. www.twinanchorsribs.com. Make no bones about it: Chicago is a meat-and-potatoes kind of town, and there are few things that native Chicagoans like more than a great slab of ribs. Choices abound, but a local favorite is Twin Anchors Restaurant and Tavern in the Old Town neighborhood just north of downtown (and a fairly short cab ride away). The menu may be limited, but the portions are generous. Be prepared for a long wait, though; this 60-seat restaurant fills up fast. Barbecue menu. Lunch, dinner. Bar. Casual attire. Valet parking. Outdoor seating. $$

WISHBONE. ★
1001 W Washington Blvd, Chicago (60607). Phone 312/850-2663. www.wishbonechicago.com. Casual Southern dishes at reasonable prices in colorful settings filled with faux-outdoor art comprise the winning combination at Wishbone. Lunches and dinners serve up bean-based hoppin' John, blackened catfish, and shrimp and grits. Breakfast offers plenty of unusual choices, such as crab cakes, to round out the egg offerings. American menu. Lunch, dinner, brunch. Casual attire. Outdoor seating. $$

Crest Hill
MERICHKA'S RESTAURANT. ★
604 Theodore St, Crest Hill (60435). Phone 815/723-9371. This classic American roadside diner with a 69-year history is still run by the same family. Locals rave about Merichka's Poor Boy sandwiches. American menu. Lunch, dinner. Casual attire. $

Joliet
TRUTH. ★★
808 W Jefferson St, Joliet (60435). Phone 815/744-5901. This restaurant serves contemporary American regional cuisine in an inviting neighborhood

KIDS' PICK

White Fence Farm has thrived for nearly 50 years serving fried chicken dinners within the confines of a homey farmhouse restaurant. Second-generation owner Bob Hastert Jr. and his mother, Doris Hastert, start with only fresh chicken, never frozen, and use a secret breading recipe milled exclusively for White Fence. Each meal comes with a potpourri of homemade sides: bean salad, coleslaw, pickled beets, and corn fritters—plus cottage cheese and choice of potato. The property itself is truly a farm and features a petting zoo and a museum containing classic cars, clocks, music boxes, and other antiques. You really need to visit the restaurant itself to get the full experience, but if you can't find time between Saturday's and Sunday's races, you can at least get a taste of the food. White Fence operates a carry-out store at 80 Barney Drive in Joliet by the Jefferson Square Mall (phone 815/744-2072). American menu. Lunch, dinner. Closed Mon; Thanksgiving, Dec 24-25; also Jan. Children's menu. Casual attire. $$ *11700 Joliet Rd, Lemont (60439). Phone 630/739-1720. www.whitefencefarm.com.*

atmosphere. American menu. Dinner. Closed Sun-Mon. Casual attire. Reservations recommended. $$

Lockport

PUBLIC LANDING. ★★
200 W 8th St, Lockport (60441). Phone 815/838-6500. Built in 1838, the building is an Illinois Historic Landmark. American menu. Lunch, dinner. Closed Mon. Bar. Casual attire. $$

Morris

R-PLACE FAMILY EATERY. ★
21 Romines Dr, Morris (60450). Phone 815/942-3690. This 24-hour restaurant is housed in a truck stop with Victorian-era décor; chandeliers, Tiffany-style lamps; an extensive collection of Americana, antique toys, mechanical puppets, and gas station memorabilia. American menu. Breakfast, lunch, dinner, late-night. Children's menu. Casual attire. $

ROCKWELL INN. ★★
2400 W Hwy 6, Morris (60450). Phone 815/942-6224. www.rockwellinn.50megs.com. The decorations in this restaurant include Norman Rockwell prints and a bar from the 1893 Columbian Exposition. American menu. Lunch, dinner, Sun brunch. Bar. Casual attire. $$

Rockdale

SYL'S RESTAURANT. ★★
829 Moen Ave, Rockdale (60436). Phone 815/725-1977. www.sylsrestaurant.com. A Joliet area landmark since 1946, Syl's Restaurant offers classic American cuisine in a stately environment. American menu. Lunch, dinner. Sun brunch. Casual attire. $$

LOCAL RECOMMENDATIONS

Elwood

MR. B'S BAR & GRILL.
23956 Rte 53, Elwood (60421). Phone 815/727-7070. Located about a half-mile south of the speedway, Mr. B's is one of only a handful of restaurants within walking distance of the track and hands-down the best. If you have a craving for a good burger or fish and chips and a beer and don't want to drive to Joliet proper, this is the place. American menu. Lunch, dinner. Casual attire. $

Joliet

CHICAGO STREET BAR & GRILL.
75 N Chicago St, Joliet (60432). Phone 815/727-7171. www.chicagost.com. An Irish pub located in downtown Joliet, Chicago Street is the only place in the country where you'll find Chicago Street Irish Amber, a beer microbrewed exclusively for the tavern. The menu consists of hearty, reasonably priced soups, salads, and sandwiches (featuring homemade spreads like creamy onion or hot-and-sweet mustard), all made from scratch. American menu. Lunch, dinner. Bar. Casual attire. $

CORNER CAFÉ.
700 Ruby St, Joliet (60435). Phone 815/726-1988. The Corner Café has the look and feel of a small-town eatery where the locals gather to swap fish stories and down a cup of coffee with their eggs. Great family place. Nothing fancy, just good food. American menu. Breakfast, lunch. Casual attire. $

HEROES & LEGENDS SPORTS BAR & GRILL.
2400 W Jefferson St, Joliet (60435). Phone 815/741-9207. www.heroesandlegends.com. Famous for its 1-pound hamburgers on oversized buns, Heroes & Legends topped the *Joliet Herald News* Reader's Choice poll for best sandwiches four years running. Forty televisions ensure you don't miss a minute of any game. American menu. Lunch, dinner. Bar. Casual attire. $

KNIGHTS OF COLUMBUS.
1813 E Cass St, Joliet (60432). Phone 815/723-3827. It may sound a little odd, but two days a week the Joliet Knights of Columbus holds one of the best fish fries (Alaskan cod and walleye) in the area, and serves a decent fried chicken as well. This is not a restaurant but the Knights of Columbus hall, so don't expect flashy signs or a refined interior. American, seafood menu. Lunch (Fri), dinner (Fri-Sat). Casual attire. $

OLD FASHIONED PANCAKE HOUSE.
2022 W Jefferson St, Joliet (60435). Phone 815/741-4666. Don't let the name fool you. Although this family-owned restaurant serves breakfast all day (try the strawberry waffle à la mode for a late-night snack), it offers an extensive menu of steaks, chicken, and seafood, with some influence from Italian and French cuisines. American menu. Breakfast, lunch, dinner. Casual attire. $$

For more dining recommendations, go to www.mobiltravelguide.com

SIDETRIP

Land of Lincoln
Springfield, IL

Take in a little more of the original Route 66—and a whole lot of history on the 16th president of the United States—by making the three-hour drive to Springfield, Illinois. The Illinois state capital and home to Abraham Lincoln for nearly 25 years added yet another piece of Lincolnia in the fall of 2004 with the opening of the **Abraham Lincoln Presidential Library and Museum** (112 N Sixth St, phone 217/524-7216). (The museum portion is actually slated to open in early 2005.)

The museum mingles high-tech with history. The exhibit "The Journey" uses forensic science to determine what Lincoln might have looked like as a boy and traces his life through his presidency and assassination. "Lincoln's Eyes" is a three-screen, 360-degree illusion effect that examines Lincoln's life and legacy from the viewpoints of supporters and detractors.

After a simulated overview of Lincoln's life, visit the places he lived and worked. Start at the **Lincoln Home National Historic Site** (426 S 7th St, phone 217/492-4241, www.nps.gov/liho), the only home the rail-splitter ever owned. The Lincoln family lived there from 1844 until their 1861 departure for Washington, DC. The home has been restored with Lincoln family furnishings, period artifacts, reproduced wallpapers, and window hangings.

Other restored Lincoln sites include: the **Lincoln Depot** (10th and Monroe sts, phone 217/544-8695), where he delivered his farewell address before departing for Washington; the **Lincoln-Herndon Law Office Building** (6th and Adams sts, phone 217/785-7289), where he practiced law; and the **Old State Capitol State Historic Site** (between 5th and 6th sts, phone 217/785-7961), where he made his famous "House Divided" speech.

Finish up, fittingly, at the **Lincoln Tomb State Historic Site** in Oak Ridge Cemetery (1500 Monument Ave, phone 217/782-2717). A monumental sarcophagus sits in the center of the domed burial chamber. Lincoln is actually buried 10 feet below to prevent grave robbers from disturbing the remains.

Stop in and pay your respects to Illinois' favorite son at the Lincoln tomb.

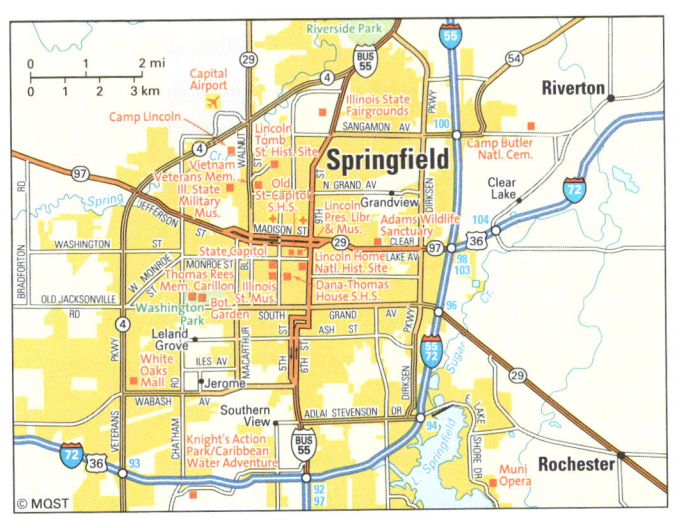

For more Springfield recommendations, go to www.mobiltravelguide.com

92

Bobby Hamilton Jr (No. 25), Casey Atwood (No. 14), and David Stremme (No. 32) jockey for position during the NASCAR Busch Series Diamond Hill Plywood Co. 200.

Darlington Raceway

Darlington, SC

5

These fans leave no doubt about what they want to see—NASCAR action under the South Carolina sun.

TRACK FACTS
DARLINGTON RACEWAY. 1301 Harry Byrd Hwy, Darlington (29532). Phone 843/395-8499. www.darlingtonraceway.com.

SECURITY. Coolers no larger than 6 x 6 x 12 inches are allowed. Other items brought into the raceway must be in an approved container: either a soft-sided insulated bag or a bag worn on a strap around the neck or clipped to the belt. Cameras are allowed.

PARKING. Free parking to accommodate a full house of 60,000 fans is available on grassy areas around the track.

FIRST AID. Paramedics staff first aid stations in the concourse areas behind the front stretch and backstretch. Doctors are on duty at the medical care facility in the infield.

CONCESSIONS. Stands are located at ground level, at the top of the grandstands, and on the concourses. They offer the usual racing menu of hot dogs, burgers, sausage, fries, barbecue, and the regional specialty, boiled peanuts.

DARLINGTON RACEWAY, SC

Race cars move into a tight turn in front of another full house of fans.

GETTING TICKETS

Tickets for the 2005 races face high demand, because the raceway is hosting just one NASCAR NEXTEL Cup race instead of two—so the pool of available tickets is much smaller. Prices range from $45 to $95 per seat. Order tickets by calling toll-free 866/459-7223 or through the track's Web site at www.darlingtonraceway.com.

RV AND CAMPING

Nothing is more convenient when visiting the track than camping on the Darlington Raceway grounds. To book a space, call toll-free 866/459-7223.

For 2005, an RV with two people costs $475 for a week of camping over the May race dates. Each extra person older than 12 is an additional $100. The tent camp is $590 for the week for four people. It costs $100 to drive your car onto the infield, plus $100 for each person in the car.

Darlington has room for 400 RVs, 132 tent camping sites, and 150 spaces for cars. Book as far in advance as possible to ensure the best choice of sites.

GETTING AROUND

If you're traveling to the track on I-95, take Exit 164 and turn right onto northbound US Rte 52. You'll travel about 5 miles to US Rte 52 bypass north. Turn left and travel about 2 miles to South Carolina Rte 151/34. Follow the exit ramp onto Hwy 151 and turn left. The track is approximately 1 1/2 miles on the left.

From I-20, take Exit 131 to northbound US Rte 401. Travel about 10 miles to the US Rte 52 bypass and turn left. Drive a short distance and turn left again on South Carolina 151/34. The track is about 1 1/2 miles ahead.

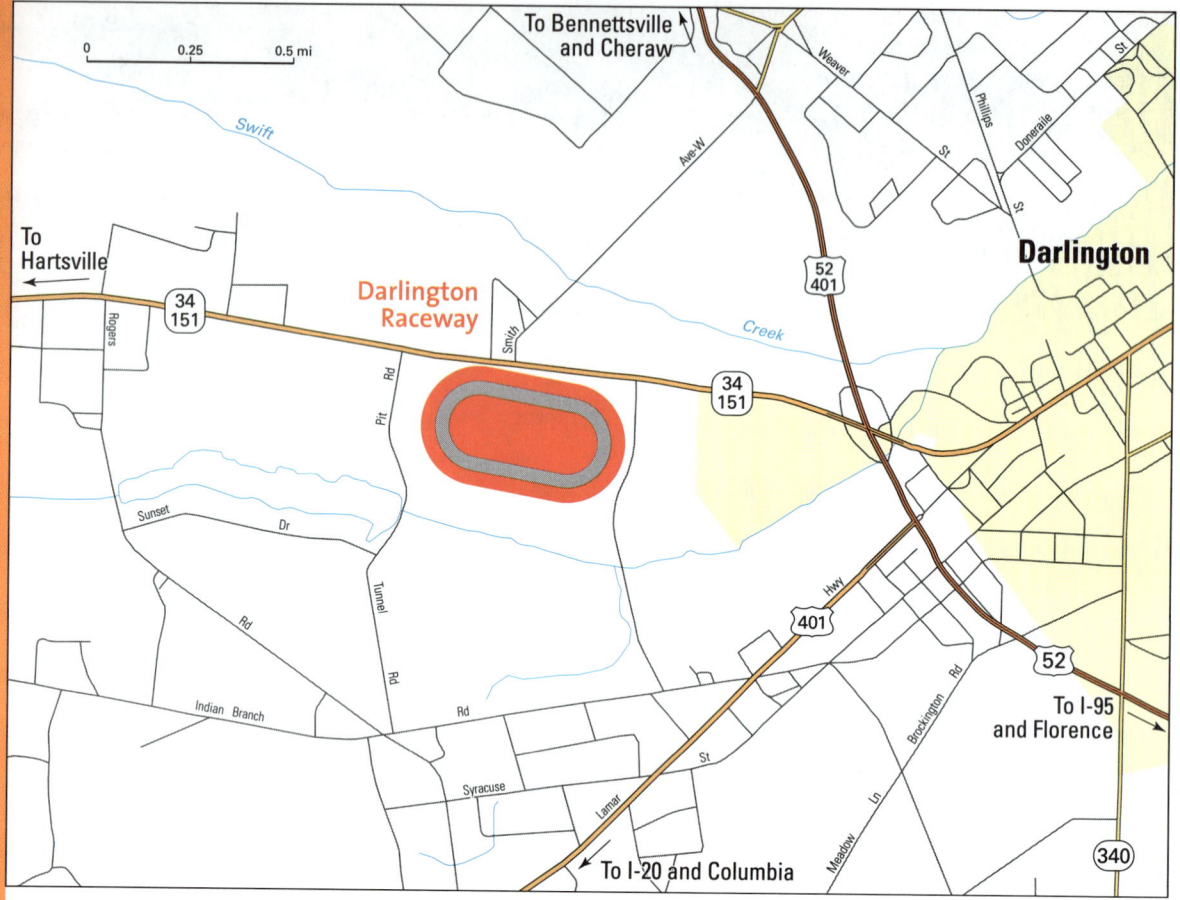

DARLINGTON POLE POSITION:
The 10 miles surrounding Darlington Raceway.

NOTHIN' BUT TRACK

The racetrack is Darlington's biggest attraction. The town is very small, with fewer than 7,000 residents, a fraction of the number of fans who pour into the facility for a race. Track officials boast the race at Darlington isn't just a vacation stop—it's so out-of-the-way, it *is* the vacation.

A trip to Darlington, insiders say, is reserved for true race fans, the ones who want to experience racing history at the first track built purely for stock car competition and those who appreciate the difficulty level of Darlington's unique track.

Across the street from the massive stadium is a sea of green fields, lush with soybeans, peanuts, cotton, and tobacco. Downtown is a square built around the Darlington County Courthouse. The blocks around downtown feature small, local stores and casual restaurants, and older Victorian homes.

Also downtown is the **Liberty Lane Walk of Fame** (100 block of Pearl St, phone toll-free 888/427-8720), where you can see the handprints of nearly 20 NASCAR drivers, including Jeff Gordon and Edward Glenn "Fireball" Roberts.

The true charm of the area is the people. When NASCAR comes to town and the population increases tenfold, locals don't grumble about the tourists. Instead, they seem eager to offer a taste of small-town hospitality, by way of directions and restaurant recommendations.

Unless you camp at the track, there aren't too many places to stay in Darlington. Nearby Florence has a host of strip malls with restaurants and motel chains, as well as a small amusement park and a minor league hockey team. The towns of Sumter and Camden have historical sites and more offbeat bed-and-breakfast options.

But the real draw of the region will always be the raceway, the track "too tough to tame."

DARLINGTON RACEWAY, SC

INSIDER'S PICK

As past president of the Darlington Raceway, **Andrew Gurtis** had his pick of the city's best eats. "We really enjoy Red Bone Alley. The overall atmosphere is vibrant and the building is unique, set in a two-story warehouse to look like an alley. The food is great and Red Bone has a wonderful children's area featuring ice cream and an old milk truck the kids can play in. It's a great place for anyone from 1 to 100 years old." *1903 W Palmetto St, Florence, 29501. Phone 843/673-0035. www.redbonealley.com.*

Don't miss out on an old-fashioned oyster roast while in Darlington.

Walk through some historic train cars at the Florence, SC, Railroad Museum.

DARLINGTON CALENDAR

MAY 5, 2005
Taste of Darlington. Located just west of Darlington at 1301 Harry Byrd Hwy (29532). Phone 843/395-2310; toll-free 888/842-7872. A variety of foods, beverages, and desserts, all locally made.

MAY 6, 2005
NASCAR Busch Series

MAY 7, 2005
NASCAR NEXTEL Cup Series. Come early for the traditional wedding ceremonies held every quarter-hour until the race starts. Call to book your own wedding.

MAY 7, 2005
Blessing of the Inlet Sound. Murrells Inlet, Myrtle Beach (20124). Phone 843/650-7677. Entertainment, exhibitions, children's activities, seafood, and arts and crafts held creek-front.

MAY 7, 2005
Riverfest. Riverfront Park and historic Columbia Canal, Columbia (29212). Phone 803/798-8502; toll-free 800/332-1000. www.epilepsysc.org. Participate in the 8K River Run, scenic bike tour, or leisurely 5K River Walk, or enjoy games, rides, live bands, and craft and food vendors.

MAY 14–15, 2005
Little River Blue Crab Festival. Historic Little River Waterfront, Mineola Ave and Riverview Dr, Little River (29566). Phone 843/385-3180. www.bluecrabfestival.org. Try a blue crab special, and enjoy other food, arts and crafts, children's activities, and live music.

DARLINGTON OUTFIELD:
The 60 miles surrounding Darlington Raceway.

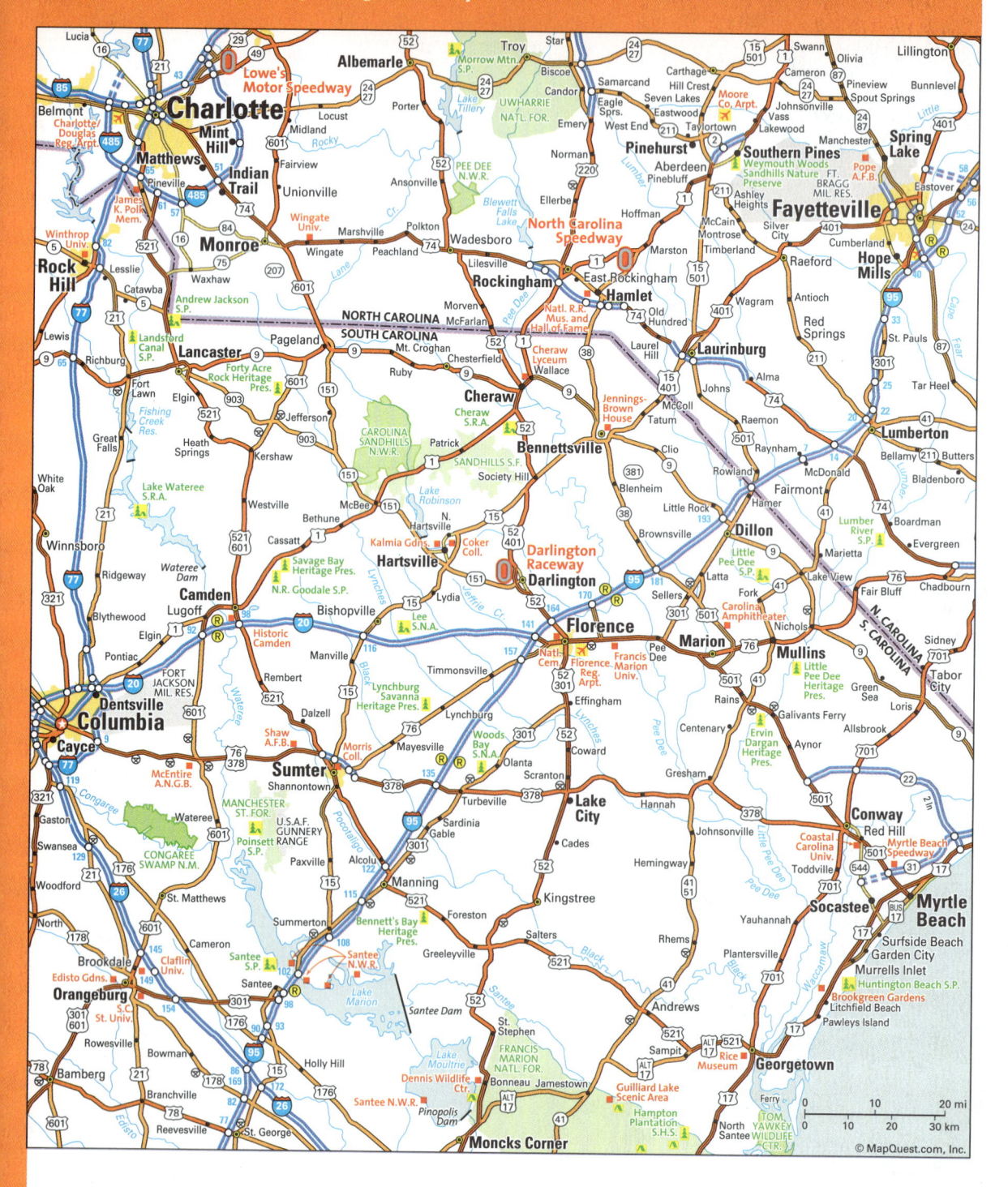

SEE

ATTRACTIONS

Camden, SC

HISTORIC CAMDEN.
Phone 803/432-9841. www.camden-sc.org. Camden offers guided tours (nominal fee) of a 107-acre outdoor museum preservation complex and variety of historic homes, some of which date back to before the Revolutionary War. The site of the Battle of Camden, a National Historic Landmark, lies 5 miles north of town.

Cheraw, SC

CHERAW HISTORICAL DISTRICT.
Phone 843/537-8425. www.cheraw.com or www.cherawchamber.com. Cheraw showcases a 213-acre historic district with several recommended walking routes. The town's roots date back to before the Revolutionary War, and Cheraw has a deep Civil War history as well. The town green (circa 1768) is the site of the small Cheraw Lyceum Museum (circa 1820). Other notable buildings are Town Hall (circa 1858), Market Hall (circa 1837), and the Inglis-McIver Law Office (circa 1830). Victorian and Revival homes dot the walking trail through the heavily wooded town. Limit your drinking: local lore has it that in the past, anyone found drunk in public in Cheraw had to plant a tree in the town limits. **FREE**

CHERAW STATE PARK.
100 State Park Rd, Cheraw (29520). Phone 843/537-9656. Located on 7,361 acres of gently rolling green sandhills, the park offers boat rentals, fishing, nature trails, an 18-hole golf course, picnic shelters, a playground, and a recreation building. You'll also find camping and cabins. **$**

Darlington, SC

DARLINGTON RACEWAY STOCK CAR MUSEUM AND NATIONAL MOTORSPORTS PRESS ASSOCIATION HALL OF FAME.
1301 Harry Byrd Hwy, Darlington. Phone 843/395-8499. www.darlingtonraceway.com. Explore Darlington's storied NASCAR history. The Hall of Fame features everyone from David Pearson and Dale Earnhardt to NASCAR'S first champion, Red Byron. Stock cars include the blue Plymouth that Richard Petty drove to victory in ten races back in 1967, a 1991 Chevy driven by Darrell Waltrip that rolled eight times during a race, and a 1971 Mercury driven by Pearson, Darlington's all-time winner. **$**

LIBERTY LANE WALK OF FAME.
100 block of Pearl St, Darlington. Phone toll-free 888/427-8720. Stroll down the Walk of Fame, which honors NASCAR stock car drivers who have won at Darlington Raceway. Compare your hands with the cement prints of NASCAR greats like Neil Bonnett, Dale Earnhardt, Bill Elliott, Harry Gant, and Richard Petty. **FREE**

Dillon, SC

LITTLE PEE DEE STATE PARK.
1298 State Park Rd (County Rd 22), Dillon (29536). Phone 843/774-8872. www.discoversouthcarolina.com/stateparks. Along the Little Pee Dee River and convenient to Interstate 95, this 835-acre park offers a tranquil setting for picnicking, fishing in the 54-acre Lake Norton, camping, or just relaxing. Roam through the small river swamp and dry sandy areas and explore the variety of flora and fauna. (Daily 9 am-6 pm) **$**

Florence, SC

FLORENCE MUSEUM OF ART, SCIENCE AND HISTORY.
558 Spruce St, Florence (29501). Phone 843/662-3351. www.florenceweb.com/museum.htm. This interesting local museum showcases rotating art exhibits, historic objects from the Florence and Pee Dee area, Southwestern pueblo pottery, African and Asian artifacts, and a new Civil War collection donated by Francis A. Lord, the author of a five-volume encyclopedia about Civil War collectibles. The museum also has an outpost Railroad Museum nearby, which allows visitors to stroll through a vintage caboose and box car filled with railroad memorabilia from Florence's days as a railroad town. (Tues-Sat 10 am-5 pm, Sun 2-5 pm; Railroad cars June-Aug Sat-Sun 3-5 pm) **$**

FLORENCE NATIONAL CEMETERY.
803 E National Cemetery Rd, Florence (29501). Phone 843/669-8783. This is the smaller of South Carolina's Civil War cemeteries, where Union captives who died at the neighboring stockade are buried. Researchers have identified many of the dead, who were originally

SEE ATTRACTIONS

buried as unknown soldiers (lists are available from the cemetery). **FREE**

FLORENCE STOCKADE.
Stockade Rd (off National Cemetery Rd near I-95), Florence (29506). The stockade was a Civil War prison that housed Union soldiers transferred from the notorious Andersonville prison. Roughly 2,800 soldiers died there over about six months of operation, including Florena Budwin, who Friends of the Florence Stockade say is the only female Civil War prisoner to die in captivity. She is buried in the adjoining cemetery. The site is a Civil War Heritage Site, and the society has put a marker along the south wall to commemorate the soldiers who died. A 1947 marker put up by the United Daughters of the Confederacy of Florence memorializes "the Confederate soldiers and the citizens of the community who in the line of duty guarded these prisoners." **FREE**

MISTER MARK'S FUN PARK.
1331 N Cashua Dr, Florence (29501). Phone 843/669-7373. www.mistermarksfunpark.com. This entertainment complex has a restaurant on site, an 18-hole miniature golf course ($), an oval sprint car track, go-kart road course ($$$$), and 8,000-square-foot arcade.

PEE DEE GOLFING.
3290 W Radio Dr, Florence (29501). Phone 843/669-0950; toll-free 800/325-9005. Pee Dee Golfing arranges packages including accommodations, breakfast, 18-hole greens fees, and cart fees. It can book times at a variety of local courses. **$$$$**

PEE DEE PRIDE MINOR LEAGUE HOCKEY TEAM.
Florence City-County Civic Center, Florence (29501). Phone 843/669-7825. www.peedeepride.com. The Pee Dee Pride team occasionally gets lost in the hoopla surrounding NASCAR, but they still attract large crowds. The arena has a full schedule of other events and some public skating hours. Find schedules and prices on the civic center Web site at www.florencecivicicenter.com.

WAR BETWEEN THE STATES MUSEUM.
107 S Guerry St, Florence (29501). Phone 843/669-1266. www.florenceweb.com/warmuseum.htm. Explore artifacts, pictures, and stories that bring you back to the Civil War. (Wed and Sat 10 am-5 pm) **$**

Hartsville, SC

HARTSVILLE MUSEUM.
222 N Fifth St, Hartsville (29550). Phone 843/383-3005. www.hartsvillemuseum.org. Founded in 1980, this local history museum is housed in a 1930s post office building. The galleries depict history, arts, and present-day events, and include Native American art and an ancient spinning wheel. After perusing the museum, head outside to wander through the sculpture courtyard. (Mon-Fri 10 am-5 pm, Sat 10 am-2 pm) **FREE**

KALMIA GARDENS OF COKER COLLEGE.
624 W Carolina Ave, Hartsville (29550). Phone 843/383-8145. www.coker.edu/kalmia. A 33-acre botanical garden with walking trails through blackwater swamp, mountain laurel thickets, uplands of pine, oak, and holly, and a beech bluff. Plantings of azaleas, camellias, and other ornamentals complement native plants. **FREE**

Hopkins, SC

CONGAREE NATIONAL PARK.
100 National Park Rd, Hopkins (29061). Phone 803/776-4396. www.nps.gov/cosw. Congaree is about a two-hour drive away from the racetrack, but as South Carolina's only national park (and the nation's newest), it's worth the trip. Roughly 22,000 acres of old-growth bottomland hardwood forest spill across a wetlands rich with wildlife, giving the lush enclave a Jurassic-era feel. There are 20 miles of hiking trails, fishing, canoeing, hiking trails, and boardwalks. Primitive camping is allowed by permit. **FREE**

Myrtle Beach, SC

NASCAR SPEEDPARK.
1820 21st Ave, Myrtle Beach (29577). Phone 843/918-8725. www.nascarspeedpark.com. Continue the racing fun with tracks you can drive, miniature golf courses, kiddie rides, an indoor climbing wall, bumper boats, an arcade, and NASCAR souvenirs. (See "Side Trip," page 105.)

Sumter, SC

SUMTER OPERA HOUSE.
21 N Main St, Sumter (29150). Phone 803/436-2500. The 1893 Opera House stands today not only as a symbol of the past but also as an active sign of the progressive spirit of the people of Sumter. The 550-seat auditorium is used for concerts, school events,

STAY

For more attractions, go to www.mobiltravelguide.com

MOBIL STAR-RATED LODGINGS

Camden, SC

GREENLEAF INN. ★★
1308 Broad St, Camden (29020). Phone 803/425-1806; toll-free 800/437-5874. www.greenleafinncamden.com. Located in the historic district of Camden, the inn features guesthouses built in 1805 and 1890 and decorated in Victorian style. 10 rooms, 2 story. Complimentary full breakfast. Check-in 3 pm, check-out 11 am. High-speed Internet access. Restaurant. $

Latta, SC

ABINGDON MANOR. ★★★
307 Church St, Latta (29565). Phone 843/752-5090; toll-free 888/752-5090. www.abingdonmanor.com. This mansion is beautifully restored in the style of an English manor with exquisite service and luxurious accommodations. It combines the attention of a small hotel with the comfort and seclusion of a grand home. Gourmet dining is a specialty, and the manor features seasonal menus to reflect the local produce. 5 rooms, 2 story. Check-in 3 pm, check-out 11 am. Children over 12 years only. Complimentary full breakfast. $

Laurinburg, NC

COMFORT INN. ★★
1705 401 Bypass S, Laurinburg (28352). Phone 910/277-7788; toll-free 800/424-6423. www.comfortinn.com. Set at the intersection of Highways 401 and 74, this award-winning hotel features cozy rooms and impeccable service. In-room amenities include high-speed Internet access, and down pillows and comforters. 80 rooms. Complimentary continental breakfast. Check-in 3 pm, check-out noon. Fitness room. Outdoor pool. $

Sumter, SC

FAIRFIELD INN. ★
2390 Broad St, Sumter (29150). Phone 803/469-9001; toll-free 800/228-2800. www.fairfieldinn.com. Close to a number of area universities and colleges, as well as the Swan Lake Iris Gardens and the Sumter Opera House, this well-appointed hotel is sure to please guests. 124 rooms, 2 story. Complimentary continental breakfast. Check-in 3 pm, check-out noon. Fitness room. Outdoor pool. Business center. $

MAGNOLIA HOUSE BED AND BREAKFAST. ★★★
230 Church St, Sumter (29150). Phone 803/775-6694; toll-free 888/666-0296. Built in 1907, this inn's architecture is reminiscent of the Old South, including a four-column front porch. The décor is antique French. Evening cocktails are served on the veranda overlooking the gardens. 4 rooms, 2 story. Pets accepted. Complimentary full breakfast. Check-in 3 pm, check-out 11 am. $

PIT PASS

Local lore has it that the owner of a peanut field used to play in a poker game at the town jail. One day, another player suggested building a race track on the site. The owner shrugged, but when he came home, he found his buddy, Harold Brasington, on a tractor, carving out a rough track in the field. "Okay," the man is rumored to have said. "Just don't ruin my minnow pond." Brasington made a few modifications to protect the prized fishing spot—which became Ramsey's Pond near Turn 4—and the result was Darlington's unique, egg-shaped track design.

LOCAL RECOMMENDATIONS

Darlington, SC

BEST VALUE INN.
705 Washington St, Darlington (29532). Phone 843/393-8990; toll-free 888/315-2378. www.bestvalueinns.com. 56 rooms, 2 story. Complimentary continental breakfast. Check-in 1 pm, check-out 11 am. **$**

Florence, SC

BEST WESTERN INN.
1808 W Lucas St, Florence (29501). Phone 843/678-9292; toll-free 800/780-7234. www.bestwestern.com. 74 rooms, 2 story. Complimentary continental breakfast. Check-in 2 pm, check-out 11 am. High-speed Internet access. Outdoor pool. **$**

COUNTRY INN AND SUITES.
1739 Mandville Rd, Florence (29501). Phone 843/317-6616; toll-free 888/201-1746. www.countryinns.com. 80 rooms, 3 story. Complimentary continental breakfast. Check-in 3 pm, check-out noon. Wireless Internet access. Outdoor pool. **$**

COURTYARD BY MARRIOTT FLORENCE.
2680 Hospitality Blvd, Florence (29501). Phone 843/662-7066; toll-free 800/321-2211. www.courtyard.com. Near shopping areas and the Florence Civic Center, this hotel boasts a courtyard with a gazebo. 90 rooms, 3 story. Check-in 3 pm, check-out noon. High-speed Internet access. Restaurant. Fitness room. Indoor pool. **$**

DAYS INN NORTH.
2111 W Lucas St, Florence (29501). Phone 843/665-4444; toll-free 800/489-4344. www.daysinn.com. With 15 restaurants within a 1-mile radius, as well as nearby shopping, museums, and movie theaters, guests will find no shortage of things to see and do in the Florence area. 103 rooms, 2-story. Complimentary continental breakfast. Check-in 2 pm, check-out 11 am. Fitness room. Outdoor pool. **$**

HAMPTON INN AND SUITES FLORENCE—CIVIC CENTER.
3000 W Radio Dr, Florence (29501). Phone 843/629-9900; toll-free 800/426-7866. www.hamptoninn.com. Located at the junction of Interstates 20 and 95, the hotel is adjacent to the Florence Civic Center, the Swamp Fox Cinemas, and across the street from Magnolia Mall and the Commons of Magnolia. 82 rooms, 3 story. Complimentary continental breakfast. Check-in 3 pm, check-out noon. High-speed Internet access. Laundry services. Fitness room. Outdoor pool. **$**

HOLIDAY INN AND SUITES HOTEL.
1819 W Lucas St, Florence (29501). Phone 843/665-4555; toll-free 866/655-4669. www.holiday-inn.com. Refurbished and renovated in 2001, this hotel includes a NASCAR-themed sports bar. 204 rooms, 2 story. Pets accepted. Check-in 3 pm, check-out noon. High-speed Internet access. Laundry services. Restaurant, bar. Fitness room. Outdoor pool. **$**

HOLIDAY INN EXPRESS HOTEL AND SUITES FLORENCE.
2101 Florence Harlee Blvd, Florence (29506). Phone 843/629-9779; toll-free 866/655-4669. www.hiexpress.com. Near the Florence Regional Airport, this hotel is in a suburban setting. 86 rooms, 4 story. Complimentary continental breakfast. Check-in 4 pm, check-out 11 am. High-speed Internet access. Fitness room. Indoor pool. Business center. **$**

SPRINGHILL SUITES BY MARRIOTT FLORENCE.
2670 Hospitality Blvd, Florence (29501). Phone 843/317-9050; toll-free 888/287-9400. www.springhillsuites.com. The Florence Civic Center and shopping area are located nearby. 95 rooms, 4 story. Complimentary continental breakfast. Check-in 3 pm, check-out noon. High speed Internet access. Fitness room. Indoor pool. **$**

WINGATE INN.
2123 W Lucas St, Florence (29501). Phone 843/629-1111; toll-free 800/228-1000. www.wingateinns.com. 84 rooms, 3 story. Complimentary continental breakfast. Check-in 2 pm, check-out 11 am. Wireless Internet access. Fitness room. Outdoor pool, whirlpool. Business center. **$**

Sumter, SC

BEST WESTERN SUMTER INN.
1050 Broad St, Sumter (29150). Phone 803/773-8110; toll-free 800/780-7234. www.bestwestern.com. 47 rooms, 1 story. Check-in noon, check-out 11 am. Outdoor pool. **$**

COMFORT SUITES SUMTER.
2500 Broad St, Sumter (29150). Phone 803/469-0200; toll-free 877/424-6423. www.comfortsuites.com. This hotel is located in the downtown area. 65 rooms, 3 story. Complimentary continental breakfast.

Check-in 3 pm, check-out noon. High-speed Internet access. Fitness room. Indoor pool, whirlpool. Business center. $

HAMPTON INN SUMTER.
1370 Broad St, Sumter (29150). Phone 803/469-2222; toll-free 800/426-7866. www.hamptoninn.com. This location is about 5 miles west of the downtown area and within a mile of several restaurants. 74 rooms, 3 story. Complimentary continental breakfast. Check-in 2 pm, check-out 11 am. High-speed Internet access. Fitness room. Outdoor pool, whirlpool. Business center. $

RV AND CAMPING
Bishopville, SC

LEE STATE NATURAL AREA.
487 Loop Rd, Bishopville (29010). Phone 803/428-5307. www.discoversouthcarolina.com/stateparks. Campsites have water, electrical hook-ups, and access to restrooms with hot showers. Sites accommodate RVs up to either 30 feet or 36 feet. There are 25 sites for family camping and 23 designated for equestrian campers. A primitive equestrian camping area near the stable is available as well. Reserved sites are $1 extra per night, while most sites rent on a first-come, first-served basis.

Cheraw, SC

CHERAW STATE PARK.
100 State Park Rd, Cheraw (29520). Phone 843/537-9656. www.discoversouthcarolina.com/stateparks. There are 17 campsites on packed gravel with individual water and electrical hook-ups. Pull-through sites accommodate RVs up to either 40 feet or 34 feet and have a dump station. Restrooms and hot showers are on site, and six sites are along Lake Juniper, the park's 360-acre lake. Boaters may set up camp at the old boat landing on the north side of the lake. Equestrian camping, which includes central water, is also available near the lake. Reserved sites are $1 extra per night, while most sites rent on a first-come, first-served basis. Cheraw State Park also has furnished one-bedroom cabins with living supplies such as bed and bath linens, and kitchen utensils and appliances, as well as outside grills.

Dillon, SC

LITTLE PEE DEE STATE PARK.
1298 State Park Rd (County Rd 22), Dillon (29536). Phone 843/774-8872. www.discoversouthcarolina.com/stateparks. Within the state park, you'll find 32 sites with water and electrical hook-ups, and 18 tent sites with individual water, but no electricity. The campground offers restroom facilities with hot showers, and dump station. Reserved sites are $1 extra per night, while most sites rent on a first-come, first-served basis.

For more lodging recommendations, go to www.mobiltravelguide.com

EAT

MOBIL STAR-RATED RESTAURANTS
Camden, SC

LUCY'S. ★★
1043 Broad St, Camden (29020). Phone 803/432-9096. This gourmet restaurant is located in a historic building. The signature dish is lightly breaded veal sautéed with mushrooms. Other dishes include salmon and grits with dill saffron sauce, or shrimp and grits

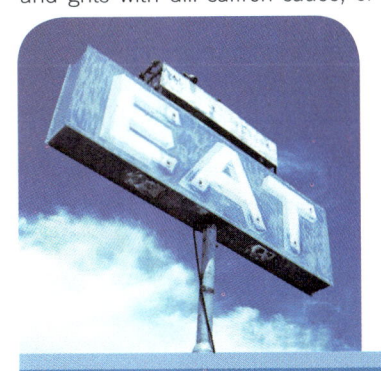

ROAD FOOD

The **Pee Dee State Farmers' Market** fills table after table with fresh produce and local cheese and honey. This is a great place for campers to find fresh food, or for race-goers to catch a break from restaurants. It's also the first stop for picnickers or hikers on their way to the region's parks. Open year-round. *US Hwy 52 between Florence and Darlington. Phone 843/665-5154.*

104 EAT MOBIL STAR-RATED RESTAURANTS

with tasso gravy. American menu. Lunch, dinner. Closed Sun-Mon; Jan 1, Thanksgiving, Dec 25. Bar. Casual attire. Reservations recommended. $$

Rembert, SC
LILIFREDS OF CAMDEN. ★★
8425 Main St, Rembert (29128). Phone 803/432-7063. A menu heavy on seafood draws diners to this low-country favorite. Seafood menu. Dinner. Closed Sun-Tues; holidays. $$

LOCAL RECOMMENDATIONS
Boykin, SC
BOYKIN'S AT THE MILL POND.
73 Boykin Mill Rd, Boykin (29128). Phone 803/425-8825. Some of the area's best high-end dining, Southern-style, is offered at this restaurant about ten minutes from Camden. The menu includes staples like grits and fried green tomatoes. American menu. Dinner. Closed Sun-Mon. Casual attire. Reservations recommended. $$

Camden, SC
THE DAILY GRIND.
1012 Broad St, Camden (29020). Phone 803/713-0033. This coffee shop offers a range of coffees and teas. American menu. Breakfast, lunch. Closed Sun. Casual attire. $

THE GREENLEAF INN OF CAMDEN.
1308 N Broad St, Camden (29020). Phone toll-free 800/437-5874. www.greenleafofcamden.com. This restaurant serves low-country specials such as shrimp and grits in a relaxed, upscale setting. American menu. Lunch, dinner. Reservations recommended. Casual attire. $$$

OLD SOUTH RESTAURANT.
402 DeKalb St, Camden (29020). Phone 803/713-0009. Hearty Southern fare is served, primarily buffet style. American menu. Breakfast, lunch, dinner. Closed Sun. Casual attire. $

Columbia, SC
BIG T BAR-B-QUE.
7535-C Garners Ferry Rd, Columbia (29209). Phone 803/776-7132. Featuring the mustard, ketchup, and vinegar combination barbecue sauce that the South Carolina midland area is known for, all of the meats at this down-home eatery are locally smoked and roasted over owner Larry Brown's barbecue pits. The selection and sauce here are touted as some of the area's best. Barbecue menu. Lunch, dinner. Casual attire. $

Darlington, SC
JEWEL'S DELUXE RESTAURANT.
32 Public Sq, Darlington (29532). Phone 843/393-5511. Friendly service and home-style cooking won this restaurant the title of "best Darlington County restaurant" in the local Pee Dee area paper. Choose from a buffet or menu items including soup, sandwiches, and salads. House specialties include baked chicken and dressing with sweet potato souffle, and macaroni and cheese. American menu. Lunch. $

Florence, SC
ROGER'S BAR-B-CUE RESTAURANT.
2004 W Second Loop Rd, Florence (29501). Phone 843/667-9291. Roger's serves vinegar-based Southern barbecue, buffet style. It's a tangy and satisfying treat. Barbecue menu. Lunch, dinner. Casual attire. Outdoor seating. $

VENUS PANCAKE HOUSE.
471 W Palmetto St (29501). Phone 843/669-9977. Breakfast and lunch are served all day at this long-time, family-owned establishment. Hang out with local college students, business folks, and neighborhood families for a hearty plate of pancakes and other breakfast and lunch specialties. American menu. Breakfast, lunch, dinner. $

Laurinburg, NC
CHAMPS FINE FOOD AND SPIRITS.
1500 Hwy 401 S, Laurinburg (28352). Phone 910/276-0632; toll-free 800/582-2106. Meat eaters will feel right at home at this restaurant, which specializes in ribs and steaks. There's also an impressive salad bar. American menu. Dinner. Closed Dec 25. Bar. Children's menu. Casual attire. $$

Myrtle Beach, SC
NASCAR CAFE.
1808 21st Ave, Myrtle Beach (29577). Phone 843/946-7223. www.nascarcafe.com. This cafe offers steaks, fried chicken, sandwiches, salads, and lots of NASCAR memorabilia. American menu. Lunch, dinner. (See "Side Trip," page 105).

For more dining recommendations, go to www.mobiltravelguide.com

SIDETRIP

Neon and Nature
Myrtle Beach, SC

South Carolina's most famous resort town is a lot of things: a stretch of pristine beach, amusement parks, scores of top-quality golf courses, and one of the biggest doses of neon hoopla this side of Las Vegas. The formula works well enough to draw millions of visitors each year.

This is a destination where tourists can explore nearby wildlife and wetlands via kayak, canoe, bike, or car, while others opt for one of the many sky-high water slides or some 50 miniature golf courses, most with wild and outlandish decorations such as lava-spewing volcanoes and menacing gorillas.

Myrtle Beach is an easy two-hour drive from Darlington. A side trip in early May means you'll experience Myrtle Beach before the hordes of visitors arrive a month later. Attractions are less crowded, though prized tee times may still be hard to get.

On one side of Ocean Boulevard is the Grand Strand, a strip of caramel-colored, hard-packed sandy beach. On the other side is a line of brightly colored hotels and motels marching for miles. It's a see-and-be-seen cruise zone in the evenings.

Among the major draws is the **Myrtle Beach Pavilion Amusement Park** (phone 843/913-5200, www.mbpavilion.com), which just added the 110-foot-tall wooden Hurricane Category 5 roller coaster to its offerings. In nearby North Myrtle Beach, **Alligator Adventure** at **Barefoot Landing** (phone 843/361-0789, www.alligatoradventure.com) is one of the largest exotic reptile parks in the world. A **NASCAR Cafe** (1808 21st Ave N, phone 843/946-7223) offers lunch and dinner for fans, and the adjacent **NASCAR SpeedPark**

There is plenty to do in Myrtle Beach for young and old alike. Myrtle Beach is 90 minutes southeast of Darlington. For more travel tips, contact the **Myrtle Beach Area Chamber of Commerce** (Phone toll-free 800/356-3015. www.mbchamber.com) or visit www.myrtlebeachonline.com.

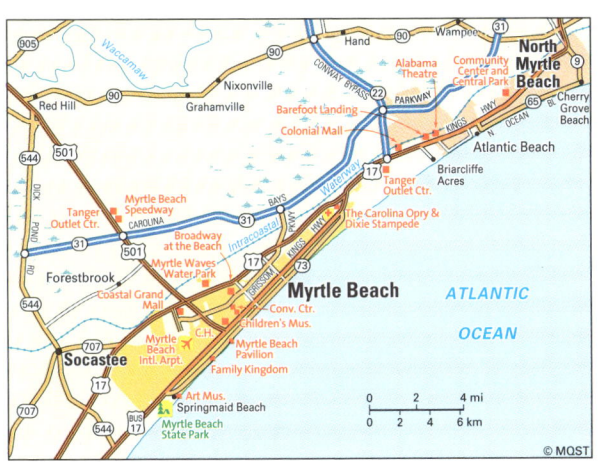

(phone 843/918-8725, www.nascarspeedpark.com) will meet your need for speed. Both the cafe and speed park are part of the **Broadway at the Beach** complex (phone toll-free 800/386-4662, www.broadwayatthebeach.com), an outdoor mall spread across 350 acres around a man-made lake. Kids will love the Build-a-Bear Workshop, where they can pick out the makings of a stuffed animal and watch workers stuff and finish it along an assembly line.

For more Myrtle Beach recommendations, go to www.mobiltravelguide.com

Pit crew members ready Michael Waltrip's Chevrolet for a return to action during the NASCAR NEXTEL Cup Series Pepsi 400.

Daytona International Speedway

Daytona Beach, FL

6

Racers begin the NASCAR NEXTEL Cup Series Pepsi 400 under the lights on a hot July night.

TRACK FACTS
DAYTONA INTERNATIONAL SPEEDWAY. 1801 W International Speedway Blvd, Daytona Beach (32114). Phone 386/253-7223. www.daytonainternationalspeedway.com.

SECURITY. Racegoers may bring in one soft-sided cooler, scanner bag, fanny pack, purse, binocular bag, or diaper bag (that's key)—but none larger than 6 x 6 x 12 inches. In addition, you can bring one clear plastic bag, no larger than 18 x 18 x 4 inches, and binoculars, scanners, headsets, and cameras worn over the neck or on a belt. Seat cushions are allowed, but insulated cups or flasks, strollers, and umbrellas are not. For more guidance, download fan guides from the track's Web site.

CHILD SAFETY. Free child safety and identification wristbands are available at information booths and at DAYTONA USA's Guest Services Desk. The wristbands leave space to list a child's name, a preselected meeting location, parent's name and phone number, and other information to ensure a quick reunion.

DAYTONA INTERNATIONAL SPEEDWAY, FL   109

Cars maneuver for position during an early stage of the NASCAR NEXTEL Cup Series Daytona 500.

PARKING. Lots open one hour before admission gates for both races. See the speedway fan guides for information about the track's parking areas and free satellite parking areas served by a shuttle service. Most stores and restaurants along International Speedway Boulevard (ISB) sell spaces in their lots. If you go this route, and are heading to Interstate 95 and Interstate 4 afterward, select a lot across from the track so you can make a right-hand turn onto ISB.

FIRST AID. First aid stations are located throughout the grandstands and infield. Fully staffed infield care centers are positioned inside the speedway and outside the front stretch at the base of the city's pedestrian bridge.

CONCESSIONS. Stands are located throughout the speedway. Permanent stands offer complimentary water and cups.

GETTING TICKETS
The speedway's Web site, www.daytonainternational speedway.com, is your best bet: the 3-D track helps you visualize where to sit (the higher the seat, the better the view). Phone 386/253-RACE (7223). The front stretch is the most exciting, but the back superstretch is a good compromise—especially with the strategically placed monitors. If you want to see several races during Speedweeks, Web site deals bundle race tickets together or with fan hospitality tickets and hotel rooms.

SUN AND SPEED

Though fans make the pilgrimage to Daytona for the racing, they also enjoy its warm weather and 23 miles of beaches. The area is made up of eight communities: Daytona Beach, Ormond Beach, Ormond-by-the-Sea, and Holly Hill to the north; and Port Orange, South Daytona, Daytona Beach Shores, and Ponce Inlet to the south. The Halifax River/Intracoastal Waterway splits the area and runs parallel to the Atlantic Ocean. This means there's a mainland fronted by the river and a barrier island with the river on one side and the ocean on the other. Getting to any of the beaches requires crossing one of the area's six bridges.

It's easy to extend your vacation here and head off for fun in any direction. Theme park-crazy Orlando is a little more than one hour southwest, St. Augustine is one hour north, and Kennedy Space Center is one hour south. Increase the mileage a little and you'll find even more big-ticket alternatives vying for your

The Ponce de Leon Lighthouse is the tallest lighthouse in Florida and the second tallest in the nation. The 175-foot climb to the top might sound daunting, but you will be rewarded with amazing views of the Florida coastline.

Family activities abound on the 23 miles of beaches that helped make Daytona famous.

attention. Or stay put and enjoy the attractions and beaches of Daytona, a town so crazy about NASCAR you'd be hard-pressed to find a person or restaurant that *doesn't* have a story about one of the drivers. In fact, one fan swears he saw Kyle Petty singing karaoke at the Checkers Cafe. So keep your eyes open. You never know who you might run into.

The Daytona area's racing history runs deep. The first sanctioned time trial was held on Ormond Beach's hard-packed sand in 1903. As more and more time trials were held, the town became known as "The Birthplace of Speed." Eventually, the trials gave way to races up and down the area's wide beaches.

One of those beach racers was "Big Bill" France Sr, who later became a successful race promoter. In December 1947, France helped organize a meeting to discuss stock car racing rules and regulations at the Streamline Hotel (which still stands on Atlantic Avenue). Out of that meeting, the National Association for Stock Car Auto Racing was born. France went on to open a wildly successful racetrack that ran half on the beach and half along Highway A1A near

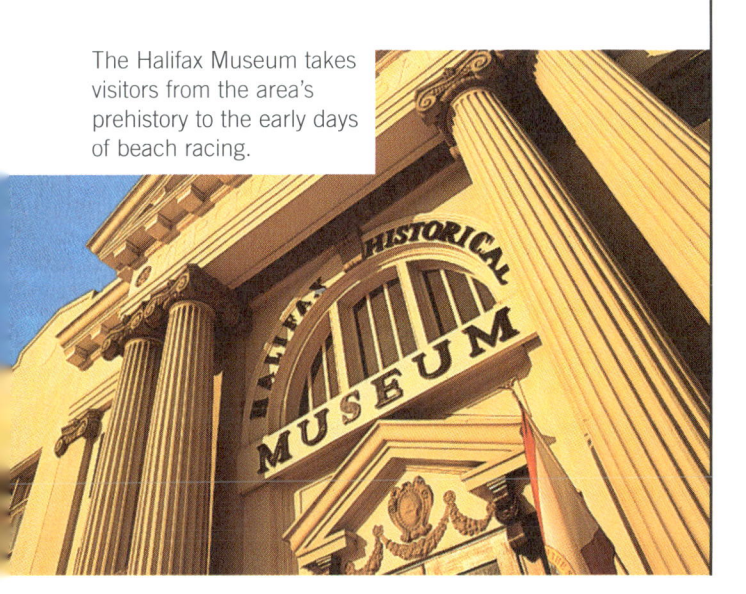

The Halifax Museum takes visitors from the area's prehistory to the early days of beach racing.

GETTING AROUND

I-4 is the main thoroughfare from Tampa all the way to Daytona, but construction, congestion, and delays are common. During racing events, the highway becomes a parking lot. Start early if you must use I-4 on a race day.

However, once you reach Orlando, it's an easy drive. Head east on I-4 to I-95 north. Merge onto I-95, and take Exit 261 (US 92/International Speedway Blvd), the next exit on the right. Head east on US 92/International Speedway Blvd a short distance and you're at the track. From Miami or Ft. Lauderdale, drive north on I-95 to Exit 261 (US 92/International Speedway Blvd), then head east. From Jacksonville or St. Augustine, drive south on I-95 to Exit 261A (US 92/International Speedway Blvd) and go east.

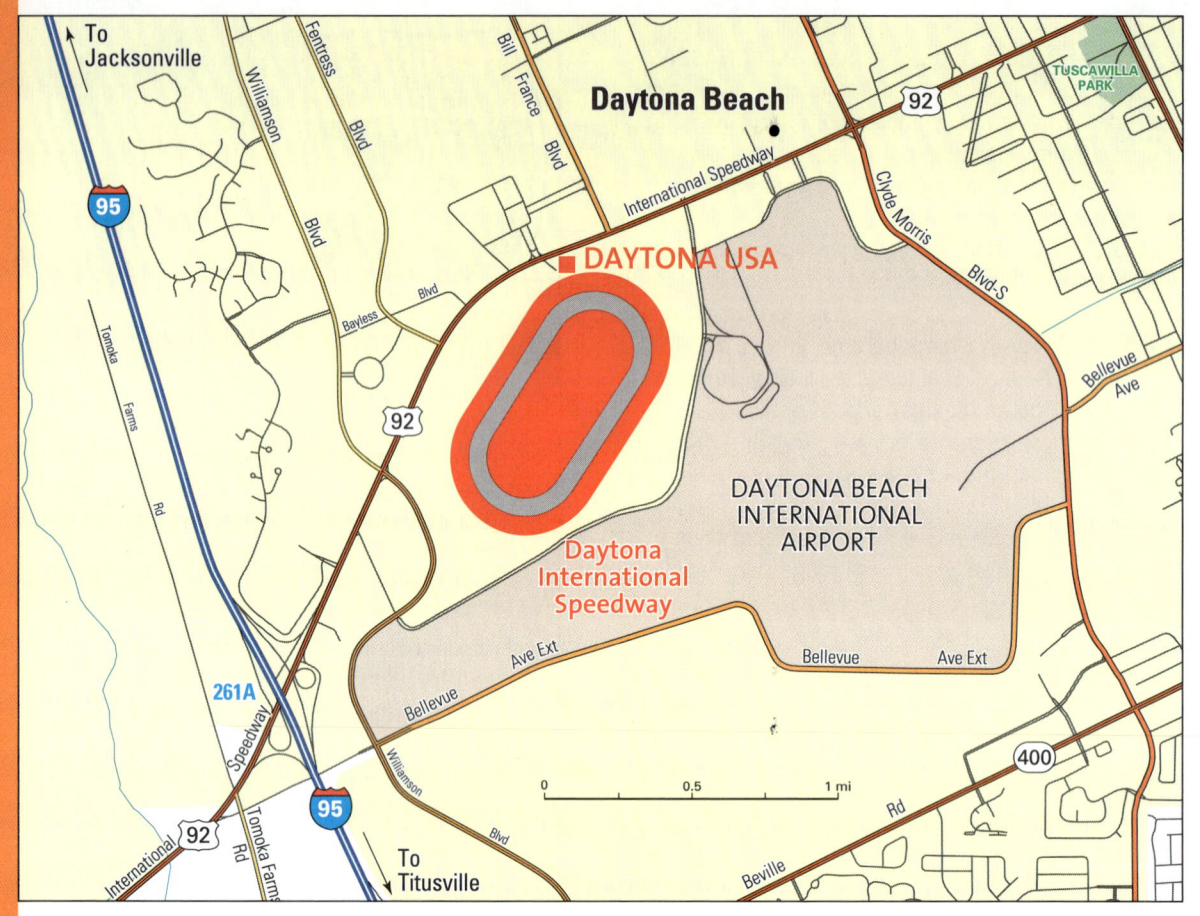

DAYTONA BEACH POLE POSITION:
The 10 miles surrounding Daytona International Speedway.

Ponce Inlet. But he dreamed of a new asphalt track. That vision came true when he opened Daytona International Speedway's steeply banked, 2 1/2-mile tri-oval "superspeedway" in 1959. Lee Petty was the track's first winner, and his son, Richard, won the first completely televised live race, the 1979 Daytona 500. Richard Petty still holds the record for most 500 wins with seven.

The track has gone through extensive renovations recently. The all new infield Fan Zone will include a Media Zone, where you can relive past races; a Garage Zone, where you can see crews and drivers as they prepare for upcoming races; and a new rooftop viewing area/walkway. The new Daytona 500 Club will overlook the new Victory Lane.

Infield campers will appreciate a new waterfront area along Lake Lloyd with docks, a boardwalk, playgrounds, a community center exclusively for campers, and new specialty vehicle parking with paved drives, parking pads, water, electricity, and cable television. Additional standard grass parking spaces will still be available.

DRIVER'S PICK

Mark Martin (Roush Racing No. 6 Ford Taurus) doesn't have to drive far from the track to get his favorite eats in Daytona. "I really like **Carrabba's Italian Grill**. They're primarily an Italian restaurant, but I love their seafood. The grilled salmon and grilled mahi-mahi is my favorite." *2200 W International Speedway Blvd, Daytona Beach (32114). Phone 386/255-3344. www.carrabbas.com.*

Crew members use foot power instead of horsepower to maneuver Joe Nemechek's car into the pits during a weather delay.

DAYTONA BEACH CALENDAR

FEBRUARY 5–20, 2005
Speedweeks. Daytona International Speedway. Phone 386/253-7223. www.daytonabeach.com/festivalseventsguide.asp. Gear up to the NASCAR NEXTEL Cup Series Daytona 500 with a parade and other race-related events.

FEBRUARY 12, 2005
NASCAR NEXTEL Cup Series

FEBRUARY 17, 2005
NASCAR NEXTEL Cup Series. NASCAR NEXTEL Cup Series drivers battle in the only qualifying race to set the Daytona 500 starting grid.

FEBRUARY 18, 2005
NASCAR Craftsman Truck Series

FEBRUARY 19, 2005
NASCAR Busch Series; season opener.

FEBRUARY 20, 2005
NASCAR NEXTEL Cup Series Daytona 500

FEBRUARY 26–27, 2005
US Cowboy Tour professional rodeo. Ocean Center, 101 N Atlantic Ave, Daytona Beach (32118). Phone 678/721-6280. www.uscowboytour.com. Watch real cowboy action.

MARCH 4–13, 2005
Bike Week. Main St, Daytona. Phone 386/255-0415; toll-free 800/854-1234. www.officialbikeweek.com. Attracts enthusiasts from around the world, and includes a race, shows, exhibits, and concerts.

JULY 1, 2005
NASCAR Busch Series

JULY 2, 2005
NASCAR NEXTEL Cup Series, followed by fireworks.

JULY 15–30, 2005
Florida International Festival. Various locations, Daytona. Phone 386/872-2331. www.fif-lso.org. This musical treat brings the London Symphony Orchestra to town, as well as dance and comedy.

DAYTONA BEACH OUTFIELD:
The 60 miles surrounding Daytona International Speedway.

SEE

ATTRACTIONS

Daytona Beach Area

ATLANTIC AVENUE.
Atlantic Avenue is filled with touristy but entertaining T-shirt and souvenir shops, the Racing 2000 memorabilia store, and several bars and restaurants—including the cheesy and fun Cruisin' Cafe at Atlantic and Main. Eat lunch in a booth made from a stock car and check out the autographed ceiling tiles.

THE BEACH.
The liveliest, most action-packed beach area is located between Seabreeze and International Speedway boulevards. The hard-packed sand that makes driving so easy is soft and textured enough to feel like you're walking on crushed velvet. This section is closed to public beach driving, but it's filled with the vehicles of vendors renting chairs, umbrellas, golf carts, and boogie boards.

After splashing around in the ocean, walk along the Boardwalk, an area packed with arcade games, go-karts, giant swinging rides, and refreshment stands, to the Daytona Beach Pier. As you walk, look down at the Salute to Speed, plaques built right into the sidewalk tracing the area's motorsports history. At the pier, catch a cool breeze aboard the gondola skyride or get a panoramic view of the area on the slowly revolving, 180-foot "Daytona 360" tower. The pier offers fishing, helicopter rides, and a full-service restaurant. Redevelopment plans include adding a second pier. Construction is expected to begin in 2005.

Sun Splash Park is south of International Speedway Boulevard and made for families. This park features an interactive water fountain, a shaded playground, picnic areas, and free parking.

During daylight hours, you can drive on 11 of the 23 miles of sand that run along the coast of the Daytona area. Follow the signs that mark the traffic lane. Remember that the days of racing on the beach are over: the speed limit is only 10 miles per hour. There is a small vehicle fee from February to November.

DAYTONA USA.
1801 W International Speedway Blvd, Daytona Beach (32114). Phone 386/947-6800. www.daytonausa.com. Located just outside the speedway's Turn 4, this theme park is like a racing fan's Disney World—with track tours, loads of memorabilia, racing simulator rides, the actual car of the latest Daytona 500 winner, and two films in the IMAX Theatre, "NASCAR 3D: The IMAX Experience" and "Daytona 500: The Movie," which depicts action during the Daytona 500. In addition, it regularly hosts appearances by drivers and other celebrities. (Daily; closed Dec 25) **$$$$**

GOLFING AND OTHER ACTIVITIES.
Daytona Beach is home to the international headquarters of the Ladies Professional Golf Association. In addition to the LPGA's two golf courses, there are more than 20 other courses in the area including the Jack Nicklaus-designed Ocean Hammock golf club by the beach. For information on all of the area's courses, log onto www.golfdaytonabeach.com.

The area also has four wildly themed miniature golf courses, four go-kart tracks, and boating and fishing tours. Visit www.daytonabeach.com for specific information.

HALIFAX HISTORICAL MUSEUM.
252 S Beach St, Daytona Beach (32114). Phone 386/255-6976. www.halifaxhistorical.org. The museum occupies a historic bank building and contains memorabilia dating from the early days of beach car racing. (Tues-Fri 10 am-4 pm, Sat 10 am-noon) **$**

LIVING LEGENDS OF AUTO RACING MUSEUM.
253 Riverside Dr, Holly Hill (32117). Phone 386/257-2828. www.livinglegendsofautoracing.com. If you enjoy NASCAR's early history, visit this museum owned by a local group whose president, Ray Fox, is a Hall of Fame car builder credited with helping Junior Johnson win the 1960 Daytona 500. Employees are full of interesting stories about past drivers, owners, and pit crews. (Wed-Sat) **FREE**

MARINE SCIENCE CENTER.
100 Lighthouse Dr, Ponce Inlet (32127). Phone 386/304-5545. www.marinesciencecenter.com. The inexpensive Marine Science Center is just around the corner from the Ponce de Leon Inlet Lighthouse. It isn't very big, but inside you'll find small alligators, snakes, a moray eel, aquariums, and environmental exhibits. In the classroom lab, kids can make craft projects

such as sea turtle paper plates and paper bag pelicans. Outside, stroll Turtle Terrace to observe the sea turtle rehabilitation area. The sea bird rehabilitation center is on the other end of the parking lot, and a nature trail is located across the street. **$**

OCEAN WALK SHOPPES @ THE VILLAGE.
250 N Atlantic Ave, Daytona Beach (32118). Phone 386/566-6876; toll-free 877/845-WALK (9255). www.oceanwalkvillage.com. Nestled between the Hilton Daytona Beach Resort (formerly Adam's Mark) and the Ocean Walk Resort, this colorful new dining, shopping, and entertainment complex offers specialty shops, Cold Stone Creamery, Bubba Gump Shrimp Co., a ten-screen movie theater, live entertainment, and more. Just to the east sits the historic oceanfront Bandshell. Built in 1937 of coquina shells, the Bandshell hosts concerts and events throughout the year. The new **Daytona Lagoon** (www.daytonalagoon.com), with a water park, arcade, and go-karts, is scheduled to open across the street from the Shoppes in 2005.

PONCE DE LEON INLET LIGHTHOUSE.
4931 S Peninsula Dr, Ponce Inlet (32127). Phone 386/761-1821. www.ponceinlet.org. The scenic town of Ponce Inlet features the country's second-tallest lighthouse, located at the southern tip of the Daytona area's barrier island. At the top is an incredible view of both the Intracoastal Waterway and the ocean, but beware: the 203-step trip can be strenuous. Once back on solid ground, explore the original homes and buildings that surround the lighthouse. Each is filled with exhibits on lighthouse, maritime, and area history—including a continuously running black-and-white video of beach races from the 1940s. (Daily) **$**

TROLLEYBOAT TOURS.
Ocean Walk Shoppes @ The Village, 250 N Atlantic Ave, Kiosk 2, Daytona Beach (32118). Phone 386/238-3738. www.daytonatrolleyboattours.net. This amphibious vehicle picks up in front of the Ocean Walk Shoppes and travels down a few streets before plunging into the Halifax River. While slowly floating along, tour guides talk about the area's history from its Native American inhabitants to the birth of NASCAR. You'll glimpse the mansion of Bill France Jr, former chairman and CEO of NASCAR—and you may spot a dolphin or two. During Speedweeks, the amphibious trolleys also go by the Halifax Harbor Marina as guides point out the boats of drivers such as Jeff Gordon, Dale Earnhardt Jr, and Mark Martin. The tour ends with a drive on the beach, but at 75 minutes long, it probably moves a little slowly for most kids. **$$$$**

New Smyrna Beach

THE BEACH AND FLAGLER AVENUE SHOPS.
www.flaglerave.com. Lovely New Smyrna Beach's small-town atmosphere is quaint and laid back. Wander through the many shops, boutiques, and galleries that pack Flagler Avenue, then head to the town's pretty beach area, on the northern tip of Canaveral National Seashore.

Orlando

Located a little more than an hour from Daytona, Orlando is the theme park capital of the world, home to Disney World's four parks, Universal Studios and Islands of Adventure, Sea World, and Discovery Cove. However, there are smaller, slightly less expensive attractions as well: Gatorland, The Holy Land Experience, Titanic The Exhibition, the upside-down building that houses hands-on exhibits at Wonder Works, and Wet 'n Wild water park. It can become almost overwhelming trying to sort through all that's offered. Here's a sampling.

DOLLY PARTON'S DIXIE STAMPEDE.
8251 Vineland Ave, Orlando (32819). Phone 407/238-4455; toll-free 866/443-4943. www.dixiestampede.com. Dolly Parton opened Orlando's newest dinner theater, her Dixie Stampede Dinner and Show, in June 2003. The 1,200-seat facility, built at a cost of $28 million, hosts an energetic North vs. South show featuring a large cast of elaborately costumed actors, live animals (including 32 horses), dramatic lighting, sound, and pyrotechnics—and don't forget the ostriches, pig races, and chicken chases. A four-course meal is served during the performance. (Showtimes vary) **$$$$**

GATORLAND.
14501 S Orange Blossom Trail, Orlando (32837). Phone 407/855-5496; toll-free 800/393-JAWS (5297). www.gatorland.com. For the quintessential Florida experience, visit this 110-acre park and wildlife preserve for thousands of alligators and crocodiles. After walking through the massive alligator head entrance, explore exhibits such as Alligator Island and Flamingo Lagoon, go through the petting zoo, and hop aboard the Gatorland Express. Shows include Jungle Crocs,

the Up Close snake show, Gator Wrestlin', and the Gator Jumparoo—where large alligators jump out of the water to grab food from a trainer's hand. (Daily 9 am-dusk) $$$$

For more attractions, go to www.mobiltravelguide.com

STAY

NOTE: At press time, some area hotels and restaurants were closed due to hurricane damage. Call ahead to check availability.

MOBIL STAR-RATED LODGINGS

Daytona Beach

BEACHCOMER DAYTONA BEACH RESORT. ★★
2000 N Atlantic Ave, Daytona Beach (32118). Phone 386/252-8513; toll-free 800/245-3575. www.beachcomerresort.com. This tall, mint-green hotel offers a large heated beachside pool and deck, hot tub, children's pool, poolside snack shop, and full-service restaurant. The recreation staff provides year-round activities such as beach volleyball, ice cream socials, and pool bingo. Private balconies and refrigerators are standard, with a game room and laundry facilities on premises. 184 rooms, 7 story. Pets accepted. Check-in 3 pm, check-out 11 am. Laundry services. Restaurant, bar. Children's activity center. Beach. Outdoor pool, children's pool, whirlpool. $

HAMPTON INN DAYTONA SPEEDWAY/AIRPORT. ★
1715 W International Speedway Blvd, Daytona Beach (32114). Phone 386/257-4030; toll-free 800/593-0344. www.hamptoninn.com. This newly renovated hotel is in a great location about three blocks from the track. It provides clean rooms with coffee makers, complimentary breakfast bar, and small fitness center. 122 rooms, 4 story. Complimentary continental breakfast. Check-in 3 pm, check-out 11 am. Fitness room. Outdoor pool, whirlpool. $

HILTON GARDEN INN DAYTONA BEACH AIRPORT. ★
189 Midway Ave, Daytona Beach (32114). Phone 386/944-4000; toll-free 877/944-4001. www.hiltongardeninn.com. The best part of this hotel is its location: it's just one block east of Daytona International Speedway, across the street from the Volusia Mall, and next to the Cancun Lagoon Bar & Grill. You can see the track from upper rooms. All rooms come with microwaves and refrigerators. 156 rooms, 3 story. Check-in 4 pm, check-out 11 am. High-speed Internet access. Fitness room. Outdoor pool, whirlpool. $

PIT PASS

If you're staying in the infield and have questions about anything, head to one of the 15 Guest Information Centers located throughout the area. Booth staffers have the Holy Grail of information: the Big Binder. This fat three-ring notebook has information on everything from the price and location of ice to the names and numbers of RV repair shops that are pre-credentialed. This means that if you have any mechanical problems, you don't have to drive out of the infield looking for help. Instead, call any of the pre-credentialed vendors available and they'll come out and service your vehicle, right at the track. You still have to pay for the service—but the convenience can't be beat.

118 STAY MOBIL STAR-RATED LODGINGS

HOLIDAY INN EXPRESS DAYTONA SPEEDWAY AND I-95. ★★
2620 W International Speedway Blvd, Daytona Beach (32114). Phone 386/258-6333; toll-free 800/377-8660. www.hiexpress.com. This hotel is a sports fan's paradise, with six tennis courts, a golf course, swimming pool, and, of course, quick access to the race track. 151 rooms, 2 story. Check-in 3 pm, check-out 11 am. Fitness room. Outdoor pool, children's pool. Golf. Tennis. Airport transportation available. $

PLAZA RESORT AND SPA. ★★
600 N Atlantic Ave, Daytona Beach (32118) Phone 386/255-4471; toll-free 800/874-7420. www.plazaresortandspa.com. 322 rooms, 14 story. Check-in 4 pm, check-out 11 am. Restaurant, bar. Children's activity center. Fitness room. Beach. Outdoor pool. $

SUN VIKING LODGE. ★★
2411 S Atlantic Ave, Daytona Beach (32118). Phone 386/252-6252; toll-free 800/815-2846. www.sunviking.com. Look for the tall building with the large Viking ship. This fun hotel is geared toward families and features a playground, big heated outdoor pool with 60-foot water slide, heated indoor pool with waterfall, exercise room, and—in case just being outside in Florida isn't enough for you—a sauna. Barbecue grills, laundry machines, and a guest recreation program are all available. Inside, you'll find microwaves and refrigerators in each cheerfully decorated room. 91 rooms, 8 story. Check-in 3 pm, check-out 11 am. Laundry services. Restaurant. Children's activity center. Fitness room. Beach. Indoor pool, outdoor pool, children's pool, whirlpool. $

Daytona Beach Shores

ACAPULCO HOTEL AND RESORT. ★★
2505 S Atlantic Ave, Daytona Beach Shores (32118). Phone 386/761-2210; toll-free 800/245-3580. www.acapulcoinn.com. Every room in this hotel has a microwave, mini refrigerator, and private balcony with an ocean view. Outside you'll find a large oceanfront deck with swimming pool, two whirlpools, children's pool, and shuffleboard. Scheduled activities are posted daily and may include sand castle contests and poolside pizza parties. The hotel sits right across from the Hawaiian Falls miniature golf course. 133 rooms, 8 story. Check-in 3 pm, check-out 11 am. Restaurant, bar. Beach. Outdoor pool, children's pool, two whirlpools. $

QUALITY INN OCEAN PALMS. ★
2323 S Atlantic Ave, Daytona Beach Shores (32118). Phone 386/255-0476; toll-free 800/874-7517. www.qualityinn.com. 110 rooms, 6 story. Pets accepted; fee. Complimentary continental breakfast. Check-in 3 pm, check-out 11 am. Beach. Outdoor pool, children's pool. $

FAN FAVORITE

It's all about the history at **Racing's North Turn Beach Bar & Grille.** This restaurant sits on the exact location of the old beach track's north turn, where racing events were held until 1958. Memorabilia and photos from this time, along with more recent items, adorn the inside, along with 20 televisions tuned to the latest race. Enjoy the burgers and fries outside and imagine what it was like to see cars racing over the sand. Some of racing's "living legends" drop in regularly, and even sign autographs during Speedweeks. Check the restaurant's Web site for upcoming event information. American menu. Lunch, dinner. Casual attire. Outdoor seating. $$. *4511 S Atlantic Ave, Ponce Inlet (32127). Phone 386/322-3258. www.racingsnorthturn.com.*

TREASURE ISLAND INN. ★★
2025 S Atlantic Ave, Daytona Beach Shores (32118). Phone 386/255-8371; toll-free 800/543-5070. www.treasureislandinn.com. 227 rooms, 11 story. Check-in 4 pm, check-out 11 am. Restaurant, bar. Children's activity center. Beach. Two outdoor pools, children's pool. Comedy club. **$**

LOCAL RECOMMENDATIONS

Daytona Beach

BEST WESTERN AKU TIKI INN.
2225 S Atlantic Ave, Daytona Beach (32118). Phone 386/252-9631; toll-free 800/258-8454. www.bwakutiki.com. This inn is located right on the beach and has a game room great for kids. Each room has a small refrigerator. 132 rooms, 5 story. Check-in 3 pm, check-out 11 am. Restaurant, bar. Beach. Outdoor pool, children's pool. **$**

BEST WESTERN LA PLAYA RESORT.
2500 N Atlantic Ave, Daytona Beach (32118). Phone 386/672-0990; toll-free 800/874-6996. www.bestwestern.com. This hotel has a restaurant and tiki bar. 238 rooms, 9 story. Pets accepted, some restrictions; fee. Check-in 3 pm, check-out 11 am. Laundry services. Restaurant, bar. Beach. Indoor pool, outdoor pool, children's pool, whirlpool. **$**

BEST WESTERN MAYAN INN BEACHFRONT.
103 S Ocean Ave, Daytona Beach (32118). Phone 386/252-2378; toll-free 800/443-5323. www.bestwestern.com. Located right by the ocean and just a few blocks south of the Pier, this yellow hotel is in a great spot. After taking a dip in the pool, drop in next door to the popular, casual Ocean Deck restaurant. Or sip something cool and enjoy the seascape in the Mayan's lounge. Most rooms have balconies and at least an ocean view. 112 rooms, 8 story. Complimentary continental breakfast. Check-in 3 pm, check-out 11 am. Laundry services. Bar. Outdoor pool. **$**

HILTON DAYTONA BEACH AT OCEAN WALK VILLAGE.
100 N Atlantic Ave, Daytona Beach (32118). Phone 386/254-8200; toll-free 800/411-8776. www.hilton.com. In the middle of all the action, this newly refurbished beachfront hotel is located between the Ocean Walk Shoppes and the Boardwalk and just two blocks north of the Pier. This sprawling resort, formerly Adam's Mark, has seven bars and restaurants, two pools, and two fitness centers. Guest rooms include high-speed Internet access and marble bathrooms. 742 rooms, 16 story. Check-in 4 pm, check-out 11 am. High-speed Internet access. Laundry services. Restaurants, bars. Fitness room. Beach. Two outdoor pools. Business center. **$$**

LA QUINTA INN & SUITES DAYTONA BEACH.
816 N Atlantic Ave, Daytona Beach (32118). Phone 386/944-0060; toll-free 800/531-5900. www.lq.com. This newly renovated limited-service hotel is a pleasant surprise. More than half of the large yet cozy rooms have private balconies with an oceanfront view. 77 rooms, 3 story. Complimentary continental breakfast. Check-in 3 pm, check-out 11 am. High-speed Internet access. Laundry services. Fitness room. Outdoor pool, whirlpool. **$**

OCEAN WALK RESORT AT THE VILLAGE.
300 N Atlantic Ave, Daytona Beach (32118). Phone 386/323-4800; toll-free 800/649-3566. www.oceanwalk.com. This luxury condo resort has one-, two-, or three-bedroom suites with their own washers and dryers. Its best feature: the almost over-the-top deck area with three outdoor pools, water slide, and 250-foot lazy river that winds around a putting green. 125 rooms, 19 story. Laundry services. Restaurant, bar. Fitness room. Two indoor pools, three outdoor pools, whirlpool. **$**

RAMADA INN SPEEDWAY.
1798 W International Speedway Blvd, Daytona Beach (32114). Phone 386/255-2422; toll-free 800/352-2722. www.ramada.com. Located across the street from Daytona International Speedway. 128 rooms, 1 story. Pets accepted, some restrictions; fee. Check-in 3 pm, check-out noon. Restaurant. Outdoor pool. **$**

Daytona Beach Shores

TROPICAL MANOR MOTEL.
2237 S Atlantic Ave, Daytona Beach Shores (32118). Phone 386/252-4920; toll-free 800/253-4920. www.tropicalmanor.com. Small, unique, and charming, this colorful motel has the feel of an old-time resort from its shuffleboard court, picnic tables, and lush landscaping to its beautifully decorated rooms, many with hand-painted murals. With names like Sweet Pea and Ocean Breeze, no two rooms are exactly alike. 71 rooms, 3 story. Check-in 3 pm, check-out noon. Outdoor pool, children's pool. **$**

STAY LOCAL RECOMMENDATIONS

Ormond Beach

BEST WESTERN MAINSAIL INN & SUITES.
281 S Atlantic Ave, Ormond Beach (32176). Phone 386/677-2131; toll-free 800/843-5142. www.bestwestern.com. 44 rooms, 4 story. Complimentary continental breakfast. Check-in 4 pm, check-out 11 am. Beach. Outdoor pool, children's pool. $

CORAL BEACH MOTEL.
711 S Atlantic Ave, Ormond Beach (32176). Phone 386/677-4712; toll-free 800/553-4712. www.coralbeachmotel.com. This popular oceanfront resort's rooms are cozy and clean, with a microwave and refrigerator. Most come with private balconies. The Pirate's Cove miniature golf course is across the street. 97 rooms, 7 story. Check-in 3 pm, check-out 11 am. Laundry services. Indoor pool, outdoor pool. $

RV AND CAMPING

Daytona Beach

INTERNATIONAL RV PARK AND CAMPGROUND.
3175 W International Speedway Blvd, Daytona Beach (32124). Phone 386/239-0249; toll-free 866/261-3698. www.internationalrvdaytona.com. This park has spacious lots in a countrylike setting, and is less than 2 miles west of the speedway. A shuttle service is typically available to races. A swimming pool, general store, laundry, and showers are available, as well as hook-ups and pull-through sites.

RACETRACK RV PARK.
270 Coral Sea Way, Daytona Beach (32174). Mailing address: 2547 Bellevue Ave, Daytona Beach (32114). Phone toll-free 877/787-2246. www.racetrackrv.com. Only open for major events such as the Daytona 500, the Pepsi 400, and Bike Week, this campground is conveniently located within easy walking distance of the speedway. Hook-ups available.

Ormond Beach

TOMOKA STATE PARK.
2099 N Beach St, Ormond Beach (32174). Phone 386/676-4050; toll-free 800/326-3521. Located near the confluence of the Tomoka and Halifax rivers, this park has fishing areas, canoe rentals, nature trails, guided tours, a boat ramp, and 100 campsites.

For more lodging recommendations, go to www.mobiltravelguide.com

EAT

MOBIL STAR-RATED RESTAURANTS

Daytona Beach

CHART HOUSE. ★★
1100 Marina Pointe Dr, Daytona Beach (32114). Phone 386/255-9022. www.chart-house.com. This beautiful restaurant serves outstanding, unique seafood dishes and steaks. It features friendly service and a gorgeous view of the Halifax Harbor Marina. It's popular with race drivers; several dock their boats at the marina during Speedweeks or stay in the condos just up the street. Due to its popularity, especially during racing events, reservations are strongly recommended. Seafood, steak menu. Dinner. Bar. Children's menu. Casual attire. Outdoor seating. $$$

MAIN STREET STEAKHOUSE. ★
601 Main St, Daytona Beach (32014). Phone 386/255-2550. This casual restaurant has outdoor seating and reasonable prices. American menu. Dinner. Closed Sun-Tues. Bar. Casual attire. Outdoor seating. $$

MARIA BONITA. ★
1435 S Ridgewood Ave, Daytona Beach (32114). Phone 904/255-3465. This authentic Mexican restaurant has become a favorite of locals for its food, good service, and prices. Mexican menu. Lunch, dinner. Bar. Children's menu. Casual attire. Outdoor seating. $$

New Smyrna Beach

NORWOOD'S RESTAURANT & WINE SHOP. ★★
400 Second Ave, New Smyrna Beach (32169). Phone 386/428-4621. www.norwoods.com. You can't go through New Smyrna without dropping in at Norwood's. With dimmed lights and an intimate setting, this restaurant has been serving up good seafood and Angus beef since 1946. It offers a free wine tasting every Friday evening. At its wine shop, browse for bottles of wine, souvenirs, and gifts. Seafood menu. Lunch, dinner. Closed Dec 25. Bar. Children's menu. Casual attire. $$

DAYTONA INTERNATIONAL SPEEDWAY, FL

LOCAL RECOMMENDATIONS

Daytona Beach

CANCUN LAGOON BAR & GRILL.
1735 W International Speedway Blvd, Daytona Beach (32114). Phone 386/255-6500. www.cancunlagoon.com. Located amid all the racing action, Cancun Lagoon is just down the street from the speedway. The main dining area has the feel of an old Mexican courtyard, complete with stucco arches and a fountain. Outside, a small thatched-roof patio looks out onto the parking lot packed with vendors and displays during racing events. And if all that's not enough for you, the inside bar features hermit crab races on Wednesday nights. An extensive takeout menu is available. Mexican, American menu. Lunch, dinner, late-night. Casual attire. Outdoor seating. $$

CARIBBEAN JACK'S RESTAURANT & MARINA.
721 Ballough Rd, Daytona Beach (32114). Phone 386/523-3000. www.caribbeanjacks.com. This colorful eatery next to the Halifax River provides fun with a tropical flair. Eat inside the large, island-inspired dining room or outside at glider picnic tables on the huge deck beside the marina's boats. Like most of Daytona's restaurants, fresh seafood and steaks are the specialty. The restaurant offers live music, daily happy-hour specials, and killer "riveritas." In addition, Caribbean Jack's is next door to the private marina where Bill France Jr docks his yacht. During Speedweeks, keep your eyes open for other drivers' boats docking. American menu. Lunch, dinner. Casual attire. Outdoor seating. $$

CRABBY JOE'S DECK & GRILL.
3701 S Atlantic Ave, Daytona Beach (32127). Phone 386/788-3364. www.sunglowpier.com. This restaurant is located on the ocean, on the Sunglow fishing pier. During Speedweeks, there's a good chance you'll catch Richard Petty dining here at least once around 5 pm. (He celebrated his birthday here in 2004.) American menu. Breakfast, lunch, dinner. Bar. Casual attire. Outdoor seating. $$

MR. GOODCENTS SUBS & PASTAS.
1808 International Speedway Blvd, Daytona Beach (32114). Phone 386/238-2368. www.mrgoodcents.com. DAYTONA USA fans flock across the street to this shop to enjoy its fresh subs. The staff puts takeout items into clear bags to ease the security process

ROAD FOOD

The family-owned **Aunt Catfish's on the River** has been named Best Restaurant by the Daytona Beach Area Convention and Visitors Bureau for the last five years, and no wonder: it serves up big portions of down-home cooking with extra-friendly service and a gorgeous view. This Port Orange eatery is popular with locals, race fans who return year after year, and drivers such as Richard Petty and Dale Jarrett. Its specialty catfish is served three ways; other seafood dishes, ribs, and rotisserie chicken are almost as good. Include a trip through the hot bar for baked beans, cornbread, and cheese grits. And enjoy drinks served in Mason jars. American menu. Lunch, dinner, brunch. Casual attire. Outdoor seating. $$ *4009 Halifax Dr (at Dunlawton Bridge). Phone 386/767-4768. www.auntcatfish.com.*

at the track—and if you and your friends want to buy one big sub, you can have it sliced to fit exactly into a regulation 6 x 6 x 12-inch cooler. Deli menu. Lunch, dinner. Casual attire. $

OCEAN DECK RESTAURANT & BEACH CLUB.
127 S Ocean Ave, Daytona Beach (32118). Phone 386/253-5224. www.oceandeck.com. You can walk into this laid-back, very popular restaurant right off the beach. About two blocks south of the Daytona Pier, the Deck's downstairs dining area serves everyone, including swimmers and sunbathers in for a break. From spicy Jamaican jerk buffalo wings to crab cakes and other seafood dishes, the salty sea breezes seem to make everything taste better. Children's menu items

EAT LOCAL RECOMMENDATIONS

are served in take-home flying discs. The upstairs area, a little nicer, is air conditioned. Listen to live reggae music nightly. American menu. Lunch, dinner. Children's menu. Casual attire. Outdoor seating. $$

THE WRECK RIVERFRONT BAR & GRILL.
115 Main St, Daytona Beach (32118). Phone 386/226-3000. www.wreckbar.com. Located on the east side of the Halifax River on the barrier island, this local favorite offers very good seafood, steaks, sandwiches, homemade desserts—even alligator bites. Or enjoy a cold drink, some live music, and the beautiful sunset views from the deck. American menu. Lunch, dinner. Casual attire. Outdoor seating. $$

New Smyrna Beach

J. B.'S FISH CAMP & RESTAURANT.
859 Pompano, New Smyrna Beach (32169). Phone 386/427-5747. www.jbsfishcamp.com. This restaurant is a real fish camp, so don't let the rustic exterior worry you when you first drive up. Some of the specials at J. B.'s, known for having the freshest seafood, depend on the catch of the day. They take their time cooking, but it's definitely worth the wait. When it's ready, dine inside or outside on the patio along the river. A boat ramp, bait shop, and tiny grocery store are located nearby. Seafood menu. Lunch, dinner. Casual attire. Outdoor seating. $$

Orlando

There are many restaurants in Orlando in all price ranges. Some of the most fun are located at Downtown Disney (**House of Blues, Rainforest Café,** and **Planet Hollywood**), the area along International Drive (**Dan Marino's Town Tavern, Bahama Breeze,** and **Boston Lobster Feast**), and Universal CityWalk (**NBA City, Emeril's,** and **Jimmy Buffett's Margaritaville**). For more information, visit www.downtowndisney.com, www.internationaldriveorlando.com, or www.citywalkorlando.com.

NASCAR CAFE.
6000 Universal Blvd, Suite 743 (inside Universal CityWalk complex), Orlando (32819). Phone 407/224-RACE (7223). www.nascarcafeorlando.com. The only officially NASCAR-sanctioned restaurant, this two-story building features full-sized stock cars, racing displays, a gift shop, and interactive games. Head upstairs for burgers, barbecued chicken, or ribs while fast-paced racing highlights play on an overhead screen. Packed with fans during race weeks, the cafe hosts events including signings with NASCAR NEXTEL Cup and Busch Series drivers. Check the Web site's events section to see what's coming up. *Note:* It costs $8 to park in the Universal parking garage, so get your money's worth by wandering around the many shops and bars in the CityWalk area. American menu. Lunch, dinner. Children's menu. Casual attire. $$

Ponce Inlet

INLET HARBOR MARINA AND RESTAURANT.
133 Inlet Harbor Rd, Ponce Inlet (32127). Phone 386/767-5590. www.inletharbor.com. More of an entertainment area than just a restaurant, the Inlet Harbor is well worth the drive south, nearly to the end of the Daytona Area's barrier island. A smiling mermaid sign welcomes you to a marina, giant outdoor bar, gift shop, and a restaurant with a tropical feel. The excellent food begins with rolls served with Key lime butter and continues with fresh seafood and steaks. While dining, enjoy the boats along the Intracoastal Waterway. Have dessert or drinks on the area's largest outdoor deck, complete with tiki torches, live music, and a dance floor. Families are welcome. American menu. Lunch, dinner. Casual attire. Outdoor seating. $$

For more dining recommendations, go to www.mobiltravelguide.com

SIDETRIP

America's Oldest City
St. Augustine, FL

Founded in 1565, the oldest city in the country is just one hour north of Daytona. Parts of beautiful and charming St. Augustine still look and feel like an old European town. Since most of its historical sites and attractions are grouped in a small area, it's easy to park the car and amble along. But first, take a sightseeing tour, the best way to get an overview of the area and an appreciation for its history.

On the **Old Town Trolley Tour** (phone 904/829-3800), you'll go by the **Old Jail** (not to be missed), **Ponce de Leon's Fountain of Youth** (kind of cheesy), the **Oldest House, Wooden Schoolhouse,** and **Drugstore** (all interesting), **Ripley's Believe It or Not** (for the kids), the **San Sebastian Winery** (for the adults), and more. The admission price lets you get off and back on at any of its 19 stops.

One of the stops worth checking out is the **Castillo de San Marcos.** Wander through the rooms of this fort completed in 1695, listen to tour guides, and watch reenactors and cannon-firing demonstrations on the weekends. The Castillo is also a good place to let the kids run around.

Another worthwhile trolley stop is the pedestrian-only **St. George Street** walking mall, in the heart of the historic district. This narrow street is packed with shops, antiques stores, restaurants, old buildings, and the **Spanish Quarter Village.** Full of friendly and talkative reenactors, the Village's old homes and buildings are set in 1740. Afterwards, get a scoop of St. Augustine Mud ice cream at **Kilwin's.**

Next, cross the Bridge of Lions to Anastasia Island and the **Alligator Farm and Zoological Park,** one of the oldest alligator parks in the country and filled with all

St. Augustine is located between Route 1 and the Atlantic Ocean. For more travel tips, go to St. Augustine Chamber of Commerce, phone 904/829-5681. www.staugustine.com/visit and www.oldcity.com.

types and sizes of crocodiles and alligators—some quite close to the walks. Don't miss the albino alligator, which looks like it's been carved out of white chocolate. If it turns its pink eyes on you, legend says it's a sign of coming good fortune.

End the day with dinner at one of the waterfront restaurants and a carriage ride. If you're really adventurous, spend the evening looking for ghosts on one of the city's many tours. Take your pick among haunted cemeteries, haunted pubs, pirate ghosts, and more.

For more St. Augustine recommendations, go to www.mobiltravelguide.com

The "Monster Mile®" at Dover primarily draws fans from the Philadelphia, Baltimore, and Washington, DC metro areas.

Dover International Speedway®

Dover, DE

7

There's plenty of action during the June 6, 2004, running of the NASCAR NEXTEL Cup Series MBNA 400: "A Salute to Heroes" race.

TRACK FACTS

DOVER INTERNATIONAL SPEEDWAY. 1131 N DuPont Hwy, Dover (19901). Phone 302/734-RACE (7223); phone toll-free 800/441-RACE (7223). www.doverspeedway.com.

SECURITY. One cooler (14 x 14 x 14 inches or smaller) per person is permitted. One clear plastic bag smaller than 18 x 18 x 4 inches is permitted (no ice). Prohibited: glass containers, liquor or wine, beer in packs, beer balls, strollers, umbrellas, and fireworks.

PARKING. Lots are free except for Sunday races ($10). Infield parking allowed Sundays only; gates open 4:30-11:30 am. There is a $40 fee for every vehicle and $40 for each person older than 12. RV lots are located south and east of the track near Old Leipsic Road.

FIRST AID. An infield care station is located by Turn 4. Other stations are at the south end of Old Leipsic Road, between Gates 7 and 8; the corner of Persimmon Tree Lane and Pit Stop Road near Lot 9; and outside the west side of the North Tent Village, across from Gate 15.

CONCESSIONS. Stands scattered throughout the speedway offer burgers, hot dogs, sausage sandwiches, pizza, nachos, beer, sodas, and water.

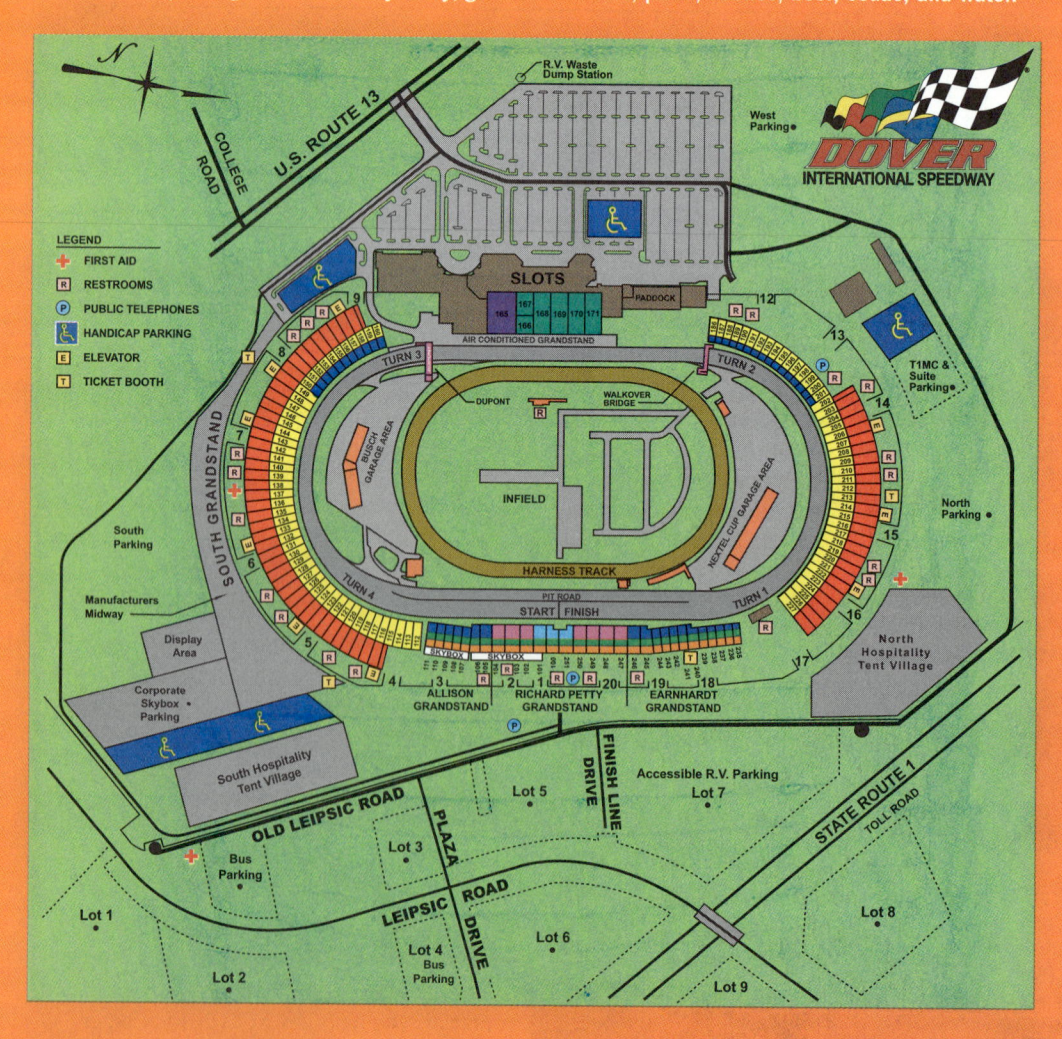

DOVER INTERNATIONAL SPEEDWAY, DE 127

When NASCAR NEXTEL Cup racing comes to town, 140,000 fans jam the 1-mile, concrete oval track.

A DELIGHTFUL DEAL

You may not have considered Delaware a vacation destination, but once you get off the main highways, you will discover many happy surprises. For one, Delaware has an impressive state park system where recreational opportunities such as boating, fishing, hiking, and swimming abound. Nearly all Delaware state parks are open all year.

There are plenty of free museums here—and don't leave without doing at least a little shopping in a state where it is tax-free. At **Tanger Outlet Center** (36470 Seaside Outlet Dr, Rehoboth, phone 302/266-9223, www.tangeroutlet.com), there are nearly 150 merchants of clothing, housewares, and more. Along Route 13, convenient to the track, you'll find plenty of hotels, shopping, and restaurants. South of Dover on Route 1, you'll find delicious seasonal fruits, vegetables, and flowers—including incredible tomatoes and peaches in the summer months and pumpkins and mums in the fall.

The town of Dover itself is a mix of old and new. Old Dover, which has served as the state capital since 1777, can be seen in the historic buildings of the downtown area. The **Old State House** and museum on the Green is administered by **Delaware State Museums** (406 Federal St, phone 302/739-4266, www.destate museums.org/vc), and offers information on attractions throughout the state (open daily except holidays). The Green itself is the hub of the downtown historic area, flanked by the Golden Fleece Tavern, where Delaware became the first state to ratify the US Constitution. At the free **Johnson Victrola Museum** (Bank and New sts, phone 302/739-4266), you can view a tribute to Eldridge Reeves Johnson, founder of the Victor Talking Machine Company; and at the **Museum of Small Town Life** (316 S Governors Ave, phone 302/739-3261), you can experience what a turn-of-the-century pharmacy, carpenter shop, general store, post office, shoemaker's shop, and printer's shop would have looked like.

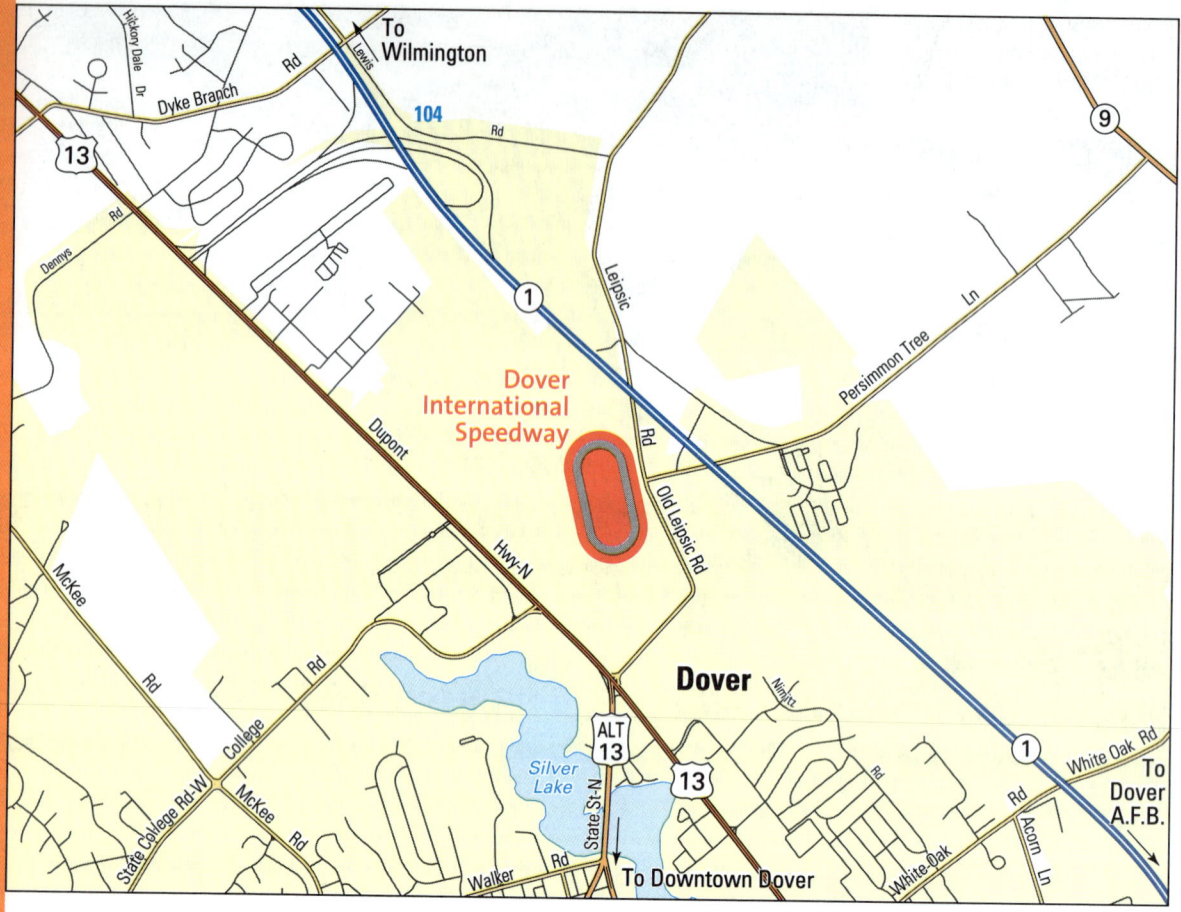

DOVER POLE POSITION:
The 10 miles surrounding Dover International Speedway.

The modern side of Dover can be enjoyed in the huge concrete and metal structure that is Dover International Speedway, and in the Dover Downs Hotel and Conference Center, which runs alongside. Modern Dover also gets much of its personality from **Dover Air Force Base.** The biggest thing in town at 3,730 acres, it has been providing airlift assistance for troops, cargo, and equipment since 1942. Huge cargo planes, including the mammoth C-5 Galaxy, can be seen on the airfield from Route 1 or, often, flying overhead.

The base's **Air Mobility Command Museum** (phone 302/677-5938, www.amcmuseum.org), located in a hangar at the base, houses more than two dozen aircraft and historical artifacts dating from World War II.

Delaware's climate is generally mild—good news for **Nassau Valley Vineyards** (32165 Winery Way, Lewes, phone 302/645-9463, www.nassauvalley.com), the state's first farm winery, where you can picnic, sample the fare, or participate in special events. Long summers are not unusual here, and there's seldom frost until late autumn. Temperatures at the shore can be 10 degrees higher in winter or lower in summer than inland temperatures.

DOVER INTERNATIONAL SPEEDWAY, DE   **129**

DRIVER'S PICK

Mike McLaughlin, driver of the No. 25 Car for Team Marines Ford in the NASCAR Busch Series, is on the road so much, what he craves is some home cooking. "Believe it or not, my favorite place to eat at Dover is my motor home. My full-blooded Italian mother cooks for me."

The C-54 aircraft is just one of the planes you can view at the Air Mobility Command Museum.

Mark Martin celebrates in Victory Lane after winning the NASCAR NEXTEL Cup Series MBNA 400: "A Salute to Heroes" in his Ford.

DOVER CALENDAR

JUNE 3, 2005
NASCAR Craftsman Truck Series

JUNE 4, 2005
NASCAR Busch Series

JUNE 5, 2005
NASCAR NEXTEL Cup Series

JUNE 6, 2005 (ALSO SEPTEMBER 26)
Monster Racing Ride Day. Dover International Speedway. Phone toll-free 800/468-6946. www.monsterracing.com. Take a ride as a passenger around the Monster Mile in a genuine NASCAR NEXTEL Cup or NASCAR Busch Grand National car, or NASCAR Craftsman truck. Reservations suggested.

JUNE 18, 2005
June Jam. G&R Campground, 2075 Gun and Rod Club Rd, Houston (19954). Phone 302/284-JUNE (5863). www.junejam.com. A huge local benefit concert for the whole family.

JUNE–AUGUST, 2005
City of Dover Arts on the Green. South State St, Dover (19901). Phone 302/736-7050. www.visitdover.com. A free concert series featuring family-style entertainers. Thursday evenings 7-8:30 pm.

SEPTEMBER 23, 2005
NASCAR Busch North Series

SEPTEMBER 24, 2005
NASCAR Busch Series

SEPTEMBER 25, 2005
NASCAR NEXTEL Cup Series

SEPTEMBER
Elvis Festival. Rusty Rudder, Dickinson St on the Bay, Dewey Beach (19971). Phone 302/227-3888. Dozens of Elvis impersonators compete for prizes. **FREE**

DOVER OUTFIELD:
The 70 miles surrounding Dover International Speedway.

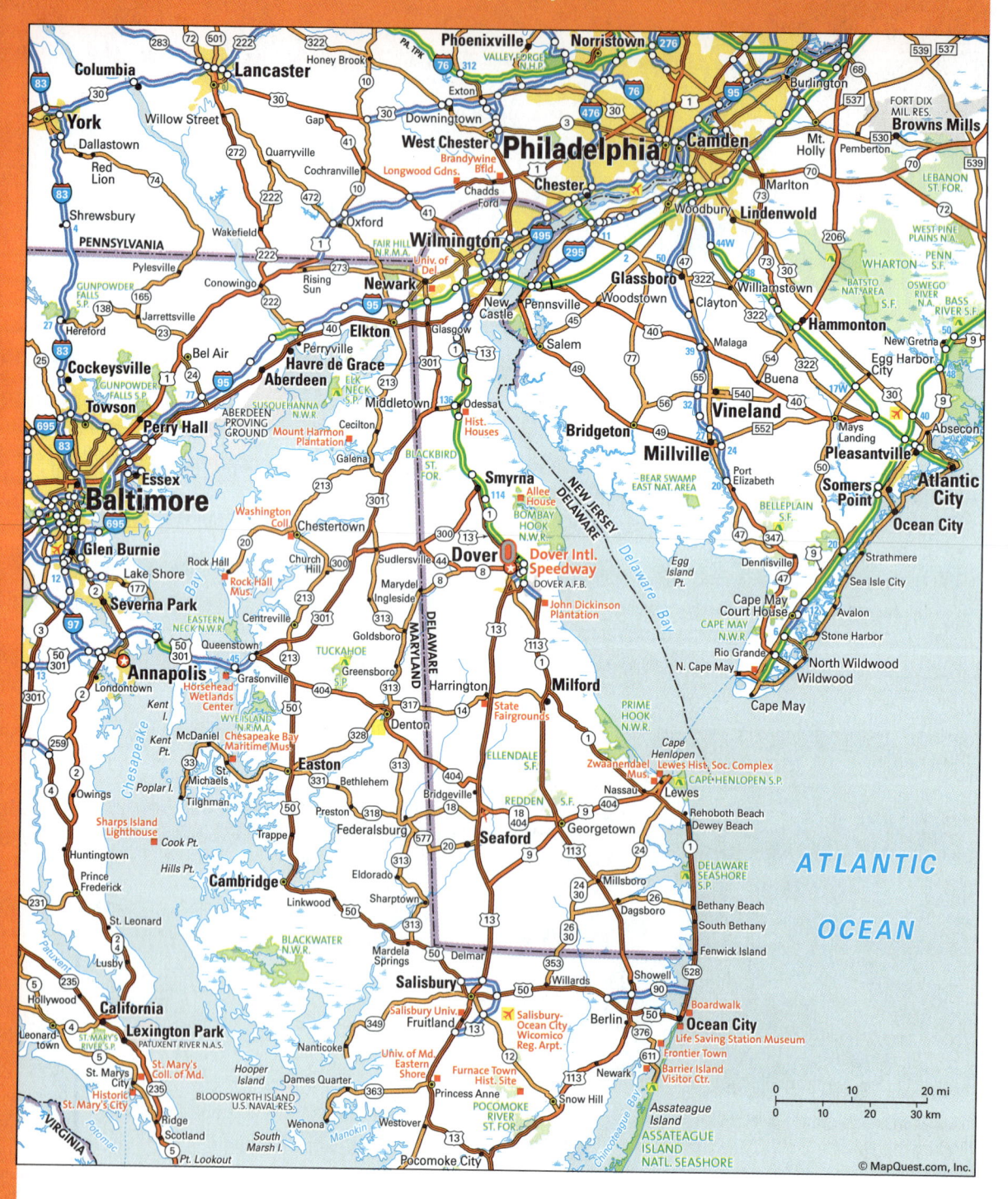

SEE

ATTRACTIONS

Dover

AIR MOBILITY COMMAND MUSEUM.
1301 Heritage Rd, Dover (19902). Phone 302/677-5938. www.amcmuseum.org. Located in a historic hangar on the south side of Dover Air Force Base, the museum houses a collection of more than two dozen aircraft and historical artifacts dating back to World War II. (Tues-Sat 9 am-4 pm; closed federal holidays) **FREE**

THE OLD STATE HOUSE.
The Green, 406 Federal St, Dover (19901). Phone 302/739-4266. www.destatemuseums.org/sh. Delaware's seat of government since 1777, the State House, restored in 1976, contains a courtroom, ceremonial governor's office, legislative chambers, and county offices. Although Delaware's General Assembly moved to nearby Legislative Hall in 1933, the State House remains the state's symbolic capitol. (Tues-Sat 10 am-4:30 pm, Sun 1:30-4:30 pm; closed holidays) **FREE**

Felton

KILLEN'S POND STATE PARK AND KILLEN'S POND WATER PARK.
5025 Killens Pond Rd, Felton (19943). Phone 302/284-4526. The water park includes water slides, interactive water features like a spouting fountain and the Floating Lily Pond Fun Walk, lap lanes, a tot pool, and areas for sunbathing and picnicking. A bathhouse with changing facilities and food concessions are available. The park offers fishing, boat rentals (summer only), game courts, ball fields, an 18-hole disc golf course, trails, a bike path, playgrounds, and picnic and camping areas. Park (Memorial Day-Labor Day). Campgrounds (year-round). **$**

Fenwick Island

FENWICK ISLAND LIGHTHOUSE.
146th St and Lighthouse Ln, Fenwick Island (19944). *Phone 302/539-4115.* Built in 1858, this popular attraction is 89 feet tall and houses a mini-museum in its base. Gift shop on premises. (Open most summer days, weather permitting) **FREE**

Rehoboth

MIDWAY SPEEDWAY.
Midway Shopping Center, Rte 1 N, Rehoboth (19971). Phone 302/644-2042. This recreational racing park features four tracks including a Super 8 Track and Family Track, eight different styles of go-karts, and a kiddie raceway and bumper boats. **$$$$**

Rehoboth Beach

JUNGLE JIM'S.
8 Country Club Rd, Rehoboth Beach (19971). Phone 302/227-8444. www.funatjunglejims.com. Fifteen acres of family fun include go-karts, batting cages, two miniature golf courses, bumper boats, rock climbing, and a water park. (Mid-June-mid-Sept: daily; late May-early June, Sept: limited hours) **$$$$**

Smyrna

BOMBAY HOOK NATIONAL WILDLIFE REFUGE.
2591 Whitehall Neck Rd, Smyrna (19977). Phone 302/653-6872. www.bombayhook.fws.gov. Annual fall and spring resting and feeding spot for migratory waterfowl, including ducks and tens of thousands of snow and Canada geese; home for bald eagles, shorebirds, deer, fox, and muskrat. Includes an auto tour route (12 miles), wildlife foot trails, and observation towers. Visitor center (spring and fall: daily; summer and winter: Mon-Fri). Refuge (daily). **$**

Wilmington

DELAWARE ART MUSEUM.
800 S Madison St, Wilmington (19807). Phone 302/571-9590. www.delart.org. Features the Howard Pyle Collection of American Illustrations with works by Pyle, N. C. Wyeth, and Maxfield Parrish; American painting collection, with works by West, Homer, Church, Glackens, and Hopper; English Pre-Raphaelite art, with works by Rossetti and Burne-Jones. Changing exhibits, children's participatory gallery; store. (Mon-Sat 10 am-8 pm, Sun 1-5 pm; closed Jan 1, Thanksgiving, Dec 25) A new, larger facility is scheduled to open in spring 2005. **$$**

132 SEE ATTRACTIONS

Winterthur

WINTERTHUR MUSEUM, GARDEN, AND LIBRARY.
Rte 52 (Kennett Pike), Winterthur (19735). Phone 302/888-4600; toll-free 800/448-3883. www.winterthur.org. Henry Francis DuPont established this world-class antiques museum, naturalistic garden, and Americana library on a 979-acre country estate in the early 1950s. Inspiring period rooms showcase thousands of objects made or used in America between 1640 and 1860. Museum and garden (Tues-Sun 10 am-5 pm; closed holidays). Library (Mon-Fri 8:30 am-4:30 pm; closed Mon, holidays). **$$$**

For more attractions, go to www.mobiltravelguide.com

STAY

MOBIL STAR-RATED LODGINGS

Dover

COMFORT INN. ★
222 S DuPont Hwy, Dover (19901). Phone 302/674-3300; toll-free 800/228-5150. www.choicehotels.com. 89 rooms, 2 story. Complimentary continental breakfast. Check-in 2 pm, check-out noon. High-speed Internet access. Outdoor pool. **$**

SHERATON DOVER HOTEL. ★★★
1570 N DuPont Hwy, Dover (19901). Phone 302/678-8500; toll-free 888/625-5144. www.sheraton.com. This hotel is conveniently located just minutes from shopping and local attractions in historic Dover. 152 rooms, 7 story. Check-in 3 pm, check-out noon. Restaurant, bar. Fitness room. Indoor pool, whirlpool. **$**

Fenwick Island

ATLANTIC COAST INN. ★
Ocean Hwy and Hwy 54, Fenwick Island (19944). Phone 302/539-7673; toll-free 800/432-8038. www.atlanticcoastinn.com. Bordering on Ocean City, Maryland, this small yet comfortable hotel is great for families looking to check out the beach and all the water sports available in the area. 48 rooms, 2 story. Closed Oct-mid-Apr. Check-in 3 pm, check-out 11 am. Outdoor pool. **$**

Lewes

INN AT CANAL SQUARE. ★★★
122 Market St, Lewes (19958). Phone 302/644-3377; toll-free 888/644-1911. www.theinnatcanalsquare.com. Adjacent to the beautiful historic district, this charming bed-and-breakfast is the only waterfront inn in Lewes. 26 rooms, 4 story. Pets accepted, some restrictions. Complimentary continental breakfast. Check-in 3 pm, check-out 11 am. Restaurant. **$$**

ZWAANENDAEL INN. ★★★
142 2nd St, Lewes (19958). Phone 302/645-6466; toll-free 800/824-8754. www.zwaanendaelinn.com. Listed in the National Historic Register, this antiques-filled inn pleases guests with its charm and elegance.

BRAKE HERE

If your kids have never watched a movie under the stars, **Diamond State Drive-In Theater** is the perfect place. Originally opened in 1949, the renovated theater started doing business again in 1995 and shows first-run family films. The snack bar serves hamburgers, hot dogs, and fries served in a cruiser-shaped container with optional cheese or Old Bay Seasoning. Open mid-spring to mid-Oct, Fri-Sun. *9720 S DuPont Hwy, Felton (19943). Phone 302/284-8307. www.dsdit.com.*

Guests can enjoy nearby antiques shopping and beaches. 26 rooms, 4 story. Check-in 2 pm, check-out 11 am. Restaurant. $

Newark

HILTON WILMINGTON/CHRISTIANA. ★★★
100 Continental Dr, Newark (19713). Phone 302/454-1500; toll-free 800/445-8667. www.hilton.com. This family- and business-friendly hotel is actually situated on a sprawling country estate, lending charm and elegance to the atmosphere and accommodations. Enjoy a meal in one of two restaurants—one casual and one more upscale—or explore shopping and dining in the surrounding area. 266 rooms, 4 story. Check-in 2:30 pm, check-out 11:30 am. High-speed Internet access. Restaurant, bar. Fitness room. Outdoor pool, whirlpool. Business center. $

HOLIDAY INN. ★★
1203 Christiana Rd, Newark (19713). Phone 302/737-2700; toll-free 800/465-4329. www.holiday-inn.com. 144 rooms, 2 story. Check-in 3 pm, check-out noon. Restaurant, bar. Outdoor pool. $

Rehoboth Beach

BOARDWALK PLAZA HOTEL. ★★★
Olive Ave and the Boardwalk, Rehoboth Beach (19971). Phone 302/227-7169; toll-free 800/332-3224. www.boardwalkplaza.com. The charm and comfort of this Victorian-style hotel on Rehoboth Beach will delight guests. Enjoy the scenic ocean views at Victoria's restaurant. 84 rooms, 4 story. Check-in 3 pm, check-out 11 am. Restaurant, bar. Fitness room. Beach. Indoor pool. $$$

BRIGHTON SUITES HOTEL. ★
34 Wilmington Ave, Rehoboth Beach (19971). Phone 302/227-5780; toll-free 800/227-5788. www.brightonsuites.com. This all-suite hotel features comfortable furnishings and a location that allows guests access to shopping, dining, entertainment, and an array of beach and water sports. 66 rooms, 4 story, all suites. Check-in 3 pm, check-out 11 am. Fitness room. Indoor pool. $

COMFORT INN. ★
4439 Hwy 1, Rehoboth Beach (19971). Phone 302/226-1515; toll-free 877/424-6423. www.comfortinn.com. 97 rooms. Complimentary continental breakfast. Check-in 4 pm, check-out noon. Outdoor pool. $

Wilmington

BRANDYWINE SUITES HOTEL. ★★
707 N King St, Wilmington (19801). Phone 302/656-9300; toll-free 800/756-0070. www.brandywinesuites.com. Located in the heart of Wilmington, this small, luxurious European-style hotel offers intimate attention to visitors, and comfortable and spacious suites. 49 rooms, 4 story, all suites. Complimentary continental breakfast. Check-in 3 pm, check-out noon. Restaurant, bar. Airport transportation available. $

COURTYARD BY MARRIOTT. ★★
1102 West St, Wilmington (19801). Phone 302/429-7600; toll-free 800/321-2211. www.courtyard.com. 125 rooms, 10 story. Check-in 3 pm, check-out noon. High-speed Internet access. Restaurant, bar. Fitness room. Airport transportation available. $$

DOUBLETREE HOTEL. ★★
4727 Concord Pike, Wilmington (19801). Phone 302/478-6000; toll-free 800/222-8733. www.doubletree.com. 244 rooms, 7 story. Check-in 3 pm, check-out noon. Restaurant, bar. Fitness room. Indoor pool, whirlpool. $$

HOTEL DU PONT ★★★
11th and Market sts, Wilmington (19801). Phone 302/594-3100; toll-free 800/441-9019. www.hoteldupont.com. The Hotel Du Pont has been a Delaware institution since it opened in 1913. Constructed in downtown Wilmington to rival the grand hotels of Europe, this palatial hotel is close to city attractions while remaining in the heart of the scenic Brandywine Valley. The guest rooms are classically decorated with mahogany and imported linens. Patrons dine on sublime French cuisine in the Green Room. The ambience of the Brandywine Room, which features contemporary American fare, resembles a private club. 217 rooms, 10 story. Pets accepted, some restrictions; fee. Check-in 3 pm, check-out noon. Restaurant,

bar. Fitness room. Airport transportation available. Business center. $$

WYNDHAM WILMINGTON HOTEL. ★★★
700 King St, Wilmington (19801). Phone 302/655-0400; toll-free 877/999-3223. www.wyndham.com. This conveniently located hotel is close to several area activities, including golf, a natural jogging trail, and an extensive fitness center, as well as a short drive to all the sights and history of Philadelphia. 219 rooms, 9 story. Check-in 3 pm, check-out noon. High-speed Internet access. Restaurant, bar. Fitness room. Indoor pool, whirlpool. Business center. $

LOCAL RECOMMENDATIONS

Denton

BEST WESTERN DENTON INN.
521 Fleetwood Rd, Denton (21629). Phone 410/479-8400. www.bestwestern.com. This hotel is located near shops, golf courses, restaurants, and many historic sites. 60 rooms, 2 story. Complimentary continental breakfast. Check-in 3 pm, check-out noon. Outdoor pool. $

Dover

BEST WESTERN GALAXY INN.
1700 E Lebanon Rd, Dover (19901). Phone 302/735-4700; toll-free 800/780-7234. www.bestwestern.com. 64 rooms, 2 story. Complimentary continental breakfast. Check-in 2 pm, check-out 11 am. Laundry services. Outdoor pool, whirlpool. $

FAIRFIELD INN.
655 N DuPont Hwy, Dover (19901). Phone 302/677-0900; toll-free 800/228-2800. www.fairfieldinn.com. 58 rooms, 4 story. Complimentary continental breakfast. Check-in 3 pm, check-out noon. Indoor pool, whirlpool. $

HAMPTON INN.
1568 N DuPont Hwy, Dover (19901). Phone 302/736-3500; toll-free 800/426-7866. www.hamptoninn.com. 77 rooms. Complimentary continental breakfast. Check-in 3 pm, check-out noon. Fitness room. Outdoor pool. $

HOLIDAY INN EXPRESS AND SUITES.
1780 N DuPont Hwy, Dover (19901). Phone 302/678-0600; toll-free 800/465-4329. www.hiexpress.com. Newest hotel in Dover. Conveniently located just minutes from Dover Downs and Dover Air Force Base. 81 rooms, 5 story. Complimentary continental breakfast. Check-in 3 pm, check-out noon. Fitness room. Outdoor pool. $

New Castle

BRIDGEVIEW INN NEW CASTLE WILMINGTON.
1612 N DuPont Hwy, New Castle (19720). Phone 302/658-8511; toll-free 800/272-6232. 120 rooms, 2 story. Complimentary continental breakfast. Check-in 2 pm, check-out noon. Outdoor pool. $

RV AND CAMPING

Bear

LUMS POND STATE PARK.
1068 Howell School Rd, Bear (19701). Phone toll-free 877/987-2757. 68 sites. Showers, sanitary facilities, dumping station, picnic tables, and grills. Six sites with electric hook-ups. No alcoholic beverages. Open Mar-Nov.

Dover

LOST LANDS RV PARK.
1741 Long Point Rd, Dover (19901). Phone 302/436-9450. Electric hook-ups. Outdoor pool, nature trails, community center. Three-night minimum stay Memorial Day weekend-Labor Day weekend.

Felton

KILLENS POND STATE PARK.
5025 Killens Pond Rd, Felton (19943). Phone 302/284-4526; office 302/284-3412. Campground. 59 sites. Tents, RVs, cabins. Electric, water, showers, dumping station. Open year-round.

Houston

G & R CAMPGROUND.
4075 Gun and Rod Club Rd, Houston (19954). Phone 302/398-8108. RVs, tents (primitive), cabins. Water, electric, sewer hook-ups, dump station. Swimming pool, picnic areas, softball field, volleyball court, basketball court, game room, play area, activity hall, general store. Open year-round.

Rehoboth Beach

3 SEASONS CAMPING RESORT.
727 Country Club Rd, Rehoboth Beach (19971). Phone 302/227-2564; toll-free 800/635-4996. 300 sites of all types. Water, electric, sewer, and cable TV hook-ups,

dump station. Laundry facilities. Picnic tables and grills. Swimming pool, miniature golf, video arcade, volleyball court, playground, summertime family activities program. RV parts and service, ice, firewood, propane. Shuttle bus to beach. Open Apr-Nov.

> **For more lodging recommendations, go to www.mobiltravelguide.com**

EAT

MOBIL STAR-RATED RESTAURANTS

Bethany Beach

MANGO'S. ★

97 Garfield Pkwy, Bethany Beach (19930). Phone 302/537-6621. www.mangomikes.com. Inside a breezy white beach house, this restaurant serves up island-inspired fare, along with great views of the beach. Relax with a tropical drink and choose from a menu that features sandwiches, salads, and a behemoth crab and lobster bake for two. Caribbean menu. Lunch, dinner. Children's menu. Casual attire. Outdoor seating. **$$**

Dover

ATWOODS. ★ ★ ★

800 N State St, Dover (19901). Phone 302/674-1776. This restaurant was formerly known as the Blue Coat Inn. Seafood, steak menu. Lunch, dinner. Closed Dec 25. Bar. Children's menu. Casual attire. **$$$**

Lewes

LIGHTHOUSE. ★

Savannah and Anglers rds, Lewes (19958). Phone 302/645-6271. www.lighthouselewes.com. Specializing in seafood caught from the harbor that lies just beyond the windows of the dining room, this restaurant boasts a following of repeat customers as well as a great varied menu. Seafood menu. Breakfast, lunch, dinner. Closed Thanksgiving, Dec 24-25. Bar. Children's menu. Outdoor seating. **$$**

Newark

KLONDIKE KATE'S. ★

158 E Main St, Newark (19711). Phone 302/737-6100. www.klondikekates.com. Housed in a building that has served many a function over the years, including a courthouse and jail, several taverns, and even a skating rink, this restaurant is now a modern eatery, serving pub fare as well as pastas and salads, with a relaxed, old-fashioned ambience. American, Southwestern menu. Lunch, dinner. Closed Thanksgiving, Dec 25. Bar. Children's menu. Outdoor seating. **$$**

Rehoboth Beach

BLUE MOON. ★ ★

35 Baltimore Ave, Rehoboth Beach (19971). Phone 302/227-6515. www.bluemoonrehoboth.com. Beyond the eclectic award-winning menu, this restaurant, open for almost 25 years, also features a monthly rotation of unique artwork by local artists. Sunday brunch is a real treat, with fresh-caught seafood and classic brunch favorites, and unlimited mimosas perfect for a group of friends. American menu. Dinner, Sun brunch. Closed three weeks in Jan. Bar. **$$$**

PIT PASS

If you want to avoid driving to and from the track, there are options. For Sunday events, a Race Express Bus (phone 302/652-3278, www.dartfirststate.com) runs from the Blue Hen Mall/Corporate Center on US Route 113 at Route 13 ($20-per-car fee includes parking and round-trip bus service). Service runs from 8 am to one hour after the race. Exact change required. Or, ride the Race Express buses from the Christiana Mall Park-n-Ride in Newark just off I-95 at Exit 4A (leave at 7:30 am; 1,000 seats available on a first-come, first-served basis; $10 per person).

136 EAT MOBIL STAR-RATED RESTAURANTS

IGUANA GRILL. ★
52 Baltimore Ave, Rehoboth Beach (19971). Phone 302/227-0948. www.iguanagrill.com. This laid-back gathering spot takes full advantage of its beach surroundings with a tropical island theme. Featuring sandwiches, seafood, and burgers, the bar also mixes a mean margarita, as well as other tropical cocktails. American, Southwestern menu. Lunch, dinner. Closed Nov-first weekend of Mar. Bar. Casual attire. Outdoor seating. **$**

Smyrna

THOMAS ENGLAND HOUSE. ★ ★
1165 S Dupont Blvd (Hwy 13), Smyrna (19977). Phone 302/653-1420. This colonial-era building housed troops during the Revolutionary War and was later a stop on the Underground Railroad. American menu. Dinner. Bar. Children's menu. Reservations recommended. **$$$**

Wilmington

KID SHELLEENS. ★
1801 W 14th St, Wilmington. (19806) Phone 302/658-4600. www.kidshelleens.com. This family-friendly pub features American favorites like burgers, sandwiches, and huge salads, as well as a fish and chips plate that's not to be missed. American menu. Lunch, dinner, late-night, Sun brunch. Closed Thanksgiving, Dec 25. Bar. Children's menu. Casual attire. Outdoor seating. **$$**

LOCAL RECOMMENDATIONS

Dover

FROGGY'S.
1036 Lafferty Ln, Dover (19901). Phone 302/678-1117. Sources say this is a popular hangout for drivers and their crews. Southwestern menu. **$**

LA TOLTECA.
247 S DuPont Hwy, Dover (19901). Phone 302/734-3444. Authentic Mexican food with an unbeatable price tag is served in a fun, casual atmosphere. Mexican menu. Lunch, dinner. **$**

MICHELE'S GOURMET RESTAURANT.
1131 N DuPont Hwy, Dover (19901). Phone 302/674-4600, ext 2120; toll-free 866/473-7378. This restaurant is located on the second floor of Dover Downs Hotel and Conference Center. Seafood, steak menu. Dinner, Sun brunch. Closed Mon. Reservations recommended. **$$$**

TANGO'S BISTRO.
1570 N DuPont Hwy, Dover (19901). Phone 302/678-0100. This bistro is a popular driver destination. American menu. Breakfast, lunch, dinner, Sun brunch. **$$**

WHERE PIGS FLY.
617 E Loockerman St, Dover (19901). Phone 302/678-0586. Baby back ribs, hickory-smoked pulled pork and pulled chicken sandwiches, and barbecued chicken are the specialties here. Barbecue menu. Lunch, dinner. **$**

Leipsic

SAMBO'S TAVERN.
283 Front St, Leipsic (19901). Phone 302/674-9724. Sambo's is a local favorite, and what's better, you're likely to see drivers here on race weekends, pounding away at some blue crabs. Jerry Nadeau's motorcoach driver has awarded Sambo's his coveted "four steering wheels" rating. Seafood menu. Lunch, dinner. **$**

Rehoboth Beach

DOG HEAD BREWINGS AND EATS.
320 Rehoboth Ave, Rehoboth Beach (19971). Phone 302/226-2739. This brew pub features wood-grilled specialties, salads, sandwiches, pizza, and seafood. American menu. Lunch, dinner. Children's menu. **$**

Smyrna

WALLY'S BAR-B-QUE.
244 S Main St, Smyrna (19977). Phone 302/653-7515. Wally's doesn't look like much from the outside, but don't be deterred. Run by native Georgian Wally Green and his wife, Arleen, it has a solid reputation as one of the best barbecue joints north of the Mason-Dixon line. The succulent Southern-style barbecue sauce is served over baby back ribs, chicken, pulled pork, or sausage. Barbecue menu. Lunch, dinner. Closed Sun-Mon. **$**

For more dining recommendations, go to www.mobiltravelguide.com

SIDETRIP

Charm, Crab, and A Constellation
Baltimore, MD

Located about 100 miles away from Dover by car, Baltimore has experienced a renaissance since the harbor's redevelopment in the 1970s. More than 13 million tourists flock to "Charm City" every year, and June and September (race dates at Dover) are great times to go, weather-wise.

One of the newer additions to the Inner Harbor area is **Port Discovery Children's Museum** (35 Market Pl, phone 410/727-8120, www.portdiscovery.org). Ranked among the nation's top five children's museums by *Child* magazine, Port Discovery offers educational exhibits geared toward ages 2-12. Activities include an enclosed three-story jungle gym, puppet shows, art studio, and a Tot Spot chock-full of Mega Blocks.

Nearby, **The National Aquarium** (501 E Pratt St, phone 410/576-3800, www.aqua.org) showcases a fascinating cast of aquatic creatures. A dolphin show, tropical rain forest tour, and rotating exhibits featuring everything from seahorses to sharks to jellyfish are both entertaining and educational. (*Note:* no strollers allowed.)

Across the harbor, **The Maryland Science Center** (601 Light St, phone 410/685-2370, www.mdsci.org) is home to kid-friendly exhibits on dinosaurs, the human body, and outer space. In the Kids Room, young children will enjoy water play, dress-up, a construction area, magnets, and more.

History lovers will enjoy a tour of the **USS *Constellation*** (Pier 1, 301 E Pratt St, phone 410/539-1797, www.constellation.org), the only Civil War-era vessel still afloat. The museum offers a self-guided audio tour along with hands-on activities and demonstrations.

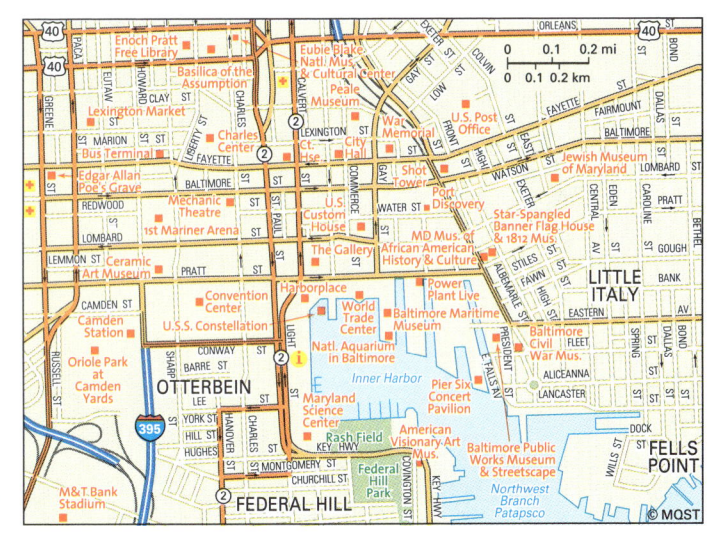

No trip to Baltimore is complete without feasting on the favorite local cuisine—steamed crabs. Two good options are quite close: **Phillips Harborplace** (301 Light St, phone 410/685-6600), located in the Light Street Pavilion, or **Obrycki's** (1727 E Pratt St, phone 410/732-6399), a favorite of celebrities and pro athletes.

One of the nation's oldest seaports, Baltimore Inner Harbor offers fantastic restaurants, entertainment, and a real sense of what Baltimore is all about.

For more Baltimore recommendations, go to www.mobiltravelguide.com

Former St. Louis Blues star Tony Twist waves the green flag to start the 2002 NASCAR Busch Series Charter Pipeline 250.

Gateway International Raceway

Madison, IL

8

The Pit Lanes fill up during the 2004 Charter 250 NASCAR Busch Series Race.

TRACK FACTS
GATEWAY INTERNATIONAL RACEWAY. 700 Raceway Blvd, Madison (62060). Phone 618/482-2400; toll-free 866/35-SPEED (tickets). www.gatewayraceway.com.

SECURITY. Fans may bring one bag or cooler (hard- or soft-sided) no larger than 8 1/2 x 8 1/2 x 12 inches. Coolers may contain ice, food, drinks including beer (no wine or liquor) in cans or plastic containers. Also allowed: umbrellas, seat cushions. Scanners, binoculars, or cameras are allowed on a strap or belt clip. No strollers or pets.

PARKING. It's best to buy your parking pass in advance, especially for the NASCAR Busch Series Race. The close-in Orange lot is best; or park in the free Blue lot near the truck stop behind the backstretch; a free shuttle is provided.

FIRST AID. First aid stations and cooling stations staffed by medical personnel are located around the track.

CONCESSIONS. Concession stands and souvenir shops are grouped in a "concession village" behind the main grandstand that stretches almost its entire length. Stands sell hot dogs, hamburgers, turkey legs, bratwursts, pizza, and chicken sandwiches. Bags of ice are for sale at the main concession stand—just ask the concessionaire.

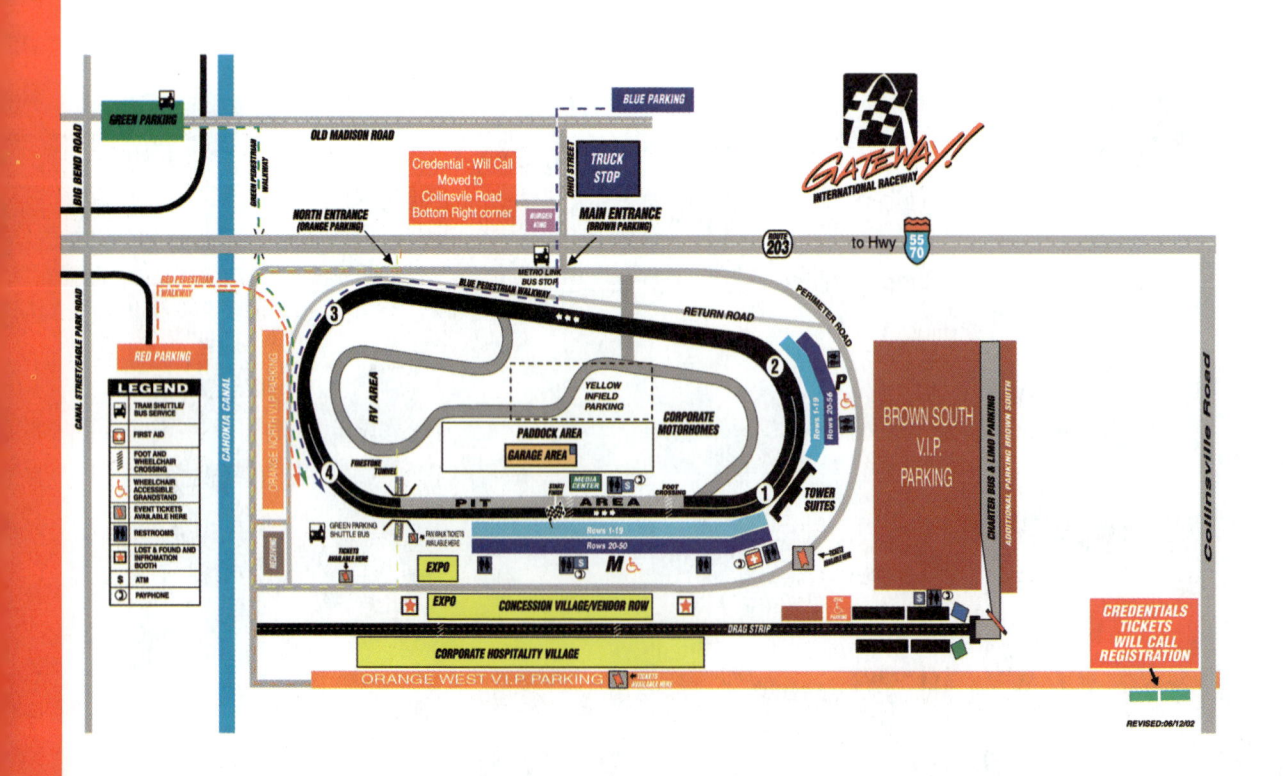

THE BEST OF EAST AND WEST

The 1997 opening of **Gateway International Raceway** (phone 618/482-2400), less than five minutes from downtown St. Louis, only enhanced what was already one of America's elite sports towns. **Cardinals** baseball (stlouis.cardinals.mlb.com), **Rams** football (www.stlouisrams.com), **Blues** hockey (www.stlouisblues.com), **Saint Louis University** college sports (www.slu.edu), and minor league baseball all add to the scene, but no other city boasts a big-time racetrack so close to its downtown.

Racing is part of St. Louis's blood. Even before Gateway emerged on the scene, the city long was home to a thriving regional racing scene on the many prominent short tracks scattered across the region. The Wallace brothers—Rusty, Kenny, and Mike—all hail from St. Louis, while Missouri also has produced Ken Schrader and Jamie McMurray, among others.

Entering the city, the first thing you might notice on the skyline is the unique **Gateway Arch** (phone toll-free 877/982-1410, www.stlouisarch.com). At 630 feet tall, it is the highest man-made monument in the United States. The arch itself, designed by famed architect Eero Saarinen, is part of a memorial to commemorate Westward expansion during the 1800s. North of the city is the part of historic Route 66 that crosses the Mississippi River. It winds along **Old Chain of Rocks Bridge** (www.trailnet.org), the longest pedestrian bridge in the world, where you'll get a great view of downtown.

Lewis and Clark wintered just north in Hartford two centuries ago before beginning their famous trek through the Northwest; learn more at the **Lewis and Clark State Historic Site** in Hartford, Illinois (phone 618/251-5811, www.greatriverroad.com), whose centerpiece is a 15,000-square-foot visitor center at the confluence of the Missouri and Mississippi rivers.

Despite the city's reputation as the "Gateway to the West," it feels much more like it belongs back East than among other cities such as Kansas City and Denver. From its mix of Industrial Age and modern architecture to its myriad cultural offerings, St. Louis balances Eastern cosmopolitanism with a folksy Middle America feel.

Fireworks explode in the background as Brendan Gaughan celebrates his victory in the 2003 NASCAR Craftsman Truck Series Ram Tough 200 race.

Drivers trail the pace car vehicle before the start of the NASCAR Craftsman Truck Series Illinois/Missouri Dodge Dealers Ram Tough 200.

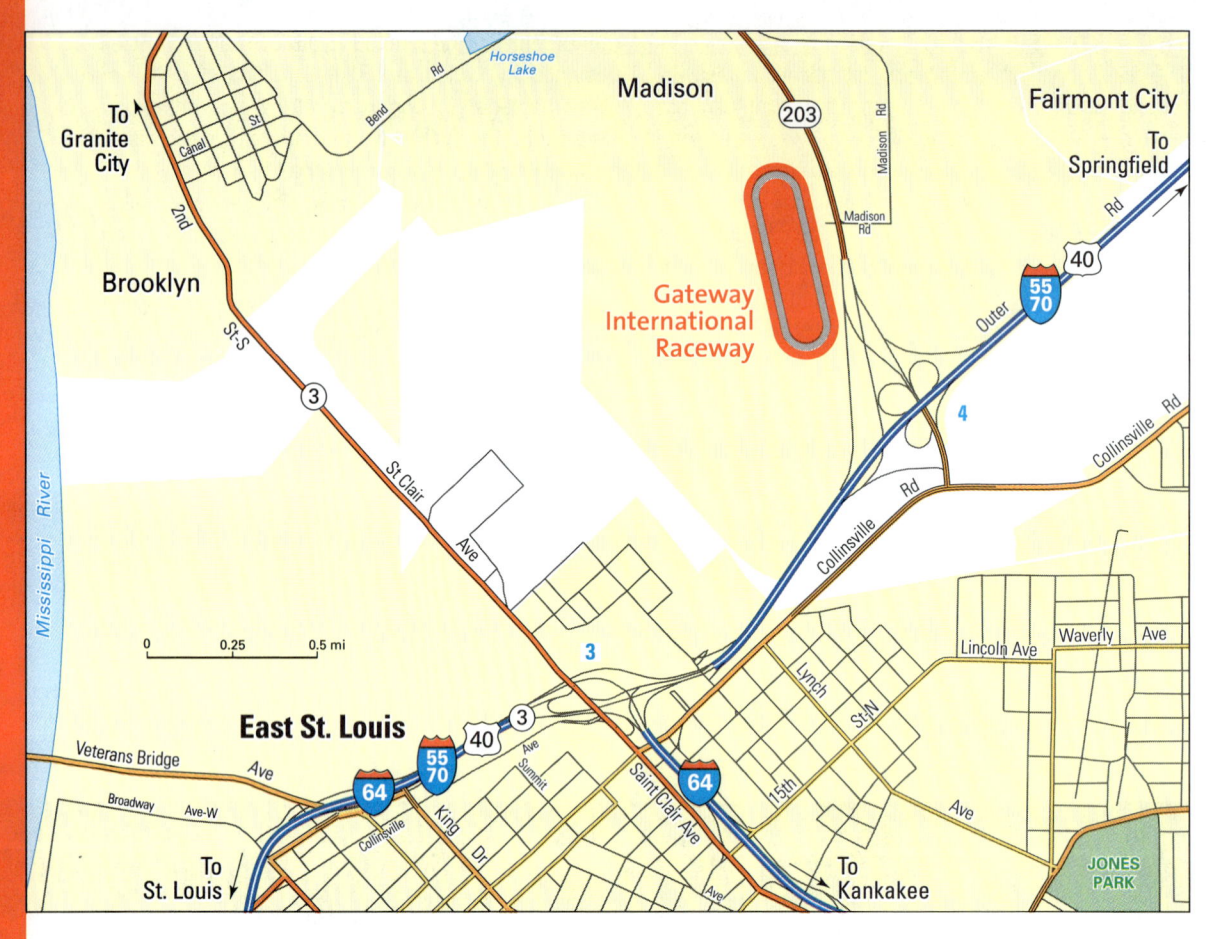

MADISON POLE POSITION:
The 10 miles surrounding Gateway International Raceway.

The result is a city that has all the challenges related to an urban setting as well as diverse attractions and charm. There are plenty of family attractions in the suburbs, but the revitalized downtown is the true draw. As the home of musicians such as Chuck Berry and Tina Turner, St. Louis has a thriving music scene with noteworthy hangouts all around town.

Laclede's Landing, on the western bank of the Mississippi, is a world-class nightlife district, while the clubs and bars of the Soulard neighborhood just south of downtown are always jumping. The charming Hill neighborhood, which serves as St. Louis's version of Little Italy, offers great options for dining. Best of all, the city itself is compact enough that all these attractions are a short drive from the racetrack.

Summer is an especially good time to visit because there's so much going on, even though the heat and humidity can be stifling at times. Start at www.explorestlouis.org and www.stltoday.com, the Web site for the *St. Louis Post-Dispatch* newspaper, and www.riverfronttimes.com. No matter where you go, before or after the competition, St. Louis is one of the best destinations in America for a well-rounded race weekend or vacation.

MADISON CALENDAR

APRIL 2–4, 2005
NCAA Men's Basketball Final Four. Edward Jones Dome, 701 Convention Plz, St. Louis, MO (63101). Phone 314/241-1888. www.stlouissports.org/events. Finals and semifinals games that decide the 2004–2005 NCAA Division I hoops kings.

THROUGH APRIL 24, 2005
"Baseball As America," Missouri Historical Society, Lindell and DeBaliviere sts, Forest Park, MO (63108). Phone 314/746-4599. www.mohistory.org. A display of more than 500 historic uniforms, balls, bats, gloves, art, and more.

APRIL 30, 2005
NASCAR Craftsman Truck Series

MAY 1, 2005
Anheuser Busch Michelob Ultra Weekend Bicycle Race. Carondelet Park. Phone 314/721-4592. www.stlbiking.com. This weekend on wheels in Carondelet Park features a series of fun rides and serious races for cruisers and competitors of all skill levels.

JULY 30, 2005
NASCAR Busch Series

JULY 30, 2005
Homegrown Tomato Challenge. Missouri Botanical Garden, 4344 Shaw Blvd, St. Louis, MO (63110). Phone 314/577-5100. www.mobot.org. See who wins the $5,000 grand prize for the best tomato.

The majestic 630-foot-tall Gateway Arch is a fixture on St. Louis's downtown skyline.

Enjoy a scenic cruise aboard an old-fashioned paddlewheel riverboat.

SHOP TALK

If watching screaming stock cars ignites a little automobile lust within your soul, this place can satisfy your craving. Located less than 10 minutes from the speedway, **Gateway Classic Cars** deals in everything from fully restored American muscle cars and street rods to genuine racers. There are cool trucks and motorcycles for sale, too, if that's more your style. Open Monday-Friday 10 am-5 pm, Saturday 9 am-5 pm, Sunday noon-5 pm. *5401 Collinsville Rd, Fairmont City, IL (62201). Phone 618/271-3000; toll-free 800/231-3616.*

MADISON OUTFIELD:
The 50 miles surrounding Gateway International Raceway.

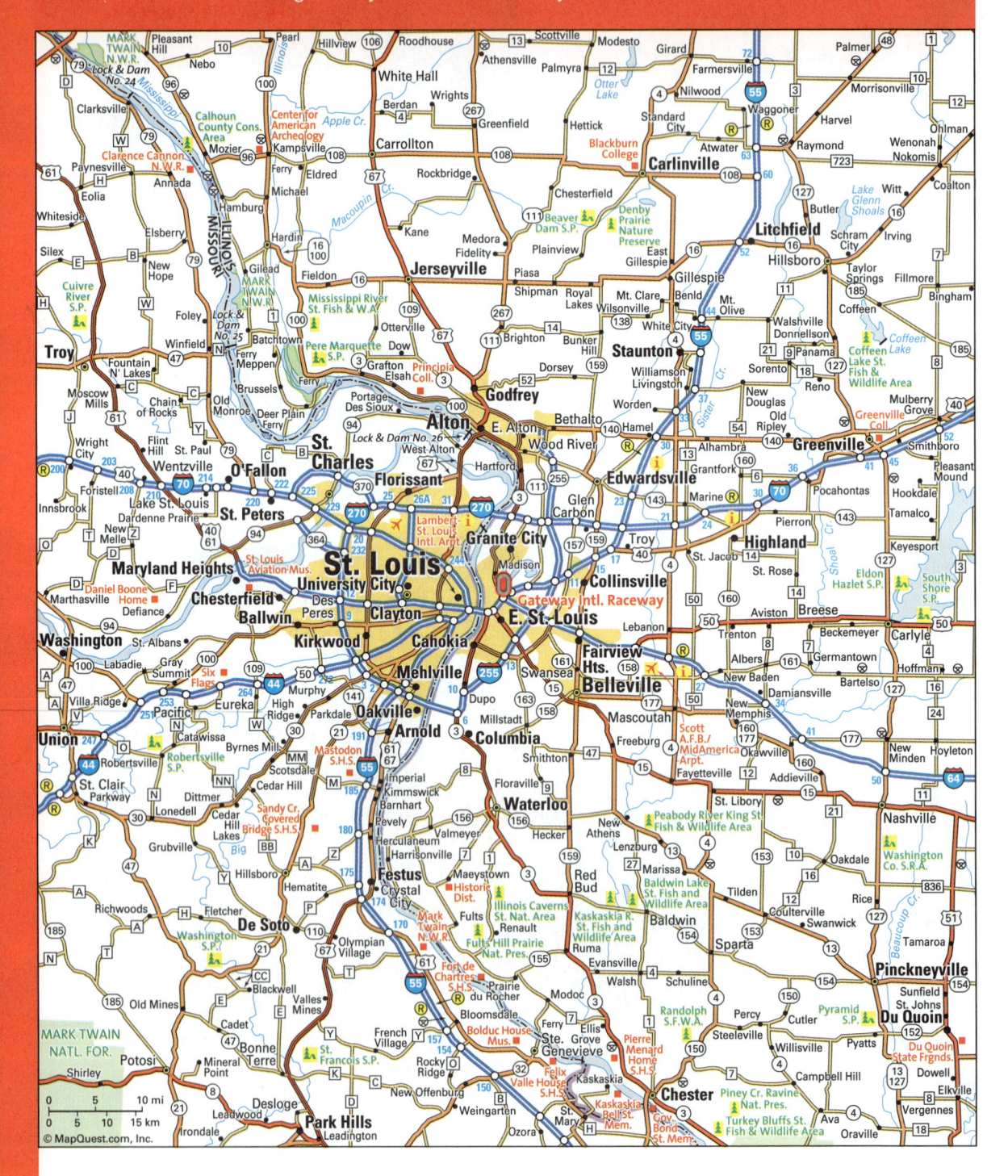

SEE

ATTRACTIONS

Eureka, MO

SIX FLAGS ST. LOUIS.
I-44, Exit 261, Eureka (63025). Phone 636/938-4800. www.sixflags.com. This edition of the theme park franchise has rides and attractions for kids and grownups, plus live shows throughout summer. Big among the two dozen or so rides here are the roller coasters, especially Batman The Ride and the Ninja. Parking (fee). (Mid-May-Labor Day: daily from 10 am; early Apr-mid-May, Labor Day-Halloween: weekends from 10 am; closing times vary) **$$$$**

Grafton, IL

RAGING RIVERS WATERPARK.
100 Palisades Pkwy, Grafton (62037). Phone 618/786-2345. www.ragingrivers.com. There are few better ways to spend a hot day than at the 500-foot swirling plumes, Endless River, or the slides and wave pools in between. Take the little ones to Itty Bitty Surf City. (Daily, times vary by season) **$$$$**

Hazelwood, MO

NASCAR SPEEDPARK.
5555 St. Louis Mills Blvd, Hazelwood (63042). Phone 314/227-5600. www.nascarspeedpark.com. This mini-amusement park northwest of downtown, and one of five now open across North America, contains everything from an arcade to a rock climbing wall to a NASCAR merchandise store. But its main draw is its multitude of race tracks. You can even climb into a mock stock car and experience centrifugal forces, turns, and crash impacts as you "drive" a full-motion NASCAR Silicon Motor Speedway simulator. (Mon-Sat 10 am-9:30 pm, Sun 11 am-7 pm; closed Easter, Thanksgiving, Dec 25) **$$$$**

BIGFOOT 4X4 INC.
6311 N Lindbergh Blvd, Hazelwood (63042). Phone 314/731-2822. www.bigfoot4x4.com. Visit the birthplace and home of Bigfoot, where the monster truck phenomenon began. This photo opportunity waiting to happen includes several trucks on display—including Bigfoot 5, the world's largest, widest, and heaviest pickup—along with an extensive souvenir collection and a factory area where monster trucks are built. (Mon-Fri 9 am-5 pm, Sat 9 am-3 pm; closed Sun) **FREE**

St. Louis, MO

ANHEUSER-BUSCH BREWERY.
12th and Lynch sts (Exit 206C), St. Louis (63118). Phone 314/577-2333. www.budweisertours.com. Trace the making of Budweiser beer from farm fields to finished product in a tour of the nation's largest brewery. Inside the 150-year-old plant, whose grounds encompass 100 acres, you'll also experience a historic brew house, beechwood aging cellars, packing facility, and Clydesdale stables. Adults can sample Bud products. (Daily, various times; closed holidays) **FREE**

GATEWAY ARCH.
Gateway Arch Riverfront, St. Louis (63102). Phone toll-free 877/982-1410. www.gatewayarch.com. At 630 feet tall, the St. Louis Arch is the tallest manmade monument in the United States. Ride a (very) small tram to the top of the arch for a spectacular view, visit exhibits on America's Westward expansion, and more. At the levee below the Arch, take an hour-long river cruise. (Labor Day-Memorial Day: daily 9 am-6 pm; rest of year: daily 8 am-10 pm; closed Jan 1, Thanksgiving, Dec 25) **$$**

INTERNATIONAL BOWLING MUSEUM AND HALL OF FAME.
111 Stadium Plz, St. Louis (63102). Phone 314/231-6340. www.bowlingmuseum.com. Bowling is enjoying a resurgence of popularity, and there's no better place to revel in the sport than in this 50,000-square-foot facility. View wacky bowling shirts and the very sublime Hall of Fame, and bowl a few frames. The museum shares the building with the **St. Louis Cardinals Museum,** which boasts an outstanding collection of Redbirds memorabilia. (Apr-Nov: daily 11 am-4 pm; Oct-Mar: Tues-Fri 11 am-4 pm; closed Jan 1, Thanksgiving, Dec 24–25, 31) **$$**

SEE ATTRACTIONS

ST. LOUIS ZOO.
1 Government Dr, St Louis (63110). Phone 314/781-0900; toll-free 800/966-8877. www.stlzoo.org. The St. Louis Zoo is widely considered one of the best in the country. Lions, cheetahs, and giraffes roam in natural African settings, while other areas showcase exotic species from the poles to the tropics. At Discovery Corner, kids can feed birds, mingle with otters, and more. There are plenty of places to eat and shop, too. (Memorial Day-Labor Day: daily 8 am-7 pm; rest of year: daily 9 am-5 pm; closed Jan 1, Dec 25) **FREE**; some attractions $

For more attractions, go to www.mobiltravelguide.com

STAY

MOBIL STAR-RATED LODGINGS

Alton, IL

HOLIDAY INN ALTON. ★★
3800 Homer Adams Pkwy, Alton (92002). Phone 618/462-1220; toll-free 866/655-4669. www.holiday-inn.com. Set between downtown St. Louis and Lambert International Airport, this comfortable, budget-friendly hotel is great for visiting families. 137 rooms, 4 story. Pets accepted; fee. Complimentary continental breakfast. Check-in 2 pm, check-out noon. High-speed Internet access. Restaurant, bars. Fitness room. Indoor pool, whirlpool. Airport transportation available. Business center. $

Fairview Heights, IL

HAMPTON INN ST. LOUIS/FAIRVIEW HEIGHTS. ★
150 Ludwig Dr, Fairview Heights (62208). Phone 618/397-9705; toll-free 800/426-7866. www.hamptoninn.com. This family-friendly hotel is removed enough from downtown for a quiet stay, yet is still convenient to St. Louis-area attractions. 62 rooms, 3 story. Complimentary continental breakfast. Check-in 3 pm, check-out noon. High-speed Internet access, wireless Internet access. Indoor pool, whirlpool. Airport transportation available. $

RAMADA INN FAIRVIEW HEIGHTS. ★★
6900 N Illinois, Fairview Heights (62208). Phone 618/632-4747; toll-free 800/272-6232. www.ramada.com. Only a 15-minute drive from St. Louis, this clean, quiet hotel offers a variety of amenities. 159 rooms, 5 story. Pets accepted, some restrictions; fee. Complimentary continental breakfast. Check-in 3 pm, check-out noon. High-speed Internet access, wireless Internet access. Restaurant, bar. Fitness room. Indoor pool, outdoor pool, whirlpools. $

St. Louis, MO

COURTYARD BY MARRIOTT ST. LOUIS DOWNTOWN. ★★
2340 Market St, St. Louis (63103). Phone 314/241-9111; toll-free 800/321-2211. www.courtyard.com. Visitors to St. Louis hoping to explore the impressively restored Union Station will find ideal accommodations here, down the street from the station, one of the city's major shopping and dining areas. 151 rooms, 4 story. Check-in 3 pm, check-out noon. Bar. Fitness room. Indoor pool, whirlpool. $

BRAKE HERE

The **Bass Pro Shops Sportsmans Warehouse** isn't just for fishermen. This hangar-sized, 70,000-square-foot store northwest of St. Louis is heaven on earth for anyone who loves the great outdoors. It's packed with fishing and boating supplies, of course, but is also loaded with outdoor clothes, footwear, and even outdoors-themed home décor items. Workshops and activities address such themes as fly fishing and camping. *1365 S Fifth St, St. Charles, MO (63301). Phone 636/688-2500. www.basspro.com.*

HAMPTON INN ST. LOUIS UNION STATION. ★

2211 Market St, St. Louis (63103). Phone 314/241-3200; toll-free 800/426-7866. www.hamptoninn.com. The downtown location of this large hotel, close to the Arch, Union Station, and sports arenas, makes it a great choice for those who plan to tackle as many local attractions as possible. 239 rooms, 11 story. Pets accepted, some restrictions. Complimentary continental breakfast. Check-in 3 pm, check-out noon. Bar. Fitness room. Indoor pool, whirlpool. $

RENAISSANCE ST. LOUIS HOTEL. ★ ★ ★

9801 Natural Bridge Rd, St. Louis (63134). Phone 314/429-1100; toll-free 800/340-2594. www.renaissancehotels.com. Located in the historic district with its own 19th-century charm, this hotel is adjacent to Lambert International Airport. 393 rooms, 12 story. Check-in 3 pm, check-out 1 pm. High-speed Internet access. Restaurant, bar. Fitness room. Indoor pool, outdoor pool, whirlpool. Airport transportation available. Business center. $$

LOCAL RECOMMENDATIONS

Collinsville, IL

BEST WESTERN PEAR TREE INN.

552 Ramada Blvd, Collinsville (62234). Phone 618/345-9500; toll-free 866/777-8133. www.bestwestern.com. This hotel is located about 10 miles east of downtown St. Louis and just a few miles south of Gateway International Raceway. 105 rooms, 2 story. Pets accepted. Complimentary continental breakfast. Check-in 3 pm, check-out noon. Outdoor pool. $

HOLIDAY INN COLLINSVILLE.

1000 Eastport Plaza Dr, Collinsville (62234). Phone 618/345-2800; toll-free 866/655-4669. www.holiday-inn.com. If one facility serves as the track's unofficial host hotel, it's here, about 5 miles east of the raceway. The place is packed with fans on race weekends, and some teams—and even drivers—stay here, too. Next to Splash Waterpark. 244 rooms, 5 story. Pets accepted. Check-in 3 pm, check-out noon. Laundry services. Restaurant, bar. Fitness room. Indoor pool, whirlpool. $

Fairview Heights, IL

BEST WESTERN CAMELOT INN OF FAIRVIEW HEIGHTS.

305 Salem Pl, Fairview Heights (62208). Phone 618/624-3636; toll-free 800/780-7234. www.bestwestern.com. This hotel is located 11 miles from downtown St. Louis just off Interstate 64, a few miles southwest of Gateway International Raceway, and three blocks from the large St. Clair Square Mall. 55 rooms, 2 story. Complimentary continental breakfast. Check-in 3 pm, check-out 11 am. High-speed Internet access. Laundry services. Indoor pool, whirlpool. $

FOUR POINTS BY SHERATON FAIRVIEW HEIGHTS.

319 Fountains Pkwy, Fairview Heights (62208). Phone 618/622-9500; toll-free 888/625-5144. www.sheraton.com. Eight miles southeast of the racetrack on Interstate 64, this new hotel is next to the St. Clair Square Mall, the largest in southern Illinois. 120 rooms, 4 story. Check-in 3 pm, check-out noon. Restaurant, bar. Indoor pool. $

Hazelwood, MO

BEST WESTERN HAZELWOOD INN.

7133 Douglas Palmer, Hazelwood (63042). Phone 314/895-8899; toll-free 800/780-7234. www.bestwestern.com. This hotel is located 13 miles northwest of downtown St. Louis just off Interstate 270 and near Lambert Airport. 70 rooms, 3 story. Complimentary continental breakfast. Check-in 3 pm, check-out 11 am. Indoor pool. $

Maryland Heights, MO

BEST WESTERN WESTPORT PARK HOTEL.

2434 Old Dorsett Rd, Maryland Heights (63043). Phone 314/291-8700; toll-free 800/780-7234. www.bestwestern.com. This hotel is located 14 miles west of downtown St. Louis, near Lambert Airport and Interstate 270. Shops and restaurants of Westport Park are nearby. 149 rooms, 4 story. Pets accepted, some restrictions. Check-in 3 pm, check-out 11 am. Restaurant, bar. Indoor pool, whirlpool. $

Pontoon Beach, IL

BEST WESTERN CAMELOT INN.

1240 E Chain of Rocks Rd, Pontoon Beach (62040). Phone 618/931-2262; toll-free 800/780-7234. www.bestwestern.com. This hotel is about 11 miles from downtown St. Louis and a few miles northeast of Gateway International Raceway. 54 rooms, 2 story.

STAY LOCAL RECOMMENDATIONS

Pets accepted; fee. Complimentary continental breakfast. Check-in 3 pm, check-out noon. Indoor pool. $

St. Charles, MO

BEST WESTERN ST. CHARLES INN.
1377 S Fifth St, St. Charles (63301). Phone 636/916-3000; toll-free 800/780-7234. www.bestwestern.com. This hotel is located 19 miles northwest of downtown St. Louis and near Interstate 70. 64 rooms, 3 story. Complimentary continental breakfast. Check-in 3 pm, check-out noon. Fitness room. Indoor pool. $

St. Louis, MO

BEST WESTERN 55 SOUTH INN.
6224 Heimos Industrial Park, St. Louis (63129). Phone 314/416-7639; toll-free 800/592-5432. www.bestwestern.com. This hotel is located 14 miles south of downtown on Interstate 55. 88 rooms, 3 story. Complimentary continental breakfast. Check-in 3 pm, check-out 11 am. Fitness room. Indoor pool, whirlpool, children's pool. $

BEST WESTERN AIRPORT INN.
10232 Natural Bridge Rd, St. Louis (63134). Phone 314/427-5955; toll-free 800/872-0070. www.bestwestern.com. This hotel is less than a mile from Lambert Airport and about 11 miles northwest of downtown. 137 rooms, 2 story. Complimentary continental breakfast. Check-in 3 pm, check-out 11 am. Laundry services. Outdoor pool. Airport transportation available. $

BEST WESTERN INN AT THE PARK.
4630 Lindell Blvd, St. Louis (63129). Phone 314/367-7500; toll-free 800/373-7501. www.bestwestern.com. Three miles from downtown in the funky turn-of-the-century Central West End area, this hotel is next to Forest Park and near dining, nightlife, and shopping. 128 rooms, 3 story. Check-in 3 pm, check-out noon. Laundry services. Restaurant. Fitness room. Outdoor pool. $

BEST WESTERN KIRKWOOD INN.
1200 S Kirkwood Rd, St. Louis (63122). Phone 314/821-3950; toll-free 800/435-4656. www.bestwestern.com. This hotel is located 12 miles southwest of downtown on Interstate 44. 113 rooms, 6 story. Pets accepted, some restrictions; fee. Complimentary continental breakfast. Laundry services. Bar. Fitness room. Outdoor pool. $

EMBASSY SUITES HOTEL.
901 N First St (in Laclede's Landing), St. Louis (63102). Phone 314/241-4200; toll-free 800/362-2779. www.embassysuites.com. This property is located in the heart of St. Louis's most popular dining and nightlife district, just across the river from the raceway. 297 rooms, 9 story. Complimentary full breakfast. Check-in 4 pm, check-out noon. Restaurant. $

HAMPTON INN GATEWAY ARCH.
333 Washington Ave (in Laclede's Landing), St. Louis (63102). Phone 314/621-7900; toll-free 800/426-7866. www.hamptoninn.com. This local outpost of the national chain opened in 2003. It's 5 miles from the track and very close to many popular St. Louis attractions. 190 rooms, 14 story. Complimentary continental breakfast. High-speed Internet access. Indoor pool, whirlpool. $

RV AND CAMPGROUND

Cahokia, IL

CAHOKIA RV PARQUE.
4060 Mississippi Ave, Cahokia (62206). Phone 618/332-7700. www.cahokiarv.com. Eight miles southwest of Gateway International Raceway at State Routes 157 and 3, this facility has pull-through and back-in sites along with 30/50-amp service, propane and dump stations, a pool, lounge, restrooms, laundry room, playground, and tent-camping area.

East St. Louis, IL

CASINO QUEEN RV PARK.
200 S Front St, East St. Louis (62201). Phone toll-free 800/777-0777. www.casinoqueen.com. Just west of Gateway International Raceway, this park has 130 full-sized spaces, pull-through sites, full hook-ups, bathhouse, laundry facility, buffet restaurant, and convenience store. And it's near the popular Casino Queen hotel and its many restaurants.

Granite City, IL

ST. LOUIS NE/GRANITE CITY KOA CAMPGROUND.
3157 W Chain of Rocks Rd, Granite City (62040). Phone 618/931-5160. www.koa.com. Eight miles north of Gateway International Raceway, this full-service campground offers full hook-ups with 30/50-amp service, LP gas, playground, swimming pool, and laundry facility.

For more lodging recommendations, go to www.mobiltravelguide.com

EAT

MOBIL STAR-RATED RESTAURANTS

Belleville, IL

FISCHER'S. ★★
2100 W Main St, Belleville (62226). Phone 618/233-1131. www.fischersrestaurant.com. This family favorite offers lighter fare such as salads and sandwiches to more substantial entrées like veal Parmesan and Hawaiian pork chops. Save room for Fischer's turtle pie. American menu. Breakfast, lunch, dinner. Closed holidays. Bar. Children's menu. Casual attire. **$$**

Fairview Heights, IL

LOTAWATA CREEK. ★
311 Salem Pl, Fairview Heights (62208). Phone 618/628-7373. www.lotawata.com. This is laid-back comfort food dining at its best—the food is filling and authentic, the service is friendly, and the restaurant can't seem to stay out of the local papers for having the biggest and best burgers, nachos, and quesadillas in town. American menu. Lunch, dinner. Closed Thanksgiving, Dec 25. Children's menu. Casual attire. **$$**

St. Louis, MO

CHUY ARZOLA'S. ★
6405 Clayton Ave, St. Louis (63139). Phone 314/644-4430. Tex-Mex menu. Lunch, dinner. Closed holidays. Bar. Children's menu. Casual attire. Outdoor seating. **$**

CROWN CANDY KITCHEN. ★
1401 St. Louis Ave, St. Louis (63106). Phone 314/621-9650. For more than 90 years, this local legend has been every ice cream lover's fantasy. Any patron who can consume five ice cream creations—sundaes, shakes, whatever you fancy—in 30 minutes or less gets them all free, but you don't have to eat nearly that much to enjoy the fare. American menu. Lunch, dinner. Closed Sun; holidays. **$**

ROAD FOOD

Although the line at the **City Coffee House and Creperie** will most likely be long, especially on a weekend morning, you'll be glad for the time to choose something from the colorful chalkboard describing more than 30 kinds of crepes, as well as quiches, salads, and sandwiches. The giant gourmet crepes range from fruit fillings to Nutella to the Brittany, with honey ham, fresh asparagus and spinach, and havarti. American menu. Breakfast, lunch. Outdoor seating. **$** *36 N Brentwood, St. Louis (63105). Phone 315/862-2489.*

CUNETTO HOUSE OF PASTA. ★★
5453 Magnolia Ave, St. Louis (63139). Phone 314/781-1135. This restaurant is located in an old Italian neighborhood. Italian menu. Lunch, dinner. Closed Sun; holidays. Bar. Casual attire. Outdoor seating. **$$**

DIERDORF AND HART'S STEAK HOUSE. ★★
323 Westport Plz, St. Louis (63146). Phone 314/421-1772. Owned by two local football legends, this steakhouse features a man's-man menu. Here, the steak is done one of four ways—tenderloin filet, New York strip, porterhouse, or ribeye, served with stalwart side dishes. Steak menu. Dinner. Closed holidays. Bar. Business casual attire. Reservations recommended. **$$$**

K.C. MASTERPIECE. ★★
16123 W Chesterfield Pkwy, St. Louis (63017). Phone 314/991-5811. www.kcmasterpiece.com. The makers of the original barbecue sauce opened the doors of their signature restaurant in 1987. Since then, it's become one of the most popular barbecue restaurants in the Midwest. Barbecue menu. Lunch, dinner. Closed Thanksgiving, Dec 25. Bar. Children's menu. $$

LEONARDO'S LITTLE ITALY. ★★
5901 Southwest Ave, St. Louis (63139). Phone 314/781-5988. This restaurant is located in an old Italian neighborhood. Italian menu. Lunch, dinner. Closed Mon; holidays. Bar. Children's menu. Business casual attire. Outdoor seating. $$

MIKE SHANNON'S. ★★
100 N Seventh St, St. Louis (63101). Phone 314/421-1540. www.shannonsteak.com. The most famous sports hangout in town is owned and operated by the popular broadcaster and former Cardinals third baseman—you may see the man himself at the bar after games. Oversized steaks, grilled chicken, and other classic American dishes are the specialty. American menu. Lunch, dinner. Bar. Closed holidays. $$

LOCAL RECOMMENDATIONS

Alton, IL

FAST EDDIE'S BON-AIR.
1530 E Fourth St, Alton (62002). Phone 618/462-5532. www.fasteddiesbonair.com. Fast Eddie's has been a retro-kitsch institution just south of downtown Alton, northwest of the track, for 80 years, thanks to its unique format. The few menu items are head-shakingly cheap. Only alcoholic drinks are served. Beef kabobs, burgers, and shrimp are your best bets. Bar menu. Lunch, dinner, late-night. Casual attire. No credit cards accepted. $$

Belleville, IL

ECKERT'S COUNTRY RESTAURANT.
951 S Green Mount Rd, Belleville (62220). Phone 618/233-0513. www.eckerts.com. The country-casual restaurant at the popular Eckert's Orchard and Country Store is known for biscuits with creamy apple butter. The down-home menu features fried chicken and family-style favorites ranging from country-fried steak to catfish fillets. Shop in the store and garden center, and buy seasonal fresh fruit grown on-site. American menu. Lunch. $

THREE-1-THREE.
313 E Main St, Belleville (62220). Phone 618/239-6885. www.three-1-three.com. Race fans looking for a little rock 'n' roll with their dinner will feel right at home in this downtown music club and restaurant, which regularly hosts local and touring bands. The menu is basic bar food, but the revolving daily specials fit the budget. Bar menu. Dinner. $

O'Fallon, IL

ANDRIA'S.
6805 Old Collinsville Rd, O'Fallon (62209). Phone 618/632-4866. www.andrias.com. This long-popular steakhouse occupies a rambling old white farmhouse framed by towering trees just north of Interstate 64, southeast of the racetrack. For unique flavor, have your steak or pork dish cooked with Andria's Brush-On Steak Sauce. Steak menu. Dinner. Closed Sun. Casual attire. $$

St. Louis, MO

ARCELIA'S.
2001 Park Ave, St. Louis (63104). Phone 314/231-9200. Arcelia's is a haul from the racetrack, but the best Mexican food in town is worth the drive. The comfortable cantina offers traditional dishes and more experimental fare, such as the highly recommended nopales salad, which contains prickly pear cactus paddles. Mexican menu. Lunch, dinner. Casual attire. Outdoor seating. $ After dinner, stroll down the street to **The Chocolate Bar** (1915 Park Ave), a great place for snacks and dessert.

SHOW-ME'S ON THE LANDING.
724 N First St (Laclede's Landing), St. Louis (63102). Phone 314/241-8245. www.showmes.com. Show-Me's is a hard-core sports bar, and probably the best place in town to find fellow race fans and sometimes even team members and drivers. Show-Me's is a reliably lively late-night hangout, and the kitchen is usually open until about midnight. Bar food. Lunch, dinner, late-night. Bar. Outdoor seating. $

For more dining recommendations, go to www.mobiltravelguide.com

SIDETRIP

Americana on the River
Hannibal, MO

Hannibal, Missouri, 120 miles north of Gateway International Raceway, is the hometown of Samuel Clemens—better known as Mark Twain, the author of such classics as *The Adventures of Tom Sawyer* and *The Adventures of Huckleberry Finn*. A day trip to this tiny slice of Americana blends history with a big Mississippi River adventure.

The annual **National Tom Sawyer Days** (phone 573/221-3231, www.hannibaljaycees.org), held around the Fourth of July, is a festival of both Mark Twain and small-town America that draws 100,000 people each year. It includes such Twain homages as fence-painting and frog-jumping contests (if you don't own a frog, you can rent one) as well as tricycle races for kids, a mud volleyball tournament for adults, fireworks, and a parade.

With quaint shops, antique stores, and restaurants, all of Hannibal (phone 573/221-2477, toll-free 1-TOMANDHUCK or 866/263-4825, www.hanmo.com or www.visithannibal.com) is worth checking out. At the **Mark Twain Boyhood Home and Museum** (phone 573/221-9010, www.marktwainmuseum.org), one fee ($6 for adults, $3 for children) lets you tour the six main Twain-related properties, including his boyhood home where he dreamed up many of the adventures that became the basis of his famous stories. Twain's father served as justice of the peace down the street. A new museum boasts Norman Rockwell paintings that

Hannibal is rich with literary history—make time to explore. The most fun way to reach Hannibal is to drive along the Great River Road, Highway 79, an America's National Scenic Byway.

illustrated special editions of the Tom Sawyer and Huck Finn books.

You'll want to see the big Huck and Tom statue on Main Street, visit the **Mark Twain Memorial Lighthouse,** and tour the **Mark Twain Cave,** which is featured in the tales of Sawyer and Finn.

For more Hannibal recommendations, go to www.mobiltravelguide.com

NASCAR Busch Series cars wait on Homestead's pit road for their chance to qualify.

Homestead-Miami Speedway®

Homestead, FL

9

Tony Stewart leads the field in the 2003 NASCAR NEXTEL Series Ford 400.

TRACK FACTS

HOMESTEAD-MIAMI SPEEDWAY. 1 Speedway Blvd, Homestead (33035). Phone 305/230-7223. www.homesteadmiamispeedway.com.

SECURITY. Each person may carry one soft-sided bag or cooler no larger than 6 x 6 x 12 inches; it may contain ice. One clear plastic bag no larger than 18 x 8 x 14 inches is allowed but not for ice. Track reentry passes are available. Binoculars, cameras, and headsets (worn around the neck) are allowed, as are seat cushions. No large bags, strollers, bikes, umbrellas, chairs, or pets allowed.

PARKING. Free during events. Overnight parking not allowed. Lots open at 6:30 am and close at dusk. Reserved parking available with some advance ticket purchases. Handicapped-accessible spaces (display credentials) in Lots A, E, L, and Blue. Weekend-long parking for RVs available with advance purchase at Palm Drive RV Lot, on south side of track.

FIRST AID. Find first aid facilities in the administrative building directly across from the speedway's main entrance and around the track; or phone 305/230-5050.

CONCESSIONS. Relax at the Rum Pavilion, or find refreshments at concession stands throughout the grandstand area. Hospitality tents offer amenities to those with exclusive tickets (phone 305/230-7223).

TROPICAL PLEASURES

The racy shores of South Beach, the marshy swamps of the Everglades, and the sultry Latin vibe of Miami combine to make South Florida a one-of-a-kind destination for every kind of traveler. If you've come for the racing thrills at Homestead-Miami Speedway and the Ford Championship weekend in November, you'll stay for the unique brand of excitement the Miami area offers—and there are plenty of options.

Homestead itself is a rural community of about 36,000. Its downtown celebrates turn-of-the-century history by preserving and renovating several buildings such as the **Redland Hotel** (5 S Flagler Ave, www.redlandhotel.com), first built in 1904, and the **Seminole Theater** (18 N Krome Ave), currently being restored. Brick streets lined with antiques shops and restaurants give the downtown its characteristic charm.

The area's long history as a farming community has attracted Hispanic workers, particularly Mexicans, who have added their own fiery flavor to the local cuisine. As a result, Homestead has earned the reputation as having the best Mexican food in the Southeast. Area farms produce a wealth of tropical fruits, including avocados, papayas, mangos and traditional citrus, strawberries, tomatoes, and corn.

The track itself is landscaped with 975 palm trees and four lakes, one deep enough to submerge a six-story building. The infield lake is stocked with peacock and largemouth bass and provides a pleasant pastime for drivers and crew. Other opportunities to cast a pole can be found along the 120-mile **Florida Keys,** famous as a sport fisherman's paradise. The Keys are only 30 miles from Homestead, which resides right at the tip of Florida's mainland.

North of the speedway's hometown is a town that also prides itself on its history and architecture: Coral Gables, whose many buildings reflect a Mediterranean influence. The suburb of Miami has two

Matt Kenseth, 2003 NASCAR champion, leads seven-time champion Richard Petty in a ceremonial pace lap.

Parrots are just a few of the colorful animals on display at Miami's MetroZoo.

golf courses, several museums, and lots of opportunities to shop, many of which are accessible by the city's vintage-style, hybrid electric trolleys. While you're in town, take a dip in the refreshing 820,000-gallon **Venetian Pool** (phone 305/460-5306, www.venetianpool.com) and bask under the Venetian-style porticos of this registered National Historic Place. To experience nature in a domesticated state, stop by the 83-acre **Fairchild Tropical Botanic Garden** (phone 305/667-1651, www.fairchildgarden.org) and tour the conservatory and tropical fruit pavilion surrounded by lakes and lily ponds.

Looking for nature in a wilder state? Miami's waterfront, at the juncture of the Miami River and the Atlantic Ocean, is home to 15 miles of beaches and unparalleled water sports. It also features two of the most unique national parks in the country: **Everglades National Park** (phone 305/242-7700, www.nps.gov/ever), where you can prowl the boardwalks and waterways—and quite possibly spot an alligator or two; and **Biscayne National Park** (phone 305/230-7275, www.nps.gov/bisc), an underwater park where you can explore the coral reef from a glass-bottom vessel or with scuba gear.

They appear to be smiling, but don't get too friendly with these inhabitants of Everglades National Park.

Get even closer to the gators at the **Everglades Alligator Farm** (40351 SW 192nd Ave, Florida City, phone 305/247-2628, www.everglades.com), which has more than 3,000 of them. Take an airboat ride through the nearby Everglades or, if you're brave enough, hold a baby alligator during one of their daily wildlife shows.

No gators, but just as much—if not more—excitement is available in Miami. Aptly named "Gateway to the Americas," the greater Miami area is home to 2.1 million citizens, many of whom have emigrated from Cuba, Mexico, and Latin America. Go to **Little Havana** (SW 8th St) for café con leche, guayabera shirts, and Miami's slice of Cuba; or head to **Little Haiti** for authentic Caribbean fare. Immigrants aren't the only ones flocking to Miami—3.5 million tourists a year come to the port of the city, granting it the title "Cruise Ship Capital of the World." But to simply come to cruise would mean you miss the city's culture and dazzle.

A must-have when in Miami—Key lime milkshakes from Robert is Here.

GETTING AROUND

From the north, take the Florida Turnpike south to Speedway Blvd (Exit 6), and continue heading south, following signs to the track. If you're arriving at the track from the south, take US Hwy 1 to Palm Dr, and head east for 2 1/2 miles. Turn left on SW 142 Ave, and follow signs to the track.

Speedway Club Seat holders may park in the Blue Lot. If you have season tickets, head for the Red Lot. The Green Lot is reserved for three-day package ticket holders. Keep in mind that Red and Green lots can be accessed through low-traffic routes; similar back roads are established for quick exit flow as well.

GETTING TICKETS

There are several ways to purchase tickets in advance: call the track at 305/230-RACE (7223) or toll-free 866/409-RACE (7223), go to www.homesteadmiamispeedway.com, or visit the track at 1 Speedway Blvd, Homestead.

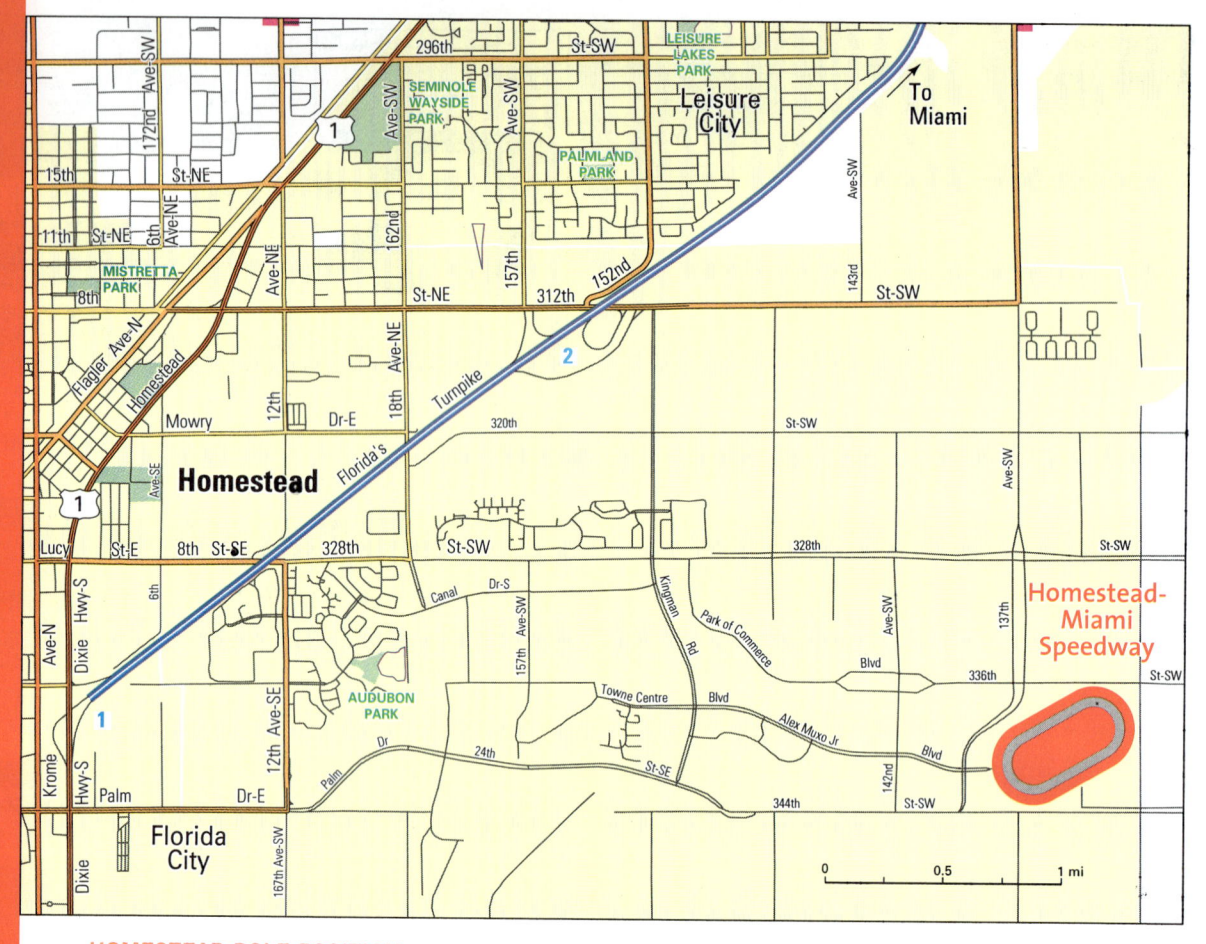

HOMESTEAD POLE POSITION:
The 10 miles surrounding Homestead-Miami Speedway.

Miami's famous **South Beach**, or "SoBe," is legendary for everything there is to enjoy during the day and night. The **Art Deco District** (1001 Ocean Dr, phone 305/531-3484) was the center for the architectural movement that brought zigzags and bold colors to buildings in the 1930s and '40s. Take a guided walking tour of some of the 800 buildings in this style throughout the Miami area. While SoBe is famous—or infamous—for a no-holds-barred beach scene, plenty of family-friendly options for enjoying surf and sand are available in northern Miami.

If it's night life you're looking for, trade in your flip-flops for dancing shoes, enjoy dinner at one of Miami's many fine restaurants, and head for the clubs. The same buildings that are art forms by day, turn on neon lights and pulsate with Latin rhythms by night, attracting celebrities such as Will Smith and Jennifer Lopez. Dance on top of a 2,000-gallon aquarium at **Club Deep** (621 Washington Ave, phone 305/532-1509) or check the score of the game on the 10-foot big screen at the **Clevelander** (1020 Ocean Dr, phone toll-free 800/815-6829).

No matter where you turn, whether it's smoldering Miami, the sunny Keys, or the sultry Everglades, Florida has something for everyone. For more information on the area, check out www.flausa.com.

HOMESTEAD CALENDAR

OCTOBER 2005–JANUARY 2006
Junior Orange Bowl Festival. Locations throughout the Miami area. Phone 305/662-1210. www.jrorangebowl.com. Middle and high school students compete in sports and artistic events.

NOV 18–21, 2005
Ford Championship Weekend. Includes NASCAR Craftsman Truck Series, NASCAR Busch Series, and NASCAR NEXTEL Cup Series.

NOVEMBER, 2005
Harvest Festival. Miami-Dade County Fair Expo Center, Coral Way and SW 112 Ave, Miami (33165). Phone 305/375-1492. www.historical-museum.org. Celebrate southern Florida's agricultural traditions with crafts, music, and reenactments.

NOVEMBER, 2005
Miami Book Fair International. Miami Dade College, Wolfson Campus, 300 NE 2nd Ave, Miami (33132). Phone 305/237-3258. www.miamibookfair.com. More than 1 million books for sale and many authors speaking.

DEC 1–4, 2005
Art Basel Miami Beach. Miami Beach Convention Center, 1901 Convention Center Dr, Miami Beach (33139). Phone 305/891-7270. www.artbaselmiamibeach.com. International art show features music, film, and more.

The famed Budweiser team of Clydesdales makes its way down the front stretch in pre-race ceremonies at the 2003 NASCAR Busch Series Ford 300.

INSIDER'S PICK

As Chairman of the Board and CEO, **Brian France** is the big fish in NASCAR's big pond. And that's what he wants for a night out on the town. "When I go down to Homestead, I enjoy dining at **Grill Fish** in Miami. It's one of my favorite spots. Everything on the menu is terrific." *1444 Collins Ave, Miami Beach (33139). Phone 305/538-9908.*

HOMESTEAD OUTFIELD:
The 50 miles surrounding Homestead-Miami Speedway.

SEE

ATTRACTIONS

Coral Gables

FAIRCHILD TROPICAL BOTANIC GARDEN.
10901 Old Cutler Rd, Coral Gables (33156). Phone 305/667-1651. www.fairchildgarden.org. This 83-acre garden was planted by Robert Montgomery with the help of his friend David Fairchild, who traveled the world collecting seeds and specimens of rare plants, many of which now thrive in this subtropical paradise. The gift shop offers treasures nearly as grand as the plants. Tram tour included with admission fee. (Daily 9:30 am-4:30 pm; closed Dec 25) **$$**

VENETIAN POOL.
2701 De Soto Blvd, Coral Gables (33134). Phone 305/460-5306. www.venetianpool.com. The pool was created in 1924 when the rock quarry used to provide native stone for local architecture filled with more than 800,000 gallons of fresh water from a natural spring. The pool is emptied each night and refilled by morning with fresh, cold water. With rock caves and palm grottoes. The pool has an on-site café. (Hours vary) **$$**

Homestead

BISCAYNE NATIONAL PARK.
9700 SW 328th St, Homestead (33033). Phone 305/230-7275. www.nps.gov/bisc. Learn about the coral reef from the visitors center, or hop aboard a tour boat to snorkel, scuba dive, or observe the reef from a glass-bottom vessel. Two islands offer camping facilities accessible by private or park boat (Nov-May). **FREE**

EVERGLADES NATIONAL PARK.
40001 State Rd 9336, Homestead (33034). Phone 305/242-7700. www.nps.gov/ever. This park allows a rare opportunity to explore the quiet "river of grass." Boardwalks, boating, canoeing, and kayaking appeal to nature lovers. Alligator sightings are practically guaranteed in this last vestige of the Everglades, protected as a national park by Harry S. Truman in 1947, but under siege by environmental hazards. (Daily, 24 hours) **$$** per car.

Miami

BAYSIDE MARKETPLACE.
401 N Biscayne Blvd, Miami (33132). Phone 305/577-3344. www.baysidemarketplace.com. A cool shopping opportunity with more than 150 stores and restaurants, many from south of the border with tropical fashions and flavors, clustered around the waterfront. Departure point for gondola and sightseeing cruises.

THE DEERING ESTATE AT CUTLER.
16701 SW 72nd Ave, Miami (33157). Phone 305/235-1668. www.deeringestate.com. Built in the early 1900s, the estate provides a glimpse of life for weathly Florida pioneers. Tour the homes and natural preserves, or explore the waterfront by kayak. (Daily 10 am-5 pm) **$$**

LITTLE HAVANA.
SW 8th St between SW 11th Ave and 27th Ave, Miami. Also known as Calle Ocho, Little Havana is the heart of Cuban culture in Miami, settled by Cuban refugees and still populated by immigrants. Delicious Cuban restaurants and cafecitas, gift shops, and art galleries bring the old home island to the mainland. Lively yet peaceful—except during the annual Calle Ocho Festival, which draws an estimated 1 million partiers to the Latin cultural celebration.

MIAMI METROZOO.
12400 SW 152nd St (Coral Reef Dr), Miami (33177). Phone 305/251-0400. www.miamimetrozoo.com. More than 900 animals prowl this 300-acre zoo park, including rare and exotic creatures such as Komodo dragons and white Bengal tigers. The largest Asian aviary in the United States provides a natural setting and home for more than 300 rare Asian birds. (Daily 9:30 am-5:30 pm) **$$$**

For more attractions, go to www.mobiltravelguide.com

STAY

Note: At press time, some area hotels and restaurants were closed due to hurricane damage. Call ahead to check availability.

MOBIL STAR-RATED LODGINGS

Coconut Grove

DOUBLETREE HOTEL. ★★
2649 S Bayshore Dr, Miami (33133). Phone 305/858-2500; toll-free 800/222-8733. www.doubletree.com. This hotel is convenient to Miami International Airport, area attractions, and Homestead-Miami Speedway. Many of the rooms and suites have bay views and terraces overlooking the marina and parks across the street. 192 rooms, 20 story. Check-in 3 pm, check-out noon. High-speed Internet access. Restaurant, bar. Fitness room. Outdoor pool, whirlpool. Business center. $$

GROVE ISLE RESORT. ★★★
4 Grove Isle Dr, Miami (33133). Phone 305/858-8300; toll-free 800/884-7683. www.groveisle.com. Situated on a secluded private island on Biscayne Bay, this resort's tropical rooms and suites have glossy, terra-cotta-tiled floors and floor-to-ceiling windows that open onto private terraces. 49 rooms, 5 story. Pets accepted. Complimentary continental breakfast. Check-in 3 pm, check-out noon. Restaurant, bar. Fitness room. Outdoor pool, whirlpool. Tennis. $$$

Coral Gables

BILTMORE HOTEL CORAL GABLES. ★★★
1200 Anastasia Ave, Coral Gables (33134). Phone 305/445-1926; toll-free 800/633-7313. www.biltmorehotel.com. First opened in 1926, this elegant, grand hotel has hosted dignitaries from around the world. The Biltmore is also home to the nation's largest hotel pool. 280 rooms, 15 story. Check-in 3 pm, check-out noon. Restaurant, bar. Fitness room, spa. Outdoor pool. Golf. Tennis. Business center. $$$

Key Largo

HOLIDAY INN. ★★
99701 Overseas Hwy, Key Largo (33037). Phone 305/451-2121; toll-free 800/843-5397. www.holidayinnkeylargo.com. This marina resort, with two relaxing waterfall pools, is on a canal 3 miles from the beach—and is the home port to the original *African Queen*, used in the Humphrey Bogart movie of the same name. 130 rooms, 2 story. Check-in 3 pm, check-out 11 am. Restaurant, bar. Fitness room. Two outdoor pools, whirlpool. Airport transportation available. $

MARRIOTT KEY LARGO BAY BEACH RESORT. ★★★
103800 Overseas Hwy, Key Largo (33037). Phone 305/453-0000; toll-free 800/228-9290. www.marriottkeylargo.com. This Key Largo resort offers Professional Association of Diving Instructors professionals for scuba diving lessons, specialty certifications, and daily dive and snorkel trips to the coral reef and marine sanctuary. 153 rooms, 4 story. Check-in 3 pm, check-out noon. Restaurant, bar. Fitness room. Outdoor pool, whirlpool. $$

PIT PASS

You can bank on wild action at Homestead-Miami since the facility underwent a $10 million reconfiguration project in 2003. The banking on the 1 1/2-mile oval was increased to a maximum of 20 degrees in the turns, largely in response to requests from fans and some NASCAR drivers. The result? Each turn has three racing "grooves" at the bottom, middle, and top of each banked curve, guaranteeing plenty of fender-to-fender action.

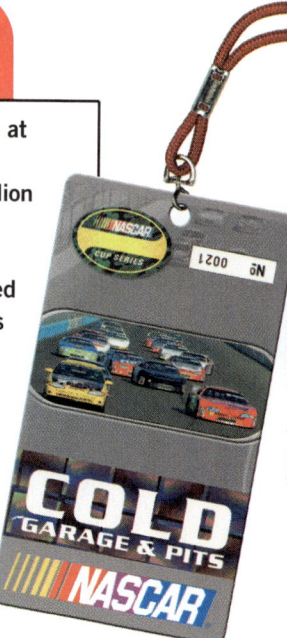

SHERATON BEACH RESORT KEY LARGO. ★★★
97000 S Overseas Hwy, Key Largo (33037). Phone 305/852-5553; toll-free 800/539-5274. www.sheraton.com. This hotel is set on 12 acres neighboring the Everglades. White sand awaits at this door to the Keys near John Pennekamp Coral Reef State Park, the only living coral reef in North America. 200 rooms, 4 story. Check-in 3 pm, check-out noon. High-speed Internet access. Restaurants, bar. Fitness room. Two outdoor pools, children's pool, whirlpool. Tennis. **$**

Miami
COURTYARD BY MARRIOTT. ★★
1201 NW LeJeune Rd, Miami (33126). Phone 305/642-8200; toll-free 800/321-2211. www.courtyard.com. 125 rooms, 5 story. Check-in 3 pm, check-out noon. Restaurant, bar. Fitness room. Outdoor pool, whirlpool. Tennis. Airport transportation available. Business center. **$**

DORAL GOLF RESORT AND SPA. ★★★
4400 NW 87th Ave, Miami (33178). Phone 305/592-2000; toll-free 800/713-6725. www.doralresort.com. You'll find five 18-hole championship courses at this 650-acre oasis in northwest Miami. Play the famous Dick Wilson and Robert von Hagge "Blue Monster" course, shop, dine, play tennis, or simply get pampered in the 168,000-square-foot spa. 793 rooms. Check-in 4 pm, check-out 11 am. Restaurant, bar. Children's activity center. Fitness room, spa. Indoor pool, five outdoor pools, children's pool, whirlpool. Golf, 90 holes. Tennis. Business center. **$$$**

HILTON MIAMI AIRPORT AND TOWERS. ★★★
5101 Blue Lagoon Dr, Miami (33178). Phone 305/262-1000; toll-free 800/445-8667. www.hilton.com. 418 rooms, 14 story. Check-out 11 am. Restaurant, bar. Fitness room. Outdoor pool, whirlpool. Tennis. Airport transportation available. Business center. **$$**

Miami Lakes
DON SHULA'S HOTEL. ★★★
6842 Main St, Miami Lakes (33014). Phone 305/821-1150; toll-free 800/247-4852. www.donshulahotel.com. Namesake of the venerable Miami Dolphins coach, Don Shula's casts a lush South Florida compound into an adrenaline addict's mecca. Dolphins photographs and bronze sculptures dedicated to baseball's Florida Marlins share 500 acres with fish ponds and tropical gardens. Two 18-hole golf courses, nine tennis courts, a well-equipped gym, and several swimming pools—including one shaped like a tennis racquet—serve athletic passions. 289 rooms, 3 story. Check-in 3 pm, check-out noon. Restaurant, bar. Fitness room, spa. Outdoor pool, whirlpool. Golf. Tennis. Business center. **$$**

LOCAL RECOMMENDATIONS
Coral Gables
BEST WESTERN CHATEAUBLEAU HOTEL.
1111 Ponce de Leon Blvd, Coral Gables (33134). Phone 305/448-2634; toll-free 888/642-6442. www.bestwestern.com. 118 rooms, 4 story. Pets accepted, some restrictions; fee. Check-in 3 pm, check-out 11 am. Laundry services. Bar. Outdoor pool. Airport transportation available. Business center. **$**

Cutler Ridge/Miami
BEST WESTERN FLORIDIAN HOTEL.
10775 Caribbean Blvd, Cutler Ridge/Miami (33189). Phone 305/253-9960; toll-free 800/371-9232. www.bestwestern.com. 150 rooms, 6 story. Pets accepted, some restrictions; fee. Complimentary continental breakfast. Check-in 3 pm, check-out noon. High-speed Internet access. Laundry services. Restaurant. Outdoor pool. **$$**

BAYMONT INN AND SUITES.
10821 Caribbean Blvd, Cutler Ridge (33189). Phone 305/278-0001; toll-free 866/999-1111. www.baymontinns.com. 100 rooms, 4 story. Pets accepted. Complimentary continental breakfast. Check-in 3 pm, check-out noon. Laundry services. Outdoor pool. **$**

Florida City
BEST WESTERN HOMESTEAD/FLORIDA CITY'S GATEWAY TO THE KEYS.
411 S Krome Ave, Florida City (3334). Phone 305/246-5100; toll-free 888/981-5100. www.bestwestern.com. 114 rooms, 2 story. Complimentary continental breakfast. Check-in 3 pm, check-out noon. Laundry services. Outdoor pool, whirlpool. **$**

STAY LOCAL RECOMMENDATIONS

COMFORT INN FLORIDA CITY.
333 SE First Ave, Florida City (33034). Phone 305/248-4009; toll-free 877/424-6423. www.comfortinn.com. 83 rooms, 2 story. Complimentary continental breakfast. Check-in 2 pm, check-out 11 am. High-speed Internet access. Laundry services. Outdoor pool. $

HAMPTON INN MIAMI/FLORIDA CITY.
124 E Palm Dr, Florida City (33034). Phone 305/247-8833; toll-free 800/426-7866. www.hamptoninn.com. This hotel is very close to the track. 120 rooms, 2 story. Complimentary continental breakfast. Check-in 3 pm, check-out noon. High-speed Internet access. Laundry services. Outdoor pool. $

Homestead

EVERGLADES INTERNATIONAL HOSTEL.
20 SW Second Ave, Homestead (33033). Phone 305/248-1122; toll-free 800/372-3874. www.everglades hostel.com. This hotel offers a special deal for NASCAR fans—along with a special contract. Fans can rent dorm suites for themselves and friends for prices ranging from $100 for four people to $275 for eight. The contract stipulates that the facilities are open for guest-only parties, and that revelers will be considerate of other guests and refrain from loud behavior late at night. Pets accepted, some restrictions; fee. Check-out 11 am. High-speed Internet access. Laundry services. $

REDLAND HOTEL.
5 S Flagler Ave, Homestead (33033). Phone 305/246-1904; toll-free 800/595-1904. www.redlandhotel.com. Built in 1904, condemned and facing the wrecking ball, the Redland Hotel was rescued by Katy and Rex Oleson and Nancy and Jerry Gust, who renovated the historic building and run the hotel today. The small, intimate inn is popular with track officials and booked long in advance. Vintage bar and restaurant with relaxing veranda. 22 rooms. Check-in 3 pm, check-out 11 am. Restaurant, bar. $

Key Largo

BEST WESTERN SUITES AT KEY LARGO.
201 Ocean Dr, Key Largo (33037). Phone 305/451-5081; toll-free 800/462-6079. www.bestwestern.com. 40 rooms, 2 story, all suites. Complimentary continental breakfast. Check-in 3 pm, check-out 11 am. Outdoor pool. $

NEPTUNE'S HIDEAWAY.
104180 Overseas Hwy, Key Largo (33037). Phone 305/451-0357; toll-free 888/251-4813. www.neptunes hideaway.com. All the cottage-style accommodations here have kitchenettes. 20 rooms. Check-in 2 pm, check-out 11 am. Beach. $

Miami

BEST WESTERN MIAMI AIRPORT WEST INN AND SUITES.
3875 NW 107th, Miami (33178). Phone 305/463-7195; toll-free 800/327-7755. www.bestwestern.com. 103 rooms, 4 story. Complimentary continental breakfast. Check-in 3 pm, check-out noon. High-speed Internet access. Laundry services. Fitness room. Outdoor pool. Business center. $

BEST WESTERN SOUTH MIAMI.
5959 SW 71st St, Miami (33143). Phone 305/667-6664; toll-free 800/780-7234. www.bestwestern.com. 117 rooms, 4 story. Complimentary continental breakfast. Check-in 3 pm, check-out noon. Laundry services. Restaurant. Fitness center. Outdoor pool. Airport transportation available. $

Miami Beach

BEST WESTERN BEACH RESORT.
4333 Collins Ave, Miami Beach (33140). Phone 305/532-3311; toll-free 800/832-8332. www.best western.com. 250 rooms, 8 story. Check-in 3 pm, check-out noon. High-speed Internet access. Beach. Outdoor pool. $

BEST WESTERN OCEANFRONT RESORT.
9365 Collins Ave, Bal Harbour (33154). Phone 305/864-2232; toll-free 800/327-1412. www.bestwestern .com. 93 rooms, 3 story, all suites. Complimentary continental breakfast. Check-in 3 pm, check-out 11 am. Laundry services. Beach. Two outdoor pools. $

BEST WESTERN ON THE BAY INN AND MARINA.
1819 79th St Causeway, North Bay Village (33141). Phone 305/865-7100; toll-free 800/624-3961. www. bestwestern.com. 116 rooms, 5 story. Check-in 3 pm, check-out 11 am. Laundry services. Outdoor pool. Airport transportation available. $

BEST WESTERN SOUTH BEACH.

1050 Washington Ave, Miami Beach (33139). Phone 305/674-1930; toll-free 888/343-1930. www.bestwestern.com. This is a renovated 1930s Art Deco hotel. 135 rooms, 3 story. Complimentary continental breakfast. Check-in 3 pm, check-out noon. High-speed Internet access. Fitness center. Outdoor pool. Business center. **$**

BEST WESTERN THUNDERBIRD BEACH RESORT.

18401 Collins Ave, Sunny Isles Beach (33160). Phone 305/931-7700; toll-free 800/327-2044. www.bestwestern.com. A renovated Rat Pack hangout, this beachfront vintage hotel includes a beauty salon and tiki bar. 180 rooms, 5 story. Check-in 3 pm, check-out 11 am. Laundry services. Bar. Fitness room. Beach. Outdoor pool, whirlpool. Business center. **$**

RV AND CAMPING

Florida City

SOUTHERN COMFORT RV RESORT.

345 E Palm Dr, Florida City (33034). Phone 305/248-6909. Locals call this "NASCAR headquarters for campers" because of its close proximity to the racetrack. With more than 200 sites, full hook-ups, phone lines, recreation hall, tiki bar, package store, and pool. **$$**

Homestead

BOARDWALK MOBILE HOME AND RV PARK.

100 NE 6 Ave, Homestead (33030). Phone 305/248-2487. Small and large RVs accommodated; no tents. Laundry, pool, clubhouse. $75 or $350 per week.

GOLD COASTER MANUFACTURED HOME AND RV RESORT.

34850 SW 187th Ave, Homestead (33034). Phone 305/248-5462; toll-free 800/465-3146. 81-acre park for 200 RVs. Swimming pool and Jacuzzi. Laundry room, showers, recreation rooms and dance hall, full hook-ups, no tents. $40, two people.

MIAMI EVERGLADES CAMPGROUND.

20675 SW 162 Ave, Miami (33187). Phone 305/233-5300; toll-free 800/917-4923. www.miamicamp.com. 331 sites, full, 30- and 50-amp hook-ups, some with phone service. Free cable, pool and hot tub, laundry, showers. Cabins, lodges, and bunkhouse. Propane station, supply store, computer and Internet service. Tent sites. $159, three days for two people; $212, four days for two people. Three-night minimum stay. $3 per person additional daily deposit required.

PALM DRIVE RV PARKING.

At Homestead-Miami Speedway during Ford Championship Weekend, Speedway Blvd, Homestead (33035). Phone 305/230-7223. Camp in the RV parking lot and walk or catch a shuttle to the speedway from this lot, which is only open during Ford Championship weekend. Water and dump stations, portable restrooms, 24-hour security. Spaces are 20 by 50 feet. $195 plus minimum purchase of two race-event tickets.

For more lodging recommendations, go to www.mobiltravelguide.com

EAT

MOBIL STAR-RATED RESTAURANTS

Coral Gables

JOHN MARTIN'S. ★

253 Miracle Mile, Coral Gables (33134). Phone 305/445-3777. www.johnmartins.com. This casual dining spot combines the atmosphere of an Irish pub with the laid-back friendliness and fresh fare of many Miami restaurants. The menu features everything from a Cuban sandwich to Gaelic steak. Irish, American menu. Lunch, dinner. Bar. Children's menu. Casual attire. Closed Dec 25. **$$**

MELODY INN. ★★

83 Andalusia Ave, Coral Gables (33134). Phone 305/448-0022. French, Swiss menu. Dinner. Closed Dec 24-25. Bar. Casual attire. Valet parking. **$$**

ORTANIQUE ON THE MILE. ★★★
278 Miracle Mile, Coral Gables (33134). Phone 305/446-7710. www.ortaniqueontheweb.com. Caribbean menu featuring authentic island fare, aptly described as the "cuisine of the sun." Tropical fruits, spices, herbs, and marinades paint poultry, beef, shellfish, and a brilliant selection of seafood to winning success. Ceviche del mar, West Indian curried crabcakes, and jerk-rubbed Sonoma foie gras are some of the kitchen's most eagerly devoured signature dishes. Lunch, dinner. Closed holidays. Valet parking. American, Caribbean menu. Casual attire. Reservations recommended. Outdoor seating. $$$

Florida City

CAPRI. ★★
935 N Krome Ave, Florida City (33034). Phone 305/247-1544. Richard Accursio's Capri has been the area's favorite Italian restaurant since 1958. Although pizza is featured, Capri is best known for its Angus beef and veal specialties, Florida lobster Fra Diavolo, and shrimp marinara. Lunch, dinner. Italian, American menu. Bar. Children's menu. Closed Sun; Dec 25. $$

MUTINEER. ★
11 SE 1st Ave, Florida City (33034). Phone 305/245-3377. Seafood, steak menu. Lunch, dinner, Sun brunch. Bar. Children's menu. $$

Miami

CASA JUANCHO. ★★
2436 SW Eighth St, Miami (33135). Phone 305/642-2452. www.casajuancho.com. Gorgeous presentation and atmosphere, as well as unique Spanish dishes, are what keep people coming back to this villa-style restaurant. For those who have never tried tapas and are feeling adventurous, 32 items grace the tapas menu, including unusual dishes like boiled octopus with paprika and roasted peppers with codfish mousse, as well as more familiar items like chicken sautéed in garlic sauce and fried calamari. Spanish menu. Lunch, dinner. Bar. Casual attire. Valet parking. $$$

MAMBO CAFÉ. ★★
3105 Commodore Plz, Miami (33133). Phone 305/448-2768. For the great Cuban-style food alone, the prices at this outdoor-seating-only restaurant are already surprisingly inexpensive. Throw in the first-rate people-watching, fun neighborhood atmosphere, and a sunny Miami day, and you couldn't ask for a better deal. Cuban menu. Lunch, dinner, late-night. Children's menu. Casual attire. Outdoor seating. $$

SNAPPERS. ★
401 Biscayne Blvd, Miami (33132). Phone 305/379-0605. On the bay in South Miami, Snappers earns raves simply for its water and marina views. But the restaurant solidifies its standing with large portions of seafood, including the eponymous snapper, as platters or sandwiches. The family-friendly, open-air setting with generous tables and efficient service is a good choice for groups, too. Seafood menu. Lunch, dinner. Bar. Children's menu. Casual attire. Reservations recommended. Outdoor seating. $$$

TUSCANY TRATTORIA. ★★
3484 Main Hwy, Miami (33133). Phone 305/445-0022. The perfect place to sit down to a fabulous Sunday brunch before hitting nearby boutiques and shops, this café serves a great mix of Italian and American favorites and has a great outdoor dining patio. Italian menu. Lunch, dinner. Bar. Children's menu. Casual attire. Outdoor seating. $$$

VERSAILLE'S. ★
3555 SW Eighth St, Miami (33135). Phone 305/445-7614. The most popular Cuban restaurant in Little Havana, this authentic restaurant has been the site of many political negotiations over café con leche, frijoles negros, and rich pastries. Cuban menu. Breakfast, lunch, dinner. Children's menu. Casual attire. Valet parking. $$

Miami Beach

BIG PINK. ★
157 Collins Ave, Miami Beach (33139). Phone 305/532-4700. Big portions and the big personalities serving them characterize Big Pink, a South Beach favorite for casual meals. The menu—also big, of course—spans eggs, burgers, sandwiches, salads, pizzas, and homemade TV dinners complete with compartmentalized trays. Generous, group-friendly booths and a boisterous sense of goodwill make this a common meeting ground for a diverse array of people. American menu. Breakfast, lunch, dinner, late-night. Bar. Children's menu. Casual attire. Outdoor seating. $$

MONTY'S STONE CRAB. ★ ★

300 Alton Rd, Miami Beach (33139). Phone 305/673-3444. Among stone crab specialists, Monty's in South Beach (the 1967 original is in Coconut Grove) has the advantage of location with a stellar view of the city skyline and yacht-filled Miami Beach Marina. The menu encompasses a globe's worth of seafood specialties, including Bahamian conch chowder, oysters Rockefeller, Maine lobster, and bouillabaisse in addition to the signature stone crabs. Several private dining rooms. Seafood menu. Dinner. Bar. Casual attire. Reservations recommended. **$$**

LOCAL RECOMMENDATIONS

Coconut Grove

SCOTTY'S LANDING.

3381 Pan American Dr, Coconut Grove (33133). Phone 305/854-2626. With fun, outdoor seating on the water at Grove Key Marina, Scotty's features fresh seafood, a full bar, and live music in a casual setting. Walk through the marina boat lot to get to the restaurant. American menu. Lunch, dinner. Casual attire. Outdoor seating. **$$**

Florida City

FARMER'S MARKET RESTAURANT.

300 N Krome Ave, Florida City (33034). Phone 305/242-0008. Simple, local homemade fare prepared with fresh fruits and vegetables, thanks to its convenient location at the area farmers distribution center. Fresh seafood is a house specialty. American menu. Breakfast, lunch, dinner. **$**

GUSTO'S GRILL AND BAR.

326 SE 1st Ave, Florida City (33034). Phone 786/243-9800. www.gustosgrillandbar.com. A Florida-born chain sports bar that's especially popular with race fans, this grill also offers a huge raw bar and friendly service. Lunch, dinner. American menu. Bar. Children's menu. Casual attire. **$**

KEYS SEAFOOD HOUSE.

404 SE 1st Ave, Florida City (33034). Phone 305/247-9456. Excellent fresh seafood is served in a casual family-style atmosphere for reasonable prices. Unbeatable fresh and frozen seafood is also available for those who wish to grill or cook their own. Lunch, dinner. **$$**

ROSITA'S RESTAURANTE.

199 W Palm Dr, Florida City (33034). Phone 305/246-3114. Praised as the most authentic of Homestead's Mexican cuisine offerings, Rosita's offers hot tamales, tostadas, flautas, huevos rancheros, beef, pork, fish, and shrimp simmered in garlic or mole sauces. Mexican menu. Breakfast, lunch, dinner. **$**

Homestead

EL TORO TACO.

1 S Krome Ave, Homestead (33033). Phone 305/245-8182. This is one of the most popular restaurants for race fans. Although the restaurant does not serve beer, wine, or liquor, diners are welcome to bring their own drinks, and many lug in coolers to tuck beneath their tables. Mexican menu. Lunch, dinner. Closed Mon. **$**

ROAD FOOD

Bring a taste of the tropics to the track from **Robert is Here,** a friendly, family-owned market that offers local fresh fruit and vegetables, seasonal samples, condiments, and fruit milk shakes. *19200 SW 344th St, Homestead (33034). Phone 305/246-1592.* Or visit the 35-acre **Fruit and Spice Park,** which cultivates more than 500 varieties of exotic fruits, herbs, spices, and nuts. Sample fruit and buy cookbooks in the gift shop. Tours daily. **$** *24801 SW 187th Ave, Homestead (33031). Phone 305/247-5727.*

168 EAT LOCAL RECOMMENDATIONS

LA QUERBRADITA TAQUERIA.
702 N Krome Ave, Homestead (33033). Phone 305/245-4586. Outdoor seating adds atmosphere to the spicy flavor of this simple Mexican café. Mexican menu. Lunch, dinner. Outdoor seating. **$$**

MAIN ST CAFÉ.
128 N Krome Ave, Homestead (33033). Phone 305/245-7575. www.mainstreetcafe.net. Sandwiches, wraps and salads by day and local folk, country, and jazz music live by night. American menu. Lunch, dinner. Closed Sun-Mon. **$**

NIKKO JAPANESE RESTAURANT.
877 N Homestead Blvd, Homestead (33033). Phone 305/242-8772. Sushi and salsa are both hits at this spot with a special Mexican roll that gives a nod to local clientele, who rave about the fresh flavors of this Asian cuisine. Japanese menu. Lunch, dinner. **$$**

SHIVER'S BAR-B-Q.
28001 S Dixie Hwy, Homestead (33033). Phone 305/248-2272. Shiver's has offered heavenly scented barbecue served at long rows of picnic tables since 1950. It's been rated "Best Miami Barbecue" by *Miami New Times*. Barbecue menu. Lunch, dinner. **$$**

Miami

TOBACCO ROAD.
626 S Miami Ave, Miami (33130). Phone 305/374-1198. www.tobacco-road.com. Established in 1912, Tobacco Road is Miami's oldest bar—first a trading post on the Miami River, today a pub featuring the best in local music and after-midnight steak dinner specials. Open until 5 am, it's a good spot to wind down after a night on South Beach. American menu. Dinner, late-night. Bar. **$**

Miami Beach

JOE'S STONE CRAB.
227 Biscayne St, Miami Beach (33139). Phone 305/673-0365. A Miami institution for decades, Joe's is a must-try for seafood fans: the stone crabs are incomparable, and so is the famous Key lime pie. Reservations are not accepted, so expect a wait. Seafood menu. Lunch, dinner. Valet parking. **$$$**

South Miami

BOUGAINVILLEA'S OLD FLORIDA TAVERN.
7221 SW 58th Ave, South Miami (33143). Phone 305/669-8577. www.floridatavern.com. A three-room tavern in a converted 1929 home built with aged Dade County pine. Live jazz and blues. American menu. Bar menu. Dinner, late-night. Bar. Closed Mon. **$$**

For more dining recommendations, go to www.mobiltravelguide.com

SIDETRIP

A Fisherman's Key to Paradise
Florida Keys, FL

November's NASCAR event at Homestead-Miami is the last race of the season, so many drivers stay over for a brief respite in the Florida Keys, which is lined with the nation's only living coral reef and a spectacular spot for scuba diving and snorkeling. Kayakers enjoy cruising the mangrove-lined shorelines, and often encounter manatees, dolphins, and sea turtles in the shallow waters along the 120-mile long string of islands.

US Highway 1 is the main road from Homestead/Florida City to Key West, with an 18-mile stretch connecting the mainland to Key Largo. Construction is scheduled in 2005. To avoid delays, take Card Sound Road off US 1 to Key Largo—and drive carefully along the two-lane highway.

Islamorada, about 45 miles from Homestead, is called the sport fishing capital of the world and offers fine dining and luxury and boutique lodgings, as well as vintage motels. **The Ragged Edge Resort** (www.ragged-edge.com) offers clean, basic lodging for those planning to spend their time on the water.

Laid back, rustic, and down-to-earth, **Marathon** is home to those who make their living from the sea. Many of the motels and resorts are geared for those with fishing in mind. Try an ocean-front property with free half-day boat use daily at **Rainbow Bend Resort** (www.rainbowbend.com); **Coconut Cay Resort and Marina** (www.coconutcay.com) for updated motel rooms and cottages with water access; **Banana Bay Resort and Marina**

Duval Street is the heart of the night life scene in Key West, which is easily accessible from the racetrack via US Highway 1.

(www.bananabay.com) for all the amenities in a peaceful hideaway, including boat rentals, tours, and a private island retreat off their Marathon Key Resort. Or try **Captain Pip's Marina and Hideaway** (www.captainpips.com), basic apartments with your own boat throughout your stay. Before hitting the water, visit **Crane Point Museum of Natural History of the Florida Keys** (www.cranepoint.org) to learn about the fragile reefs and special care needed to protect this amazing ecosystem, and to see remants of a pirate ship.

For more Florida Keys recommendations, go to www.mobiltravelguide.com

170

Jeff Gordon and crew perform the traditional "Kissing of the Bricks" after Gordon's 2004 NASCAR NEXTEL Cup Brickyard 400 victory at Indianapolis Motor Speedway.

Indianapolis Motor Speedway
Indianapolis Raceway Park

Indianapolis, Indiana

10

Fans flock to their seats at the Indianapolis Motor Speedway.

TRACK FACTS

INDIANAPOLIS MOTOR SPEEDWAY (IMS). 4790 W 16th St, Indianapolis (46222). Phone 317/492-6700. www.indianapolismotorspeedway.com.

SECURITY. All items carried into the track are subject to a search—and search, they do. IMS prohibits entry with glass containers and bottles, but allows personal coolers—hard and soft-sided—with a size restriction of no larger than 14 x 14 x 14 inches. Personal bags and backpacks are allowed at any size, but for your comfort and those around you, they should be small enough to fit under your seat. Other permitted items: binoculars, scanners, cameras (and their cases), strollers, lawn chairs, and umbrellas. Other prohibited items: bikes, inline skates, skateboards, scooters, and pets. Tailgating is OK in the lots adjacent to the track and in the infield, but no cooking or open-flame heat sources.

FIRST AID. IMS has 15 first aid stations around the track—ten on the perimeter and five in the infield, including the 17-bed Clarian Emergency Medical Center, the hub of the operation. All are clearly marked in the race-day Fan Guide with a symbol of a red cross inside a yellow square. The CEMC is staffed with emergency doctors and nurses, and works with Methodist Hospital in Indianapolis if full trauma care is needed.

CONCESSIONS. How about these stats: on race day, IMS sells more than 6 1/2 miles of dogs and brats, more than 8 tons of Track Fries, and more than 10,000 pounds of Brickyard Burgers. The gotta-have-it menu item is jumbo pork tenderloin. Purchase one (or maybe two) at the Plaza Café next to the Pagoda, and at 14 other locations around the track. Or enjoy your meal without missing a turn on the track by ordering a box lunch before race day. Visit www.brickyardboxlunch.com and place your order online, or call 317/492-6483. You'll receive a voucher with the pickup location. Then simply collect your lunch when you get to the track, and you're good to go.

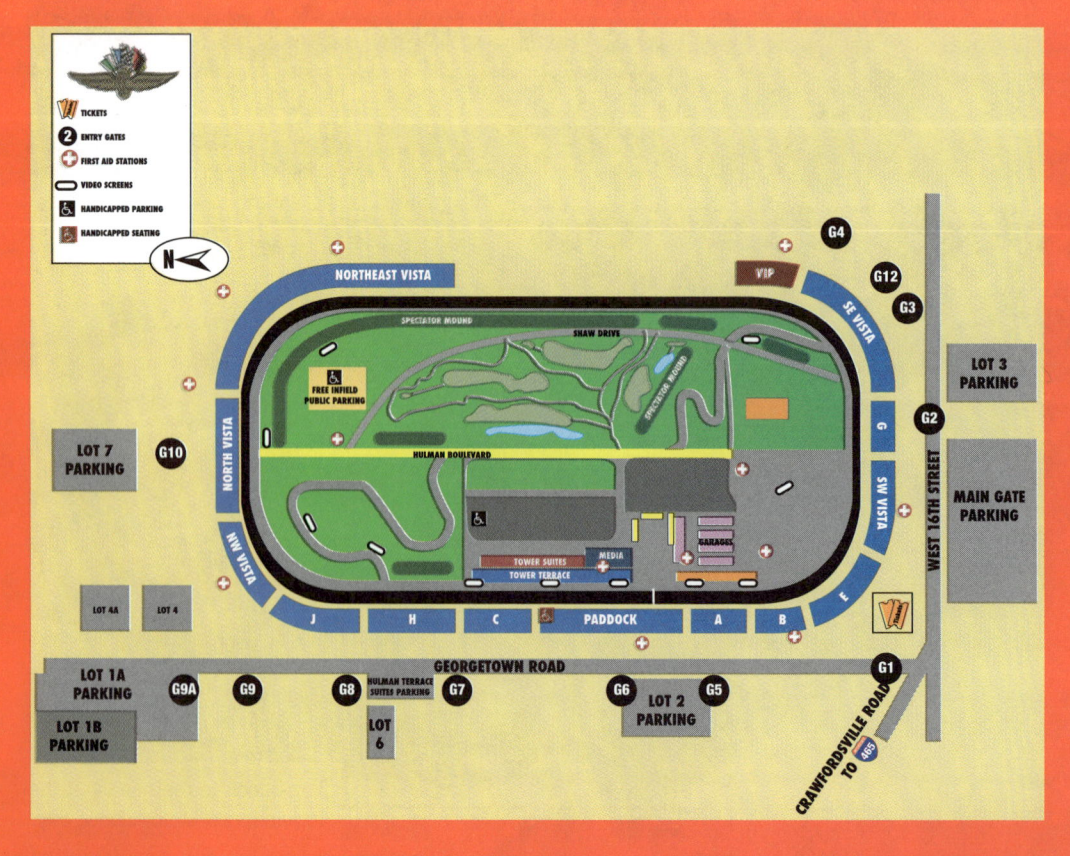

A CITY OF TWO TRACKS

IMS. It's THE racing hub for fans worldwide. It's got a race day excitement factor of about a million, and it's immense. With a 2 1/2-mile oval and the largest seating capacity of any sports venue in the world, IMS does not disappoint. "There's something about being there live—the sound, the energy," says Niki Taylor, supermodel and honorary Grand Marshal of the 2004 NASCAR NEXTEL Cup Brickyard 400. "The atmosphere is definitely God, Family, and Country, with hundreds of thousands of people in totally organized chaos. That just shows how great the Indianapolis track organizers are."

The track itself, though, is another story. No whole-track view here. Cars have to line up parade-style, as their size and speed on the relatively flat-banked track means they have to brake into the turns, enter low, and swing high toward the wall on the way out. But straightaway sprints create a battle royal among cars and make anything possible at Indy.

There simply is no bigger goose-bump-feeling than when you hear, "Gentlemen, start your engines" and see the green flag wave from high atop the "Yard of Bricks" at this hallowed home of racing.

GETTING IMS TICKETS. Like Indy-style cars, tickets go incredibly fast, but you can get them at www.indianapolismotorspeedway.com or by calling the ticket office toll-free at 800/822-INDY (4639), at least a month ahead of time. Consider ordering a parking pass together with your tickets. You'll pay just as much for yard parking near the speedway, but if you pop for the package up front, you're guaranteed a spot closer to the entrance.

A full field thunders down Indy's famed front straightaway.

TRACK FACTS

INDIANAPOLIS RACEWAY PARK (IRP). 10267 E Hwy 136, Indianapolis (46234). Phone 317/291-4090. www.irponline.com.

SECURITY. IRP allows coolers up to 14 x 14 x 14 inches in the grandstands for all oval events, and 14 x 14-inch coolers for the Mac Tools US nationals. No glass containers are allowed at any events, and no alcohol is allowed at the Mac Tools event. All items carried into the track are subject to search.

FIRST AID. First aid is located in three areas: on the north side of the event office, closest to Gate 7 (northwest side of the drag strip), in the pit area on the southwest side of the drag strip, and in the pit area across from the grandstands on the southeast side of the drag strip, next to the concession stands north of Parks Tower. From IRP, the closest hospital is Methodist Hospital, 7 miles from the track.

CONCESSIONS. Besides filling your coolers with snacks, you can always purchase a variety of food and beverages at the Mac Tools Concourse west of the drag strip, in the northwest corner of the oval pit area (across from the grandstands), and behind the oval's main straightaway grandstands.

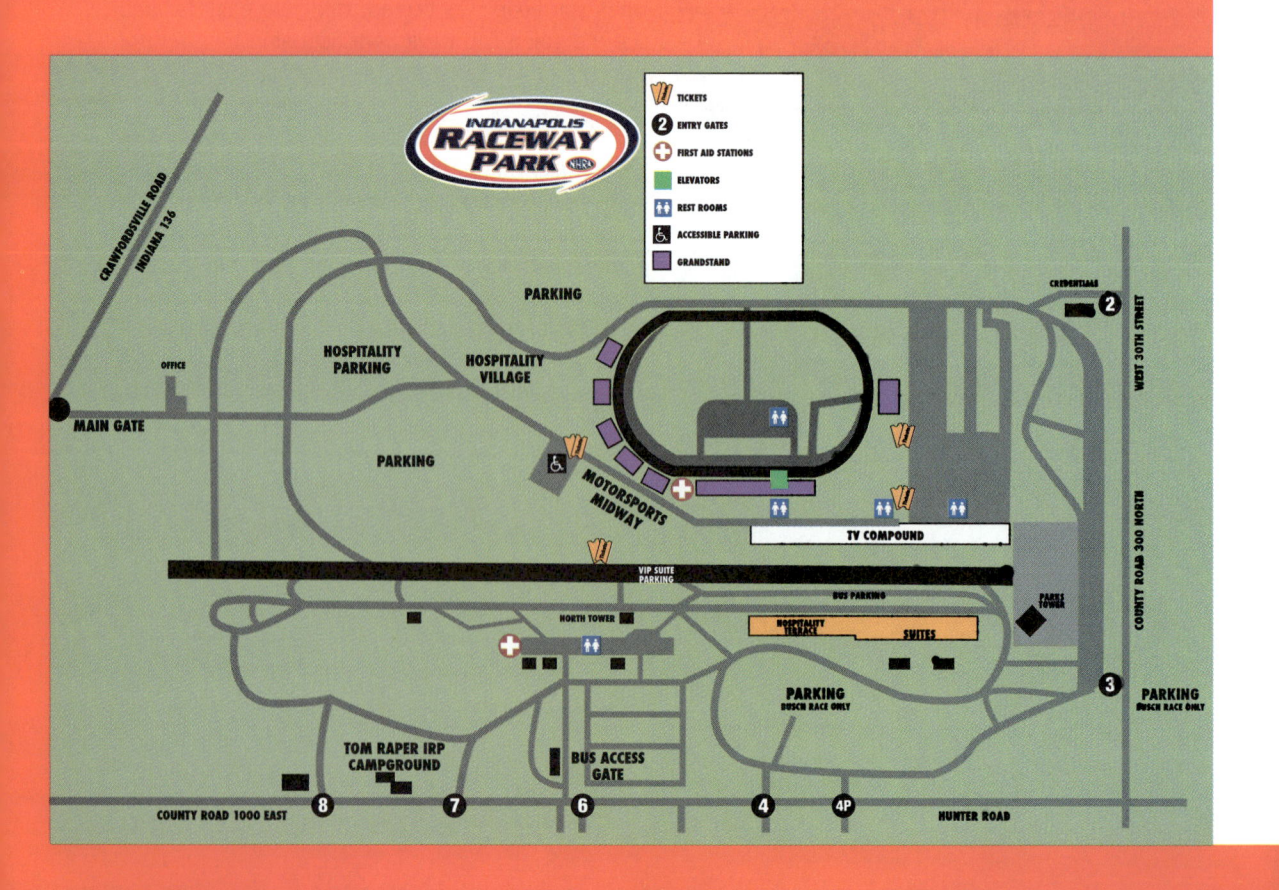

INDIANAPOLIS MOTOR SPEEDWAY/INDIANAPOLIS RACEWAY PARK, IN 175

Trucks are on view prior to the start of the NASCAR Craftsman Truck Series Power Stroke Diesel 200 at Indianapolis Raceway Park.

IRP. Just up the road from IMS is Indianapolis Raceway Park. This National Hot Rod Association-owned raceway opened in 1960, and it boasts its own trifecta of racing fun: a 0.686-mile oval, a quarter-mile drag strip, and a 12-turn, 2 1/2-mile road course.

GETTING IRP TICKETS. Get tickets online at www.ticketmaster.com, call the ticket office toll-free at 800/884-6472, or stop by the main ticket plaza at the track (off the main road on the northwest side of the oval, across from Turn 4). For exact pricing, check out the tickets section of www.irponline.com. IRP may offer Express parking passes with tickets, depending on the event.

Indianapolis is home to the world's largest children's museum. The museum offers something for visitors of all ages. Dig for fossils, ride a turn-of-the-century carousel, try your skills at rock climbing, or sail through space at the SpaceQuest Planetarium.

HIGH OCTANE—LOW HASSLE

Founded in 1821, Indianapolis lies in the center of Indiana, a true heartland city in almost every way: from its food to its farming past to its racing. Although it's the state's largest city, as well as its capital, you'd hardly notice. At just over 800,000 people, America's 12th-largest city is smaller than its fellow Midwestern metropolitan cities of Chicago and Detroit. It's also more negotiable by car and walkable on foot, and arguably more friendly and laid-back. More highways crisscross this city than any other in the nation, hence its fitting nickname, the "Crossroads of America." No wonder they know their driving.

Weather around Brickyard time is an average of 84 degrees Fahrenheit by day, 63 by night, but it can

Visitors and residents alike enjoy the renovated Central Canal area with its array of paved sidewalks, lagoons, fountains, pedestrian bridges, monuments, and beautiful landscaping.

get super-sticky with humidity, so be prepared. Thank goodness the dress code is also laid-back; locals hoof around town in shorts and jeans, with few exceptions, so feel free to follow suit.

MORE THAN MOTORING

In addition to its double-the-rubber fun of two NASCAR tracks, Indy residents root for other sports as well: the Colts, the Pacers, and the International League Indianapolis Indians baseball team.

A scenic canal runs through Indy, complete with pedalboats, and a biking and walking path. Traveling with kids? Don't miss the **Children's Museum of Indianapolis** (3000 N Meridian St, phone 317/334-3322, www.childrensmuseum.org), ranked the best children's museum in the nation by *Child* magazine in 2002. Or make a stop at **Conner Prairie** (13400 Allisonville Rd, Fishers, phone toll-free 800/966-1836, www.connerprairie.org), an indoor-outdoor living history museum with a Native American wigwam, Victorian farm, and pioneer village.

Suspended seven stories above a busy downtown intersection is the Indianapolis Artsgarden. This unusual structure is connected directly to Circle Centre, the $319.5 million retail and entertainment complex.

GETTING AROUND

IN and OUT of IMS: IMS sits just inside Indy's I-465 "beltway" that circles the city. IMS is on the west side of town, about 2 miles from the highway on the northeast corner of Crawfordsville and Georgetown roads, smack in the middle of a residential neighborhood.

The easiest way to get there is from I-465. Exit at Crawfordsville Road (Exit 16A) east, which leads you toward the speedway. Police direct traffic on this route in three different directions, all of which lead to the track.

There are two alternate routes from I-465. You can exit at 38th Street (Exit 17), and go south on Moller Road, then east on 30th Street. Or take 10th Street (Exit 14A) east to Lynhurst Drive. Head north on Lynhurst, then east on 16th Street toward the speedway.

IN and OUT of IRP: IRP is 3 miles west of the town of Clermont. From I-465 take the Crawfordsville Road exit (Exit 16A). Turn west, and continue through Clermont. The track is on the south (left) side of the road.

You can also take the Brownsburg exit (Exit 66). At the stoplight, turn south onto Route 267, then east onto Northfield Drive. Turn south onto Route 136 from Northfield Drive. The track is on the right side of Route 136.

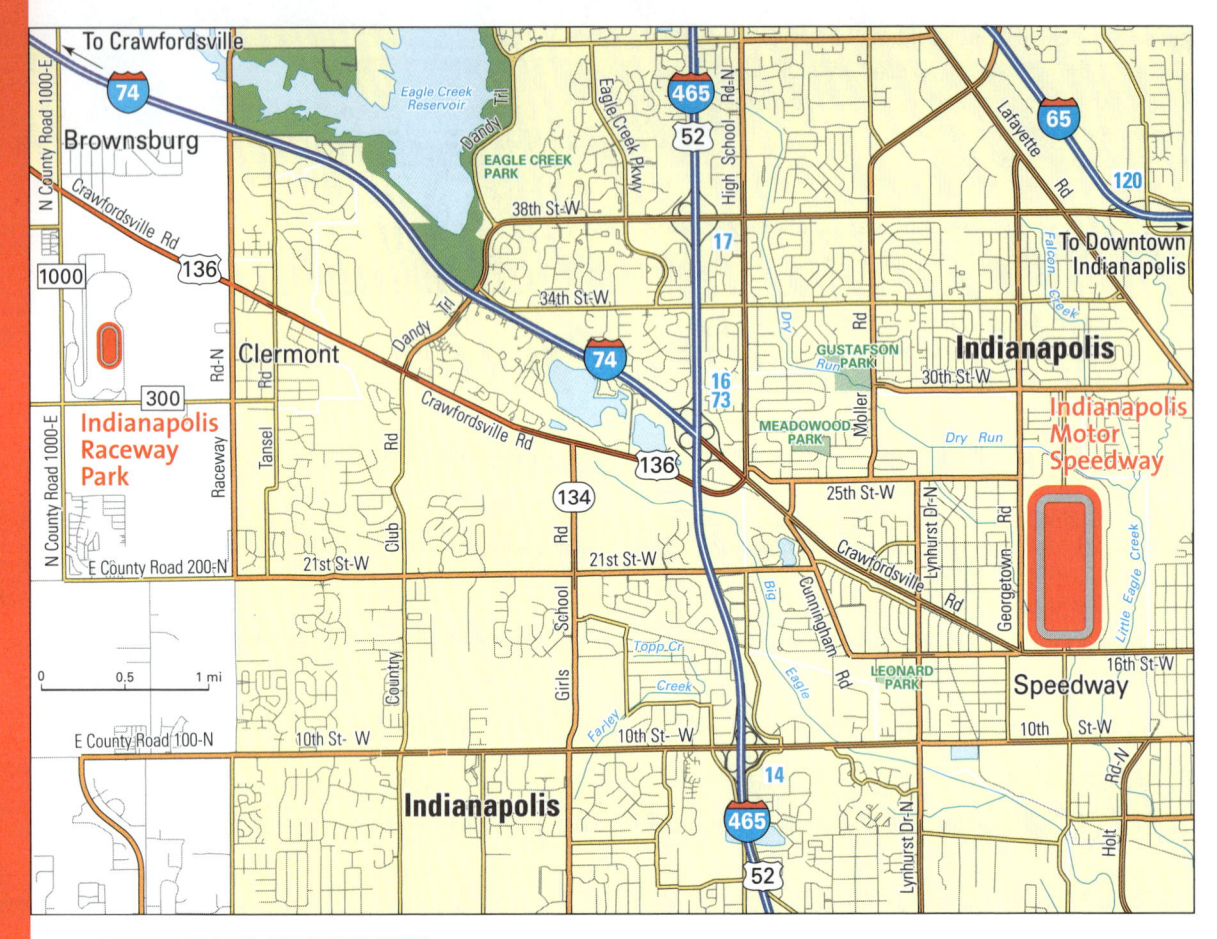

INDIANAPOLIS POLE POSITION:
The 6 miles between Indianapolis Motor Speedway and Indianapolis Raceway Park.

Not far from the speedways is the 250-acre **White River State Park** (801 W Washington St, phone toll-free 800/665-9056, www.in.gov/whiteriver). It offers the standard state park romping and picnicking opportunities, and it's also home to the NCAA Hall of Champions, Victory Field, Eiteljorg Museum of American Indians and Western Art, White River Gardens botanical gardens, the Indianapolis Zoo, the Indiana State Museum, and an IMAX movie theater.

Monument Circle anchors downtown and offers panoramic views from the 284-foot Soldiers' and Sailors' Monument, built in 1902 to honor Indiana residents who served in the Spanish-American and Civil wars. From there, it's just a few steps to **Circle Centre Mall,** (49 W Maryland St, phone 317/681-8000, www.circle-centre.com) with more than 100 shops in a European market setting. Eateries abound, along with a nine-screen movie theater.

Circle Centre located in the heart of downtown, features more than 100 specialty retailers, restaurants, nightclubs, a cinema, and a food court.

INDIANAPOLIS CALENDAR

JULY 30–31, 2005
Hot Dog Festival. Main St, Frankfort (46041). Phone 765/654-4081. www.accs.net/mainstreet. Celebrate America's favorite summer food, along with arts and crafts booths, live music, a classic car show, and a great weiner cookoff.

AUGUST 4, 2005
WIBC's Dodge Racers on the Circle. Downtown, Monument Circle, Indianapolis (46204). Phone 317/684-8755. 4-8 pm. Food, music, and Dodge NASCAR driver autographs.

AUGUST 4–6, 2005
Kroger SpeedFest. Indianapolis Raceway Park. NASCAR Craftsman Truck Series and Busch Series.

AUGUST 5–7, 2005
Brickyard 400 weekend. Indianapolis Motor Speedway. NASCAR NEXTEL Cup Series.

AUGUST 10–21, 2005
Indiana State Fair. Indiana State Fair Grounds, 1202 E 38th St, Indianapolis (46208). Phone 317/927-7500. www.indianastatefair.com. Bring the whole family for live performances from top country artists, livestock nursery, barn tours, an interactive kid-sized farm, and a mini Indy Speedway.

AUGUST 26–27, 2005
Amish Country Market And Preview Party & Sale. Hamilton County Fairgrounds, 2003 E Pleasant St, Noblesville (46060). Phone 317/941-2205. www.juliancenter.org. The preview party includes dinner and a silent auction. At the market, you can purchase antiques, baskets, pottery, clothing, folk art, furniture, and more. Or place a bid in the live auction.

Monument Circle is a popular landmark in downtown Indianapolis.

DRIVER'S PICK

St. Elmo Steak House ★★ is the oldest Indiana restaurant still in its original location (downtown since 1902). Driver of the No. 45 NASCAR NEXTEL Cup Dodge **Kyle Petty** agrees with many Hoosiers about this classic. "St. Elmo's in Indianapolis is the best place for steaks. They're also famous for their shrimp cocktail." $$$ *127 S Illinois St, Indianapolis (46225). Phone 317/637-1811. www.stelmos.com.*

INDIANAPOLIS OUTFIELD:
The 50 miles surrounding Indianapolis Motor Speedway and Indianapolis Raceway Park.

SEE

ATTRACTIONS

Camby

HEARTLAND CROSSING GOLF LINKS.
6701 S Heartland Blvd, Camby (46113). Phone 317/630-1785. www.heartlandcrossinggolf.com. One of the state's premiere public golf courses, Heartland Crossing features 18 challenging holes that zig-zag across a verdant landscape of rolling hills, deep bunkers, and pristine greens. The course, designed by Steve Smyers and Nick Price, is a 15-minute drive south of downtown Indianapolis, off State Road 67. **$$$$**

Fishers

CONNER PRAIRIE.
13400 Allisonville Rd, Fishers (46038). Phone toll-free 800/966-1836. www.connerprairie.org. Conner Prairie, an open-air living history museum, is located in a quiet suburb northeast of Indianapolis. Costumed interpreters depict the life and times of early settlers in this 1836 village, which contains about 40 buildings, including a Federal-style brick mansion constructed by fur trader William Conner. The 1,400-acre property is divided into five distinct historic areas. Kids enjoy the hands-on activities, games, and toys in the PastPort Area. (Tues-Sat 9:30 am-5 pm, Sun 11 am-5 pm; closed holidays; also Tues in Apr and Nov) **$$$**

Indianapolis

ACTION DUCKPIN BOWL.
1105 Prospect St, Indianapolis (46203). Phone 317/686-6006. This quirky and fun twist on conventional bowling entails rolling a small marble ball at ten pint-size pins. Action Duckpin Bowl, with a retro interior that harkens back to the 1930s, appeals to children and adults alike. The alley is located on the fourth floor of the historic Fountain Square Theatre Building, a few blocks southeast of downtown. Remember: in duckpin bowling, as in auto racing, it's important to stay in your lane. (Daily) **$$**

BRICKYARD CROSSING GOLF COURSE.
4400 W 16th St, Indianapolis (46222). Phone 317/484-6572. www.brickyardcrossing.com. This 18-hole course, redesigned by heralded links architect Pete Dye, lies at the east end of the Indianapolis Motor Speedway's grounds and includes four holes inside the track. During time trials, views of the track from the fairways allow fans of both golf and racing to indulge in two passions at once. (Mar-Oct) **$$$$**

CHILDREN'S MUSEUM OF INDIANAPOLIS.
3000 N Meridian St, Indianapolis (46208). Phone 317/334-3322. www.childrensmuseum.org. The largest of its kind, this outstanding children's museum has ten major galleries. Exhibits cover science, culture, space, history, and exploration. Kids especially love the SpaceQuest Planetarium (additional fee), the 33-foot-high Water Clock, the Playscape hands-on gallery for preschoolers, the old-fashioned indoor carousel, and the new Dinosphere exhibit. (Mar-Labor Day: daily 10 am-5 pm; Labor Day-early Feb: Tues-Sun 10 am-5 pm; closed Easter, Thanksgiving, Dec 25) **$$**

CIRCLE CENTRE MALL.
49 W Maryland St, Indianapolis (46204). Phone 317/681-8000. www.circle-centre.com. Indianapolis's sprawling downtown mall offers more than 100 shopping, dining, and entertainment options. Anchor stores, Nordstrom and Parisian, are flanked by popular chains such as Gymboree, Banana Republic, and Yankee Candle in this four-story structure that spans two city blocks. (Mon-Sat 10 am-9 pm, Sun noon-6 pm; closed Thanksgiving, Dec 25) While at the mall, check out **Sega GameWorks Studio** (phone 317/226-9267), a 27,000-square-foot virtual reality funfest, featuring a simulated roller coaster, full-size Indy car racing, and hundreds of arcade games. (Daily; closed Thanksgiving, Dec 25)

INDIANAPOLIS MOTOR SPEEDWAY HALL OF FAME MUSEUM.
4790 W 16th St, Indianapolis (46222). Phone 317/492-6784. www.indianapolismotorspeedway.com. You'll want to set aside plenty of time to peruse the Hall of Fame Museum, located on the grounds of the Indianapolis Motor Speedway. Designated a National Historic Landmark, the museum displays approximately 75 cars, including a 1957 SSI Corvette and the Marmon "Wasp," which, with Ray Harroun behind the wheel, won the first-ever Indy 500 in 1911. Track tours also are available. **$**

SEE ATTRACTIONS

WHITE RIVER STATE PARK.
801 W Washington St, Indianapolis (46204). Phone toll-free 800/665-9056. www.in.gov/whiteriver. Situated on downtown Indy's west side, White River State Park is home to some of the city's most popular attractions, including the Eiteljorg Museum of American Indian and Western Art, the Indianapolis Zoo, White River Gardens, the NCAA Hall of Champions, an IMAX Theater, the Indiana State Museum, Victory Field, and the Congressional Medal of Honor Memorial.

One of the finest collections of Native American artifacts in the country, the **Eiteljorg Museum of American Indian and Western Art** (www.eiteljorg.org) is reminiscent of the culture of the American West even in its distinctive exterior architecture. The Eiteljorg has artifacts and art from almost every Native American tribal group, from the Plains to the Southwest. The museum also displays artwork and artifacts from cultures of the Pacific Northwest and Alaska. (Memorial Day-Labor Day: Mon-Sat 10 am-5 pm, Sun noon-5 pm; rest of year: Tues-Sat 10 am-5 pm, Sun noon-5 pm; closed Jan 1, Thanksgiving, Dec 25) **$$**

The 64-acre **Indianapolis Zoo** (phone 317/630-2001, www.indyzoo.com) boasts the state's largest aquarium, an enclosed dolphin pavilion, and more than 350 species from around the world. The Encounters area houses domesticated animals, and a 600-seat outside arena offers daily programs and demonstrations. Living Deserts of the World is a conservatory covered by an 80-foot-diameter transparent dome. (Hours vary by season) **$$$**

White River Gardens (phone 317/630-2001, www.whiterivergardens.com) is a 3.3-acre botanical attraction, with more than 1,000 plant varieties on display. The on-site Hilbert Conservatory hosts rotating exhibits, such as live butterflies and a display of bonsai trees. (Hours vary by season) **$$**

The **NCAA Hall of Champions** (www.ncaa.org/hall_of_champions) celebrates intercollegiate athletics through photographs, video presentations, and displays covering 22 sports and all NCAA championships. The 25,000-square-foot facility contains two levels of interactive displays and multimedia presentations. Three theaters present videos about topics such as the Final Four and coaching, while the Hall of Honor salutes individuals who have been honored with an NCAA award. Visitors can grab a basketball and test their jump-shooting skills in an "old-school" gymnasium, much like the one featured in the movie *Hoosiers*. (Tues-Sat 10 am- 5 pm, Sun noon-5 pm; closed holidays) **$**

The only **IMAX Theater** (phone 317/233-IMAX, www.imax.com/indy) in the state allows you to watch special 3-D movies, as well as mainstream 2-D Hollywood releases, on a six-story-high screen. Located in the Indiana State Museum. (Daily) **$$$**

Transportation Tip: Everything in downtown Indy is a short walk away. That said, if your dogs are barking, take a load off on the **Blue Line Circulator,** a color-splashed bus that carries passengers throughout downtown and White River State Park. Street signs identify the pick-up/drop-off points, and the fare will only set you back 50 cents.

For more attractions, go to www.mobiltravelguide.com

STAY

MOBIL STAR-RATED LODGINGS

Carmel

DOUBLETREE GUEST SUITES. ★★
11355 N Meridian St, Carmel (46032). Phone 317/844-7994; toll-free 800/222-8733. www.doubletree.com. This hotel is located in a burgeoning suburb north of Indianapolis. The oversized guest suites here provide visitors with amenities such as pullout sleeper sofas, refrigerators, and microwave ovens. If you have the time, drive south on Meridian Street to 38th Street, a trip that will take you past a long stretch of stately mansions, including the governor's official residence at 4750 N Meridian St. 137 rooms, 3 story. Check-in 3 pm, check-out noon. Restaurant, bar. Fitness room. Indoor pool, outdoor pool, whirlpool. **$**

Greenfield

LEES INN GREENFIELD. ★
2270 N State St, Greenfield (46140). Phone 317/462-7112; toll-free 800/733-5337. www.leesinn.com. This clean and comfortable hotel is a good choice for

budget-conscious race fans traveling to Indianapolis from the east on Interstate 70. It's a minimum 30-minute trip from the hotel to the racing venues on the west side of town. Still, you're likely to get a better value at this hotel; lodgings near the tracks charge a hefty premium on race weekends. 100 rooms, 2 story. Complimentary continental breakfast. Check-in 3 pm, check-out noon. Pets accepted, some restrictions. $

Indianapolis

CANTERBURY HOTEL. ★★★

123 S Illinois St, Indianapolis (46225). Phone 317/634-3000; toll-free 800/538-8186. www.canterburyhotel.com. The European charm and elegance of the Canterbury Hotel make you feel like you've been transported across the Atlantic Ocean. Since its opening as the Lockerbie Hotel in 1928, the property has stood as the city's most prestigious and refined hotel, the place where celebrities and dignitaries stay. The Canterbury provides visitors with a convenient downtown location and private access to the adjacent Circle Centre shopping mall, filled with upscale stores and restaurants. Mahogany furniture and traditional artwork complete the classic décor in the guest rooms. 99 rooms, 12 story. Complimentary continental breakfast. Check-in 3 pm, check-out noon. Wireless Internet access. Restaurant, bar. Fitness room. $$

COURTYARD BY MARRIOTT DOWNTOWN. ★★

501 W Washington St, Indianapolis (46204). Phone 317/635-4443; toll-free 800/321-2211. www.courtyard.com. If you're planning to visit the top attractions in downtown Indianapolis, you definitely should consider staying at this hotel, located in the heart of White River State Park, a short walk from the NCAA Hall of Champions, Indianapolis Zoo, Eiteljorg Museum, and IMAX Theater. An on-site TGI Friday's restaurant ensures you'll never go hungry during your stay. 235 rooms. Complimentary continental breakfast. Check-in 3 pm, check-out noon. Outdoor pool. Business center. $

CROWNE PLAZA HOTEL UNION STATION. ★★★

123 W Louisiana St, Indianapolis (46225). Phone 317/631-2221; toll-free 888/303-1746. www.crowneplaza.com. Nowhere else can you sleep in one of 26 authentic Pullman sleeper train cars, each one named for and decorated to recall a famous personality from the early 1900s. The hotel is noted also for the life-size "ghosts" (fiberglass figures in period dress) who inhabit the hotel reflecting travelers from a bygone era. Combining old-world charm and modern convenience, this hotel boasts charming stained-glass windows and soaring archways. The Crowne Plaza connects to the functioning train station, and it is within walking distance of downtown eateries, and sports and cultural hot spots. 275 rooms, 3 story. Check-in 4 pm, check-out noon. Restaurant. Fitness room. Indoor pool, whirlpool. $$

HAMPTON INN INDIANAPOLIS—DOWNTOWN CIRCLE CENTRE. ★

105 S Meridian St, Indianapolis (46225). Phone 317/261-1200; toll-free 800/426-7866. www.hamptoninn.com. 180 rooms, 9 story. Complimentary continental breakfast. Check-in 3 pm, check-out 11 am. Fitness room. $

SHOP TALK

Indiana's association with speed is well known. But the state was once home to some of the best-known automobile brand names in the nation and some of the most exotic and expensive cars. Remember that heritage with a collection of coffee mugs decorated with cars built in the Hoosier State: a 1902 Haynes, 1926 Stutz, 1929 Duesenberg, 1933 Auburn, 1936 Cord, and a 1950 Studebaker from the **Indiana Historical Society's History Market.** *450 W Ohio St, Indianapolis (46202). Phone 317/234-0026. www.indianahistory.org/historymarket/store.*

STAY MOBIL STAR-RATED LODGINGS

MARRIOTT DOWNTOWN. ★★★
350 W Maryland St, Indianapolis (46225). Phone 317/822-3500; toll-free 877/640-7666. www.marriott.com. Superior customer service is the hallmark of this downtown hotel. Guest rooms are tastefully appointed with modern furnishings. The on-site Champions Sports Bar features more than 30 TVs, making it the perfect spot to watch a big race or game. 615 rooms, 19 story. Pets accepted. Check-in 4 pm, check-out 11 am. Restaurant, bar. Fitness room. Indoor pool, whirlpool. Business center. $$

LOCAL RECOMMENDATIONS

Brownsburg

COMFORT SUITES.
500 W Northfield Dr, Brownsburg (46112). Phone 317/852-2000; toll-free 877/424-6423. www.comfortsuites.com. This hotel offers all the amenities of home: in-room microwaves, refrigerators, and coffeemakers; high-speed Internet access in all rooms and common areas; and guest laundry facilities. If you're bringing the kids, you'll appreciate the nearby bowling alley and movie theater, as well as the many restaurants that are a short walk away. 70 rooms, 3 story, all suite. Complimentary continental breakfast. Check-in 3 pm, check-out 11 am. High-speed Internet access. Laundry services. Fitness room. Indoor pool. $

HOLIDAY INN EXPRESS INDIANAPOLIS-BROWNSBURG (I-74W).
31 Maplehurst Dr, Brownsburg (46112). Phone 317/852-5353; toll-free 800/377-8660. www.hiexpress.com. This hotel's west-side location, a short drive from both Indianapolis Motor Speedway and Indianapolis Raceway Park, makes it a convenient lodging choice for race fans. Guest rooms include free high-speed Internet access. Suites are available with microwaves, refrigerators, and whirlpool tubs. 75 rooms, 2 story. Complimentary continental breakfast. Check-in 4 pm, check-out 11 am. High-speed Internet access. Fitness room. Outdoor pool. $

Indianapolis

BEST WESTERN AIRPORT SUITES.
55 S High School Rd, Indianapolis (46241). Phone 317/246-1505; toll-free 800/780-7234. www.bestwestern.com. Flying to Indianapolis for a race? You should check out this all-suite hotel; it's a mere

PIT PASS

Many great seating options exist at IMS. One great view is high in the grandstands across from the start/finish line. These seats can run about $80-$140, but you'll get full view of the pits, the start/finish, and more of Turns 1 and 4. One great option is a high seat in one of the turns for a wide-angle view with some straightaway. Try Stand or Penthouse E in Turn 1, the Southeast Vista, sections 20-30 in Turn 2, the Northeast Vista, sections 8-18 in Turn 3, or Section J, sections 27-30, the Northwest Vista, sections 1-10 or Tower Terrace, section 79 in Turn 4. Remember: there is no full-track view at IMS.

2 miles from Indianapolis International Airport, 3 miles from the Motor Speedway, and 7 miles to the Raceway Park. Ideal for families, each suite has a refrigerator, microwave, two 25-inch TVs, and a sofa sleeper bed. 55 rooms, 3 story, all suite. Complimentary continental breakfast. Check-in 3 pm, check-out 11 am. High-speed Internet access. Laundry services. Fitness room. $

BEST WESTERN CASTLETON INN.
8300 Craig St, Indianapolis (46250). Phone 317/842-9190; toll-free 800/232-5757. www.bestwestern.com. This hotel, located off I-69 on the city's northeast side, should appeal to shopping lovers, given its proximity to more than 100 stores at Castleton Mall. If you're traveling with the family dog or cat, this Best Western deserves consideration; it's one of the few local hotels that allows pets. 113 rooms, 3 story. Pets accepted; fee. Complimentary continental breakfast. Check-in 3 pm, check-out noon. Outdoor pool. $

BEST WESTERN CITY CENTRE HOTEL & SUITES.

410 S Missouri St, Indianapolis (46225). Phone 317/822-6400; toll-free 800/780-7234. www.bestwestern.com. Downtown Indianapolis's most popular shops and restaurants are a short walk away from this hotel, centrally located one block south of the Convention Center. You can choose an executive suite or standard guest room. The hotel offers coin-operated laundry facilities, meaning you can wash the kids' (and maybe your own) Dale Jr T-shirts after returning from a hot day at the track so they can wear them again the next day. 108 rooms, 6 story. Complimentary continental breakfast. Check-in 3 pm, check-out 11 am. Laundry services. Indoor pool, whirlpool. $

BEST WESTERN COUNTRY SUITES.

3871 W 92nd St, Indianapolis (46268). Phone 317/879-1700; toll-free 800/780-7234. www.bestwestern.com. The interior of this north-side hotel evokes the cozy feel of a New England bed-and-breakfast, its lobby appointed with rich hardwood floors, a two-story brick fireplace, and comfy chairs. All rooms are suites, with two TVs, two phone lines, and separate living room and sleeping areas. Rooms also include refrigerators and microwaves, making it easy to prepare a pre- or post-race snack. 40 rooms, 2 story, all suite. Complimentary continental breakfast. Check-in 3 pm, check-out noon. Fitness room. $

BEST WESTERN INDIANAPOLIS SOUTH.

4450 Southport Crossing Dr, Indianapolis (46237). Phone 317/888-5588; toll-free 800/780-7234. www.bestwestern.com. As its name indicates, this Best Western is located on Indianapolis's south side, which makes it a convenient spot if you're arriving from Kentucky or other parts south. The hotel's game room keeps kids entertained while parents can relax in the heated indoor pool or work off stress in the fitness room. 64 rooms, 2 story. Complimentary continental breakfast. Check-in 3 pm, check-out 11 am. High-speed Internet access. Fitness room. Indoor pool. $

AMERISUITES INDIANAPOLIS KEYSTONE.

9104 Keystone Crossing, Indianapolis (46240). Phone 317/843-0064; toll-free 877/774-6467. www.amerisuites.com. This all-suite hotel shoulders Interstate 465 on the city's north side, a hop, skip, and a jump away from the upscale Keystone at the Crossing shopping mall. Guest rooms include a refrigerator and microwave. The hotel offers a complimentary breakfast buffet, but you should consider strolling over to Café Patachou where they serve up the tastiest omelets and cinnamon toast in town. 126 rooms, 6 story, all suite. Pets accepted, some restrictions. Complimentary continental breakfast. Check-in 3 pm, check-out noon. Laundry services. Fitness room. Outdoor pool. $

BRICKYARD CROSSING GOLF RESORT INN.

4400 W 16th St, Indianapolis (46222). Phone 317/241-2500. www.brickyardcrossing.com. Looking for a room as close as possible to the Indianapolis Motor Speedway? If so, this is the place for you. Brickyard Crossing Inn sits just outside Turn 2 of the world's most famous racetrack. If you want to add golf to your itinerary, you'll appreciate the short walk from the hotel to the 18 challenging holes at the Brickyard Crossing Golf Course. 108 rooms, 2 story. Pets accepted. Check-in 3 pm, check-out noon. Laundry services. Restaurant, bar. Pool. Golf. $

Westfield

BEST WESTERN WESTFIELD INN.

17650 Hwy 31 N, Westfield (46074). Phone 317/867-5678; toll-free 800/780-7234. www.bestwestern.com. Tidy rooms and friendly service await guests at this hotel north of Indianapolis. From Westfield, you can expect a minimum 45-minute drive to either the Motor Speedway or Raceway Park. What the hotel lacks in convenience for race-goers, it makes up for with pleasant accommodations at a low price. 54 rooms, 3 story. Complimentary continental breakfast. Check-in 3 pm, check-out 11 am. Laundry services. Fitness room. Indoor pool, whirlpool. $

For more lodging recommendations, go to www.mobiltravelguide.com

EAT

MOBIL STAR-RATED RESTAURANTS

Indianapolis

ARISTOCRAT PUB. ★

5212 N College Ave, Indianapolis (46220). Phone 317/283-7388. Dark wood and art-glass windows make the Aristocrat feel like a classic pub. The good-sized menu, complimented by a nice selection of drinks, runs the gamut from salads to sandwiches to steaks and pasta dishes. Despite its location on a busy street, the outdoor tables out front are popular on balmy evenings. American menu. Lunch, dinner, Sun brunch. Closed Jan 1, Thanksgiving, Dec 25. Children's menu. Casual attire. Outdoor seating. $$

CAFE PATACHOU. ★

4911 N Pennsylvania St, Indianapolis (46205). Phone 317/925-2823. www.cafepatachou.com. Locals flock to this bustling neighborhood spot on the city's north side for omelets, heaping bowls of hearty oatmeal, homemade granola, and heavenly cinnamon toast made from thick, fresh-baked bread. Lunch items at this hip hangout, where local artwork adorns the brightly colored walls, include chicken salad sandwiches and a chock-full salad Niçoise. Expect to wait for a table on weekends. American menu. Breakfast, lunch, brunch. Casual attire. $

CHANTECLAIR. ★ ★ ★

2501 S High School Rd, Indianapolis (46241). Phone 317/243-1040. French menu. Dinner. Closed Sun. Bar. Jacket required. Reservations recommended. $$$

DADDY JACK'S. ★ ★

9419 N Meridian St, Indianapolis (46260). Phone 317/843-1609. American menu. Lunch, dinner. Closed Sun; holidays. Casual attire. Outdoor seating. $$

HOLLYHOCK HILL. ★ ★

8110 N College Ave, Indianapolis (46240). Phone 317/251-2294. Hollyhock Hill, north of downtown, is easy to miss; it's in the middle of a residential area and inhabits what looks like a private residence. Inside, you may just feel like you've landed at Grandma's for dinner. The kitchen serves up homey dishes like skillet-fried chicken and mashed potatoes, family style. The place fills up with large groups, so it's wise to call ahead for reservations, especially on weekends. (If Hollyhock Hill is full, try **Dodd's Town House,** a similar restaurant at 5694 N Meridian St.) American menu. Lunch (Sun only), dinner. Closed Mon. Bar. Children's menu. Casual attire. $$

PALOMINO. ★ ★

49 W Maryland St, Indianapolis (46204). Phone 317/974-0400. www.palomino.com. One of the most vibrant and popular restaurants in downtown Indianapolis, Palomino offers a varied menu, ranging from steaks to seafood to pasta dishes, that should appeal to even the most persnickety of palates. For dessert, don't miss the decadent tiramisu. Reservations are a must on Friday and Saturday nights, particularly if a sporting event is being hosted at the RCA Dome or Conseco Fieldhouse, both of which are just a few blocks away. Mediterranean menu. Lunch, Dinner. Closed Sun. Children's menu. Casual attire. Reservations recommended. Outdoor seating. $$

RESTAURANT AT THE CANTERBURY. ★ ★ ★

123 S Illinois St, Indianapolis (46225). Phone 317/634-3000. Decorated more like an English club than a restaurant, this elegant, tranquil hotel dining room serves American Continental cuisine, focusing on game dishes. Lunch can be very reasonable, and don't miss the afternoon tea service with live piano music. International/Fusion menu. Breakfast, lunch, dinner, Sun brunch. Bar. Jacket required. Valet parking. $$$

RICK'S CAFE BOATYARD. ★★
4050 Dandy Trail, Indianapolis (46254). Phone 317/290-9300. International/Fusion menu. Lunch, dinner, Sun brunch. Bar. Children's menu. Business casual attire. Outdoor seating. **$$**

Plainfield

PLAINFIELD DINER. ★
3122 E Main St, Plainfield (46168). Phone 317/839-9464. One of the oldest historic roadside diners in Indiana. Diner. Breakfast, lunch, dinner. Casual attire. **$**

LOCAL RECOMMENDATIONS

Brownsburg

BOULDER CREEK DINING COMPANY.
1551 N Green St, Brownsburg (46112). Phone 317/858-8100. www.bouldercreekdiningcompany.com. This family-friendly suburban spot, modeled after a mountain lodge, has a menu that's sure to please all tastes—burgers, wood-roasted pizzas, steaks and chops, seafood, and pasta selections. American menu. Lunch, dinner. Bar. Casual attire. Outdoor seating. **$$**

YATS.
1430 N Green St, Brownsburg (46112). Phone 317/858-1312. www.yatscajuncreole.com. It's 820 miles from Indianapolis to New Orleans. Fortunately, you don't have to travel nearly that far to get good Cajun food. Yats serves up jambalaya, chili, and a red beans and rice dish that's so spicy and delicious, you'll think you've entered an eatery down on the bayou. Yats is located in the west-side suburb of Brownsburg, a quick car trip away from either of the tracks. The restaurant sits a quarter-mile north of Interstate 74 at the exit for State Road 267. Cajun/Creole menu. Lunch, dinner. Casual attire. Outdoor seating. **$**

Indianapolis

BROAD RIPPLE BREW PUB.
840 E 65th St, Indianapolis (46220). Phone 317/253-2739. Since the Broad Ripple Brew Pub opened its doors in 1990 as the state's first brew pub, plenty of others have opened around the city, but the original maintains its head (pun intended) above the rest. This convivial gathering spot is dark and smoky, with tin ceilings and dartboards. Completing the British character, the kitchen serves up Scotch eggs, fish and chips, and a few pasta specials in addition to its beloved ales, usually a choice of about eight. Parking is scarce, and the service is not always super-attentive, but the warm ambience and smooth brews more than make up for any shortcomings. Try the delicious veggie chips instead of fries. American menu. Lunch, dinner. Casual attire. Outdoor seating. **$$**

MUG 'N BUN DRIVE-IN.
5211 W 10th St, Indianapolis (46224). Phone 317/244-5669. Combine your love of cars with your love of food at the Mug 'N Bun, Indy's first drive-in. You'll get the whole deal at this beloved classic—curbside

FAN FAVORITE

Combine an English-inspired pub with a healthy dose of racing fever, and you have **Union Jack Pub's** Speedway location. (There's another outpost in Broad Ripple on Indy's north side.) About 2 miles from the Indianapolis Motor Speedway, it's a great place to grab a beer before or after the race; they have more than 70 brews from around the world. You'll also find typical pub fare like wings, nachos, and burgers, along with a decent Chicago-style pizza. American menu. Lunch, dinner. Bar. Children's menu. Casual attire. **$$** *6225 W 25th St, Speedway (46224). Phone 317/243-3300.*

service, frosted mugs of homemade draft root beer, and crispy onion rings, along with a Hoosier favorite, breaded tenderloin sandwiches. No indoor tables. Located near the Indianapolis Motor Speedway. American menu. Lunch, dinner. Casual attire. Outdoor seating. No credit cards accepted. **$**

THE RATHSKELLER.

401 E Michigan St, Indianapolis (46204). Phone 317/636-0396. www.rathskeller.com. This restaurant and beer hall, tucked away in the basement of the 1894 Athenaeum Building, is the city's oldest restaurant still in operation. If you're craving schnitzel, wurst, and sauerkraut, this is the place to indulge—German favorites dominate the menu here, paired with an incredible array of German, Belgian, and other beers. Those who prefer stateside fare have plenty of options as well. In summer, the outdoor biergarten is a popular spot for live entertainment. German menu. Lunch, dinner. Bar. Casual attire. Reservations recommended. Outdoor seating. **$$**

SHAPIRO'S DELICATESSEN.

808 S Meridian St, Indianapolis (46225). Phone 317/631-4041. www.shapiros.com. Shapiro's brings a taste of New York to the Circle City. Open since 1905, this cafeteria-style deli prides itself on its time-tested recipes and no-nonsense preparations of Jewish deli favorites. Hot pastrami and corned beef are piled high between thick slices of homemade bread. Stuffed cabbage, meatloaf, and potato pancakes are just the way Mama used to make them. Save room for a sinful slice of fresh-baked pie or cake. American menu. Breakfast, lunch, dinner. Casual attire. **$$**

SLIPPERY NOODLE INN.

372 S Meridian St, Indianapolis (46225). Phone 317/631-6974. www.slipperynoodle.com. The Slippery Noodle is a downtown Indianapolis institution. Although it's had many different names since it opened in 1850, it is considered the state's oldest continuously operating bar—beer was made in the basement even during Prohibition. Music lovers come for the nightly live blues—performers have included greats like Edgar Winter and James Cotton—and they stay for the decent steaks, seafood, and of course, a few noodle dishes. American menu. Lunch, dinner. Bar. Casual attire. **$$**

THAI HOUSE.

8431 N Michigan Rd, Indianapolis (46268). Phone 317/871-0023. Don't let its modest exterior and low prices fool you; this restaurant prepares authentic Thai cuisine that's every bit as creative and flavorful as the fare offered at more upscale eateries in town. The extensive dinner menu includes more than 60 entrées, the favorite, perhaps predictably, being the pad Thai, a dish termed "the ultimate food" by one restaurant regular. Thai House is located on the city's northwest side, roughly a mile south of Interstate 465. Thai menu. Lunch, dinner. Closed Mon. Casual attire. **$$**

For more dining recommendations, go to www.mobiltravelguide.com

SIDETRIP

Brown County
Nashville, IN

Looking for a change of pace after your high-octane, high-traffic race weekend? About an hour and a half south of Indianapolis, Brown County and Nashville, Indiana, can refuel the entire family. Depending on your preference and energy level, this getaway offers everything from fishing at a quiet stream to shopping your heart out to hammering down mountain bike trails.

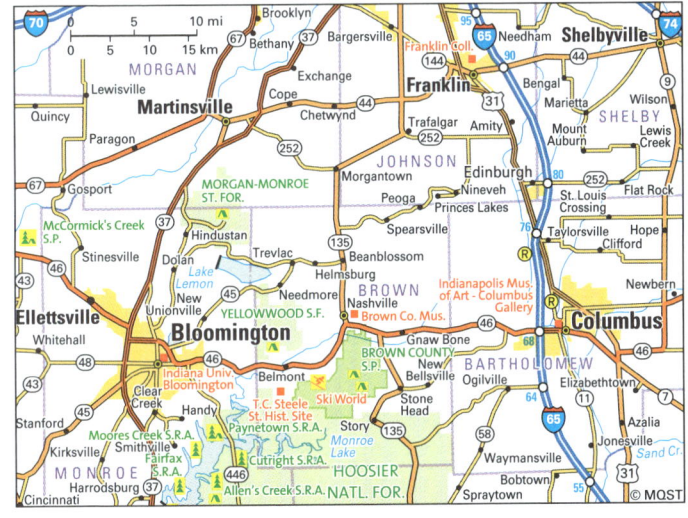

Driving from Indy, southern Indiana's rolling landscape unfolds mile after mile of pastoral beauty, complete with covered bridges. Brown County calls itself the "Art Colony of the Midwest," and, indeed, more than 100 artisans and crafters call it home. But it is much more than craft shows and antiques. An estimated 3 1/2 million families head to "the other Nashville" each year for local food, big-name entertainment, tons of outdoor activities in Indiana's largest state park, and interesting places to stay, like log cabins by a lake, a rustic lodge, a haunted inn, and Nashville's Rawhide Ranch (www.browncountylodging.com).

Brown County State Park (www.browncountystatepark.com) measures 16,000 acres, encompassing two lakes, 12 miles of hiking trails, camping, fishing, swimming (in the park pool only), horseback riding, clean facilities (including showers), abundant wildlife, and, in the fall, an awesome spectacle of foliage that you can view from the famous fire watch tower lookout. Check into the park's 86-room, rustic Abe Martin Lodge or one of the 20 year-round housekeeping cabins for an overnight.

Or stay in nearby Story, Indiana, where the population is the number of guests at the Story Inn, the town's famous haunted hotel. Story's star attraction: the Blue Lady—a playful ghost rumored to haunt the inn. Go for the food, catch its regular events, listen to the legend, and get satisfyingly spooked (phone toll-free 800/881-1183, www.storyinn.com).

If you are looking to take a break from the big city, head out to this nature lover's paradise.

For more Nashville recommendations, go to www.mobiltravelguide.com

Jamie McMurray catches some air on the road course at Infineon Raceway.

CA

Infineon Raceway

Sonoma, CA

11

An aerial view of Infineon Raceway's left and right turns.

TRACK FACTS

INFINEON RACEWAY. 29355 Arnold Dr, Sonoma (95476). Phone toll-free 800/870-RACE (7223). www.infineonraceway.com.

SECURITY. Coolers and packs (no larger than 15 x 15 x 15 inches) can be brought into any seating area, but are subject to search. Cans, glass containers, and alcohol are prohibited, but fans may bring food or other drinks in plastic bottles. No pets are allowed.

PARKING. Parking is free. Attendants will direct you to a parking space. Some parking is far from the track, but free shuttles deliver racegoers to the track entrance.

FIRST AID. Located underneath the main grandstand, Fan Care offers first aid, as do first aid stations situated at Turns 2, 3, 7, and 9.

The Sonoma Valley Hospital (347 Andrieux St, Sonoma) is 12 miles away.

CONCESSIONS. Infineon offers an array of fun activities and food for fans. Check out Margarita Beach (located above Turns 8-9), where you'll find a sand volleyball court, music, and, of course, margaritas. The Carneros Marketplace offers a taste of the Sonoma Valley, trackside, where you can choose from an assortment of local foods, fresh fruit, and wines. You can purchase ice for coolers at the Raceway Café.

RESTROOMS. The facilities beneath the main grandstand are by far the best. Plentiful stalls mean little time is lost standing in line. Diaper changing facilities are available in the grandstand restrooms only. There are additional permanent restrooms near Turns 2 and 10. All other bathroom facilities are temporary.

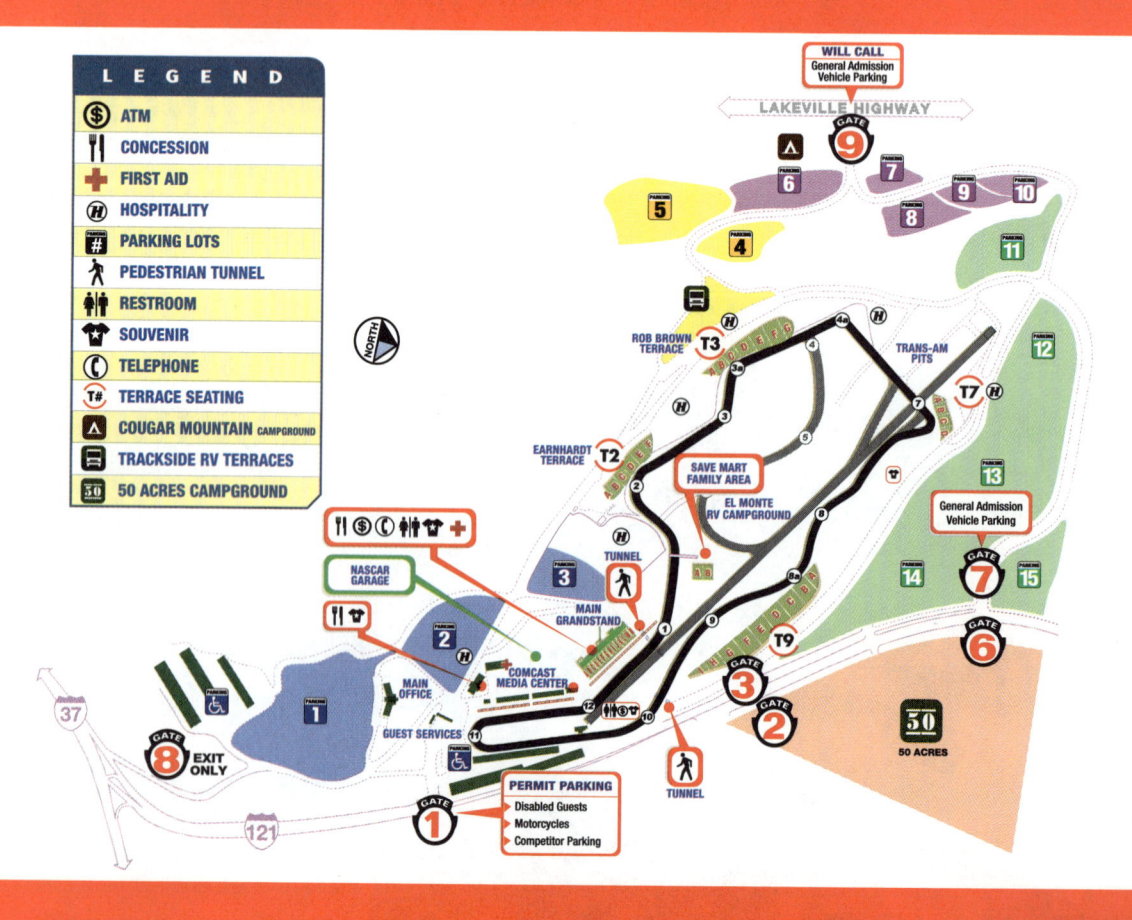

INCREDIBLE INFINEON

A recent $60 million modernization of Infineon Raceway—one of NASCAR's two road courses—made an incredible 70 percent of the raceway visible from every seat in the facility. But even with such great views, the fans at this road course still clamor for their preferred seats. Turns 7 and 9 are favored by track regulars as some of the best spots in the house (several critical passes have taken place on Turn 7 in past NASCAR events). The start/finish grandstand offers fans the opportunity to view the race on a large screen, watch the action in the pits, and see the post-race festivities in the Winner's Circle.

Race car drivers come to Infineon Raceway prepared to tackle both left- and right-hand turns as they maneuver through the winding road course. Visitors touring the region surrounding Infineon Raceway have the opportunity to make a few twists and turns of their own. Cruise the winding Highway 1 and watch the Pacific Ocean crash onto shore, or crank the wheel to make the tight turns of brick-lined Lombard Street in San Francisco. Shift gears, and explore the rolling hillsides of Sonoma Valley, enjoy the solitude at area parks, or hob-nob with the in crowd in Napa Valley.

INFINEON FOR FAMILIES

Located just above Turn 1, below the lap leader board, is the Save Mart family area. Here, families can enjoy a children's playground and family-friendly concessions. The area is an alcohol-free zone and smoking is prohibited. Handicap seating is available in the family area, with room for one accompanying individual.

GETTING TICKETS

To purchase tickets, call toll-free 800/870-RACE (7223) or visit www.infineonraceway.com. General admission tickets cannot be purchased in advance; they may be available at the gate on race day. However, it's best to call well in advance to secure reserved seats. The Web site's virtual tour of the raceway allows fans to see seating options. Wheelchair-accessible viewing is available at the hillside terraces at Turns 2, 3, 7, and 9, and at the main grandstand. There are some shady seats available in the upper part of the main grandstand.

RACEWAY CLUB. For $250, you'll get a weekend-long event pass, catered lunch on Saturday and Sunday, complimentary drinks, preferred parking, and reserved seating. The most valuable part of this package, however, may be access to the Raceway Club and a reprieve from the sun.

FANS WITH DISABILITIES. Physically handicapped fans should enter the facility through Gate 1 (show a handicapped placard or special identification license plate or have a handicapped identification card and matching driver's license). A shuttle service offers transportation around the facility.

Jimmie Johnson leads the field around the famous curves at Infineon Raceway.

Make time to tour a winery or two—your trip to Wine Country wouldn't be complete without it.

FERTILE VALLEYS, VIBRANT CITIES

Award-winning vintages and a pastoral setting invite people from around the world to sample the good life in the Napa and Sonoma valleys. If fine wine is your thing, you've come to the right neighborhood. Easily identified by the endless vineyards and wineries that line busy roads, the areas are similar in that both regions offer up some fabulous wine, gourmet foods, and spectacular scenery.

There are subtle differences, though. Napa Valley tends to be more upscale; many of the lodging and restaurant options are high-end, making it a challenge to visit on a budget. While the Sonoma Valley has its fair share of finery, the area seems to remain closer to its agricultural roots; a farm truck parked outside a tasting room is just as common as a limousine. Another difference: you're more likely to pay for wine tasting in the Napa Valley. That's not to say there aren't wineries with tasting fees in Sonoma Valley, but the chardonnay may flow more freely across the county line.

If you want to sample or purchase some of the region's finest wines while in the area, a few options include the **Buena Vista Winery** (18000 Old Winery

With the crowd in the background in the Turn 2 Dale Earnhardt Terraces, Dale Earnhardt Jr gets ready to crest Turn 3a.

GETTING AROUND

NASCAR events at Infineon Raceway can cause traffic jams. With only two entrances to the parking areas, there are usually delays, so allow plenty of time.

Arrive early and stay late to avoid traffic (some fans show up at 7 am with a tailgate breakfast). Track officials have taken the "stay late" plan to heart: Infineon has added a Trans-Am race about 30 minutes after the **NASCAR NEXTEL** Cup race, thus extending the window for exiting the track.

Gate 9 (off Lakeville Hwy) offers the easiest entrance to the parking area if you are arriving from the North Bay. The best exit point from the parking area is Gate 8, taking you directly onto Hwy 37. Tune to 87.9 FM for raceway traffic information.

Infineon Raceway's Ride the Bus program offers several pick-up locations throughout the Bay Area. This program includes premium reserved seating at the track and transportation to and from the raceway. For more information, phone toll-free 800/870-RACE (7223).

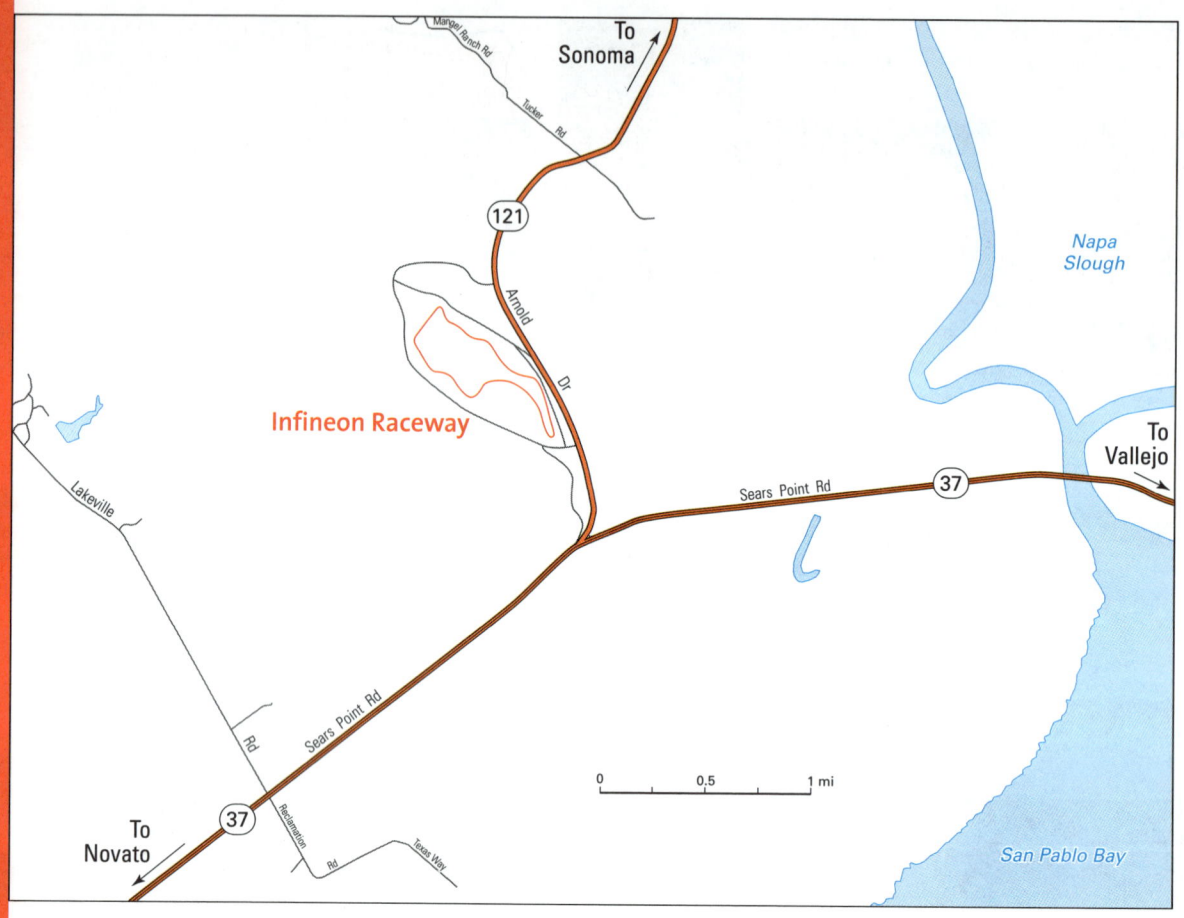

SONOMA POLE POSITION:
The 10 miles surrounding Infineon Raceway.

Rd, Sonoma, phone 707/938-1266); **Gloria Ferrer Champagne Caves** (23555 Hwy 121, Sonoma, phone 707/996-7256); and **Sebastiani Sonoma Cask Cellars** (389 4th E, Sonoma, phone 707/938-5532).

If your tastes lean more to the hustle and bustle of a big city, take a day or two to explore the Bay Area. In San Francisco, admire the view from atop Coit Tower, enjoy some amazing Italian food in North Beach, or sample fresh clam chowder served in a bread bowl at **Fisherman's Wharf** (Embarcadero and Jefferson at the foot of Taylor St, phone 415/705-5500) for a true taste of San Francisco. Sports fans can take in a baseball game—the San Francisco Giants and the Oakland A's call the Bay Area home. Of course, a visit to the City by the Bay wouldn't be complete without a walk across the **Golden Gate Bridge** (US Hwy 101, San Francisco).

In nearby Vallejo, visitors can get their thrills at Six Flags Marine World or visit the Vallejo Naval & Historical Museum at Mare Island, though there is little else here to entertain visitors. If the premium room rates in San Francisco are more than your bank account can handle, Vallejo is a less expensive alternative. **The Baylink Ferry** (www.baylinkferry.com), with departure times throughout the day, offers a great shortcut to San Francisco and a fun way to avoid the headache of parking in the city.

SONOMA CALENDAR

JUNE, 2005
Silverado Concours d' Elegance. Mare Island. www.silveradoconcours.com. Phone 707/552-3400. A classic car show featuring street rods and modifieds, as well as vintage military vehicles, antique cars, and motorcycles. First Sunday of June.

JUNE 24–26, 2005
NASCAR NEXTEL Cup Series

JULY 3–4, 2005
Sonoma County Hot Air Balloon Classic. Keiser Park, Windsor (95492). Phone 707/837-1884. www.schabc.org. Arrive before sunrise to watch the 5 am liftoff of more than 25 multicolored balloons. Then stick around to see them float into the sky. Crafts, food, and entertainment round out the day.

JULY 4, 2005
Kenwood Fourth of July Celebrations and World Pillow Fighting Championships. Plaza Park, Warm Springs Rd, Kenwood (95452). Phone 707/833-2440. www.kenwoodpillowfights.com. Competitors straddle a pole suspended over a muddy pit, and do their darndest to hang on.

JULY 4 WEEKEND, 2005
Napa County Fair. Napa County Fairgrounds, Calistoga (94515). Phone 707/942-5111. www.napacountyfairgrounds.com. Enjoy fireworks, country music concerts, rides, a barbecue contest, exhibits, and a festive country fair atmosphere.

The Bear Flag Monument commemorates the events of the Bear Flag Revolt of 1846, when settlers revolted against Mexican rule and brought the area under US control.

OWNER'S PICK

Famed NASCAR championship car owner **Jack Roush** puts the pedal to the metal to get to a blue Victorian building directly overlooking the water with a great view of San Francisco. "When we go out to Infineon Raceway, one of my favorite places to dine is **Scoma's of Sausalito.** ★★ I'm particularly fond of their swordfish. It's tops. That area of California is beautiful, too, and it just adds to the experience." *588 Bridgeway, Sausalito (94965). Phone 415/332-9551. www.scomasausalito.com.*

SONOMA OUTFIELD:
The 50 miles surrounding Infineon Raceway.

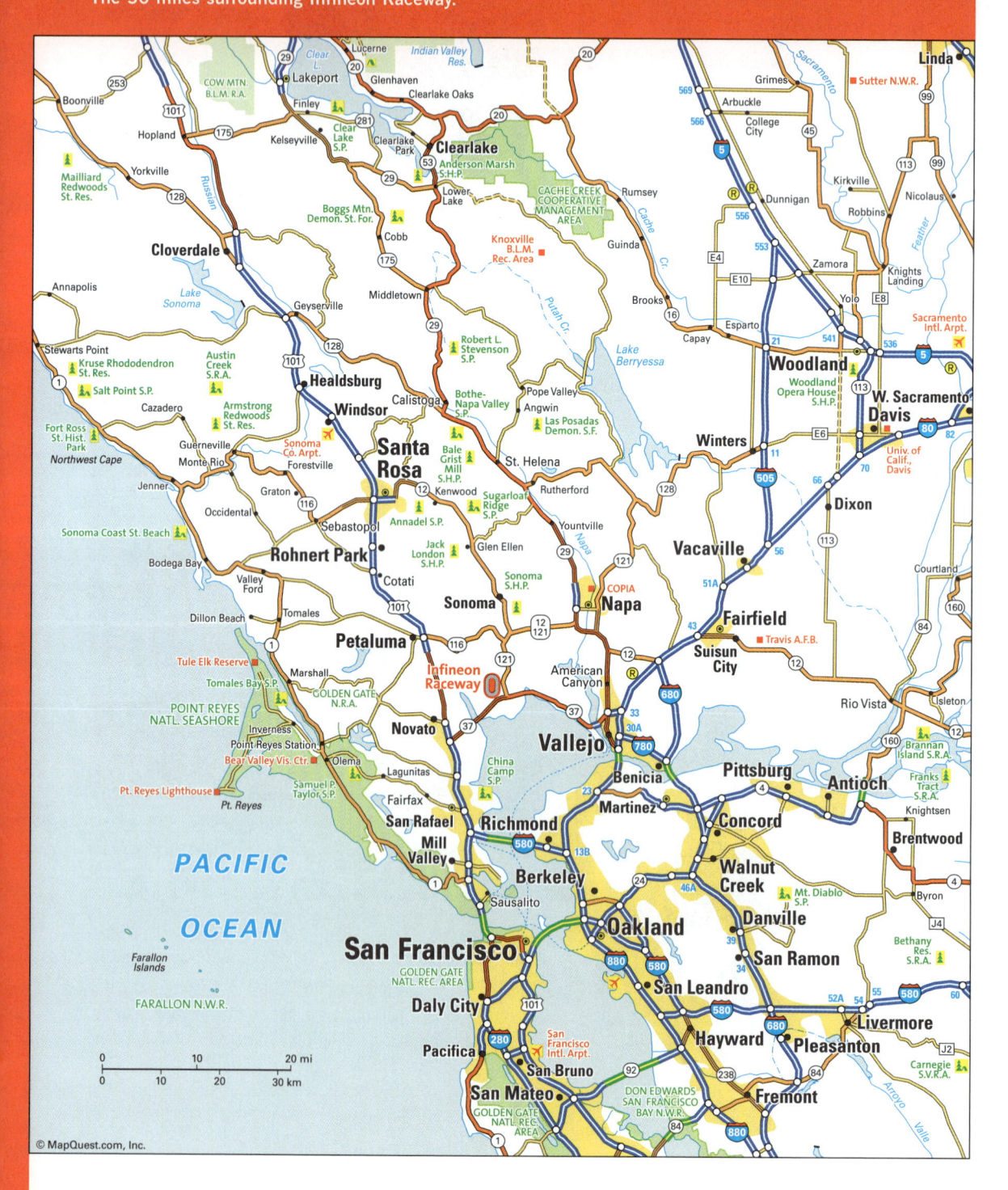

SEE

ATTRACTIONS

BAY AREA

Fairfield

JELLY BELLY FACTORY TOURS.
One Jelly Belly Ln, Fairfield (94533). Phone toll-free 800/522-3267. www.jellybelly.com. With more than 150 flavors of jellybeans and guided tours that lead visitors through the Jelly Belly-making process, this is a can't-miss diversion for those with a sweet tooth. Follow your tour with a trip to the Jelly Belly sampling bar and the gift shop. On weekends, videos replace the busy candy-making scene. There is a restaurant and picnic area on-site. (Daily 9 am-5 pm; closed holidays) **FREE**

San Francisco

MARITIME MUSEUM.
Beach and Polk sts, San Francisco (94109). Phone 415/561-7100. www.maritime.org. Situated on San Francisco Bay across from Ghirardelli Square, this museum offers a peek into the history of West Coast vessels. Don't miss the hands-on radio room where you can explore communication technology, from signal flags to Morse Code. The sandy beach at Aquatic Park is right outside the back door. (Daily 10 am-5 pm; closed Jan 1, Thanksgiving, Dec 25) **FREE**

Vallejo

SIX FLAGS MARINE WORLD.
2001 Marine World Pkwy, Vallejo (94589). Phone 707/643-6722. www.sixflags.com/parks/marineworld. Part of the Six Flags chain, this marine park specializes in animal and water shows, but also has enough rides to shake up the whole family. There are also plenty of tamer rides and a guided Sunset Safari where you can meet the animals up close. (Memorial Day-Labor Day: daily; Mar-Memorial Day and Labor Day-Oct: weekends; hours vary; call or visit Web site for schedule) **$$$$**

NAPA VALLEY

Calistoga

OLD FAITHFUL GEYSER OF CALIFORNIA.
1299 Tubbs Ln, Calistoga (94515). Phone 707/942-6463. www.oldfaithfulgeyser.com. One of only three regularly erupting geysers in the world, Old Faithful spews approximately every 30 minutes for about three minutes at a time. Fed by a lava-heated underground river, vapor and steam escape to heights of 60 feet. A favorite of families, the site also features picnic grounds. (Daily 9 am-6 pm) **$$**

THE PETRIFIED FOREST.
4100 Petrified Forest Rd, Calistoga (94515). Phone 707/942-6667. www.petrifiedforest.org. Some 3 million years ago, a volcanic eruption toppled and petrified the giant redwoods that covered this land. Turned to solid quartz and stone, these prehistoric behemoths measure up to 105 feet long and 8 feet in diameter. A short, shady hike takes visitors past the petrified trees. The museum and rock shop offer a close-up look at some geological wonders. (Daily 9 am-6 pm; to 5 pm in winter; closed Dec 25) **$**

NORTH BAY

Santa Rosa

REDWOOD EMPIRE ICE ARENA.
1667 W Steele Ln, Santa Rosa (95403). Phone 707/546-7147. www.snoopyshomeice.com. Built by Charles M. Schulz, the creator of the Peanuts comic strip, this ice arena, known as Snoopy's Home Ice, is a great place to cool off on a hot summer day. The rink offers skate rentals and has a restaurant on site (call ahead for skating hours). Next door is the Charles M. Schulz Museum. It's great for comic aficionados, but young children may find it less than exciting. (Mon, Wed-Fri, noon-5 pm; Sat-Sun, 10 am-5 pm) **$$**

SAFARI WEST WILDLIFE PRESERVE.
3115 Porter Creek Rd, Santa Rosa (95404). Phone toll-free 800/616-2695. www.safariwest.com. Board a safari vehicle and head into the hills in search of the more than 400 exotic mammals and birds that call this place home. Tours (daily). (Spring-fall, 9 am, 1 pm, and 4 pm; winter, 10 am and 2 pm) **$$$$**

SEE ATTRACTIONS

Sebastopol

PATRICK AMIOT'S ART.
Florence St, Sebastopol (95472). www.patrickamiot-brigittelaurent.com. Just blocks from Sebastopol's Main Street, turn-of-the-century homes mingle with sculptures such as a giant caveman and a replica of an old Oliver tractor. Made of what some of us might call junk, Amiot's art is on display in an unusual venue—his neighbors' yards. Walk the street to get an up-close look at the clever artwork. **FREE**

SONOMA VALLEY

Glen Ellen

JACK LONDON STATE HISTORIC PARK.
2400 London Ranch Rd, Glen Ellen (95442). 8 1/2 miles W on Hwy 12, then 1 1/2 miles W of Glen Ellen on London Ranch Rd. Phone 707/938-5216. www.jacklondonpark.com. A memorial to author Jack London, the park is located in the Valley of the Moon. Just before its completion, fire consumed London's magnificent dream home. See the rock-wall ruins of the Wolf House, the Pig Palace, and the House of Happy Walls, now a museum. Hiking trails traverse the park. Museum (daily 10 am-5 pm; closed Jan 1, Thanksgiving, Dec 25). Park (early Apr-Oct: 9:30 am-5 pm; rest of year: 10 am-5 pm). **$$**

Sonoma

SONOMA TRAIN TOWN.
20264 Broadway, Sonoma (95476). Phone 707/938-3912. www.traintown.com. Young children will find Train Town enchanting. Miniature trains take visitors on a 20-minute ride through a landscaped park with animals, waterfalls, and historic replica structures. (June-Sept: daily 10 am-5 pm; rest of year: Fri-Sun 10 am-5 pm; closed Thanksgiving, Dec 25) **$**

> For more attractions, go to www.mobiltravelguide.com

BRAKE HERE

Both kids and adults with a fascination for all things mechanical will find the **Cable Car Museum** a must-see attraction. A viewing area allows visitors to see part of the network of tunnels, cables, and sheaves that guide the cable car system from under the streets. Antique cable cars (including the front of one of the original cars), vintage photographs, historic displays, and a real cable car bell that you can ring complete the experience. (Apr-Sept: daily 10 am-6 pm; Oct-Mar: daily to 5 pm; closed Jan 1, Thanksgiving, Dec 25) **FREE** *1201 Mason St, San Francisco (94108). Phone 415/474-1887. www.cablecarmuseum.com.*

STAY

MOBIL STAR-RATED LODGINGS

BAY AREA

Fairfield

HAMPTON INN FAIRFIELD/NAPA VALLEY. ★
4441 Central Pl, Fairfield (94585). Phone 707/864-1446; toll-free 800/426-7866. www.hamptoninn.com. 57 rooms, 3 story. Complimentary continental breakfast. Check-in 4 pm, check-out noon. Wireless Internet access. Fitness room. Outdoor pool. **$**

San Francisco

COURTYARD BY MARRIOTT SAN FRANCISCO DOWNTOWN. ★★
299 Second St, San Francisco (94105). Phone 415/947-0700; toll-free 800/321-2211. www.courtyard.com. Situated in the heart of the South of Market business district, guests will find this property convenient to SBC Park, Union Square, and other

area attractions. 405 rooms, 18 story. Check-in 4 pm, check-out noon. High-speed Internet access. Restaurant, bar. Fitness room. Indoor pool. $$

CROWNE PLAZA HOTEL SAN FRANCISCO—UNION SQUARE. ★★★
480 Sutter St, San Francisco (94108). Phone 415/398-8900; toll-free 888/303-1746. www.crowneplaza.com. Well situated for tourists and business travelers alike, this Crowne Plaza is one block from Union Square. The Powell Street cable car conveniently stops at the hotel's corner. 403 rooms, 30 story. Pets accepted; fee. Check-in 3 pm, check-out noon. High-speed Internet access. Two restaurants, bar. Fitness room. Business center. $$

HYATT AT FISHERMAN'S WHARF. ★★★
555 North Point St, San Francisco (94133). Phone 415/563-1234; toll-free 888/591-1234. www.hyatt.com. One of the best choices in the Fisherman's Wharf area, this Hyatt is a few blocks from Ghirardelli Square and the Hyde Street cable car line, which chugs past the crooked part of Lombard Street. The outdoor pool is a rarity in this city. 313 rooms, 5 story. Check-in 3 pm, check-out noon. Restaurant, bar. Children's activity center. Fitness room. Outdoor pool, whirlpool. Business center. $$

NORTH BAY

Santa Rosa

HILTON SONOMA COUNTY/SANTA ROSA. ★★★
3555 Round Barn Blvd, Santa Rosa (95403). Phone 707/523-7555; toll-free 800/445-8667. www.hilton.com. Hilton Sonoma, situated on the crest of a hill, offers the perfect stay for any guest. It is centrally located to more than 140 world-class Sonoma County wineries and golf courses. Picturesque towns and state parks are close by, offering hiking, biking, and sailing. 244 rooms, 3 story. Check-in 3 pm, check-out noon. Restaurant, bar. Fitness room. Outdoor pool, whirlpool. Business center. $$

HYATT VINEYARD CREEK HOTEL—SONOMA COUNTY. ★★★
170 Railroad St, Santa Rosa (95401). Phone 707/636-7100; toll-free 800/633-7313. www.hyatt.com. Located close to Sonoma wine country, this hotel is convenient to the area's many wineries as well as the racetrack. A full-service spa is located within the hotel. 155 rooms, 2 story. Pets accepted, some restrictions; fee. Check-in 3 pm, check-out noon. High-speed Internet access. Restaurant, bar. Fitness room, spa. Outdoor pool, whirlpool. Airport transportation available. Business center. $$

LOCAL RECOMMENDATIONS

BAY AREA

Benicia

BEST WESTERN HERITAGE INN.
1955 E 2nd St, Benicia (94510). Phone 707/746-0401; toll-free 800/937-8376. www.bestwestern.com. 99 rooms, 3 story. Pets accepted; fee. Complimentary continental breakfast. Check-in 3 pm, check-out 11 am. High-speed Internet access. Outdoor pool, whirlpool. $

Fairfield

BEST WESTERN CORDELIA INN.
4373 Central Pl, Fairfield (94534). Phone 707/864-2029; toll-free 800/422-7575. www.bestwestern.com. 60 rooms, 2 story. Complimentary continental breakfast. Check-in 3 pm, check-out noon. High-speed Internet access. Outdoor pool, whirlpool. $

Novato

BEST WESTERN NOVATO OAKS INN.
215 Alameda Del Prado, Novato (94949). Phone 415/883-4400; toll-free 800/625-7466. www.bestwestern.com. 107 rooms, 3 story. Complimentary continental breakfast. Check-in 3 pm, check-out noon. Fitness room. Outdoor pool, whirlpool. $

Vallejo

BEST WESTERN INN AT MARINE WORLD.
1596 Fairgrounds Dr, Vallejo (94589). Phone 707/554-9655; toll-free 800/780-7234. www.bestwestern.com. 117 rooms, 3 story. Complimentary continental breakfast. Check-in 3 pm, check-out 11 am. Outdoor pool, whirlpool. $

HOLIDAY INN VALLEJO—NAPA VALLEY GATEWAY.
1000 Fairgrounds Dr, Vallejo (94589). Phone 707/644-1200; toll-free 800/533-5753. www.holiday-inn.com. Across from Six Flags Marine World Theme Park.

165 rooms. Pets accepted. Check-in 3 pm, check-out noon. Fitness center. Outdoor pool, whirlpool. $

NAPA VALLEY

Calistoga

BEST WESTERN STEVENSON MANOR INN.
1830 Lincoln Ave, Calistoga (94515). Phone 707/942-1112; toll-free 800/780-7234. www.bestwestern.com. 34 rooms, 2 story. Complimentary continental breakfast. Check-in 3 pm, check-out 11 am. Fitness room. Outdoor pool, whirlpool. $

Napa

BEST WESTERN ELM HOUSE INN.
800 California Blvd, Napa (94559). Phone 707/255-1831; toll-free 888/849-1997. www.bestwestern.com. 22 rooms, 3 story. Complimentary full breakfast. Check-in 3 pm, check-out noon. High-speed Internet access. $$

BEST WESTERN INN AT THE VINES.
100 Soscol Ave, Napa (94559). Phone 707/257-1930; toll-free 877/846-3729. www.bestwestern.com. 68 rooms, 3 story. Complimentary full breakfast. Check-in 4 pm, check-out 11 am. Pool, whirlpool. $$

NORTH BAY

Petaluma

BEST WESTERN PETALUMA INN.
200 S McDowell Blvd, Petaluma (94954). Phone 707/763-0994; toll-free 800/297-3846. www.bestwestern.com. Located in the charming riverfront town of Petaluma near dining, shopping, and museums. 73 rooms, 2 story. Check-in 2 pm, check-out 11 am. Outdoor pool. $

Rohnert Park

BEST WESTERN INN.
6500 Redwood Dr, Rohnert Park (94928). Phone 707/584-7435; toll-free 800/780-7234. www.bestwestern.com. 144 rooms, 2 story. Pets accepted, some restrictions. Complimentary continental breakfast. Check-in 3 pm, check-out noon. Restaurant. Outdoor pool, whirlpool. $

Santa Rosa

BEST WESTERN GARDEN INN.
1500 Santa Rosa Ave, Santa Rosa (95404). Phone 707/546-4031; toll-free 800/780-7234. www.bestwestern.com. 78 rooms, 2 story. Pets accepted, some restrictions; fee. Check-in 2 pm, check-out noon. Outdoor pool. $

SONOMA VALLEY

Sonoma

BEST WESTERN SONOMA VALLEY INN.
550 2nd St W, Sonoma (95476). Phone 707/938-9200; toll-free 800/334-5784. www.bestwestern.com. 80 rooms, 2 story. Pets accepted, some restrictions, fee. Complimentary continental breakfast. Check in 2 pm, check-out noon. Fitness room. Pool. Business center. $

RV AND CAMPING

BAY AREA

Vallejo

TRADEWINDS RV PARK.
239 W Lincoln Rd, Vallejo (94590). Phone 707/643-4000. 78 sites, full and partial hook-ups. Showers, restrooms, laundry.

NAPA VALLEY

Calistoga

RV PARK AT THE NAPA COUNTY FAIRGROUNDS.
1435 Oak St, Calistoga (94515). Phone 707/942-5221. 72 RV and tent sites, some with full hook-up. Dump station on-site. Pets accepted, some restrictions. ($22 per night, $25 with sewer hook-up)

Napa

BOTHE-NAPA VALLEY STATE PARK.
3801 St. Helena Hwy, Napa (94515). Located 5 miles N of St. Helena and 4 miles S of Calistoga on Hwy 29/128. Phone 707/942-4575; toll-free 800/444-7275. www.parks.ca.gov. 1,800 acres of pine and redwood groves invite visitors to explore the natural beauty of the Napa Valley. 50 tent and RV sites; no hook-ups. Restrooms, showers. Hiking, day use.

NORTH BAY

Bodega Bay

DORAN REGIONAL PARK.
201 Doran Beach Rd, Bodega Bay (94923). Phone 707/565-2267. Just a short walk from Doran Beach. 132 sites, 5 handicap accessible sites. No hook-ups. Showers, restrooms. Dump site. Hiking, day use. ($17/night)

Olema

OLEMA RANCH CAMPGROUND.
10155 Hwy 1, Olema (94950). Phone 415/663-8001; toll-free 800/655-2267. www.olemaranch.com. Situated near six national and state parks. 203 RV sites with full and partial hook-ups. 175 tent sites. Hot showers. Pets accepted, restrictions. ($35 RV, $25 tent)

Petaluma

PETALUMA KOA.
20 Rainsville Rd, Petaluma (94952). Phone 707/763-1492; toll-free 800/992-2267. www.petalumakoa.com. 300 spaces on 60 acres. Tents, RV hook-ups, Kamping Kabins.

SONOMA VALLEY

Glen Ellen

SUGARLOAF RIDGE STATE PARK.
2605 Adobe Canyon Rd, Glen Ellen (95452). Phone 707/833-5712. 50 tent and RV sites; no hook-ups. Restrooms. Hiking, day use.

> For more lodging recommendations, go to www.mobiltravelguide.com

EAT

MOBIL STAR-RATED RESTAURANTS

BAY AREA

San Francisco

FRANCISCAN. ★ ★
Pier 43 1/2 Embarcadero, San Francisco (94133). Phone 415/362-7733. Fresh fish and crab cakes are the draw at this restaurant in touristy Fisherman's Wharf serving contemporary California cuisine. Tables boast wide-lens views of San Francisco Bay, and the dining and bar areas offer tiered seating to provide patrons with unencumbered vistas. Seafood menu. Lunch, dinner. Closed Thanksgiving, Dec 25. Bar. Children's menu. Outdoor seating. $$$

MO'S GOURMET HAMBURGERS. ★
1322 Grant Ave, San Francisco (94133). Phone 415/788-3779. North Beach takes a break from Italian fare at this hamburger joint, which beckons with its neon signage. Mo's is still willing to serve a "bloody," high-quality burger (if you want it that way), along with thick fries and milkshakes. Colorful folk-art murals and a large framed photo of the Three Stooges observe as you indulge. American menu. Breakfast, lunch, dinner. Closed Thanksgiving, Dec 25. Casual attire. $

NAPA VALLEY

Calistoga

PACIFICO. ★
1237 Lincoln Ave, Calistoga (94515). Phone 707/942-4400. www.pacificorestaurant.com. Vividly colored décor invites visitors to relax and enjoy a taste of the true flavors of Mexico. Mexican menu. Dinner, brunch. Closed Thanksgiving, Dec 24-25. Bar. Children's menu. $$

PIT PASS

If you've ever ached to fulfill your need for speed, the ESPN Russell Racing School at Infineon Raceway offers several classes for race enthusiasts. The Cadet Karting Course ($300) is a half-day program that emphasizes basic kart handling skills and places kids aged 8-12 behind the wheel of real racing karts, scaled down to fit younger children. Adults and teens learn about kart safety and racing theory in the one-day Techniques of Karting Course ($445). Both courses include safety gear. For more information, call toll-free 800/733-0345, www.espnrussellracing.com.

204 EAT MOBIL STAR-RATED RESTAURANTS

Napa

RUFFINO'S. ★★

645 1st St, Napa (94559). Phone 707/255-4455. As soon as you see the family photos lining the walls of this family-owned Italian restaurant in downtown Napa, it's clear that it has been a local favorite for years. Serving traditional Italian fare in a comfortable, yet elegant setting, the restaurant has consistently been voted by local radio and newspapers as the best in the area. It is set in a quiet neighborhood, near the American Center for Wine, Food, and the Arts. Italian menu. Lunch, dinner. Closed Mon; holidays. Bar. Children's menu. **$$**

NORTH BAY

Bodega Bay

BAY VIEW. ★★

800 Hwy 1, Bodega Bay (94923). Phone 707/875-2751. True to its name, this restaurant promises a fantastic view for every table in its warm, elegant dining room, accented with beamed ceilings and a cozy fireplace. The menu features recipes highlighting California cuisine, and takes advantage of the fresh produce, seafood, and poultry that has made Sonoma County well-known in the world of food fanatics. California menu. Dinner. Closed Mon-Tues. Bar. Children's menu. Outdoor seating. **$$**

LUCAS WHARF. ★

595 Hwy 1, Bodega Bay (94923). Phone 707/875-3522. www.lucaswharf.com. On the waterfront of Bodega Bay, this simple, rustic seafood restaurant features great views of the Bay and the fishing boats that catch the fish and shellfish served here every day. With an open kitchen, nautical décor, and a working fireplace, the atmosphere is airy and comfortable. Seafood menu. Lunch, dinner. Closed Thanksgiving, Dec 25. Bar. Children's menu. Casual attire. Outdoor seating. **$$**

Novato

CACTI. ★★

1200 Grant Ave, Novato (94945). Phone 415/898-2234. What makes this Marin County restaurant particularly intriguing is the fact that it is set in what used to be a church, complete with high, open-beamed ceilings and hardwood floors. Southwestern menu. Lunch, dinner. Closed Jan 1, Thanksgiving, Dec 25. Bar. Children's menu. Outdoor seating. **$$**

Petaluma

DE SCHMIRE. ★

304 Bodega Ave, Petaluma (94952). Phone 707/762-1901. At first glance, one might underestimate this little bistro on Petaluma's central west end, with its small sign and tucked-away location. However, step inside and you'll realize you've found a local gem that has been serving fine California fare to local devotees for about 30 years. California, French menu. Dinner. Closed July 4, Dec 24-25. **$$**

GRAZIANOS. ★

170 Petaluma Blvd N, Petaluma (94952). Phone 707/762-5997. In historic downtown Petaluma, this northern Italian restaurant has been a local favorite for more than 20 years. With a wine list that includes both California and Italian wines, the menu features an array of pasta, seafood, and steak dishes, as well as decadent desserts. Italian menu. Dinner. Closed Mon; holidays. Bar. **$$**

Sausalito

HORIZONS. ★★

558 Bridgeway, Sausalito (94965). Phone 415/331-3232. For the best view of the Bay Bridge outside of San Francisco, head to this casual bayside restaurant which also offers full views of Tiburon and Angel Island. If you can take your eyes off the shimmering water, you'll notice the dining room's creative nautical theme. California, seafood menu. Breakfast, lunch, dinner, brunch. Closed Dec 25. Bar. Children's menu. Valet parking. Outdoor seating. **$$**

SONOMA VALLEY

Sonoma

CAFÉ LAHAYE. ★★

140 E Napa St, Sonoma (95476). Phone 707/935-5994. Artwork from a neighboring art gallery hangs throughout this cozy restaurant, just off the main square in Sonoma. Diners rave about the upscale, yet fun atmosphere, comparing the restaurant to a friend's dining room—a friend, that is, who also happens to be a phenomenal cook. The menu items are made with locally grown and produced meats, cheeses, and fruits and vegetables, resulting in what the chef calls "home-grown cuisine." California menu. Lunch, dinner. Closed Mon; holidays. Reservations recommended. Outdoor seating. **$$**

DEUCE. ★★
691 Broadway, Sonoma (95476). Phone 707/933-3823. The atmosphere and menu at this chef-owned restaurant are diverse: looking out onto an English garden, the dining room is lit by unique Italian lights, while guests peruse creative American cuisine options. With great outdoor dining, seasonal menus, and friendly and knowledgeable service, it's not surprising that both locals and tourists keep coming back. American menu. Lunch, dinner. Closed Dec 24-25. Bar. Children's menu. Outdoor seating. **$$**

SADDLES STEAKHOUSE. ★★
29 E MacArthur St, Sonoma (95476). Phone 707/933-3191. Magically managing to stay very much on the good side of the tasteful-to-tacky spectrum, this downright elegant Western-themed steakhouse at the MacArthur Place Hotel sits among lush, peaceful gardens. The décor is decidedly "cowboy," with antique boots, saddles, and cowboy hats throughout the restaurant, but the food is decidedly delicious, featuring excellent steaks and seafood. Steak menu. Lunch, dinner. Bar. Children's menu. Outdoor seating. **$$$**

LOCAL RECOMMENDATIONS

BAY AREA

San Francisco

LORI'S DINER.
149 Powell St, San Francisco (94102). Phone 415/677-9999. www.lorisdiner.com. Situated near Union Square, Lori's Diner brings back the fabulous '50s with the classic cars on display (including a '56 Chevy Bel Air) and jukebox music. American menu. Breakfast, lunch, dinner. **$**

NAPA VALLEY

Napa

PICCOLINO'S ITALIAN CAFÉ.
1385 Napa Town Center, Napa (94559). At First and Franklin sts. Phone 707/251-0100. Old-world Italian meals such as pasta mix with entrées like portabella torta and broiled eggplant sandwich. If your family can agree on one entrée, Poppa's family-style dinners are a good value and serve four to five hungry people. Italian menu. Lunch, dinner. **$$**

KIDS' PICK

Kids may recognize the **Screamin' Mimi's** name of this fun ice-cream parlor from the Judy Moody books—author Megan McDonald lives in Sebastopol. Try out Mimi's Mud—a decadent blend with fudge, Oreo cookies, and chocolate chips in espresso-based ice cream. **$** *6902 Sebastopol Ave, Sebastopol (95472). Phone 707/823-5902.*

ZUZU.
829 Main St, Napa (94558). Phone 707/224-8555. www.zuzunapa.com. In the heart of Napa's old town, Zuzu serves up an assortment of tapas made with locally grown organic ingredients. Traditional Mediterranean appetizers fused with California cuisine create a unique dining experience at a reasonable price (most tapas are under $10). Be aware that street parking is often difficult, and Zuzu does not take reservations. Spanish, tapas menu. Lunch (Mon-Fri), dinner. **$$**

Novato

HILLTOP CAFÉ.
850 Lamont Ave, Novato (94945). Phone 415/892-2222. www.htnet.com. In the late 1930s, the Hilltop Café (then called the Maison Marin) served filet mignon with soup and salad for $1.75. It may cost a little more nowadays ($28), but the view is still beautiful. The 11 varieties of fresh fish, 15 meat or steak entrées, and (of course) an extensive wine list provide an elegant meal without the trip into San Francisco. Lunch (Mon-Sat), dinner, Sun brunch. **$$**

EAT LOCAL RECOMMENDATIONS

Occidental

UNION HOTEL.
3731 Main St, Occidental (95465). Phone 707/874-3444. www.unionhotel.com. The friendly waitresses at the Union Hotel serve up traditional Italian food in a family-style setting. The raviolis are particularly good. A local favorite since 1879, the restaurant has changed little over the years; the red-checked tablecloths and black-and-white photos of old Occidental still work for this family-owned restaurant. Italian menu. Lunch, dinner. Outdoor seating. $$

Petaluma

JOHNNY GARLIC'S CALIFORNIA PASTA GRILL.
840 Petaluma Blvd N, Petaluma (94952). Phone 707/781-9111. www.johnnygarlics.com. Specializing in grilled fare and pastas, they also offer a large selection of local wines and microbrews. American menu. Lunch, dinner. $$

Santa Rosa

CATTLEMENS RESTAURANT.
2400 Midway Dr, Santa Rosa (95401). Phone 707/546-1446. www.cattlemensrestaurants.com. A casual steakhouse with a Western attitude and a separate bar. You'll find generous portions and the locally famous "bean girl," with her ever-full crock of beans. Steak menu. Dinner. $$

Sebastopol

COFFEE CATZ.
6761 Sebastopol Ave, Sebastopol (95472). Phone 707/829-6600. The coffee is roasted on site at this casual café. Simple fare includes homemade soups and sandwiches. American menu. Breakfast, lunch, dinner. $

Windsor

POWELL'S SWEET SHOPPE.
720 McClelland Dr, Windsor (95492). Phone 707/836-0808. Not so much a place to eat a meal as it is a place to feed your nostalgic soul, this old-fashioned candy store is the next best thing to Willie Wonka's Chocolate Factory. Oversized peppermint sticks mingle with gourmet chocolates and confections that baby boomers will recognize from their childhood. Open daily. $

NORTH BAY

Bodega Bay

SANDPIPER DOCKSIDE CAFÉ & RESTAURANT.
1410 Bay Flat Rd, Bodega Bay (94923). Phone 707/875-2278. You're more likely to dine with locals here than tourists. Adjacent to Spud Point Marina, watch as the boats unload the catch of the day. Seafood menu. Breakfast, lunch, dinner. $$

Graton

WILLOW WOOD MARKET CAFÉ.
9020 Graton Rd, Graton (95444). Phone 707/823-0233. The recently renovated small town of Graton (just a few miles from Sebastopol) is home to this funky little restaurant that serves up some unique entrées. Try the Open Egg Sandwich, an unexpected blend of egg salad and pesto—it's fabulous. American menu. Breakfast, lunch, dinner. $

Healdsburg

BEAR REPUBLIC BREWING COMPANY.
345 Healdsburg Ave, Healdsburg (95448). Phone 707/431-7258. www.bearrepublic.com. In addition to specialty beers, Bear Republic has a full menu, but start with an appetizer, known here as the Bear Necessities. Customize a burger with choices such as beef, turkey, chicken breast, or vegetarian. American menu. Lunch, dinner. Outdoor seating. $$

SONOMA VALLEY

Sonoma

SONOMA CHEESE FACTORY.
2 Spain St, Sonoma (95476). Phone 707/996-1931; toll-free 800/535-2855. Sample numerous varieties of cheeses, such as pepper jack or Mediterranean, all made on-site. Pick up a picnic lunch or order a burger to enjoy on the outside patio. Peek through a window into the cheese-making facility. Deli menu. Lunch. Outdoor seating. $

For more dining recommendations, go to www.mobiltravelguide.com

SIDETRIP

California's Gold Country
Placerville, CA

In 1848, James Marshall plucked a gold nugget from the American River, setting in motion one of the greatest migrations in the history of the United States. Mining towns popped up overnight. Today, many of those old towns remain, offering visitors a glimpse of California in the 1850s. Traveling scenic Highway 49 (a highway in name only), you'll pass through old mining towns and near enough to a number of state parks to warrant a stop (www.parks.ca.gov, unless otherwise noted).

In Coloma, visitors to **Marshall Gold Discovery State Historic Park** will find a full-size reconstruction of Sutter's Mill. Modern-day treasure seekers can try their hand at panning for gold in the American River—an occasional visitor gets lucky.

Nine miles south of Coloma, Placerville's main street boasts **Placerville Hardware** (phone 530/622-1151). In operation for more than 150 years, the store boasts original wood floors and an eclectic assortment of hardware and household items. Downtown Placerville offers a couple of great places to eat; sample the fabulous oversized cinnamon rolls at **Sweetie Pies** (phone 530/642-0128) or check out the gourmet potpies at **Z Pie** (phone 530/621-2626). The **El Dorado County Historical Museum** (www.co-el-dorado.ca.us/museum) is nearby.

Jackson is a good place to fill the gas tank or stop for groceries. Eight miles east of Jackson is **Indian Grinding Rock State Historic Park** (use Hwy 88), where you'll see a reconstructed Miwok village, Native American petroglyphs, and an outcropping of marbleized limestone with an amazing 1,185 mortar holes.

Named for legendary guide Kit Carson, Carson Pass offers visitors amazing views of the Sierra Nevada mountain range.

Back on Highway 49, head south toward Angels Camp. A good half-day diversion is **Calaveras Big Trees State Park,** 4 miles northeast of Arnold along Highway 4. This 6,500-acre state park features groves of giant sequoias and mixed conifer forests, as well as opportunities for hiking and camping. Wrap up your tour of Gold Country with visits to **Columbia State Historic Park,** a restored 1850s gold town, and **Railtown 1897 State Historic Park** (www.csrmf.org/railtown), home to one of America's last authentic operating railroad roundhouses.

For more Placerville recommendations, go to www.mobiltravelguide.com

NASCAR followers are riveted by the action as racers roar through Turn 1 at the speedway.

Kansas Speedway

Kansas City, KS

12

Ryan Newman celebrates his 2003 NASCAR NEXTEL Cup Series Banquet 400 victory by smoking his tires in the front stretch.

TRACK FACTS

KANSAS SPEEDWAY. 400 Speedway Blvd, Kansas City (66111). Phone 913/328-7223. www.kansasspeedway.com.

SECURITY. No coolers, ice, glass containers, alcohol, umbrellas, folding chairs, strollers, bicycles, or outside food or beverages allowed. You may bring in one soft-sided 6 x 6 x 12-inch bag (purse, camera bag, etc.).

PARKING. Parking lots, which are free, open at 6 am. Motorcyclists park on Watkins Glen Drive off State Avenue. Guests with disabilities may park in Lots 2, 3, and 7. Your state-issued hangtag serves as a pass; otherwise, call the racetrack. Shuttles operate to and from the ADA-compliant track. Tow vehicles, available from 7:30 am to 5 pm, help with lockouts, flat tires, and minor repairs. Ask track staff or visit the main security office in Lot 25 (northeast side).

FIRST AID. Medical help is available at street level beneath the grandstand, one under Sections 122/222 and the other under Sections 121/221. An infield care center is available. The nearest hospital is Providence Medical Center (8929 Parallel Pkwy, phone 913/596-4000).

CONCESSIONS. Regulars tailgate for breakfast because by 10 am, the track is jam-packed. Get fixin's the night before to save time. The nearest convenience store is at Phillips 66, 110th Street and Parallel Avenue (phone 913/788-0950). Don't miss the barbecue at the many concession stands scattered throughout the speedway.

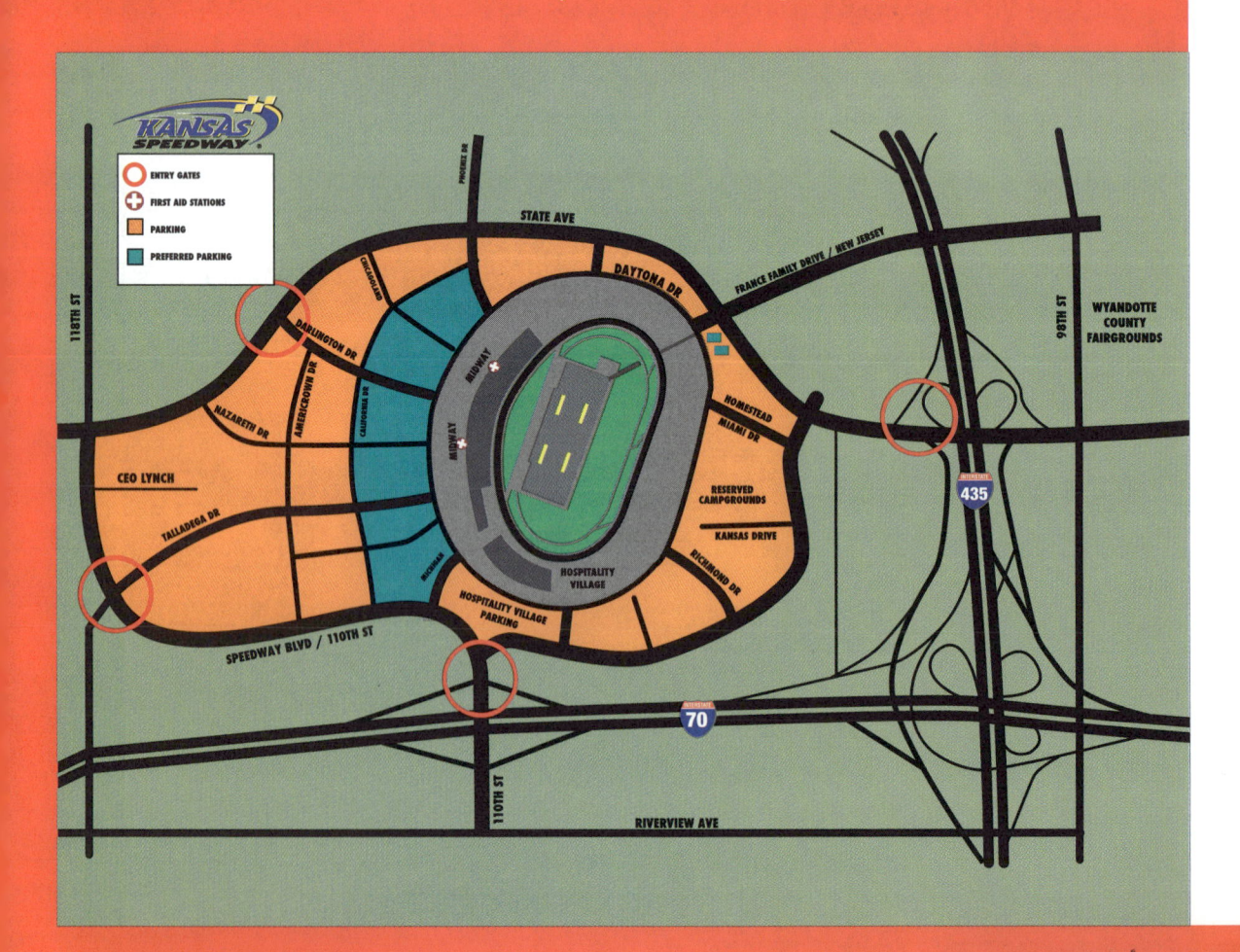

KANSAS SPEEDWAY, KS 211

An aerial view of the track once the race has gotten underway.

GETTING TICKETS

Tickets can only be purchased for the entire season. It's possible to buy them online at www.kansasspeedway.com or by calling 913/328-7223; toll-free 866/460-7223.

The grandstands at Kansas, which can accommodate almost 82,000 fans, are packed for the NASCAR NEXTEL Cup Series Banquet 400.

GETTING AROUND

The speedway has three main entrances: Talladega Dr, off Speedway Blvd, and Darlington and Nazareth drives off State Ave. Before the event on race days, all these streets run one way toward the track. Conversely, they will run one way from the track after the race.

Traffic on race days will be heavy, but it's especially thick between 7 am and 10 am. Since the parking lots are open at 6 am, many fans arrive early and tailgate for breakfast. The grandstand gates swing open at 8 am.

From I-70, take the 110th St exit and follow the instructions of traffic control officers to Speedway Blvd all the way to the track. From Hwy 7, take State Ave east to the track. From I-435, take I-70 W to 110th St.

If you're arriving for the race on a motorcycle, the track has special parking on Watkins Glen Dr. A shuttle will ferry fans to the front gates of the speedway.

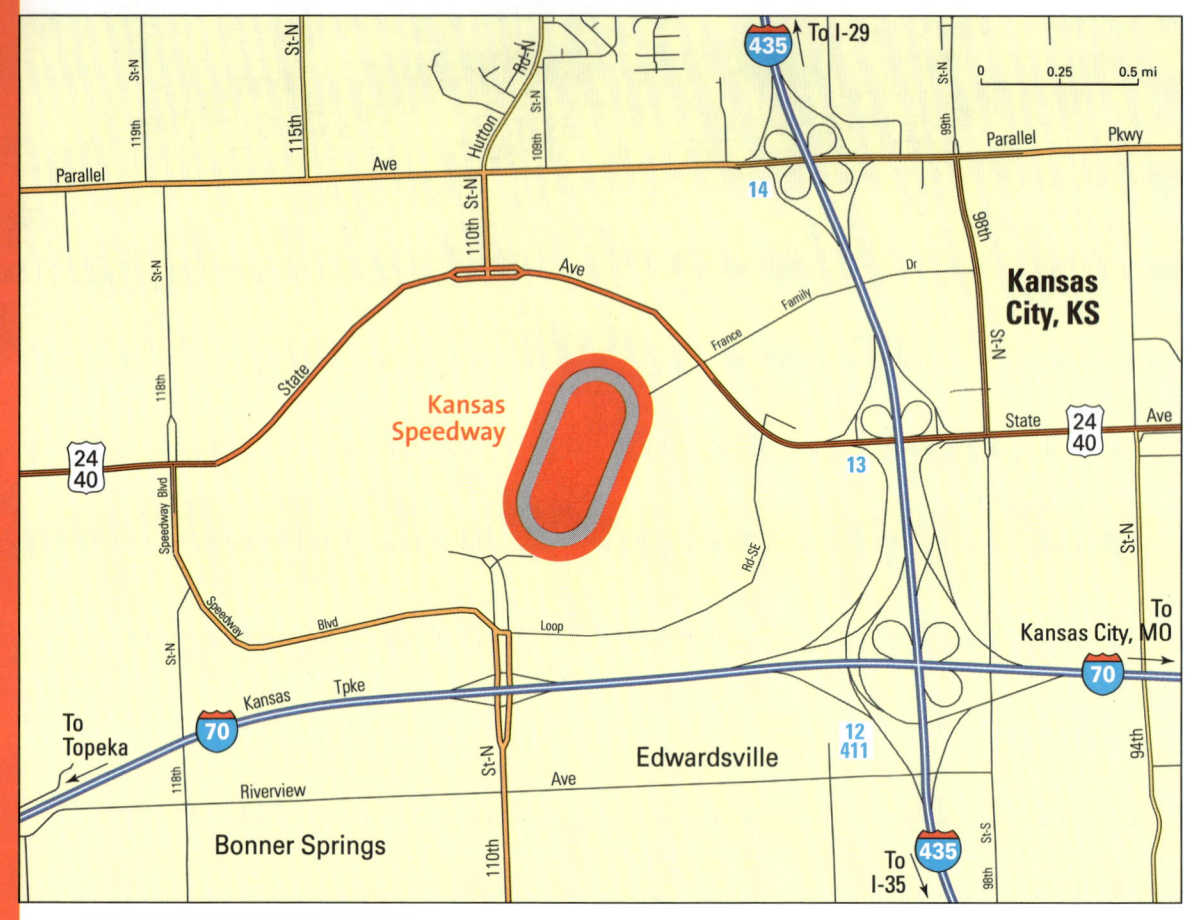

KANSAS CITY POLE POSITION:
The 10 miles surrounding Kansas Speedway.

ONE CITY, TWO STATES

Driving into the Kansas City area, you'll pass through miles and miles of waving wheat and picturesque farms before reaching the more metropolitan area. Comprising 1,200 acres, the Kansas Speedway is at the intersection of Interstates 435 and 70, just 15 miles west of downtown Kansas City, providing plenty of nearby options for pre- and post-race sightseeing, dining, and recreation.

July is hotter than a race car engine, so drink plenty of water and protect your skin. Summer's average highs are 90 degrees and evenings are only slightly cooler—hey, the Kansas state motto isn't "To the stars through difficulties" for nothing. It's not unheard of in October to come home from the track with an unexpected sunburn, so keep sunblock handy but layer up: temperatures reach the high 60s and drop to the upper 40s. Light snow is also possible.

NOT IN KANSAS ANYMORE

With few cabs and little public transportation, Kansas City is no place to be without a car. Rent one or bring your own.

Downtown Kansas City closes up at 5 pm when all the government workers go home, so you won't find too many dining and lodging options in the city proper. If you want to stay up late, visit other neighborhoods like the 18th and Vine District, home to blues and jazz clubs. One highlight is the **Blue Room,** which is part of the **American Jazz Museum** (1616 E 18th St, Kansas City, phone 816/474-8463; call for ticket information).

KANSAS CITY CALENDAR

JULY 2, 2005
NASCAR Craftsman Truck Series

JULY 15–16, 2005
Amelia Earhart Festival. Santa Fe Depot, Atchison, KS (66002). Phone 913/367-2427. www.atchisonhistory.org. Carnival rides, fireworks, ice cream socials, outdoor concerts, and a fun run.

OCTOBER, 2005
Renaissance Festival. Adjacent to Agricultural Hall of Fame, Bonner Springs, KS (64111). Phone 816/561-8005; toll-free 800/373-0357. www.kcrenfest.com. Period costumes, games, entertainment, food, jousts, and pony rides. Weekends through Oct 16.

OCTOBER 8, 2005
NASCAR Busch Series

OCTOBER 9, 2005
NASCAR NEXTEL Cup Series

OCTOBER 26–NOVEMBER 3, 2005
Neewollah Festival. Riverside Park, downtown Independence, KS (67301). Phone 620/331-2005. www.neewollah.com. Chili cook-off, live blues, parades, street acts, a musical, and a grand ball.

OCTOBER 28–31, 2005
Boo at the Zoo. Kansas City Zoo, 6800 Zoo Dr, Kansas City, MO (64108). Phone 816/513-5700. www.kansascityzoo.org. Safe trick-or-treating, hands-on crafts, not-very-scary haunted house.

SHOP TALK

Shopping is getting a lot easier for racing fans since the **Village West** retail complex opened in 2003. You can't beat the proximity—it's right across the street from the speedway—and the number of stores continues to grow. Cabela's, one of the largest sporting goods retailers in the world, offers a wide array of camping gear and accessories. Nebraska Furniture Mart sprawls over 712,000 square feet and offers hundreds of electronic products. More retailers are on the way. *1601 Village West Pkwy, Kansas City (66111). www.villagewest.us.*

There are plenty of places to hear some great musicians in Kansas City.

KANSAS CITY OUTFIELD:
The 60 miles surrounding Kansas Speedway.

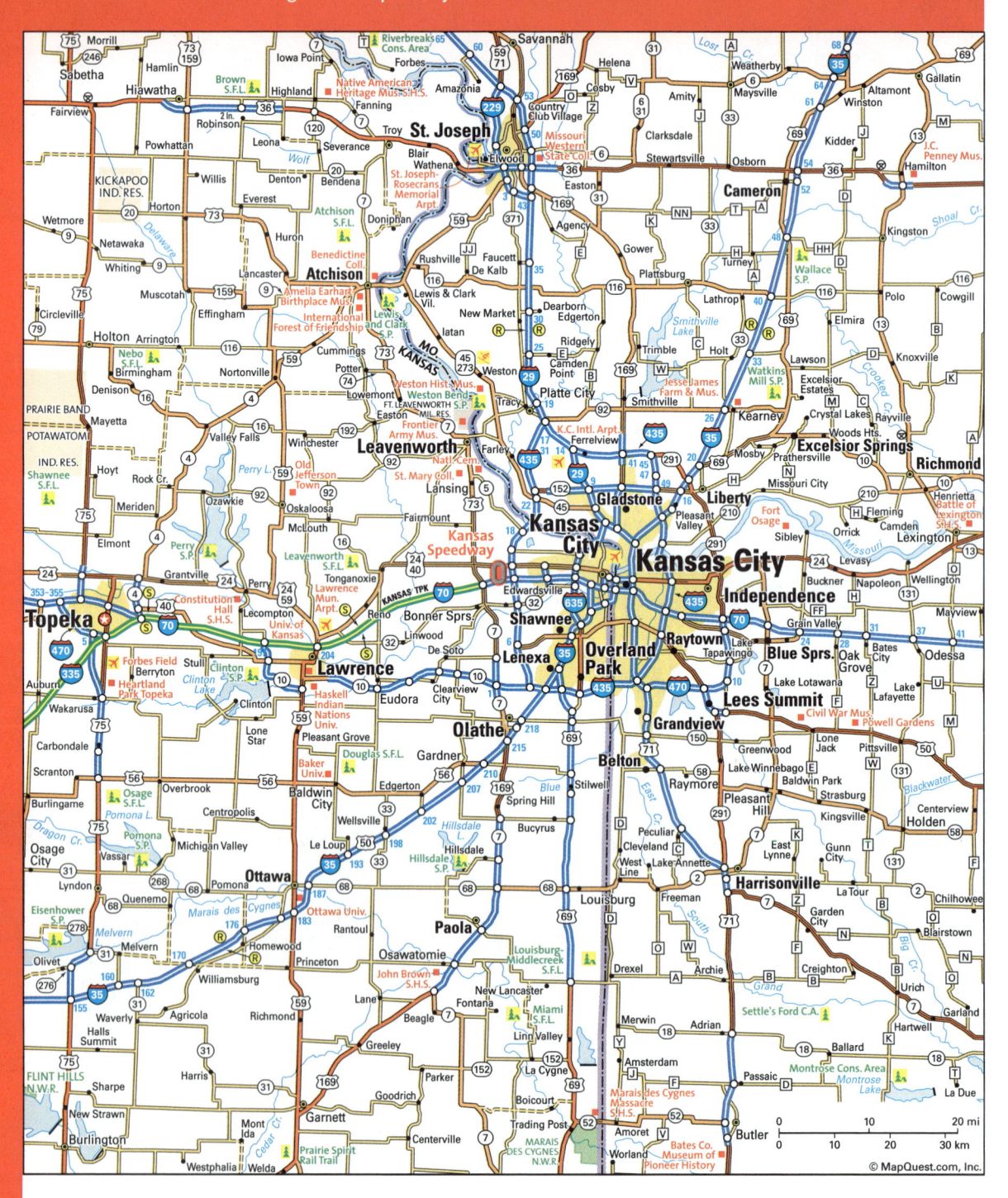

SEE

ATTRACTIONS

Kansas City, KS

LAKESIDE SPEEDWAY.
5615 Wolcott Dr, Kansas City (66109). Phone 913/299-2040. www.lakesidespeedway.net. Lakeside Speedway, located about 8 miles from Kansas Speedway, is a 1/2-mile oval that was converted from asphalt to dirt in 2000. Lakeside hosts the NASCAR Dodge Weekly Series on Friday nights from April to mid-September.

THE WOODLANDS.
9700 Leavenworth Rd, Kansas City (66109). Phone 913/299-3434; toll-free 800/695-7223. www.woodlandskc.com. Check out greyhound racing year-round and thoroughbred and quarterhorse racing in summer and autumn. At the Weiner Dog Nationals, 64 randomly chosen dachshunds compete for the Grand Champion title. RV parking and camping available (fee; phone 913/596-5978; shuttle runs from facility to campgrounds). Call for race dates and post times. **FREE**

Kansas City, MO

KANSAS CITY ZOO.
I-435 and Hwy 71 at Swope Park, 6800 Zoo Dr, Kansas City (64132). Phone 816/516-5700. www.kansascityzoo.org. Explore 200 acres landscaped to resemble natural animal habitats. Sea lion and wild bird shows; IMAX Theater on grounds. (Daily 9:30 am-5 pm; closed holidays). **$$**

UNION STATION.
30 W Pershing Rd, Kansas City (64108). Phone 816/460-2020. Train aficionados will enjoy the history of this refurbished station while kids explore Science City, an interactive museum. Munch on a treat from the Rocky Mountain Chocolate Factory. (Daily 6 am-midnight. Individual shop times vary) **$$**

WORLDS OF FUN/OCEANS OF FUN.
4545 Worlds of Fun Ave, Kansas City (64161). Phone 816/454-4545. www.worldsoffun.com. An amusement park adjacent to a water park: don't say we didn't warn you about the ThunderHawk. (Apr-May, Sept-Oct: Mon-Fri 10 am-10 pm, Sat-Sun 10 am-8 pm; June-Aug: Mon-Fri 10 am-10 pm, Sat-Sun 10 am-midnight) **$$$$**

Leavenworth, KS

FRONTIER ARMY MUSEUM.
7th and Metropolitan aves, Leavenworth (66048). Reynolds Ave within Fort Leavenworth. Phone 913/684-3191. Discover the history of Fort Leavenworth and the United States Regular Army on the Frontier. See historic army uniforms, weapons, and equipment, including a 1917 JN4D Jenny biplane and the carriage that Abraham Lincoln traveled in when he visited in 1859. (Mon-Fri 9 am-4 pm, Sat 10 am-4 pm; closed Sun, holidays)

Olathe, KS

THE GREAT MALL OF THE GREAT PLAINS.
20700 W 151st St, Olathe (66061). Take exit 215 off I-35. Phone 913/829-6277. www.greatmallgreatplains.com. Kansas's largest outlet mall offers entertainment for children and adults, great food, great shopping, and more. (Mon-Sat 10 am-9 pm, Sun noon-6 pm)

Overland Park, KS

DEANNA ROSE CHILDREN'S FARMSTEAD.
138th St and Switzer, Overland Park (66221). Phone 913/897-2360. Feed and pet farm animals, hop on a horse-drawn wagon, and walk through a replica of an early 1900s Kansas farmhouse. Playground equipment. (Oct-May: daily 9 am-5 pm; June-Sept: daily 9 am-8 pm) **FREE**

Topeka, KS

GAGE PARK.
9635 SW Gage Blvd, Topeka (66603). Phone 785/368-3700. Tennis, swimming, softball, and volleyball facilities are available here, along with playground equipment for different ages and abilities. The newly restored carousel was built in 1908 and operates from 10 am to 8 pm (75 cents) during the summer and on weekends only in September and October. A mini-train ($) runs along the park for a pretty view. Park (sunrise-sunset). Home to the Topeka Zoo (phone 785/368-9180; daily 9 am-5 pm). **FREE**

SEE ATTRACTIONS

LAKE SHAWNEE RECREATIONAL AREA.
3137 SE 29th St, Topeka (66605). Phone 785/267-1156. Lake Shawnee, covering more than 400 acres, offers fishing, boating, sailing, and swimming and is surrounded by more than 1,500 acres of parkland with foot trails, a golf course, a marina, tennis courts, shelter houses, ball diamonds, and gardens. (Sunrise-sunset) **FREE**

For more attractions, go to www.mobiltravelguide.com

STAY

MOBIL STAR-RATED LODGINGS

Kansas City, MO

FAIRMONT KANSAS CITY AT THE PLAZA. ★★★
401 Ward Pkwy, Kansas City (64112). Phone 816/756-1500; toll-free 800/257-7544. www.fairmont.com. This elegant and contemporary hotel is located within the exclusive Plaza shopping and dining area. Guest rooms and suites are comfortably stylish and are equipped with modern amenities and luxurious details. A 24-hour business center and fitness center with outdoor pool and spa treatments are among the additional perks. The Oak Room restaurant features steaks and chops. 366 rooms, 12 story. Pets accepted; fee. Check-in 3 pm, check-out noon. High-speed Internet access. Restaurant, bar. Fitness room. Outdoor pool, children's pool. Airport transportation available. Business center. **$$**

HOTEL PHILLIPS. ★★★
106 W 12th St, Kansas City (64105). Phone 816/221-7000; toll-free 800/433-1426. www.hotelphillips.com. Located in the heart of downtown, this intimate boutique hotel is a convenient base for business travelers. Seductive Art Deco furnishings and gracious service make this hotel a standout. While the historic integrity of this 1931 landmark has been preserved, modern amenities have been added to the plush rooms and suites. 217 rooms, 20 story. Check-in 3 pm, check-out noon. High-speed Internet access. Two restaurants, two bars. Fitness room. Airport transportation available. Business center. **$**

HOTEL SAVOY. ★★
219 W 9th St, Kansas City (64105). Phone 816/842-3575; toll-free 800/728-6922. This restored 1888 landmark building features original architectural details such as stained and leaded glass, tile floors, and tin ceilings. The Savoy Grille is located on the property, and there are many attractions nearby. 22 rooms, 6 story. Complimentary full breakfast. Check-in 3 pm, check-out 1 pm. Restaurant, bar. **$**

HYATT REGENCY CROWN CENTER. ★★★
2345 McGee St, Kansas City (64108). Phone 816/421-1234; toll-free 888/591-1234. www.hyatt.com. Connected to the Crown Complex by an elevated walkway and near the Truman Sports Complex, an amusement park, and the international airport, this hotel is convenient and comfortable. 731 rooms, 42 story. Pets accepted, some restrictions. Check-in

---

PIT PASS

For race weekend, the **Pit Stop Pub** at the Kansas Speedway serves up catered meals and icy cold ones. The Pub changes themes annually, so every race season there's something new. You can even participate in question-and-answer periods with NASCAR NEXTEL Cup and NASCAR Busch Series drivers, plus get a tour of Pit Road (not something your average fan experiences). Limited spaces available, and it's kinda pricey: expect to spend $300 per person for the weekend. To purchase a Pit Stop package, call 913/328-3317.

3 pm, check-out noon. High-speed Internet access, wireless Internet access. Five restaurants, bar. Fitness room. Outdoor pool, whirlpool. Tennis. Airport transportation available. Business center. **$$**

MARRIOTT KANSAS CITY DOWNTOWN. ★★★
200 W 12th St, Kansas City (64105). Phone 816/421-6800; toll-free 800/228-9290. www.marriott.com. This large hotel is located downtown near the city market, family attractions, and more. 983 rooms, 22 story. Pets accepted. Check-in 3 pm, check-out noon. High-speed Internet access, wireless Internet access. Two restaurants, two bars. Fitness room (fee). Indoor pool. Airport transportation available. Business center. **$$**

THE RAPHAEL HOTEL. ★★★
325 Ward Pkwy, Kansas City (64112). Phone 816/756-3800; toll-free 800/695-8284. www.raphaelkc.com. This hotel is located in the midtown area near shops, restaurants, and other attractions for visitors to the area. 123 rooms, 9 story. Check-in 4 pm, check-out 1 pm. High-speed Internet access. Restaurant, bar. Fitness room. Airport transportation available. Business center. **$$**

Lawrence, KS

ELDRIDGE HOTEL. ★★★
7th and Massachusetts sts, Lawrence (66044). Phone 785/749-5011; toll-free 800/527-0909. www.eldridgehotel.com. This historic inn, with its unique history dating back to the Civil War, is located near the University of Kansas. Built in 1855 as a Free State hostelry for abolitionists, many fights during the Civil War took place here. 48 rooms, 5 story. Check-in 3 pm, check-out noon. Wireless Internet access. Restaurant, bar. **$**

Overland Park, KS

EMBASSY SUITES HOTEL KANSAS CITY—OVERLAND PARK. ★★
10601 Metcalf Ave, Overland Park (66212). Just off I-435. Phone 913/649-7060; toll-free 800/362-2779. www.embassysuites.com. This hotel is located in the heart of the south Kansas City business district. 199 rooms, 7 story, all suites. Complimentary full breakfast. Check-in 3 pm, check-out noon. Restaurant, bar. Fitness room. Indoor pool, whirlpool. Business center. **$**

HOLIDAY INN OVERLAND PARK—WEST. ★★
8787 Reeder Rd, Overland Park (66214). Phone 913/888-8440; toll-free 800/465-4329. www.holiday-inn.com. This hotel resides at a quiet location in the suburbs with restaurants and taverns nearby. 191 rooms, 8 story. Check-in 3 pm, check-out noon. Restaurant, bar. Fitness room. Indoor pool, outdoor pool, whirlpool. Airport transportation available. Business center. **$**

LOCAL RECOMMENDATIONS

Kansas City, KS

BEST WESTERN INN AND CONFERENCE CENTER.
501 Southwest Blvd, Kansas City (66103). Phone 913/677-3060; toll-free 800/780-7234. www.bestwestern.com. This hotel is close to the convention center and Kemper and American Royal arenas. 113 rooms, 2 story. Complimentary continental breakfast. Check-in 1 pm, check-out noon. Outdoor pool, whirlpool. Airport transportation available. **$**

Independence, MO

BEST WESTERN TRUMAN INN.
4048 S Lynn Ct, Independence (64055). Phone 816/254-0100; toll-free 800/780-7234. www.bestwestern.com. This hotel is just a short drive from all the area attractions including the Truman Home & Museum. 105 rooms, 2 story. Complimentary continental breakfast. Check-in 2 pm, check-out 11 am. Outdoor pool. **$**

Kansas City, MO

BEST WESTERN COUNTRY INN AIRPORT.
11900 NW Plaza Cir, Kansas City (64153). Phone 816/464-2002; toll-free 800/780-7234. www.bestwestern.com. Located just 1 mile from the Kansas City International Airport, this modern hotel features up-to-date amenities with country charm. 43 rooms, 2 story. Complimentary continental breakfast. Check-in 3 pm, check-out noon. Airport transportation available. **$**

BEST WESTERN COUNTRY INN NEAR WORLDS OF FUN.
7100 NE Parvin Rd, Kansas City (64117). Phone 816/453-3355; toll-free 800/780-7234. www.bestwestern.com. This cozy hotel provides a friendly staff and a relaxed atmosphere in contrast to the action at nearby Worlds of Fun and the Kansas Speedway.

STAY LOCAL RECOMMENDATIONS

86 rooms, 2 story. Complimentary continental breakfast. Check-in 3 pm, check-out 11 am. Outdoor pool, whirlpool. $

BEST WESTERN COUNTRY INN NORTH.
2633 NE 43rd St, Kansas City (64117). Phone 816/459-7222; toll-free 800/780-7234. www.bestwestern.com. The combination of great value, great amenities, and a comfortable, homey atmosphere make this an ideal place for business travelers and families. 44 rooms, 2 story. Complimentary continental breakfast. Check-in 3 pm, check-out 11 am. Outdoor pool. $

BEST WESTERN SEVILLE PLAZA HOTEL.
4309 Main St, Kansas City (64111). Phone 816/561-9600; toll-free 800/780-7234. www.bestwestern.com. Freshly renovated, the downtown location of this upgraded hotel makes it a natural choice for those wanting to get out and see the city. Within walking distance is the upscale Country Club Plaza shopping center. 77 rooms, 4 story. Complimentary continental breakfast. Check-in 3 pm, check-out 11 am. High-speed Internet access. Laundry services. Fitness room. Business center. $

CHATEAU AVALON.
701 Village West Pkwy, Kansas City (66111). Phone 913/596-6000; toll-free 877/522-8256. www.chateauavalon.net. 62 rooms, 3 story. No children allowed. Complimentary continental breakfast. Check-in 5 pm, check-out 11 am. Restaurant. $

HAMPTON INN.
1051 N Cambridge, Kansas City (64120). Phone 816/483-7900; toll-free 800/426-7866. www.hamptoninn.com. This hotel is 7 miles from downtown Kansas City and even closer to the Historic River Market. 131 rooms, 1 story. Complimentary continental breakfast. Check-in 3 pm, check-out noon. Wireless Internet access. Laundry services. Outdoor pool, whirlpool. $

Kearney, MO

BEST WESTERN KEARNEY INN.
601 Centerville Ave, Kearney (64060). Phone 816/628-5000; toll-free 866/626-5005. www.bestwestern.com. Stay here and get the best of both worlds: convenience to Kansas City in a serene setting near Smithville Lake, with its 175 miles of shoreline and close proximity to area attractions. 39 rooms, 2 story. Complimentary continental breakfast. Check-in 2 pm, check-out 11 am. High-speed Internet access. Indoor pool. $

Platte City, MO

BEST WESTERN PRAIRIE VIEW INN & SUITES.
2512 NW Prairie View Rd, Platte City (64079). Phone 816/858-0200; toll-free 800/780-7234. www.bestwestern.com. Set among a beautiful prairie landscape, this hotel features a cozy lodgelike lobby, updated rooms, and an ideal location near the Kansas Speedway, Fort Leavenworth, and historic Weston. 72 rooms, 3 story. Pets accepted, some restrictions; fee. Complimentary continental breakfast. Check-in 4 pm, check-out 11 am. Laundry services. Indoor pool, whirlpool. $

➤ For more lodging recommendations, go to www.mobiltravelguide.com

EAT

MOBIL STAR-RATED RESTAURANTS

Independence, MO

V'S ITALIANO. ★★
10819 Hwy 40 E, Independence (64055). Phone 816/353-1241. www.vsrestaurant.com. Forty years ago, this place started off as a little café, but my, how it's grown. A little off the beaten path, it's worth the drive. American, Italian menu. Lunch, dinner. Closed Thanksgiving, Dec 25. Bar. Children's menu. Casual attire. $$

Kansas City, MO

BERLINER BEAR. ★
7815 Wornall Rd, Kansas City (64114). Phone 816/444-2828. German menu. Lunch, dinner. Closed Mon; holidays. Bar. Children's menu. Casual attire. $$

CALIFORNOS. ★★
4124 Pennsylvania, Kansas City (64111). Phone 816/531-7878. www.californos.com. American menu. Lunch, dinner. Closed Sun; holidays. Bar. Casual attire. Reservations recommended. Valet parking. Outdoor seating. $$

CASCONE'S ITALIAN RESTAURANT. ★★
3733 N Oak, Kansas City (64116). Phone 816/454-7977. www.cascones.com. Italian menu. Lunch, dinner. Closed holidays. Bar. Children's menu. Casual attire. Reservations recommended. Outdoor seating. **$$**

CHAPELL'S. ★★
323 Armour Rd, North Kansas City (64116). Phone 816/421-0002. This place has an enormous collection of sports memorabilia and is a hit with the college kids. You can while away many a post-race hour gawking at the surroundings. Steak menu. Lunch, dinner. Closed Jan 1, Thanksgiving, Dec 25. Bar. Children's menu. Casual attire. **$$**

CLASSIC CUP CAFÉ. ★★
301 W 47th St, Kansas City (64112). Phone 816/753-1840. www.classiccup.com. This casual, European-style bistro and wine cellar is located in downtown's Country Club Plaza. American menu. Breakfast, lunch, dinner, Sun brunch. Closed holidays. Bar. Casual attire. Outdoor seating. **$$**

FIORELLA'S JACK STACK BAR-B-Q. ★★★
13441 Holmes St, Kansas City (64145). Phone 816/942-9141; toll-free 877/419-7427. www.jackstackbbq.com. Barbecue menu. Lunch, dinner, brunch. Closed Thanksgiving, Dec 25. Children's menu. Casual attire. Reservations recommended. Outdoor seating. **$$**

GOLDEN OX. ★★
1600 Genessee, Kansas City (64102). Phone 816/842-2866. www.goldenox.com. Another classic, down in the old stockyard area of the West Bottoms. The Ox has been serving steaks to hungry Kansas Citians for 55 years—they must be doing something right. Steak menu. Lunch, dinner. Closed Jan 1, Dec 25. Bar. Children's menu. Casual attire. **$$$**

JESS & JIM'S STEAKHOUSE. ★★
517 E 135th St, Kansas City (64145). Phone 816/941-9499. www.jessandjims.com. Steak menu. Lunch, dinner. Closed holidays. Bar. Children's menu. Casual attire. Reservations recommended. **$$$**

O'DOWD'S LITTLE DUBLIN. ★★★
4742 Pennsylvania Ave, Kansas City (64112). Phone 816/561-2700. www.odowdslittledublin.com. This authentic Irish pub, built in Ireland then shipped here, serves the best fish and chips in town. Irish menu. Lunch, dinner, late-night. Closed Memorial Day. Bar. Children's menu. Casual attire. Reservations recommended. Outdoor seating. **$**

PLAZA III—THE STEAKHOUSE. ★★★
4749 Pennsylvania Ave, Kansas City (64112). Phone 816/753-0000. www.dineoutkc.com/plaza3. The epitome of the Kansas City steakhouse, with USDA prime aged cuts of Midwestern beef, chops, fresh fish, and lobster. Lunch includes their famous steak soup. Steak menu. Lunch, dinner. Closed holidays. Bar. Children's menu. Business casual attire. Reservations recommended. Valet parking. **$$$**

Overland Park, KS

DICK CLARK'S AMERICAN BANDSTAND GRILL. ★
10975 Metcalf Ave, Overland Park (66210). Phone 913/451-1600. www.crghospitality.com/abgrill. The pictures and memorabilia on the walls depict eras of rock and roll. American menu. Lunch, dinner, late-night. Closed Thanksgiving, Dec 25. Bar. Children's menu. Casual attire. **$$**

K.C. MASTERPIECE. ★★
10985 Metcalf Ave, Overland Park (66210). Phone 913/345-1199. www.kcmrestaurants.com. Barbecue menu. Lunch, dinner, brunch. Closed Thanksgiving, Dec 25. Bar. Children's menu. Casual attire. **$$**

FAN FAVORITE

The best souvenir available at Kansas Speedway? An actual tire used by a race car that day for about $10, less than a T-shirt would set you back at some other sports event. To get yours, go to the infield about an hour after the race, when crews are packing up.

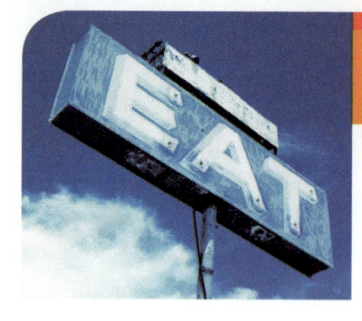

ROAD FOOD

With all the barbecue here, Kansas City is no place to be a vegetarian. Don't leave without tasting **Arthur Bryant's** ★ can't-miss barbecue, located at the speedway. Barbecue menu. Lunch, dinner. $ *1702 Village West Pkwy, Kansas City, KS (66111). Phone 913/788-7500. Also at 1727 Brooklyn Ave, Kansas City, MO (64127). Phone 816/231-1123. www.arthurbryantsbbq.com.* You'll also want to gnaw on some ribs at **Gates Bar-B-Q**, which offers wet and dry versions. Barbecue menu. Lunch, dinner. $ *1026 State Ave, Kansas City, KS (66102). Phone 913/621-1134. www.gatesbbq.com.*

LOCAL RECOMMENDATIONS

Kansas City, MO

BRAVO CUCINA ITALIANO.
7301 NW 87th St, Kansas City (64138). Phone 816/741-4114. www.bravoitalian.com. The open kitchen lets you see what's cooking. Menu choices for families and every diet, even carb counters (yes, at an Italian restaurant). Choose terrace seating, weather permitting. Italian menu. Lunch, dinner. Casual attire. Outdoor seating. **$$**

GOJO JAPANESE STEAK HOUSE.
4163 Broadway St, Kansas City (64111). Phone 816/561-2501. Sit around the grill and enjoy the chef's meticulous preparations—be ready to catch a shrimp or two thrown your way (in your mouth, not your hand). Good for lone rangers—you'll be seated with other diners who always end up talking. Japanese, steak menu. Lunch, dinner. Casual attire. Reservations recommended. **$$**

HEREFORD HOUSE.
2 E 20th St, Kansas City (64108). Phone 816/842-1080. www.herefordhouse.com. The Hereford House has been serving great steaks for 44 years. American menu. Lunch, dinner. Casual attire. Reservations recommended. **$$$**

MANNY'S.
207 Southwest Blvd, Kansas City (64108). Phone 816/474-7696. Downtown workers crowd this homey spot at lunchtime but you can usually snag a spot—and the freshly prepared food is worth the wait. Mexican menu. Lunch, dinner, brunch. Closed Sun. Bar. Children's menu. Casual attire. Reservations recommended. **$**

MIKE KELLEY'S WESTSIDER.
1515 Westport Rd, Kansas City (64111). Phone 816/931-9417. For Cajun fun, don't miss the Bon Ton Soul Accordian Band on Saturday nights. Even if you've never heard the word zydeco, you'll find your toe tapping along to these tunes. Cajun/Creole menu. Lunch, dinner, late-night. Closed Sun. Casual attire. **$$**

PONAK'S MEXICAN KITCHEN.
2856 Southwest Blvd, Kansas City (64108). Phone 816/753-5577. This eatery gets a thumbs-up for food although the waitstaff is a bit inconsistent. You're here for the food, and it's some of the best Mexican around. Mexican menu. Lunch, dinner. Bar. Casual attire. **$**

TANNER'S BAR AND GRILL.
420 NW Englewood Rd, Kansas City (64118). Phone 816/452-5252. A little pricier, but this sports venue, which attracts mostly the over-25 crowd, is one of the best-kept secrets in town. American menu. Lunch, dinner, late-night. Bar. Casual attire. **$**

Leawood, KS

YAHOOZ.
4701 Town Center Dr, Leawood (66211). Phone 913/451-8888. Yahooz offers "contemporary cowboy cuisine." The wood-burning fireplaces and leather furniture create a cozy atmosphere and the lively menu, with kids' choices, makes this a unique steakhouse. American, steak menu. Lunch, dinner. Bar. Children's menu. Reservations recommended. **$$$**

For more dining recommendations, go to www.mobiltravelguide.com

SIDETRIP

The Live Music Show Capital of the World
Branson, MO

Branson, Missouri, the thriving resort community considered the "Live Music Show Capital of the World," is about 225 miles from the speedway in the foothills of the Ozarks. Crowds and traffic won't stop you from having a great time. Choose from as many as 70 different shows, from Charley Pride, Doug Kershaw, and Kenny Rogers to Acrobats of China and Yakov Smirnoff. Some favorites include the Dixie Stampede, Dolly Parton's dinner and show with 32 horses and a cast of, seemingly, thousands. Shoji Tabuchi and Mickey Gilley in concert are not to be missed.

Prices for the shows range from $12 to $50 per person. Most shows are closed on Mondays. For information and details, call the Branson Tourism Center toll-free at 800/524-0222.

If your ears need a rest from music, go to the races—not NASCAR, though. Here, it's ostriches. Or take a brunch cruise with **American Star**, visit the **Hollywood Wax Museum**, take in an **IMAX** show, believe it or not at **Ripley's**, wander through the **Roy Rogers-Dale Evans Museum**, or watch the **Shepherd of the Hills Homestead** show.

Other picks, especially if the kids are along, include **Silver Dollar City** (399 Indian point Rd, Branson, phone toll-free 800/475-9370, www.silverdollarcity.com), a theme park that seeks to re-create daily life in the 1880s. It boasts nearly 20 rides, 60 shops, daily concerts, and festivals throughout the year. **White Water** park offers loads of attractions and rides.

For lodging, try the Best Westerns—either Center Pointe Inn or Music Capital Inn (phone toll-free 800/WESTERN). For campers: **America's Best Campground** (phone toll-free 800/671-4399); for RVers: **Branson Stagecoach RV Park** (phone toll-free 800/446-7110).

Three main lakes—Table Rock Lake, Bull Shoals Lake, and Lake Taneycomo—offer fishing, boating, water-skiing, and cruising, plus nature trails for outdoor enthusiasts.

After all that activity, you're bound to be hungry. Head to the **Branson Café, Mesquite Charlie's Steakhouse,** or **The Shack.**

Branson has more than 40 theaters offering live entertainment nightly. Historic Downtown Branson is at the junction of Hwy 376 and Hwy 76. For more details, go to www.branson.com.

For more Branson recommendations, go to www.mobiltravelguide.com

222

The annual NASCAR Busch Series race is the largest motorsports event in Kentucky and one of the largest annual events in the Greater Cincinnati/Northern Kentucky area.

www.mobiltravelguide.com 223

Kentucky Speedway

Sparta, Kentucky

13

Fireworks explode behind Kyle Busch, who celebrates his second career win at Kentucky Speedway in the 2004 NASCAR Busch Series Meijer 300 Presented by Oreo.

TRACK FACTS

KENTUCKY SPEEDWAY. 5120 Sparta Pike, Sparta (41086). Phone 859/567-3400. www.kentuckyspeedway.com.

SECURITY. Coolers and beverage containers of all types are prohibited. Noisemaking devices, video cameras, umbrellas, folding chairs, and pets are forbidden. Scanners and binoculars are fine. All bags are subject to search.

PARKING. Track parking can accommodate more than 30,000 cars, but it's tightly controlled, so don't expect a choice of spaces, and watch for mud on a rainy race day. Neighboring farmers turn fields into reasonably priced parking lots that may allow a quicker exit after races.

FIRST AID. Fan care centers are found on the main concourse behind Grandstands 2 and 4. A trauma center is located in the infield. Carroll County Hospital (309 11th St, Carrollton, phone 502/732-4321) is about 30 minutes away.

CONCESSIONS. Food and beverage stands are located at gates throughout the arena. Outback Steakhouse facilities are behind grandstands and in the infield. For driver merchandise, visit the fan center gift shop located in Turn 3. NASCAR souvenir trailers are grouped in front of the grandstand entrance. If you need to recharge your wallet, head for mobile ATMs near the main entrances at Gates 15 and 16.

Kentucky Speedway Location Map

KENTUCKY SPEEDWAY, KY **225**

Campers enjoy a unique view of the action when they choose to set up in the backstretch area of the speedway.

GETTING TICKETS

Tickets are available at the track's Turn 3 Fan Center and the main ticket office in nearby Fort Mitchell (2216 Dixie Hwy, Suite 200) or purchase at Meijer retail stores in the region. An easier option is to order via the Web (www.tickets.com) or by phone (toll-free 888/652-7223). Buy tickets early: prices rise $5 at the gate on race day. Ticket offices are located in the fan center and main entrances at Gates 15 and 16.

RV AND CAMPING

Many fans avoid traffic by simply camping at the speedway. About 2,000 general camping spaces are available off Speedway Boulevard ($30 per weekend). For $175 per weekend, 300 larger, reserved camping spaces sit outside of Turns 1 and 2, an easy walk to the grandstands. Pets are allowed here. Private RV parking is on the backstretch; spaces must be reserved for the entire season and there's often a waiting list, so call early.

GETTING AROUND

The speedway is located on I-71, just before the I-71 and I-75 split. Finding it is easy but backups start early on race day.

The most direct route is I-71 to Sparta. Signs direct cars to Exit 57 and RVs to Exit 55. From Exit 57, turn onto Hwy 35 north to speedway entrances. From Exit 55, turn onto Rte 1039 and follow directions. From Florence, head south on Hwy 42 to Warsaw and pick up Hwy 35 to the speedway. The surrounding area is rural and poorly lit at night, so stick with slow, sure highway traffic rather than trying to find your way out on country roads.

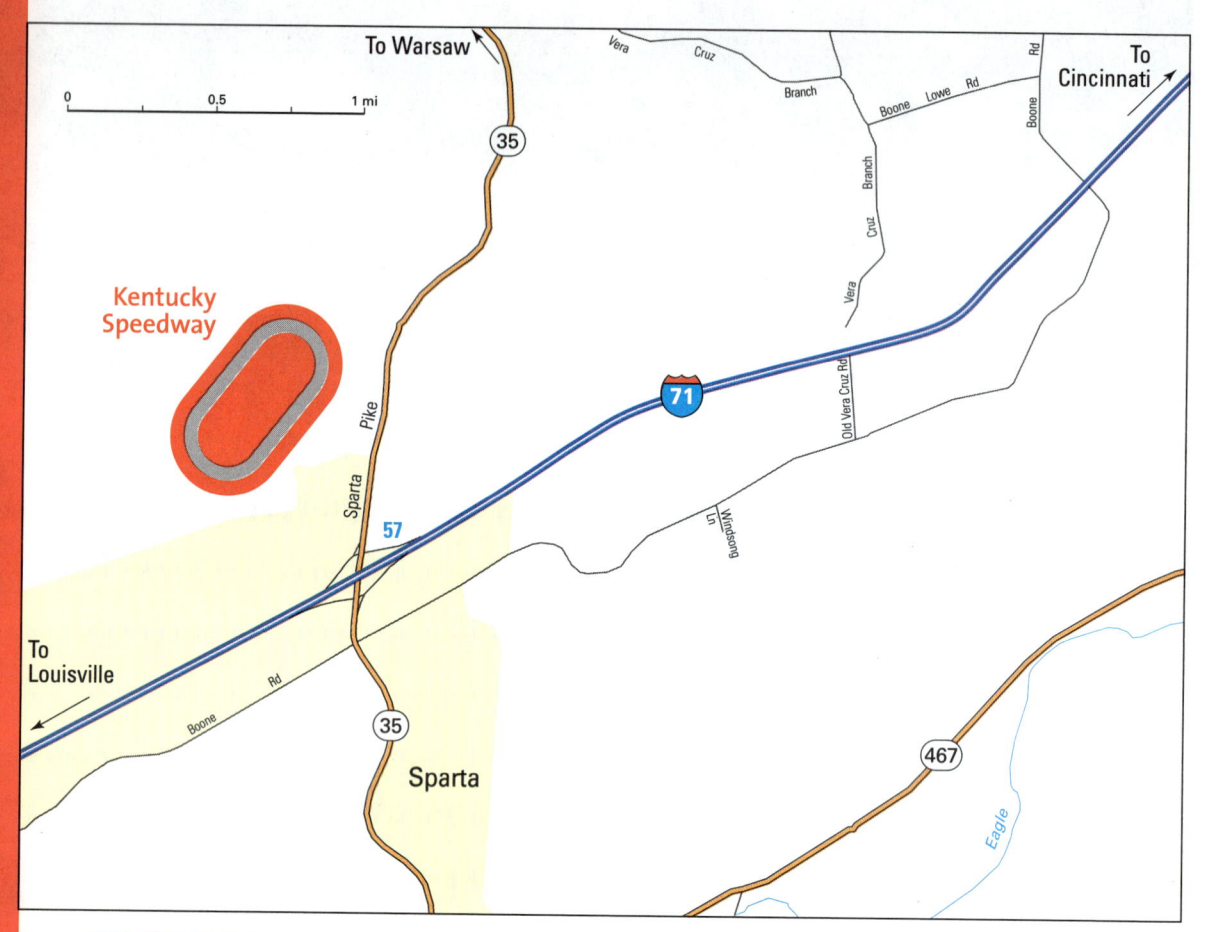

SPARTA POLE POSITION:
The 10 miles surrounding Kentucky Speedway.

FROM BLUEGRASS FARMS TO ROARING CARS

Northern Kentucky has been known for farmers and horse breeders since the 1800s, and they are still an important part of the landscape, so the region surrounding the Kentucky Speedway is dotted with small communities that enjoy a slower pace and quieter lifestyle than many other NASCAR cities. On a sell-out day at the track, Sparta, population 230, becomes the third-largest city in Kentucky behind Lexington and Louisville.

The speedway opened in June 2000 and sits on 1,000 acres of former farmland off Interstate 71. With a 1 1/2-mile tri-oval track and grandstands that seat more than 66,000, the state-of-the-art facility has become a big draw for seasoned race fans and newcomers alike, in part because of its modern design.

The facility has a bowl-like structure, with the track sitting 22 feet below the first row of seats. That's good news for fans, because it allows a clear view of the entire track from virtually every seat.

Outside the track, you'll have to travel a bit to find similar fast-paced excitement. Cincinnati, Louisville, and Lexington are the nearest places to enjoy big-city amenities, but it'll take you about an hour to get to most of them. Instead, look to the smaller cities in the area, many of which offer some fun and unique attractions. Because the area is so rural, traveling is easy and traffic isn't much of an issue anywhere you might choose to go, except in the hours before a race.

On the banks of the Ohio River at the northernmost tip of Kentucky, Covington and Newport have fun and reasonably priced family attractions including riverboat restaurants, the wildly popular Newport on the Levee entertainment center, and MainStrasse Village, a historic district that pays tribute to its original German residents. It's about 50 miles from the track, but it's an easy trip and worth it if you have the time.

Many fans head to Florence on race weekends, about 30 miles north of the track. It's one of the larger towns in the area and has plenty to see and do, from movies, bowling, and active endeavors to restaurants to suit every taste.

Or, slow down and savor the charm of historic Madison, Indiana, also about 30 miles from the track on the banks of the Ohio River. All 133 blocks of the downtown area are listed on the National Register of Historic Places, and it seems as if time has stood still in many of them. The town's dedication to preserving its heritage shows in every area, from the historic homes, antiques shops, and museums to the general southern hospitality of the place.

No matter where you're headed, be prepared for a variety of weather. Summer in the Ohio River Valley can get unbearably hot and muggy, and thunderstorms and heavy rains can pop up at any time. But it's also not unheard of for temperatures to fall into the 50s at night during colder spells, so equip yourself for both ends of the spectrum.

SPARTA CALENDAR

JUNE 17–18, 2005
NASCAR Busch Series

JUNE, 2005
Stargazer Amphitheatre. 2737 Clifty Dr, Madison, IN (47250). Phone 812/265-6400. www.stargazeramphitheatre.com. Grab a blanket and picnic and enjoy the sounds of country, rock and roll, blues, bluegrass, and '80s. Check the Web site for dates and times.

JULY 4, 2005
Regatta and Governor's Cup Race. Madison, IN (47250). Phone 812/265-2956. Watch the competition of hydroplanes on the Ohio River. Late June-early July.

JULY 8–9, 2005
NASCAR Craftsman Truck Series

JULY 15–16, 2005
Bluegrass Festival. Point Park, Carrollton (41008). Phone 502/732-7036. Blues bands entertain throughout the day and night. Primitive camping is available.

JULY 17, 2005
MainStrasse Village Classic Car Show. Sixth Street Promenade, Covington (41011). Phone 859/491-0458. www.mainstrasse.org. Admire more than 250 classic cars.

Cars aren't the only things cruising in Kentucky. You can cruise along the Ohio River on an elegant BB Riverboat.

SPARTA OUTFIELD:
The 50 miles surrounding Kentucky Speedway.

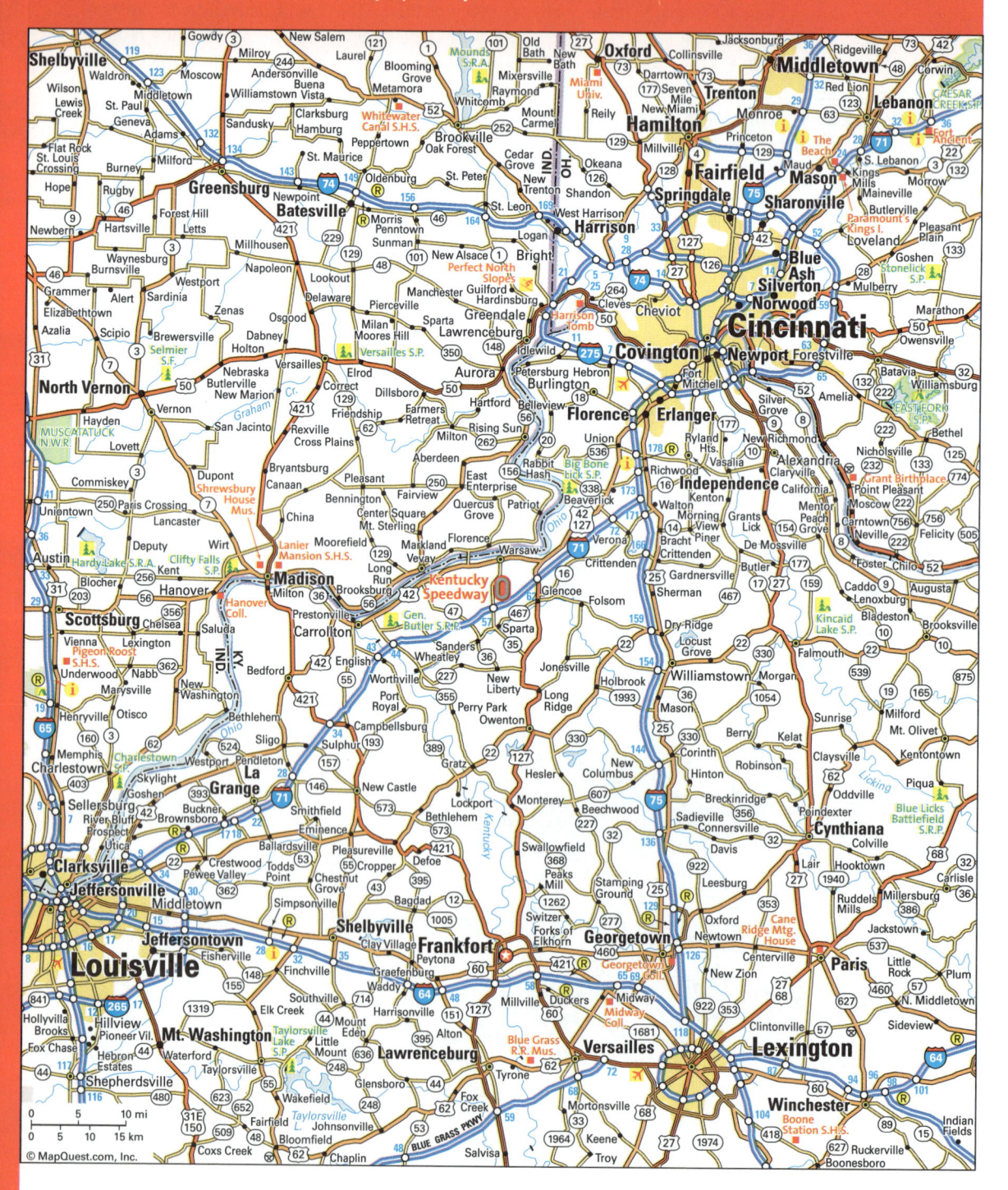

SEE

ATTRACTIONS

Carrollton, KY

GENERAL BUTLER STATE RESORT PARK.
1608 Hwy 227, Carrollton (41008). 2 miles S on Hwy 227, Exit 44. Phone 502/732-4384. www.state.ky.us /agencies/parks/genbutlr.htm. This 795-acre park is a memorial to William O. Butler, Carrollton native and battle hero. Swim, fish, and boat (rentals available) at the 30-acre lake, or play nine-hole golf (fee) or tennis. Cottages, lodge, dining room, tent, and trailer camping also available (daily, standard fees).

Covington, KY

JILLIAN'S.
522 W 12th St, Covington (41011). Phone 859/491-5388. www.jillians.com. A former brewery converted into a massive entertainment and dining complex, Jillian's features restaurants, video and arcade games, a billiards lounge, bowling, dancing, live music, and plenty of TVs to catch the game. (Sun-Wed 11 am-midnight, Thurs-Sat 11-2 am)

MAINSTRASSE VILLAGE.
406 W 6th St, Suite 201, Covington (41011). Phone 859/491-0458. www.mainstrasse.org. Approximately five square blocks in Covington's old German area offer a historic district of residences, shops, and restaurants in more than 20 restored buildings dating from the mid- to late 1800s. (Mon-Sat 11 am-5 pm, Sun noon-5 pm)

RIVERBOAT CRUISES.
BB Riverboats, 1 Madison Ave, Covington (Cincinnati Airport Area) (41011). Phone 859/261-8500. For a moving view of the Ohio River, sightseeing cruises are available, with lunch, dinner, and moonlight cruises as options. Full-day and half-day cruises by appointment. **$$$$**

Florence, KY

FLORENCE CINEMAS.
7685 Florence Mall Rd, Florence (41042). Phone 513/699-1500. This theater offers nine screens and is located close to restaurants and shopping. Call for show times.

WORLD OF SPORTS.
7400 Woodspoint Dr, Florence (41042). Phone 859/371-8255. This family entertainment complex includes an 18-hole golf course, 25-station lighted practice range and nine covered tees, miniature golf course, billiard hall, snack bar, and video arcade, as well as five racquetball/wallyball courts and three slam-dunk basketball courts. (Sun-Fri 9 am-11 pm, Sat 9-1 am)

Fort Mitchell, KY

VENT HAVEN MUSEUM.
33 W Maple, Fort Mitchell (41011). Phone 859/341-0461. This unique museum features more than 500 ventriloquist figures from 20 countries, and pictures and collectibles related to ventriloquism. (By appointment only, May-Sept) **$**

Madison, IN

CLIFTY FALLS STATE PARK.
1501 Green Rd, Madison (47250). 1 mile W on Hwy 56. Phone 812/273-8885. This 1,460-acre park offers a view of the Ohio River and its traffic, as well as hills on the Kentucky shore. It contains waterfalls, fossil beds, and a regional winter vulture roost. Swimming pool (Memorial Day-Labor Day; fee); tennis; picnicking (shelters, fireplaces); concession; playground. **$$**

JEFFERSON COUNTY TRAIN STATION MUSEUM.
615 W First St, Madison (47250). Phone 812/265-2335. This eight-sided railroad station from the late 19th century features original stained-glass windows and includes train memorabilia. (May-Nov, daily; rest of year, Mon-Fri) **$$**

SCHOFIELD HOUSE.
217 W Second St, Madison (47250). Phone 812/265-4759. This two-story tavernhouse, made of handmade, sun-dried brick, was built in the early Federal style between 1809 and 1816. (Apr-Oct, Mon-Tues, Thurs-Sun) **$$**

SEE ATTRACTIONS

Newport, KY

NEWPORT ON THE LEVEE.
1 Levee Way, Suite 1113, Newport (41071). Phone toll-free 866/538-3359. www.newportonthelevee.com. This 10-acre entertainment district on the river includes a trendy shopping center; 12 stylish restaurants; a state-of-the-art, 20-screen movie theater; and the highly acclaimed Newport Aquarium. (June-Aug: Mon-Thurs 10 am-9 pm, Fri-Sat 10 am-10 pm, Sun noon-6 pm; closed Easter, Thanksgiving, Dec 25)

Union, KY

BIG BONE LICK STATE PARK.
Hwy 42 and Rte 338, Union (41094). 7 miles W on Hwy 338. Phone 859/384-3522. www.state.ky.us/agencies/parks/bigbone.htm. On the grounds of this 547-acre park are a museum and diorama explaining prehistoric mammal life preserved in the soft sulphur spring earth around the salt lick (daily) and displays of Ice Age formations. Swimming pool is open for campers only (camping demands a standard fee). Tennis (free) and picnicking available. $

For more attractions, go to www.mobiltravelguide.com

STAY

MOBIL STAR-RATED LODGINGS

Carrollton, KY

GENERAL BUTLER STATE RESORT PARK. ★★
Hwy 227, Carrollton (41008). Phone 502/732-4384; toll-free 800/325-0078. Open year-round, this resort features beach games, golf, tennis, hiking trails, and large recreational areas. Plan a conference in one of the many meeting rooms. 77 rooms, 3 story. Check-out noon; cottages 11 am. Restaurant. Children's activity center. Outdoor pool, children's pool. Golf, 9 holes. Tennis. Business center. State-owned; all facilities of state park. $

HOLIDAY INN EXPRESS. ★
141 Inn Rd, Carrollton (41008). Phone 502/732-6661; toll-free 800/465-4329. www.holiday-inn.com. 62 rooms, 2 story. Complimentary continental breakfast. Check-in 3 pm, check-out noon. $

Florence, KY

ASHLEY QUARTERS. ★
4880 Houston Rd, Florence (41042). Phone 859/525-9997; toll-free 888/525-9997. www.ashleyquarters.com. 70 rooms, 2 story. Pets accepted; fee. Check-out noon. Outdoor pool. Business center. $

HILTON GREATER CINCINNATI AIRPORT. ★★★
7373 Turfway Rd, Florence (41042). Phone 606/371-4400; toll-free 800/932-3322. www.hilton.com. 206 rooms, 5 story. Check-out noon. Restaurant, bar. Fitness room. Outdoor pool. Tennis. Airport transportation available. $

RAMADA LIMITED CINCINNATI AIRPORT/FLORENCE. ★
30 Cavalier Ct, Florence (41042). Phone 859/371-0081; toll-free 800/272-6232. www.ramada.com. 123 rooms, 2 story. Complimentary continental breakfast. Check-in 2 pm, check-out noon. Outdoor pool. Airport transportation available. Business center. $

Fort Mitchell, KY

DRAWBRIDGE INN. ★★
2477 Royal Dr, Fort Mitchell (41017). Phone 859/341-2800; toll-free 800/354-9793. www.drawbridgeinn.com. The Oldenberg brewery is adjacent. 505 rooms, 4 story. Check-out noon. Restaurant, bar. Fitness room. One indoor pool, two outdoor pools, whirlpool. Tennis. Airport transportation available. $

Williamstown, KY

DAYS INN. ★
211 Hwy 36 W, Williamstown (41097). Phone 859/824-5025; toll-free 800/329-7466. www.daysinn.com. 51 rooms, 2 story. Pets accepted, some restrictions; fee. Complimentary continental breakfast. Check-in 1 pm, check-out 11 am. Pool. $

LOCAL RECOMMENDATIONS

Carrollton, KY

BEST WESTERN EXECUTIVE INN.
10 Slumber Ln, Carrollton (41008). Phone 502/732-8444; toll-free 800/780-7234. www.bestwestern.com. 53 rooms, 2 story. Pet accepted, some restrictions; fee. Complimentary continental breakfast. Check-in 3 pm, check-out 11 am. Outdoor pool. Tennis. $

DAYS INN.
Jct I-71 and Hwy 227, Exit 44, Carrollton (41008). Phone 502/732-9301; toll-free 800/329-4667. www.daysinn.com. 84 rooms, 2 story. Complimentary continental breakfast. Check-in 3 pm, check-out 11 am. Outdoor pool. $

HAMPTON INN.
7 Slumber Ln, Carrollton (41008). Phone 502/732-0700; toll-free 800/426-7866. www.hamptoninn.com. 60 rooms, 3 story. Complimentary continental breakfast. Check-in 3 pm, check-out noon. Indoor pool. $

Florence, KY

WILDWOOD INN.
7809 Hwy 42, Florence (41042). Phone 859/371-6300; toll-free 800/758-2335. www.wildwood-inn.com. Call early to reserve the Speedway Suite, which features an actual car, checkered tile flooring, authentic race car seats for chairs, more than 50 race car models, racing memorabilia, posters, and authentic signage. Other suites available range from the Wild West to an arctic cave; also a tropical dome features a heated waterfall and a family activity area. 124 rooms, 2 story. Complimentary continental breakfast. Check-in 4 pm, check-out noon. Indoor pool. 25 minutes from the Kentucky Speedway. $

Fort Mitchell, KY

BEST WESTERN FORT MITCHELL INN.
2100 Dixie Hwy, Fort Mitchell (41011). Phone 859/331-1500; toll-free 800/780-7234. www.bestwestern.com. This hotel, close to both downtown and the airport, features many services with families and children in mind. 210 rooms, 2 story. Pets accepted, some restrictions; fee. Complimentary continental breakfast. Check-in 4 pm, check-out 11 am. Restaurant. Fitness room. Indoor pool, whirlpool. Airport transportation available. $

Sparta, KY

RAMADA LIMITED & SUITES.
3 Dale Dr, Sparta (41086). Phone 859/567-7223; toll-free 800/272-6232. www.ramada.com. A favorite spot with the race team support staff. 78 rooms, 4 story. Complimentary continental breakfast. Check-in 3 pm, check-out noon. Indoor pool. Half-mile from the Kentucky Speedway. $

Williamstown, KY

BEST VALUE INN & SUITES—WILLIAMSTOWN.
10 Skyway Dr, Williamstown (41097). Phone 859/824-7177; toll-free 888/315-2378. www.bestvalueinn.com. 38 rooms, 2 story. Pets accepted, some restrictions; fee. Complimentary continental breakfast. Check-in 3 pm, check-out noon. Restaurant. Outdoor pool. $

RV AND CAMPING

Madison, IN

CLIFTY FALLS STATE PARK.
1501 Green Rd, Madison (47250). Phone 812/265-1331. The park features 165 primitive and developed campsites with a pool, tennis, gift shop, a nature center, and a campground store. For more comfortable accommodations, the Clifty Inn has 63 guest rooms, 4 suites, and a restaurant on-site.

PIT PASS

The speedway's 97-acre infield has 104 private garage stalls, all of which are angled toward the grandstands so fans seated there can watch as teams prepare for the race. For a closer look, $20 will buy your way into the cold pit area, which allows access to the area around victory circle, as well as some contact with the drivers. Discounted tickets are available for children.

STAY LOCAL RECOMMENDATIONS

Sparta, KY

EDGE OF SPEEDWAY CAMPGROUND.
4125 Kentucky Hwy 1130, Sparta (41083). Phone 859/576-2161. This well-manicured, fan-friendly campground overlooks the track and has space for 200 campers. Gravel roads and large sites set it apart from other camping spots in the area; city water is free and hot showers are available for a $5 fee. It's about a half-mile walk to track shuttle buses, or a 1 1/2-mile drive to the track parking area. Parking is $10 per vehicle; RVs and tents run $25 per night.

Walton, KY

OAK CREEK CAMPGROUND.
Rte 16 and Oak Creek Rd, Walton (41094). Phone 859/485-9131; toll-free 877/604-3503. Twenty miles from the track, this highly regarded, family-run campground has 99 sites with water and electric and four primitive tent areas. Modern restrooms with air conditioning and heat, showers, laundry, and swimming pool are available.

For more lodging recommendations, go to www.mobiltravelguide.com

EAT

MOBIL STAR-RATED RESTAURANTS

Covington, KY

DEE FELICE CAFE. ★★
529 Main St, Covington (41011). Phone 859/261-2365. www.deefelice.com. This is a neighborhood spot featuring Cajun classics such as shrimp Creole and jambalaya; large portions, reasonable prices. American menu. Lunch, dinner. Closed holidays. Outdoor seating. $$

MIKE FINK. ★★
1 Ben Berstein Pl, Covington (41011). Phone 859/261-4212. www.mikefink.com. This restaurant is housed in a permanently moored old paddlewheel steamer. Seafood menu. Lunch, dinner, brunch. $$

RIVERVIEW. ★★
668 W 5th St, Covington (41011). Phone 859/491-5300. Located on the 18th floor of the Radisson Hotel Cincinnati Riverview, this revolving eatery offers a panoramic view of downtown Cincinnati and northern Kentucky. American menu. Lunch, dinner, Sun brunch. Closed Dec 25. $$

WATERFRONT. ★★★
14 Pete Rose Pier, Covington (41011). Phone 859/581-1414. www.jeffruby.com. This bustling "steak and lobster house" has a stunning view of the Cincinnati skyline and a sit-down sushi bar. Seafood, steak menu. Dinner. Closed Sun. Valet parking. Outdoor seating. $$

Dry Ridge, KY

COUNTRY GRILL. ★
21 Taft Hwy, Dry Ridge (41035). Phone 859/824-6000. A good variety of reasonably priced traditional American offerings includes freshly made biscuits, homemade soups, and fried chicken. American menu. Breakfast, lunch, dinner. Closed holidays. Children's menu. $$

Fort Mitchell, KY

ORIENTAL WOK. ★
317 Buttermilk Pike, Fort Mitchell (41017). Phone 859/331-3000. Chinese, American menu. Lunch, dinner. Closed Thanksgiving, Dec 25. Outdoor seating. $

Madison, IN

KEY WEST SHRIMP HOUSE. ★
117 Ferry St (Hwy 56), Madison (47250). Phone 812/265-2831. The Shrimp House, in a century-old building just across the Ohio River in historic Madison, is known for its down-home hospitality. American, seafood menu. Lunch, dinner. Closed Mon. $

LOCAL RECOMMENDATIONS

Carrollton, KY

CHURCHILL MANOR.
1408 Highland Ave, Carrollton (41008). Phone 502/732-5082. Reminiscent of the highway roadhouse diners of yesteryear, the Manor is a casual spot for relaxing. American menu. Breakfast, lunch, dinner. $

KIDS' PICK

Once you take a look at the menu here at **Rafferty's,** you might wish you were still 12 years old and could order from the less-intimidating kids' menu. The main menu offers every kind of soup, salad, burger, sandwich, and entrée imaginable. Just make sure to order an appetizer to hold you over—you'll need it for all the time you'll spend just deciding what to have for your meal. American menu. Lunch, dinner. Casual attire. $ *7379 Turfway Rd, Florence (41042). Phone 859/371-1140.*

THE LODGE.
Hwy 227, Carrollton (41008). Phone 502/732-4384. Located in the lodge at General Butler State Resort Park, the restaurant serves traditional American fare and old-fashioned southern cooking. American menu. Breakfast, lunch, dinner. $

REIFFEN'S.
1968 Park Ave, Carrollton (41008). Phone 502/732-5570. Visit this traditional American steak house for its hand-cut steaks, signature pasta dishes, and fried green tomatoes. American menu. Lunch, dinner. $$$

Cold Spring, KY

COLD SPRING ROADHOUSE.
4210 Alexandria Pike, Cold Spring (41076). Phone 859/441-3508. Hand-cut steaks are cooked over a wood-burning fire in this casual eatery. Try the award-winning barbecue sauce, which is slow-cooked in iron pots, on the tender baby back ribs. American menu. Dinner. $$

Covington, KY

BARTON ON PARK PLACE.
129 Park Pl, Covington (41011). Phone 859/291-7275. This casual deli offers a tailgater's choice of homemade soups, sandwiches, and pizza. American menu. Lunch. Closed Sat-Sun. $

BEHLE STREET CAFÉ.
50 E RiverCenter Blvd, Covington (41011). Phone 859/291-4100. Enjoy upscale pub food in a casual, comfortable atmosphere adorned with local and movie memorabilia. American menu. Lunch, dinner. Outdoor seating. $$

EL COYOTE SOUTHWESTERN GRILLE.
3041 Dixie Hwy, Covington (41017). Phone 859/331-6767. Mexican menu. Dinner. $$

WERTHEIM'S.
516 W 6th St, Covington (41011). Phone 859/261-1233. Located amid the old-world charm of Covington's MainStrasse Village, this friendly restaurant serves a wide selection of German specialties such as wienerschnitzel, sauerkraut, and bratwurst. For those less adventurous, but no less hungry for a good meal, the menu also includes standard American fare. German, American menu. Lunch, dinner. $$

WILLIE'S SPORT CAFÉ.
401 Crescent Ave, Covington (41011). Phone 859/581-1500. Willie's is an upscale sports café with a view of Cincinnati's skyline across the Ohio River. The dining room offers steak, pasta, and seafood dishes. American menu. Lunch, dinner. Bar. Casual attire. $$

Dry Ridge, KY

LITTLE SHRIMP RESTAURANT.
20 Broadway St, Dry Ridge (41035). Phone 859/824-5000. This family-friendly casual spot offers burgers, coneys (chili dogs), sandwiches, and ice cream. American menu. Breakfast, lunch, dinner. Closed Sun. $

Florence, KY

CATHAY KITCHEN.
8049 Connector Dr, Florence (41042). Phone 859/282-0770. Chinese menu. Lunch, dinner. $

FAMOUS DAVE'S BAR-B-QUE.
4931 Houston Rd, Florence (41042). Phone 859/647-7788. Serving a vast variety of pit-smoked meats, united under the Famous Dave's name by one fabulous barbecue sauce, this restaurant touts its ribs and "'cue" as St. Louis-style, although Dave's first establishment began in Minneapolis in 1994. The menu also has salads and sandwiches for lighter appetites, and a family-style barbecue meal for hungry groups. Barbeque menu. Lunch, dinner. **$**

KARLO'S BISTRO ITALLIA.
4911 Houston Rd, Florence (41042). Phone 859/282-8282. Offering more imaginative dishes than your average Italian joint, this laid-back restaurant also features friendly and knowledgeable service. Try the grilled chicken Milanese in smooth gorgonzola sauce or the chopped salad, but not both, unless you're planning to share with a friend—the portions are more than generous. Italian menu. Lunch, dinner. **$**

Fort Mitchell, KY

GATEHOUSE TAVERN.
2477 Royal Dr, Fort Mitchell (45217). Phone 859/341-7535. The Gatehouse, in the Drawbridge Inn, resembles a cozy English castle—complete with moat and live music. American menu. Dinner. Closed Mon-Tues. **$$**

GREYHOUND TAVERN.
2500 Dixie Hwy, Fort Mitchell (41017). Phone 859/331-3767. Northern Kentucky's oldest continuous operating restaurant, this spot began as an eatery for trolley passengers. A casual, nostalgic atmosphere complements traditional American fare including prime beef, seafood, pastas, soups, salads, sandwiches, and other regional favorites. American menu. Lunch, dinner. **$$**

Fort Wright, KY

WALT'S HITCHING POST.
3300 Madison Pk, Fort Wright (41011). Phone 859/331-0494. This Kentucky institution is housed in an authentic log cabin. Walt's is famous for its open-pit barbecued ribs and signature sauce. American menu. Lunch, dinner. Casual attire. **$$**

Newport, KY

CLADDAGH IRISH PUB.
1 Levee Way, Newport (41071). Phone 859/581-8888. Irish music fills the air in this lively bar and the restaurant resembles an authentic Irish pub and serves traditional fare including fish and chips, shepherd's pie, and corned beef and cabbage. Irish menu. Lunch, dinner, brunch. Casual attire. **$$**

HOFBRAUHAUS.
Third St and Saratoga Ave at the Levee, Newport (41071). Phone 859/491-7200. This celebratory spot was the first American rendition of the famous beer hall in Munich, Germany. Featuring authentic fare and beers. An indoor hall and outdoor garden seats more than 700 revelers. German menu. Lunch, dinner. Casual attire. **$$**

Sparta, KY

PIT STOP GRILLE.
101 Kentucky Hwy 465, Sparta (41086). Phone 859/643-3100. The family eatery in front of this restaurant, a half-mile from the track, offers standard diner fare, including burgers, sandwiches, and a children's menu. Parents, note that a separate entrance leads to Racers Premiere Gentlemen's Club in the building. Diner menu. Lunch, dinner. Children's menu. **$**

For more dining recommendations, go to www.mobiltravelguide.com

SIDETRIP

Mammoth Cave National Park
Mammoth Cave, KY

For a relaxing contrast to the roar of the speedway, return to nature at **Mammoth Cave National Park** in south central Kentucky (phone 270/758-2190, www.nps.gov/maca). Located two hours from the track (take Interstate 71 south to Interstate 65 south to Exit 53 at Cave City; follow signs to park visitor center), the park is home to the longest recorded cave system in the world, with more than 360 miles of explored and mapped passages.

The labyrinth offers a dozen ranger-guided and self-guided tours for all levels of skill and endurance. Tours can sell out in summer, so make reservations, especially for the more difficult programs ($4-$46 for adults; $2.50-$18 youths). Bring a jacket, as cave temps stay around 54 °F.

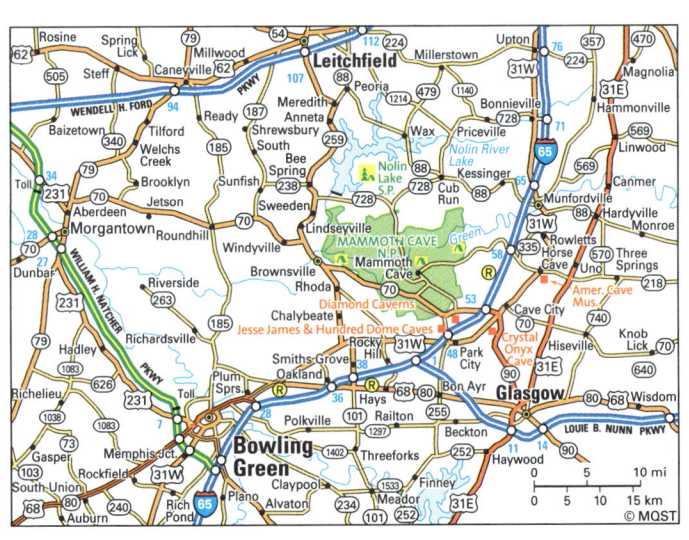

The park has three campgrounds and the **Mammoth Cave Hotel** (phone 270/758-2225), adjacent to the cave entrance, offering guest rooms, cottages, and pet kennels.

Above ground, there are more than 52,000 acres offering camping, hiking, canoeing, horseback riding, boating, and fishing. Pick up the park brochure at the visitors center for information. You can travel by car to most places in the park.

Other nearby attractions add down-home fun to your trip. **Kentucky Action Park,** on the way to the cave (phone toll-free 800/798-0560), features a 1/4-mile alpine slide, horseback riding, miniature golf course, bumper cars and boats, and a go-kart track.

In the early morning, fog drifts eerily at the entrance to the caves of Mammoth Cave National Park. For more details on touring Mammoth Cave, go to www.nps.gov/maca.

Guntown Mountain, next to Interstate 65 in Cave City, is a re-creation of an Old West frontier town, complete with gunfights, can-can dancers, a country and Western music theater, carnival rides, and a haunted house (phone 270/773-3530). **Kentucky Down Under** is an Australian-themed animal park where you can walk through an open field with kangaroos and emus, or discover what life is like on an Australian sheep station (phone 270/786-2634).

For more Mammoth Cave recommendations, go to www.mobiltravelguide.com

236

Dale Earnhardt Jr, driving the No. 8 Chevrolet, heads down pit road for some mid-race service.

Las Vegas Motor Speedway

Las Vegas, NV

14

Race leaders head down Las Vegas Motor Speedway's pit road.

TRACK FACTS

LAS VEGAS MOTOR SPEEDWAY. 7000 Las Vegas Blvd N, Las Vegas (89115). Phone toll-free 800/644-4444. www.lvms.com.

SECURITY. Fans should expect random bag searches. Folding chairs, umbrellas, noisemakers, coolers, or outside food are not permitted, but scanners, binoculars, and other such devices are welcome.

FIRST AID. First aid and rescue stations are located at Gate F, behind Section 3 in Midway, behind Section 1 in Midway, and at the Infield Care Center. The speedway's mobile medical teams patrol the grounds at all times in carts marked with Red Cross symbols. If you have a pre-existing condition, ask a gate attendant to point out the locations of the first aid kiosks as you enter.

TICKETS AND SEATING. Race fans can get the best for their buck by purchasing seats in the Red Section 2. The $125 seats include tickets for Saturday and Sunday's races, plus free admission for Friday's qualifying day. Red Section 2 is directly across from the pit road. Also, check out www.sportstravel.com/lasvegas400.html, a travel agency with tickets and hotel packages starting at $415 per person—a good price considering how much you could shell out for a hotel room alone during race weekend.

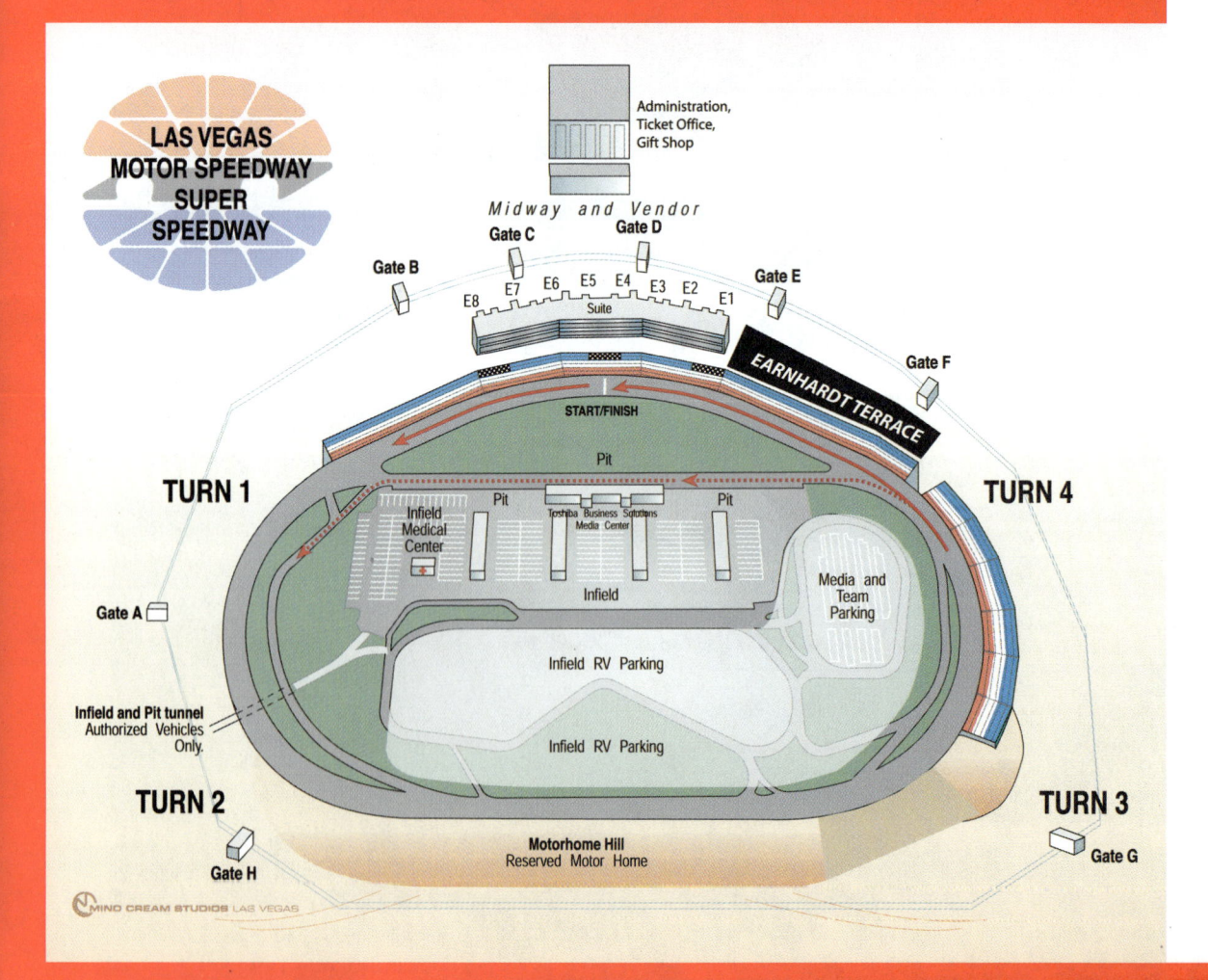

CONCESSIONS. Souvenir and food vendors pitch their wares in a carnival-like atmosphere on Midway Plaza between Gates B and E, with options that range from hotdogs and beer to Mexican and barbecue. Guests are allowed to enter the track with any food bought here. Inside, several concession counters are scattered around the facility. Those sitting in the Clubhouse seats—the black-and-white checkered sections between Gates C and E—can access an indoor buffet and bar or ask servers to bring them beverages as part of the ticket price. Scanners are available to rent at merchandise stands located throughout the speedway grounds.

Near the track, there's a Petro Stopping Center with an Iron Skillet Restaurant just off Interstate 15. The Stopping Center convenience store carries a wide range of sundries. There's also a Wal-Mart Supercenter about 4 miles south at 4350 North Nellis Boulevard, Las Vegas (89115). Phone 702/643-1500.

PARKING. General parking is free and there are shuttles roaming about to deliver you to the stadium door. One great alternative is the $45, three-day Lucky 7 Preferred Parking pass, which allows you to bypass exit traffic to Interstate 15 through an alternative route.

A similar alternative is to take Interstate 15 north to US Highway 95 north to 215 east and then reunite with Interstate 15. That's shorter and probably just as efficient, but US Highway 95 is one of the valley's busiest arteries anyway and it's less predictable than the 215.

The need for speed at Las Vegas Motor Speedway.

Fans in the NASCAR NEXTEL Cup garage on Sunday morning.

Las Vegas comes alive at night.

A NEON OASIS IN THE DESERT

The famous boast, "what happens in Vegas, stays in Vegas," may be true, but everybody has some pretty good ideas of what goes on here, anyway. This is, after all, one of the world's most famous cities, an eye-popping neon oasis drawn improbably and fabulously on a desert canvas that has evolved over a century from quiet railroad depot to Entertainment Capital of the World. The pulsing lights that replace the cloudless blue skies at night can be quite alluring, and any city known both for sin and Celine Dion is sure to amuse just about anyone.

In 1998, the NASCAR gods gifted the city with a place in their NASCAR Series, and now the springtime NEXTEL Cup race at the Las Vegas Motor Speedway is the year's largest sporting event west of Texas. It's such a huge success that in 2004, the Las Vegas Motor Speedway added 15,000 more seats wih the construction of the Dale Earnhardt Terrace, a stunning $85.4 million non-gaming boost to the regional economy. The choice of March for the NASCAR NEXTEL Cup race was a stroke of genius; the breezy mid-70s temperatures make it among the most comfortable times in the otherwise scorching desert to take in an outdoor event.

In hindsight, it's a wonder Las Vegas and NASCAR didn't get hitched sooner. NASCAR is now the tourist mecca's most profitable single-day event all year. Be aware that the biggest resorts charge upwards of $400 a night over NASCAR weekend and are largely sold out months in advance even at that. Still, with 129,000 hotel rooms and thousands of RV sites, there's always a place to lay your head.

Today's Vegas, like NASCAR, is all grown up. After an attempt in the early 1990s to market itself as a primarily family destination, Vegas has settled in

Push your own limits—ride the roller coaster that is perched atop the Stratosphere.

as a destination for 35 million people who come for expensive celeb-chef cuisine and inexpensive buffets; top-tier concerts and glitzy impersonations of old legends; rows of elegant, fantastical megaresorts; and clusters of low-frills gaming halls. It's hard to believe that there's an adult or child alive who could be bored by all that sensational neon, all those inventive swimming pools, death-defying thrill rides, and exotic animal exhibits. If that doesn't grab you, just stand on a pedestrian bridge and watch the diverse group of tourists.

The era of dirt-cheap buffets is largely over and even Gladys Knight costs more than $65 a seat, but the best of Las Vegas is totally, gloriously free. You can't really say you've visited the city if you come and go without ever watching the Las Vegas Strip's **Fountains of Bellagio** (3600 S Las Vegas Blvd S, phone 702/693-7111, www.bellagio.com) on the famed resort's streetside 3-acre lake. It goes off every 15 minutes each night 7 pm-midnight and every half-hour 3-7 pm on weekdays and noon-7 pm on weekends.

After that, duck inside Bellagio's lobby to gawk at the **Fiori di Como chandelier,** made up of 2,000 hand-blown glass flowers. Then wander through the plethora of exotic plants at the **Bellagio Conservatory.**

A few more free favorites include the waterfall that goes volcanic every 15 minutes starting at 7 pm outside **The Mirage** (3400 S Las Vegas Blvd S, phone 702/791-7111, www.mirage.com); the statues that come to life for 10 minutes at the top-of-the-hour light and fire shows at either end of **Caesars Palace's**

Sneak in a few holes during the race weekend.

GETTING AROUND

Las Vegas Motor Speedway is a long oval planted largely in the middle of empty desert, bounded on the west by Interstate 15 and on the east by Las Vegas Boulevard North, and 12 miles north of the Interstate 15 and US Highway 95 interchange known as the Spaghetti Bowl. Most racegoers approach the track from the south.

The most underutilized way to avoid the backup is the new Las Vegas Beltway, a.k.a. the 215. From the Strip vicinity, take Interstate 15 south to the 215 west. Take the 215 all the way to Interstate 15 north—but don't merge with traffic on Interstate 15 as you're only a mile south of the track and are permitted to drive on the shoulder. What you add in mileage, you save in frustration and time.

If you prefer to commute without your car, the easiest way is by the Citizen Area Transit's special NASCAR bus service, which gets traffic preferences arriving at and leaving the speedway and on Interstate 15. You'll have to take public transportation to the Downtown Transportation Center, where you hop specially marked NASCAR buses, but it's really simple, especially from the Strip, where you take the ubiquitous 301 bus to the depot. It's also incredibly cheap, at $5 each way. Buy a four-day pass in advance for $25 by visiting www.catride.com. Visit the Web site or call toll-free 800/229-3911 with questions.

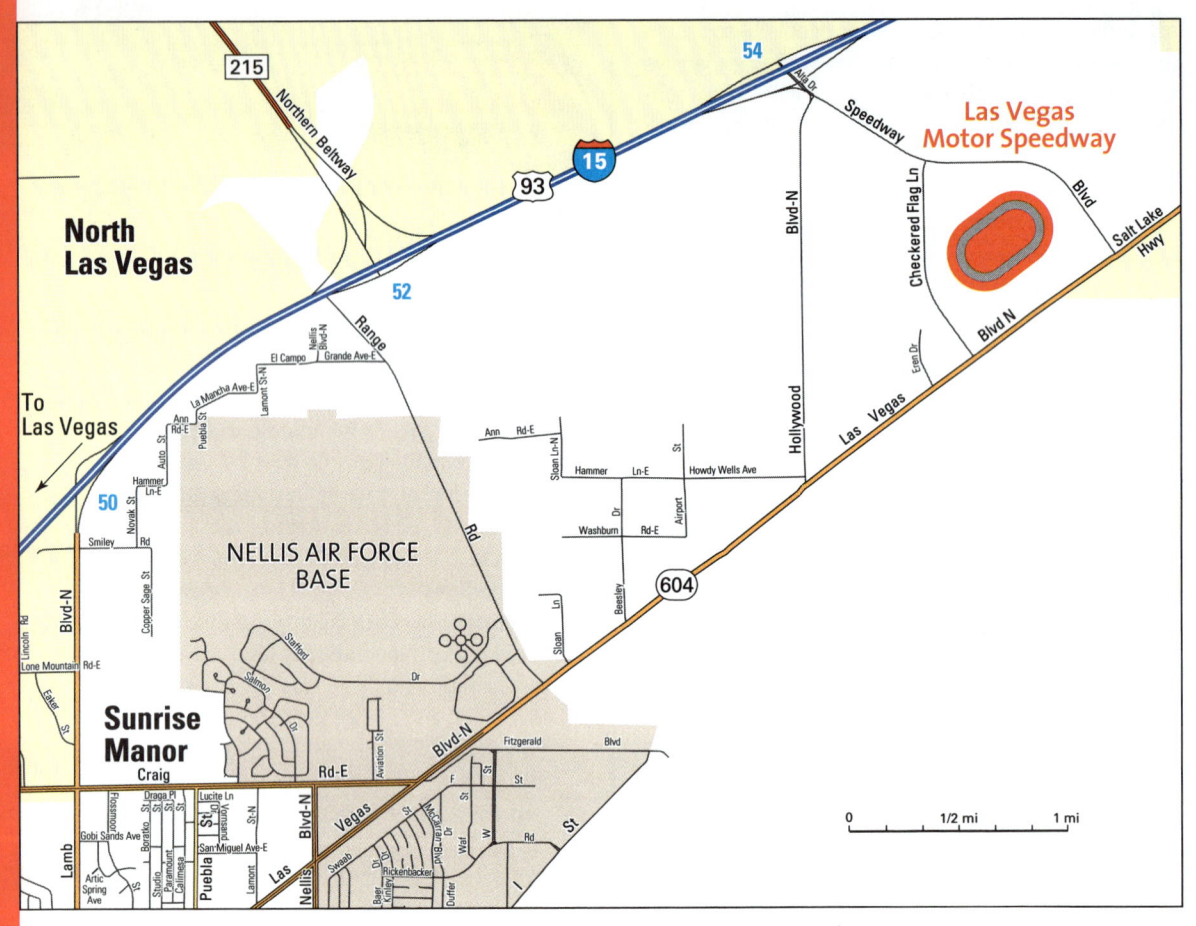

LAS VEGAS POLE POSITION:
The 10 miles surrounding Las Vegas Motor Speedway.

Forum Shops (3570 Las Vegas Blvd S, phone toll-free 877/427-7243); and the amazing hourly video and music production show known as the **Fremont Street Experience** (425 Fremont St, phone 702/678/5600, www.vegasexperience.com) that appears on the largest LED screen in the world—which is also the underside of the Fremont Street 4 1/2-block-long metal canopy.

Plus, enjoy a free preview and opine on upcoming TV shows before they air at the **CBS Television City Research Center** inside MGM Grand (3799 Las Vegas Blvd S, phone toll-free 800/646-7787) or at the **MRC Group Research Institute** inside the Venetian Resort (3355 Las Vegas Blvd S, phone toll-free 877/883-6423).

On a more serious note, **A Permanent Tribute to Heroes** at the New York-New York Hotel & Casino (3790 Las Vegas Blvd S, phone toll-free 888/696-9887, www.nynycasino.com) is a September 11 memorial plaza in front of its replica of the Statue of Liberty, complete with display cases showing some of the thousands of T-shirts, notes, and other mementos left by mourning tourists in the months following the terror attacks.

LAS VEGAS CALENDAR

FEBRUARY 25–27, 2005
Home & Garden Show. Cashman Center, 850 Las Vegas Blvd N (89101). Phone 702/386-7100. www.plusevents.com. Browse more than 400 booths featuring everything from roofs to floors, windows to doors.

MARCH 12, 2005
NASCAR Busch Series

MARCH 13, 2005
NASCAR NEXTEL Series

APRIL 7–9, 2005
International Billiard & Home Recreation Expo at the Las Vegas Convention Center. www.bca-pool.com. Get in the game with hundreds of billiard tables and accessories, as well as darts, foosball, novelty items, video games, and more.

SEPTEMBER, 2005
Giant Garage Sale. Black Mountain Recreation Center, 599 Greenway Rd, Henderson (89015). Phone 702/267-4070. www.visithenderson.com. Find treasures of clothes, toys, books, and other items among the dozens of booths. Mid-September.

SEPTEMBER 24, 2005
NASCAR Craftsman Truck Series

Grab a bite to eat at the NASCAR Cafe.

DRIVER'S PICK

When in Vegas, 1961 Daytona 500 winner, **Marvin Panch,** who was voted one of NASCAR's 50 Greatest Drivers, heads to the strip. "My wife Bettie and I like **The Steak House at Circus Circus** ★★ in Las Vegas. The steaks there are exceptional. The lamb chops are great, too, and the ice cream is better than homemade." $$$ *2880 Las Vegas Blvd S, Las Vegas (89109). Phone 702/794-3767. www.circuscircus.com/dining/steakhouse.php.*

LAS VEGAS OUTFIELD:
The 50 miles surrounding Las Vegas Motor Speedway.

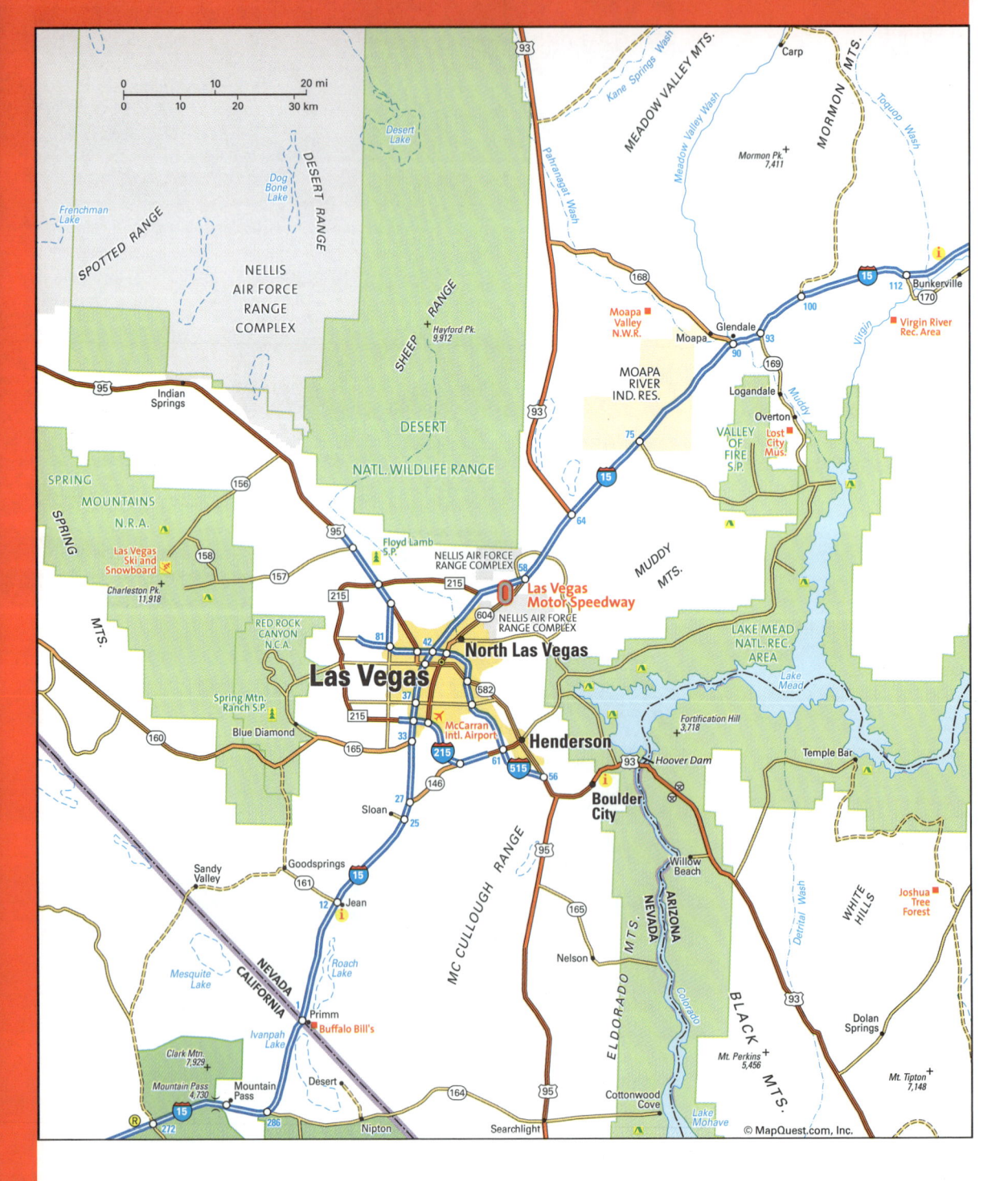

SEE

ATTRACTIONS

HOOVER DAM.
At the Nevada-Arizona border on US Hwy 93. Phone 702/597-5970; toll-free 866/291-8687. www.usbr.gov/lc/hooverdam. A million people a year visit this monument to American technological ingenuity and daring and take a rather thoughtful guided subterranean tour, thereby proving that not every attraction in the Las Vegas area is merely mindless entertainment. While you're there, note the huge white stain on the canyon walls of Lake Mead—evidence of the dwindling water level caused by the ongoing worst drought on record. Parking (fee). (Spring, summer: daily 9 am-5 pm; fall, winter 9 am-4:30 pm) **$$**

VALLEY OF FIRE STATE PARK.
About 50 miles N of Las Vegas and 40 miles N of the Las Vegas Motor Speedway. Phone 702/397-2088. www.parks.nv.gov/vf.htm. You'll simply never know how gorgeous the seemingly barren southern Nevada area is until you drive through this valley flanked by huge beet-red rock formations that seem to sprout from nowhere. There are several easy hikes and areas for kids to climb small boulders with little risk. Camping on-site is first-come, first-served for 51 spaces with water and restrooms but no hook-ups ($14/night/vehicle). Park (daily dawn to dusk). Visitor Center (8:30 am-4:30 pm). $6 per car per day.

Las Vegas

LIBERACE MUSEUM.
1775 E Tropicana Ave, Las Vegas (89119). Phone 702/798-5595. www.liberace.com. Looking for a taste of Old Vegas? The Liberace Museum was once a confusing jumble of artifacts and leftovers from the musician of remarkable stage presence, but it was recently reconfigured to lead visitors through a coherent history of the legend's ascendance to fame. You actually get a sense of how Liberace's lust for gaudy costumes and rhinestone-encrusted pianos made him a star. The professionalism and earnestness of this place makes it worth a visit. (Mon-Sat 10 am-5 pm, Sun noon-4 pm) **$$$**

SHARK REEF, MANDALAY BAY RESORT & CASINO.
3950 Las Vegas Blvd S, Las Vegas (89119). Phone 702/632-4555. www.mandalaybay.net. There are lots of impressive animal exhibits in Las Vegas, but this dazzling 95,000-square-foot aquarium swims to the very top as proved by its American Zoo and Aquarium Association accreditation. Shark Reef houses more than 2,000 animals, including the recent introduction of the great hammerhead shark, the only one in a closed-system aquarium in the world and the only one on display in the United States. Also notable: a 12,000-gallon aquarium housing 200 fish from 40 species in the hotel's lobby is free to view 24 hours a day. (Daily 10 am-11 pm, last admission at 10 pm) **$$$$**

THRILL RIDES ATOP THE STRATOSPHERE HOTEL.
2000 Las Vegas Blvd S, Las Vegas (89104). Phone toll-free 800/998-6937. www.stratospherehotel.com. How brave are you? Let's see you go 1,149 feet up to the top of the tallest freestanding building west of the Mississippi, and then have the Big Shot ($$) toss you another 160 feet at 45 mph. Or ride the X-Scream ($$) and let a mechanical arm dangle you off the side like a cruel see-saw. Can't handle that? The High Roller's ($) for the more easygoing among us, a comfortable roller coaster wrapping around the Stratosphere's needle that's more like a horizontal Ferris wheel affording the best aerial views of Vegas. (Sun-Thurs 10-1 am, Fri-Sat 10-2 am)

For more attractions, go to www.mobiltravelguide.com

STAY

MOBIL STAR-RATED LODGINGS

Henderson

GREEN VALLEY RANCH RESORT & SPA. ★★★
2300 Paseo Verde Pkwy, Henderson (89052). Phone 702/617-7777; toll-free 866/617-7777. www.greenvalleyranchresort.com. You've seen it featured on Discovery Channel's *American Casino* series, now

check it out for yourself. The Whiskey Beach pool area is a wonder; it seems to go on forever with pools and gardens. 201 rooms. Pets accepted, some restrictions. Check-in 3 pm, check-out noon. High-speed Internet access. Wireless Internet access. Six restaurants, four bars. Fitness room, spa. Beach. Outdoor pool, children's pool, whirlpool. Tennis. Airport transportation available. Business center. Casino. $$

Las Vegas Strip and Vicinity

EMBASSY SUITES HOTEL LAS VEGAS. ★★

4315 Swenson St, Las Vegas (89119). Phone 702/795-2800; toll-free 800/362-2779. www.embassysuites.com. Across the street from the perpetual party at the Hard Rock Hotel, this hotel offers a serene environment to unwind peacefully. The non-gaming lobby is a sweeping atrium framed by balconies overflowing with greenery around an indoor water garden and swans. 65 rooms. Complimentary full breakfast. Check-in 3 pm, check-out noon. High-speed Internet access. Restaurant, bar. Outdoor pool, two whirlpools. Airport transportation available. $$

FAIRFIELD INN. ★

3850 Paradise Rd, Las Vegas (89109). Phone 702/791-0899; toll-free 800/228-2800. www.fairfieldinn.com. Located east of the heart of the Vegas scene, this quiet hotel is an affordable and simple choice for road-trippers, economy travelers, or those who require accommodations near the airport. This four-story inn is definitely limited service, with no gaming or dining. A free shuttle is available most of the day to and from nearby McCarran Airport. 129 rooms, 4 story. Check-in 3 pm, check-out noon. Wireless Internet access. Outdoor pool, whirlpool. Airport transportation available. $

FLAMINGO LAS VEGAS. ★★

3555 Las Vegas Blvd S, Las Vegas (89109). Phone 702/733-3111; toll-free 800/732-2111. www.flamingolv.com. During NASCAR weekend in Vegas, the Flamingo charges less than some other casinos, around the $220-a-night level. The pool area itself is a kids' fave, with slides and waterfalls galore. 3,655 rooms, 28 story. Pets accepted, some restrictions. Check-in 3 pm, check-out noon. Restaurant, bar. Fitness room, spa. Outdoor pool. Tennis. Business center. Casino. $

LA QUINTA INN LAS VEGAS CONVENTION CENTER. ★

3970 Paradise Rd, Las Vegas (89109). Phone 702/796-9000; toll-free 800/531-5900. www.laquinta.com. Offering convenient airport access and a quiet environment with friendly, courteous staff, this budget-friendly hotel is ideal for families, especially those hoping to visit the Las Vegas Strip, the Cirque du Soleil, and the nearby NASCAR track. 251 rooms, 3 story. Pets accepted, some restrictions. Complimentary continental breakfast. Check-in 3 pm, check-out noon. Outdoor pool. Airport transportation available. $

LUXOR HOTEL AND CASINO. ★★★

3900 Las Vegas Blvd S, Las Vegas (89119). Phone 702/262-4000; toll-free 888/777-0188. www.luxor.com. In a sea of box-shaped hotels dressed up with a themed "skin," the pyramidal Luxor stands out as a rare example of daring architecture. Try to get a room in the main building and not in the ordinary-shaped towers if only so you can ride the "inclinator," a diagonal elevator, to your floor. Legend has it that the booming light pouring skyward from the top of the Luxor can be seen in outer space. It certainly can be easily seen from the racetrack as the sun sets. 4,400 rooms, 30 story. Check-in 3 pm, check-out 11 am. Restaurant, bar. Fitness room, spa. Outdoor pool, children's pool. Business center. Casino. $

ORLEANS HOTEL AND CASINO. ★★

4500 W Tropicana Ave, Las Vegas (89103). Phone 702/365-7111; toll-free 800/675-3267. www.orleanscasino.com. Slightly west of the Strip, this New Orleans-themed hotel is a huge favorite of NASCAR fans because it has a 70-lane bowling alley and frequently plays host to popular country and vintage '60s acts in its intimate 830-seat showroom. The hotel offers a 9,000-square-foot Kid's Tyme play area for kids up to 12 years old, essentially a babysitting service that costs $5 per hour, maximum three hours a day. 1,426 rooms. Check-in 3 pm, check-out noon. High-speed Internet access. Restaurant, bar. Children's activity center. Fitness room, spa. Outdoor pool, children's pool, whirlpool. Business center. Casino. $$

SAHARA HOTEL AND CASINO. ★★

2535 Las Vegas Blvd S, Las Vegas (89109). Phone 702/737-2111; toll-free 888/696-2121. www.sahara

vegas.com. An obvious favorite for NASCAR fans because of the NASCAR Cafe, where drivers will undoubtedly pop in during the big weekend. Plus, there are thrill rides, a roller coaster, and a Las Vegas Cyber Speedway simulation ride. 1,720 rooms, 27 story. Check-in 3 pm, check-out noon. Five restaurants, bar. Outdoor pool, children's pool. Business center. Casino. $

Off-Strip/Downtown Las Vegas

GOLDEN NUGGET HOTEL AND CASINO. ★★★

129 E Fremont St, Las Vegas (89101). Phone 702/385-7111; toll-free 800/846-5336. www.goldennugget.com. If you must stay downtown, this is the nicest and largest property you can choose. Despite embarrassing itself as the focus of an awful Fox reality series, *The Casino,* the place is a standard-bearer. The Golden Nugget is along the Fremont Street Experience, so don't miss the hourly light show on the underside of the canopy. 1,907 rooms, 22 story. Check-in 3 pm, check-out noon. Five restaurants, two bars. Fitness room, spa. Indoor pool, outdoor pool. Business center. Casino. $

LOCAL RECOMMENDATIONS

Las Vegas Strip and Vicinity

BEST WESTERN MARDI GRAS HOTEL & CASINO.

3500 Paradise Rd, Las Vegas (89109). Phone 702/731-2020; toll-free 800/634-6501. www.mardigrasinn.com. All the rooms here are suites, an unusual configuration for this chain, but then again a casino in a Best Western is a novelty in itself. The hotel is also feet from the Las Vegas Monorail station at the Las Vegas Convention Center, so it affords great access to the Strip. 314 rooms, 3 story. Check-in 3 pm, check-out 11 am. Restaurant. Outdoor pool, whirlpool. $

BEST WESTERN MCCARRAN INN.

4970 Paradise Rd, Las Vegas (89119). Phone 702/798-5530; toll-free 800/626-7575. www.bestwestern.com. Here's a no-frills way to be close to the Strip without being on top of it or having to march across acres of green-felt tables. Located just outside of McCarran Airport, a free shuttle takes you to the MGM Grand Hotel, from where you can easily walk the boulevard or ride the monorail. 99 rooms, 3 story. Complimentary continental breakfast. Check-in 2 pm, check-out noon. Outdoor pool. Airport transportation available. $

North Las Vegas

CANNERY CASINO AND HOTEL.

2121 E Craig Rd, North Las Vegas (89030). Phone 702/507-5700; toll-free 800/999-4899. www.cannerycasinos.com. This dull little property has a 1940s theme and is also the largest casino near the Las Vegas Motor Speedway and capitalizes on its proximity by offering a $10 discount to anyone who asks for the "racer's rate" when calling up. 201 rooms, 3 story. Check-in 3 pm, check-out noon. Five restaurants. Outdoor pool. $

HOLIDAY INN EXPRESS.

4540 Donovan Way, North Las Vegas (89031). Phone 702/649-3000; toll-free 800/465-4329. www.hiexpress.com. Perhaps because it's right off Interstate 15 and 5 miles south of the speedway, this site attracts a

If you think the Strip is only for luxury hotels, think again. Circus Circus Hotel & Las Vegas KOA RV PARK isn't much to look at, but it may be the best deal on the Strip. The average space goes for about $30 a night, a shocking steal. This is a great property for families with children because of its terrific Adventuredome theme park. The hotel has 3,770 rooms, and the tallest of its several buildings is 35 stories. Check-in 3 pm, check-out 11 am. Outdoor pool. Seven restaurants. The RV park has 399 sites with full-service utility hook-ups. Check-in 3 pm, check-out 11 am. Outdoor pool. Seven restaurants. Hotel: *2880 Las Vegas Blvd S, Las Vegas (89109). Phone 702/734-0410; toll-free 800/634-3450. www.circuscircus.com.* RV Park: *Phone 702/733-9707; toll-free 800/562-7270. lasvegas@koa.net.*

STAY LOCAL RECOMMENDATIONS

regular crowd of NASCAR devotees who carpool or rent shuttle buses to the race together. It's not hard to see why they like it here; they probably all met munching on free milk and Otis Spunkmeyer cookies from 6-8 pm in the lobby. 74 rooms, 2 story. Pets accepted; fee. Check-in 3 pm, check-out noon. High-speed Internet access. Laundry services. Outdoor pool. $

Off-Strip/Downtown Las Vegas

BEST WESTERN MAIN ST INN.
1000 N Main St, Las Vegas (89101). Phone 702/382-3455; toll-free 800/851-1414. www.bestwestern.com. The Fremont Street Experience area, the oldest section of the city, is only 1/2 mile from this hotel. 91 rooms, 3 story. Pets accepted; fee. Check-in 3 pm, check-out noon. Laundry services. Outdoor pool. $

BEST WESTERN NELLIS MOTOR INN.
5330 E Craig St, Las Vegas (89115). Phone 702/643-6111; toll-free 800/546-1119. www.bestwestern.com. A smart choice for bypassing traffic heading back into the city after the race, this hotel sits in the far northeast reaches of the valley, close to Lake Mead. 52 rooms, 2 story. Pets accepted. Complimentary continental breakfast. Check-in 4 pm, check-out 11 am. Laundry services. Outdoor pool. $

BEST WESTERN PARKVIEW INN.
921 Las Vegas Blvd N, Las Vegas (89101). Phone 702/385-1213; toll-free 800/548-6122. www.bestwestern.com. This place is perfect for folks who want to be nearby, but avoid the casinos. The Parkview Inn is north of US Highway 95 and only about a mile from the seedy hubbub of the Fremont Street Experience, but it's a world away. If you drive, be aware that this is one of the few hotels in Las Vegas that charges for parking ($7 a day). 42 rooms, 2 story. Check-in 3 pm, check-out noon. Laundry services. Outdoor pool. $

LAQUINTA NELLIS.
4288 N Nellis Blvd, Las Vegas (89115). Phone 702/632-0229; toll-free 800/531-5900. www.laquinta.com. This hotel is the absolute closest to the Las Vegas Motor Speedway—literally right around the corner—but there's no shuttle to get you anywhere else and it's a solid 20 miles north of the Strip. The lobby walls boast an intriguing collection of old photos reflecting the history of the base. 59 rooms, 3 story. Complimentary continental breakfast. Check-in 2 pm, check-out noon. Laundry services. Indoor pool, whirlpool. $

RV AND CAMPING

Las Vegas

SAM'S TOWN RV PARK.
5111 Boulder Hwy, Las Vegas (89122). Phone 702/456-7777; toll-free 800/634-6371. There are actually two RV areas here, one along Boulder Highway and the other on the South Nellis Boulevard part of the property that also includes the hotel-casino. Together, they total 452 full hook-ups. Pool. Laundry services. Showers. Pet runs. BBQ areas.

SILVERTON HOTEL CASINO RV PARK.
3333 Blue Diamond Rd, Las Vegas (89139). Phone 702/263-7777; toll-free 800/588-7711. www.silvertoncasino.com. The great advantage of the Silverton is that it's right off Interstate 15 at the Blue Diamond exit and is far enough away from both the Strip (6 miles) and the Las Vegas Motor Speedway (30 miles) to possibly be kinder to your pocketbook. RVers can use the property's pool and spa. 300 rooms, 3 floors. Check-in for hotel 3 pm, check-out noon. RV park has 300 spaces, full hook-up, showers, laundry services, mini-mart, and pool access. The office is open from 7 am to 7 pm, but you can pay the next day if you arrive late and grab a space.

For more lodging recommendations, go to www.mobiltravelguide.com

EAT

MOBIL STAR-RATED RESTAURANTS

Las Vegas Strip

THE BUFFET AT THE BELLAGIO. ★
Bellagio Las Vegas, 3600 Las Vegas Blvd S, Las Vegas (89109). Phone 702/693-8111. www.bellagiolasvegas.com. Even at a classy hotel like the Bellagio, the hordes must be fed. Ergo the buffet, a crowd-feeding staple at many Strip and off-Strip hotels. But like everything else at the Bellagio, the buffet redefines the standard. You'll find mounds of jumbo cocktail shrimp, Japanese sushi rolls, made-to-order dishes,

and ethnic fare from China to Italy. Prices are higher than at rival spreads, but so is the quality. To make the best of it, go very hungry. American menu. Breakfast, lunch, dinner. **$$**

COYOTE CAFÉ. ★★

MGM Grand Hotel and Casino, 3799 Las Vegas Blvd S, Las Vegas (89109). Phone 702/891-7777. www.mgmgrand.com. Celebrated chef Mark Miller runs this spin-off of his Santa Fe original just off the casino floor in the MGM Grand. Despite his status, Miller's food is highly approachable, beginning with his zesty homemade salsas and potent margaritas. Mexican standards like quesadillas, tacos, and enchiladas gain a Southwestern accent in blue corn tortillas and New Mexican chiles. Drop into the lively, casual café or make a reservation to dine in the adjacent Grill Room, which serves more upscale versions of Miller's fare. Southwestern menu. Breakfast, lunch, dinner. Valet parking. **$$$**

ORTANIQUE. ★★

Paris Las Vegas, 3655 Las Vegas Blvd S, Las Vegas (89109). Phone 702/967-7999. www.parislasvegas.com. A trip to the French Caribbean in the all-things-French Paris Las Vegas, Ortanique conjures the culinary tropics. Chef Cindy Hutson spins off a Vegas version of her Miami hotspot, preparing sun-kissed dishes like curried crab cakes, "rasta pasta" with jerk shrimp, Jamaican-spiced ahi, and Caribbean bouillabaisse. Jazz, steel drum, and reggae music keep the island beat. Look for Ortanique in the walkway en route to Bally's next door. French-Caribbean menu. Dinner. **$$**

PHARAOH'S PHEAST. ★

Luxor Hotel and Casino, 3900 S Las Vegas Blvd, Las Vegas (89119). Phone 702/262-4772. www.luxor.com. Catering to the mass of Luxor hotel guests and gamblers, Pharaoh's Pheast lays out a buffet suitable for Tutankhamun himself. Amid the Egypt-inspired room, a vast bank of kitchen-side serving stations lays out options highlighted by a 30-foot salad bar, homemade pizzas, carved-to-order meats, and made-to-order omelets. Save room for a trip through the enticing dessert section, which offers sugarless versions for those watching their waistlines. The all-you-can-eat prices are quite reasonable, ranging from about $10 per person at breakfast to around $17 at dinner. American menu. Breakfast, lunch, dinner. **$$**

SAM WOO BBQ. ★

4215 Spring Mountain Rd, Las Vegas (89102). Phone 702/368-7628. This local secret is a no-frills, economically friendly culinary adventure that's open till the wee hours. And if the ducks, chickens, and pigs hanging in the front window were not indication enough, this carnivore's heaven is no place to bring your vegetarian friends. The BBQ here is heavy on meat, big on grease, and easy on the wallet. Chinese menu. Breakfast, lunch, dinner. Casual attire. **$**

LOCAL RECOMMENDATIONS

Las Vegas Strip

NASCAR CAFE.

Sahara Hotel and Casino, 2535 Las Vegas Blvd S, Las Vegas (89109). Phone 702/737-2760. www.nascar

ROAD FOOD

For the perfect sack lunch en route to the race, you can't go wrong grabbing a delicious—and huge—sub at one of **Capriotti's** nondescript storefronts, just off the Strip or near US 95, depending on your route to the speedway. Capriotti's trademark is the "Bobbie," using the basic ingredients of Thanksgiving leftovers: hand-pulled turkey, cranberries, and stuffing with mayo. Check out the "Slaw Be Jo," which combines roast beef, cole slaw, provolone cheese, and Russian dressing. **$** *Near the Strip: 322 W Sahara Ave, Las Vegas (89102). Phone 702/474-0229. Near US 95 in the northwest: 7440 W Cheyenne Ave, Suite 103, Las Vegas (89129). Phone 702/656-7779. Near US 95 in the southeast: 3830 E Flamingo Rd, Las Vegas (89121). Phone 702/454-2430. www.capriottis.com.*

cafelasvegas.com. Obviously, this is local ground zero for all things NASCAR, so expect large crowds on race weekends. The menu offers burger varieties and several dishes named for NASCAR drivers. Looming over the bar is the Carzilla, the world's largest stock car, which weighs more than 3 tons and measures 408 square feet. A visit here should include a hop on the Speed roller coaster, which vrooms up to 70 mph, and the Las Vegas Cyber Speedway, a simulated-motion ride where riders feel like they're in a car blasting around the track. American menu. Lunch, dinner, Sun brunch. $$

BOOTLEGGER BISTRO.

7700 Las Vegas Blvd S, Las Vegas (89123). Phone 702/736-4939. www.bootleggerlasvegas.com. Here's one of those only-in-Vegas stories: this Italian local favorite happens to be owned by the family of former lounge singer-turned-current Nevada Lieutenant Governor Lorraine Hunt. What's more, Hunt can even be caught crooning by the concert piano when she's not up in Carson City. And her 84-year-old mother, Maria Perry, still oversees her time-honored recipes as executive chef, just as she did 55 years ago. Such Vegas stars as Clint Holmes, Sheena Easton, and Gladys Knight have been known to pop in after 10 pm on Mondays to sing karaoke. Open 24 hours. Italian menu. Breakfast, lunch, dinner, late-night. Bar. Children's menu. $

HARLEY-DAVIDSON CAFÉ.

3725 Las Vegas Blvd S, Las Vegas (89109). Phone 702/740-4555. www.harley-davidsoncafe.com. With obvious NASCAR appeal, this eatery serves up the predictable array of burgers and other comfort foods amid an overwhelming collection of motorcycle memorabilia and noise. The walls are decked with portraits of celebrities on their Hogs, and even the waiters look like bikers. The raspberry bread pudding is a show-stopper. American menu. Lunch, dinner. $$

PARADISE GARDEN BUFFET.

Flamingo Las Vegas, 3555 Las Vegas Blvd S, Las Vegas (89109). Phone 702/733-3111; toll-free 800/732-2111. www.flamingolv.com. Let's face it: most buffets are roughly the same—until you get to the offensively expensive ones. But the Flamingo's has something none of the others have at any price: a view of their beautiful 15-acre wildlife preserve where pink flamingos and brown African penguins frolic and colorful fish swim in the waters just below the window. Ask for a window seat and go during daylight hours. American menu. Breakfast, lunch, dinner. $

North Las Vegas

CANNERY ROW BUFFET.

Cannery Casino and Hotel, 2121 E Craig Rd, North Las Vegas (89030). Phone 702/507-5700; toll-free 866/999-4899. www.cannerycasinos.com. At this, the closest major casino property to the Las Vegas Motor Speedway, you'll find a genuinely cheap, pretty good buffet. With most pushing closer and closer to $20 a head elsewhere, the champagne brunch on Sundays is a reasonable alternative, complete with a carving station, Mexican and Chinese offerings, and made-to-order omelets. It's a nice space, too, with lots of World War II imagery on the walls, but this is a "locals" casino, so they don't go too bonkers with the theme. American menu. Lunch, dinner, Sun brunch. $

Off-Strip

COFFEE PUB.

2800 W Sahara Ave, Las Vegas (89102). Phone 702/367-1913. This 20-year-old spot west of the Strip, tucked a bit confusingly inside a strip mall, is where the powerbrokers of Las Vegas eat breakfast. It's worth the search, if only for the best banana pancakes anywhere. American menu. Breakfast, lunch. $

LINDO MICHAOCAN.

2655 E Desert Inn, Las Vegas (89121). Phone 702/735-6828. www.lindomichaocan.com. The menu at this homespun eatery run by an immigrant family from the central Mexican state of Michaocan runs beyond the ordinary: you'll find chicken breasts cooked in red chilis and orange juice, and shrimp stuffed with cheese and wrapped in bacon. Las Vegas natives, among them Andre Agassi, were delighted when this institution reopened in 2004 following a devastating 2002 fire. Mexican menu. Lunch, dinner, brunch. $$

PAYMON'S MEDITERRANEAN CAFÉ AND HOOKAH LOUNGE.

4147 S Maryland Pkwy, Las Vegas (89119). Phone 702/731-6030. www.paymons.com. The best Greek food is found at this site west of the Strip opened by a pair of brothers who saved up their money from jobs as busboys and dishwashers. Don't miss the spicy Athens fries. Adjacent is the ancient Persia-decked Hookah Lounge, where you can inhale smoke from a water bong with fruit-flavored tobacco coursing through it. Greek menu. Lunch, dinner, brunch. $$

For more dining recommendations, go to www.mobiltravelguide.com

SIDETRIP

Zion National Park
Springdale, UT

Need a break from the hurried pace of the race? Spend some time communing with nature at Zion National Park where you can recharge your batteries.

Those who grew up watching old coyote-and-roadrunner cartoons expect nothing from the desert but sandy cliffs, sagebrush, and dull brown desolation, but the American Southwest's unexpected beauty is constantly astounding. Just 160 miles northeast of Las Vegas, Zion National Park's 229 square miles of colorful rock formations reflect 240 million year's of geological history set against the cliffs and canyons cut through by the Virgin River.

Kolob Arch, at 310 feet, is the largest natural arch in North America as well as one of the only attractions here. The half-mile hike at Lower Emerald Pool takes you to the edge of sensational waterfalls and the 3 1/2-mile Par'us Trail, which begins near the Visitors Center and winds along the river, providing a stunning sampler of the looming red-rock formations around the region. The Zion Human History Museum offers a 22-minute orientation film that explains the geological history and significance of the region.

March, before the region is overrun by tourists, is one of the best times to visit. Motorists can still drive through the park ($20 per vehicle) while the weather is warm enough to enjoy the outdoors. (From April through October, the six-mile Zion Canyon Scenic Drive is closed to private vehicles; a shuttle from the Visitors Center lets guests off at various trailheads, scenic attractions, the Zion Lodge, and the Zion Human History Museum.) However, in the winter months, ranger-led activities are not available and some parts of the park are closed because it's still too cold, particularly in higher elevations.

For more Zion National Park recommendations, go to www.mobiltravelguide.com

Jimmie Johnson burns up his tires after winning the NASCAR NEXTEL Cup Series UAW-GM Quality 500.

Lowe's Motor Speedway

Concord, NC

15

The night comes to life at Lowe's Motor Speedway for the NASCAR NEXTEL Cup Series UAW-GM Quality 500.

TRACK FACTS

LOWE'S MOTOR SPEEDWAY. 5555 Concord Pkwy S, Concord (28027). Phone toll-free 800/455-3267. www.lowesmotorspeedway.com.

SECURITY. Prohibited items: umbrellas, strollers, glass bottles, firearms, pets (except for guides for the disabled), bicycles, grills, open flames, skateboards, inline skates, golf carts, ATVs, fireworks, folding chairs, golf cars, coolers larger than 14 x 14 x 14 inches, balloons, and beach balls.

PARKING. Race event parking is free in unreserved Lowe's Motor Speedway-owned lots surrounding the track. The earlier you get there, the better your choices. Be warned: it usually takes between two and three hours to clear the parking lots after a race.

FIRST AID. Medical teams patrol the area, but the fastest way to reach them is to ask a speedway staff member for help. Carolinas Medical Center has a fully staffed infield care center at races to treat emergencies. There are EMS stations under every major grandstand.

CONCESSIONS. Offerings consist of the usual hot dogs, hamburgers, nachos, and beer, though some independent vendors sell food outside the track. If you're seeking easier access to food stands and restrooms, consider buying tickets in the underutilized Diamond Tower Terrace. It lacks a view of the pits, but has more stands and bathrooms than older sections of the track.

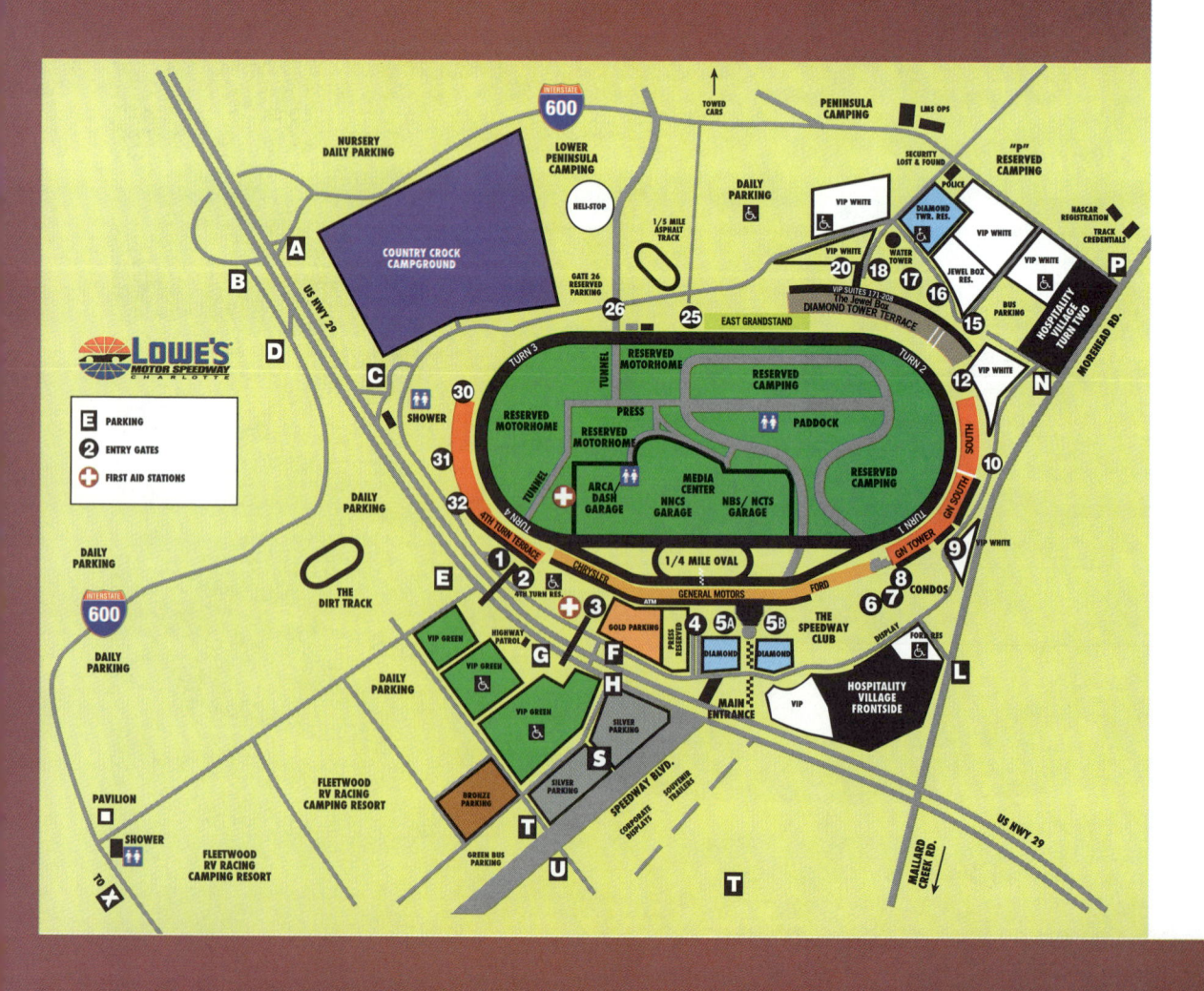

GETTING TICKETS

Lowe's Motor Speedway offers the cheapest ticket in NASCAR NEXTEL Cup Series racing: $19. The most expensive outdoor seats are in the new ten-story Ford Tower Grandstand: be prepared for nosebleeds. Good medium-priced options: the South Grandstand, between Turns 1 and 2, and the Fourth Turn Terrace both offer good views. For $99, you can buy a Superticket that covers four nights of racing during the October Race Week. Buy tickets by calling toll-free 800/455-FANS (3267), or at www.lowesmotorspeedway.com.

HOME BASE FOR DRIVERS

Here's a secret that newly minted NASCAR fans might not know, but drivers certainly do: Lowe's Motor Speedway, and greater Charlotte, is home.

Dale Earnhardt Jr. is perhaps Charlotte's most renowned home-town boy these days, but he's not the only one who hails from here. In fact, most NASCAR drivers, current and veteran, live around Charlotte. And 90 percent of NASCAR's race teams are based within a two-hour drive of Lowe's. In nearby Concord and Kannapolis, Junior's late pop, Dale Earnhardt, is everywhere—in statues, park names, street signs, and definitely many hearts. Across from Lake Norman, Mooresville touts itself as "RACE CITY, USA," and offers tours of race shops and restaurants full of driving memorabilia.

Rusty Wallace waves to the crowd during a pre-race event.

Kyle Busch in the No. 5 Car crosses the finish line after a dominating performance in the NASCAR Busch Series CARQUEST 300.

For nightlife, dining, and possibly a driver spotting, head to downtown (called "uptown") Charlotte.

Speed along the tracks of a roller coaster at Paramount's Carowinds theme park.

In other words, racing fans, there is no place where you are more likely to run into drivers than in Charlotte. Maybe you'll spot one fishing on Lake Norman or simply dining out in one of the area restaurants. Even if you don't, you can always surround yourself by all things NASCAR at the many race shops and racing museums. In all, there are more than 400 motor sports-related businesses in greater Charlotte.

HUMBLE HOST

Lowe's is one of NASCAR's oldest speedways, hosting races since 1960, and one of only two tracks that still boasts three NASCAR NEXTEL Cup races. Until the Carolina Panthers went to the 2004 Super Bowl, NASCAR was the only professional sport with real buzz. Despite its duly respected past and present, the Queen City is no haughty host. It embraces NASCAR—and NASCAR fans—as an old friend and a home-grown regional sport.

To celebrate in style, Charlotte pulls out all the stops for race weekends. The biggest party, the Food Lion Speed Street Festival in downtown Charlotte, coincides with May's Race Week. On weekend evenings, Tryon Street bustles with traffic and revelers, and hotels that cater to weekday business travelers happily host racing fans on weekends.

When it's not focused on NASCAR, Charlotte offers plenty of other attractions, including the Carolinas' biggest tourist draw: Concord Mills outlet mall, located just next to the speedway. Not into shopping till you drop? Besides NASCAR, other sports spectacles are gaining fans. Since the Panthers' stint at the Super Bowl, every home game draws crowds to Bank of America stadium. Although the Hornets left, the Bobcats, an expansion basketball team, is setting up shop. Outside the city, Charlotte has charms as well. Paramount's Carowinds, one of the biggest amusement parks in the Carolinas, is a 20-minute drive away, and so is massive Lake Norman, a perfect spot for boating, kayaking, swimming, and hiking.

In downtown (called "uptown") Charlotte, an enormous new basketball arena is being built, another step toward raising Charlotte's profile beyond NASCAR. Further altering Charlotte's skyline are two skyscrapers, which house the banking headquarters of Wachovia and Bank of America. Banking has brought new life to the city's once-dormant uptown neighborhood. Developers are lining up to build luxury condos, and more restaurants and bars are opening to serve the young professionals who are buying them.

GETTING AROUND

There's a reason why no one holds races on I-85. Traffic isn't moving.

The locals know better than to get stuck there. Skip I-85, and instead head for the brand new I-485. The eastern part, running from the speedway in Concord to southern Mecklenburg and Union County, just opened, and it's too new to be crowded. Alternatively, take US 29 and NC 49. Yes, there are more stoplights, but considerably fewer cars. The best advice of all: get there early. In addition to missing the throngs of cars, trucks, and RVs, you can enjoy one of the pre-race shows for which Lowe's is well known.

Besides coin collections, this former US Mint houses exhibits on pottery, maps, costumes, and American art.

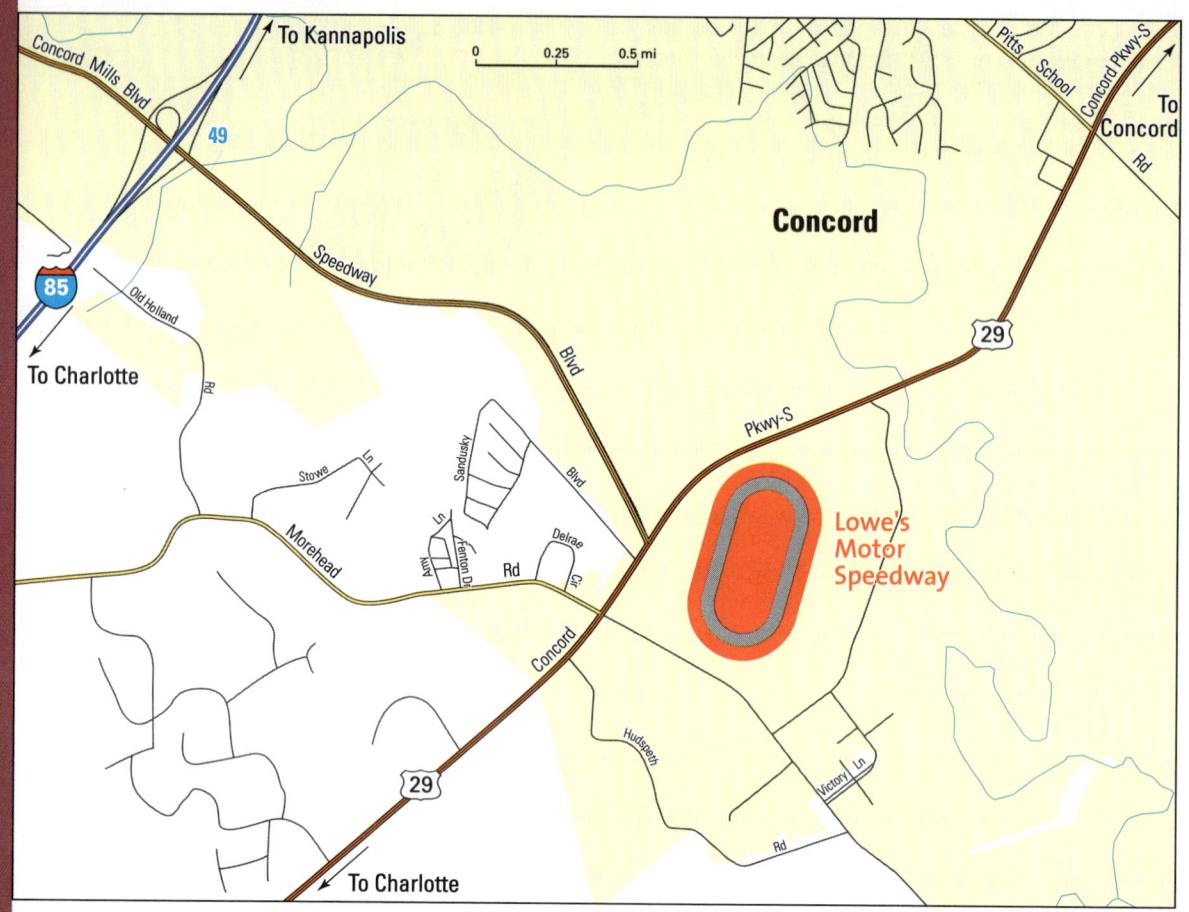

CONCORD POLE POSITION:
The 10 miles surrounding Lowe's Motor Speedway.

The influx of young, professional residents is sparking more than bars and restaurants. The SouthPark Mall now includes upscale stores such as Nordstrom and Anthropologie. The once-quiet NoDa neighborhood is home to new galleries and live music venues. Older neighborhoods such as Dilworth and Elizabeth are also experiencing renewal. These areas, beloved for their tree-lined boulevards and parks, now have new boutiques and upscale restaurants, many of them housed in old homes.

TRADITIONAL CHARLOTTE

One of Charlotte's esteemed traditions is the University of North Carolina at Charlotte, which got its start in 1946 as an evening college. The grounds are tucked away off a street of strip malls and big box stores, meandering over 1,000 acres of green space and botanical gardens.

Charlotte also has a thriving religious community, and churches number more than 700. The city's legendary barbecue and superior Southern cooking are not to be overlooked, either.

Traditions Charlotte is not so happy about? Speedway traffic and hot, muggy weather. Even in May, temps can be pretty hot. Still, you aren't a true NASCAR fan until you've seen a race at Lowe's Motor Speedway—keep an eye out for Humpy's Bump, a notoriously tricky spot by Turn 4. If you don't see Dale Jr. in person, you're sure to see him at the track.

LOWE'S MOTOR SPEEDWAY, NC **259**

CONCORD CALENDAR

MAY 20, 2005
NASCAR Craftsman Truck Series, Infineon 200.

MAY 21, 2005
NASCAR NEXTEL All-Star Challenge

MAY 26–28, 2005
Food Lion Speed Street Festival. Tryon between Stonewall and 7th sts, Charlotte (28202). Phone 704/455-6814. www.600festival.com. Get in the racing mood with music, food, driver appearances, and more.

MAY 28, 2005
NASCAR Busch Series CARQUEST Auto Parts 300

MAY 29, 2005
NASCAR NEXTEL Cup Series Coca-Cola 600

OCTOBER, 2005
Charlotte Shout! Festival. Various locations, Charlotte. Phone 704/332-2227. www.charlotteshout.com. This music and art event also includes a food festival, with barbecue cookoff, wine tastings, and ice carving. Throughout October.

OCTOBER 1–30, 2005
Carolina Renaissance Festival. 16445 Poplar Tent Rd, Huntersville (28078). Phone 704/896-5544; toll-free 877/896-5544. www.royalfaires.com/carolina. Join the jousters for a jubilant medieval celebration and arts fair. Weekends.

OCTOBER 14, 2005
NASCAR Busch Series Charlotte 300

OCTOBER 15, 2005
NASCAR NEXTEL Cup Series UAW-GM Quality 500

The pit crew for the No. 48 Lowe's Chevrolet of NASCAR NEXTEL Cup Series driver Jimmie Johnson pulls off an impressive pit stop en route to a dominating win in the NASCAR NEXTEL Cup Series Coca-Cola 600.

DRIVER'S PICK

For a veteran of 173 NASCAR Cup Series events, from 1955 to 1967, convenience is king. When at Lowe's, **Johnny Allen** doesn't stray far. "When I'm in Concord, I like to eat at the **Red Lobster** across from the track. I order the shrimp trio plate. It has shrimp scampi, fried shrimp, and shrimp pasta. The best." *8012 Concord Mills Blvd, Concord (28027). Phone 704/979-1160. www.redlobster.com.*

CONCORD OUTFIELD:
The 50 miles surrounding Lowe's Motor Speedway.

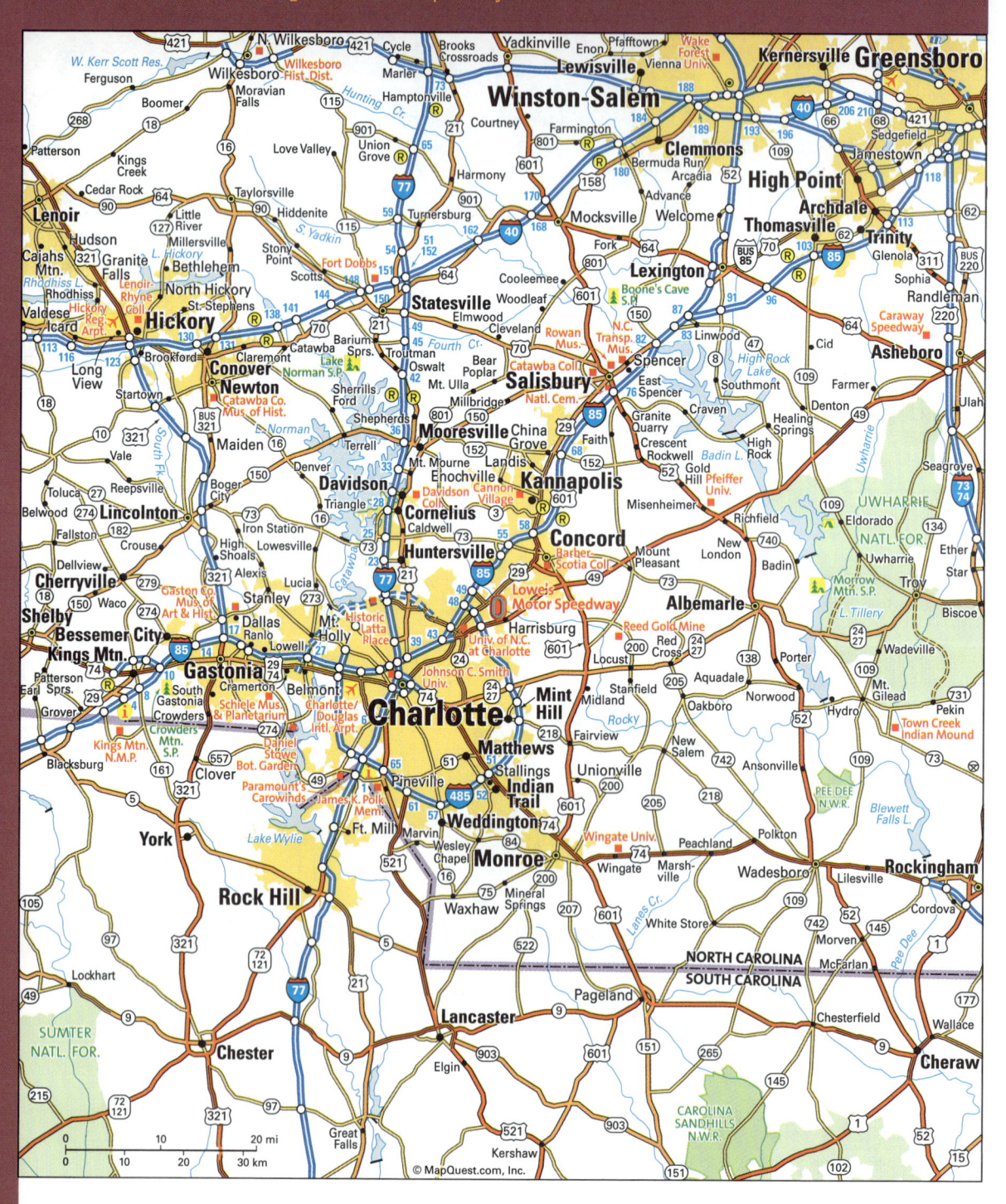

SEE

ATTRACTIONS

There are plenty of racing-affiliated attractions around Concord, Charlotte, Kannapolis, and Mooresville, but that's not all. Gold was discovered here even before the famous California gold rush sent prospectors west, and the museum offerings in Charlotte are some of the best in the South. When all else fails, head outside—the area's natural beauty is a nice break from the speedway.

Charlotte

LEVINE MUSEUM OF THE NEW SOUTH.
200 E 7th St, Charlotte (28202). Phone 704/333-1887. www.museumofthenewsouth.org. The museum chronicles the history of the post-Civil War South with an ever-changing series of exhibits featuring industry, ideas, people, and historical eras such as the civil rights movement. **$$**

MINT MUSEUM OF ART.
2730 Randolph Rd, Charlotte (28207). Phone 704/337-2000. First branch of the US Mint operated in the building from 1837 to 1861 and 1867 to 1913, and in 1933 it was chartered as an art museum. Collections include European and American art from Renaissance to contemporary; fine pottery and porcelain; maps; period costumes; pre-Columbian and African artifacts; and an exhibition of coins. (Tues-Sun; closed holidays) **$$$**

PARAMOUNT'S CAROWINDS.
14523 Carowinds Blvd, Charlotte (28207). Exit 90 off I-77, at state line. Phone 704/588-2600; toll-free 800/888-4386. www.carowinds.com. This 100-acre family theme park has more than 40 rides, shows, and attractions including the 12-acre water entertainment complex WaterWorks; Nickelodeon Central children's area; Drop Zone stunt tower; and roller coasters. The 13,000-seat Paladium Amphitheater hosts special events. (June-late Aug, daily; Mar-May and Sept-Oct, weekends) **$$$$**

Concord

CONCORD MILLS.
8111 Concord Mills Blvd, Concord (28027). Phone 704/979-3000. www.concordmills.com. This outlet mall has more than 200 stores and draws more tourists on an annual basis than any other attraction in the Carolinas.

CONCORD MOTORSPORT PARK.
7940 US Hwy 601 S, Concord (28025). Phone 704/782-4221. www.concordmotorsportpark.com. The NASCAR Dodge Weekly Series runs Saturday nights from April through October at this 1/2-mile asphalt tri-oval 30 miles northeast of Charlotte, in the heart of NASCAR country. The grandstands seat 8,000, and there are spots for 28 RVs at Turn 3. **$$$$**

NASCAR SPEEDPARK, CONCORD MILLS.
8461-G1 Concord Mills Blvd, Concord (28027). Phone 704/979-6770. www.nascarspeedpark.com. A 7-acre race-themed amusement park with five racetracks, a state-of-the-art interactive arcade, one 18-hole miniature golf course, kiddie rides, Lazer Tag, and a snack bar. **$$$$**

RICHARD PETTY DRIVING EXPERIENCE.
Lowe's Motor Speedway, 5555 Concord Pkwy S, Concord (28027). Phone 800/237-3889. www.1800bepetty.com. Always wanted to rip a stock car around the curves at Lowe's Motor Speedway? This is the largest of the driving schools that takes fans right out onto the track. For anywhere between $99 for a ride-along to almost $3,000 for an "advanced racing experience," you can live your dream. **$$$$**

SAM BASS GALLERY.
6104 Performance Dr SW, Concord (28027). Phone 704/455-6915; toll-free 800/556-5464. www.sambass.com. Sam Bass is the first officially licensed artist of NASCAR. His gallery sells NASCAR artwork and is down the road from the track. (Mon-Sat 10 am-5 pm)

Gastonia

SCHIELE MUSEUM OF NATURAL HISTORY & PLANETARIUM.
1500 E Garrison Blvd, Gastonia (28052). Phone 704/866-6900. www.schielemuseum.org. Habitat settings showcasing more than 75,000 mounted birds, mammals, reptiles, fish; rocks and minerals, Native

262 SEE ATTRACTIONS

American arts and crafts; forestry exhibits; and 28-acre nature park. Major exhibits on the Southeast and North Carolina; special exhibits and events, films; and a restored mid-1700s pioneer farm with living history programs. Planetarium programs. (Daily) $

Huntersville

LATTA PLANTATION NATURE CENTER AND PRESERVE.

5226 Sample Rd, Huntersville (28078). I-77, exit 16 B (Sunset Rd W), right at Beattie's Ford Rd 5 miles, then left at Sample Rd. Phone 704/875-1391. www.lattaplantation.org. Approximately 1,200-acre nature preserve on Mountain Island Lake. Interpretive Center, Carolina Raptor Center, Audubon Bird Sanctuary, Equestrian Center (fees apply for some). Bridle paths, hiking trails, fishing, picnicking, canoe access. (Daily) **FREE**

Kannapolis

DALE EARNHARDT TRIBUTE.

Dale Earnhardt Plaza (intersection of Dale Earnhardt Blvd and Hwy 3 at Main and "B" sts), Kannapolis (28081). The people of Kannapolis have preserved the memory of their favorite son, Dale Earnhardt, in 900 pounds of bronze. The statute is near murals depicting Earnhardt's career.

Mooresville

MEMORY LANE MOTORSPORTS & HISTORIC AUTOMOTIVE MUSEUM.

769 River Hwy, Mooresville (28117). Phone 704/662-3673. www.memorylaneautomuseum.com. One-of-a-kind vehicles from race cars to vintage cars and motorcycles are on display at the museum, in addition to toys, memorabilia, and more. $$

NORTH CAROLINA AUTO RACING HALL OF FAME.

119 Knob Hill Rd, Mooresville (28117). I-77 exit 36. Phone 704/663-5331. www.ncarhof.com. As Mooresville's official visitor's center, the museum offers a large display of more than 35 cars dedicated to all types of auto racing, and provides free race shop guides and maps to fans. Fans can savor racing's greatest moments at the Goodyear Mini-Theater, or marvel at the artistry of some of motorsport's top artists. The gift shop is also the official "RACE CITY, USA" merchandise headquarters, and carries a wide selection of racing memorabilia. $

Winston-Salem

BOWMAN GRAY STADIUM.

1250 S Martin Luther King Jr. Dr, Winston-Salem (27107). Phone 336/727-2900. www.bowmangrayracing.com. Bowman Gray Stadium is a multi-use public arena that hosts Winston-Salem State Rams college football games, and features a 1/4-mile asphalt oval. Part of the city's Lawrence Joel Veterans Memorial Coliseum Complex, Bowman Gray has been hosting races for more than 50 years, making it the longest operating NASCAR short track in the country. The stadium is about an hour away from Lowe's Motor Speedway and seats 17,000.

For more attractions, go to www.mobiltravelguide.com

STAY

MOBIL STAR-RATED LODGINGS

Charlotte

COURTYARD BY MARRIOTT CHARLOTTE UNIVERSITY. ★★

333 W W. T. Harris Blvd, Charlotte (28262). Phone 704/549-4888; toll-free 800/321-2211. www.courtyard.com. Many of the 152 rooms in this four-story hotel have views of the university area. All rooms have work desks and ergonomic chairs, reflecting the hotel's efforts to cater to businesspeople. 152 rooms, 4 story. Check-in 3 pm, check-out noon. High-speed Internet access. Restaurant, bar. Fitness room. Outdoor pool, whirlpool. $

DOUBLETREE HOTEL. ★★

895 W Trade St, Charlotte (28202). Phone 704/347-0070; toll-free 800/222-8733. www.doubletree.com. Convenient to downtown and the convention center, as well as shopping and dining options. 187 rooms, 8-story. Check-in 3 pm, check-out noon. Internet access. Restaurant, bar. Fitness room. Outdoor pool, whirlpool. $

HILTON CHARLOTTE CENTER CITY. ★★★
222 E 3rd St, Charlotte (28202). Phone 704/377-1500; toll-free 800/445-8667. www.hilton.com. Located in the financial district downtown, near shopping and restaurants. 407 rooms, 22 story. Check-in 3 pm, check-out noon. High-speed Internet access. Restaurant, bars. Business center. **$$**

HILTON UNIVERSITY PLACE CHARLOTTE. ★★★
8629 J. M. Keynes Dr, Charlotte (28262). Phone 704/547-7444; toll-free 800/445-8667. www.hilton.com. The official hotel of Lowe's Motor Speedway. Guest rooms and suites have great views of the university area. Relax over dinner at the Lakeside Restaurant or in the Lakeside Lounge, enjoy the pool, or take advantage of the many nearby attractions. 393 rooms, 12 story. Check-in 3 pm, check-out noon. Wireless Internet access. Restaurant, bar. Fitness room. Outdoor pool. **$$**

MARRIOTT CHARLOTTE CITY CENTER. ★★★
100 W Trade St, Charlotte (28202). Phone 704/333-9000; toll-free 800/228-9290. www.marriott.com. Located in the central uptown business district, this hotel is only blocks from the New Charlotte Convention Center and Bank of America Stadium. 442 rooms, 19 story. Check-in 3 pm, check-out noon. High-speed Internet access. Four restaurants, three bars. Fitness room. Indoor pool, whirlpool. Business center. **$$**

OMNI CHARLOTTE HOTEL. ★★★
132 E Trade St, Charlotte (28202). Phone 704/377-0400; toll-free 800/843-6664. www.omnihotels.com. This downtown hotel is located near a science center, performance and cultural center, and other attractions. 374 rooms, 15 story. Pets accepted. Check-in 3 pm, check-out noon. High-speed Internet access. Wireless Internet access. Restaurant, bar. Fitness room. Outdoor pool. Business center. **$$**

PARK HOTEL. ★★★
2200 Rexford Rd, Charlotte (28211). Phone 704/364-8220; toll-free 800/334-0331. www.theparkhotel.com. South of the business district in the elegant South Park neighborhood, the hotel offers a quiet getaway for travelers, with amenities that include a nine-hole putting green and a Charles Grayson Day Spa. 192 rooms, 6 story. Check-in 4 pm, check-out noon. High-speed Internet access. Wireless Internet access. Restaurant, bar. Fitness room. Outdoor pool. Business center. **$$**

SUMMERFIELD SUITES BY WYNDHAM—CHARLOTTE. ★
4920 S Tryon St, Charlotte (28217). Phone 704/525-2600; toll-free 877/999-3223. www.summerfieldsuites.com. Located about 5 miles from downtown and near convention facilities. 144 rooms, 5 story, all suites. Pets accepted, some restrictions; fee. Check-in 3 pm, check-out noon. High-speed Internet access. Fitness room. Outdoor pool, whirlpool. Airport transportation available. Business center. **$**

BRAKE HERE

When you hear the phrase "There's gold in them thar hills," you probably think "California." But this coast has its own stockpile of the natural wonder. In fact, the **Reed Gold Mine State Historic Site** boasts the first documented discovery of gold in the United States way back in 1799, long before those California 'forty-niners hit the mines. Stop and check out the underground mine tours, history trail, working machinery, demonstrations, exhibits, visitor center, and film, or enjoy the panning area, and see what you find. Picnic areas are available for a pre- or post-tour meal. 9621 Reed Mine Rd, Midland (28107), 10 miles SE on US 601 and NC 200 to Georgeville, then 2 miles S on NC 1100. Phone 704/721-4653. Panning area (Apr-Oct, daily; fee) (Tues-Sat) **FREE**

Cornelius

COMFORT INN & SUITES. ★
19521 Liverpool Pkwy, Cornelius (28031). Phone 704/896-7622; toll-free 800/228-5150. www.comfortinn.com. Minutes from Lake Norman and 2 miles from Davidson College. 64 rooms, 4 story. Check-in 3 pm, check-out 11 am. Fitness room. Outdoor pool, whirlpool. $

HAMPTON INN LAKE NORMAN. ★
19501 Statesville Rd, Cornelius (28031). Phone 704/892-9900; toll-free 800/426-7866. www.hamptoninn.com. Located just off Interstate 77, near the popular Lake Norman area. 116 rooms, 55 story. Complimentary continental breakfast. Check-in 3 pm, check-out noon. Fitness room. Outdoor pool. $

HOLIDAY INN CHARLOTTE—LAKE NORMAN. ★ ★
19901 Holiday Ln, Cornelius (28031). Phone 704/892-9120; toll-free 800/465-4329. www.holiday-inn.com. Near Davidson College and between Lake Norman and downtown Charlotte. 119 rooms, 2 story. Pets accepted. Check-in 3 pm, check-out 11 am. Restaurant, bar. Fitness room. Outdoor pool. $

Gastonia

HAMPTON INN GASTONIA. ★
1859 Remount Rd, Gastonia (28054). Phone 704/866-9090; toll-free 800/426-7866. www.hamptoninn.com. Conveniently located for travelers passing through the area. 109 rooms, 5 story. Check-in 3 pm, check-out noon. Fitness room. Outdoor pool. $

LOCAL RECOMMENDATIONS

Charlotte, NC

BEST WESTERN AIRPORT INN.
4040 I-85 at Little Rock Rd, Charlotte (28208). Phone 704/394-4111; toll-free 800/780-7234. www.bestwestern.com. 111 rooms, 2 story. Pets accepted, some restrictions; fee. Complimentary continental breakfast. Fitness room. Outdoor pool. Airport transportation available. $

BEST WESTERN STERLING HOTEL & SUITES.
242 E Woodlawn Rd, Charlotte (28217). Phone 704/525-5454; toll-free 800/780-7234. www.bestwestern.com. 81 rooms, 3 story. Complimentary continental breakfast. Fitness room. Airport transportation available. $

Concord, NC

HAMPTON INN.
612 Dickens Pl N, Concord (28025). Phone 704/793-9700; toll-free 800/426-7866. www.hamptoninn.com. 102 rooms, 5 story Complimentary continental breakfast. High-speed Internet access. Outdoor pool. Airport transportation available. $

HAMPTON INN AND SUITES—CHARLOTTE AT CONCORD MILLS.
9850 Weddington Rd, Concord (28027). Phone 704/979-5600; toll-free 800/426-7866. www.hamptoninn.com. 125 rooms, 6 story. Complimentary continental breakfast. Check-in 3 pm, check-out 11 am. Outdoor pool. $

HOLIDAY INN EXPRESS.
7772 Gateway Ln NW, Concord (28027). Phone 704/979-7900; toll-free 800/377-8660. www.hiexpress.com. 79 rooms, 4 story. Check-in 3 pm, check-out 11 am. Fitness room. Outdoor pool. $

KIDS' PICK

Discovery Place is a hands-on science museum that gives kids (and adults who like to play) a chance to learn about electricity, weather, rocks, minerals, and other scientific wonders. Visit the aquarium, science circus, life center, rain forest, collections gallery, and OMNIMAX theater, as well as major traveling exhibits. (Daily; closed Easter, Thanksgiving, Dec 24-25) *301 N Tryon St, Charlotte (28202). Phone 704/372-6261; toll-free 800/935-0553. www.discoveryplace.org.*

SPRINGHILL SUITES CHARLOTTE CONCORD MILLS/SPEEDWAY.
7811 Gateway Ln, Concord (28027). Phone 704/979-2500; toll-free 888/287-9400. www.springhillsuites.com. 95 rooms, 5 story. Complimentary full breakfast. Indoor pool, whirlpool. $

Cornelius, NC
BEST WESTERN LAKE NORMAN.
19608 Liverpool Pkwy, Cornelius (28031). Phone 704/896-0660; toll-free 888/207-0666. www.bestwestern.com. 80 rooms, 4 story. Pets accepted, some restrictions; fee. Complimentary continental breakfast. Check-in 3 pm, check-out 11 am. Fitness room. Outdoor pool, whirlpool. $

Fort Mill, SC
BEST WESTERN CAROWINDS.
229 Carowinds Blvd, Fort Mill (29708). Phone 803/548-8400; toll-free 800/780-7234. www.bestwestern.com. 50 rooms, 3 story. Complimentary continental breakfast. Check-in 2 pm, check-out 11 am. Outdoor pool. $

Gastonia, NC
BEST WESTERN EXECUTIVE INN.
360 Best Western Ct, Gastonia (28054). Phone 704/868-2000; toll-free 800/780-7234. www.bestwestern.com. 63 rooms, 3 story. Complimentary continental breakfast. Restaurant. Outdoor pool. $

COURTYARD BY MARRIOTT GASTONIA.
1856 Remount Rd, Gastonia (28054). Phone 704/852-4411; toll-free 800/321-2211. www.courtyard.com. About 15 miles east of Charlotte near Interstate 85, this hotel offers a boatload of amenities. 130 rooms, 4 story. Pets accepted. Check-in 3 pm, check-out noon. High-speed Internet access. Restaurant. Fitness room. Indoor pool. $

MICROTEL INN.
1901 Broadcast St, Gastonia (28052). Phone 704/810-6622; toll-free 888/771-7171. www.microtelinn.com. Easy access to Interstate 85 and the proximity to a large number of nearby restaurants are part of the draw. 61 rooms, 2 story. Check-in 3 pm, check-out noon. $

Kannapolis, NC
BEST WESTERN KANNAPOLIS.
2808 Lane St, Kannapolis (28083). Phone 704/983-5080; toll-free 800/780-7234. www.bestwestern.com. 43 rooms, 2 story. Complimentary continental breakfast. Check-in 2 pm, check-out 11 am. Outdoor pool. $

FAIRFIELD INN BY MARRIOTT.
3033 Cloverleaf Pkwy, Kannapolis (28083). Phone 704/795-4888; toll-free 800/228-2800. www.fairfieldinn.com. 84 rooms. 4 story. Complimentary continental breakfast. Outdoor pool. $

Monroe, NC
BEST WESTERN INN & SUITES—MONROE.
2316 Hanover Dr, Monroe (28110). Phone 704/283-4746; toll-free 800/780-7234. www.bestwestern.com. 64 rooms, 2 story. Complimentary continental breakfast. Check in 3 pm, check-out 11 am. Fitness room. Outdoor pool. $

Mooresville, NC
FAIRFIELD INN BY MARRIOTT.
120 Consumer Square Dr, Mooresville (28117). Phone 704/663-6100; toll-free 800/228-2800. www.fairfieldinn.com. 97 rooms, 3 story. Complimentary continental breakfast. High-speed Internet access. Fitness center. Outdoor pool, whirlpool. $

Pineville, NC
BEST WESTERN CROWN SUITES.
9705 Leitner St, Pineville (28134). Phone 704/540-8500; toll-free 800/780-7234. www.bestwestern.com. 85 rooms, 5 story. Complimentary continental breakfast. Check-in 2 pm, check-out 11 am. Fitness room. Outdoor pool. $

Rock Hill, SC
BEST WESTERN INN.
1106 N Anderson Rd, Rock Hill (29730). Phone 803/329-1330; toll-free 800/780-7234. www.bestwestern.com. 60 rooms, 2 story. Complimentary full breakfast. Check-in 2 pm, check-out 11 am. Outdoor pool, whirlpool. $

RV AND CAMPING
Concord
APOLLO MOBILE HOME AND TRAVEL PARK.
4275 Morehead Rd, Concord (28027). Phone 704/455-2409. Just a few minutes walk from the track, this site offers about 100 full hook-ups including both 30- and 50-amp outlets. Shaded areas allow for camping unhampered by the hot Carolina sun. It costs $60 per

STAY RV AND CAMPING

night for two adults with an extra $5 per night for each additional person. Three-night minimum stay. Sites are rented on a first-come, first-served basis.

FLEETWOOD RV RACING RESORT AT CHARLOTTE, LOWE'S MOTOR SPEEDWAY.
5555 Concord Pkwy S, Concord (28027). Phone 704/455-4445. 463 sites with full hook-up, $500 per site for a week during Race Week, $20-$25 a night the rest of the year; more than 7,000 primitive sites, $75-$100 per site, available during Race Week only. You can't stay any closer to the speedway. The prices are far from dirt cheap, but nearby hotels raise the rates for Race Week, and this is one of the more affordable options near the speedway.

The primitive camping sites are near a bathhouse, and there are shuttles to the race. Lowe's officials warn that the full hook-up sites sell out quickly before both the May and October races; book early for the best selection of camping sites. At the primitive sites, wagons are available to empty sewage and/or refill water tanks for $20 per service. Generators are allowed, but must be turned off from midnight to 7 am, unless there is a medical reason to keep them on. The fee for the sites allow one tent or "camping unit" and one vehicle per site, a rule speedway officials attribute to fire marshals.

✈ *For more lodging recommendations, go to www.mobiltravelguide.com*

EAT

MOBIL STAR-RATED RESTAURANTS

Charlotte

FUSE BOX. ★★
227 W Trade St, Suite 1200, Charlotte (28202). Phone 704/376-8885. Sushi, pan-Asian menu. Lunch, dinner. Closed Sun. Casual attire. $$

HEREFORD BARN STEAK HOUSE. ★★
4320 N I-85 Service Rd, Charlotte (28206). Phone 704/596-0854. The rustic, homey atmosphere of this restaurant, set in an old restored barn, is what keeps diners coming back. A warm fireplace, quaint bushel-basket lights, and huge barrels of red delicious apples adorn the entranceway, where diners wait to sit at tables set with red-and-white checked cloths. Steak menu. Dinner. Closed Sun-Mon; holidays. Bar. Children's menu. Casual attire. $$

THE KABOB HOUSE. ★★
6432 E Independence Blvd, Charlotte (28212). Phone 704/531-2500. Middle-Eastern menu. Lunch, dinner. Closed Mon. Casual attire. Reservations recommended. $$

LAVECCHIA'S SEAFOOD GRILLE. ★★★
225 E 6th St, Charlotte (28202). Phone 704/370-6776. www.lavecchias.com. Located in the heart of downtown Charlotte, LaVecchia's is a festive spot for lovers of sea-faring entrées like sea bass and seared yellowfin tuna. This restaurant is a local favorite, packed with a stylish crowd. It's decked out in a modern, urban, marine-themed design. Seafood menu. Dinner. Closed Sun. Bar. $$$

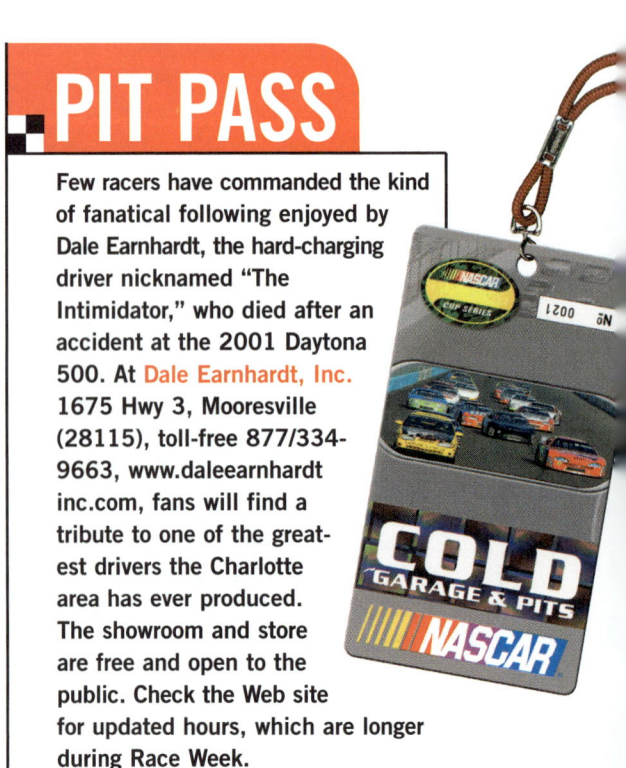

▶ PIT PASS

Few racers have commanded the kind of fanatical following enjoyed by Dale Earnhardt, the hard-charging driver nicknamed "The Intimidator," who died after an accident at the 2001 Daytona 500. At **Dale Earnhardt, Inc.** 1675 Hwy 3, Mooresville (28115), toll-free 877/334-9663, www.daleearnhardt inc.com, fans will find a tribute to one of the greatest drivers the Charlotte area has ever produced. The showroom and store are free and open to the public. Check the Web site for updated hours, which are longer during Race Week.

MERT'S HEART AND SOUL. ★
214 N College St, Charlotte (28202). Phone 704/342-4222. The super laid-back atmosphere of this neighborhood favorite is clear the moment you walk through the door—you're greeted by the smells of soul food simmering in the kitchen and eclectic décor in red, purple, and beige. Southern/Soul menu. Lunch, dinner. Casual attire. Outdoor seating. **$**

RAINBOW CAFÉ. ★
201 S College St, Charlotte (28031). Phone 704/372-2256. The clean and simple décor of this second-floor eatery can be deceiving, as the lunch hour here is mobbed with hungry business people—sometimes the kitchen turns out up to 300 lunches a day. But don't be intimidated—the restaurant is popular for a reason and worth braving the crowds. American menu. Lunch, dinner, late-night. Closed Sat-Sun; holidays; also week of July 4, week after Christmas. Bar. Children's menu. Casual attire. **$**

RANCH HOUSE. ★
5614 Wilkinson Blvd, Charlotte (28208). Phone 704/399-5411. Seafood, steak menu. Dinner. Closed Sun; holidays. Children's menu. Casual attire. **$$**

RHEINLAND HAUS. ★ ★
2418 Park Rd, Charlotte (28203). Phone 704/376-3836. www.rheinlandhaus.com. Charlotte's first and only German restaurant is everything you could ask for in a traditional German establishment—fantastic dark wood paneling, traditional bands for their Oktoberfest celebration, and of course, famous apple strudel. The restaurant has been open for almost 40 years, and the excellent European dishes prove why. German menu. Lunch, dinner. Closed Sun. Bar. Children's menu. Casual attire. Outdoor seating. **$$**

SMOKY'S GRILL. ★ ★ ★
2200 Rexford Rd, Charlotte (28211). Phone 704/364-1346. Located in the Park Hotel (see) on Rexford Road, this eatery has well-prepared and varied meals that are beautifully presented. American menu. Breakfast, lunch, dinner. Business casual attire. Valet parking. Outdoor seating. **$$**

Huntersville

CAPTAIN'S GALLEY. ★
105 Statesville Rd # J, Huntersville (28078). Phone 704/875-6038. Seafood menu. Lunch, dinner. Closed Sun; holidays. Children's menu. **$$**

LOCAL RECOMMENDATIONS

Charlotte

AMALFI'S.
8542 University City Blvd, Charlotte (28078). Phone 704/547-8651. Italian menu. Lunch, dinner. **$$**

BILL SPOON'S BARBECUE.
5524 South Blvd, Charlotte (28217). Phone 704/525-8865. Only Eastern North Carolina barbecue is on the menu here. Barbecue menu. Lunch (Mon-Fri). **$**

ROAD FOOD

Located in a large, older house, **Cajun Queen** takes diners to New Orleans with every serving of its Cajun and Creole dishes. Barbecued shrimp are soaked in a Creole sauce while spicy fried oysters come with a sharp dipping sauce. Other favorites include crawfish, chicken, and shrimp entrées served at various levels of hot. Specials change nightly. After dinner, consider hanging around to enjoy the lively crowd and the live music in the upstairs dining area. Cajun menu. Dinner. Bar. Children's menu. **$** *1800 E 7th St, Charlotte (28204). Phone 704/377-9017. www.cajunqueen.com.*

268 EAT LOCAL RECOMMENDATIONS

FLYING SAUCER DRAFT EMPORIUM.
9605 N Tryon St, Charlotte (28262). Phone 704/717-8179. www.beerknurd.com. This restaurant offers salads, soft pretzels, wings, burgers—and more than 200 beers in bottles and on tap. American menu. Lunch (Fri-Sun), dinner, late-night. Bar. **$**

GREEK ISLES.
200 E Bland St, Charlotte (28203). Phone 704/444-9000. Here you'll find some of the best ethnic food in Charlotte. The perfect spinach pie makes a great meal, as does any of the perfectly done seafood dishes. For an appetizer, go for the traditional flaming cheese soaked in brandy, and yell "Opa!" when it arrives at your table. Greek menu. Lunch, dinner. **$$**

KNIFE & FORK.
2531 N Sharon Amity Rd, Charlotte (28205). Phone 704/568-9711. This is the closest thing to a New York diner in Charlotte. A good brunch menu, along with sandwiches, salads, seafood, and a friendly proprietor. American menu. Lunch, brunch. **$**

LUPIE'S CAFÉ.
2718 Monroe Rd, Charlotte (28205). Phone 704/374-1232. Hot chili, spaghetti with meat sauce, macaroni and cheese, and banana pudding—the menu is small, but there are so many highlights. Simple, filling, inexpensive fare. Italian menu. Lunch, dinner. **$$**

MAMA FU'S ASIAN HOUSE.
1600 E Woodlawn, Charlotte (28209). Phone 704/714-5080. www.mamafus.com. This chain restaurant specializes in noodle dishes and salads with chicken, beef, shrimp, tofu, or all veggie. Pan-Asian menu. Lunch, dinner. Outdoor seating. **$**

PRESTO BAR AND GRILL.
445 W Trade St, Charlotte (28202). Phone 704/334-7088. Presto is really a bistro with a wide-ranging, well-executed menu. Good choices include the salmon club sandwich, chicken marsala, and any of the salads. American menu. Lunch, dinner. **$$**

RED STAR TAVERN.
1315 East Blvd, Charlotte (28203). Phone 704/333-3393. This chain restaurant is in a large complex in the old, tree-lined Dilworth neighborhood. The bar area is a hot after-work spot, and the American menu offers capably done comfort fare—macaroni and cheese, burgers, steaks, ribs. American menu. Lunch, dinner. Bar. **$$**

Concord

GEORGE WASHINGTON BOOKSTORE & TAVERN.
16 Union St S, Concord (28025). Phone 704/788-1561. www.georgewashingtonbookstoreandtavern.com. The menu features hearty soups, sandwiches, and salads with Southern twists: fried-green tomatoes, candied pecans, lowcountry shrimp and grits. The bookstore is home to frequent musical concerts and readings; check the Web site for updated info. American menu. Lunch, dinner. **$$**

THE SPEEDWAY CLUB AT LOWE'S MOTOR SPEEDWAY.
Speedway Blvd, Concord (28075). Phone 704/455-3216. The Speedway Club is open year-round for lunch and dinner. American menu. Lunch, dinner. Reservations recommended. **$$**

Greensboro

NASCAR CAFE.
2101 Four Seasons Blvd, Greensboro (27407) Phone 336/323-0313. www.nascarcafe.com. Steaks, fried chicken, sandwiches, salads and lots of NASCAR memorabilia. American menu. Lunch, dinner. **$$**

Mooresville

THE PRICKLY PEAR.
761 N Main St, Mooresville (28115). Phone 704/799-0875. Enjoy Mexican food in a restored Catholic church. Dishes range from the standard tacos and burritos to more adventurous sauces and seafoods. Mexican menu. Lunch, dinner. **$$**

VINNIE'S SARDINE GRILL AND RAW BAR.
643 Williamson Rd, Mooresville (28117). Phone 704/799-2090. Raw oysters and wings both make the menu here, and the bar has a lively evening scene that's been known to draw NASCAR drivers and crew who live in the Lake Norman area. Seafood menu. Lunch, dinner. **$$**

For more dining recommendations, go to www.mobiltravelguide.com

SIDETRIP

A Cool Mountain Retreat
Asheville, NC

Only a couple of hours from Charlotte, Asheville feels like it's days from NASCAR and the New South. North Carolina's coolest city is nestled in the beautiful Blue Ridge Mountains, where the climes are moderate and the setting is stunning.

Its historic downtown, gorgeous backdrop, and thriving artistic community have drawn travelers since before the Jazz Age. Asheville is known for its artists, especially potters, and is the center of a lively local music scene.

The city of Asheville has created an **"Urban Trail,"** a self-guided tour through the city's downtown historic district and its Art Deco buildings. Another district has more than 200 homes from the beginning of the century. In 2002, the city restored and reopened the historic **Grove Arcade Public Market,** a galleria of public shopping that was built in 1929.

A monument to the city's most famous son—the home of turn-of-the-century writer **Thomas Wolfe**—reopened after a devastating fire almost destroyed it. After six years of work, expert restorers saved much of the furniture and original items damaged in the fire.

The **Wolfe Memorial's Visitor Center** is downtown, part of a web of narrow streets and small, locally owned galleries and shops. Restaurants, pubs, bistros, and cafés are on every corner. Coffee houses and bars offer live music.

Biltmore Estate, just off Interstate 40, has a 250-room French chateau, a winery, formal gardens, and a hotel on the premises (www.biltmore.com). The 19th-century mansion, built by George Vanderbilt, was one of the most advanced homes of its time. It is still a popular site for weddings and events.

Outside the city, adventurers can find whitewater rafting on rivers to both the west and the south. The **Appalachian Trail** passes through nearby, and the Asheville Convention and Visitors Bureau (www.exploreasheville.com) offers information about hiking and biking trails, as well as places to rent equipment.

Asheville is about 120 miles west of Charlotte, at the intersection of Interstates 26 and 40, but a more leisurely, scenic route is following Route 74 through small towns and the foothills. For more local information, go to www.asheville.com, www.exploreasheville.com, or www.asheville-nc.com.

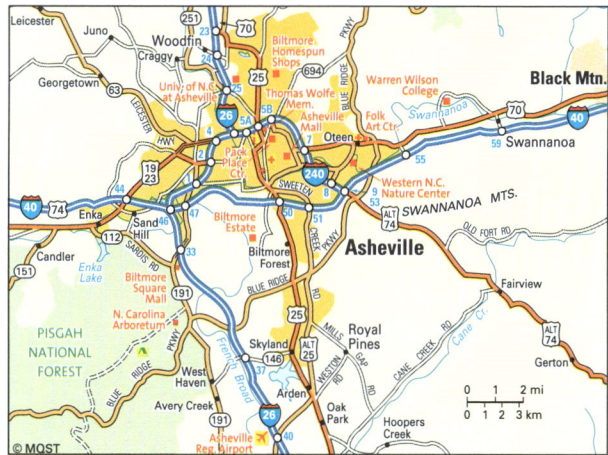

For more Asheville recommendations, go to www.mobiltravelguide.com

270

Jack Sprague, the eventual winner of the inaugural NASCAR Craftsman Truck Series UAW/GM Ohio 250 on May 16, 2004, leads the field into Turn 1 after a late race restart.

Mansfield Motorsports Speedway

Mansfield, OH

16

Fans get three times the excitement as the No. 99 Truck driven by Carl Edwards moves inside on David Reutimann and Hank Parker Jr. during the first NASCAR Craftsman Truck Series UAW/GM Ohio 250.

TRACK FACTS

MANSFIELD MOTORSPORTS SPEEDWAY. 400 Crall Rd, Mansfield (44903). Phone 419/525-7223. www.mansfield-speedway.com.

SECURITY. Coolers, video cameras, food, beverages, and firearms are all prohibited. Scanners and binoculars are allowed, but carry them in mesh or see-through bags to keep the lines moving smoothly during security checks. All bags must be able to fit underneath the seats inside the track.

PARKING. On nice days, track parking is ample and accessible, but wet weather can turn things messy in the grass parking areas. The track has free parking for approximately 6,500 vehicles on-property and within walking distance, but a good portion of that is set aside for VIP, Official, and Reserved Seating parking. More spots are available at neighboring Mansfield Lahm Airport and some nearby industrial sites (all are clearly marked). These remote parking lots may charge a fee, but the speedway will provide free shuttles to the racetrack. Off-premise, private parking is also on hand for a reasonable fee, or simply head down State Route 545, the residential street leading to the track, where many homeowners will be happy to let you park in their driveways or yards for a nominal fee.

FIRST AID. The track operates a first aid station and fully staffed medical units during race events. MedCentral/Mansfield Hospital is 15 minutes away (335 Glessner Ave, Mansfield (44903); phone 419/526-8000). Thirty minutes away is Samaritan Regional Health System (1025 Center St, Ashland (44805); phone 419/289-0491). Both are full-service facilities.

CONCESSIONS. Concessions are located around the perimeter of the seating areas within the gates, and consist of your basic track foods: pizza, burgers, fries, chicken wings, etc. Specialty trailers provide a few other offerings, but don't look for anything especially out of the ordinary. Avoid the huge lines that form at the concessions nearest to the entrance. Chances are you'll find a food stand much closer to your seat with a much shorter line.

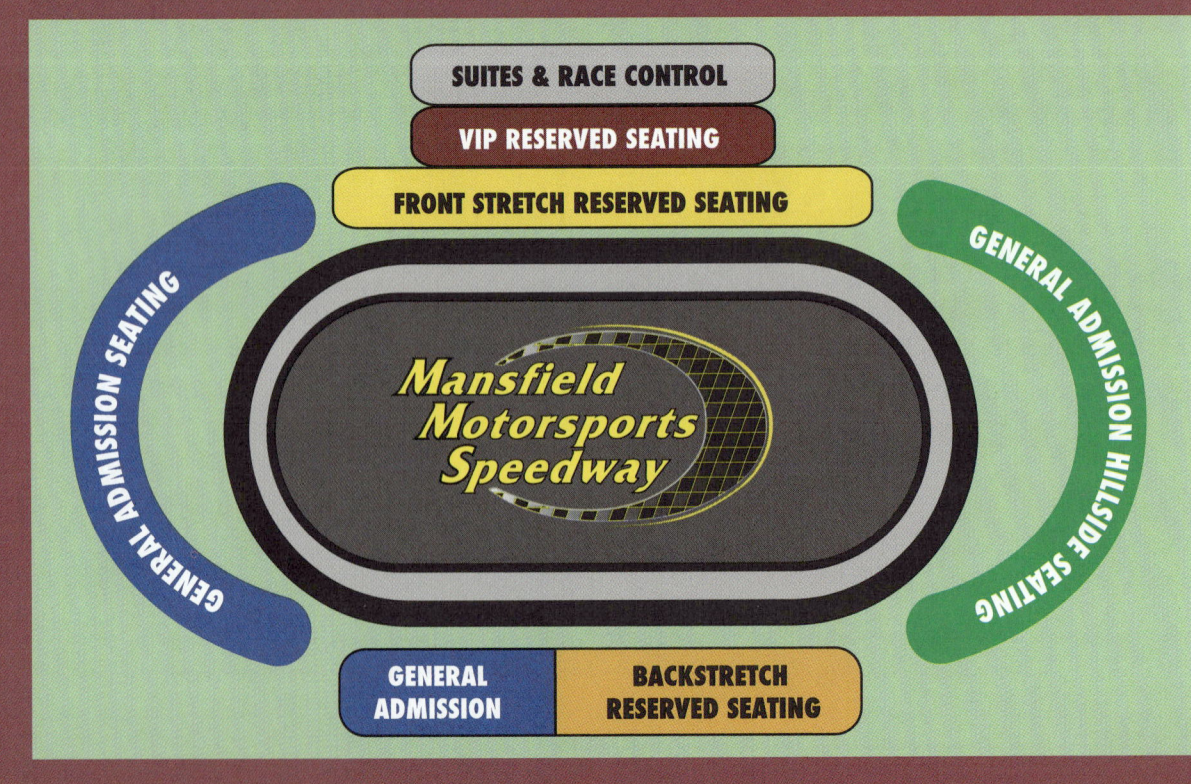

GETTING TICKETS

Purchase tickets (available only through the track itself) as early as possible. It's unlikely any will be available the day of the event. Ticket holders from last year's event have the first shot at this year's seats, but others can call the track (phone 419/525-7223) for ticket availability.

The main grandstands seat 6,000 and run from the exit to Turn 4 to the entrance to Turn 1. Temporary grandstands also line the track from Turn 1 through the end of the back straightaway. Views from the grandstands are largely similar and encompass the entire track.

There is a general-admission grass seating area on a hill between Turns 3 and 4 that can accommodate 500-600 people. It's very popular among families, but be forewarned that when cars are in the short stretch between those turns, spectators will briefly lose sight of them.

APPLE TREES, AMISH, AND AUTO RACES

Halfway between Columbus and Lake Erie in North Central Ohio sits Mansfield, which boasts a population of roughly 51,000.

Travelers to the area enjoy temperate weather in the spring and summer, but since this is the Midwest, it can be unpredictable, so be prepared for a pop-up storm. Expect moderate, cooler temperatures in the 50s and

GETTING AROUND

The track, which sits 5 miles north of downtown Mansfield, is easy to get to thanks to plentiful event signage. From the west, take US 30 E to SR 545 and head north for several miles. Follow signs to the track. If you're coming from the east, take US Rte 30 W to the SR 13 N exit. Go approximately 3 miles and follow signs. From the northeast, take I-71 S to 30 W. From the north, take SR 13 and follow signs. And from the south, take I-71 to 30 and head west as described above. Arrive at the track early and avoid the crush of cars that arrives an hour before race time.

When leaving, traffic funnels out the same way. There simply aren't enough roads to offer alternate routes.

The No. 59 Truck driven by Mark McFarland, who placed sixth in the NASCAR Craftsman Truck Series UAW/GM Ohio 250, is trailed by the truck driven by Brad Keslowski and other racers as McFarland booms down the front stretch.

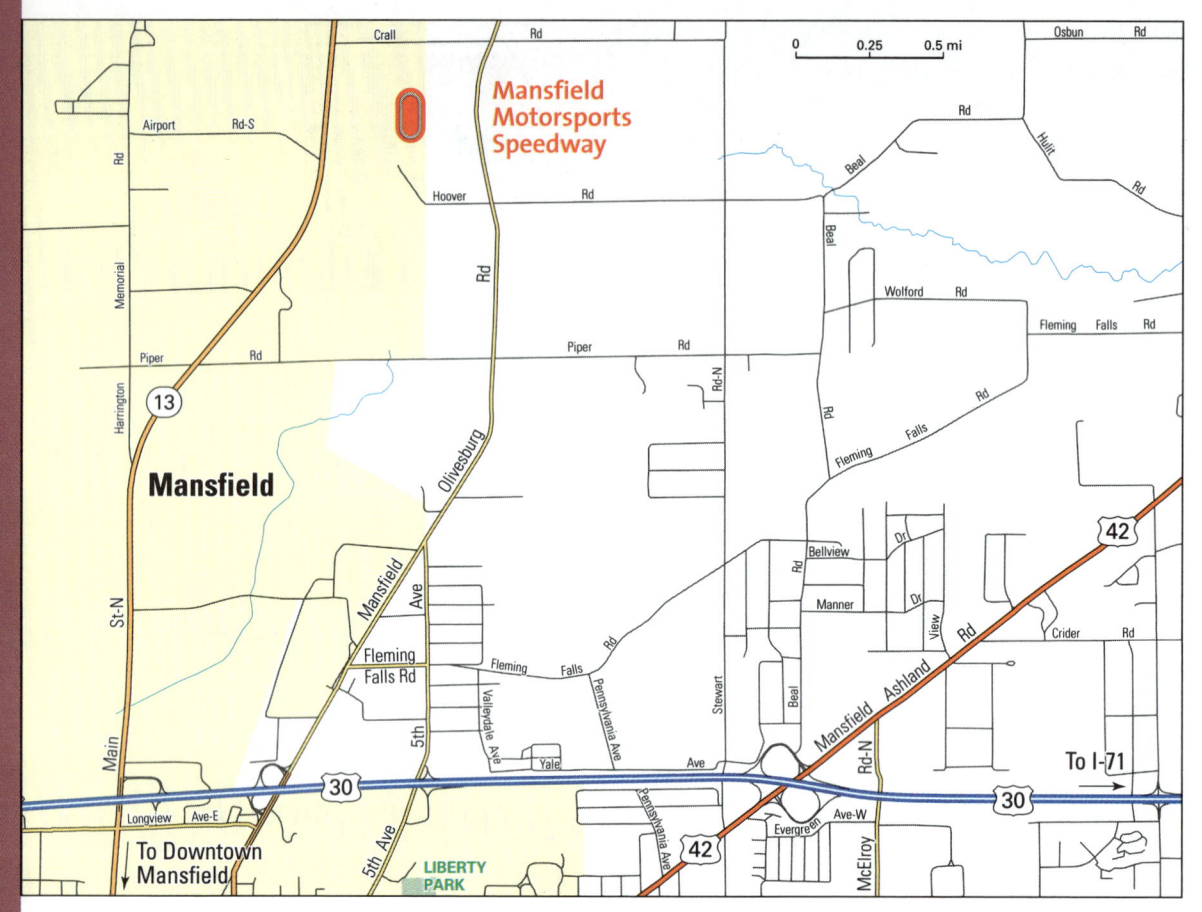

MANSFIELD POLE POSITION:
The 10 miles surrounding Mansfield Motorsports Speedway.

60s in the spring, and summer days that range from the upper 70s during the day to the upper 50s at night.

This region was the legendary home of John "Appleseed" Chapman, and the neighborliness Johnny Appleseed was known for is still evident today.

Much of the new growth in Mansfield has spread to the suburbs, particularly Ontario and Lexington. One exception is the **Historical Carrousel District,** a revitalized area located on Main Street, just north of the city's main square. In addition to the namesake **Richland Carrousel Park** (75 N Main St, Mansfield; phone 419/522-4223, www.richlandcarrousel.com)—the first new, hand-carved carrousel to be built and operated in the United States since the 1930s—the district features shops, galleries, and restaurants in restored Victorian buildings.

The region is also home to the world's largest Amish population. This area is a popular destination, where travelers can enjoy the scenic farmland and learn about Amish culture while shopping for Amish goods or touring a local farm.

A new attraction is the **Johnny Appleseed Outdoor Historical Drama** (2179 Rte 603, Ashland; phone toll-free 800/642-0388, www.jahci.org), a production that takes spectators back to the days when the agricultural steward roamed the countryside barefoot, planting apple trees and befriending Native Americans and settlers alike.

Be sure to stick to the posted speed limits. Locals say the city's proximity to the Amish communities (and their slow-moving horse-drawn buggies) tend to make area law enforcement quick to ticket speeders.

MANSFIELD CALENDAR

MAY 7–8, 2005
Civil War Show. Richland County Fairgrounds, 750 N Home Rd, Mansfield (44906). Phone 419/747-3717. www.richlandcountyfair.com. Browse items, relics, and other Civil War memorabilia.

MAY 14–15, 2005
Spring Plowing Days. Malabar Farm, 4050 Bromfield Rd, Lucas (44843). Phone 419/892-2784. www.malabarfarm.org. Watch the unique competitions of plowing, log-skidding, and an obstacle course.

MAY 15, 2005
NASCAR Craftsman Truck Series

MAY–JUNE, 2005
Marion County Fair. Marion County Fairgrounds, 220 E Fairground St, Marion (43302). Phone 740/382-2558. Activities at this two-month event include horse shows, pig sales, and dog obedience.

JUNE 15–18, 2005
Miss Ohio Festival. Renaissance Theatre, 138 Park Ave W, Mansfield (44902). Phone 419/522-6677. www.missohio.org. Watch who's chosen to go on to the Miss America Pageant.

JULY 31, 2005
NASCAR Elite Midwest Touring Series for MMS

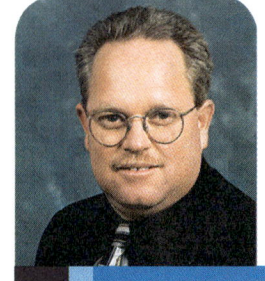

See the world's largest free-standing steel cell block on a tour of the historic Ohio State Reformatory.

Ride one of 52 wild animals or a chariot on the hand-painted Richland Carrousel.

INSIDER'S PICK

Wayne Auton, *Director of the NASCAR Craftsman Truck Series, gets in gear to go to a local favorite eatery. "I like to eat at* **Mama's Touch of Italy** *in downtown Mansfield. They have a great lunch buffet with a great selection. All their Italian dishes are good." 275 Park Ave W, Mansfield (44902). Phone 419/526-5099.*

MANSFIELD OUTFIELD:
The 40 miles surrounding Mansfield Motorsports Speedway.

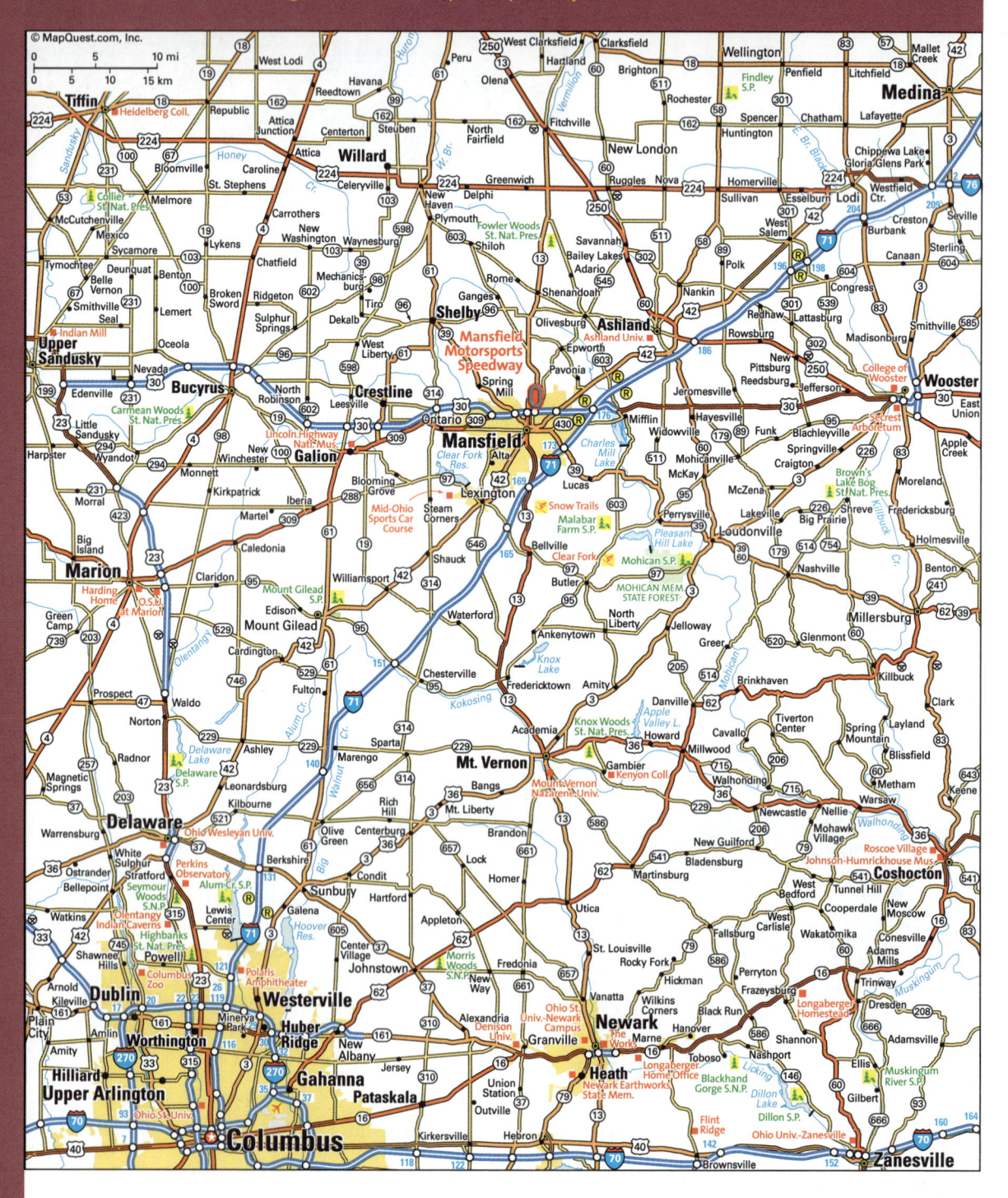

SEE

ATTRACTIONS

Amherst

LORAIN SPEEDWAY.
Rte 58 just S of Rte 113, Amherst (44001). Phone 440/986-7223. www.lorainspeedway.com. Formerly known as the Lorain County Speedway, this 3/8-mile semi-banked oval track is about 55 miles north of Mansfield. It runs late models, modifieds, grand nationals, and spectator stocks every Saturday night from mid-April to mid-September as part of NASCAR Dodge Weekly Series. A recorded message gives the lowdown on races and times.

Ashland

JOHNNY APPLESEED OUTDOOR HISTORICAL DRAMA.
2179 Rte 603, Ashland (44805). Phone 419/525-4759; toll-free 800/642-0388. www.jahci.org. This live, two-hour outdoor performance tells the story of the famed Johnny "Appleseed" Chapman and the challenges that he and others faced in North Central Ohio during the early 1800s. 1,600-seat amphitheater. Nightly performances mid-June-late Aug: Tues-Sun at 8 pm. Tickets/reservations required. **$$$$**

Bellevue

HISTORIC LYME VILLAGE.
5001 Rte 4, Bellevue (44811). www.lymevillage.com. 2 miles E on Hwy 113 then S on Rte 4. Phone 419/483-4949. The John Wright Victorian mansion is featured with several other buildings that have been moved here and restored to create a village depicting 19th-century life. Several events throughout the year. (June-Aug: Tues-Sun 11 am-4 pm; May, Sept: Sun 1-4 pm) **$$**

MAD RIVER AND NKP RAILROAD SOCIETY MUSEUM.
253 S West St, Bellevue (44811). Phone 419/483-2222. View a display of various old railroad cars, artifacts; gift shop. (Memorial Day-Labor Day: daily 1-5 pm; May, Sept-Oct: weekends) **$**

SENECA CAVERNS.
15248 E Thompson Township Rd 178, Bellevue (44811). 3 miles S on Hwy 269, then 2 miles W on Thompson Township Rd 178. Phone 419/483-6711. www.senecacavernsohio.com. One of Ohio's largest natural caverns and a Registered Natural Landmark, it is actually a unique "earth crack" created by undetermined geologic forces. Seven rooms on seven levels; Old Mist'ry River flows at the lowest level (110 feet); electrically lighted. One-hour guided tours; constant temperature of 54°F. Pan for gemstones and minerals (additional fee). (Memorial Day-Labor Day: daily 9 am-7 pm; May, Sept-mid-Oct: weekends 10 am-5 pm) **$$**

Delaware

ALUM CREEK STATE PARK.
3615 Old State Rd, Delaware (43015). 6 miles E on Hwy 36, which then becomes 37. Phone 740/548-4631. On 8,000 acres. The versatile topography and character of lake provide for abundance of activities. Swimming, water-skiing, fishing, boating; hunting, hiking and bridle trails, snowmobiling, camping. Nature programs. (Daily) **FREE**

DELAWARE STATE PARK.
5202 US 23 N, Delaware (43015). Phone 740/369-2761. This 1,686-acre park, with a 1,330-acre lake, features 211 electric sites suitable for tents or trailers; flush toilets, showers, and laundry facilities. Swimming, bathhouse, fishing, boating (rentals, ramp); hiking, picnicking, concession, camping. Pets permitted at designated sites. (Daily) **FREE**

OLENTANGY INDIAN CAVERNS AND OHIO FRONTIERLAND.
1779 Home Rd, Delaware (43015). Phone 740/548-7917. The natural limestone cave is 55-105 feet below ground on three levels with various rock strata and fossils; it once was a refuge for the Wyandot. Tours (35 minutes) guided and self-guided (Apr-Oct from 9:30 am-5 pm). Also re-creation of Ohio frontierland and Native American dwellings (Memorial Day-Labor Day) **$$**

Lexington

THE INFIELD.
176 E Main St, Lexington (44904). Phone 419/884-4386. Features a go-kart track, batting cages, miniature golf, and arcade. Buck's Bar & Grill is on site. Open seasonally.

Lucas

MALABAR FARM STATE PARK.
4050 Bromfield Rd, Lucas (44843). About 10 miles SE of Mansfield. Phone 419/892-2784. www.malabarfarm.org. Louis Bromfield's farm and house are within this 875-acre park. Fishing, hiking, bridle trails, equestrian camp, picnicking. Tractor-drawn wagon tour of farm and house. Tour hours vary greatly by season, so call ahead. **$$**

Mansfield

KINGWOOD CENTER.
900 Park Ave W, Mansfield (44906). Phone 419/522-0211. www.kingwoodcenter.org. The center has 47 acres of landscaped gardens, greenhouses, and wooded property. French Provincial mansion with horticultural library (Easter-early Nov: Tues-Sun; rest of year: Tues-Sat; closed holidays). Greenhouses and gardens (daily). Flower and art shows, special lectures, workshops throughout the year. **FREE**

OAK HILL COTTAGE.
310 Springmill St, Mansfield (44902). Phone 419/524-1765. With seven gables, five double chimneys, and seven marble fireplaces, as well as all original period furnishings of the 1800s, this restored 1847 house is considered one of the most perfect Gothic houses in the nation. (Apr-Dec: Sun 2-5 pm; closed holidays) **$$**

THE OHIO STATE REFORMATORY.
Hwy 545 and Hwy 30, Mansfield (44905). Phone 419/522-2644. www.mrps.org. Listed on the National Register of Historic Places and in the *Guinness Book of World Records,* the prison boasts the world's largest free-standing steel cell block. The site was used in such films as *The Shawshank Redemption* and *Air Force One.* In addition to regular tours, the reportedly haunted site offers overnight ghost hunts twice monthly as well as haunted ghost tours Thursday-Sunday evenings in October. (June-Aug: Tues-Fri 2 pm; late May-late Sept: Sun 1-4 pm) **$$$**

RICHLAND CARROUSEL PARK.
75 N Main St, Mansfield (44902). 4th and Main sts. Phone 419/522-4223. www.richlandcarrousel.com. Features a wooden, hand-carved, hand-painted, turn-of-the-century-style carousel with 52 animals and two chariots. (Daily; call for holiday hours; may be closed for private functions) **$**

Milan

THE EDISON BIRTHPLACE MUSEUM.
9 Edison Dr, Milan (44846). Phone 419/499-2135. www.tomedison.org. This is the two-story red brick house where the inventor spent his first seven years; contains some original furnishings, inventions, and memorabilia. Guided tours. (Tues-Sun; hours vary by month) **$$**

GALPIN WILDLIFE AND BIRD SANCTUARY.
Edison Dr and Berlin Rd, Milan (44846). 1/2 mile SE on Edison Dr. Phone 419/499-4909. Woodland with many varieties of trees, wildflowers, and birds; nature trail. (Daily) **FREE**

Mount Gilead

MOUNT GILEAD STATE PARK.
Mount Gilead (43338). 1 mile E on Hwy 95. Phone 419/946-1961. www.ohiodnr.com/parks. More than 170 acres. Fishing, boating (electric motors only); hiking, picnicking (shelter), camping (electricity but no running water). (Daily)

For more attractions, go to www.mobiltravelguide.com

STAY

MOBIL STAR-RATED LODGINGS

Akron

CROWNE PLAZA HOTEL AKRON QUAKER-SQUARE.
★★★
135 S Broadway St, Akron (44308). Phone 330/253-5970; toll-free 888/303-1746. www.crowneplaza.com. Constructed from 19th-century silos and mills, this historic hotel with round guest rooms, built in 1932 for the Quaker Oats Company, is a landmark for the business sector of Akron. Also housed here are a large entertainment complex, restaurants, shops, and much more. 190 rooms, 8 story. Pets accepted; fee. Check-in 3 pm, check-out noon. High-speed Internet

access. Four restaurants, two bars. Fitness room. Indoor pool. Airport transportation available. Business center. $

Mansfield

COMFORT INN NORTH—MANSFIELD. ★
500 N Trimble Rd, Mansfield (44906). Phone 419/529-1000; toll-free 800/918-9189. www.comfortinn.com. 114 rooms, 2 story. Pets accepted; fee. Complimentary continental breakfast. Check-in 3 pm, check-out noon. Bar. Indoor pool. $

HOLIDAY INN HOTEL & SUITES—MANSFIELD CONFERENCE CENTER. ★ ★
116 Park Ave W, Mansfield (44902). Phone 419/525-6000; toll-free 866/655-4669. www.holiday-inn.com. 149 rooms, 7 story. Check-in 3 pm, check-out noon. Restaurant, bar. Fitness room. Indoor pool, whirlpool. $

Marion

COMFORT INN. ★
256 James Way, Marion (43302). Phone 740/389-5552; toll-free 877/424-6423. www.comfortinn.com. 56 rooms, 2 story. Pets accepted; fee. Complimentary continental breakfast. Check-in 3 pm, check-out 11 am. Indoor pool, whirlpool. $

Milan

COMFORT INN. ★
11020 Milan Rd, Milan (44846). Phone 419/499-4681; toll-free 877/424-6423. www.comfortinn.com. 102 rooms, 2 story. Check-in 2 pm, check-out noon. Indoor pool, outdoor pool, whirlpool. $

Mount Vernon

HISTORIC CURTIS INN ON THE SQUARE. ★ ★
6-12 Public Sq, Mount Vernon (43050). Phone 740/397-4334. 72 rooms, 2 story. Pets accepted, some restrictions; fee. Check-out noon. Restaurant, bar. $

LOCAL RECOMMENDATIONS

Ashland

AMERIHOST INN.
741 Hwy 250 E, Ashland (44805). Phone 419/281-8090; toll-free 800/434-5800. www.amerihostinn.com. 60 rooms. Complimentary continental breakfast. Check-in 3 pm, check-out 11 am. Indoor pool. $

DAYS INN ASHLAND.
1423 County Rd 1575, Ashland (44805). Phone 419/289-0101; toll-free 800/329-7466. www.daysinn.com. 61 rooms, 2 story. Pets accepted; fee. Complimentary continental breakfast. Check-in 3 pm, check-out 11 am. Restaurant. $

Bellville

COMFORT INN & SUITES.
855 Comfort Plaza Dr, Bellville (44813). Phone 419/886-4000; toll-free 877/424-6423. www.comfortinn.com. Nicely appointed rooms and lobby. Game room; pool in tropical atrium with a retractable roof. Family fun package includes pizza and game tokens. 100 rooms. Complimentary continental breakfast. Check-in 3 pm, check-out noon. Indoor/outdoor pool. $

QUALITY INN & SUITES.
1000 Comfort Plaza Dr, Bellville (44813). Phone 419/886-7000; toll-free 800/272-6232. www.qualityinn.com. Clean, attractive rooms nestled in a scenic river valley. 66 rooms, 3 story. Complimentary

FAN FAVORITE

It seems impossible, but it is true: a college-owned hotel that offers more than dorm-style service. **The Wooster Inn** ★ ★ ★ is a quaint country inn offering comfortable rooms and elegant dining experiences. Enjoy American-style fare served in the restaurant or a nightcap in the billiard parlor over a game of pool on the vintage table. Colonial décor. Owned and operated by College of Wooster; on campus. 15 rooms, 2 story. Closed early Jan, Dec 25-26. Pets accepted; fee. Check-out 11 am. Restaurant. Golf, 9 holes. $$ *801 E Wayne Ave, Wooster (44691). Phone 330/263-2660. http://woosterinn.wooster.edu.*

continental breakfast. Check-in 3 pm, check-out 11 am. Indoor pool, whirlpool. $

Mansfield

BAYMONT INN & SUITES.
120 Stander Ave, Mansfield (44903). Phone 419/774-0005; toll-free 877/229-6668. www.baymontinns.com. Minutes from the track. 87 rooms, 4 story. Pets accepted. Complimentary full breakfast. Check-in 3 pm, check-out noon. Indoor pool. $

COUNTRY INN & SUITES.
2069 Walker Lake Rd, Mansfield (44906). Phone 419/747-2227; toll-free 800/456-4000. www.countryinns.com. Warm, country atmosphere. 67 rooms, 3 story. Complimentary continental breakfast. Check-in 3 pm, check-out noon. Fitness room. Indoor pool, whirlpool. $

FAIRFIELD INN ONTARIO MANSFIELD.
1065 N Lexington-Springmill Rd, Mansfield (44906). Phone 419/747-2200; toll-free 800/228-2800. www.fairfieldinn.com. 62 rooms, 3 story. Complimentary continental breakfast. Check-in 3 pm, check-out noon. Indoor pool, whirlpool. $

SPRUCE HILL INN & COTTAGES.
3230 O'Possum Run Rd, Mansfield (44903). Phone 419/756-2200. www.sprucehillinn.com. Choose from rooms in an elegant Victorian inn, a rustic lodge house, or individual cottage units. Quiet, relaxing atmosphere. 36 rooms. Complimentary continental breakfast. Check-in 3 pm, check-out 11 am. $

Millersburg

INN AT HONEY RUN.
6920 County Rd 203, Millersburg (44654). Phone 330/674-0011; toll-free 800/468-6639. www.innathoneyrun.com. An arts-centered inn on 60 acres in the heart of Amish Country. Bird-watching, nature trails, and other outdoor activities. 39 rooms, 3 story. Complimentary continental breakfast. Check-in 4:30 pm, check-out noon. $$

Mount Gilead

BEST WESTERN EXECUTIVE INN.
3991 County Rd 172, Mount Gilead (43338). Phone 419/768-2378; toll-free 800/780-7234. www.bestwestern.com. 33 rooms, 2 story. Complimentary continental breakfast. Check-in 3 pm, check-out noon. Outdoor pool. $

RV AND CAMPING

Butler

BUTLER MOHICAN KOA.
6918 Bunker Hill Rd S, Butler (44822). Phone 419/883-3314; toll-free 800/562-8719. www.koa.com. More than 100 tent and RV sites. Fishing lake, swimming pool, convenience store, laundry.

Loudonville

MOHICAN CAMPGROUND AND CABINS.
3058 Hwy 3 S, Loudonville (44842). Phone 419/994-2267; toll-free 888/909-7400. A great spot for families. Primitive, group, or full RV hook-up sites. Modern bath and shower house with hot water. Swimming pool. Sand volleyball, miniature golf, and go-karts. Convenience store and laundry within walking distance.

Mansfield

CHARLES MILL LAKE PARK.
1271 Hwy 430, Mansfield (44903). Phone 419/368-6885. More than 500 campsites (with and without

SHOP TALK

Lehman's Hardware, a general store that specializes in non-electric home products, was originally established to serve the neighboring Amish community. These days, however, the store is a mecca for non-Amish shoppers, too. Anyone with a fondness for all things old-fashioned will be dazzled. Thousands of traditional products, from liniments to laundry hand wringers, make it equal parts tourist attraction and store. (Mon-Sat 8 am-5:30 pm, Thurs until 8 pm). *One Lehman Cir, Kidron (44636). Phone 330/857-5757; toll-free 888/438-5346.*

EAT

For more lodging recommendations, go to www.mobiltravelguide.com

MOBIL STAR-RATED RESTAURANTS

Akron

LANNING'S. ★★★
826 N Cleveland-Massillon Rd, Akron (44333). Phone 330/666-1159. www.lannings-restaurant.com. On the banks of Yellow Creek, this fine-dining room, offering fresh fish and hand-cut steaks, has been in business for more than 25 years. Everything is made in-house, including all dressings, sauces, soups, breads, and desserts. American menu. Dinner. Closed Sun. Reservations recommended. Valet parking. $$$

TANGIER. ★★★
532 W Market St, Akron (44303). Phone 330/376-7171. This local gem attracts visiting dignitaries, as well as the best of contemporary music. Noted as one of Ohio's most unique locations, it offers wonderful music by some of the top jazz and light rock artists, as well as an eclectic spin on Middle Eastern cuisine. Accommodates large parties and catered events. Steak menu. Lunch, dinner. Closed Sun. Reservations recommended. Outdoor seating. $$$

Bellevue

MCCLAIN'S. ★★
137 E Main St, Bellevue (44811). Phone 419/483-2727. Seafood, steak menu. Lunch, dinner. Closed Sun; holidays. $$

Delaware

BRANDING IRON. ★
1400 Stratford Rd, Delaware (43015). Phone 740/363-1846. Barbecue, steak menu. Dinner. Closed Mon; Jan 1, Dec 24-25; also first two weeks in Aug. Bar. $$

BUN'S OF DELAWARE. ★
6 W Winter St, Delaware (43015). Phone 740/363-3731. American menu. Breakfast, lunch, dinner. Closed Mon; holidays. $$

MICHAEL OLIVER'S. ★★
351 S Sandusky St, Delaware (43015). Phone 740/363-1262. Italian menu. Dinner. Casual attire. $$

Milan

HOMESTEAD INN. ★★
12018 Hwy 250 N, Milan (44846). Phone 419/499-4271. This restaurant is located in an 1883 Victorian house. American menu. Breakfast, lunch, dinner. Closed holidays. $$

Wooster

TJ'S. ★★
359 W Liberty St, Wooster (44691). Phone 330/264-6263. American menu. Lunch, dinner. Closed Sun; holidays. $$

WOOSTER INN. ★★★
801 E Wayne Ave, Wooster (44691). Phone 330/263-2660. woosterinn.wooster.edu. Nestled in peaceful Amish country, this inn has an intimate dining option. The 14-room property serves dinner in the main dining room, which overlooks a nine-hole golf course and driving range. In the summer, enjoy the local opera company and return in the fall for the guest chef's series. American menu. Lunch, dinner. Closed Dec 25-26; also early Jan. $$

LOCAL RECOMMENDATIONS

Ashland

THE CABIN.
2106 Hwy 603, Ashland (44805). Phone 419/368-4457. This quaint ribs, steak, and seafood joint is in a casual, rustic setting. American menu. Dinner. Closed Sun. Outdoor seating. $$

Bellville

DUTCH HERITAGE RESTAURANT.
720 Hwy 97, Bellville (44813). Phone 419/886-7070. Located in the scenic Pleasant Valley area, this restaurant serves up traditional Amish food and features a bakery and gift shop. American, Amish menu. Breakfast, lunch, dinner. Closed Sun. $$

Bucyrus

HIDEAWAY COUNTRY INN.
1601 Hwy 4, Bucyrus (44820). Phone 419/562-3013; toll-free 800/570-8233. American menu. Breakfast, lunch, dinner. Reservations recommended. $$

Lexington

BUCK'S BAR & GRILL.
192 E Main St, Lexington (44904). Phone 419/884-2825. This racing-themed casual spot features huge burgers, wraps, and sandwiches, as well as traditional American entrées. American menu. Lunch, dinner. Closed Sun. $$

Loudonville

LEGENDS AT THE CASTLE RESTAURANT.
561 Hwy 3352, Loudonville (44842). Phone 419/994-3427; toll-free 800/291-5501. Casual fine dining with an emphasis on fresh ingredients. American menu. Lunch, dinner. $$$

Mansfield

BRUNCHES CAFÉ.
103 N Main St, Mansfield (44902). Phone 419/526-2233. This café serves traditional breakfasts, soups, sandwiches, and quiche. American menu. Breakfast, lunch. $$

CONEY ISLAND DINER.
98 N Main St, Mansfield (44902). Phone 419/526-2669. Floats, malts, coneys, and burgers are served at this vintage diner located in a historic building. Diner. Breakfast, lunch, dinner. $

EL CAMPESINO.
1971 W 4th St, Mansfield (44906). Phone 419/529-5330. Mexican menu. Lunch, dinner. Children's menu. Casual attire. $

FLYING TURTLE CAFÉ MANSFIELD.
2100 Harrington Memorial Rd, Mansfield (44903). Phone 419/524-2404. This café sits beside the runway at Mansfield Lahm Airport. American menu. Breakfast, lunch, dinner. $$

FORK & FINGERS RESTAURANT.
54 Park Ave W, Mansfield (44902). Phone 419/526-2321. Mexican, Tex-Mex menu. Lunch, dinner. Casual attire. $$

PAPA'S GONDOLA.
3080 Park Ave W, Mansfield (44906). Phone 419/529-5005. Traditional Italian fare, including pastas and pizza, is served at this casual, cozy spot. Italian menu. Dinner. Closed Sun-Mon. No credit cards accepted. $$

ROCKY'S PUB.
22 Park St S, Mansfield (44902). Phone 419/522-1342. This cozy bistro offers seafood, steaks, and pasta in a turn-of-the-century building on the city's main square. American menu. Dinner. Closed Sun-Tues. $$

SKYWAY EAST.
2461 Emma Ln, Mansfield (44903). Phone 419/589-9929. Candlelight and crisp linens create a romantic and elegant ambience at this upscale, casual supper club. Seventy-five menu items include traditional steaks, seafood, veal, and pasta. American menu. Dinner. Closed Sun. Reservations recommended. $$$

SWEENEY'S TOO.
777 Lexington Ave, Mansfield (44907). Phone 419/756-2858. This casual yet upscale supper club is known for its steaks and generous portions. Steak menu. Dinner. Reservations recommended. $$

Ontario

THE BROWN DERBY ROADHOUSE.
3895 Park Ave W, Ontario (44862). Phone 419/529-2959. American menu. Lunch, dinner. Casual attire. $$

STEVE'S DAKOTA GRILL—ONTARIO.
3101 Park Ave W, Ontario (44862). Phone 419/529-9064. www.stevesdakotagrill.com. Casual dining in a lodge atmosphere featuring traditional American steaks, seafood, prime rib, and St. Louis-style barbecue ribs. American menu. Lunch, dinner. $$

Perrysville

THE MALABAR INN.
3645 Pleasant Valley Rd, Perrysville (44864). Phone 419/938-5205. www.malabarfarm.org. Traditional home cooking is served in a restored 1820s stagecoach stop. American menu. Lunch, dinner. Closed Mon in Nov-Apr. $$

For more dining recommendations, go to www.mobiltravelguide.com

SIDETRIP

Cedar Point Amusement Park/Resort
Sandusky, OH

Satisfy your own need for speed about an hour and a half's drive north of the speedway in Sandusky, Ohio, home to **Cedar Point Amusement Park/Resort.**

The historic park has been around since 1870, but state-of-the-art attractions help maintain its status as one of the highest-rated amusement parks in the world. Admission at the gate is a costly $43.95 for adults, but this park truly has something for everyone, from the smallest to the tallest.

Of course, the main draw is the rides—68 in all, including 16 roller coasters designed to leave you hoarse by day's end. Coaster enthusiasts love the variety at this park, from the classic wooden Blue Streak to the Top Thrill Dragster, one of the tallest and fastest roller coasters on the planet, which peaks at a scream-inducing 120 miles per hour.

There are four children's areas with nearly 30 rides just for the younger set, including coasters of their own. Some rides even have specially designed seats so parents can ride with their children.

There are more leisurely attractions, too, including a paddleboat excursion or a spin on one of three carousels. In addition to the rides, there is live entertainment, a crafts area, restaurants, shopping, and even a museum that chronicles the history of the park. For a break from the commotion, head over to the mile-long **Cedar Point Beach** for some sand-castle building or a walk on the boardwalk.

Test your speed-demon quotient on one of 16 roller coasters at the amusement park. From the speedway, drive north on Route 13 to US 250, which will take you directly into Sandusky.

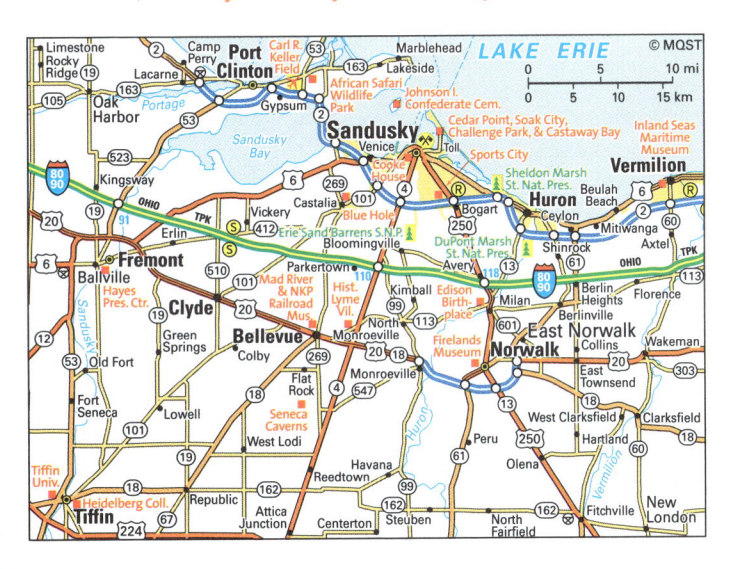

The park is open daily from early May through Labor Day; only Friday nights, Saturdays, and Sundays after Labor Day and through October. Phone 419/627-2350. www.cedarpoint.com. **$$$$**

For more Sandusky recommendations, go to www.mobiltravelguide.com

284

Dale Earnhardt Jr. (No. 8 Car) and Kevin Harvick head for the track as they make their way through the Martinsville pit area.

Martinsville Speedway

Martinsville, VA

17

With 800-foot straights and turns banked at only 12 degrees, Martinsville has been dubbed "two drag strips with a turnaround on each end."

TRACK FACTS

MARTINSVILLE SPEEDWAY. 340 Speedway Rd, Martinsville (24112), P.O. Box 3311, Martinsville (24115). Phone toll-free 877/722-3849. www.martinsvillespeedway.com.

SECURITY. The speedway is revising its policy on backpacks and coolers, so check the Web site for updates before your visit. What's prohibited: umbrellas, pets, baby strollers, glass containers, liquor, and lawn chairs. Beer is allowed, but only in cans.

PARKING. All 200 acres of free public parking lies outside the track; allow two to three hours to leave once the race is over.

FIRST AID. There are two first aid stations: one at the exit near Turn 2 and one under the Blue Ridge Tower about midway down. For more serious help, the closest hospital is Martinsville Memorial Hospital (320 Hospital Dr, Martinsville, phone 276/666-7200).

CONCESSIONS. There are 13 concession stands located throughout the track. Souvenir vendors are located next to the track; while lapel pins are the hottest seller, the 1947 commemorative khaki ball caps are the coolest souvenir.

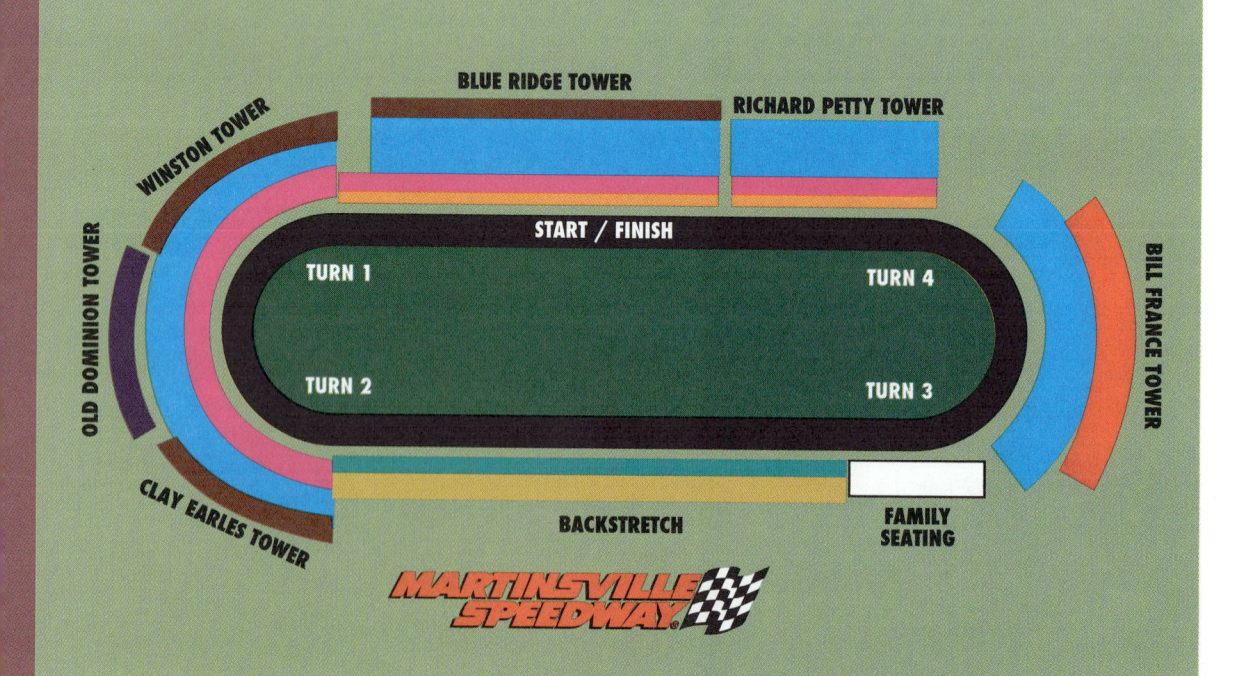

The infield is full of team haulers, and the pit area is abuzz with activity as a sell-out crowd awaits the start of the NASCAR NEXTEL Cup Series 2004 Advance Auto Parts 500.

COURTLY SOUTHERN CHARM

Think Mayberry with a little sass, and you'll peg Martinsville. The town is nestled among rolling hills an hour from the **Blue Ridge Parkway** (www.blueridgeparkway.org), one of the most scenic drives in the country. The speedway is about 5 miles south of Martinsville on Highway 220, which winds through Virginia's lush farm country to North Carolina. Everyone from the short-order cooks at the convenience store grills to the newspaper editor greets visitors with gentle good humor, generosity, and the down-home friendliness characteristic of this part of Virginia.

It wasn't always this way, however. In the early years of the track, which was founded in 1947, the tourists who attended races at the Martinsville Speedway generated about as much local enthusiasm as an oil change, but now visitors are treated like long-lost kin. The reason is economic: when manufacturers, the major players in the local job market, started moving overseas in the late 1990s, unemployment began to erode local incomes. As the sport of NASCAR became more and more popular, tourists to the track found themselves worth their weight in NASCAR NEXTEL cups.

Martinsville and neighboring Collinsville hug one another like a two-piece puzzle, forming a single metro area. The speedway spills across a splash of flat green land surrounded by the natural beauty of Virginia's foothills. From parks to the racing headquarters of one of NASCAR's stars, there's plenty to engage the senses of even the most demanding traveler.

Before you leave the area, make a side trip to Stuart and the **Wood Brothers Racing Museum** (phone 276/694-2121), which celebrates the longest-running racing team sponsorship in NASCAR history (they are currently backing Ricky Rudd). Or camp at **Fairy Stone State Park** (phone 276/930-2424) outside Stuart and take a glittering opportunity to relax and enjoy nature. The park is named after the shiny staurolites (or "fairy stones") found on its southern border.

There's plenty happening in this part of the Old Dominion State. If you're a Civil War buff, consider moseying down US 58 toward Danville, Virginia, which features the **Danville Museum of Fine Arts**

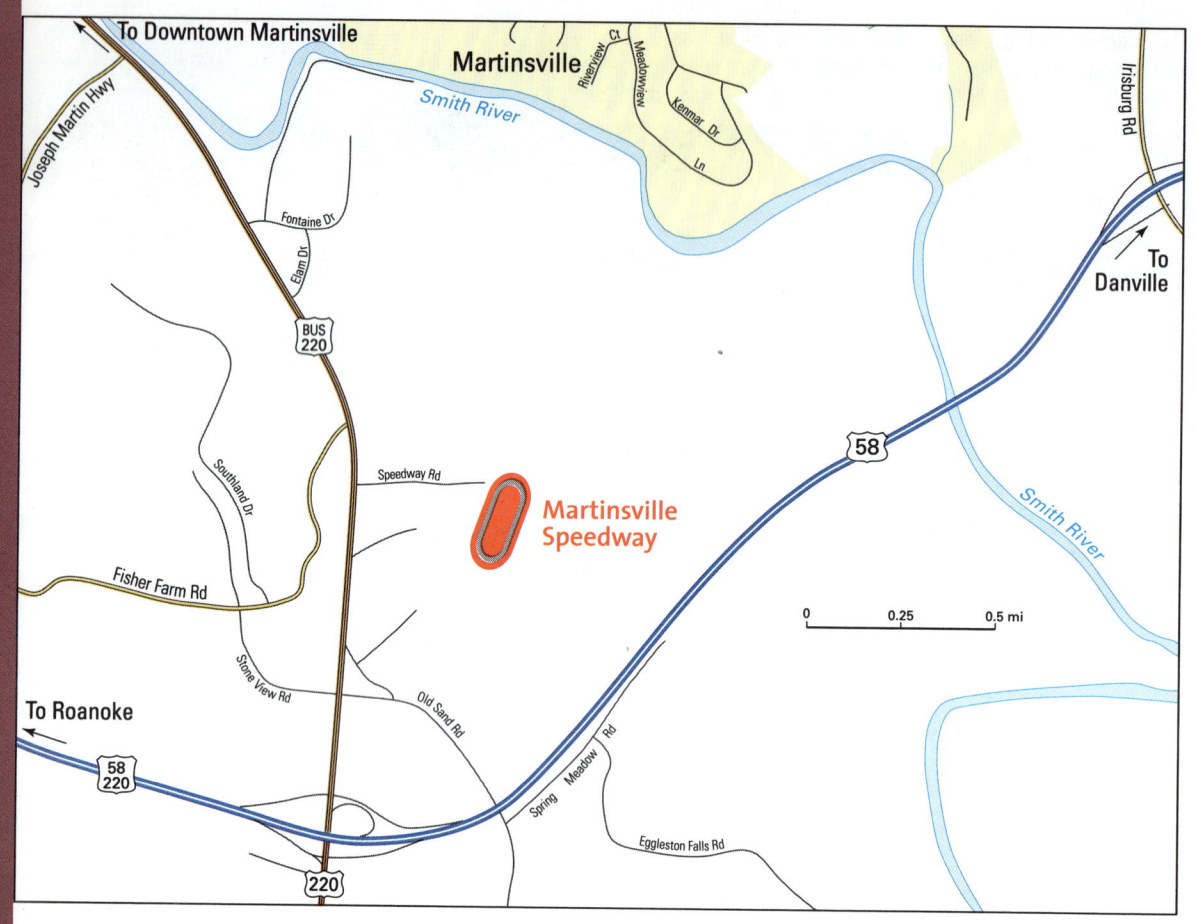

MARTINSVILLE POLE POSITION:
The 10 miles surrounding Martinsville Speedway.

and History (phone 434/793-5644). Located in the Sutherlin mansion, this fine home hosted Jefferson Davis during his last days as the Confederacy's president. Danville also boasts an interesting string of historic buildings, including homes and churches—just right for a leisurely drive or walk.

If your fancy turns to shopping, duck into the **Dan River Factory Outlet Store** (phone 434/799-7205), where you'll find towels, sheets, and other bedding at bargain prices. Danville also has **Piedmont Mall** (phone 434/792-0400), with more than 70 stores and a food court.

Traveling farther south another 48 miles into North Carolina takes you to Greensboro, which, along with Winston-Salem and High Point, forms the Triad cities, an area that's family-friendly and rich with activities. For a history fix, try the **Greensboro Historical Museum** (phone 336/373-2043), with vintage cars and Revolutionary War exhibits. Then check out the **Natural Science Center of Greensboro** (phone 336/288-3769), with a planetarium that'll please even the littlest kids.

Anywhere you visit in this area, you'll be in luck: the NASCAR NEXTEL Cup Series races run during two of the area's lushest seasons. Spring in this part of Virginia features an explosion of flowers and greenery, and the autumn foliage dazzles, with its profusion of colorful leaves that bank every road leading to the speedway. April can be cool in these parts, especially at night, so bring a jacket or sweater. Late October is crisp during the day and nippy at night—perfect Halloween weather.

MARTINSVILLE CALENDAR

APRIL, 2005
Fifth Annual Triad Area Spring Pottery Festival. Greensboro Farmer's Curb Market, 501 Yanceyville St, Greensboro (27405). Phone 336/574-3547. www.ci.greensboro.nc.us/leisure/curbmarket. Watch potters at work, buy handmade pottery.

APRIL 8, 2005
Racin' and Tastin'. 629 Craghead St, Danville (24540). Phone 434/793-4636. www.danvillechamber.com. Get your fill of the all-you-can-eat barbecued chicken and pork while enjoying live band performances. Ticket prices include an open bar.

APRIL 9, 2005
NASCAR Craftsman Truck Series

APRIL 10, 2005
NASCAR NEXTEL Cup Series

SEPTEMBER, 2005
Danville Pittsylvania County Fair. Danville Pittsylvania County Fairgrounds, 2400 Cavalier Rd, Ringgold (24586). Phone 434/822-6850. www.dpcfairgrounds.com. A weeklong fair with free music, petting zoo, demolition derby, and more.

SEPTEMBER 24, 2005
Annual Harvest Jubilee and Wine Festival. Avoca Museum, 1514 Main St, Altavista (24517). Phone 434/369-1076. www.avocamuseum.org/wine-festival.htm. Music, wine tasting, games for kids.

Get a glimpse of history at the Museum of Fine Arts, housed in the Sutherlin mansion, built in the mid-1800s.

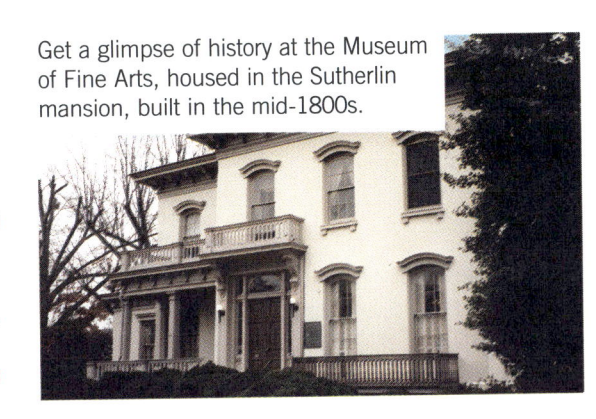

OCTOBER 22, 2005
NASCAR Craftsman Truck Series

OCTOBER 23, 2005
NASCAR NEXTEL Cup Series

NOVEMBER 12-13, 2005
Holiday Living Craft Show. Halifax County High School, South Boston (24592). Phone toll-free 877/663-9102. www.oldhalifax.com. This arts and crafts show features 130 artisans.

DECEMBER 4, 2005
Danville Riverview Rotary Christmas Parade. Main St, Danville (24541). Phone 434/793-4636. Be there for Santa's official arrival. www.visitdanville.com.

Take a walk through Danville's beautifully preserved Historic District.

SHOP TALK

If you run out of anything—anything at all—you can probably find it at the **Wal-Mart Supercenter.** Open 24 hours a day, it sells groceries, pharmaceuticals, automotive supplies, camping gear, and everything else necessary to fully enjoy a race weekend. Be advised: the store's pharmacy operates Monday-Friday 8 am-8 pm, Saturday 8 am-6 pm, and Sunday 11 am-5 pm. *976 Commonwealth Blvd, Martinsville. Phone 276/634-5110.*

MARTINSVILLE OUTFIELD:
The 50 miles surrounding Martinsville Speedway.

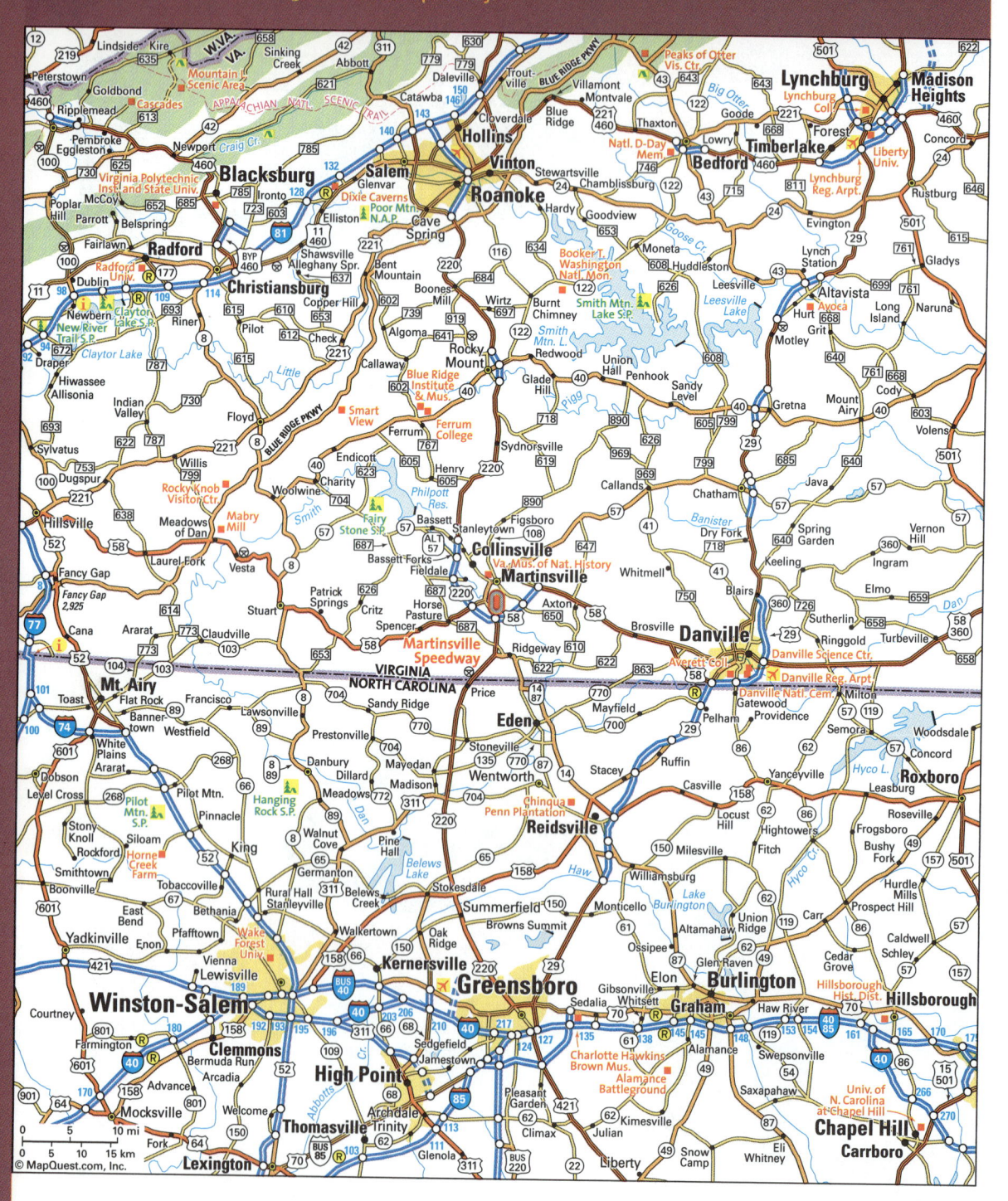

SEE

ATTRACTIONS

Danville, VA

DANVILLE HISTORIC DISTRICT.
Downtown, Danville (24541). www.visitdanville.com. Take a self-guided walking tour of Danville's Historic District, including old tobacco buildings and "Millionaire's Row," with its eclectic mix of architectural styles dating from pre-Civil War times. **FREE**

DANVILLE MUSEUM OF FINE ARTS AND HISTORY.
975 Main St, Danville (24541). Phone 434/793-5644. www.danvillemuseum.org. Built in the mid-1800s, the museum was the last residence of the Confederate leadership at the end of the Civil War. Featured here are historic and artistic items from the region's past. (Tues-Fri 10 am-5 pm, Sat-Sun 2-5 pm; closed holidays) **FREE**

Greensboro, NC

GREENSBORO HISTORICAL MUSEUM.
130 Summit Ave, Greensboro (27401). Phone 336/373-2043. www.greensborohistory.org. Housed in an 1892 building in the downtown area, the museum features displays on the Revolutionary War, First Lady Dolly Madison, and writer O. Henry, among others. (Tues-Sat 10 am-5 pm, Sun 2-5 pm; closed holidays) **FREE**

NATURAL SCIENCE CENTER OF GREENSBORO.
4301 Lawndale Dr, Greensboro (27455). Phone 336/288-3769. www.natsci.org. This hands-on science center for kids features a zoo and planetarium. Check out the 36-foot-tall Tyrannosaurus rex model. (Mon-Sat 9 am-5 pm, Sun 12:30-5 pm) **$$**

Martinsville, VA

VIRGINIA MUSEUM OF NATURAL HISTORY.
1001 Douglas Ave, Martinsville (24112). Phone 276/666-8600. www.vmnh.net. Younger kids will appreciate this small museum, housed in an old school. Exhibits featuring wild animals, butterflies, nature, and science are a few they'll enjoy along with a model of a giant sloth and a computer-activated, car-sized Triceratops. The museum's new 89,000-square-foot home will open in mid-2006. (Mon-Sat 10 am-5 pm, Sun 1-5 pm; closed Jan 1, Thanksgiving, Dec 25) **$**

South Boston, VA

SOUTH BOSTON SPEEDWAY.
1188 James D. Hagood Hwy, South Boston (24592). Phone 434/572-4947; toll-free 877/440-1540. www.southbostonspeedway.com. Affectionately known as SoBo to its fans, the 4/10th-mile South Boston Speedway celebrates its 48th anniversary in 2005, although it's only been NASCAR-sanctioned since 1960. Joe Mattioli III, whose family founded and owns Pocono Raceway, purchased SoBo in 2000 and implemented upgrades that include children's attractions. The track, about 60 miles from Martinsville Speedway, seats more than 8,000 and has hosted a number of NASCAR Busch Series events.

Stuart, VA

FAIRY STONE STATE PARK AND PHILPOTT LAKE.
Hwy 346 N, Stuart (24171). Phone 276/930-2424. www.dcr.state.va.us. Located in the foothills of the Blue Ridge Mountains, the park features a number of cabins and campsites as well as swimming, a boathouse, boating (launch, rentals, electric motors only), hiking and biking trails, picnic facilities, and a concession stand. Fishing is allowed (license required), and a dump station and electrical hook-ups are available. The legendary "fairy stones" found in the park come from staurolite stones, a combination of silica, iron, and aluminum.

WOOD BROTHERS RACING MUSEUM.
21 Performance Dr, Stuart (24171). Phone 276/694-2121. www.woodbrothersracing.com. This racing museum chronicles the Wood Brothers—the current sponsors of driver Ricky Rudd—and their many contributions to the sport. (Mon-Fri 9 am-noon, 1-5 pm; also Sat of Martinsville Speedway races) **FREE**

For more attractions, go to www.mobiltravelguide.com

STAY

MOBIL STAR-RATED LODGINGS

Danville, VA

HOLIDAY INN EXPRESS. ★

2121 Riverside Dr, Danville (24540). Phone 434/793-4000; toll-free 800/377-8660. www.hiexpress.com. Clean and comfortable, there's nothing fancy about these lodgings, but they're quiet and offer access to numerous restaurants. Prices higher on race weekends. 98 rooms, 3 story. Complimentary continental breakfast. Check-in 4 pm, check-out noon. Outdoor pool. $

STRATFORD INN. ★★

2500 Riverside Dr, Danville (24540). Phone 434/793-2500; toll-free 800/326-8455. www.stratford-inn.com. 151 rooms, 2 story. Pets accepted; fee. Complimentary full breakfast. Check-in 3 pm, check-out noon. Restaurant, bar. Fitness room. Outdoor pool, children's pool, whirlpool. $

Roanoke, VA

CLARION HOTEL ROANOKE AIRPORT. ★★

3315 Ordway Dr NW, Roanoke (24017). Phone 540/362-4500; toll-free 877/424-6423. www.clarionhotel.com. Close to downtown Roanoke, the National D-Day Memorial, and the Roanoke Airport, and with on-site tennis, volleyball, and basketball courts, this hotel offers its guests plenty of activities both on and off the property. 154 rooms, 5 story. Pets accepted, some restrictions; fee. Check-in 4 pm, check-out 11 am. High-speed Internet access. Restaurant, bar. Fitness room. Indoor pool, outdoor pool, whirlpool. Tennis. Airport transportation available. Business center. $

HOLIDAY INN ROANOKE-TANGLEWOOD. ★★

4468 Starkey Rd, Roanoke (24014). Phone 540/774-4400; toll-free 866/655-4669. www.holiday-inn.com. 196 rooms, 5 story. Pets accepted; fee. Check-out noon. Restaurant, bar. Outdoor pool. Airport transportation available. $

HOTEL ROANOKE AND CONFERENCE CENTER. ★★

110 N Shenandoah Ave, Roanoke (24016). Phone 540/985-5900; toll-free 800/222-8733. www.hotelroanoke.com. This vintage 1882 hotel has been lovingly restored to its rich, 19th-century elegance and is listed in the National Register of Historic Places. It is just a short walk across the Market Square Bridge to downtown Roanoke. 332 rooms, 7 story. Check-in 4 pm, check-out noon. Wireless Internet access. Two restaurants, bar. Fitness room. Outdoor pool, whirlpool. Airport transportation available. Business center. $

LOCAL RECOMMENDATIONS

Chatham, VA

SIMS-MITCHELL HOUSE B&B.

242 Whittle St SW, Chatham (24531). Phone toll-free 800/967-2867. www.victorianvilla.com/sims-mitchell/index.htm. It can comfortably accommodate eight people but can—in a pinch—host a few extras. This regal home overlooks the tiny town, which writer and owner Henry Mitchell says, "has not expanded in all these years." Guests at Sims-Mitchell B&B are made to feel like part of the family, and the Mitchells are happy to recount the area's history to visitors. 2 rooms. $

THE VILLA JIDIOT.

158 S Main St, Chatham (24531). Phone 434/432-3919. Renovated from top to bottom and crammed full of antiques, this gorgeous old home is the pet project of transplanted New Yorkers. Touches such as a famous gourmet breakfast featuring made-to-order omelets garnished with fresh herbs grown on the premises, served on freshly laundered and starched Irish linen tablecloths, make each morning special. The owners strive to give guests "as beautiful an experience possible." 2 rooms. Pets accepted. Children over 12 years only. Complimentary full breakfast. Fitness room. $

Collinsville, VA

DUTCH INN/QUALITY INN.

2360 Virginia Ave, Collinsville (24078). Phone 276/647-3721; toll-free 800/424-6423. www.dutchinn.com. After a fire, the owners of the Dutch Inn rebuilt and renovated the hotel. It's cozy, attractive, and spotless with an attentive and pleasant staff. The on-site restaurant serves steaks and seafood and is noted for its ice cream bar. Locals say to opt for the prime rib—and don't be surprised if you spot a driver or pit crew dining here on race weekends. The treasure is the upstairs lounge (over 21 only), the Flying Dutchman. The ceiling is painted to look like a night sky, replete with twinkling "stars." Entertainment ranges from a live band to karaoke. 146 rooms, 2 story. Pets accepted; fee. Check-in 3 pm, check-out noon. Restaurant, bar. Fitness room. $

Danville, VA

BEST WESTERN WINDSOR SUITES.
2006 Veasley St, Danville (27407). Phone 336/294-9100; toll-free 800/780-7234. www.bestwestern.com. This all mini-suite hotel offers some with Jacuzzis to pamper weary travelers after a day of sightseeing or after the race. 76 rooms, 3 story, all suites. Pets accepted, some restrictions; fee. Complimentary continental breakfast. Check-in 3 pm, check-out 11 am. Fitness room. Outdoor pool, whirlpool. $

HAMPTON INN.
2130 Riverside Dr, Danville (24540). Phone 434/793-1111; toll-free 800/426-7866. www.hamptoninn.com. The Hampton Inn sits on one of Danville's main drags, surrounded by lots of places to eat and shop. A favorite with business travelers, the Hampton has immaculate rooms and a well-presented continental breakfast. Beds have luxurious linens and are piled high with fluffy pillows. For light sleepers, this place is a keeper—it's quiet and restful. The executive rooms are the best buys for the money. 58 rooms, 3 story. Complimentary continental breakfast. Check-in 3 pm, check-out noon. Fitness room. Outdoor pool. $

Greensboro, NC

BEST WESTERN DEEP RIVER.
7800 National Service Rd, Greensboro (27409). Phone 336/454-0333; toll-free 800/780-7234. www.bestwestern.com. This hotel is located close to the airport and major highways. 61 rooms, 4 story. Complimentary continental breakfast. Check-in 2 pm, check-out 11 am. Fitness center. Outdoor pool. Airport transportation available. $

PIT PASS

In 2004, Martinsville Speedway installed new safety barriers made of steel tubes and pads of hard foam. Attached to the concrete walls, the barriers absorb some of the energy produced during contact, lessening the danger of injury to the driver. Installing the barriers and repaving the track surface is expected to promise even more competitive races.

BEST WESTERN WENDOVER PLAZA.
1103 Lanada Dr, Greensboro (27407). Phone 336/297-1055; toll-free 800/780-7234. www.bestwestern.com. The Wendover is only 8 miles from the airport and 700 feet from the interstate and features a multilingual staff. 114 rooms, 5 story. Complimentary continental breakfast. Check-in 3 pm, check-out noon. Fitness room. Outdoor pool. $

Martinsville, VA

BEST WESTERN MARTINSVILLE INN.
1755 Virginia Ave, Martinsville (24112). Phone 276/632-5611; toll-free 800/780-7234. www.bestwestern.com. This hotel was completely renovated in 2003 and boasts the area's largest swimming pool. Booked years in advance on race weekends, it's hard to score a room here. But if you're lucky enough to get in, you'll find yourself rubbing elbows with one of the pit crews—NASCAR rents half the rooms at this hotel during NASCAR events. The restaurant is changing its name and has a new chef/manager, but those in the know say the tiramisu's the thing to order. The restaurant offers room service. 97 rooms, 2 story. Pets accepted, some restrictions. Check-in 3 pm, check-out noon. Restaurant, bar. Fitness room. Outdoor pool, children's pool. $

STAY LOCAL RECOMMENDATIONS

Pilot Mountain, NC

BEST WESTERN ROYAL INN AND SUITES.
711 S Key St, Pilot Mountain (27041). Phone 336/368-2237; toll-free 800/780-7234. www.bestwestern.com. Nestled between Pilot Mountain and the scenic Blue Ridge Parkway, the location of this lodgelike hotel provides guests with countless activities. For the history buff, Mount Airy is nearby with many notable attractions, while outdoorsy folks can revel in the breathtaking surroundings with hiking, rock-climbing, and river rafting. For those who just like to kick back and relax, the Blue Ridge Parkway provides an excellent day-trip drive, and local shopping and dining areas are also nearby. 56 rooms, 2 story. Check-in 2 pm, check-out 11 am. High-speed Internet access. Outdoor pool. Business center. **$**

Ridgeway, VA

DAYS INN OF MARTINSVILLE.
3841 Greensboro Rd, Ridgeway (24148). Phone 276/638-3914; toll-free 800/329-7466. www.daysinn.com. With the hotel's location just a half-mile from the Martinsville Speedway—and only a ten-minute walk—guests can forget about long lines of cars waiting to park at the track. The hotel also features budget-friendly rates and a 24-hour front desk. 50 rooms, 2 story. Pets accepted; fee. Complimentary continental breakfast. Check-in noon, check-out 11 am. Outdoor pool. **$**

Roanoke, VA

BEST WESTERN INN AT VALLEY VIEW.
5050 Valley View Blvd, Roanoke (24012). Phone 540/362-2400; toll-free 800/780-7234. www.bestwestern.com. 85 rooms, 3 story. Pets accepted; fee. Complimentary continental breakfast. Check-in 3 pm, check-out noon. Indoor pool. Airport transportation available. **$**

RV AND CAMPING

Axton, VA

DAVID AND JULIA'S RV PARK.
Beckham Church Rd (take exit 650 from US 58 E and drive 2 1/2 miles to campground). Phone 276/632-8718 or 276/632-6856. www.rvnetlinx.com/dba/dba.php3?id=2764. Small park with pond, provides bathhouse. Open April-Oct. Dump station. Prices climb on race weekends. RV slots are usually booked, although those in tents might still score a campsite. No credit cards accepted.

Ridgeway, VA

TOM JOHNSON CAMPING CENTER CAMPGROUND.
Martinsville Speedway, Speedway Rd (Hwy 220 S), Ridgeway (24128). Phone toll-free 877/722-3849. www.martinsvillespeedway.com. If you have an RV or camper, save yourself some big bucks and park as close to the action as the racers by staying at the Martinsville Speedway. The speedway occupies 200 acres outside Martinsville, much of which is rented out to campers. The campgrounds open eight days before race weekend and race officials say as many as 300 campers wait for the grounds to open. No electrical hook-ups available; one car pass per spot; no bicycles, ATVs, dirt bikes, or golf carts. Available: dumping station (fee); drinking water; grocery stores, convenience stores close by. Campers are allowed on the grounds at 8 am on Saturday one week before the race. The campgrounds open at 8 am. Campers are held two hours after the race to reduce congestion.

Stuart, VA

FAIRY STONE STATE PARK.
967 Fairystone Lake Dr, Stuart (24171). Phone toll-free 800/933-7275. www.dcr.state.va.us/parks/fairyst.htm. Named for the sparkling stones found on the park's southern edge, Fairy Stone offers swimming, boating, camping, and both cabins and a lodge at budget prices. The cabins and lodge have high- and low-season rates and charge more for non-Virginia residents. Some facilities have lake views; cabins and lodge come with kitchen utensils and linens. Firewood is available for $3 a bundle at the park. Both RV and tent sites have electric and water hook-ups. There is a bathhouse with hot running water.

For more lodging recommendations, go to www.mobiltravelguide.com

EAT

MOBIL STAR-RATED RESTAURANTS

Greensboro, NC

GATE CITY CHOP HOUSE. ★★

106 S Holden St, Greensboro (20407). Phone 336/294-9977. www.chophouserestaurants.com. Enjoy a drink at the circular oak bar while waiting for seating in one of the five dining areas. American menu. Lunch, dinner. Bar. Closed Sun; July 4, Thanksgiving, Dec 24-25. Outdoor seating. **$$$**

Roanoke, VA

BILLY'S RITZ. ★★

102 Salem Ave SE, Roanoke (24011). Phone 540/342-3937. Under the same family ownership for more than 25 years, this restaurant in downtown Roanoke attracts locals and not-so-locals for its excellent steak and seafood, not to mention its unique atmosphere. There are four dining areas, each with a decidedly different theme—one room has the feel of a European bistro, another takes diners back to the 19th century, yet another has a Southwestern desert theme, and the outdoor patio lets diners enjoy fresh breezes and great food. Seafood, steak menu. Dinner. Closed Tues; holidays. Casual attire. Reservations recommended. Outdoor seating. **$$**

KABUKI JAPANESE STEAK HOUSE. ★★

3503 Franklin Rd SW, Roanoke (24014) Phone 540/981-0222. Just beyond this restaurant's private drive lies not only an excellent dining experience, but a fun one as well. Diners are seated at rectangular tables, each with its own chef cooking delicious Japanese specialties to each guest's liking on a hibachi grill. A note: each table in the two dining rooms seats eight people, so if you have a party of four people, for example, be prepared to make some friends. Japanese menu. Dinner. Closed July 4, Thanksgiving, Dec 25. Casual attire. Reservations recommended. **$$**

LOCAL RECOMMENDATIONS

Collinsville, VA

DUTCH INN RESTAURANT.

Hwy 220 N, Collinsville (24078). Phone 276/647-3721. This restaurant, ideal for an elegant meal, is located in a hotel frequented by both racers and pit crews. Prime rib is the house specialty. Don't fill up too much—the ice cream bar goes with the buffet and the restaurant also serves lots of delicious cakes and cobblers. American menu. Breakfast, lunch, dinner. Casual attire. **$$**

ROAD FOOD — don't miss it

If you want to eat where the pit crews and drivers do, drive over to **Clarence's Steak & Seafood House,** a family-owned restaurant 2 miles east of the track. The likes of Morgan Shepherd, Ricky Craven, Rusty Wallace, Darrell Waltrip, Sterling Marlin, and Jimmy Spencer have all chowed here. Expect a line that stretches out the door on race weekends. Once you're inside the no-frills eatery, leave room for the creamy pineapple cheesecake. Open 6 am-10 pm. No checks or credit cards accepted. *6636 Greensboro Rd, Ridgeway (24148). Phone 276/956-3400.*

296 EAT LOCAL RECOMMENDATIONS

EL RANCHITO.
3069 Virginia Ave, Collinsville (24078). Phone 276/647-4330. There are lots of options at this Mexican eatery, which features a menu that also accommodates those looking for "gringo" options. Dynamite margaritas. The entire menu is available for carryout. Mexican menu. Lunch, dinner. Casual attire. **$**

Danville, VA

DOMINIC'S WATERSIDE GRILL.
2575 Hwy 29 N, Danville (24541). Phone 434/836-5700. This is the place to take your sweetie for a romantic evening out. Locals say there's not an off dish in the house and that the prime rib and steaks are especially good. Weekly specials are featured. American menu. Dinner, Sun brunch. Casual attire. **$$$**

REUBEN'S.
5000 Riverside Dr, Danville (24541). Phone 434/822-2013. If you're looking for what locals say is the best hamburger in the area, then Reuben's is the place to go. This hamburger joint's been around for decades, serving burgers and fries to local teens and families. Order the special: a large burger, fries, and a drink for about half the price of a movie ticket. Hot dogs and a variety of sandwiches are also available. American menu. Lunch, dinner. Casual attire. **$**

SHORT SUGAR'S.
2215 Riverside Dr, Danville (24541). Phone 343/793-4800. If it's barbecue you want, then Short Sugar's is for you. This family-oriented, sit-down restaurant sits on Riverside Drive smack in the middle of a stretch of restaurants and hotels. Here, everything from ribs to sandwiches comes up barbecued—the restaurant has its own sauce recipe—but it also has dishes for those who shy away from this Virginia-style delicacy. Barbecue menu. Lunch, dinner. **$$**

Martinsville, VA

COUNTRY COOKIN'.
Liberty Fair Mall, 240 Commonwealth Blvd, Martinsville (24112). Phone 276/666-0768. www.countrycookin.com. This small buffet-style restaurant does a booming business with mall shoppers and locals alike. Diners order an entrée from the menu, then load up their plates from the vegetable, salad, bread, and dessert bars. The hot bread pudding is nicely spiced; kids will love the make-your-own sundae ice cream bar. Prices linger on the low side, and the restaurant offers three meals a day. The staff couldn't be more cheerful and accommodating—they make the meal a true pleasure. American menu. Breakfast, lunch, dinner. Casual attire. **$**

MACARENA'S RESTAURANT.
Best Western Martinsville Inn, 1755 Virginia Ave, Martinsville (24112). Phone 276/632-5611. The low lighting and leather banquettes add to the laid-back ambience at Macarena's, which recently changed management. The chef is known for his excellent American-style food, so order just about anything and you'll be sure to enjoy it. Insiders say the tiramisu is made from scratch and sure to please. Don't be surprised to find a pit crew chowing down here, since NASCAR crews rent out half the hotel on race weekends. American menu. Breakfast, lunch, dinner. Casual attire. **$$**

TEXAS STEAKHOUSE.
283 W Commonwealth Blvd, Martinsville (24112). Phone 276/632-7133. This restaurant offers delicious steaks and salads in a setting that's equally attractive for lunch or dinner. Appetizers are a favorite of race fans and racers alike, so keep an eye out for the famous or soon-to-be-famous on race weekends. Steak menu. Lunch, dinner. Casual attire. **$$**

YAMATO'S JAPANESE RESTAURANT.
810 Commonwealth Blvd, Martinsville (24112). Phone 276/638-2743. The Japanese hibachi-style food featured here is cooked right at the table. Japanese menu. Lunch, dinner. Casual attire. Reservations recommended. **$$**

For more dining recommendations, go to www.mobiltravelguide.com

MARTINSVILLE SPEEDWAY, VA **297**

SIDETRIP

The Scenic Route
Blue Ridge Parkway, VA/NC/TN

Even NASCAR drivers take it slow on the **Blue Ridge Parkway** (phone 828/298-0398, www.blueridgeparkway.org). Located about an hour's drive from Martinsville Speedway, the 469-mile parkway connects the breathtaking mountain passes of two national parks—Virginia's Shenandoah and the Great Smoky Mountains in North Carolina and Tennessee.

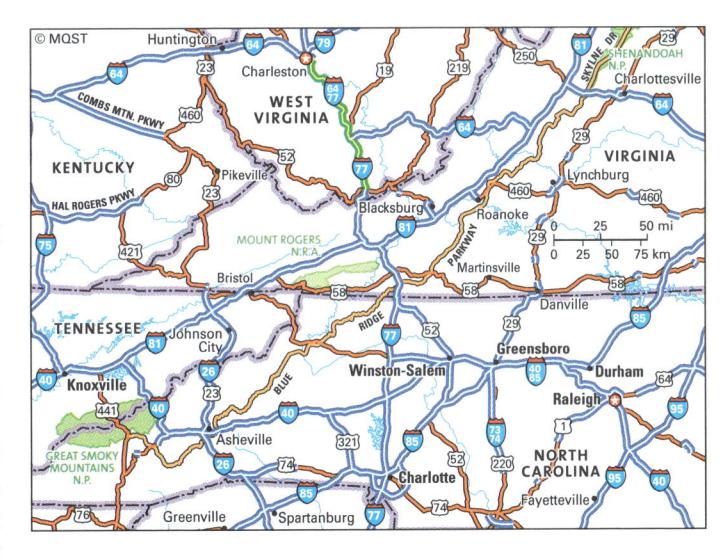

Construction of the route, which carves its way through ranges that include the Southern Appalachian and Black mountains, took more than 50 years. Birds, squirrels, foxes, opossums, chipmunks, skunks—even bobcat, deer, and bear—all roam the mountainsides.

Camp at one of nine recreational campgrounds (open May-Oct, no reservations required). Two adult campers pay $14 per night to stay up to 21 days at the same campsite. Children, accompanied by an adult, camp free. There are no showers, laundry facilities, or electrical hook-ups, but drinking water, comfort stations, and dump stations for RVs are provided. Campsite elevations can top 5,000 feet, which makes for cool nights, even in July. Campers can fish in parkway waters with a state fishing license.

Hotels and bed-and-breakfasts dot the parkway perimeter. Many fill up during peak foliage periods in the fall and on holidays, so reserve in advance. Cabins, accessible to Martinsville at Marker 174.1,

After a drive along the scenic Blue Ridge Parkway, consider staying overnight at one of the nine campsites.

can also be rented (phone 540/593-3503). Along the way, you'll find opportunities to experience mountain life and music and purchase traditional crafts.

For more Blue Ridge Parkway recommendations, go to www.mobiltravelguide.com

298

There's action along pit road in front of Grandstand G during the NASCAR Busch Series Sam's Town 250.

Memphis Motorsports Park

Memphis, TN

18

NASCAR great Bill Elliott (third from left) unveils the Elvis Presley "He Dared To Rock" Dodge at Sun Studios in Memphis during a July 2004 event commemorating the 50th anniversary of the birth of rock 'n' roll.

TRACK FACTS
MEMPHIS MOTORSPORTS PARK. 5500 Taylor Forge Dr, Memphis (38053). Phone 901/358-7223; toll-free 866/40-SPEED (77333). www.memphismotorsportspark.com.

SECURITY. Expect security screenings. Each person may carry: one cooler 14 x 14 x 14 inches or smaller; one clear plastic bag up to 18 x 18 x 4 inches, and one bag, purse, camera, or scanner bag up to 6 x 6 x 12 inches. Food must fit into approved containers. Wear binoculars, scanner, headset, or camera around your neck or attached to your belt. Seat cushions permitted. Umbrellas, glass bottles, and pets are prohibited. Beer in coolers is allowed, but wine and liquor are prohibited.

PARKING. On Taylor Forge Drive, the street along the track, turn right for general parking. If you've purchased $49 MMP Club passes ahead of time (not available on race days), turn left into preferred lots. Passes allow access to the hospitality area and include a special race-day program and a souvenir gift.

FIRST AID. A first aid station staffed by paramedics and the fire department is available in each grandstand. Methodist North Hospital (3960 New Covington Pike, Memphis, phone 901/384-5200) is 6 miles from the track.

CONCESSIONS. Bargain hunters stock up on ice and refreshments before arriving at the track, but food stands and souvenir kiosks are located in both grandstands.

MEMPHIS MOTORSPORTS PARK, TN 301

The 3/4-mile oval track is a favorite of drivers and fans because it generates so much "rubbin' racin' " once the competition begins.

GETTING TICKETS

Order single-day tickets several ways: call 866/40-SPEED or 901/358-7223; fax requests to 901/358-7274; visit the track ticket office from 8 am to 5 pm Monday through Friday; mail your order to the track (5500 Taylor Forge Dr, Memphis, 38053); or order online at www.memphismotorsportspark.com/tickets.html. The Season Ticket includes admission to the two NASCAR NEXTEL Cup races. Renew season tickets by mail, fax, or in person at the ticket office. Take photo identification to collect tickets at the "will call" window behind the track's main offices.

Bobby Hamilton earns his first win in his home state with a victory in the 2004 NASCAR Craftsman Truck Series O'Reilly 200.

Join throngs of visitors for a peek into the life of Elvis on a tour of Graceland.

BLUE MUSIC, MUDDY WATER

As the unofficial capital of the Mississippi Delta region, Memphis serves as the central metropolis for the corners of Tennessee, Arkansas, and Mississippi that meet at the Mississippi River. You can trace the fortunes of Memphis by following its tracks.

The river drew Chickasaw Indians and, later, Spanish explorer Hernando de Soto to this region. Andrew "Old Hickory" Jackson and other settlers borrowed the name of Memphis from the Egyptian city (it means "place of good abode") after deciding that the Mississippi reminded them of the Nile River.

Memphis grew into one of the largest ports in the United States, especially for traders of cotton and slaves. (Even today, almost half of America's raw cotton moves through the city's markets.) Union forces captured the city in 1862 and Reconstruction efforts after the war put an end to plantation life. The city actually lost its charter in 1879, when a yellow fever epidemic decimated its population. More recently, the Rev. Dr. Martin Luther King Jr was shot in 1968 at the city's Lorraine Motel, now preserved by the **National Civil Rights Museum** (phone 901/521-9699) alongside it.

Memphis's musical history—a crossroads of blues, rock, and country music—is complex and fascinating. Blues legend W. C. Handy wrote many of his famous songs, like "Memphis Blues," in his house on **Beale Street** (phone 901/526-0110). More than 400 rock and R&B hit songs—including "Theme from Shaft," "Great Balls of Fire," "Think," "Sittin' on the Dock of the Bay," and "Let's Stay Together"—were recorded in Memphis, and 24 of the 97 stars honored in the Rock and Roll Hall of Fame and Museum were born within 100 miles of the city. In 1953, years before he earned the moniker "the King of Rock and Roll," Elvis Presley walked into **Sun Studio** (phone 901/521-0664) just to see what his voice sounded like on a record. Other iconic musicians, such as Johnny Cash, B. B. King, and Roy Orbison, also recorded at this modest studio, which is now a National Historic Landmark.

Elvis and his lavish home, **Graceland** (phone toll-free 800/238-2000)—the most popular attraction in Memphis, and the second-most visited residence in the United States after the White House—are draws for tourists, many of whom leave mementos for Presley. NASCAR driver Ron Hornaday swears he left race-day tickets for the King under the door at Graceland before a 1999 race. "I'm not sure if he made it, but I know he was there in spirit," he says.

So stay for the music, even if you come for the track, which has a history of its own.

Memphis Motorsports Park opened in 1986 with a drag strip, go-kart track, and a dirt track where, 11 years later, the owners constructed a tri-oval course with 11 degree banks and turns for NASCAR. Drivers like Travis Kvapil and Matt Crafton will tell you that the track still feels like a down-home race, with cars racing side by side and bumper to bumper even at the back of the pack in front of 35,000 charged-up fans.

Beyond the track's reputation for hard-fought races, many spectators say it's one of the most fan-friendly tracks in the NASCAR world.

On race days, you can collect candid driver photos and autographs along the "Memphis Fan Walk"—a designated walking path that runs behind the pit road and in front of the garage area. The track also organizes a pre-race "Fanfest" autograph session with top drivers.

Modern Memphis continues to dominate the Delta region. It's the largest city in Tennessee, drawing millions of people each year from surrounding communities to its museums, universities, and shopping centers. Memphis made a big splash in the national sports spotlight when more than 30,000 people attended the open house for the **FedExForum,** the new home of the Memphis Grizzlies NBA basketball team. Another bright spot in the hearts of Memphians is **St. Jude Children's Research Hospital,** one of the world's largest medical centers dedicated to researching and treating childhood illnesses. (Memphis Motorsports Park hosts the annual NASCAR Busch Series Sam's Town 250 race that benefits the hospital.)

In many ways, though, it retains the slow, sleepy pace of the typical river town. (You'll understand if you've seen any of the movies based on John Grisham novels set in Memphis: *The Firm, The Client,* and *The Rainmaker.)* The summertime humidity levels are

GETTING AROUND

You'll have little trouble getting to the races if you follow I-40 or I-240 around the city center. Approaching Memphis from the east, take I-40 to Exit 24 (Paul Barrett Pkwy); exit at Raleigh Millington Rd and turn left at the bottom of the exit ramp; continue south for 3 miles; turn right onto Fite Rd; turn right onto Taylor Forge Dr. From the west, take I-240 to Exit 6 (Warford Rd); continue north for 6 miles; turn left onto Raleigh Millington Rd; turn left on Fite Rd; turn right on Taylor Forge Dr.

Try your pipes at Sun Studio, where Elvis, Jerry Lee Lewis, Carl Perkins, and Johnny Cash recorded memorable music.

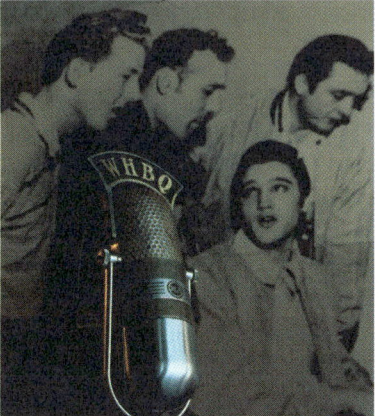

Head to famous Beale Street for some authentic live blues, whether you hit a club like B. B. King's or just listen to the street musicians.

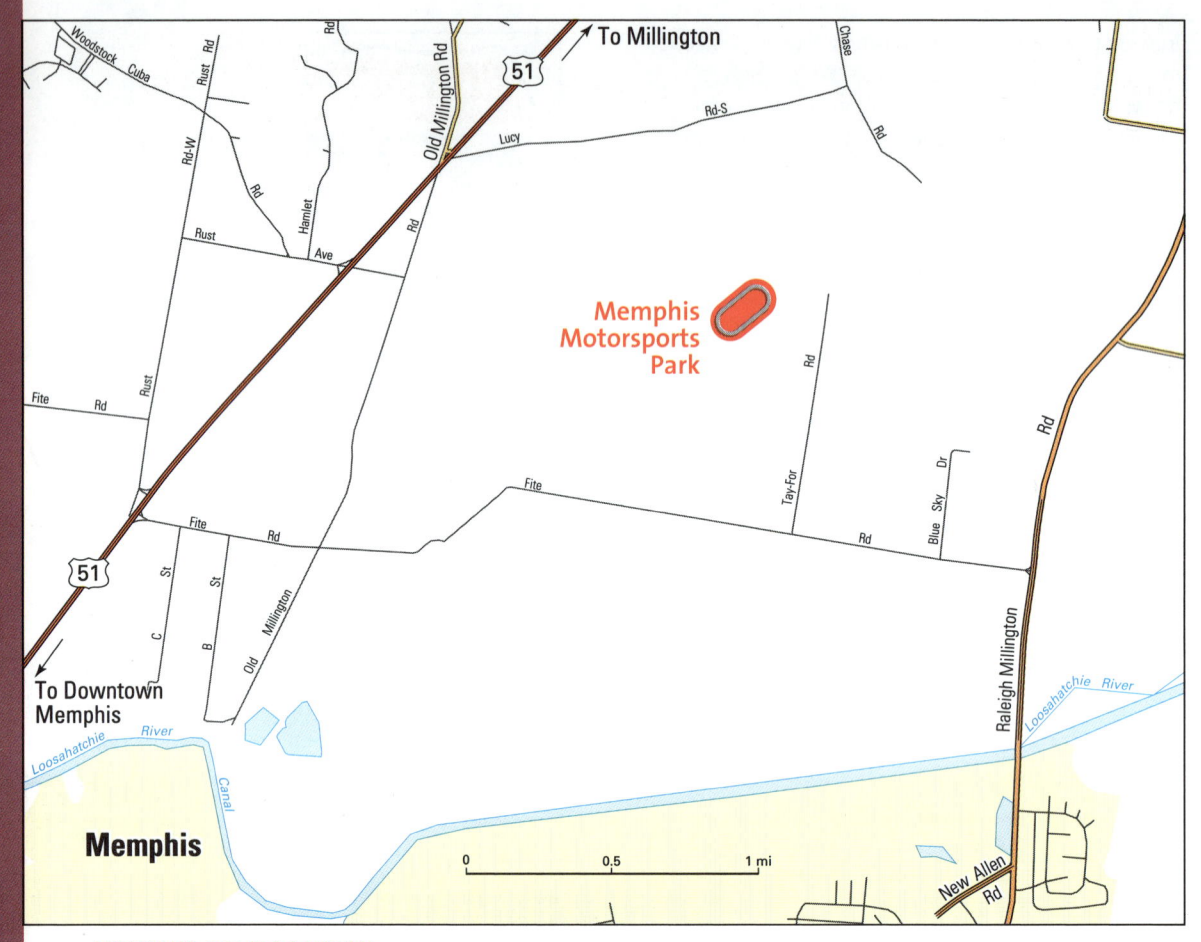

MEMPHIS POLE POSITION:
The 10 miles surrounding Memphis Motorsports Park.

legendary, and the city posts more sunny days than many parts of Florida. Even the ducks at **The Peabody Memphis** hotel (phone 901/529-4000) take their time padding through the hotel's lobby on their twice-daily treks (take the kids to see this, if you can spare the time).

Local restaurants serve sweet tea over ice—a hearty brew mixed with sugar as the tea steeps—to take the edge off the summer heat after a long day at the races.

You can't go wrong in this city where the original Welcome Wagon started in 1928, the world's largest Christmas gift-wrap maker produces 2 billion feet of paper a year, and City Hall holds a record five trophies from national competitions for America's cleanest city.

Like most Southern cities, your best bet for navigating Memphis is to drive your own vehicle. Interstate 240 circles the entire city of Memphis, converging on the northern side of town with Interstate 40, which links Memphis to Nashville on the east and to Little Rock on the west. Interstate 40 offers several exits on the western edge of Memphis (Riverside Dr, 2nd and 3rd sts, and Danny Thomas Blvd) that will take you straight downtown. Just west of the city, Interstate 55 runs north to south from Mississippi across the river to Arkansas. Parking garages in Memphis run from $5 to $10 a day.

If you're adventurous, try the not-always-reliable Main Street Trolley system along Main Street between Auction and Patterson streets (50¢ each way, exact change required). You'll also find cabs downtown.

MEMPHIS CALENDAR

JULY 4, 2005
Beale Street Fourth of July. Tom Lee Park, Riverside Dr and Beale St (38103). Phone 901/529-0999. Watch fireworks explode over the Mississippi.

JULY 23, 2005
NASCAR Craftsman Truck Series, O'Reilly 200

JULY 23, 2005
WEVL FM 90 Blues on the Bluff. Held at the National Ornamental Metal Museum, 374 Metal Museum Dr (38106). Phone 901/528-0560. www.wevl.org. Get some real Memphis blues at this annual festival, with views of the Mississippi River.

AUGUST 8–16, 2005
Elvis Week. Throughout Memphis; check Web site for locations and times. Phone 901/332-3322; toll-free 800/238-2000. www.elvis.com. Commemorate the music, magic, and memories of Elvis Presley and attend the famous Candlelight Vigil.

OCTOBER 21–22, 2005
NASCAR Busch Series, Sam's Town 250

OCTOBER 28, 2005
Halloween on the Square. Collierville (38017). Phone 901/853-3225; toll-free 888/853-1949. www.colliervilleparks.org. Held in conjunction with the Historic Square Merchants Association, the annual event for children 8 and younger, features games, crafts, face painting, candy, prizes, and two moonbounces.

Revisit a tumultuous period of the nation's history at the Civil Rights Museum.

DRIVER'S PICK

Kyle Busch, driver of the Lowe's No. 5 Chevrolet in the NASCAR Busch Series, has one thing on his taste buds when he heads to Memphis: barbecue. "I love ribs, and my favorite place for ribs is Corky's in Memphis." **Corky's Ribs & BBQ.** 5259 Poplar Ave, Memphis (38119). Phone 901/685-9744. www.corkysbbq.com.

MEMPHIS OUTFIELD:
The 50 miles surrounding Memphis Motorsports Park.

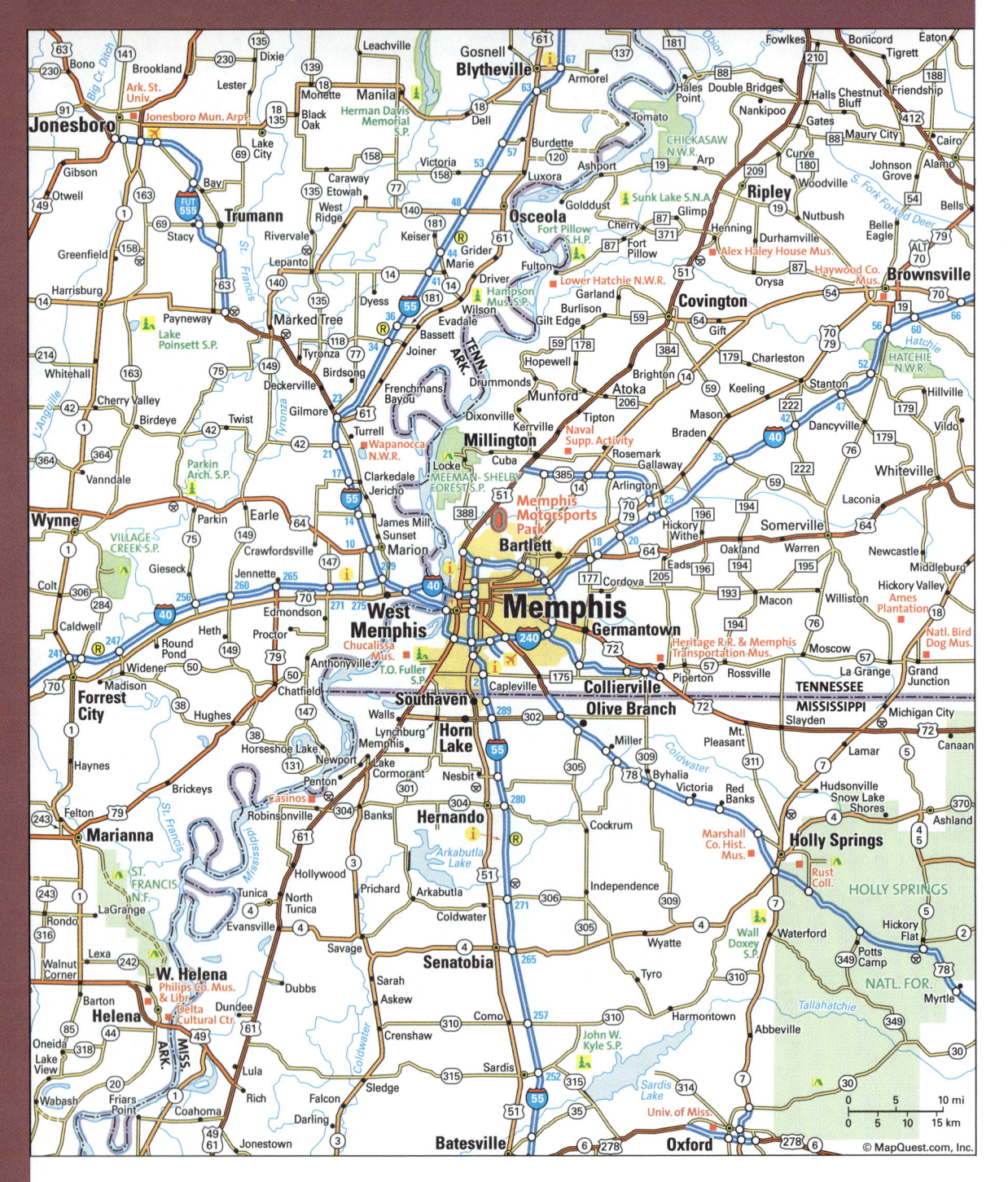

SEE

ATTRACTIONS

Memphis

BEALE STREET ENTERTAINMENT DISTRICT.
Phone 901/526-0110. www.bealestreet.com. The blues live on in this three-block section of Memphis, stretching from 4th to 2nd streets. Tour the Gibson Guitar plant, visit the statue of blues legend W. C. Handy at 3rd and Beale streets (his house sits at 352 Beale St), and enjoy late-night street musicians and bar shows where authentic blues music lives on.

GRACELAND.
3734 Elvis Presley Blvd, Memphis (38186). Phone 901/332-3322; toll-free 800/238-2000. www.elvis.com. Set aside three to four hours for touring Elvis's 14-acre estate. The "Platinum Tour" includes admission to the mansion, car museum, airplanes, and the Sincerely Elvis Museum. You'll laugh at the "jungle" room but appreciate the Meditation Garden. (Mar-Oct: Mon-Sat 9 am-5 pm, Sun 10 am-4 pm; Nov-Feb: Mon, Wed-Sun 10 am-4 pm; closed Jan 1, Thanksgiving, Dec 25) **$$$$**

LIBERTYLAND.
940 Early Maxwell Blvd, Memphis (38104). Phone 901/274-1776; toll-free 800/552-7275. www.libertyland.com. Older kids will enjoy the thrill rides (the Rebellion free-fall ride, a log flume, the Kamikaze pendulum ride); younger kids will like the water slide and carousel. (Mid-June-mid-Aug: Wed-Fri, Sun noon-8 pm, Sat and holidays 10 am-8 pm; late Apr-mid-June and mid-Aug-Labor Day: Sat 10 am-8 pm, Sun noon-8 pm) **$$**

MEMPHIS ROCK 'N' SOUL MUSEUM.
191 Beale St (FedExForum), Memphis (38103). Phone 901/205-2533. www.memphisrocknsoul.org. Showcasing Memphis as the crossroads of blues, rock 'n' roll, and country music, this museum features exhibits such as B. B. King's first "Lucille" guitar and Dick Clark's podium from "American Bandstand." (Daily 10 am-7 pm) **$$**

MEMPHIS ZOO.
2000 Prentiss Pl, Memphis (38112). Phone 901/333-6500; toll-free 800/290-6041. www.memphiszoo.org. The Cat Country exhibit features meerkats along with lions, tigers, and cheetahs. The zoo also boasts two giant pandas in its China exhibit and an interactive "Once Upon a Farm" area that's a huge step up from the traditional petting zoo. (Mar-Oct: daily 9 am-6 pm; Nov-Feb: daily 9 am-5 pm; closed Thanksgiving, Dec 24-25) **$$**

NATIONAL CIVIL RIGHTS MUSEUM.
450 Mulberry St, Memphis (38103). Phone 901/521-9699. www.civilrightsmuseum.org. America's first civil rights museum preserves the Lorraine Motel, the site where the Rev. Dr. Martin Luther King Jr was assassinated in 1968, as well as the nearby rooming house where the fatal shot was fired. Displays and exhibits document the key events of US civil rights history. (June-Aug: Mon, Wed-Sat 9 am-6 pm, Sun 1-6 pm; rest of year: Mon, Wed-Sat 9 am-5 pm, Sun 1-5 pm; closed Jan 1, Thanksgiving, Dec 25) **$$**

THE STAX MUSEUM OF AMERICAN SOUL MUSIC.
926 E McLemore Ave, Memphis (38106). Phone 901/946-2535. www.soulsvilleusa.com. This museum is built on the original headquarters site of Stax Records, the Memphis-based record label that launched the careers of Otis Redding, Isaac Hayes, Sam and Dave, and other stars of the 1960s and 1970s. Featured here are more than 2,000 exhibits, including Hayes's gold-trimmed, peacock-blue "Superfly" Cadillac. (Mar-Oct: Mon-Sat 9 am-4 pm, Sun 1-4 pm; Nov-Feb: Mon-Sat 10 am-4 pm, Sun 1-4 pm; closed Jan 1, Easter, Thanksgiving, Dec 25) **$$**

SUN STUDIO.
706 Union Ave, Memphis (38103). Phone 901/521-0664. www.sunstudio.com. Music legends like Elvis Presley, Jerry Lee Lewis, Johnny Cash, B. B. King, Roy Orbison, and Carl Perkins made their first recordings in this small studio. The 45-minute tour is worth the stop, and you can make your own custom recording. (Daily 10 am-6 pm; last tour begins 30 minutes before closing; closed Thanksgiving, Dec 25) **$$**

For more attractions, go to www.mobiltravelguide.com

STAY MOBIL STAR-RATED LODGINGS

FAN FAVORITE

You don't have to be behind the wheel of a car to enjoy the landscape of Memphis. The expert pilots of **Belle Aire Biplane Rides** offer sightseeing rides for two aboard a 1930s-style biplane over the Mississippi River. *Charles W. Baker Airport, 3870 Fite Rd, Millington (38053). Phone 901/481-1935. www.bellairetours.com.* Or troll the river on one of the **Memphis Queen Line Riverboats.** Sightseeing cruises daily Mar-Nov; dinner cruises May-Oct, Fri-Sat. *45 Riverside Dr, Memphis (38103). Phone 901/527-5694. www.memphisqueen.com.*

STAY

MOBIL STAR-RATED LODGINGS

Memphis

COURTYARD BY MARRIOTT MEMPHIS PARK AVENUE EAST. ★★
6015 Park Ave, Memphis (38119). Phone 901/761-0330; toll-free 800/321-2211. www.courtyard.com. 146 rooms, 3 story. Check-in 3 pm, check-out noon. Restaurant, bar. Fitness room. Outdoor pool, whirlpool. $

EMBASSY SUITES. ★★
1022 S Shady Grove Rd, Memphis (38120). Phone 901/684-1777; toll-free 800/362-2779. www.embassysuites.com. 220 rooms, 5 story, all suites. Complimentary full breakfast. Check-in 3 pm, check-out noon. Restaurant, bar. Fitness room. Indoor pool, whirlpool. $

FRENCH QUARTER SUITES INN. ★★
2144 Madison Ave, Memphis (38104). Phone 901/728-4000; toll-free 800/843-0353. www.memphisfrenchquarter.com. This hotel sets itself apart from other city properties with its classical French décor and atmosphere. Its unique location also gives guests access to sights such as Graceland, Beale Street, and the downtown area. 105 rooms, 4 story, all suites. Check-in 3 pm, check-out noon. Restaurant, bar. Outdoor pool. $

HILTON MEMPHIS. ★★★
939 Ridge Lake Blvd, Memphis (38120). Phone 901/684-6664; toll-free 800/445-8667. www.hilton.com. Towering 27 stories above the Memphis area, this newly renovated hotel looks ultramodern on the outside but proves very bright and roomy on the inside. The hotel is set in the entertainment and business district, just minutes from downtown Memphis, guaranteeing a host of opportunities for sightseeing and experiencing the city. 408 rooms, 27 story. Check-in 3 pm, check-out noon. Restaurant, bar. Fitness room. Outdoor pool, whirlpool. Airport transportation available. $

HOLIDAY INN SELECT MEMPHIS—DOWNTOWN (BEALE ST). ★★
160 Union St, Memphis (38103). Phone 901/525-5491; toll-free 866/655-4669. www.holiday-inn.com. This downtown hotel is near many restaurants and attractions, including the IMAX, the zoo, and Mud Island River Park. 192 rooms, 15 story. Check-in 3 pm, check-out 11 am. High-speed Internet access. Restaurant, bar. Fitness room. Outdoor pool. Airport transportation available. Business center. $

MARRIOTT MEMPHIS DOWNTOWN. ★★★
250 N Main St, Memphis (38103). Phone 901/527-7300; toll-free 888/557-8740. www.marriott.com. This hotel, offering spacious guest rooms, is located 20 minutes from the Memphis International Airport and near shopping, museums, the world-famous

Beale Street, and Mud Island. 400 rooms, 19 story. Pets accepted, some restrictions. Check-in 4 pm, check-out noon. High-speed Internet access. Restaurant, bar. Fitness room. Indoor pool, whirlpool. Business center. $

THE PEABODY MEMPHIS. ★★★
149 Union Ave, Memphis (38103). Phone 901/529-4000; toll-free 800/732-2639. www.peabodymemphis.com. The Peabody is a downtown Memphis landmark. Perhaps best known for its signature ducks who march twice daily to splash in the hotel's fountain, this grand hotel is equally well known as a shopping destination and the home of Lansky's, Elvis's favorite clothing store. This full-service hotel caters to vacationing travelers with a comprehensive health club, indoor pool, and Gould's Day Spa and Salon. Club-level rooms come with benefits including nightly cocktails, hors d'oeuvres, and personalized services. Italian cuisine is prepared at Capriccio Restaurant, Bar & Grill, while classic French dishes are updated at Chez Philippe. 468 rooms, 13 story. Pets accepted, some restrictions; fee. Check-in 4 pm, check-out 11 am. Restaurant, bar. Fitness room, spa. Indoor pool, whirlpool. Business center. $$

RADISSON HOTEL. ★★
185 Union Ave, Memphis (38103). Phone 901/528-1800; toll-free 888/201-1718. www.radisson.com. This hotel is two blocks from the famous Beale Street, near many restaurants and the downtown entertainment district. 280 rooms, 10 story. Check-in 3 pm, check-out noon. Restaurant, bar. Fitness room. Outdoor pool, whirlpool. $

LOCAL RECOMMENDATIONS

Marion, AR

BEST WESTERN REGENCY MOTOR INN.
3635 I-55 and Hwy 64, Marion (72364). Phone 870/739-3278; toll-free 800/528-1234. www.bestwestern.com. 60 rooms, 2 story. Check-in noon, check-out noon. Outdoor pool. $

Memphis, TN

BEST WESTERN BENCHMARK HOTEL.
164 Union Ave, Memphis (38103). Phone 901/527-4100; toll-free 800/380-3236. www.bestwestern.com. If you prefer staying in downtown Memphis, this hotel offers the best value with its location (within walking distance of Beale Street and Mud Island). 124 rooms, 5 story. Check-in 3 pm, check-out noon. Restaurant, bar. Fitness room. $

BEST WESTERN EXECUTIVE INN.
3105 Millbranch Rd, Memphis (38116). Phone 901/312-7000; toll-free 800/528-1234. www.bestwestern.com. 58 rooms, 2 story. Check-in 3 pm, check-out 11 am. Complimentary continental breakfast. Fitness room. Outdoor pool. $

BEST WESTERN SUITES.
6045 Macon Cove, Memphis (38134). Phone 901/385-1999; toll-free 800/528-1234. www.bestwestern.com. This property features large suites with coffee makers, refrigerators, and microwaves. 38 rooms, 4 story. Complimentary continental breakfast. Check-in 2 pm, check-out 11 am. Fitness room. Outdoor pool. $

BEST WESTERN TRAVELERS INN.
5024 Hwy 78, Memphis (38118). Phone 901/363-8430; toll-free 800/528-1234. www.bestwestern.com. 52 rooms, 1 story. Pets accepted, some restrictions; fee. Complimentary continental breakfast. Check-in 2 pm, check-out 11 am. Restaurant. Outdoor pool. $

BEST WESTERN WEST MEMPHIS INN.
3401 Service Loop Rd, Memphis (72301). Phone 870/735-7185; toll-free 800/528-1234. www.bestwestern.com. 39 rooms, 2 story. Pets accepted, some

PIT PASS

The Memphis track offers two primary seating choices: Grandstand G (six sections) and Grandstand J (21 sections). Grandstand G always sells out first because it sits right on the start/finish line, but track insiders will tell you that Grandstand J is the better choice. From there you can view the entire front stretch on every lap. With unobstructed views on all sides, of course, you can see the entire oval, and there's not a bad seat in either grandstand.

310 STAY LOCAL RECOMMENDATIONS

restrictions. Complimentary continental breakfast. Check-in 2 pm, check-out 11 am. Restaurant. Outdoor pool. $

ELVIS PRESLEY'S HEARTBREAK HOTEL.
3677 Elvis Presley Blvd, Memphis (38116). Phone 901/332-1000; toll-free 877/777-0606. www.epheartbreakhotel.com. Fans of the King cannot miss the chance to stay in this kitschy hotel (a former Wilson World Hotel property taken over by Presley's estate in 1998). You'll find 1950s-style lobby furniture, animal prints and sequins in the Jungle Room bar, a heart-shaped pool, and photos of Elvis everywhere. Elvis movies run free 24 hours a day in your room. 128 rooms, 2 story. Complimentary continental breakfast. Check-in 3 pm, check-out noon. Restaurant, bar. Fitness room. Outdoor pool. $

HAMPTON INN—SYCAMORE VIEW.
1585 Sycamore View, Memphis (38134). Phone 901/388-4881; toll-free 800/426-7866. www.hamptoninn.com. 117 rooms, 2 story. Check-in 3 pm, check-out noon. Outdoor pool. $

HOLIDAY INN SELECT MEMPHIS AIRPORT.
2240 Democrat Rd, Memphis (38132). Phone 901/332-1130; toll-free 866/655-4669. www.holiday-inn.com. 374 rooms, 5 story. Check-in 3 pm, check-out 11 am. Restaurant, bar. Fitness room. Outdoor pool. Tennis. $

HOLIDAY INN—SYCAMORE VIEW.
6101 Shelby Oaks Dr, Memphis (38134). Phone 901/388-7050; toll-free 866/655-4669. www.holiday-inn.com. This hotel offers complimentary passes to the adjacent Six50 Sportsplex recreational facility. 175 rooms, 4 story. Pets accepted. Check-in 3 pm, check-out noon. Restaurant, bar. Fitness room. Indoor pool, whirlpool. $

WYNDHAM GARDEN.
300 N Second St, Memphis (38105). Phone 901/525-1800; toll-free 800/996-3426. www.wyndham.com. 230 rooms, 11 story. Check-in 3 pm, check-out noon. Restaurant, bar. Fitness room. Outdoor pool. $

Millington, TN

BEST WESTERN INN.
7726 Hwy 51 N, Millington (38053). Phone 901/873-2222; toll-free 800/528-1234. www.bestwestern.com. 68 rooms, 2 story. Check-in 2 pm, check-out 11 am. Complimentary continental breakfast. Outdoor pool. $

THE ADMIRALTY OF PLANTATION OAKS.
6656 Hwy 51 N, Millington (38053). Phone 901/872-8000; toll-free 888/422-1459. www.admiraltyinns.com. For families desiring to stay as close to the racetrack as possible, this well-maintained property fits the bill (especially with a one- or two-bedroom suite). 54 rooms, 2 story. Check-in 3 pm, check-out 11 am. Fitness room. $

MAGNOLIA INN.
8193 Hwy 51 N, Millington (38053). Phone 901/873-4400; toll-free 877/874-4340. www.smithinvest.com. 55 rooms, 2 story. Complimentary continental breakfast. Check-in 2 pm, check-out 11 am. Outdoor pool. $

Southhaven, MS

BEST WESTERN SOUTHHAVEN.
8945 Hamilton Rd, Southhaven (38671). Phone 662/393-4174; toll-free 800/528-1234. www.bestwestern.com. 93 rooms, 2 story. Complimentary continental breakfast. Check-in 2 pm, check-out noon. Outdoor pool. $

RV AND CAMPING

Marion, AR

BEST HOLIDAY TRAV-L-PARK MEMPHIS.
7037 I-55, Marion (72364). Phone 870/739-4801; toll-free 888/857-4890. www.tldirectory.com. 110 sites, 68 full hook-ups (34 with water and electricity). Laundry, public phone, groceries, ice. Outdoor pool. Recreation room, basketball and volleyball courts, playground.

Memphis, TN

MEMPHIS-GRACELAND RV PARK & CAMPGROUND.
3691 Elvis Presley Blvd, Memphis (38116). Phone 901/396-7125; toll-free 866/571-9236. 91 sites, 72 full hook-ups (16 with water and electricity). Laundry, public phone, groceries, ice. Outdoor pool. Basketball and volleyball courts, playground.

West Memphis, AR

TOM SAWYER'S MISSISSIPPI RIVER RV PARK.
1286 S Eighth St, West Memphis (72301). Phone 870/735-9770. 80 sites, 80 full hook-ups. Laundry, public phone, ice. Pavilion.

For more lodging recommendations, go to www.mobiltravelguide.com

EAT

MOBIL STAR-RATED RESTAURANTS

Memphis

ALFRED'S. ★
197 Beale St, Memphis (38103). Phone 901/525-3711. www.alfreds-on-beale.com. If you want great live music, tasty Southern cuisine, and a place to let your hair down, you have to check out Alfred's, located on world-famous Beale Street. It has nightly live music, a huge dance floor, DJs, karaoke, and outdoor patios. American menu. Lunch, dinner, late-night. Bar. Casual attire. Reservations recommended. Outdoor seating. **$$**

ROAD FOOD

If you enjoy a good mess of catfish—fillets dusted with flour and cornmeal, fried and presented with coleslaw, hush puppies, pickle relish, and refills of sweet tea—then stop at **Miss Sipps Catfish Saloon.** You'll smell the catfish from the parking lot (the sign of a busy place). Nothing fancy—fishing gear and an albino raccoon pelt hang from the tin walls. Lunch, dinner. Closed Sun-Mon; Thanksgiving, Dec 25. Bar. **$** *7838 Church St, Millington (38053). Phone 901/873-4746.*

AUTOMATIC SLIM'S TONGA CLUB. ★
83 S Second St, Memphis (38103). Phone 901/525-7948. The fare is American and spicy Caribbean, and the décor straight from the islands at this hip restaurant, which offers a view of The Peabody hotel and seating on the mezzanine. Caribbean menu. Lunch, dinner. Closed Sun. Casual attire. Reservations recommended. Outdoor seating. **$$**

CHARLIE VERGOS RENDEZVOUS. ★
52 S Second St, Memphis (38103). Phone 901/523-2746. www.hogsfly.com. This restaurant is a Memphis favorite for wet barbecued ribs—served with beans and slaw, of course. Located in an 1890s building and decorated with fun Memphis memorabilia and collectables, this family-run business has been going strong since 1948. Southern/Soul menu. Lunch, dinner. Closed Sun-Mon; holidays; also the first week in Jan. Bar. Casual attire. No credit cards accepted. **$**

THE CUPBOARD. ★★
1400 Union Ave, Memphis (38104). Phone 901/276-8015. www.cupboardrestaurant.com. This restaurant has been around since 1943 and has been at its new location since 2000. Be prepared to wait in line at lunchtime—The Cupboard is always crowded. Once seated, try the popular "meat and three," macaroni and cheese, or eggplant casserole. And don't leave without tasting the corn pudding. Southern/Soul menu. Lunch, dinner. Casual attire. **$**

ERLING JENSEN. ★★★
1044 S Yates Rd, Memphis (38119). Phone 901/763-3700. www.ejensen.com. This cutting-edge restaurant is one of the most popular in Memphis. Savor the shrimp and lobster terrine trimmed with mesclun greens and champagne vinaigrette, the quail and red cabbage, or the rich creamy bisques and fois gras preparations. International menu. Dinner. Closed holidays. Business casual attire. Reservations recommended. Valet parking. **$$$**

RONALDO GRISANTI AND SONS. ★★★
2855 Poplar Ave, Memphis (38111). Phone 901/323-0007. Everything is freshly prepared at this restaurant, including the seafood, which is flown in daily. Specialties of the northern Italian menu include Gorgonzola-stuffed filets, fresh sea bass, and pasta a la elfo, with shrimp, garlic, and mushroom. Italian menu. Dinner. Closed Sun. Bar. Casual attire. Reservations recommended. **$$$**

LOCAL RECOMMENDATIONS

Memphis

B. B. KING'S BLUES CLUB.
143 Beale St, Memphis (38103). Phone 901/524-5464. www.bbkingbluesclub.com. While the food is nothing to write home about—the standard ribs and barbecue that you'll find in a hundred places around Memphis—the music will keep you sitting at your table for a while. The club has a strong list of regulars who perform R&B, rock, and blues, but you're just as likely to see world-famous musicians on their way through town who have decided to drop by and sit in with the band. Southern menu. Lunch, dinner. Closed Thanksgiving, Dec 25. Bar. Casual attire. $

BUCKLEY'S FINE FILET GRILL.
5355 Poplar Ave, Memphis (38119). Phone 901/683-4538. www.buckleysgrill.com. If you love steak, don't miss the specialty of this locally owned house: the Buckley's Filet, 8 ounces of tenderloin grilled in garlic butter, served with garlic mashed potatoes. American menu. Dinner. Closed Thanksgiving, Dec 24-25. Bar. Casual attire. $

DIXIE CAFÉ.
4699 Poplar Ave, Memphis (38117). Phone 901/683-7555. Try this local favorite of many Memphis families who value authentic home cooking in a friendly atmosphere. The menu is built on Southern favorites (with 17 different vegetables every day), and you can't leave without a treat from the soda fountain. Southern/Soul menu. Lunch, dinner. Casual attire. $

EAST END GRILL.
7547 Hwy 64, Memphis (38133). Phone 901/937-1392. Locals recommend this casual eatery for its laid-back patio and "happy hour" drink specials. American menu. Lunch, dinner. Closed Thanksgiving, Dec 25. Bar. Casual attire. Outdoor seating. $

THE GREAT WALL RESTAURANT.
8361 Hwy 64, Memphis (38134). Phone 901/385-2088. You can fill up the entire family with a few laps around the buffet in this comfortable and affordable restaurant, which boasts everything from General Tso's chicken and kung pao beef to Szechuan shrimp (and even pepperoni pizza slices). Chinese, American menu. Lunch, dinner. Closed Dec 25. Casual attire. $

MOLLY GONZALES' LA CASITA.
2006 Madison Ave, Memphis (38104). Phone 901/726-1873. This locally owned Mexican eatery gets it right: great service (bowls of tortilla chips refilled without asking), a wide-ranging menu of favorites at reasonable prices, and a relaxed atmosphere. Mexican menu. Lunch, dinner. Closed Dec 25. Bar. Casual attire. $

NEELY'S BAR-B-QUE.
670 Jefferson St, Memphis (38105). Phone 901/521-9798. www.memphisbarbecue.com. Think you could polish off a full-pound pork shoulder sandwich—seasoned with the famous Neely "dry rub" or dripping with the 20-ingredient barbecue sauce that requires five hours of constant simmering over an open flame? The four Neely brothers invite you to their restaurant to give it a try. Barbecue menu. Lunch, dinner. Closed Sun; Thanksgiving, Dec 25. Casual attire. $

For more dining recommendations, go to www.mobiltravelguide.com

FAN FAVORITE

If you get jealous watching the pros have all the fun, test your skills behind the wheel of a NASCAR vehicle around the 3/4-mile paved tri-oval track at Memphis Motorsports Park (on non-race days, of course) at **Race-On Driving Experience.** Season runs from March to November, but times and dates vary, so call for a schedule. 525 N Main St, Memphis (38105). Phone 901/527-6174; toll-free 866/472-2366. www.4raceon.com.

SIDETRIP

Little-Known Secret
Little Rock, AK

In November 1992, the eyes of the world fell upon this sleepy state capital 139 miles west of Memphis, when native son Bill Clinton celebrated his election as America's 42nd president. In November 2004, Little Rock threw another party, this time for the opening of the **Clinton Presidential Center** (1200 President Clinton Ave), a must-see featuring a library shaped like a glass bridge. It houses the largest archival collection of presidential memorabilia in US history.

If you enjoy Civil War history and antebellum architecture, tour the **MacArthur Park Historic District,** the city's oldest neighborhood, which boasts more than two dozen restored houses. The **Villa Marre** house, built in 1881, was featured in the opening credits of the late '80s TV show *Designing Women*.

Another picture-perfect stop is the **Old Mill** (Lakeshore Dr and Fairway Ave N, phone 501/758-1424), a historically accurate recreation of a 19th-century water-powered grist mill. In 1998, federal officials designated **Little Rock Central High School** (2125 Daisy L. Gatson Bates Dr)—the site of tortured integration struggles in 1957—a National Historic Site.

If you still want more Southern history, take the walking tour of the **Governor's Mansion** (by appointment only; phone 501/324-9805). However, the double-wide trailer in which the first family lived while renovations were underway is long gone.

Little Rock offers several top-notch family-fun attractions. **The Little Rock Zoo** (1 Jonesboro Dr, phone 501/666-2406, www.littlerockzoo.com) features a very rare black rhino—one of fewer than 750 left in the world today—and habitats for apes and big cats. **Gator Park** (11411 W Baseline Rd, phone 501/455-3750) combines two 18-hole miniature golf courses with go-karts, bumper boats, and batting cages. If the summer heat gets to you, try two old-fashioned water parks: **Wild River Country** (6820 Crystal Hill Rd, phone 501/753-8600) and **Willow Springs** (3903 Willow Springs Rd, phone 501/888-4148).

Part of Little Rock's past involves the integration struggles of the 1950s, now highlighted at the Central High School National Historic Site and Museum.

Little Rock is a two-hour drive from Memphis, with most of the driving down Interstate 40. For more details on Little Rock, go to www.littlerock.com.

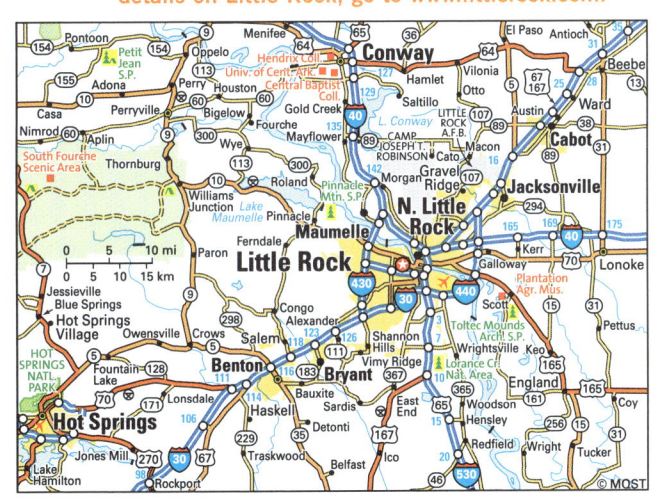

For more Little Rock recommendations, go to www.mobiltravelguide.com.

314

Scott Wimmer obliges a group of NASCAR NEXTEL Cup fans by signing autographs in pit road before making his qualifying run for the NASCAR NEXTEL Cup DHL 400.

Michigan International Speedway®

Brooklyn, MI

19

Ryan Newman smokes his tires during a celebratory burnout after winning the NASCAR NEXTEL Cup DHL 400.

TRACK FACTS

MICHIGAN INTERNATIONAL SPEEDWAY. 12626 US Hwy 12, Brooklyn (49230). Phone toll-free 800/354-1010. www.mispeedway.com.

SECURITY. Fans may enter the facility with one soft-sided container (cooler, diaper bag, etc.), 6 x 6 x 12 inches or smaller, and one clear plastic bag, 18 x 18 x 4 inches or smaller (no ice or freezer packs in this bag); binoculars, scanners, etc., with straps; and seat cushions. Glass containers, strollers, umbrellas, bicycles, and pets are prohibited.

PARKING. Park and enter the facility area based on the side of the track closest to your seats. On race day, traffic control will prevent you from circling the track, so choose a route that puts you on the correct side from the get-go. A free tram service gets fans to the grandstands.

FIRST AID. Emergency medical/air ambulance support teams stand by at the track. Physicians staff on-site care centers beneath the grandstands. The Infield Care Center is open 24 hours a day on race weekends.

CONCESSIONS. Souvenir and concession stands are scattered within the raceway; some concessionaires sell ice. For essentials, visit Buddy's Mini-Mart, which operates convenience stores in the infield and Brooklyn Highway Campground. Buddy's sells firewood, pop, beer, ice, diapers, and propane (tank trade-ins). Note that Michigan prohibits the sale of beer before noon on Sunday, so stock up beforehand.

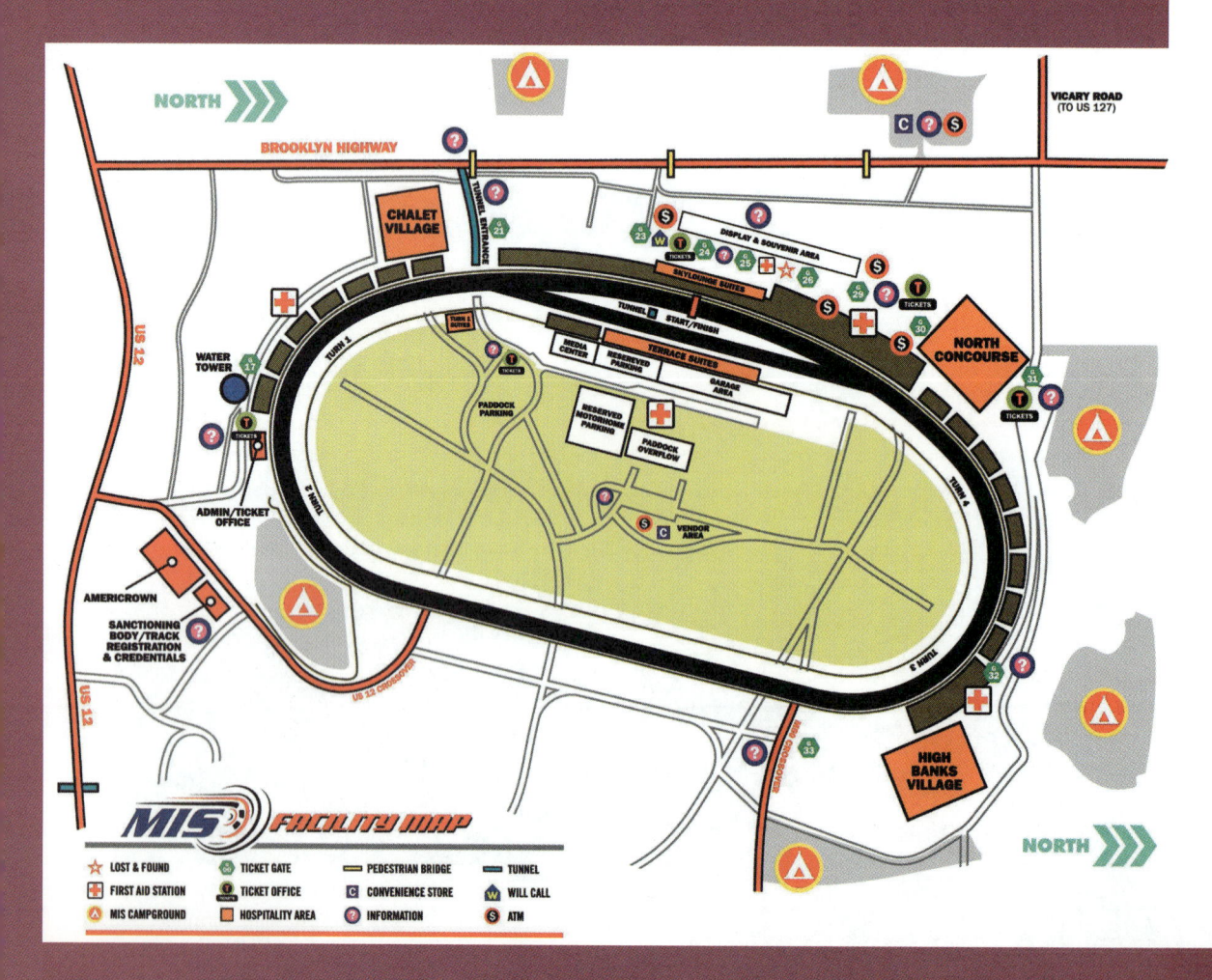

The rumble of engines reverberates through the speedway as the pack exits pit road.

A VIEW OF THE ACTION

Of the 136,373 seats at Michigan International Speedway, nearly all provide a great view of the action (if your seat is backless, bring a cushion with a back for extra comfort). If you have a choice, try for Section 1, Row 25 or higher. Seats 1-2 are particularly good because they provide a clear sight line. But any of the seats in this area gives you a tremendous view of the start-finish line, plus Turns 1 and 4. If you can tear your eyes away from the action on the track (and are seated high enough), you can see lakes on the horizon in several directions.

Fans dependent on wheelchairs and service dogs are offered a number of spots, along with tram transportation to parking and camping (call the speedway toll-free at 800/354-1010 to make arrangements).

GETTING TICKETS

To buy high-level tickets or snag a desirable campground space, place a refundable $50-per-seat or campground deposit in August. This guarantees a shot at seats that become available in early December because previous ticket holders have failed to renew or have upgraded to something better, before those tickets go on sale to the general public on February 12, 2005. Staying on top of the process is a must—it's first come, first served, and there's no calendar set in advance. Call the track toll-free at 800/354-1010 or visit www.mispeedway.com to purchase tickets.

LAND OF LAKES

Michigan International Speedway sits on nearly 1,600 acres surrounded by 52 lakes in Michigan's Irish Hills. ("Hills" are a misnomer—the elevation in this area is about 600 feet.) The lakes are pristine and full of fish, in a region long recognized as a moderately priced resort for Detroiters and vacationers from northern Ohio.

The 2-mile, D-shaped oval track, with seating for 25,000, was built in 1967 by Detroit-based owner-developer Lawrence H. LoPatin, who chose the site because of its proximity to the Motor City and Chicago.

Natural beauty abounds in Michigan; make some time to enjoy it.

Fit in some time to stop at the local farmers' market to get the freshest fruits and vegetables.

MICHIGAN INTERNATIONAL SPEEDWAY, MI

It was a good choice but at the wrong time: the first race at the speedway, on October 13, 1968, was held three days after the Detroit Tigers beat the St. Louis Cardinals in the World Series. By 1973, in the midst of the gas crisis, LoPatin, who had spent an estimated $6 million on the venture, went bankrupt and sold the track. Racing entrepreneur Roger Penske was the high bidder at $2 million; he made the track what it is today by expanding seating and improving the surface (International Speedway Corp. bought the track in 1999).

Over the last decade, Michigan International Speedway has added tens of thousands of seats to accommodate the rising number of fans and made numerous upgrades to ensure a great day at the races. However, access to the track area

GETTING AROUND

The best way to avoid traffic is to get to the track early on race day (parking lots open at 5 am) and relax until the race starts. If you want to beat the crowds exiting, leave a few laps before the race is over. A limited number of trams transport able-bodied parkers to the track.

Leave plenty of time before a race starts to get to the track. You can only go so far on major roads—then all entering traffic is limited to a two-lane road. Remember: the entrance you use to get onto speedway grounds is the same one you use when you leave.

White-tailed deer are just some of the beautiful animals you will see in Michigan.

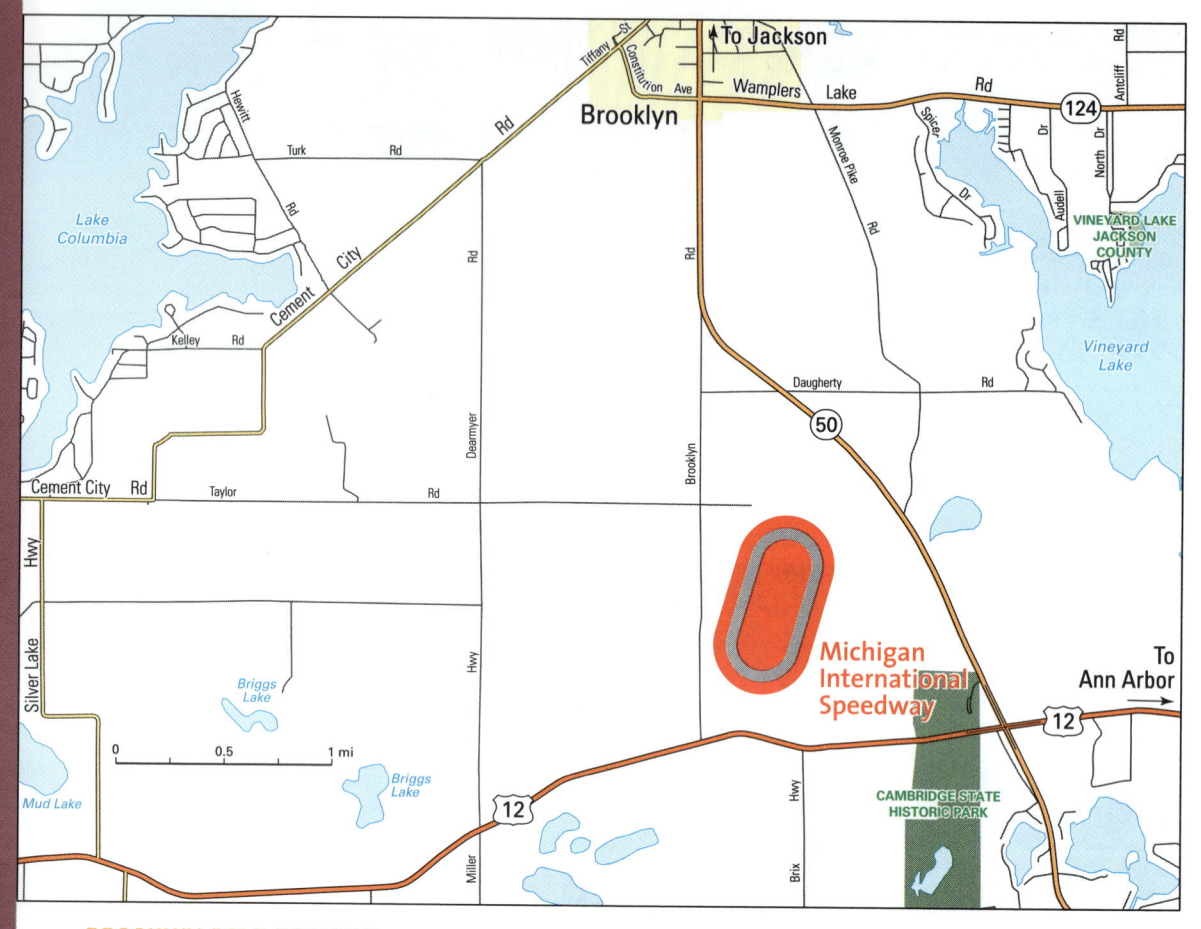

BROOKLYN POLE POSITION:
The 10 miles surrounding Michigan International Speedway.

is limited to two-lane roads, which get swamped on race days; the earlier you go, the better. You'll see experienced racegoers relaxing in lawn chairs with a grill, cooler, and the Sunday paper, waiting until race time.

Coming or going, you may spend some time on Route 12, the Old Chicago Road, which begins on Michigan Avenue in Detroit and ends, almost 300 miles later, on the street of the same name in Chicago. Built between 1829 and 1836, it was considered a modern highway and the best way to make the six-day journey.

If you're coming to the speedway from the east along Route 12, you'll pass the remnants of the resort style of a different era. The narrow road winds past private lakes surrounded by summer cottages, custard stands, go-kart tracks, and miniature golf.

If you're coming on Route 12 from the west, you'll see cows and plowed fields, with a break in-between for Jonesville, which has its own automotive claim to fame: it was home to the Deal Buggy factory, established in 1865 by J. J. Deal. As you drive through town on your way to seeing modern machines tear around a fast track, you'll be reminded of how far cars have come when you see one of only two remaining 1907 Deal automobiles on display in the Town Hall window.

BROOKLYN CALENDAR

JUNE 18, 2005
NASCAR Craftsman Truck Series

JUNE 18–19, 2005
Motor Muster. Greenfield Village, Dearborn (48124). Phone 313/271-1620. www.thehenryford.org. Hundreds of American cars from the 1930s through the 1970s. Father's Day weekend.

JUNE 19, 2005
NASCAR NEXTEL Cup Series

JULY 15–17, 2005
Detroit APBA Gold Cup. Detroit River, Belle Isle. Phone 586/774-0980. www.gold-cup.com. Watch boats, hydroplanes race at speeds up to 200 mph.

JULY 20–23, 2005
Ann Arbor Art Fairs. Ann Arbor. Phone 734/663-6511. annarbor.org/artfair2005. Four simultaneous, award-winning, juried art fairs on city streets.

AUGUST 20, 2005
NASCAR Busch Series

AUGUST 20, 2005
Woodward Dream Cruise. Woodward Ave from Eight Mile to Huron St, Detroit (48220). Phone 248/288-4694, toll-free 800/DETROIT. www.woodwarddreamcruise.com. A 20-mile-long parade, car show, and festival.

AUGUST 21, 2005
NASCAR NEXTEL Cup Series

SHOP TALK

You're not out of luck if you've forgotten any essentials on your trip to Michigan's Irish Hills. For all those family must-haves, from road trip snacks to a rain jacket, there's a **Sam's Club**, about 30 minutes from Michigan International Speedway. *3600 Oneil Dr, Jackson (49202). Phone 517/788-6075.* Also one half-hour from the track is a **Home Depot**, another good place to find that last-minute soft-sided cooler for race day. *1400 N Wisner Rd, Jackson (49202). Phone 517/817-5401.*

Crew members line up on pit road for the singing of the National Anthem.

BROOKLYN OUTFIELD:
The 70 miles surrounding Michigan International Speedway.

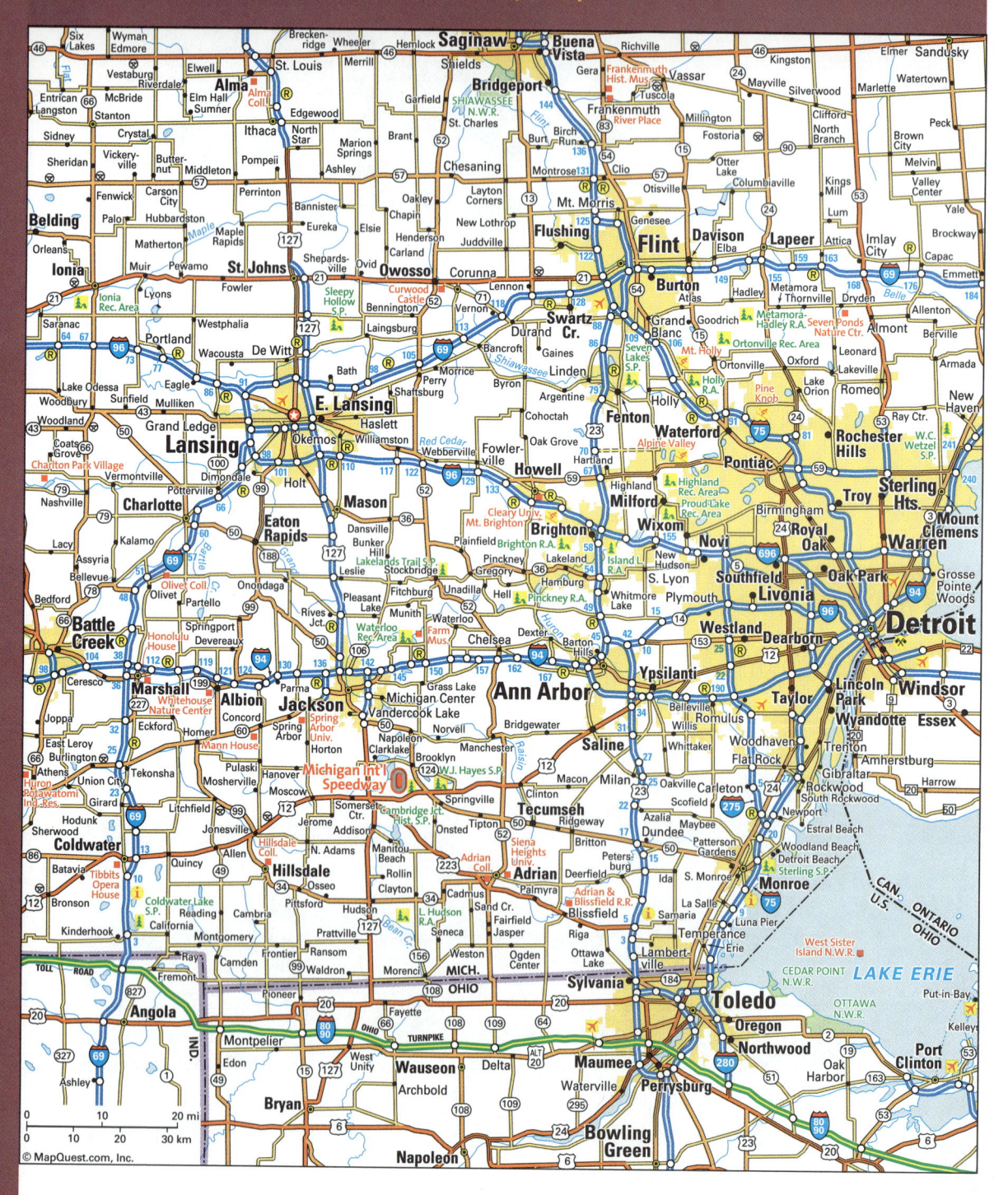

SEE

ATTRACTIONS

Brooklyn

ANTIQUES.
The 50-mile drive west from Saline to Somerset Center with a side trip up Highway 50 to Brooklyn is known locally as Antique Alley, and it makes for a great day of shopping. **Turn of the Century Lighting Co.** *(116 W Michigan Ave, Clinton; phone 517/456-6019)* features gas and electric lighting fixtures from the Victorian era and period lampshades. **Irish Hills Antiques and Outdoor Market** *(10600 Rte 12, Brooklyn; 1 mile E of Hwy 50, phone 517/467-4646)* sells antique wood and coal-burning parlor and kitchen stoves, brass cash registers, porcelain signs, and gasoline pumps. **Brick Walker Tavern Antiques** *(11705 Rte 12, Brooklyn, phone 517/467-6961)*, in an 1854 building constructed as a three-story along the Detroit-Chicago Pike, features collectable glassware, pottery, and china.

CAMBRIDGE JUNCTION HISTORIC STATE PARK/WALKER TAVERN HISTORIC COMPLEX.
13220 M-50, Brooklyn (49230). Phone 517/467-4414. Walker's farmhouse and tavern, a Federal-style white clapboard home and farm, is a museum interpreting Michigan's history as a frontier settlement. The house was a favorite stopping point for stagecoaches making the arduous trip to Chicago from 1836 to 1855. (May-Oct) **FREE**

FISHING.
The speedway is surrounded by 52 lakes, many public with very good fishing spots. These public-access lakes are the best bet for catching enough to make it fun, according to veteran anglers and the Michigan State Department of Fisheries and Wildlife: **Allen:** *off US 12, about 2 miles E of Hwy 50.* Rainbow trout, bluegill, perch. **Deep:** *off Brix Hwy, about 1 1/2 miles S of US 12, W of Hwy 50.* Trout, largemouth bass, bluegill, northern pike. **Devils:** *just S of US 223.* Large- and smallmouth bass, walleye, northern pike, bluegill, sunfish. **Iron Lake:** *on Rte 12 E of Hwy 50,* below Wamplers Lake. Large- and smallmouth bass; good night fishing. **Sand:** *Pentecost Hwy between Hwy 50 and Rte 12.* Large-, smallmouth bass. Troll slowly for 7-8 pound walleye. Crappies. **Vineyard:** *along M-124 just E of Hwy 50.* Largemouth bass, walleye, bluegill, sunfish. **Wamplers:** *N of Rte 12; access from Hayes State Park.* Largemouth bass, walleye.

Two bait and tackle shops around Brooklyn provide updated area fishing conditions and licenses. **Knutson's.** *Hwy 50 and M-124. Phone toll-free within Michigan 800/292-0857; outside the state, 800/248-9318.* **Three Lakes Supply.** *Hwy 50 about a mile S of Rte 12. Phone 517/467-2468.*

GOLFING.
With 22 public golf courses, Jackson County boasts more public golf holes per person than any other community in the country except Sarasota, Florida. Tee times are relatively easy to get and reasonably priced. Here are some courses close to the track: **Clark Lake Golf Course.** *5535 Wesch Rd, Brooklyn. Phone 517/592-6259.* Public course with 27 holes. **Greenbriar Golf Course.** *14820 Wellwood Rd, Brooklyn. Phone 517/592-9657.* Public course with 18 holes. **Hills Heart of the Lakes Golf Course.** *500 Case Rd, Brooklyn. Phone 517/592-2110.* Public course with 18 holes. **Silver Lake Golf Course.** *15649 Rte 12, Brooklyn. Phone 517/592-8036.*

Tipton

HIDDEN LAKE GARDENS.
6280 W Munger Rd (Hwy 50), Tipton (49287). Phone 517/431-2060. www.cpp.msu.edu/hlg. These "gardens" are spread over nearly 800 acres and feature the Harper collection of dwarf and rare conifers with more than 500 varieties. Hidden Lake also has an 8,000-square-foot tropical plant conservatory and 6 miles of paved roads through the hilly, oak-hickory woods, meadows, and landscaped areas that are good for hiking. (Apr-Oct: daily 9 am-dusk; Nov-Mar: daily 9 am-4 pm; closed Jan 1, Thanksgiving, Dec 25) **$**

IRISH HILLS FUN CENTER.
5600 Rte 12, Tipton (49287). Phone 517/431-2214. www.irishhillsgokarts.com. Go-karts and sprint cars for rent, batting cages, miniature golf, and paintball arena. Enough to keep the kids occupied for an afternoon. (Apr: Sat-Sun 1-6 pm; June-Aug: daily 10 am-10 pm; May and Sept: Sat-Sun noon-7 pm) **$** per attraction

For more attractions, go to www.mobiltravelguide.com

STAY

MOBIL STAR-RATED LODGINGS

Ann Arbor

BELL TOWER HOTEL. ★★
300 S Thayer St, Ann Arbor (48104). Phone 734/769-3010; toll-free 800/562-3559. www.belltower.com.
This elegant boutique hotel boasts a perfect location on the University of Michigan-Ann Arbor's campus. Guests can take in concerts, theater productions, and shops on or near university grounds. After a long day, come back to plush surroundings and special details like down comforters and pillows in guest rooms. 66 rooms, 4 story. Complimentary continental breakfast. Check-in 4 pm, check-out noon. Restaurant. $$

DAHLMANN CAMPUS INN ANN ARBOR. ★★
615 E Huron St, Ann Arbor (48104). Phone 734/769-2200; toll-free 800/666-8693. www.campusinn.com.
This inn is located near the University of Michigan's campus. The property is near many local shops, galleries, and restaurants. 208 rooms, 15 story. Check-in 4 pm, check-out 11 am. Restaurant, bar. Fitness room. Outdoor pool. $$

FOUR POINTS BY SHERATON ANN ARBOR. ★★
3200 Boardwalk, Ann Arbor (48108). Phone 734/996-0600; toll-free 888/625-5144. www.sheraton.com. Savor a breakfast buffet in the morning at this spacious, comfortable hotel, and then head out for a day in the Ann Arbor area. Ideally located 1 mile from downtown Ann Arbor, guests will find no end of nearby events and activities. For NASCAR fans, Michigan International Speedway is only about an hour's drive away. 197 rooms, 6 story. Check-in 3 pm, check-out noon. Restaurant, bar. Fitness room. Indoor pool, outdoor pool, whirlpool. Business center. $

THE KENSINGTON COURT HOTEL ANN ARBOR. ★★★
610 Hilton Blvd, Ann Arbor (48108). Phone 734/761-7800; toll-free 800/227-6963. www.kcourtaa.com.
This hotel is located 2 miles from the University of Michigan and next to a regional shopping center. Guests will enjoy spacious and handsomely appointed guest rooms, and exceptional service. 200 rooms, 3 story. Check-out 11 am. Restaurant, bar. Fitness room. Indoor pool, whirlpool. $$

RESIDENCE INN BY MARRIOTT ANN ARBOR. ★
800 Victors Way, Ann Arbor (48108). Phone 734/996-5666; toll-free 888/236-2427. www.residenceinn.com.
Ideal for longer stays, this hotel features studios, one- and two-bedroom suites, and bilevel penthouses. The rooms have been organized with separate living and sleeping areas. The hotel is located only 3 miles from downtown Ann Arbor. 114 rooms, 3 story. Pets accepted; fee. Complimentary full breakfast. Check-in 3 pm, check-out noon. Fitness room. Outdoor pool, whirlpool. $

WEBER'S INN. ★★★
3050 Jackson Ave, Ann Arbor (48103). Phone 734/769-2500; toll-free 800/443-3050. www.webersinn.com.
This hotel offers 48 poolside guest rooms and suites,

FAN FAVORITE

Pit passes are available for all three days through the speedway's ticket hotline *(phone toll-free 800/354-1010)*. **Access is particularly open during qualifying on Friday, with most drivers signing autographs after they've qualified. Even on race day, fans can wander through the pits and even stick their heads into the garages. The pits close an hour before the race starts. Children younger than 18 are allowed into the pit area on Sunday morning only.**

and is located near the University of Michigan, 30 minutes outside downtown Detroit. 160 rooms, 4 story. Complimentary continental breakfast. Check-in 4 pm, check-out noon. Restaurant, bar. Fitness room. Indoor pool, whirlpool. Business center. $

Jackson

COUNTRY HEARTH INN JACKSON. ★
1111 Boardman Rd, Jackson (49202). Phone 517/783-6404; toll-free 800/267-5023. www.countryhearth.com. 73 rooms, 2 story. Complimentary continental breakfast. Check-in 3 pm, check-out noon. $

LOCAL RECOMMENDATIONS

Adrian

DAYS INN ADRIAN.
1575 W Maumee St, Adrian (49221). Phone 517/263-5741; toll-free 800/329-7466. www.daysinn.com. This hotel is located 11 miles from the speedway and requires a two-night minimum stay during race weeks. 77 rooms. Pets accepted; fee. Complimentary continental breakfast. Check-in 3 pm, check-out 11 am. Outdoor pool. $

Ann Arbor

BEST WESTERN EXECUTIVE PLAZA.
2900 Jackson Rd, Ann Arbor (48103). Phone 734/665-4444. www.bestwestern.com. 38 miles from the track. 150 rooms, 4 story. Pets accepted, some restrictions. Check-in 3 pm, check-out noon. Laundry services. Restaurant, bar. Fitness room. Indoor pool, outdoor pool, whirlpool. $

Brooklyn

BUFFALO INN.
10845 Rte 12, Brooklyn (49230). Phone 517/467-6521. Bedrooms have private and shared baths. Minimum three-day stay during race weeks. Only 1/4 mile from the track. 5 rooms. $

TWIN GABLES MOTEL.
10500 Rte 12, Brooklyn (49230). Phone 517/467-8178. Located just 1 mile from the speedway, the motel also rents a double-wide trailer that sleeps eight (parked off Highway 50, just past Gate 1). 12 rooms. Pets accepted, some restrictions. $

Tecumseh

TECUMSEH INN MOTEL.
1445 Chicago Blvd, Tecumseh (49286). Phone 517/423-7401. www.tecumsehinn.com. 14 miles from the track. 61 rooms. Pets accepted. Restaurant, bar. $

Tipton

WHISPERING LAKES RESORT.
12900 Mull Hwy, Tipton (49287). Phone 517/431-2416. www.whisperinglakesresort.com. Each unit in this hotel has a kitchen, bathroom, and sleeps six to eight comfortably. Tent sites also available. The lakes are great for both fishing and swimming. 20 rooms. $$

PIT PASS

The flags at Michigan International Speedway aren't the only things that are color-coded. Employees at the track wear vests color-coded based on responsibilities: parking attendants wear orange, ushers wear yellow, program sellers wear purple, medical representatives wear royal blue, and security personnel wear red. Admission gate attendants wear yellow and white, while guest service ambassadors are in red and white. Look for attendants in medium blue vests if you're disabled and want assistance; in the camper line-up, attendants wear green.

RV AND CAMPING

On-speedway campgrounds

The preferred place to stay at Michigan International Speedway is on the speedway grounds, which have 8,346 campsites. Additional sites are planned over the next several years. The most popular sites are the 2,600 spots in the infield. Most of the sites are a piece of grassy pastureland with access to water, portable toilets, and free shower trailers. No pets permitted.

BROOKFEST.
Just outside Turn 4, off Hwy 50 at Daugherty Rd. Opens 8 am on Tues of race week; closes Mon at noon after the race. 20-by-40-foot site, $125; 20-by-50-foot site, $150.

BROOKLYN HIGHWAY CAMPGROUND.
Across the street from the speedway on Brooklyn Hwy. The campground opens at 8 am Sat before race week for NASCAR NEXTEL Cup races and closes Mon at noon after the race. Amenities include water spigots and a tent-only area. 20-by-50-foot site, $125.

CABELA'S CAMPGROUND.
Behind Turn 3 off Hwy 50. Opens Mon at 8 am of NASCAR NEXTEL race weeks. 20-by-40-foot site, $125.

INFIELD.
Enter the infield beginning Tues at 6 pm of race week. All sites are reserved, and the infield sites are hardest to snag; be first in line at the sales or upgrade opportunities each autumn. Everyone older than 12 who plans to watch the race from an infield campsite also needs an infield ticket—the least expensive way to take kids to the race. Grandstand tickets are not valid for infield admission for NASCAR NEXTEL Cup weekends. 15-by-40-foot interior site, $125; guardrail site, $175.

NORTHWOODS AND NORTHFIELD.
This wooded, pleasant site is across the street from Tunnel Entrance. Opens Wed morning. Limited to pop-up campers, tents, and vans. No motor homes or travel trailers. 18-by-35-foot site or 20-by-30-foot site, $125.

TREE FARM.
Just outside Turns 3 and 4 off Hwy 50. Offers shade and spacious sites. Opens Wed of race week and remains open 24 hours a day. 20-by-45-foot site, $200; 20-by-55-foot site, $225.

BRAKE HERE

Many private lakefront cottages in the Irish Hills are available to rent during race week—some within walking distance to the track. Expect to pay at least $1,000 for the weekend only and substantially more for the entire week. More than one family sharing an accommodation is usually permitted. Often, parking recreational vehicles or camping on the grounds is permitted as well. For more information, visit the Brooklyn/Irish Hills Chamber of Commerce site at www.brooklynmi.com/cottage.

WALT MICHAEL'S RV SUPER STORE TURN 2 CAMPGROUND.
Each of the 147 motorcoach-only sites has electric and water hook-ups. Opens 8 am on Sat before race week and remains open 24 hours a day. Closes Mon at noon following the race. 25-by-60-foot site, $400.

Off-speedway campgrounds

Brooklyn

GREENBRIAR CAMPGROUND.
14820 Wellwood Rd, Brooklyn (49230). Phone 517/592-6952. www.michcampgrounds.com/greenbriar. All 100 sites have water and electric hook-ups. 18-hole golf course, swimming pool, basketball, volleyball, horseshoes, playground, children's fishing pond (catch and release), laundry room. Some pets permitted.

JUNIPER HILLS, INC.
13500 Rte 12, Brooklyn (49230). Phone 517/592-6803. www.juniperhills.com. Overhead walkway to speedway gate. More than 2,000 sites, with restrooms and hot showers. Prices vary. No pets.

TED RANCH CAMPGROUND.
12985 Monroe Pike, Brooklyn (49230). Phone 517/592-8879. Ten sites within easy walking distance of the track. Water/electric hook-ups. No pets permitted.

TURN 3 ALL NITE PARKING AND CAMPING.
12801 Hwy 50, Brooklyn (49230). Phone 517/592-CAMP (2267). www.racecamping.org. Directly across from Turn 3 grandstand. Portable toilets, water and dump station. More than 130 24-by-56-foot sites. Prices vary; higher on race week. No pets.

VICTORY FAMILY CAMPGROUND (WORD OF LIFE FELLOWSHIP).
13191 Hwy 50, Brooklyn (49230). Phone 517/592-2128. www.victorycampground.com. Fourteen campsites a half-mile from the track. Portable toilets, water. No alcohol; no pets.

Cement City

IRISH HILLS RESORT KAMPGROUND.
16230 Rte 12, Cement City (49233). Phone 517/592-6751. www.irishhillskampground.com. Most of the more than 130 sites have water and electric; swimming pool. Pets permitted.

Onsted

WJ HAYES STATE PARK.
1220 Wamplers Lake Rd, Onsted (49265). Phone 517/467-7401. All of the 185 sites have electric hook-ups; bathhouses with flush toilets and hot showers, two lakes, wooded sites, pets, and fires permitted.

For more lodging recommendations, go to www.mobiltravelguide.com

EAT

MOBIL STAR-RATED RESTAURANTS

Ann Arbor

PAESANO'S. ★
3411 Washtenaw Ave, Ann Arbor (48104). Phone 734/971-0484. www.paesanosannarbor.com. Lucky for you, this rustic Italian restaurant's entire menu is available for take-out. Each dish combines regional tastes of Italy, resulting in fascinating new flavors. Enjoy seasonal flavors such as pumpkin and amaretto ravioli and stuffed chicken with fall wild mushrooms and farmer cheese. Italian menu. Lunch, dinner. Closed Jan 1, Thanksgiving, Dec 25. Bar. Children's menu. Outdoor seating. $$

Jackson

KNIGHT'S STEAKHOUSE AND GRILL. ★★
2125 Horton Rd, Jackson (49203). Phone 517/783-2777. This steakhouse has a no-frills flair that attracts both locals and out-of-towners. The great selection and value of the menu are probably the area's best-kept secret. Steak menu. Dinner. Closed Sun; holidays. Bar. Children's menu. $$

Marshall

CORNWELL'S TURKEYVILLE. ★
18935 15 1/2 Mile Rd, Marshall (49068). Phone 269/781-4293. www.turkeyville.com. Take the half-comatose, half-blissful feeling after a Thanksgiving meal and multiply it by about 20 (the number of all-turkey items on the menu), and you're in Turkeyville. With everything from turkey dogs and turkey sandwiches to old-fashioned turkey dinners and turkey ranch wraps, poultry lovers everywhere will, ahem, flock here. With a gift shop and, of all things, a dinner theater, this restaurant is a destination in itself. American menu. Lunch, dinner. Children's menu. Outdoor seating. $

EAT MOBIL STAR-RATED LODGINGS

SCHULER'S OF MARSHALL. ★★
115 S Eagle St, Marshall (49068). Phone 269/781-0600. www.schulersrestaurant.com. In addition to the delicious food and spectacular service, this restaurant has become a local institution during its 95 years of business. Schuler's takes on new recipes every week or so and sponsors and organizes local events like the Schuler's Fly-In and Etiquette Day. Beneath all that, though, lies a charming, comfortable atmosphere. American menu. Lunch, dinner, Sun brunch. Closed Dec 25. Children's menu. Outdoor seating. $

LOCAL RECOMMENDATIONS

Brooklyn

HAROLD'S PLACE.
10625 Rte 12, Brooklyn (49230). Phone 517/467-2064. At this family-style restaurant, the tasty breakfasts include country ham and light-as-air biscuits. American menu. Breakfast, lunch, dinner. $

JERRY'S PUB AND RESTAURANT.
650 Egan Hwy, Brooklyn (49230). Phone 517/467-4700. Good bar food, pasta, ribs, and burgers. Located on the south shore of Wamplers Lake, Jerry's deck is a fine spot for relaxing and sipping while watching the water. Bar menu. Lunch, dinner. Closed Mon. $$

POPPA'S PLACE.
208 S Main St, Brooklyn (49230). Phone 517/592-4625. Poppa's features big breakfasts and all-you-can-eat dinner specials. The Monday night Goulash is a winner. American menu. Breakfast, lunch, dinner. $

Cement City

ARTESIAN WELLS.
Rte 12 and Hwy 127, Cement City (49233). Phone 517/547-8777. At this biker-friendly bar where pizza, burgers, and lots of appetizers are served, the owners not only ride, they own the Harley-Davidson store next door. Bar menu. Breakfast (Fri-Sun), lunch, dinner. $$

Chelsea

COMMON GRILL.
112 S Main St, Chelsea (48118). Phone 734/475-0470. www.commongrill.com. Salads, sandwiches, pasta, lots of fish, including fresh walleye. The grill also features a superior wine list. Vegetarian menu. Lunch, dinner. Closed Mon. $$$

Clark Lake

BEACH BAR.
3505 Ocean Beach Rd, Clark Lake (49234). Phone 517/529-4211. The Beach Bar is locally famous for soups, pizza, and sandwiches. It's a great place to relax and watch the boats. American menu. Lunch, dinner. Outdoor seating. No credit cards accepted. $$

Manchester

DAN'S RIVER GRILL.
223 W Main St, Manchester (48158). Phone 734/428-9500. dansrivergrill.com. Dan serves a little bit of everything—from hamburgers to frogs' legs, jambalaya, steaks, and pasta. Ask for a seat by the window overlooking the water. Steak, seafood menu. Lunch, dinner. Closed Sun. $$

Onsted

GOLDEN NUGGET RESTAURANT.
7305 Rte 12, Onsted (49265). Phone 517/467-2190. Cozy and filled with antiques, some people call this eatery romantic—and you may walk away feeling something akin to love for the hamburgers, chicken, seafood, and steak. American menu. Lunch, dinner. Closed Mon. $$

Saline

MAC'S ACADIAN SEAFOOD SHACK.
104 E Michigan, Saline (41876). Phone 734/944-6227. Fried Louisiana farm-raised catfish, peel-and-eat Cajun shrimp, jambalaya, and shrimp Creole. Cajun/Creole menu. Lunch, dinner. Closed Sun. $$

Tipton

TOP O' THE HILL TRUCK STOP AND FAMILY RESTAURANT.
5140 Rte 12, Tipton (49287). Phone 517/456-7220. Between the yummy grilled sticky buns, tasty omelets, and big breakfast platters, you won't walk away hungry. Burgers, sandwiches, and soup are featured for lunch. Friday night walleye fish fry. American menu. Breakfast, lunch, dinner. Children's menu. No credit cards accepted. $

For more dining recommendations, go to www.mobiltravelguide.com

SIDETRIP

Gearhead Getaway
Detroit, MI

If you're crazy about cars, you will love Detroit.

One annual event guaranteed to keep a car lover enthralled is the **Woodward Dream Cruise** (www.woodwarddreamcruise.com), a vintage car event held each August.

Cars travel down the region's main drag, Woodward Avenue, from the Detroit city line at Eight Mile Road for 16 miles to the city of Pontiac. Each town along the way offers entertainment, car shows, food, and arts and crafts, as thousands of muscle and collectible car owners cruise the street. Grab a lawn chair and claim a spot. The cruise is usually held during the August race weekend at Michigan International Speedway.

Consider a trip to **The Henry Ford** (20900 Oakwood Blvd, Dearborn, phone 313/982-6100, toll-free 800/835-5237, www.hfmgv.org), the world's largest indoor-outdoor museum The "Automobile in American Life" exhibit has acres of historic cars, including the first US-built car to win an international race (in 1908) and the limo in which JFK was assassinated. Don't leave without touring the amazing and massive Ford Rouge factory.

Also worth a visit is the **Walter P. Chrysler Museum** (1 Chrysler Dr, Auburn Hills, phone 248/944-0001, toll-free 888/456-1924, www.chryslerheritage.com), which celebrates Chrysler's performance-car history, including the 1957 Plymouth Fury, the 1964 "Color Me Gone" Dodge Ramcharger 300, and the sporty

"Automobile in American Life" exhibit at the Henry Ford Museum offers a fascinating look at how developments in transportation have influenced life in the United States.

1970 Plymouth Hemi 'Cuda. Or stop at the **Motor Sports Hall of Fame of America** (43700 Expo Center Dr, Novi, phone toll-free 800/250-7223, www.mshf.com). See and touch the history of racing at this museum, which features more than 30 race cars and other high-performance vehicles.

For more Detroit recommendations, go to www.mobiltravelguide.com

330

The crowd fills the new grandstands at the start of the 2003 NASCAR Busch Series race.

The Milwaukee Mile

West Allis, WI

20

Fans follow the action intently as NASCAR Busch Series cars barrel off into Turn 1 during the 2004 Alan Kulwicki 250, presented by Forest County Potawatomi Racing.

TRACK FACTS

THE MILWAUKEE MILE. 7722 W Greenfield Ave, West Allis (53214). Phone 414/453-8277. www.milwaukeemile.com.

SECURITY. Leave your fireworks and beach balls at home, because they're not welcome in the grandstand and bleacher seating areas. Other forbidden items include coolers (any size), food or beverages (alcoholic and non), umbrellas, noisemakers, helium balloons, glass containers, weapons, and folding chairs.

PARKING. There's a dual-pay parking system here. Because the speedway is on the Wisconsin State Fair Park grounds, you'll first pay a $5 charge to enter or park on the grounds (gates are on 84th St and Greenfield Ave). If you want to park on the infield, get to the speedway the morning of the race; people start lining up the night before. There's also an additional $10 fee, and all passengers must have an event ticket or credentials. Only passenger-type vans, automobiles, pick-up trucks, and motorcycles are allowed into the track and infield area. Special handicapped accessible parking areas are located off Gates 1, 4, and 6.

FIRST AID. The main first aid station is on Grandstand Avenue, with the secondary one in the paddock area's Infield Care Center near Victory Lane. For extreme emergencies, call the Wisconsin Capitol Police at 414/266-7033.

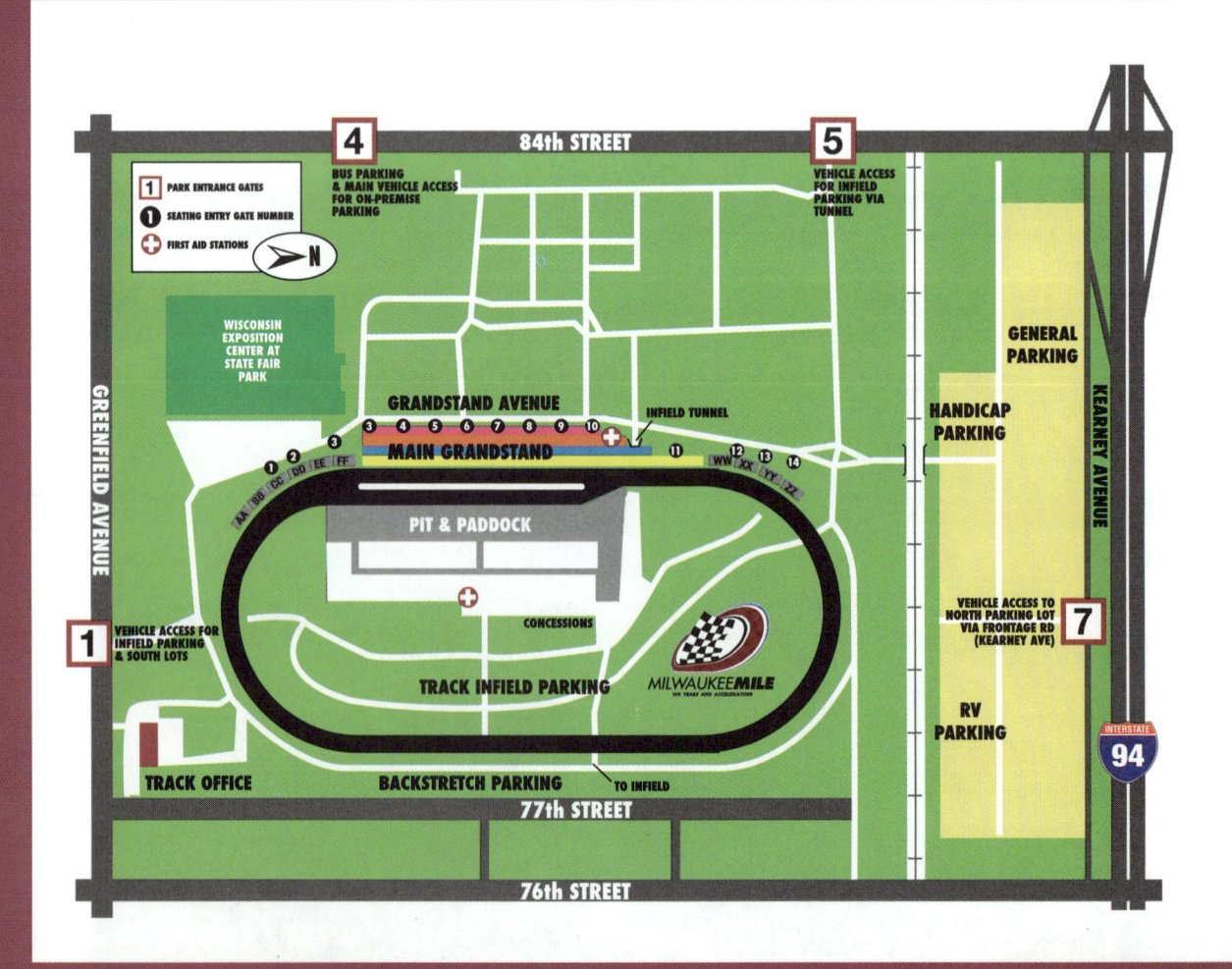

CONCESSIONS. More than a dozen concession stands along Grandstand Avenue sell typical festival fare such as hot dogs, bratwurst, barbecue sandwiches, lemonade, and cotton candy. Stands are open until on-track activity concludes for the day.

RESTROOMS. Head for the restrooms on the second level of the grandstands; they're usually empty. Other restrooms can be found under the grandstands, in the infield, and near the vendors. There are also Port-A-Johns throughout the infield.

PIT/PADDOCK PASSES. A big perk at The Mile: you can purchase three-day Pit/Paddock Passes ($50) during the NASCAR Craftsman Truck and Busch Series, affording you limited access to the team work areas. (At most NASCAR events, the garage area is off-limits to fans.) Spectators must be 18 or older and wear long pants, closed-toe shoes, and shirts covering their shoulders.

GETTING TICKETS

Life is easiest if you order tickets after January 1 and have them mailed to you before the race. (*Hint:* some of the best views are actually from the less costly bleacher seats in Section CC by the first turn.) Check The Mile's Web site for special deals and package options. If you don't order ahead, the ticket office is open Monday through Friday from 9 am to 5 pm and Saturday from 11 am to 3 pm. On race weekends, it's easiest to buy tickets at the speedway ticket booth on Grandstand Avenue between Gates 7 and 8.

There are no ticket refunds. If an event is postponed, the race will be run the next suitable day, as determined by the sanctioning body. Children two and under are free, although they must sit on an adult's lap in the reserved seating area. Handicapped accessible seating is available (Row 1 of South Terrace Sections AA through FF; Row 1 of North Terrace Sections WW through YY and Rows 1, 19, and 41 of the main grandstand). Will Call is at the Main Grandstand Ticket Booth.

Ted Musgrave (No. 1) duels with David Reutimann (No. 17) during the 2004 NASCAR Craftsman Truck Series BlackCat Fireworks 200.

David Stremme (No. 32) and Kyle Busch (No. 5) start the NASCAR Busch Series Alan Kulwicki 250, presented by Forest County Potawatomi Racing.

Extend your trip for some adventurous whitewater rafting.

Rent a boat at one of the area's many marinas.

BREW TOWN ON THE LAKE

Milwaukee is often overshadowed by Chicago, its bigger, glitzier sister to the south. But this city of 600,000 that hugs the Lake Michigan shoreline has plenty of charm, spunk, and sizzle of its own.

Native Americans first called this area Millioki, or "gathering place by the waters," in reference to its spot on the west shore of Lake Michigan where the Milwaukee, Menomonee, and Kinnickinnic rivers meet. Millioki served as a French trading post and convenient resting place between Chicago to the south and Green Bay to the north before being settled in 1813 by French trader Solomon Juneau. Europeans flooded into the city shortly after, namely Germans and Poles.

It was largely thanks to the German settlers that Milwaukee soon became synonymous with beer. At one point, there were scores of breweries in the city, including five of the nation's largest. Today, **Miller Brewing** (4251 W State St, phone 414/931-2337) is the only major brewery left, although the city also contains several microbreweries and brew pubs, and beer is still a significant cultural component of the town.

Not surprisingly, the city that loves its beer also appreciates sports and manufacturing.

Residents get their fill of sports by watching one of four professional teams: the Milwaukee Bucks (National Basketball Association), the Milwaukee Brewers (Major League Baseball), the Milwaukee Admirals (American Hockey League), and the Milwaukee Wave (Major Indoor Soccer League). And although US manufacturing jobs have declined over the years, Milwaukee is still a blue-collar stronghold, home to Fortune 1000 manufacturing powerhouses such as Briggs & Stratton, Harley-Davidson Inc., Johnson Controls, Rockwell Automation, and A.O. Smith Corporation.

Find out what goes into making a Harley then feel what it's like to sit on one at the Harley facility in Wauwatosa.

GETTING AROUND

Luckily for fans, there aren't usually major traffic problems getting to The Mile. Just hop on I-94 and you'll be there in a flash. If you're coming from Milwaukee (east of the speedway), take I-94 west to the 84th St Exit (#306). Exit and turn left onto 84th St. The Wisconsin State Fair Park grounds and 84th St parking gates are on the left. If you're coming from the west, take I-94 east to the 84th St Exit (#306). Exit and turn right onto 84th St. The Wisconsin State Fair Park grounds and 84th St parking gates are on the left.

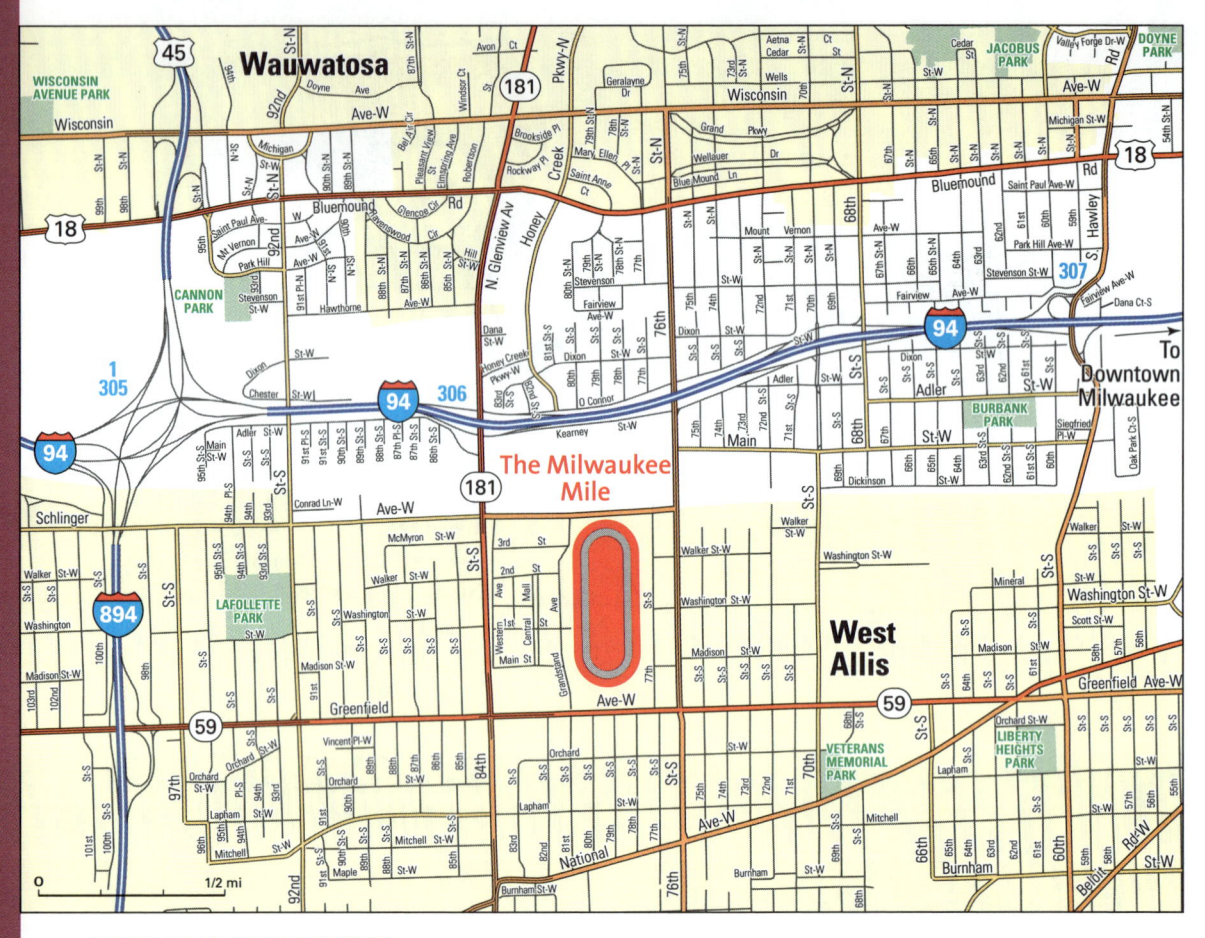

WEST ALLIS POLE POSITION:
The 10 miles surrounding The Milwaukee Mile.

But don't let this beer-swilling, Harley Hog-and-sports-loving populace fool you into thinking Milwaukee isn't chic. Sure, the feel here is more of a big little city—you won't find much pretension among residents. But that's part of the charm. And it doesn't mean Milwaukee can't compete with the big boys. The city has a fabulous art museum, for one, sporting a winglike moving sunscreen designed by world-renowned architect Santiago Calatrava. Its botanical gardens and horticultural conservatory are impressive, and the city boasts several stunning historic churches, such as the **Basilica of St. Josaphat** (2333 S Sixth St, phone 414/645-5623), a national landmark; the **Cathedral of St. John the Evangelist** (812 N Jackson St, phone 414/276-9814); and the 15th-century **St. Joan of Arc Chapel** (Marquette University, phone 414/288-6873) transported from France. Milwaukee has also been celebrating the city's diversity for decades through myriad summer ethnic festivals, long before diversity was on everyone's radar screen.

If Milwaukee has one drawback, it's the weather. Lake Michigan fiercely controls the climate, often keeping things chilly by the lake in summer. While the city's summer temperatures average a pleasant 78° F, you can subtract five or ten from that figure if you're talking about average lakeside temps.

For visitor information, contact the Greater Milwaukee Convention & Visitors Bureau, 101 West Wisconsin Avenue, Suite 425, 53203, phone 414/273-3950, toll-free 800/231-0903, www.officialmilwaukee.com.

Lightning strikes all the time at the Discovery World museum, with 150 kid-oriented interactive exhibits.

WEST ALLIS CALENDAR

JUNE 3–5, 2005
RiverSplash. Downtown Milwaukee, Pere Marquette Park, between Old World Third St and the river, Milwaukee (53203). Phone 414/297-9855. www.riversplash.com. Take part in this ten-block free festival featuring live music, food, and fireworks in downtown Milwaukee and the RiverWalk.

JUNE 24, 2005
NASCAR Craftsman Truck Series

JUNE 25, 2005
NASCAR Busch Series

JUNE 25–26, 2005
Cedarburg Strawberry Festival. Washington Ave, Cedarburg (53012). Phone 262/377-9620; toll-free 800/237-2874. www.cedarburgfestivals.org. Have a berry good time at this festival featuring strawberry treats, contests, crafts, and entertainment.

JUNE 30–JULY 10, 2005
Summerfest. Henry Maier Festival Grounds, 200 N Harbor Dr, Milwaukee (53202). Phone toll-free 800/273-3378. www.summerfest.com. Join the annual summer bash with 13 different music stages, rides, games, and food.

JULY 14–17, 2005
Bastille Days. Cathedral Square Park, Jefferson and Wells sts, Milwaukee (53202). Phone 414/271-1416. www.easttown.com. Celebrate French history and culture with street entertainers, a marketplace, sidewalk cafés, and the annual "Storm the Bastille" 5K fun run/2-mile walk.

DRIVER'S PICK

NASCAR fans head to see races at America's Legendary Oval, but other visitors head to this city on the lake for Summerfest, an annual weeklong celebration of music, beer, and brats. NASCAR Craftsman Truck Series driver of the No. 5 Toyota, **Mike Skinner**, is no exception. "We race in Milwaukee about the time the city holds its Summerfest. We like to go over to see the sights and get some of those great brats and cheeses. Real health food." Summerfest runs June 30 through July 10, 2005. *Henry Maier Festival Grounds, 200 N Harbor Dr, Milwaukee (53202). Phone 414/273-3378; toll-free 800/273-3378. www.summerfest.com.*

WEST ALLIS OUTFIELD:
The 50 miles surrounding The Milwaukee Mile.

SEE

ATTRACTIONS

Kenosha

BRISTOL RENAISSANCE FAIRE.
12550 120th Ave, Kenosha (53142). Phone 847/395-7773. www.renfair.com/bristol. Step back into a 16th-century European marketplace filled with richly gowned ladies, tattered beggars, and soldiers at the Bristol Renaissance Faire. As you stroll the grounds, stop in at a comedy show, swordfight, or thrilling jousting competition. Open nine weekends beginning July 9, plus Labor Day. (Sat-Sun 10 am-7 pm) **$$-$$$$**

Milwaukee

BETTY BRINN CHILDREN'S MUSEUM.
929 E Wisconsin Ave, Milwaukee (53202). Phone 414/390-5437. www.bbcmkids.org. Kids ten and under will have a blast at this interactive museum, where they can enter a digestion tunnel and hear what their body sounds like as it's digesting food or create their own racetrack and test drive golf ball-shaped push carts on different road surfaces. (Tues-Sat 9 am-5 pm, Sun noon-5 pm, also Mon in June-Aug 9 am-5 pm) **$**

THE BREW CITY QUEEN.
1137 N Old World Third St, Milwaukee (53203). Boat Location: Pier Marquette Park on Third St between State and Kilbourn sts. Phone 414/283-9999. www.riverwalkboats.com. In Milwaukee, brewery tours are a must. Hit three at once by hopping on *The Brew City Queen* pontoon boat, which motors up and down the Milwaukee River with pit stops at Lakefront Brewery (1872 N Commerce), the Milwaukee Ale House (233 N Water), and Rock Bottom Brewery (740 N Plankinton) for tours and tastings. The three-hour trip is available Saturdays and Sundays from mid-May through August and Saturdays only in September, depending on the weather. Board at one of the three breweries. Riverwalk Boat Rentals, which operates the tours, also rents pontoon and paddleboats by the hour, half-day, and full day. **$$$$**

DISCOVERY WORLD: THE JAMES LOVELL MUSEUM OF SCIENCE, ECONOMICS AND TECHNOLOGY.
815 N James Lovell St, Milwaukee (53233). Phone 414/765-9966. www.discoveryworld.org. Discovery World, aimed at kids 14 and under, is filled with 150 interactive exhibits. At the 4Cast Center, try your hand at weather forecasting with live Doppler Radar, the Lightning Track, and a seismograph. In the Gears & Linkages section, figure out the simple mechanics behind pulleys and other tools. (Daily 9 am-5 pm; closed July 4, Thanksgiving, Dec 25) **$$**

MILLER BREWERY TOUR.
4251 W State St, Milwaukee (53208). Phone 414/931-2337; toll-free 800/944-5483. www.millerbrewing.com. Milwaukee is synonymous with beer, so you've got to take the one-hour guided tour of Miller Brewing Company, Milwaukee's sole remaining large-scale brewery and the nation's second largest. Disappointingly, most of what you see is through windows. But you do get to see some equipment up close in the brew house, and the Caves Museum, a small showcase of brewery memorabilia housed in hand-dug tunnels once used to store beer, is cool. At the end, adults receive three beer samples while kids get root beer. Everyone also gets a packet of pretzels and a postcard. (Labor Day-Memorial Day: Mon-Sat 10 am-5 pm; rest of year: 10 am-5:30 pm; closed holidays) **FREE**

MILLER PARK TOUR.
One Brewers Way, Milwaukee (53214). Phone 414/902-4005. www.brewers.mlb.com. One of baseball's newest ballparks—and home of the Milwaukee Brewers—Miller Park is the only ballpark in North America with a fan-shaped, convertible roof and natural grass playing field. Seventy-minute tours showcase the dugout, luxury suites, clubhouse, press box, Bob Uecker's broadcast booth, and more. Tours meet in the Brewers Fan Zone Store in Miller Park's Hot Corner down the left field line; tickets can be purchased in the ticket booth just outside the store. Wheelchair accessible. General parking (fee). (Daily 10:30 am, 1:30 pm, and 3 pm during baseball season; no tours on home game days; closed holidays) **$$**

MILWAUKEE COUNTY ZOO.
10001 W Blue Mound Rd, Milwaukee (53226). Phone 414/771-3040 or 414/771-5500 (information line). www.milwaukeezoo.org. See 2,500 mammals, birds, reptiles, and fish at the Milwaukee County Zoo,

SEE ATTRACTIONS

renowned for displaying predators next to their normal prey. The zoo recently opened an animal health center with a public viewing area; make sure to catch a treatment procedure or surgery (mornings are best). Sea lion show, miniature zoo train, zoomobile with guided tours, and carousel available for a fee. Parking (fee). Stroller rental available. (May-Sept: daily 9 am-5 pm; rest of year: 9 am-4:30 pm) $$

WISCONSIN LAKE SCHOONER.
Pier Wisconsin, 500 N Harbor Dr, Milwaukee (53202). Phone 414/276-7700. www.pierwisconsin.org. Three-masted schooners aren't just the province of the oceans. Here on Lake Michigan, you can sail on the 137-foot S/V *Denis Sullivan*, the first tall ship built in Wisconsin in more than 100 years. The ship is a re-creation of a typical 19th-century Great Lakes schooner. Two-and-a-half-hour tours are typically held on select dates from May through September. *Note*: There might be a new docking site in 2005 because the group is constructing a new building. $$$$

Wauwatosa

HARLEY-DAVIDSON TOUR.
11700 W Capitol Dr, Wauwatosa (53222). Phone 414/343-7850; toll-free 877/883-1450. www.harleydavidson.com. Milwaukee is Hog Heaven, so it's only fitting to tour the propeller-factory-turned-Harley-facility and see transmission and engine assembly from start to finish, plus some engine remanufacturing. The one-hour tour also features a video on company history and a peek at the assembly line. Tickets are handed out at 9 am on a first-come, first-served basis; it's strongly recommended to arrive early. To be eligible for the tour, you must be 18; wear fully enclosed, low-heeled shoes; show a valid government-issued photo ID or passport; complete a registration card; and pass through a metal detector. Backpacks, camera bags, camcorders, and pocketknives are prohibited on the factory floor. (Mon-Fri 9:30 am-1 pm) **FREE**

For more attractions, go to www.mobiltravelguide.com

STAY

MOBIL STAR-RATED LODGINGS

Milwaukee

COURTYARD BY MARRIOTT—DOWNTOWN. ★ ★
300 W Michigan St, Milwaukee (53203). Phone 414/291-4122; toll-free 800/321-2211. www.courtyard.com. Guests will find no shortage of things to see and do near this pleasant, comfortable hotel, which is connected to downtown Milwaukee's impressive Grand Avenue Mall and within walking distance to the river and many dining options. 169 rooms, 6 story. Check-in 3 pm, check-out noon. High-speed Internet access. Restaurant. Fitness room. Indoor pool, whirlpool. Airport transportation available. Business center. $$

FAN FAVORITE

A trip to **American Serb Memorial Hall** for a traditional Wisconsin fish fry dinner is a must if you're in town on a Wednesday or Friday. On a typical Friday night, Serb Hall serves more than 2,000 fish dinners, typically deep-fried or baked cod, although perch, pollock, and walleye are also available. Dining is in a cavernous banquet room, but if you're in a hurry, the drive-through window is handy. American menu. Lunch, dinner. Open only Friday for dining and Wednesday for drive-through and carry-out. Children's menu. Casual attire. Reservations recommended. $$ 5101 W Oklahoma Ave, Milwaukee (53219). Phone 414/545-6030. www.serbhall.com.

HILTON MILWAUKEE CITY CENTER. ★★★

509 W Wisconsin Ave, Milwaukee (53203). Phone 414/271-7250; toll-free 800/445-8667. www.hilton.com. Your kids will beg you to stay at the Hilton Milwaukee City Center because it contains the 20,000-square-foot Paradise Landing, the nation's first urban indoor water park. 730 rooms, 25 story. Check-in 4 pm, check-out 11 am. Wireless Internet access. Two restaurants, bar. Fitness room. Indoor pool, children's pool, whirlpool. $$

HOLIDAY INN MILWAUKEE—DOWNTOWN. ★★

611 W Wisconsin Ave, Milwaukee (53203). Phone 414/273-2950; toll-free 800/465-4329. www.holiday-inn.com. Located right across from Milwaukee's massive Midwest Express Center, this recently renovated hotel features a rooftop pool and sundeck on its second level. Families will enjoy the restaurant on the ground floor and the option of adjoining rooms, while business travelers can take advantage of the hotel's business services and downtown location. 247 rooms, 10 story. Check-in 3 pm, check-out noon. Restaurant, bar. Fitness room. Outdoor pool. Business center. $

HYATT REGENCY MILWAUKEE. ★★★

333 W Kilbourn Ave, Milwaukee (53203). Phone 414/276-1234; toll-free 888/591-1234. www.hyatt.com. The hotel is connected by skywalk to the Grand Avenue Mall shopping center. The hotel delights its guests with Milwaukee's only revolving rooftop restaurant, which affords panoramic views of the city's skyline. 484 rooms, 22 story. Check-in 3 pm, check-out noon. Restaurant, bar. Fitness room. Business center. $$

THE PFISTER HOTEL. ★★★

424 E Wisconsin Ave, Milwaukee (53202). Phone 414/273-5026; toll-free 800/558-8222. www.pfisterhotel.com. The Pfister, in the heart of downtown Milwaukee, has been a perennial favorite of discerning travelers since 1893. All of the city's treasures, from businesses and restaurants to shops and attractions, are within walking distance of this historic landmark. The hotel embraces its past with a museum-quality collection of Victorian artwork. The views of the city and Lake Michigan are particularly alluring, and the restaurants and lounges are the places to see and be seen in the city. 307 rooms, 23 story. Check-in 3 pm, check-out noon. Three restaurants, two bars. Fitness room. Indoor pool. Airport transportation available. $$

WYNDHAM MILWAUKEE CENTER. ★★★

139 E Kilbourn Ave, Milwaukee (53202). Phone 414/276-8686; toll-free 877/999-3223. www.wyndham.com. Nestled in Milwaukee's charming theater district, this elegant hotel is located within the same building complex as the Milwaukee Repertory and Pabst theaters. Well-appointed rooms overlook the Milwaukee River, and guests are within walking distance of the Marcus Center, City Hall, and plenty of shopping and dining. 220 rooms, 10 story. Check-in 3 pm, check-out noon. High-speed Internet access. Restaurant, two bars. Fitness room. Whirlpool. Airport transportation available. $$

Wauwatosa

HOLIDAY INN EXPRESS MILWAUKEE—WEST MEDICAL CENTER. ★

11111 W North Ave, Wauwatosa (53226). Phone 414/778-0333; toll-free 800/377-8660. www.hiexpress.com. This hotel is located about ten minutes from The Mile. 122 rooms, 3 story. Complimentary continental breakfast. Check-out noon. Wireless Internet access. Indoor pool. $

LOCAL RECOMMENDATIONS

Brookfield

BEST WESTERN MIDWAY HOTEL.

1005 S Moorland Rd, Brookfield (53005). Phone 262/786-9540; toll-free 877/664-3929. www.bestwestern.com. The official hotel of The Milwaukee Mile, the Best Western Midway is just minutes from the racetrack off Interstate 94. Nearby is the Milwaukee County Zoo and Miller Park. 125 rooms, 2 story. Check-in 3 pm, check-out 11 am. Wireless Internet access. Fitness room. Indoor pool, whirlpool. $

COUNTRY INN & SUITES BY CARLSON.

1250 S Moorland Rd, Brookfield (53005). Phone 262/782-1400; toll-free 800/456-4000. www.countryinns.com. Close to The Mile and loaded with amenities. 149 rooms, 3 story. Pets accepted. Complimentary continental breakfast. Check-in 3 pm, check-out 11 am. Wireless Internet access. Restaurants. Fitness room. Indoor pool, whirlpool. Business center. $

HAMPTON INN MILWAUKEE/BROOKFIELD.

575 N Barker Rd, Brookfield (53045). Phone 262/796-1500; toll-free 800/426-7866. www.hamptoninn.com. One of the best deals close to the track is the Hampton

Inn Milwaukee/Brookfield, just off Interstate 94 and minutes from The Mile. 120 rooms, 4 story. Complimentary continental breakfast. Check-in 2 pm, check-out noon. Wireless Internet access. Fitness room. Indoor pool, whirlpool. $

Mequon

BEST WESTERN QUIET HOUSE & SUITES.

10330 N Port Washington Rd, Mequon (53092). Phone 262/241-3677; toll-free 800/780-7234. www.bestwestern.com. 54 rooms, 2 story. Pets accepted, some restrictions; fee. Complimentary continental breakfast. Check-in 2 pm, check-out 11 am. High-speed Internet access. Fitness room. Indoor pool, outdoor pool, whirlpool. Airport transportation available. $

Milwaukee

BEST WESTERN INN TOWNE HOTEL.

710 N Old World Third St, Milwaukee (53203). Phone 414/224-8400; toll-free 800/780-7234. www.bestwestern.com. 96 rooms, 12 story. Pets accepted, some restrictions; fee. Check-in 3 pm, check-out noon. Restaurant. Fitness room. $

BEST WESTERN MILWAUKEE AIRPORT HOTEL & CONFERENCE CENTER.

5105 S Howell Ave, Milwaukee (53207). Phone 414/769-0064; toll-free 800/780-7234. www.bestwestern.com. 139 rooms, 3 story. Complimentary continental breakfast. Check-in 3 pm, check-out noon. High-speed Internet access. Restaurant, bar. Fitness room. Indoor pool, whirlpool. Airport transportation available. $

BEST WESTERN WOODS VIEW INN.

5501 W National Ave, Milwaukee (53214). Phone 414/671-6400; toll-free 800/780-7234. www.bestwestern.com. 61 rooms, 3 story. Complimentary continental breakfast. Check-in 3 pm, check-out 11 am. High-speed Internet access. Restaurant, bar. Indoor pool, whirlpool. Airport transportation available. $

RADISSON HOTEL MILWAUKEE WEST.

2303 N Mayfair Rd, Milwaukee (53226). Phone 414/257-3400; toll-free 800/333-3333. www.radisson.com. You might spy some drivers at the more upscale Radisson Hotel Milwaukee West, which features Mission-style furnishings, ergonomic desk chairs, and upgraded bath products. 150 rooms, 8 story. Check-in 3 pm, check-out noon. Wireless Internet access. Restaurant, bar. Fitness room. Indoor pool. Airport transportation available. $

Pewaukee

BEST WESTERN WAUKESHA GRAND.

2840 N Grandview Blvd, Pewaukee (53072). Phone 262/524-9300; toll-free 800/367-3935. www.bestwestern.com. 97 rooms, 3 story. Pets accepted. Complimentary continental breakfast. Check-in 3 pm, check-out noon. High-speed Internet access. Fitness room. Indoor pool. $

Sturtevant

BEST WESTERN GRANDVIEW INN.

910 S Sylvania Ave, Sturtevant (53177). Phone 262/886-0385; toll-free 800/780-7234. www.bestwestern.com. 48 rooms, 2 story. Pets accepted. Complimentary continental breakfast. Check-in 3 pm, check-out noon. Indoor pool. $

RV AND CAMPING

Calendonia

YOGI BEAR'S JELLYSTONE PARK.

8425 Hwy 38, Calendonia (53108). Phone 262/835-2565. www.campjellystone.com. This facility is just a half-hour from The Mile. If features 247 campsites and cabins, a 400-foot water slide, horseshoe pit, game room, heated outdoor pools, mini-golf, movies, playground, pedal karts, sand volleyball court, laundry facilities, and RV storage. Open mid-Apr-mid-Oct. $18-$45 for tents and sites (4 people); $79-$95 for cabins. Miscellaneous additional charges may apply. Wristband for mini-golf and water slides: $14. Individual fees: $1 water slide ride; $4 for mini-golf.

Milwaukee

PROSSER RV/CRUISE AMERICA

6146 S Howell Ave, Milwaukee (53207). Phone 414/766-1079. www.prosserrv.com. $181 per day for Class C motor homes; $475 per week for pop-ups; prices are subject to change.

Mukwonago

COUNTRY VIEW CAMPGROUND.

S110 W26400 Craig Ave, Mukwonago (53149). Phone 262/662-3654. Milwaukee County's only campground is about a half-hour from The Mile and has 175 sites, both wooded and open. Amenities include a 30-amp electrical service, a heated pool, playground, laundry facilities, camp store, game room, restrooms, showers, and a dump station. Pets accepted. Open mid-Apr-mid-Oct. $20-$25.

West Allis

BADGERLAND RV RENTAL LLC
1126 S 72nd St, West Allis (53214). Phone 414/687-4847; toll-free 888/561-8199. www.badgerlandrv.com. $165 per day with a three-day minimum rental required.

RECREATIONAL VEHICLE PARK.
601 S 76th St, West Allis (53214). Phone 414/266-7035. www.wistatefair.com. Metro Milwaukee's sole RV park just happens to be 300 yards behind Turn 3 of the speedway on the Wisconsin State Fair Park grounds (enter at Gate 8). If you want a site for the 2005 NASCAR race, make a reservation as soon as possible since reservations usually fill up in early January (three-night minimum stay required during race weekends). The RV Park offers 70 full-service sites, electric-only sites, restrooms with showers, laundry facilities, dumping and potable water stations, and security personnel. Propane is sold on site. Leashed pets allowed. No tent camping. $44 (full-service) or $33 (electric) during auto races and special events; $27.50 or $22 all other times.

> For more lodging recommendations, go to www.mobiltravelguide.com

EAT

MOBIL STAR-RATED RESTAURANTS

Milwaukee

BALISTRERI'S BLUE MOUND INN. ★
6501 W Blue Mound Rd, Milwaukee (53207). Phone 414/258-9881. Italian, American menu. Lunch, dinner. **$$**

KARL RATZSCH'S. ★★
320 E Mason St, Milwaukee (53202). Phone 414/276-2720. www.karlratzsch.com. This restaurant features a collection of rare steins and glassware. German menu. Lunch, dinner. Closed Sun; holidays. Bar. Children's menu. Casual attire. Valet parking. **$$$**

PIT PASS

Do you suffer from a bad case of RV envy during race weekends? No more. Just rent your own motor home or pop-up and join the crowds behind Turn 3 in Milwaukee's RV Park. Milwaukee has two great RV rental companies, one of which is right near The Mile and the other is conveniently near the airport. Both offer late-model vehicles (generally 2003s to 2005s) for rent.

If you go with **Badgerland RV Rental** near the track, your RV will be waiting for you at the RV Park when you arrive in town. Only 31-foot Class C motor homes are available, though, and there's a three-day minimum rental required.

Prosser RV/Cruise America has both 30-foot Class C motor homes and pop-ups available. The motor homes and pop-ups have a three-day minimum rental requirement. Prosser RV is near the airport, which is convenient if you're flying in. If not, you'll have to pick up your motor home or pop-up at their place or pony up an additional $50 delivery fee to the RV Park.

THE SAFE HOUSE. ★★
779 N Front St, Milwaukee (53202). Phone 414/271-2007. www.safe-house.com. It can be a bit tricky to get into The Safe House, a spy-themed restaurant and bar in downtown Milwaukee. But don't let that stop you, because the joint is worth the hassle. A few tips: the establishment is in a building marked International Exports Ltd., and you need a password to get inside. (Ask a local before you go.) If you don't know it, you'll have to perform a silly trick to get in. Once in, feast on the tasty grub—burgers, salads, sandwiches, steak, and killer chicken tortilla soup—then wander around

The Safe House to discover all of its spy gadgets: secret mirrors, surveillance equipment, and even a CIA "cover" phone booth with 99 background sounds to provide you with an instant alibi as to your whereabouts. When you're ready to leave, pay 25 cents to use the secret exit. American menu. Lunch, dinner. Closed holidays. Bar. Children's menu. Casual attire. $$

SAZ'S STATE HOUSE. ★

5539 W State St, Milwaukee (53208). Phone 414/453-2410. www.sazs.com. This uber-popular rib joint, located in a 1905 roadhouse, is consistently rated Milwaukee's best. Try the sour cream and chive fries, a local favorite. American, barbecue menu. Lunch, dinner, brunch. Closed Dec 24-25. Bar. Children's menu. Casual attire. Reservations recommended. Outdoor seating. $$

LOCAL RECOMMENDATIONS

Brookfield

MAMA MIA'S.

18880 W Bluemound Rd, Brookfield (53045). Phone 262/789-0277. Shelve the Atkins Diet and fat-free eating for a day and head to Mama Mia's, where Milwaukeeans flock to chow down on garlic bread dripping with butter. It's a bit greasy, but oh-so-delicious. Lasagna and pizza are also popular at this casual Italian eatery in the Galleria Plaza. Italian menu. Lunch, dinner. Children's menu. Casual attire. $

Hales Corners

ANN'S ITALIAN RESTAURANT.

5969 S 108th Pl, Hales Corners (53130). Phone 414/425-5040. Don't get frustrated if you can't find Ann's at first. Housed in a converted home, it's somewhat hidden by the Holz Chervolet auto dealership on Highway 100, but it's worth the search, if just for unbelievably fresh cannoli. Be prepared to wait for a table if you don't have a reservation. Italian menu. Dinner. Casual attire. Reservations recommended. Outdoor seating. $

Milwaukee

GILLES FROZEN CUSTARD.

7515 W Bluemound Rd, Milwaukee (53213). Phone 414/453-4875. www.gillesfrozencustard.com. Popular Gilles, Milwaukee's oldest custard stand, has been serving up the delectable frozen treat since 1938. Back then, vanilla custard, hot dogs, and a small root beer were the only items on the menu. Today, Bud Selig, Major League Baseball commissioner, stops in for a grilled cheese sandwich and diet soda almost daily. American menu. Lunch, dinner. Children's menu. Casual attire. Outdoor seating. $

KELLY'S BLEACHERS.

5128 W Bluemound Rd, Milwaukee (53208). Phone 414/258-9837. Sports fans love noshing at Kelly's Bleachers, which is a stone's throw away from Miller. Head there when you're really hungry so you can try to down its legendary 4-pound hamburgers. If you're in town on a Tuesday night, try the free country line-dancing lessons. American menu. Lunch, dinner. Casual attire. Outdoor seating. $

---

don't miss it

ROAD FOOD

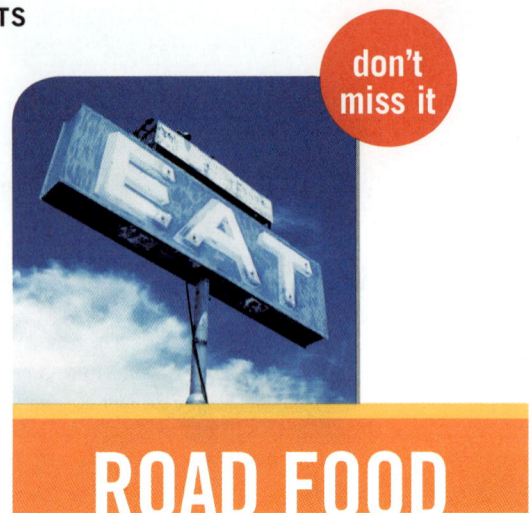

Hamburgers are a staple in the American diet, and Milwaukeeans know one of the best burgers in town can be found at family-run **Mazo's Fine Foods**, founded in 1934. Every morning the Mazos trim and grind sirloin to create the eatery's signature 6-ounce patties. Later in the day, they are grilled, then topped with butter and raw or fried onions. The restaurant also serves breakfast. Unfortunately for its fans, the restaurant only has 13 tables, is closed Sundays and Mondays, and accepts cash only. Open for breakfast, lunch, and dinner. Handicapped accessible. $ *3146 S 27th St, Milwaukee (53215). Phone 414/671-2118.*

For more dining recommendations, go to www.mobiltravelguide.com

SIDETRIP

Wisconsin Dells
Wisconsin Dells, WI

Get tickets to a water-skiing show or slip on some skis and try it for yourself.

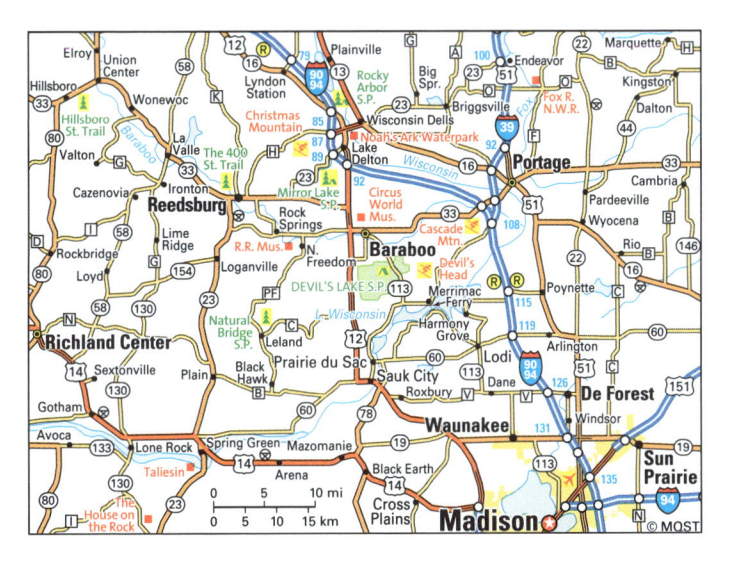

The Midwest's number one vacation destination, Wisconsin Dells, is less than two hours from The Milwaukee Mile. An odd mixture of natural beauty and man-made tackiness, it's definitely a unique spot worthy of a visit.

The Dells is perched on a scenic bend of the Wisconsin River lined with impressive Cambrian sandstone cliffs. Visitors first began flocking here in the mid-1800s to gawk at the cliffs and admire the river. A few years later, acclaimed landscape photographer Henry Hamilton Bennett began snapping pictures of the area, further popularizing the destination.

For a dollop of natural beauty, hop on an amphibious **Original Wisconsin Duck®**, which will take you up and down Roller Coaster Hill, through lush Fern Dell, and between the towering cliffs lining the Wisconsin River. A **Dells Boat Tour** is also a good choice. Top off this portion of your visit with a stop at the **H.H. Bennett Studio & History Center**, a state historic site featuring landscape photography of the Dells and Bennett's restored 1875 studio.

Now it's time for the thrilling, commercialistic side of the Dells. Hit **Noah's Ark,** an outdoor water park on the Dells' Vegas-like Strip. With three-dozen-plus water slides and water activities, not to mention mini-golf, bumper boats, and arcades, you can easily spend a day here. If a water park is too tame for you, bungee jump or ride the 110-foot skycoaster at **Extreme World.**

If you're staying overnight, try **RainTree Resort & Conference Center** or **Chula Vista Theme Resort.** Both feature modest indoor water parks, providing a good value for your money. If you want to stay at one of the major indoor water park resorts, be prepared to drop a big chunk of change.

For free Wisconsin Dells travel information, call toll-free 800/223-3557 or visit www.wisdells.com.

For more Wisconsin Dells recommendations, go to www.mobiltravelguide.com

It's rolling thunder time under the lights as fans fill the speedway to see NASCAR action at night.

Nashville Superspeedway

Lebanon, TN

21

Michael Waltrip circles the track en route to winning the Pepsi 300 NASCAR Busch Series race after the four cars leading the race tangled with two laps remaining.

TRACK FACTS

NASHVILLE SUPERSPEEDWAY. 4847-F McCrary Rd, Lebanon (37090). Phone 615/547-7500; toll-free 866/RACE-TIX (722-3849). www.nashvillesuperspeedway.com

SECURITY. What's allowed: one cooler or other bag not larger than 8.5 x 12 inches; one clear plastic bag up to 18 x 18 x 14 inches, and one seat cushion. Wear a headset, scanner, camera, or binoculars around your neck or on a belt. Beer in a cooler is allowed—but no wine or liquor. Prohibited: umbrellas, glass containers, baby strollers, and pets.

PARKING. Twelve lots are free for general admission tickets; one is for Premium Plus ticket holders (handicapped accessible spots are located here, but you must display ADA license plate or hang tag). General RV parking is first-come, first-served; call the track for information.

FIRST AID. Two first aid stations are located on ground level of the main grandstands; one is next to the elevator lobby and the other is in the Infield Care Center, which focuses primarily on driver injuries. University Medical Center (1411 W Baddour Pkwy, Lebanon) is about 15 minutes from the track.

CONCESSIONS. Concession stands in the main grandstands on ground and mezzanine levels offer the basics. Souvenir trailers are located behind Sections 127 through 133 in the main grandstands.

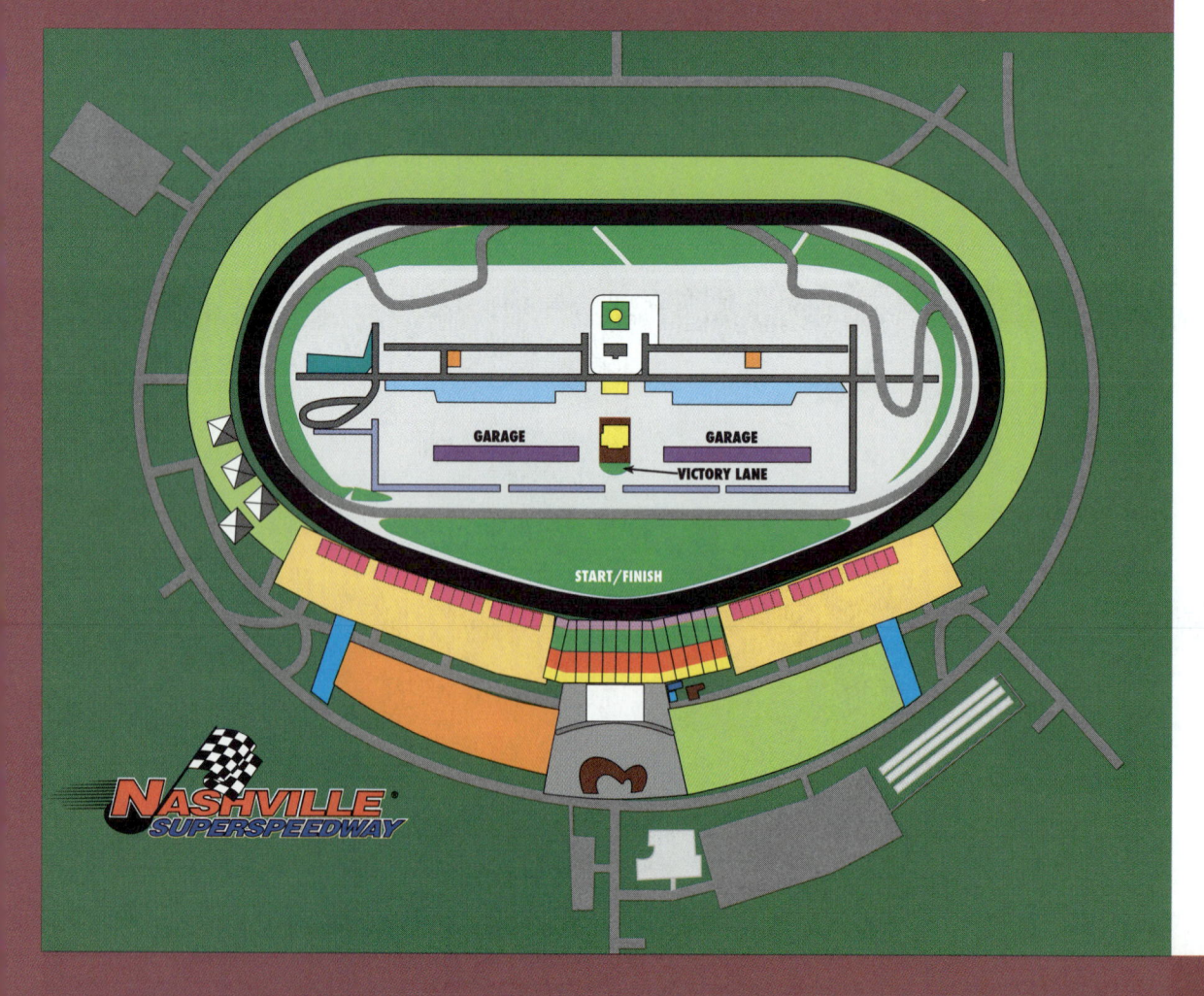

GETTING TICKETS

To order single-event tickets, call 866/RACE-TIX, fax 615/547-7225, visit the superspeedway's ticket office Monday-Friday 8 am-5 pm, mail your order to the ticket office (PO Box 330, Gladeville, TN 37071), or order online at www.nashvillesuperspeedway.com/tickets.html.

An exuberant Michael Waltrip celebrates his Pepsi 300 NASCAR Busch Series race victory at Nashville.

Round out your race weekend with some Nashville tunes at the Country Music Hall of Fame and Museum.

RHINESTONES ON THE BIBLE BELT

Nashville stands at the crossroads of the Old and New South. The city celebrates its heritage from its founding on Christmas Eve, 1779, when settlers built the log stockade at Fort Nashborough. Sixty-four years later, it became Tennessee's final state capital. Andrew "Old Hickory" Jackson built his home and spent his post-White House days here. And, of course, a small radio show begun in 1925 as the "WSM Barn Dance" grew into the "Grand Ole Opry," spawning Nashville's worldwide legacy as the birthplace of country music.

In recent years, however, the city has worked hard to expand its image beyond rhinestone cowboys, with an enormous economic development campaign that's drawn teams from the National Football League (the Tennessee Titans) and the National Hockey League (the Nashville Predators) along with giants in the insurance, banking, and printing industries. That growth gave the green light for Dover Motorsports to build the Nashville Superspeedway on the eastern outskirts of town. It's this contrast—"the buckle on the Bible Belt," living side by side with late-night dancing at the **Wildhorse Saloon** (120 Second Ave N, phone 615/902-8200)—that draws more than 10 million visitors a year.

The Nashville where President Theodore Roosevelt coined the slogan "Good to the last drop" after enjoying a cup of coffee is the same city chosen by major household names such as Cracker Barrel, Dollar General, and Gaylord Entertainment Company as their corporate headquarters.

For a US city with slightly more than half a million people, Nashville boasts a surprisingly large menu of entertainment options. Music runs the gamut from slickly packaged concerts at the **Grand Ole Opry** (2802 Opryland Dr, phone 615/871-OPRY, www.opry.com) or **Starwood Amphitheatre** to gritty, greasy country or blues jams in a hole-in-the-wall bar in the downtown Printers Alley district. If you're looking for a little culture in the "Athens of the South," you can go highbrow—the **Cheekwood Botanical Garden and Museum of Art,** a 55-acre oasis in Music City (1200 Forrest Park Dr, phone 615/356-8000, www.cheekwood.org) or lowbrow—the kitschy **Music Valley Wax**

Museum, with life-size wax images of country music stars (2515 McGavock Pike, phone 615/883-3612).

Two events stand out in Nashville's packed calendar. In June, the Country Music Association organizes the **CMA Music Festival,** billed as country music's biggest party. (In 2005, it runs June 9-12; phone toll-free 800/CMA-FEST, visit www.cmafest.com.) More than 500 singers and songwriters man autograph tables throughout the week at the Nashville Convention Center (schedules aren't posted in advance, so you have to keep your eyes open), and most stars will perform live for their loyal fans.

In November and December, the city displays its holiday spirit with "A Country Christmas" at the **Gaylord Opryland Resort and Convention Center** (2800 Opryland Dr, phone toll-free 888/777-OPRY). This annual attraction features two shows (the "Music City Holiday Spectacular," complete with aerialists and a gingerbread-men hoedown, and the "Linda Davis Family Christmas Dinner Show") as well as one of the world's largest nativity scenes, daily Yule log ceremonies, carriage rides, and a display of nearly 2 million Christmas lights.

One constant when you visit Nashville is middle-of-the-road weather, with temperatures ranging from 46° F in January to 90° F in July. During the fall months, the changing leaves can be spectacular, and the city gets very little snowfall in most years.

Have you driven in major cities where the streets are laid out logically, with lots of easy-to-read signs, so that you can find your way around even with a few wrong turns? Well, that's not Nashville. Streets begin and end and change names with little warning. And the city has grown so much in recent years that the resulting sprawl can leave you guessing where you are—and where you're going. Three interstate highways (24, 40, and 65) feed traffic into the metropolitan area, but there's no true "ring" road or connector that easily links them. The result? Confusing interchanges and heavy rush-hour traffic that can work your last nerve if you don't have excellent driving directions in your hands.

Your best bet for a stress-free driving weekend at the Nashville Superspeedway is to choose a hotel in Lebanon, the sleepy town nearest the track, or on the east side of Nashville (for example, hotels along Briley Parkway, a major Nashville road that leads straight to Interstate 40 and the track).

GETTING AROUND

From the north, take I-65 south; then take I-24 east to I-40 east; continue 30 miles on I-40 to Exit 235 (SR 840 W); go 10 miles to Exit 65 (superspeedway); turn left at top of exit. From the south, take I-65 north to Exit 59-A (SR 840 E); drive 34 miles to Exit 65 (superspeedway); turn right at top of exit. From the west on I-40, continue east to downtown Nashville, then continue for 30 miles to Exit 235 (SR 840 W); drive 10 miles to Exit 65 (superspeedway); turn left at top of exit. From the east, take I-40 west to Exit 235 (SR 840 W); drive 10 miles to Exit 65 (superspeedway); turn left at top of exit. From the west on I-24 east, take I-24 east, then continue to I-40 east; continue 36 miles to Exit 235 (SR 840 W); travel 10 miles to Exit 65 (superspeedway); turn left at top of exit.

You're in the country music capital—why not pick up a Gibson guitar and try your picking fingers?

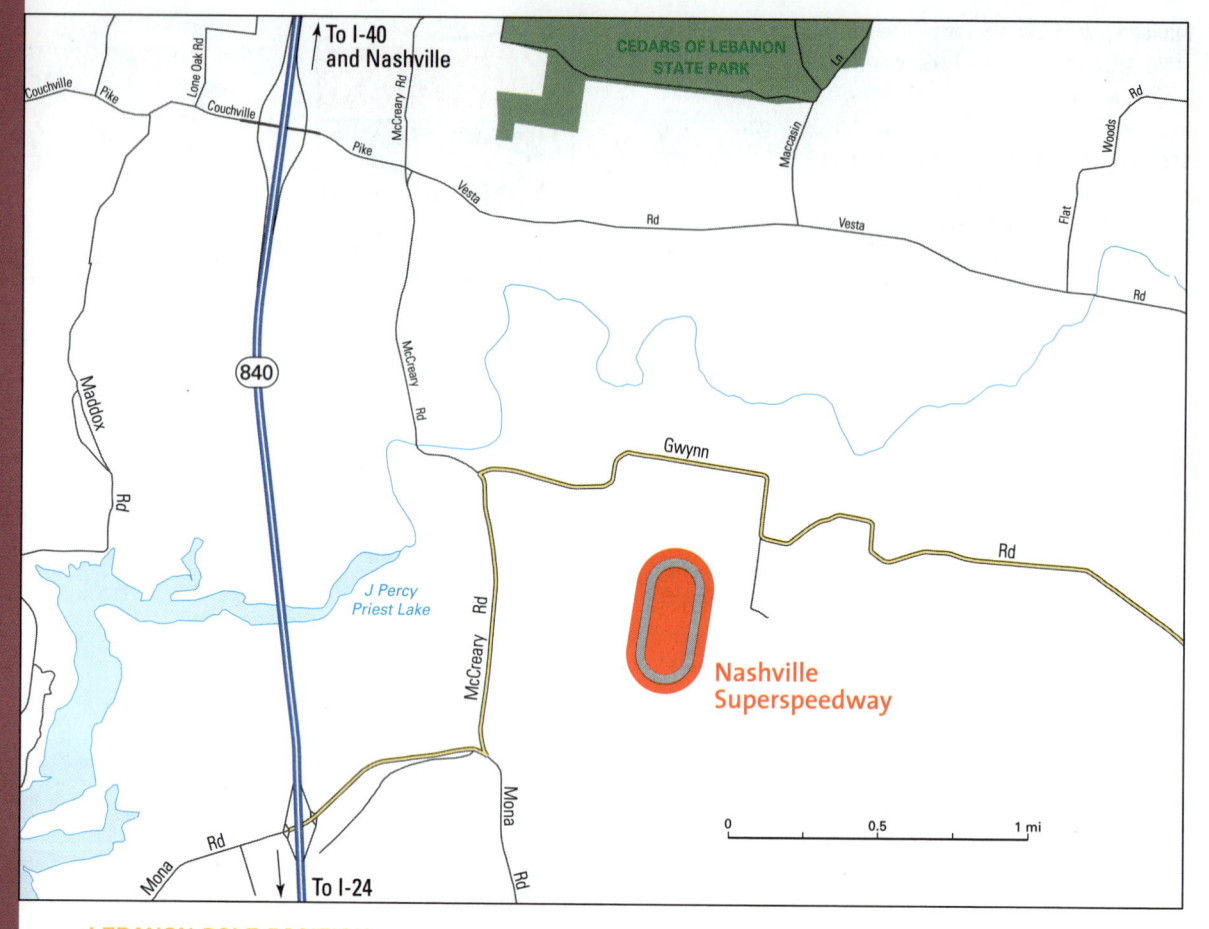

LEBANON POLE POSITION:
The 10 miles surrounding Nashville Superspeedway.

With that advice in mind, however, don't skip the sights in the downtown area and other parts of town. Most city streets have a speed limit of 30-35 mph (increasing to 55 mph on state highways and 70 mph on the interstates). You will find generous amounts of on-street parking that's metered (25 cents per half hour), with parking garages as well that run $5 up to $20 in the central downtown area.

Don't always count on the city-run buses and trolleys to get around town, or even cabs (you'll almost always have to call a taxi in advance). You'll need your car at all times while you're in Music City USA.

If you're flying into Nashville, you're in luck: the Nashville International Airport boasts service from 17 US airlines, including major low-fare carriers like Southwest and Independence Air, and the airport itself is modern and well run. You'll find complimentary shuttles for many nearby hotels, as well as paid shuttles from $11 for a one-way run downtown to more than $20 for outlying hotels.

Before you leave Nashville—"America's Friendliest City," according to *Travel & Leisure* magazine—pick up a six-pack box of GooGoo Clusters for the road. Purists dispute the origins of the unusual name; while some say the initials stand for "Grand Ole Opry," the official line from Nashville's Standard Candy Company is that this candy bar is so good that people ask for it from birth. Who cares about the name, when enjoying this mound of milk chocolate, marshmallow, peanuts, and caramel?

NASHVILLE SUPERSPEEDWAY, TN **353**

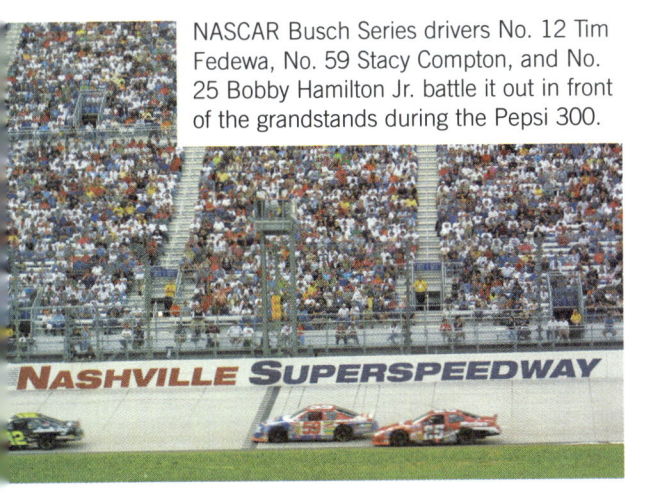

NASCAR Busch Series drivers No. 12 Tim Fedewa, No. 59 Stacy Compton, and No. 25 Bobby Hamilton Jr. battle it out in front of the grandstands during the Pepsi 300.

You can't miss this striking statue of Andrew Jackson, who made his home in Nashville after his presidency ended.

LEBANON CALENDAR

MARCH 26, 2005
NASCAR Busch Series

APRIL 9–13
Gospel Music Week. Various locations, Nashville. Phone 615/242-0303. www.gospelmusic.org. You'll be inspired by the many performances. The event concludes with the Dove Awards ceremony April 13.

JUNE 9–12
Country Music Association Music Festival. Throughout Nashville. Phone toll-free 800/262-3378. www.cmafest.com. Formerly called Fan Fair, this is country music's biggest party with celebrities performing and signing autographs throughout the event.

JUNE 11, 2005
NASCAR Busch Series

AUGUST 7, 2005
Miss Martha's Ice Cream Crankin'. First Presbyterian Church of Nashville, 4815 Franklin Rd (37220). Phone 615/254-1791. www.marthaobryan.org. You won't need to scream for ice cream at this festival with children's games, music, food, ice cream-making contests, and all the ice cream you can eat.

AUGUST 13, 2005
NASCAR Craftsman Truck Series

SHOP TALK

When Ernest Tubb and the Texas Troubadours weren't out touring in a big silver bus, the country music star was tending to his other love, the **Ernest Tubb Record Shop.** The original "E.T." died in 1984, but the store continues to sell nothing but country music releases. Offerings range from hard-to-find rarities to the newest smash hits. The store on Music Valley Drive also features the Texas Troubadour Theatre, home of the Midnight Jamboree every Saturday. *417 Broadway, Nashville (37203). Phone 615/255-7503.* Additional location at *2416 Music Valley Dr, Nashville (37214). Phone 615/889-2474. www.etrecordshop.com.*

LEBANON OUTFIELD:
The 50 miles surrounding Nashville Superspeedway.

SEE

ATTRACTIONS

Nashville

BELLE MEADE PLANTATION.
5025 Harding Rd, Nashville (37205). Phone 615/356-0501; toll-free 800/270-3991. www.bellemeadeplantation.com. This 1853 Greek Revival mansion and the nearby gabled Carriage House capture the grace of the antebellum world, with guides in period costumes leading you through the lavish grounds of the "Queen of the Tennessee Plantations." A reproduction of a slave cabin stands on the grounds. (Mon-Sat 9 am-5 pm, Sun 11 am-4 pm; last tour begins daily at 4 pm; closed Jan 1, Thanksgiving, Dec 25) **$$**

COUNTRY MUSIC HALL OF FAME AND MUSEUM.
225 5th Ave S, Nashville (37203). Phone 615/416-2001; toll-free 800/852-6437. www.countrymusichalloffame.com. This stop is "Ground Central" for NASCAR fans who love country music. The $37 million complex includes displays with costumes and instruments donated by country music legends from Minnie Pearl to George Jones. The rotunda's bronze plaques commemorating hall of fame members can cause goosebumps. Another $10 buys entrance to the restored Historic RCA Studio B, where more than 1,000 "top 10" hits from Elvis Presley, Willie Nelson, and other stars were recorded. (Daily 9 am-5 pm; closed Jan 1, Thanksgiving, Dec 25) **$$$$**

GENERAL JACKSON SHOWBOAT.
2812 Opryland Dr, Nashville (37214). Phone 615/458-3900. www.generaljackson.com. Named after the first steamboat working the Cumberland River as far back as 1817, this 300-foot paddlewheel riverboat—the world's largest showboat these days—offers lunch cruises (buffet plus country music show) and elegant dinner cruises (includes a Broadway-style show). Call for times. **$$$$**

GRAND OLE OPRY.
2802 Opryland Dr, Nashville (37214). Phone 615/871-6779. www.opry.com. You haven't made it in Music City USA as a country star until you've graced the stage of the world's longest-running radio show. Every weekend, the Opry showcases the best of bluegrass, country, gospel, swing, and Cajun. Part of the thrill for the audience is never knowing which stars who happen to be in Nashville will make a surprise appearance. (In January and February, shows originate from the Ryman Auditorium; from March to December, they're at the Grand Ole Opry House.) (Apr-Dec: Tues 7 pm, Fri 7:30 pm, Sat 6:30 pm and 9:30 pm)

NASHVILLE ZOO.
3777 Nolensville Rd, Nashville (37211). Phone 615/833-1534. www.nashvillezoo.org. At the Nashville Zoo, designers have gone to great lengths to make it seem as if you're simply walking through the woods and stumbling upon otters, cheetahs, apes, macaws, and other animals. (Apr-Oct: daily 9 am-6 pm; Nov-Mar: daily 9 am-4 pm; closed Jan 1, Thanksgiving, Dec 25) **$$**

OPRY MILLS.
433 Opry Mills Dr, Nashville (37214). Phone 615/514-1000; toll-free 877/746-7386. www.oprymills.com. Sure, Opry Mills collects more than 200 off-price and specialty retailers in one place, including the huge Bass Pro Shops Outdoor World and the NASCAR Silicon MotorSpeedway—but a part of Nashville's heart died when the beloved Opryland theme park was leveled to make way for this outlet mall. (Mon-Sat 10 am-9:30 pm, Sun 11 am-7 pm; closed Easter, Thanksgiving, Dec 25)

RYMAN AUDITORIUM.
116 Fifth Ave N, Nashville (37219). Phone 615/458-8700. www.ryman.com. The "Mother Church of Country Music" underwent an $8.5 million facelift in the 1990s. Now, this National Historic Landmark hosts concerts and a new museum that tells its story. (Don't—repeat, don't—leave without buying a box of GooGoos in the museum gift shop.) Tour of auditorium available. Museum (daily 9 am-4 pm; evening show times vary; closed Jan 1, Thanksgiving, Dec 25). **$$**

WILDHORSE SALOON.
120 Second Ave N, Nashville (37201). Phone 615/902-8200. www.wildhorsesaloon.com. It's Country Music Television come to life—66,000 square feet of bars, tables (full menu for lunch and dinner), and the largest dance floor in Nashville. Children younger than 18 allowed with parents. Daily (full-service restaurant 11 am-midnight; club 11-2 am).

For more attractions, go to www.mobiltravelguide.com

STAY

MOBIL STAR-RATED LODGINGS

Lebanon

HAMPTON INN. ★

704 S Cumberland St, Lebanon (37087). Phone 615/444-7400; toll-free 800/426-7866. www.hampton inn.com. This chain hotel offers the basics—it's clean and comfortable—with one big advantage: it's the closest property to the track that accepts pets. 87 rooms, 2 story. Pets accepted, some restrictions; fee. Complimentary continental breakfast. Check-in 3 pm, check-out 11 am. Fitness room. Outdoor pool, whirlpool. $

Murfreesboro

DOUBLETREE MURFREESBORO. ★★

1850 Old Fort Pkwy, Murfreesboro (37129). Phone 615/895-5555; toll-free 800/222-8733. www.double tree.com. This hotel is conveniently located within minutes of business centers, hundreds of Tennessee attractions, and the interstate system. 168 rooms, 5 story. Pets accepted; fee. Complimentary continental breakfast. Check-in 3 pm, check-out noon. Wireless Internet access. Restaurant, bar. Fitness room. Indoor pool, outdoor pool, whirlpool. Business center. $$

HAMPTON INN MURFREESBORO. ★

2230 Armory Dr, Murfreesboro (37129). Phone 615/896-1172; toll-free 800/426-7866. www.hampton inn.com. 114 rooms, 2 story. Pets accepted. Complimentary full breakfast. Check-in 3 pm, check-out noon. Wireless Internet access. Outdoor pool. $

HOLIDAY INN MURFREESBORO. ★★

2227 Old Fort Pkwy, Murfreesboro (37129). Phone 615/896-2420; toll-free 800/465-4329. www.holiday-inn.com. 179 rooms, 4 story. Pets accepted; fee. Check-in 4 pm, check-out 11 am. Two restaurants, bar. Fitness room. Indoor pool, outdoor pool, whirlpool. Airport transportation available. $

BRAKE HERE

Remember the 2000 Bush vs. Gore election? Before the Civil War, Andrew Jackson also lost the US presidency despite winning the popular vote (he did capture the White House later). **The Hermitage,** a restored 1837 mansion, was the home of Jackson and his wife Rachel for many years. Locals enjoy the "Hauntings at the Hermitage" programs in October. (Daily 9 am-5 pm; closed Thanksgiving, Dec 25, also third week in Jan) $$$ 4580 Rachel's Ln, Nashville (37076). Phone 615/889-2941. www.thehermitage.com

Nashville

COURTYARD BY MARRIOTT. ★★

1901 West End Ave, Nashville (37203). Phone 615/327-9900; toll-free 800/245-1959. www.courtyard.com. 223 rooms, 8 story. Check-in 3 pm, check-out noon. Restaurant, bar. Fitness room. Outdoor pool, whirlpool. $

DOUBLETREE HOTEL. ★★

315 Fourth Ave N, Nashville (37219). Phone 615/244-8200; toll-free 800/222-8733. www.double tree.com. Offering Southern charm along with modern luxuries and conveniences, this hotel is located steps from the state capitol, historic buildings, galleries, and a busy nightlife. 338 rooms, 9 story. Check-in 3 pm, check-out noon. Restaurant, bar. Fitness room. Indoor pool. Business center. $

EMBASSY SUITES. ★★
10 Century Blvd, Nashville (37214). Phone 615/871-0033; toll-free 800/362-2779. www.embassysuites.com. The suites in this hotel encircle a large atrium with waterfalls and exotic birds, and is just two minutes from the airport and ten minutes from the Grand Ole Opry. 296 rooms, 9 story, all suites. Pets accepted, some restrictions; fee. Complimentary full breakfast. Check-in 4 pm, check-out noon. Restaurant, bar. Children's activity center. Fitness room. Indoor pool, whirlpool. Airport transportation available. $$

FAIRFIELD INN BY MARRIOTT NASHVILLE OPRYLAND. ★
211 Music City Cir, Nashville (37214). Phone 615/872-8939; toll-free 800/228-2800. www.fairfieldinn.com. 109 rooms, 3 story. Complimentary continental breakfast. Check-in 3 pm, check-out noon. Fitness room. Indoor pool. Airport transportation available. $

GAYLORD OPRYLAND RESORT AND CONFERENCE CENTER. ★★★
2800 Opryland Dr, Nashville (37214). Phone 615/889-1000; toll-free 888/777-6779. www.gaylordhotels.com. You can't visit Nashville without staying at least once at this amazing property. Among many amenities, the hotel boasts three indoor gardens spanning 9 acres—the Conservatory, the Cascades, and the Delta (which features a river with flatboats to give guests a guided tour). With its parent company's ties to many Nashville attractions, the hotel usually offers package deals combining your room rate with admissions to the Opry and other stops. 2,881 rooms, 6 story. Check-in 3 pm, check-out 11 am. Seven restaurants, bars. Fitness center. Two outdoor pools, two wading pools. Business center. $

THE HERMITAGE HOTEL. ★★★
231 Sixth Ave N, Nashville (37219). Phone 615/244-3121; toll-free 888/888-9414. www.thehermitagehotel.com. This hotel is the pride of Nashville. Opened in 1910, this glorious hotel recalls the grace and charm of a former time. Its lobby virtually defines magnificence, with vaulted ceilings of stained glass, dazzling arches decorated with frescoes, and intricate stonework. When this hotel first opened, it represented the finest America could offer, and that tradition of excellence continues today. 123 rooms, 10 story. Complimentary continental breakfast. Check-in 3 pm, check-out noon. High-speed Internet access. Restaurant, bar. Fitness room. Airport transportation available. Business center. $$$

MILLENNIUM MAXWELL HOUSE NASHVILLE. ★★★
2025 Metro Center Blvd, Nashville (37228). Phone 615/259-4343; toll-free 866/866-8086. www.millenniumhotels.com. With a historic pedigree, this fully modern hotel offers personalized service and excellent accommodations. Just five minutes from downtown and 15 minutes from the Grand Ole Opry. 289 rooms, 10 story. Check-in 3 pm, check-out noon. Restaurant, bar. Fitness room. Outdoor pool, whirlpool. Tennis. $

SHERATON MUSIC CITY HOTEL. ★★★
777 McGavock Pike, Nashville (372140). Phone 615/885-2200; toll-free 800/325-3535. www.sheraton.com. With $8 million invested in 2003 to renovate its guests rooms, this property (designed to look like a Deep South mansion) is the closest full-service hotel to the Nashville Superspeedway. It's also extremely convenient to Nashville proper—3 miles from the airport, 5 miles from Opry Mills, and 7 miles from downtown. 410 rooms, 4 story. Pets accepted, some restrictions; fee. Check-in 3 pm, check-out 11 am. Restaurant, bar. Fitness room. Indoor pool, outdoor pool, whirlpool. Tennis. Business center. $$

PIT PASS

For $10 a day, race fans can get access to the area between the garage and pit road at the track by purchasing a **First Tennessee Fan Walk Pass.** The area is a great spot to catch drivers for autographs. If you're looking for a family experience at the track, the place for you is the **First Tennessee Family Seating Section** of the main grandstands. The area is alcohol- and tobacco-free, and there's no extra charge for seats there.

358 STAY MOBIL STAR-RATED LODGINGS

WYNDHAM UNION STATION HOTEL. ★★★
1001 Broadway, Nashville (37203). Phone 615/726-1001; toll-free 877/999-3223. www.wyndham.com. This hotel is located only a few blocks from Second Avenue and Music Row. Built in a renovated historic train station (circa 1897), it boasts a stained-glass roof and offers a unique place to stay with all the comforts and luxuries of a modern hotel. 124 rooms, 7 story. Pets accepted, some restrictions; fee. Check-in 3 pm, check-out noon. Restaurant, bar. Business center. $$

LOCAL RECOMMENDATIONS

Antioch

BEST WESTERN MUSIC CITY INN.
13010 Old Hickory Blvd, Antioch (37013). Phone 615/641-7721; toll-free 800/780-7234. www.bestwestern.com. 137 rooms, 2 story. Complimentary continental breakfast. Check-in 3 pm, check-out 11 am. Outdoor pool. $

Goodlettsville

BEST WESTERN FAIRWINDS INN.
100 Northcreek Blvd, Goodlettsville (37072). Phone 615/851-1067; toll-free 800/780-7234. www.bestwestern.com. 103 rooms, 3 story. Pets accepted, some restrictions; fee. Complimentary continental breakfast. Check-in 2 pm, check-out 11 am. Outdoor pool. $

Lebanon

BEST WESTERN EXECUTIVE INN.
631 S Cumberland St, Lebanon (37087). Phone 615/444-0505; toll-free 800/780-7234. www.bestwestern.com. 88 rooms, 2 story. Pets accepted, some restrictions. Complimentary continental breakfast. Check-in 3 pm, check-out 11 am. Indoor pool, outdoor pool. $

COMFORT SUITES.
904 Murfreesboro Rd, Lebanon (37090). Phone 615/443-0027; toll-free 877/424-6423. www.choicehotels.com. This all-suite property easily qualifies as the best lodging value nearest the track. It's perfect for families that need the extra space to spread out before and after the races. 85 rooms, 3 story, all suites. Complimentary continental breakfast. Check-in 2 pm, check-out 11 am. Fitness room. Indoor pool, whirlpool. $

COUNTRY INN AND SUITES.
140 Dixie Ave, Lebanon (37087). Phone 615/470-1001; toll-free 888/201-1746. www.countryinns.com. 85 rooms, 3 story. Pets accepted, some restrictions; fee. Check-in 2 pm, check-out noon. Fitness room. Indoor pool. $

HOLIDAY INN EXPRESS.
641 S Cumberland St, Lebanon (37087). Phone 615/444-7020; toll-free 800/377-8660. www.hiexpress.com. 58 rooms, 2 story. Check-in 3 pm, check-out noon. Fitness room. Outdoor pool. $

Nashville

BEST WESTERN AIRPORT INN.
701 Stewarts Ferry Pike, Nashville (37214). Phone 615/889-9199; toll-free 800/780-7234. www.bestwestern.com. 80 rooms, 3 story. Pets accepted, some restrictions; fee. Complimentary continental breakfast. Check-in 2 pm, check-out 11 am. Outdoor pool. $

BEST WESTERN DOWNTOWN/CONVENTION CENTER.
711 Union St, Nashville (37219). Phone 615/242-4311; toll-free 800/780-7234. www.bestwestern.com. 100 rooms, 5 story. Complimentary continental breakfast. Check-in 3 pm, check-out 11 am. Fitness room. $

BEST WESTERN MUSIC ROW INN.
1407 Division St, Nashville (37203). Phone 615/242-1631; toll-free 800/780-7234. www.bestwestern.com. 102 rooms, 5 story. Pets accepted, some restrictions; fee. Check-in 3 pm, check-out noon. Outdoor pool. $

BEST WESTERN SUITES NEAR OPRYLAND.
201 Music City Cir, Nashville (37214). Phone 615/902-9940; toll-free 800/780-7234. www.bestwestern.com. 100 rooms, 5 story, all suites. Complimentary continental breakfast. Check-in 3 pm, check-out noon. Fitness room. Outdoor pool. $

RV AND CAMPING

Lebanon

COUNTRYSIDE RV RESORT.
2100 Safari Camp Rd, Lebanon (37090). Phone 615/449-5527. www.countrysideresort.com. 120 sites, 68 full hook-ups (52 with water and electricity). Laundry, public phone, full-service store, ice. Outdoor pool. Pavilion, basketball/tennis/horseshoe/volleyball courts, playground.

Nashville

HOLIDAY-NASHVILLE TRAVEL PARK.
2572 Music Valley Dr, Nashville (37214). Phone 615/889-4225; toll-free 800/547-4480. 256 sites,

168 full hook-ups (67 with water and electricity). Laundry, public phone, full-service store, ice. Outdoor pool. Recreation room, basketball, volleyball, shuffleboard courts, playground.

NASHVILLE KOA KAMPGROUND.

2626 Music Valley Dr, Nashville (37214). Phone 615/889-0282; toll-free 800/562-7789. 426 sites, 291 full hook-ups (77 with water and electricity). Laundry, public phone, full-service store, ice. Outdoor pool, wading pool. Recreation hall, basketball and horseshoe courts, playground.

TWO RIVERS CAMPGROUND.

2616 Music Valley Dr, Nashville (37214). Phone 615/883-8559. www.tworiverscampgrounds.com. 105 sites, 78 full hook-ups (27 with water and electricity). Laundry, public phone, full-service store, ice. Outdoor pool. Recreation room, playground.

For more lodging recommendations, go to www.mobiltravelguide.com

EAT

MOBIL STAR-RATED RESTAURANTS

Nashville

DARFONS RESTAURANT AND LOUNGE. ★★

2810 Elm Hill Pike, Nashville (37214). Phone 615/889-3032. American, Italian menu. Lunch, dinner. Closed Sun. Reservations recommended. Outdoor seating. $$

DRUNKEN FISH. ★★

123 2nd Ave, Nashville (37201). Phone 615/254-5550. Original seafood-oriented cuisine in a clubby atmosphere. International/Eclectic menu. Lunch. Closed Sat-Sun. $$

LOVELESS CAFÉ. ★

8400 Hwy 100, Nashville (37221). Phone 615/646-9700. This Nashville institution is a can't-miss local favorite. Breakfast is the most popular meal, but you can't go wrong if you order the brittle-crusted fried chicken for lunch. You might spot some celebrities also. House specialties include award-winning country ham and red-eye gravy and scratch biscuits with homemade preserves. There is also a catalog of food items packed to go. American menu. Breakfast, lunch, dinner. Closed Jan 1, Thanksgiving, Dec 25. Outdoor seating. $$

MARIO'S RISTORANTE. ★★★

2005 Broadway, Nashville (37203). Phone 615/327-3232. www.mariosfinedining.com. This wonderful dining spot, with its creaky chairs and opulent art, has charmed Nashville for 30 years. Italian menu. Dinner. Closed Sun; also Jan 1, Dec 25. Bar. Casual attire. $$$

MONELL'S. ★

1235 Sixth Ave N, Nashville (37208). Phone 615/248-4747. If you're craving an old-fashioned, like-Grandma-used-to-make meal, be sure to visit Monell's. Located

ROAD FOOD

At the **Bluebird Cafe,** it's a given the servers here carry demo tapes in their pockets. Singer-songwriters looking to make it big perform original songs seven nights a week (early shows are free, others have an eat/drink minimum or cover) at this down-home Nashville institution. Garth Brooks and Sweethearts of the Rodeo got their starts at Bluebird, which seats only 100 patrons. With the emphasis on the music, the food is surprisingly good. Reservations strongly recommended. American menu. Dinner. Bar. Casual attire. $$ *4104 Hillsboro Rd, Nashville (37215). Phone 615/383-1461. www.bluebirdcafe.com.*

in a mid-1880s Victorian brick home in Germantown, this down-home eatery features Southern regional cooking. Service is family style, and you can eat as much as you want—all empty dishes are quickly refilled by the staff. Southern/Soul menu. Breakfast, lunch, dinner. $

TIN ANGEL. ★★
3201 West End Ave, Nashville (37203). Phone 615/298-3444. American menu. Lunch, dinner, Sun brunch. Closed holidays. Bar. Children's menu. Casual attire. Valet parking. $$

TOWN HOUSE TEA ROOM AND RESTAURANT. ★
165 Eighth Ave N, Nashville (37203). Phone 615/254-1277. This restaurant is located in a historic 24-room mansion (1840s) with fireplaces, oak floors, antiques, and paintings. American menu. Breakfast, lunch. Closed Sat-Sun; holidays. Reservations recommended. $

LOCAL RECOMMENDATIONS

Lebanon

COZUMEL'S GRILL.
1418 W Main St, Lebanon (37023). Phone 615/443-7123. After a long day at the track, this family-friendly restaurant offers hearty servings of Mexican food in a fun setting with a great staff. Mexican menu. Lunch, dinner. $

SUNSET RESTAURANT.
640 N Hwy 231, Lebanon (37087). Phone 615/444-9530. Ask Nashville Superspeedway employees for the best locally owned restaurant, and they'll steer you to this meat-and-vegetables eatery that's been operated by the same family for more than 35 years. American menu. Lunch, dinner. $

Nashville

BOURBON STREET BLUES AND BOOGIE BAR.
220 Printer's Alley, Nashville (37201). Phone 615/242-5837. www.bourbonstreetblues.com. Even though B.B. King has opened a club in Nashville, this bar is one of the city's oldest and purest venues for blues music. The menu features spicy Cajun cuisine—with the emphasis on spicy. Cajun/Creole menu. Dinner. $$

BUFFALO BILLIARDS AND HAVANA LOUNGE.
154 Second Ave N, Nashville (37201). Phone 615/313-7665. www.buffalobilliards.com. If your driver wins at Nashville, celebrate with a cigar and an excellent Southwest-style dinner at this 1940s-style lounge and restaurant. The entrées are pricey but well worth it, and you can stretch your legs later around one of the 40 professional-quality billiard tables. Southwest menu. Lunch, dinner. $$

ELLISTON PLACE SODA SHOP.
2111 Elliston Pl, Nashville (37203). Phone 615/327-1090. Picture the Nashville version of Pop's ice cream shoppe, where Archie, Jughead, and the gang might have hung out, and you'll get an image of this local landmark near Vanderbilt University. Order a burger and a shake—that's all you'll need. American menu. Breakfast, lunch, dinner. $

HOG HEAVEN.
115 27th Ave N, Nashville (37203). Phone 615/329-1234. At this outpost for barbecue excellence, you can order your pork, beef, and chicken plates and eat at the picnic tables outside. American menu. Lunch, dinner. $

NASHVILLE PALACE RESTAURANT AND DINNER THEATER.
2400 Music Valley Dr, Nashville (37214). Phone 615/885-1540. Before Lorrie Morgan and Alan Jackson were household names, they started with shows in the legendary main dining room of this Nashville institution. If it's packed, you can eat dinner in the bar—try the catfish. American menu. Dinner. $$$

NORMAN COUSER'S COUNTRY COOKING.
3754 Nolensville Rd, Nashville (37211). Phone 615/781-8270. The husband-and-wife owners have run this restaurant for more than half a century. It's the homiest place in Nashville to feed the family a complete Southern-style dinner. American menu. Lunch, dinner. $

OLD HEIDELBERG.
423 Union St, Nashville (37219). Phone 615/256-9147. If your system can handle authentic schnitzels, bratwurst, and sauerkraut, head downtown to this festive (some might say loud) German beer hall. German menu. Lunch, dinner. $$

For more dining recommendations, go to www.mobiltravelguide.com

SIDETRIP

Lookout Here
Chattanooga, TN

Sitting 135 quick miles from downtown Nashville, Chattanooga (the name comes from the Creek Indian word that means "rock coming to a point," describing nearby Lookout Mountain) makes a perfect stop for families before or after a race.

Downtown Chattanooga sits between the city's two primary tourist attractions. The **Chattanooga Choo Choo** (1400 Market St) is a renovated 1909 train station now housing a hotel, restaurants, and shops with a turn-of-the-century look. The station takes its name from Glenn Miller's 1941 hit song. Your kids will enjoy the model railroad and free electric shuttle that links the station with the town's other major attraction: the **Tennessee Aquarium** (1 Broad St, phone toll-free 800/262-0695, www.tennesseeaquarium.org), billed as the world's largest freshwater aquarium.

You'll ride an escalator to the top of the building and come down through exhibits that re-create ecosystems from the Tennessee River, Mississippi Delta, and other major rivers. To feel what it's like living inside a river, stand in the aquarium's 60-foot central canyon. Purchase combination tickets for the aquarium and the IMAX 3-D Theater (201 Chestnut St).

Conductors will punch your tickets aboard steam- or diesel-powered passenger trains at the **Tennessee Valley Railroad** (4119 Cromwell Rd), the South's largest operating historic railroad. Your 6-mile ride will cross three bridges and pass through the tunnel built in 1858 that runs under the Missionary Ridge battleground from Civil War days.

As Chattanooga is choo-choo town, how about hopping a ride on a real steam- or diesel-powered passenger train at the Tennessee Valley Railroad. Chattanooga is a two-hour drive from Nashville, if you head south on Interstate 24. For more details, go to www.chattanoogafun.com.

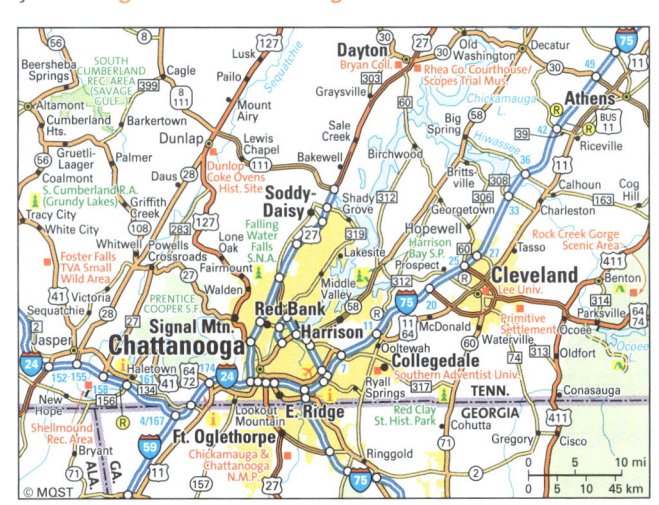

Don't leave without visiting **Lookout Mountain,** the 1,700-foot peak that towers over the city. **Rock City Gardens** features 14 acres of natural rock formations and gardens. **Lookout Mountain Caverns** includes a waterfall 1,120 feet below ground. And ride the **Lookout Mountain Incline Railway,** which will carry you at a 72.7-degree angle to the top of the mountain to enjoy the view from the observation deck.

For more Chattanooga recommendations, go to www.mobiltravelguide.com

Fans enjoy some beautiful weather as they sit on a pit road wall waiting for pre-race ceremonies.

New Hampshire International Speedway

Loudon, NH

22

Race cars roar into Turn 1 before a packed house at the NASCAR NEXTEL Cup Series SYLVANIA 300.

TRACK FACTS
NEW HAMPSHIRE INTERNATIONAL SPEEDWAY. 1122 Rte 106 N, Loudon (03307). Phone 603/783-4931. www.nhis.com.

SECURITY. Coolers 14 inches and smaller in all dimensions are permitted. No glass containers, transporters, umbrellas, or pets allowed. Unregistered motorcycles, mopeds, private golf carts, ATVs, and scooters are not allowed.

PARKING. Parking is free for cars. Free shuttle buses are offered at lots off the property. Parking is available for self-contained RVs and campers at $100 each if you order tickets before July 1 (after July 1, $125). RVs and campers must have self-contained bathroom and water facilities. No tents allowed.

FIRST AID. First aid stations are located in the main, Concord, and Laconia grandstands. Concord Hospital (250 Pleasant St, Concord, phone 603/225-2711) staffs a Level Two Trauma Center in the infield for serious medical attention. Concord Hospital is located about 14 miles from the Speedway.

CONCESSIONS. Concession stands feature staples like burgers, hot dogs, chicken, sausage, and ice cream. You'll often find restrooms right next to concession stands. Picnic tables are scattered throughout the shade under the grandstand. On race days, the area behind the grandstands is packed with souvenir trailers.

An aerial view shows the speedway on a typical day of NASCAR-sanctioned racing.

GETTING TICKETS

The speedway rewards loyalty. NASCAR NEXTEL Cup events typically sell out, but if you buy tickets in advance to any of the Friday or Saturday events at the track, you'll get a form to fill out to gain the opportunity to purchase any available NASCAR NEXTEL Cup tickets. Forms will be processed on a first-come, first-served basis. Once you get the tickets, they're yours for life if you want them.

FREEDOM RINGS

New Hampshire is one of those places where the amount of things to see and do can be downright overwhelming. It's a pretty place, with mountains, lakes, streams, ocean, and, of course, world-famous foliage (if you time it right). Its changeable weather makes packing a bit of a challenge, but, in general, if you're prepared for rain and cooler days, you won't be caught off guard.

New Hampshire loves its NASCAR fans, as evidenced by the "Welcome Race Fans" banners flying on signposts and businesses along the way to the track. The New Hampshire International Speedway, nestled among somewhat rural, lush farmlands, is reasonably close to just about everything the state has to offer.

The speedway, fondly known as the Magic Mile, prides itself on its welcoming, family-friendly atmosphere. Owners Bob, Sandy, and Gary Bahre sign more than 30,000 Christmas cards for speedway guests each year. It's that kind of attitude that keeps fans coming back to NHIS year after year.

Still, make no mistake about the fact that New Hampshire values individualism and independence. The state motto—"Live Free or Die"—makes that abundantly clear. The state was the first to declare its independence from England and the first to adopt its own constitution, and that independent and trend-setting spirit lives on in New Hampshire's residents today. As host of the first primary election in each presidential race, the rest of the world watches as New Hampshire casts its votes. It's also the little touches, like the lack of a seatbelt use law for adults and the lack of a state sales tax, that remind you that New Hampshire residents take their individual freedoms very seriously.

If you're interested in learning more about the state's rich history and colorful characters, be sure to visit the **Museum of New Hampshire History** in nearby Concord (phone 603/228-6688, www.nhhistory.org), which includes a variety of exhibitions on the heritage, traditions, and history of New Hampshire, as well as the Hands-on History Family Center designed specifically with children in mind.

Concord, the state capital and closest city to the speedway, has kept its small-town feel and offers much to do and see, especially for history buffs. If you're driving through on Route 93, you can't miss the shiny gold dome of **New Hampshire's State House** (phone 603/271-2154), which holds the oldest continuously used legislative chambers. Other historic sites worth checking out include the **Mt. Kearsarge**

Catch a tour of the historic Canterbury Shaker Village, a reminder of New Hampshire's Shaker past.

Indian Museum (phone 603/456-3244, www.indianmuseum.org) in nearby Warner and the **Kimball-Jenkins Estate** in Concord (phone 603/225-3932, www.kimballjenkins.com), a historic brick Victorian mansion that is now home to the Kimball-Jenkins School of Art.

The city also honors a New Hampshire hero at the **Christa McAuliffe Planetarium** (2 Institute Dr, phone 603/271-7831, www.starhop.com), which offers shows on space in its theater.

A few minutes north of Concord, in the Lakes Region—famous for its annual Laconia Motorcycle Week in June—you'll find everything you'd expect in a lake resort community, including dining, boating, amusements, and beaches. Cruise around Lake Winnipesaukee, the largest lake in the state, via **Mount Washington Cruises** (phone 603/366-5531, toll-free 888/843-6686, www.cruisenh.com), and stop in ports like Weirs Beach, Wolfeboro, Meredith, Alton Bay, and Center Harbor. Add to that spectacular mountain views and an abundance of fellow NASCAR fans, and you've got the perfect place to relax and let loose.

You could spend a whole day at **Funspot** (Rte 3, Weirs Beach, phone 603/366-4377, www.funspotnh.com), which has more than 500 games, an indoor golf center, bowling, kids' rides, and an on-site tavern and restaurant.

If you'd like to add a city feel to your stay, head down to Manchester, which offers dining, theater, and the **Currier Museum of Art** (201 Myrtle Way, phone 603/669-6144, www.currier.org), featuring works by famous artists like Picasso and Monet. Canterbury pays homage to its heritage at the **Canterbury Shaker Village** (288 Shaker Rd, phone 603/783-9511, www.shakers.org). Established in 1792, the site of one of the state's most vital religious communities is now a historical museum dedicated to preserving the legacy of the Canterbury Shakers.

In keeping with its spirit of individuality, New Hampshire also offers ample opportunities to try something new. Want to try your hand at mineral collecting? Visit **Ruggles Mine** in Grafton (phone 603/523-4275, www.rugglesmine.com), where you might find one of more than 150 different minerals on site, including specimens of beryl, amethyst, mica, and smokey quartz. Or, get in touch with your inner cowboy or cowgirl and visit the **Chebacco Dude Ranch** in Effingham (phone 603/522-3211,

GETTING AROUND

Gates open at 6 am, and track officials encourage fans to arrive early. To avoid traffic on Rte 9, stay on I-93 until Exit 20, then take Rural Rte 140 through the village of Belmont (follow signs to the speedway). Exit traffic is well controlled through a five-lane perimeter road. From the South Gate, all traffic must turn left and go south on Rte 106; from the North Gate, all traffic must turn right and go north on Rte 106. But traffic jams aren't all bad—one NASCAR fan recently found himself stuck in traffic next to No. 15 Michael Waltrip, who chatted amiably with him for a few minutes.

Take advantage of the many lakes and the incredible autumn scenery to do some recreational fishing.

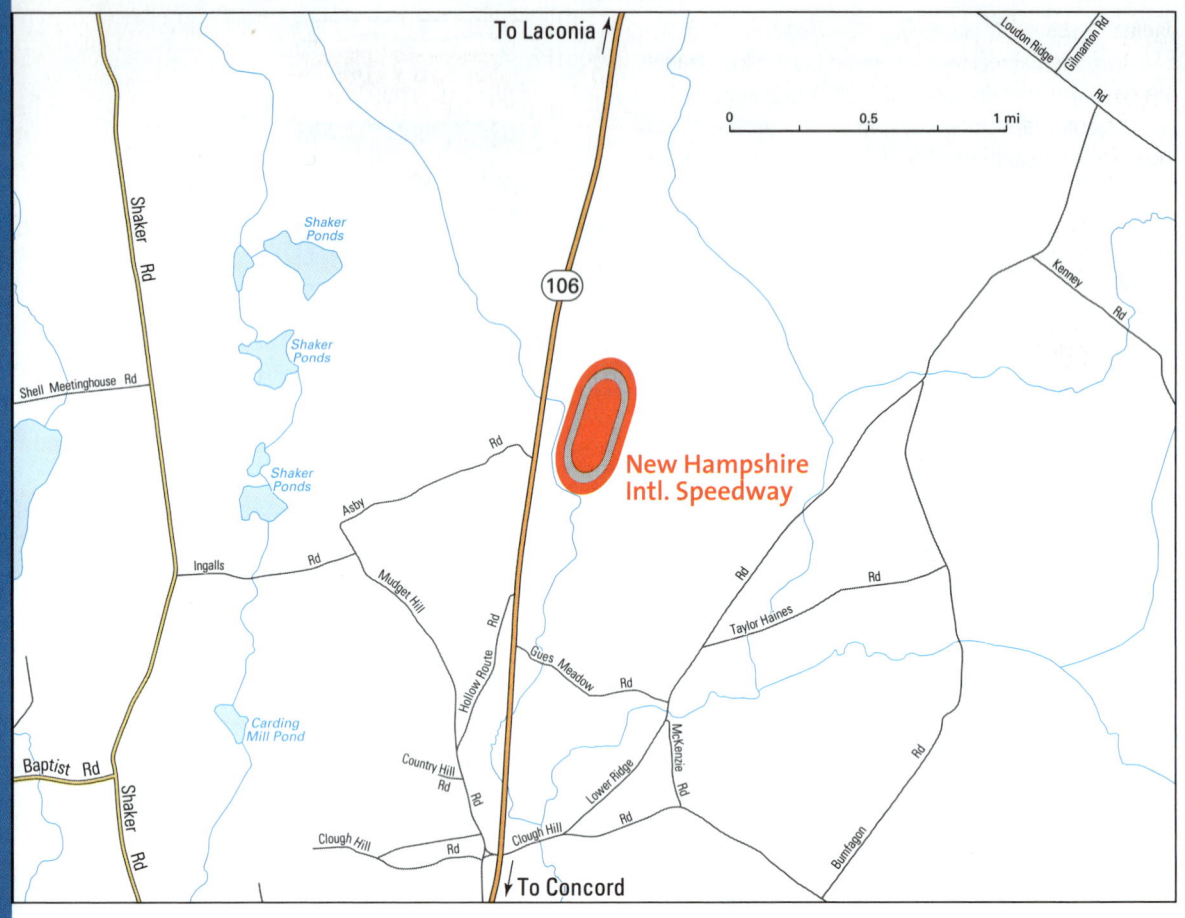

LOUDON POLE POSITION:
The 10 miles surrounding New Hampshire International Speedway.

www.chebaccoduderanch.com), where you can ride a quarter horse along a scenic wooded trail. New Hampshire is famous for its outdoor recreation opportunities, whether it's swimming in a mountain lake or on the beaches of the seacoast region, or hiking, rock climbing, river rafting, kayaking, canoeing, boating, tubing, snowshoeing, ice climbing, snowmobiling, snowboarding, bicycling, or downhill skiing.

If you're traveling with kids, New Hampshire ranks right up there as a family destination. Kid-friendly restaurants, amusement parks, arcades, and train rides will keep young ones happy and grown-ups peaceful. And if you'd like to appreciate nature's beauty, the White Mountains region offers an abundance of opportunities to do just that: take a scenic drive up the **Mt. Washington Auto Road** (phone 603/466-3988, www.mtwashingtonautoroad.com), experience the gravity-defying chug of the **Mount Washington Cog Railway** (phone toll-free 800/922-8825, www.mtwashingtoncograilway.com), spot the occasional moose, deer, or wild turkey along the Kancamagus Scenic Highway, or enjoy the breathtaking artistry of Mother Nature at Franconia Notch and Crawford Notch. For bargain-hunters, tax-free New Hampshire is loaded with factory outlet centers and antiques shops.

While NASCAR is huge in New Hampshire, there's certainly no shortage of activities beyond the speedway, in any season, and for all ages.

Several towns around Loudon host spectacular balloon festivals throughout the year.

SHOP TALK

Founded in 1927 by a Greek immigrant, **Granite State Candy Shoppe** is an old-fashioned candy store that has been delighting sweet tooths ever since with the motto, "We're in the happiness business." Now owned by his grandchildren, many of the founder's original copper kettles are still in use, and each chocolate is dipped one by one. Sure, you can buy these treats on the Internet, but nothing beats a visit to the store where it all began. *13 Warren St, Concord (03301). Phone 603/225-2591; toll-free 888/225-2531. www.nhchocolates.com.*

LOUDON CALENDAR

JULY 14–17, 2005
Hillsborough Balloon Festival and Fair. Grimes Field, US Hwy 202 and State Hwy 9, Hillsborough (03244). Phone 603/428-8337. www.balloonfestival.org. Hot air balloon launch, parade, road race, draft horse pull, and more.

JULY 16, 2005
NASCAR Busch Series

JULY 17, 2005
NASCAR NEXTEL Cup Series

JULY, 2005
Market Days and Summer Music Festival. Main St, downtown Concord (03301). Phone 603/226-2150. www.mainstreetconcord.com. Shop, eat, and relax listening to live music. Mid-July.

SEPTEMBER 17, 2005
NASCAR Craftsman Truck Series

SEPTEMBER 18, 2005
NASCAR NEXTEL Cup Series

SEPTEMBER 24–OCTOBER 1, 2005
Third Annual Wolfeboro Scarecrow Festival. 32 Central Ave, Wolfeboro (03894). Various locations throughout Wolfeboro. Phone 603/569-2200. www.wolfeborochamber.com. Pick up a map at the Chamber of Commerce, which points out the locations of more than 60 scarecrows created by area merchants and individuals. On the weekend, a trolley gives visitors a ride.

SEPTEMBER, 2005
Schnitzelfest. Downtown Hillsborough (03224). Phone 603/464-5858. www.hillsboroughnhchamber.com. Feast on grilled pork schnitzel, German potato salad, bratwurst, knackwurst, and more. Late September.

LOUDON OUTFIELD:
The 40 miles surrounding New Hampshire International Speedway.

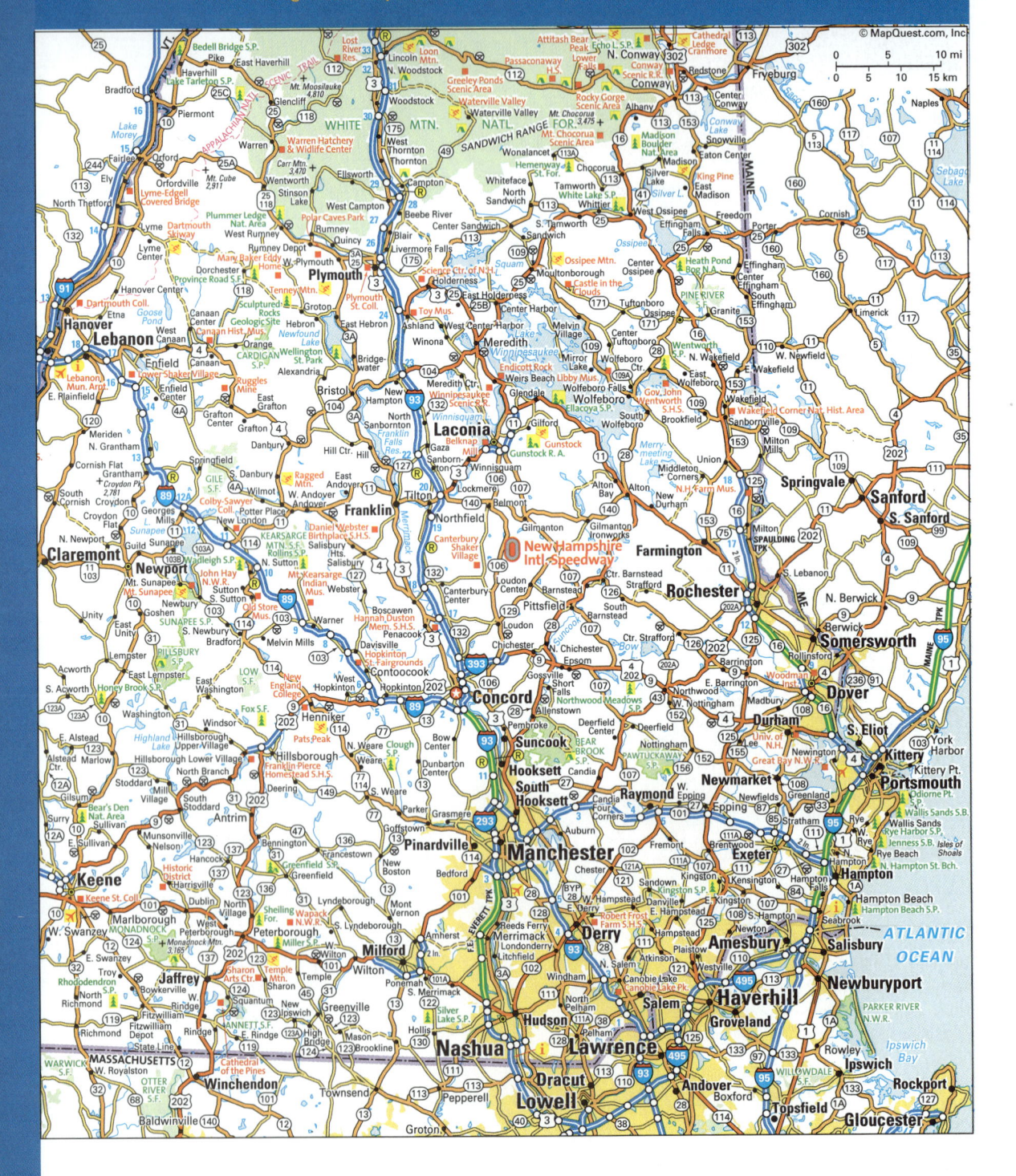

SEE

ATTRACTIONS

Canterbury

CANTERBURY SHAKER VILLAGE.
288 Shaker Rd, Canterbury (03224). Phone 603/783-9511. www.shakers.org. Pay homage to New Hampshire's Shaker heritage with a visit to this National Historic Landmark museum that offers guided and self-guided tours and a variety of exhibits. (Mid-May-late Oct: daily 10 am-5 pm; Nov-Dec: Sat-Sun 10 am-4 pm; closed Thanksgiving, Dec 25) **$$$**

Concord

CHRISTA MCAULIFFE PLANETARIUM.
2 Institute Dr, Concord (03301). Phone 603/271-7831. www.starhop.com. This living memorial to New Hampshire teacher Christa McAuliffe, who died aboard the US space shuttle *Challenger* on January 28, 1986, offers a variety of shows designed for all ages in a 92-seat theater. "Our Place in Space" is aimed at the very young while "Destination: Mars" boasts 3-D computer graphic effects likely to wow anyone. (Daily; call or visit Web site for show schedule) **$$**

Epping

STAR SPEEDWAY.
Rte 27, Epping (03042). Phone 603/679-5306. www.starspeedway.com. NASCAR awarded Star Speedway its New England Region "Team Player" Award in 2004 to honor the track's outstanding promotional efforts and achievements. In 2004, however, a building code dispute with the town of Epping stalled the start of the Saturday night NASCAR Dodge Weekly Series for more than a month, until late May. The 1/4-mile semi-banked oval, about 50 miles from New Hampshire International Speedway, is expected to open on schedule again in 2005. It seats about 5,000.

Holderness

SQUAM LAKES NATURAL SCIENCE CENTER.
23 Science Center Rd, Holderness (03245). Phone 603/968-7194. www.nhnature.org. If this attraction looks familiar, perhaps you'll recognize it as the site where the 1981 movie *On Golden Pond* with Henry Fonda and Katharine Hepburn was filmed. Walking through the woods, you'll see black bear, bobcats, otters, foxes, and mountain lions in enclosed trailside exhibits. You can also take a Golden Pond boat tour. (May-Nov: daily 9:30 am-4:30 pm) **$$$**

Laconia

DAYTONA FUN PARK.
Rte 11B, Laconia (03246). Phone 603/366-5461. www.daytonafunpark.com. Unleash your inner NASCAR driver by challenging family and friends to miniature racing on the go-karts. There's also a climbing wall, batting cages, and miniature golf. (Daily 10 am-11 pm) **$$**

Salem

CANOBIE LAKE PARK.
Rte 93, exit 2, Salem (03079). Phone 603/893-3506. www.canobie.com. Bring your bravery—and a change of clothes—for rides such as the Boston Tea Party Shoot-the-Chute water ride; the Corkscrew Coaster, which features two upside-down spins; and the Starblaster, which simulates a blast into outer space. You'll also find tamer options like bumper cars and kiddie rides. (Apr-Sept; call for hours) **$$$$**

Tilton

TANGER FACTORY OUTLET CENTER.
120 Laconia Rd, Tilton (03276). Phone 603/286-7880. www.tangeroutlet.com. A large factory outlet center featuring familiar retailing names like Gap, Wilsons Leather, and Reebok. (Mon-Sat 10 am-9 pm, Sun 10 am-6 pm)

Weirs Beach

FUNSPOT.
Rte 3, Weirs Beach (03246). Phone 603/366-4377. www.funspotnh.com. A favorite among staffers from the speedway, Funspot offers more than 500 new and classic games, an indoor golf center, bowling, kiddie rides, mini-golf, a driving range, and an on-site tavern

SEE ATTRACTIONS

and restaurant. (June-Labor Day: daily 9 am-midnight; rest of year: Sun-Thurs 10 am-10 pm, Fri-Sat 10 am-11 pm) $ per attraction

HALF MOON AMUSEMENT ARCADES.
240-260 Lakeside Ave, Weirs Beach (03246). Phone 603/366-4315. www.weirsbeach.com. This old-fashioned arcade, just across the street from the scenic Weirs Beach boardwalk, includes a penny arcade, a family fun center, and bumper cars. Revisit your teen years with classic games like Pac-Man, Asteroids, Space Invaders, and Pole Position, or let a new generation of game players discover Skeeball and pinball. (Daily, hours vary) $ per attraction

MOUNT WASHINGTON CRUISES.
Phone 603/366-5531; toll-free 888/843-6686. www.cruisenh.com. Cruise the waters of Lake Winnipesaukee (win-e-puh-SAW-kee), the largest lake in New Hampshire, and enjoy scenic mountain views aboard the M/S *Mount Washington,* which offers daily scenic cruises and dinner dance cruises. Ports of call include Weirs Beach, Wolfeboro, Meredith, Alton Bay, and Center Harbor. (Mid-May-Oct; check Web site or call for schedule and rates)

For more attractions, go to www.mobiltravelguide.com

STAY

MOBIL STAR-RATED LODGINGS

Concord

COMFORT INN CONCORD. ★
71 Hall St, Concord (03301). Phone 603/226-4100; toll-free 877/424-6423. www.comfortinn.com. Perfect for budget-conscious families, this hotel provides a number of amenities, including a Nintendo 64 station in each room. 100 rooms, 3 story. Pets accepted, some restrictions; fee. Complimentary continental breakfast. Check-in 3 pm, check-out noon. Indoor pool, whirlpool. $

Laconia

BARTON'S MOTEL. ★
1330 Union Ave, Laconia (03246). Phone 603/524-5674. www.bartonsmotel.com. Located on the shores of Lake Winnipesaukee and minutes from Weirs Beach attractions, Barton's Motel offers scenic water views as well as swimming and relaxing on its private beach. Amenities include free paddleboats and rowboats, free dockage for boat owners, and an on-site bookstore. 41 rooms. Check-out 11 am. Beach. Outdoor pool. $

Manchester

FAIRFIELD INN BY MARRIOTT MANCHESTER. ★
860 S Porter St, Manchester (03103). Phone 603/625-2020; toll-free 800/228-2800. www.fairfieldinn.com. Only minutes from the Manchester Airport, this hotel offers complimentary shuttle service to and from the airport. 112 rooms, 4 story. Complimentary continental breakfast. Check-in 3 pm, check-out noon. Outdoor pool. $

FOUR POINTS BY SHERATON MANCHESTER. ★★
55 John Devine Dr, Manchester (03103). Phone 603/668-6110; toll-free 888/625-4988. www.fourpoints.com/manchester. This hotel is conveniently located near Manchester Airport, the Mall of New Hampshire, and historic downtown Manchester. 121 rooms, 4 story. Check-in 2 pm, check-out noon. High-speed Internet access. Restaurant, bar. Indoor pool, whirlpool. Airport transportation available. $

RADISSON HOTEL MANCHESTER. ★★
700 Elm St, Manchester (03101). Phone 603/625-1000; toll-free 800/333-3333. www.radisson.com. With the hotel's location near downtown Manchester, guests can enjoy everything this quaint New England city has to offer, such as shopping, dining, live theater, and museums. 250 rooms, 12 story. Check-in 3 pm, check-out 11 am. Restaurant. Fitness room. Indoor pool, whirlpool. Airport transportation available. Business center. $

Tilton

SUPER 8 MOTEL TILTON/LAKE WINNIPESAUKEE. ★
7 Tilton Rd, Tilton (03276). Phone 603/286-8882; toll-free 800/800-8000. www.super8.com. Close to all the outdoor activities and entertainment around Lake Winnipesaukee, this budget-friendly hotel puts guests in convenient proximity to swimming, boating, and fishing. 63 rooms, 2 story. Check-in 3 pm, check-out 11 am. **$**

LOCAL RECOMMENDATIONS

Bradford

MOUNTAIN LAKE INN.
2871 Rte 114, Bradford (03221). Phone 603/938-2136; toll-free 800/662-6005. www.mountainlakeinn.com. You'll find the Mountain Lake Inn just west of Concord, in Bradford. Housed in a building built in 1760—with an addition built in the 1930s—the Mountain Lake Inn is perfect for a quiet getaway. Across the road is the inn's private beach on Lake Massasecum. The inn sits on 168 wooded acres, and behind the building is a walking trail (take lots of bug spray). Innkeepers Bob and Tracy Foor love NASCAR fans and for several years they've welcomed back a fan named Bill, who leads an official caravan of NASCAR guests from the inn to the Speedway. 10 rooms. Pets accepted, some restrictions; fee. Complimentary full breakfast. Check-in 4-9 pm, check-out 11:30 am. **$**

Concord

BEST WESTERN CONCORD INN AND SUITES.
97 Hall St, Concord (03301). Phone 603/228-4300; toll-free 800/528-1234. www.bestwestern.com. This hotel, located 4 miles from the speedway and 25 miles from the Weirs Beach area, offers a complimentary deluxe continental breakfast each morning. Tax-free outlet shopping is also close by. 66 rooms, 3 story. Pets accepted; fee. Complimentary continental breakfast. Check-in 2 pm, check-out 11 am. Laundry services. Fitness room. Indoor pool, whirlpool. **$**

Gilford

B MAE'S RESORT INN AND SUITES.
Rte 11 at 11B, Gilford (03249). Phone 603/293-7526; toll-free 800/458-3877. www.bmaesresort.com. B Mae's Resort Inn and Suites is located at Lake Winnipesaukee and is close to all Weirs Beach attractions. All rooms have a deck or patio. 83 rooms, 2 story. Complimentary continental breakfast. Check-in 3 pm, check-out 11 am. Restaurant, bar. Fitness room. Indoor pool, outdoor pool, whirlpool. **$**

Laconia

THE MARGATE ON WINNIPESAUKEE.
76 Lake St, Laconia (03246). Phone 603/524-5210; toll-free 800/627-4283. www.themargate.com. With a white sand beach only steps away, Wave Runner rentals, indoor and outdoor pools, and a tanning salon, there is never a shortage of things to do while staying at The Margate. 141 rooms. Check-in 4 pm, check-out 11 am. Indoor pool, outdoor pool. **$**

THE NASWA RESORT.
1086 Weirs Blvd, Laconia (03246). Phone 603/366-4341; toll-free 888/556-2792. www.naswa.com. If you've decided to turn your race experience into a full-blown vacation, consider the Naswa Resort. Located right on Lake Winnipesaukee, the Naswa—with its lively Beach Bar and Grill—manages to combine a happening beach scene with an old-fashioned feel. Several NASCAR

BRAKE HERE

If you've forgotten to stock up on necessities, but already are close to the speedway, keep your eye out for the **Beanstalk** *(577 Rte 106 N)*. The family-run supermarket, just 8 miles down the road on Route 106 in Loudon, is used to catering to the last-minute needs of racing fans. You can also find must-haves like food, gasoline, ice, and diapers at the **Big Apple** convenience store *(904 Rte 106 N)*.

drivers and crews—including those of Rusty Wallace and Ryan Newman—have stayed at the Naswa over the years, as did Kenny Irwin during what would be his last race at the speedway. The Naswa offers many lodging options, including motel efficiency suites, the inn, several cottages, and its main motel units. If you're looking for peace and quiet, avoid units overlooking the water or beach bar. Naswa guests can use kayaks, canoes, and paddleboats, or rent a Jet Ski. Guests can also dock their boats free. The restaurant serves Italian country and American entrées for dinner, as well as a full breakfast menu in the morning. 82 rooms. Restaurant, bar. $$

Loudon

RED ROOF INN.
519 SR 106 S, Loudon (03307). Phone 603/225-8399; toll-free 800/733-7663. www.redroof.com. This hotel is located less than 8 miles from the speedway. 73 rooms. Pets accepted, some restrictions. Complimentary continental breakfast. Check-in 3 pm, check-out 11 am. Laundry services. Indoor pool. $

Manchester

BEST WESTERN EXECUTIVE COURT INN AND CONFERENCE CENTER.
13500 S Willow St, Manchester (03103). Phone 603/627-2525; toll-free 877/627-2525. www.bestwestern.com. The Best Western Executive Court Inn and Conference Center, located just minutes from Manchester Airport and the Mall of New Hampshire, is set on 20 wooded acres about 20 miles from the speedway. 135 rooms, 4 story. Complimentary continental breakfast. Check-in 3 pm, check-out 11 am. Laundry services. Fitness room. Indoor pool, whirlpool. Airport transportation available. $

THE HIGHLANDER INN.
2 Highlander Way, Manchester (03103). Phone 603/625-6426; toll-free 800/548-9248. www.highlanderinn.com. This English-style inn is located at Manchester Airport and convenient to downtown attractions. 66 rooms. Check-in 3 pm, check-out 11 am. Restaurant, bar. Outdoor pool, whirlpool. Airport transportation available. $

TAGE INN MANCHESTER AIRPORT.
2280 Brown Ave, Manchester (03103). Phone 603/641-6466; toll-free 800/322-8243. www.tageinn.com. The Tage Inn Manchester Airport is close to movie theaters, nightclubs, and restaurants and is just 20 miles from the speedway. 96 rooms. Complimentary continental breakfast. High-speed Internet access. Fitness room. Indoor pool, whirlpool. $

Weirs Beach

CHRISTMAS ISLAND RESORT.
630 Weirs Blvd, Weirs Beach (03246). Phone 603/366-4378; toll-free 800/832-0631. www.christmasresort.com. Located in New Hampshire's Lakes Region, Christmas Island Resort offers two private beaches, complimentary rowboat and paddleboat use, and a close proximity to many local events and attractions. 45 rooms, 2 story. Check-in 3 pm, check-out 11 am. Restaurant, bar. Indoor pool, whirlpool. $

RV AND CAMPING

Ashland

YOGI BEAR'S JELLYSTONE PARK.
Rte 132, Ashland (03256). Phone 603/968-9000. www.jellystonenh.com. Unleash your inner child and join the fun with Yogi, BooBoo, and Cindy bears. It's kitsch galore here, but the kids will love it. Amenities include organized activities, playground, a picnic table and fire ring at each site, swimming pool, showers, restrooms, boat rentals, theaters, snack bar, mini-golf, and hot tub. More than 275 sites, plus cabins. Pets permitted, but strongly discouraged.

Gilford

GUNSTOCK CAMPGROUND.
Rte 11A, Gilford (03249). Phone 800/GUNSTOCK. www.gunstock.com/summer. A favorite among NASCAR fans, Gunstock is close to Lakes Region attractions. Amenities include restrooms, hot showers, in-ground pool, camp store, coin laundry, scheduled activities, and propane filling station. Approximately 300 sites. Pets allowed with documentation of vaccinations.

Weirs Beach

WEIRS BEACH TENT AND TRAILER PARK.
198 Endicott St N, Weirs Beach (03246). Phone 603/366-4747. www.ucampnh.com/WeirsBeach. Amenities include restrooms, hot showers, camping supplies and cable TV (limited sites). More than 180 sites. Pets allowed if leashed.

For more lodging recommendations, go to www.mobiltravelguide.com

EAT

MOBIL STAR-RATED RESTAURANTS

Belmont

HICKORY STICK FARM. ★★
66 Bean Hill Rd, Belmont (03220). Phone 603/524-3333. The interior is a converted colonial farmhouse. The outdoor dining area in idyllic New England surroundings is perfect for breezy summer nights, so see if you can score a table to enjoy the evening. American menu. Dinner, Sun brunch. Closed Mon. Bar. Outdoor seating. $$

Manchester

COLBY HILL INN. ★★
The Oaks, Henniker (03242). Phone 603/428-3281. A part of the Colby Hill Inn bed-and-breakfast in the New Hampshire countryside, this restaurant features a surprisingly cosmopolitan menu that combines familiar favorites with more contemporary variations. Rustic game meats appear as pepper-crusted duck breast with cranberry-orange syrup and fig-and-sage-glazed venison osso bucco. International/Fusion menu. Dinner. Closed Dec 24-25. $$$

THE PURITAN BACKROOM. ★
245 Hooksett Rd, Manchester (03104). Phone 603/669-6890. www.puritanbackroom.com. This local favorite serves everything from burgers made from black Angus ground beef to veal parmigiana. There's also a kids' menu (try the smiley-face French fries). Grown-up fans may appreciate the Backroom's extensive beer and wine list and its full bar. Homemade ice cream is also on the menu. The casual atmosphere, with its wood-paneled walls, low lighting, and framed folk art, is welcoming to race fans and doesn't require dressing up. Its easy access from Route 93 makes it a convenient stop on your way to or from the speedway. American menu. Lunch, dinner. Closed Thanksgiving, Dec 25. Bar. Children's menu. $$

Meredith

HART'S TURKEY FARM. ★★
Hwys 3 and 104, Meredith (03253). Phone 603/279-6212. www.hartsturkeyfarm.com. If you feel like a little family-style Thanksgiving during your trip, check out Hart's turkey dinners with all the trimmings. You'll also find turkey potpies, turkey croquettes, and even turkey burgers. Hart's is the speedway's official caterer, creating everything from lobster bakes to—of course—turkey dinners. Speedway staff members think the world of Hart's, which sent a chef to cook Thanksgiving dinner for staff and crew members working on Thanksgiving to prepare for a race moved to the day after the holiday in the aftermath of the September 11 attacks in 2001. American menu. Lunch, dinner. Children's menu. $$

LOCAL RECOMMENDATIONS

Concord

ANGELINA'S RISTORANTE ITALIANO.
11 Depot St, Concord (03301). Phone 603/228-3313. www.angelinasrestaurant.com. Angelina's offers a variety of antipasti, salads, pasta specialties, entrées,

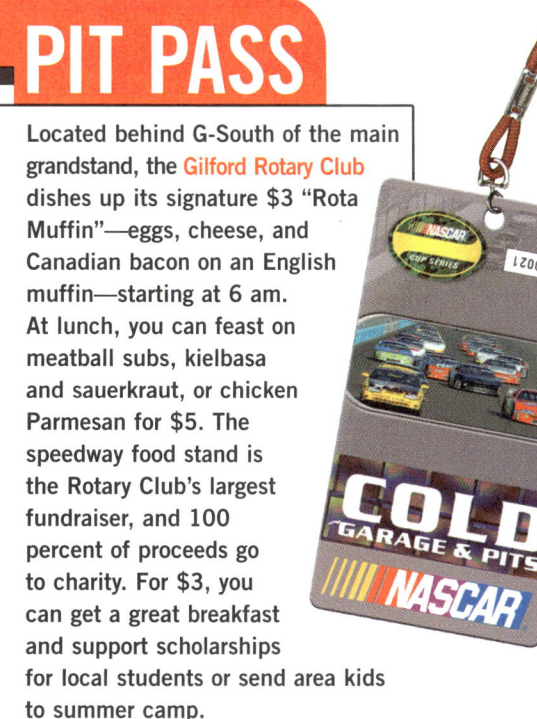

PIT PASS

Located behind G-South of the main grandstand, the **Gilford Rotary Club** dishes up its signature $3 "Rota Muffin"—eggs, cheese, and Canadian bacon on an English muffin—starting at 6 am. At lunch, you can feast on meatball subs, kielbasa and sauerkraut, or chicken Parmesan for $5. The speedway food stand is the Rotary Club's largest fundraiser, and 100 percent of proceeds go to charity. For $3, you can get a great breakfast and support scholarships for local students or send area kids to summer camp.

grilled items, and desserts, as well as a full wine list, in an upscale setting. Italian menu. Lunch, dinner. Closed Sun. **$$**

ARNIE'S PLACE.

164 Loudon Rd, Concord (03301). Phone 603/228-3225. www.arniesplace.com. Arnie's Place serves old-fashioned favorites in a nostalgic atmosphere. You'll find classics like char-grilled hamburgers and a full rack of Boss Hawg's pork spareribs; sides are extra. American menu. Lunch, dinner. Closed mid-Oct-late Feb. Outdoor seating. **$**

LONGHORN STEAKHOUSE.

217 Loudon Rd, Concord (03301). Phone 603/228-0655. www.longhornsteakhouse.com. This chain steakhouse is a speedway staff favorite, thanks to a variety of entrées including steaks, seafood, ribs, chops, and chicken. Steak menu. Lunch, dinner. **$$**

MAKRIS LOBSTER AND STEAK HOUSE.

354 Sheep Davis Rd (Hwy 106), Concord (03301). Phone 603/225-7665. www.eatalobster.com. NASCAR drivers love to eat lobster when they're in New Hampshire and rumor has it that Makris is the place that supplies 'em. Located just a short distance from the speedway, Makris features a menu of land and sea favorites like lobster dinners and prime rib. You'll also find plenty of chicken and pasta dishes on the menu. Steak, seafood menu. Lunch, dinner. Closed Sun. **$$**

RED BLAZER RESTAURANT AND PUB.

72 Manchester St, Concord (03301). Phone 603/224-4101. www.redblazer.cc. A speedway staff favorite, the Red Blazer Restaurant and Pub features an entrée menu with upscale items like filet mignon and pastry-baked chicken as well as pub fare such as a Greek souvlaki platter, fried chicken strips, and buffalo tenders. American menu. Lunch (Sun), dinner. **$$**

Laconia

THE NASWA BEACH BAR AND GRILL.

1086 Weirs Blvd, Laconia (03246). Phone 603/366-4341. www.naswa.com. The Naswa Beach Bar and Grill offers a menu of appetizers, nachos, salads, sandwiches, and burgers, as well as a full bar, in a fun lakefront atmosphere at the Naswa Resort. Live bands and special events are featured. American menu. Lunch, dinner. **$$**

Loudon

BOAR'S TAVERN.

Rtes 106 and 129, Fox Pond Plaza, Loudon (03307). Phone 603/798-3737. www.boarstavern.com. Boar's Tavern offers a variety of sandwiches, appetizers, soups, salads, and dinners, as well as a full bar, in an atmosphere that features pool tables and a band area. American menu. Breakfast (Sat-Sun), lunch, dinner. **$$**

Tilton

TILT'N DINER.

Rte 93, exit 20, Tilton (03276). Phone 603/286-2204. www.thecman.com. If you're in the mood for some fun with your food, visit the Tilt'n Diner, located a few minutes from the speedway. With its classic diner exterior and funky retro interior, the Tilt'n Diner is a downright fun place to eat. Fortunately, the food is good, too—options range from hamburgers and hot-dogs to White Mountain meatloaf or roasted turkey. American menu. Breakfast, lunch, dinner. No credit cards accepted. **$$**

Weirs Beach

WILLOW'S STEAK AND SPIRITS.

Rte 11B, Dexter Plaza, Weirs Beach (03247). Phone 603/366-5403. Rumor has it that Jeff Gordon and Jimmie Johnson like to reserve the private function room at Willow's when they're in New Hampshire. The upscale casual atmosphere includes a non-smoking bar upstairs and a non-smoking open dining area downstairs with a gorgeous floor-to-ceiling mural painted by a local artist. Chef Michael Moore, who co-owns Willow's with his wife, Victoria Makris, spent years in NASCAR as a cook for Ford and Texaco. American menu. Dinner. **$$**

For more dining recommendations, go to www.mobiltravelguide.com

SIDETRIP

A Peak Experience
White Mountains, NH

About one hour north of the speedway is New Hampshire's stunning White Mountains region. Between the breathtaking views, entertaining interludes, and affordable lodging and dining, you won't run out of things to do.

In the Lincoln area, visit **Clark's Trading Post** (phone 603/745-8913, www.clarks tradingpost.com) and ride a steam train through "Wolfman" territory, stroll through Americana museums, and climb the Old Man Tower. Don't miss the bear show—the Clark family has been training black bears for more than 60 years.

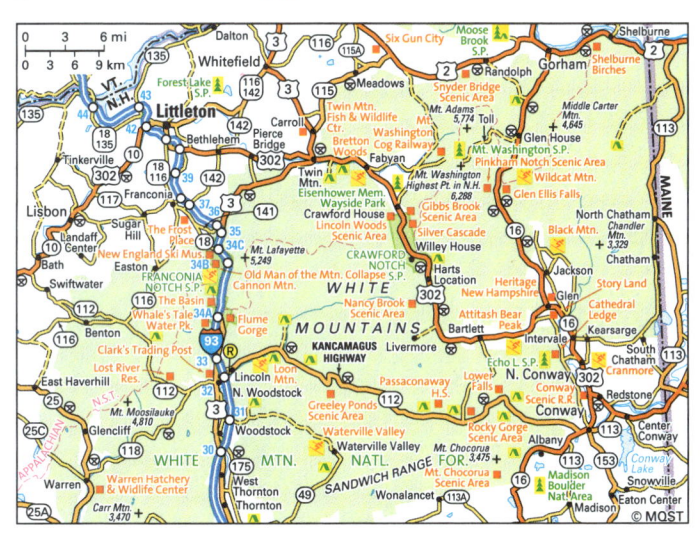

Kancamagus Scenic Byway, part of State Highway 112, runs through the **White Mountain National Forest** (www.fs.fed.us/r9/white) and features amazing views along an ear-popping ride complete with steep hills, hairpin turns, black bears, deer, and moose (it's pitch black at night and could be frightening for the fainthearted).

Follow the highway into **Conway** and the **Conway Scenic Railroad** (phone 603/356-5251, toll-free outside the state 800/232-5251, www.conwayscenic.com), as well as tax-free factory outlets just a short distance up Route 16 in North Conway. You can also visit **Story Land** (phone 603/383-4186, www.storylandnh.com), in the town of Glen, a fairy-tale-themed amusement park ideal for young children.

Route 302 through **Crawford Notch State Park** (phone 603/374-2272) brings you to the base of Mt. Washington, the highest elevation in the Northeast. Drive the Mt. Washington Auto Road to the peak, or climb aboard the Mt. Washington Cog Railway for a three-hour chug to the summit and back—you won't soon forget the view from the top.

Interstate 93 north heads through **Franconia Notch State Park** (phone 603/745-8391), where you can take a scenic hike past fantastic waterfalls and caves (sturdy shoes are a must). The park is also home to the Cannon Mountain Aerial Tramway, Echo Lake Beach, and the Old Man of the Mountain historic site.

The White Mountains are 60-plus miles from Loudon, with the majority of the drive rolling along Interstate 93. For more details on the White Mountains, go to www.visitwhitemountains.com.

For more White Mountains recommendations, go to www.mobiltravelguide.com

Jimmie Johnson signs autographs at the 2003 NASCAR NEXTEL Cup Phoenix race.

Phoenix International Raceway®

Avondale, AZ

23

Phoenix fans have the option of perching atop the hillside for a panoramic view of the speedway and Arizona's sprawling desert.

TRACK FACTS

PHOENIX INTERNATIONAL RACEWAY. 125 S Avondale Blvd, Avondale (85323). Phone 623/463-5400. www.phoenixraceway.com.

SECURITY. Forget about hard-sided coolers, thermoses and insulated cups. Each fan is allowed one soft-sided bag or cooler, no larger than 6 x 6 x 12 inches, i.e., a soft-sided insulated cooler, scanner bag, fanny pack, purse, diaper bag, or binocular bag. You're also allowed one clear plastic bag each, no larger than 18 x 18 x 4 inches. Coolers may contain ice, but clear plastic bags may not. Bring binoculars, scanners, headsets, and cameras separately, not in a bag. Make sure seat cushions don't have hollow metal tube construction. No strollers, umbrellas, scooters, skateboards, or pets.

PARKING. If you arrive early to avoid traffic, you'll be tempted to grab a spot close to the entrance. Park near the exit and you'll avoid the inevitable bottlenecks getting out. Better yet, for $7 per carload, take the Park-N-Ride shuttle. Shuttles are waved through traffic jams in and out of parking lots. Get there off the I-10 at the 83rd Avenue exit; go north to **Cricket Pavilion** (2121 N 83rd Ave), between McDowell Road and Thomas Road; enter Park-N-Ride parking from the 83rd Avenue entrance.

FIRST AID. Registered nurses man three fully equipped care centers: beneath section CC of the Bryan Grandstand, under the Oasis building outside of Turn 2, and in the infield. Doctors man the infield care center. Paramedics are available anywhere by ambulance or golf cart. **West Valley Hospital** (13677 W McDowell Ave, Goodyear) is the closest full trauma center.

Cars lined up for the start of the NASCAR NEXTEL Cup Series Checker Auto Parts 500.

CONCESSIONS. You'll find souvenir vendors and food stands near every section. Bashas' Supermarkets sets up a full grocery store at the track for all NEXTEL events. They'll even make you a cake in the style of your favorite driver. Kids activities are set up in a different location every year.

GETTING TICKETS

The best seats sell quickly and the NASCAR NEXTEL Cup events sell out every year. Order early by phoning toll-free 866/408-7223 or at www.phoenixraceway.com; or visit PIR's ticket office at the **Arizona Center** (455 N 3rd St, Phoenix, phone 602/271-4000).

The west grandstand near Turns 1 and 2 has a great view of the dogleg on the backstretch and gets more shade. The cheap seats are on the dirt hill above Turns 3 and 4. The view isn't as stellar and you're looking into the sun, but it's warm on chilly mornings. Some fans consider the backstretch bleachers the best bang for the buck.

GETTING AROUND

They say Phoenix International Raceway, where Tom Cruise burned it up in *Days of Thunder,* is the fastest 1-mile track around. The NASCAR NEXTEL Cup Series Checker Auto Parts 500 race is the largest one-day sporting event in Arizona, drawing almost 100,000 spectators, so getting there can be slow.

To avoid the worst traffic, get there via Vineyard Road. It takes you into the major parking area with a right turn rather than a left turn across traffic flow. Tune your car radio to 550 AM for traffic updates and watch for special roadway message boards. (While you're at it, set a button for KXAM 1310 AM and listen to *Racing Roundup,* 7-9 pm live and local Monday nights.)

FROM I-10 WESTBOUND: take Litchfield Rd Exit 128 left (south). Right (west) on Rte 85. Left (south) on Bullard Ave. Left (east) on Vineyard Rd.

FROM AZ 202 WESTBOUND: take Estrella Pkwy Exit 128 left (south). Left (east) on Vineyard Rd.

FROM I-10 EASTBOUND: take Cotton Ln Exit 124, right (south). Left (east) on Rte 85. Right (south) on Estrella Pkwy. Left (east) on Vineyard Rd.

The sun sets over the Phoenix skyline.

SUNSHINE AND URBAN SPRAWL

As Arizonans continue to raze hills, arroyos, and desert flora to build malls and golf courses, there's less to recognize of the old Southwest. Roads are wider now, too—to accommodate more SUVs—and there are more of them, so getting around the metropolitan area takes time. Still, with more than 300 days of low humidity and warm sunshine annually, chances are any weekend at the races will be spectacular.

Just 20 minutes from the excitement of NASCAR-sanctioned racing in Avondale you'll find a fan's shopping paradise. Along with restaurants, shops, and other activities, the **Arizona Center** (455 N 3rd St, Phoenix, phone 602/271-4000, www.arizonacenter.com) in downtown Phoenix is home to Phoenix International Raceway headquarters. There you'll find the latest motorsport merchandise and memorabilia. If there's a NASCAR race going on, you'll likely see drivers on Saturday nights, making promotional appearances and signing autographs.

You'll find plenty to do on Mill Avenue in Tempe or Fifth Avenue in downtown Scottsdale, and the area known as the Camelback Corridor east of Central Avenue in Phoenix is always hopping. The dress is casual for comfort, except in upscale Scottsdale, where a certain element dresses to be noticed, but few restaurants require jackets or ties.

Phoenix, Scottsdale, and Tempe bustle with culture, including the **Phoenix Art Museum** (1625 N Central Ave, phone 602/257-1222, www.phxart.org); **Heard Museum,** (2301 N Central Ave, phone 602/252-8848, www.heard.org); **Herberger Theater Center** (222 E Monroe, phone 602/252-8497, www.herbergertheater.org); **Symphony Hall** (phone toll-free 800/776-9080, www.phoenixsymphony.org); **Heritage Square** (phone 602/262-5071); **Scottsdale Center for the Arts** (7380 E 2nd St, Scottsdale, phone 480/994-2787); **Tempe Town Lake** (80 W Rio Salado Pkwy, Tempe, phone 480/350-8625, www.tempetownlake.com); and Arizona State University's **Gammage Auditorium** (phone 480/965-3434). The **Phoenix Zoo** (455 N Galvin Pkwy, Phoenix, phone 602/273-1341, www.phoenixzoo.org) and **Desert Botanical Garden** (1201 N Galvin Pkwy, Phoenix, phone 480/941-1217, www.dbg.org) are favorites with tourists.

Sports fans will find something going on at one of the professional arenas, including Phoenix Suns basketball at **America West Arena;** Arizona Diamondbacks baseball at **Bank One Ballpark** (with its swimming pool and a retractable roof); Arizona

Only in Phoenix do golf, cacti, and biking mix well.

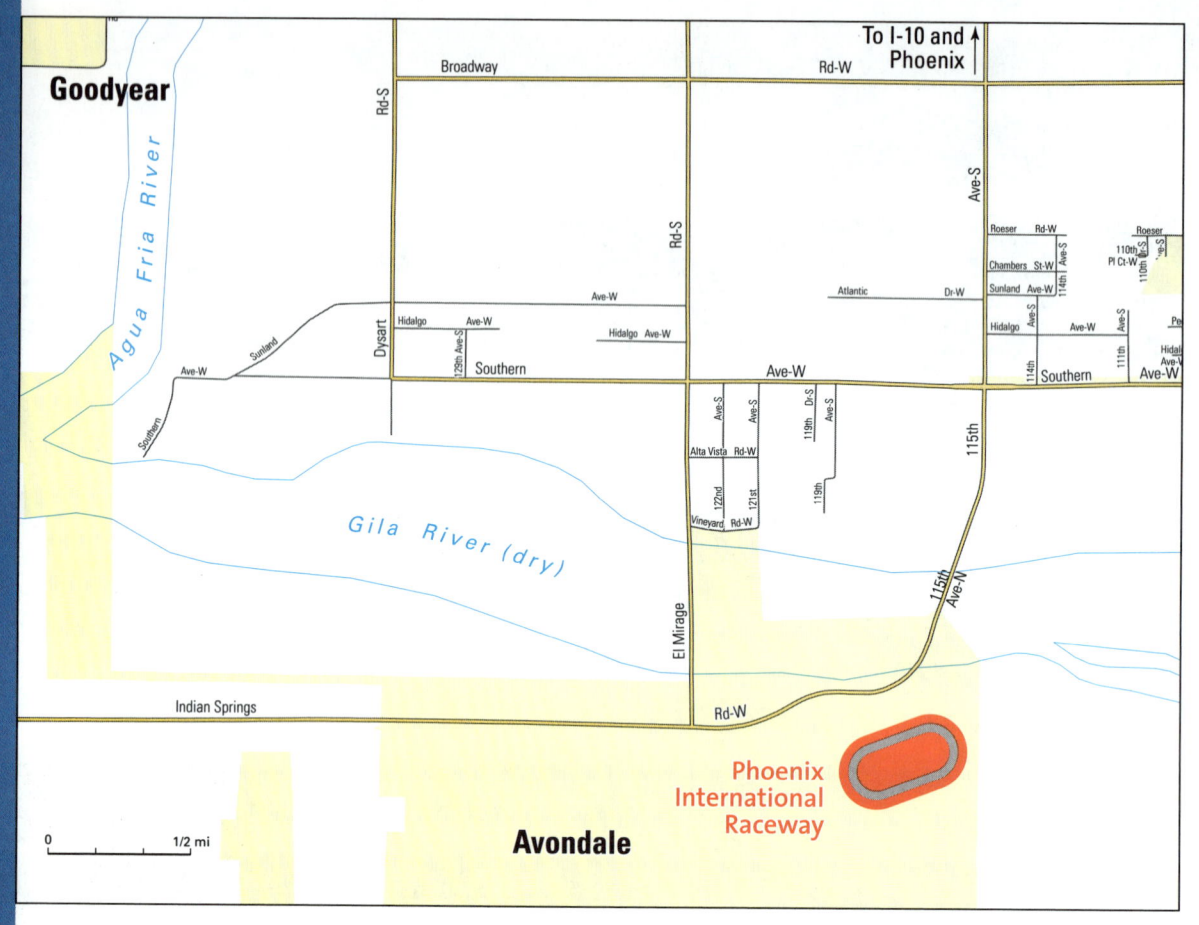

AVONDALE POLE POSITION:
The 10 miles surrounding Phoenix International Raceway.

Cardinals football at Arizona State University's **Sun Devil Stadium** or the new **Cardinals Stadium;** Phoenix Coyotes hockey at **Glendale Arena;** greyhound racing at **Phoenix Greyhound Park;** and thoroughbred racing at **Turf Paradise,** among others.

You can make like a native and golf yourself into oblivion at one of more than 275 golf courses. Or lose yourself at a hundred shopping locations, including more than a dozen 500,000-square-foot malls within a 40-mile radius.

Even the biggest automobile fans may welcome the opportunity to enjoy Arizona's wide open spaces on two wheels. Thanks to nearby Tempe's **bicycle program** (20 E 6th St, 3rd floor, Tempe, phone 480/350-2775, www.tempe.gov/bikeprogram), you can pedal more than 150 miles of bikeways along streets and through parks. Most major destinations provide bicycle racks, some designed by local artists. If you get tired, city buses are equipped with bike racks to take you where you're going. Several bicycle shops offer rentals for as little as $15 per day, including free bikeway maps.

For real drama, leave the cities behind and venture out to the mountains, lakes, and rolling deserts. A road trip to outlying areas demonstrates Arizona hasn't lost her awesome wild side, after all.

AVONDALE CALENDAR

APRIL 12–17, 2005
Scottsdale Culinary Festival. Various locations, Scottsdale. Phone 480/945-7193. www.scottsdaleculinaryfestival.org. Feast your way through this festival, with events day and night including the Great Arizona Picnic with tastings from more than 50 area restaurants, and the spectacular beer garden featuring more than 200 specialty beers.

APRIL 22, 2005
NASCAR Busch Series

APRIL 23, 2005
NASCAR NEXTEL Cup Series

APRIL 29–30, 2005
Cinco de Mayo Fiesta. Pioneer Park, 529 E Main St, Mesa (85203). Phone 480/644-5040. www.ci.mesa.az.us. Celebrate the sounds, sights, and tastes of Mexico at this festive event.

NOVEMBER 11, 2005
NASCAR Craftsman Truck Series

NOVEMBER 12, 2005
NASCAR Busch Series

NOVEMBER 12–13, 2005
Big Chalk Weekend. Heritage and Science Park, 6th St and Monroe (85004). Phone 602/327-3786. www.openvenue.org. Watch artists bring the sidewalks to life. Volunteers help kids create their own contemporary street art.

NOVEMBER 13, 2005
NASCAR NEXTEL Cup Series

INSIDER'S PICK

As president of Phoenix International Raceway, **Bryan Sperber** knows the city's best restaurants. "I enjoy **Tarbell's**. It's at 32nd and Camelback. The dishes are very creative and the food is exceptional. The menu is constantly changing, and each time you go there, it's like a new restaurant. Never the same twice. Very unique." *3213 E Camelback Rd, Phoenix (85018). Phone 602/955-8100. www.tarbells.com.*

The field for the NASCAR NEXTEL Cup Series Checker Auto Parts 500 takes the green flag.

AVONDALE OUTFIELD:
The 30 miles surrounding the Phoenix International Raceway.

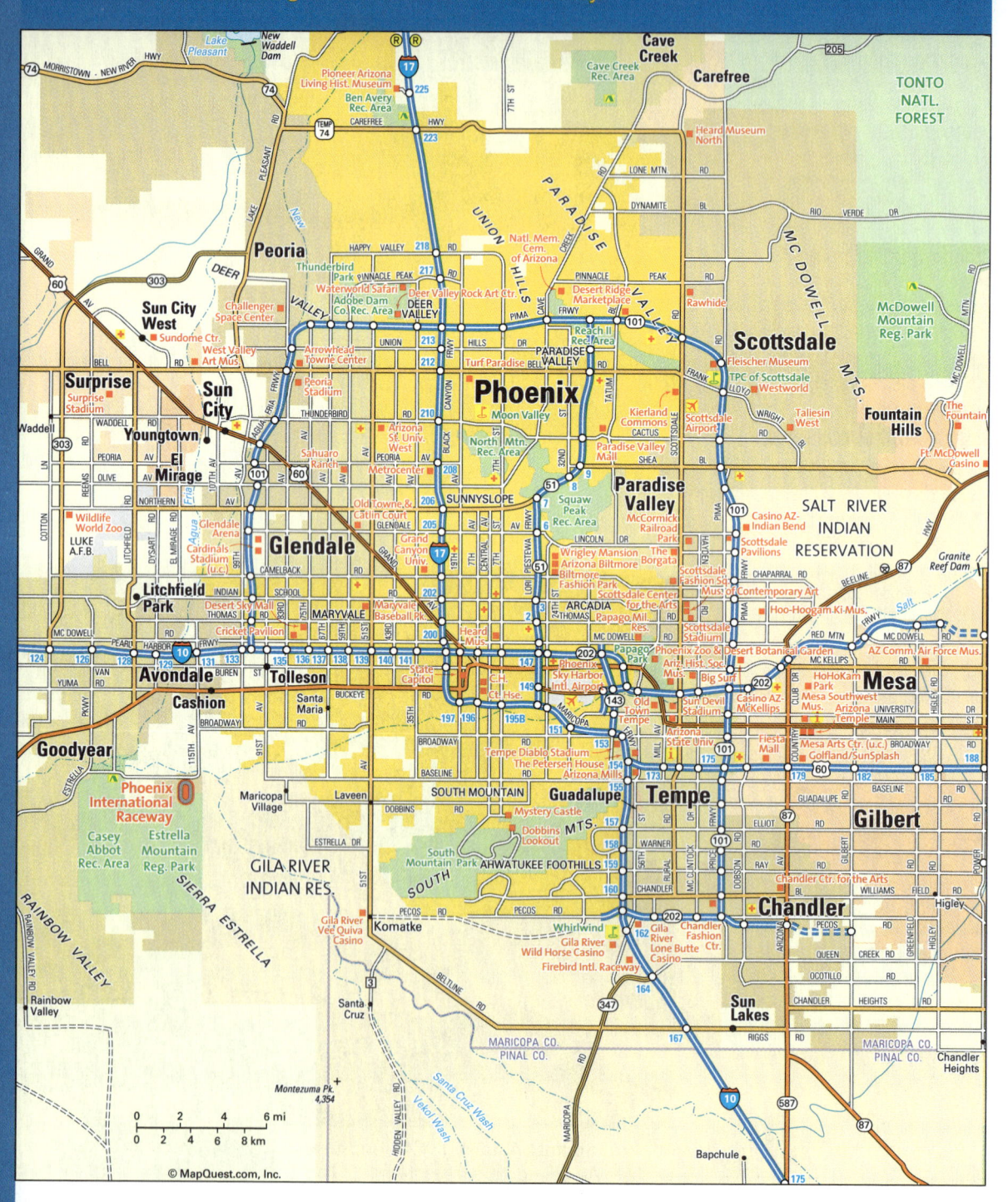

SEE

ATTRACTIONS

Glendale

GLENDALE ARENA.
9400 W Maryland Ave, Glendale (85305). Phone 623/772-3200. www.glendalearenaaz.com. Glendale Arena is home to the Phoenix Coyotes NHL ice hockey team. Located on 223 acres west of downtown Glendale, it's also a great place to go for entertainment on the west side of Phoenix. Call for a schedule of concerts, family shows, boxing, and wrestling. Convenient access from AZ Loop 101, off of I-10, and only 13 miles from the racetrack.

Goodyear

ESTRELLA MOUNTAIN RANCH GOLF CLUB.
11800 S Golf Club Dr, Goodyear (85338). Phone 623/386-2600. www.estrellamtnranch.com/golf. Jack Nicklaus II designed this 72-par, 18-hole championship course, and it's open to the public. You can whack balls over natural rolling desert fairways and enjoy views of the **Sierra Estrella Mountains.** Rates change depending on the season. The club is located off South Estrella Parkway, only 10 miles from the racetrack. Group and private lessons available. Check with the golf shop for fees and scheduling.

Phoenix

ARIZONA CENTER.
455 N 3rd St, Phoenix (85004). Phone 602/271-4000. www.arizonacenter.com. Shop, dine, dance, play, or chill out after the races at this downtown open-air marketplace boasting specialty shops, kiosks, restaurants, nightclubs, movie theaters, and more. Watch for NASCAR racer promos on Saturday night. With 3 1/2 acres of Phoenix fun, you'll never get bored. Park at the corner of 5th Street and Fillmore and get your ticket validated at the movie theater or any restaurant. (Daily; closed Jan 1, Thanksgiving, Dec 25)

DESERT BOTANICAL GARDEN.
1201 N Galvin Pkwy, Phoenix (85008). Phone 480/941-1217. www.dbg.org. Need an alternative to the noisy crowds? Stroll these peaceful paths and you'll see hundreds of natural desert plants, including colorful wildflowers and prickly cacti—a few that bloom only at night. Interactive displays show the many ways Native Americans once used the plants. Enjoy a relaxing lunch at the outdoor café surrounded by blooms. **Music in the Gardens** features performances by local bands, many playing jazz, on Friday evenings from February through June, and Saturday evenings from October through mid-November. (Oct-Apr: daily 8 am-8 pm; May-Sept: daily 7 am-8 pm; closed July 4, Dec 25) **$$**

HEARD MUSEUM.
2301 N Central Ave, Phoenix (85004). Phone 602/252-8848. www.heard.org. Immerse yourself in the culture and art of the Southwest at this internationally acclaimed Native American museum. The 130,000-square-foot attraction has unique Native American art and exhibits in ten separate galleries along with a working-artist studio. Its collection of 32,000 works includes contemporary Native-American fine art, historic Hopi Kachina dolls, important Navajo and Zuni jewelry, and prize-winning Navajo textiles. The Heard Museum also provides artist demonstrations, music and dance performances, and hands-on activities. (Daily 9:30 am-5 pm; closed holidays) **$$**

THE PHOENIX ZOO.
455 N Galvin Pkwy, Phoenix (85008). Phone 602/273-1341. www.phoenixzoo.org. If you love animals, this one has 1,300 of them—more than 400 mammals, 500 birds, and 500 reptiles and amphibians. The zoo also holds special events, educational programs, and outdoor recreational activities. Walk, rent bicycles, or take a train ride around the park. Concessions are typical junk food fare, so bring your own if you're picky. (Sept-May: daily 9 am-5 pm; June-Aug: daily 7 am-4 pm; closed Dec 25) **$$**

Scottsdale

CRUISE NIGHT AT SCOTTSDALE PAVILIONS.
9175 E Indian Bend Rd, Scottsdale, (85250). Phone 480/905-9111. While Scottsdale Pavilions may be one of the largest and most attractive shopping centers in the country, with its gorgeous contemporary Southwestern architecture and spectacular water

features, Saturday nights bring more people to the parking lot than the shops. They come for the hot rods: muscle cars, custom cars, street rods, antique roadsters, vintage trucks, motorcycles, and even a few finely tuned imports. Order a milkshake at McDonald's and groove to old tunes while you ogle the chrome with this informally gathered group of gear heads. (Starts about 5:30 pm, generally winds down around 9 pm) **FREE**

MCCORMICK-STILLMAN RAILROAD PARK.

7301 E Indian Bend Rd, Scottsdale (85250). Phone 480/312-2312. www.therailroadpark.com. The Railroad Park is a great place to take kids, or anyone who loves trains. Take a ride around this 30-acre city park aboard the **Paradise and Pacific Railroad,** a 5/12-scale reproduction of a Colorado narrow-gauge railroad. Then head over to the 1950s carousel, or to one of two well-equipped playgrounds. Railroad aficionados won't want to miss the 1928 **Roald Amundsen Pullman Car,** used by four US presidents: Herbert Hoover, Franklin D. Roosevelt, Harry S Truman, and Dwight D. Eisenhower. The park sells hot dogs, yogurt, and soft drinks. (Daily; closed Thanksgiving, Dec 25) **$**

Tempe

TEMPE TOWN LAKE.

80 W Rio Salado Pkwy, Tempe (85281). Phone 480/350-8625. www.tempetownlake.com. Tempe Town Lake on the Rio Salado, near the Mill Avenue shopping and dining district, is a 224-acre, 2-mile waterway that charters cruises and rents rowboats, pedal boats, kayaks, and canoes. It also hosts a variety of events and activities. The nicely renovated 1931 **Tempe Beach Park** has shaded picnic groves, sandy play areas, a grassy amphitheater, and the popular **Splash Playground** water park (closed Sept to spring). Take the tour, or take advantage of the 4 1\2 miles of shoreline for walking or people-watching.

> For more attractions, go to www.mobiltravelguide.com

STAY

MOBIL STAR-RATED LODGINGS

Chandler

FAIRFIELD INN. ★

7425 W Chandler Blvd, Chandler (85226). Phone 480/940-0099; toll-free 888/236-2427. www.fairfield inn.com. 66 rooms, 3 story. Complimentary continental breakfast. Check-in 3 pm, check-out noon. Outdoor pool, whirlpool. **$**

PRIME HOTEL & SUITES PHOENIX/CHANDLER. ★★

7475 W Chandler Blvd, Chandler (85226). Phone 480/961-4444. www.primehotelsandresorts.com. 159 rooms, 4 story. Check-in 3 pm, check-out noon. High-speed Internet access. Restaurant, bar. Fitness room. Outdoor pool, whirlpool. **$**

FAN FAVORITE

Located at the Arizona Center near Bank One Ball Park and America West Arena, **Majerle's Sports Grill** is an easy stop for pub grub on the way to and from a game, or for happy hour. Owned and operated by former Suns basketball player Dan Majerle, the place is full of energy, activity, and cheesy sports memorabilia. Watch three TV screens at once, or watch the parade of people going by. American menu. Brunch, lunch, dinner, late-night. **$** *24 N 2nd St, Phoenix (85004). Phone 602/253-0118. www.majerles.com.*

Litchfield Park

THE WIGWAM RESORT AND GOLF CLUB. ★★★
300 Wigwam E Blvd, Litchfield Park (85340). Phone 623/935-3811; toll-free 888/382-8610, 800/327-0396; fax 623/935-3737. www.wigwamresort.com. Once a haughty hangout for Goodyear Tire Company honchos, the upscale Wigwam now welcomes road warriors here to see the rubber meet the road at the racetrack, a mere 11 miles away. Whitewashed wood furniture, slate floors, ceramic tiles, and traditional Santa Fe touches are so thoughtfully designed you'll feel like you're walking into a rich relative's Mexican mansion. The resort has three award-winning golf courses, nine tennis courts, two pools, a waterslide, fitness center, spa, and fine restaurants. Outside tours and activities arranged with frequent pickups. 331 rooms, 2 story. Pets accepted, some restrictions; fee. Check-in 4 pm, check-out noon. Four restaurants, bar. Children's activity center. Fitness room. Two outdoor pools, whirlpools. Golf. Tennis. Airport transportation available. Business center. $$$

Phoenix

DOUBLETREE GUEST SUITES PHOENIX GATEWAY CENTER. ★★
320 N 44th St, Phoenix (85008). Phone 602/225-0500; toll-free 800/222-8733. www.doubletree.com. This 242-room hotel is just 2 miles north of Sky Harbor Airport and minutes from restaurants, shopping, sporting events, and golf. Guest suites have microwaves and refrigerators. 242 rooms, 6 story, all suites. Complimentary full breakfast. Check-in 3 pm, check-out noon. High-speed Internet access. Restaurant, bar. Fitness room. Outdoor pool, whirlpool. Airport transportation available. Business center. $$

EMBASSY SUITES HOTEL PHOENIX—BILTMORE. ★★
2630 E Camelback Rd, Phoenix (85016). Phone 602/955-3992; toll-free 800/362-2779. www.embassysuites.com. Just off Camelback Road and adjacent to the upscale shopping and dining of Biltmore Fashion Park, this family-friendly hotel is tucked in Phoenix's most renowned residential area. The dramatic lobby features cascading waterfalls and koi fish pools, along with four-story murals of the Southwest. 232 rooms, 5 story, all suites. Pets accepted; fee. Complimentary full breakfast. Check-in 3 pm, check-out 1 pm. Wireless Internet access. Restaurant, bar. Fitness room. Outdoor pool. $

POINTE SOUTH MOUNTAIN RESORT. ★★★
7777 S Pointe Pkwy, Phoenix (85044). Phone 602/438-9000; toll-free 877/800-4888. www.pointesouthmtn.com. This upscale property—the largest all-suite resort in Arizona—offers a delightful intermingling of space and elegance and a place to play just about anything. The Oasis water park boasts a wave pool and an eight-story waterslide. Guests have the option of tennis on lighted courts, volleyball in water or sand, ping pong, pool, racquetball, croquet, or golf on the resort's own 18-hole course. Get outta Dodge on horseback from the resort's own stables, or hike or bike the South Mountain Preserve right out the back door. 640 rooms, 5 story. Check-in 4 pm, check-out noon. Restaurant, bar. Children's activity center. Fitness room, spa. Seven outdoor pools, children's pool, seven whirlpools. Golf. Tennis. $

Scottsdale

THE FAIRMONT SCOTTSDALE PRINCESS. ★★★
7575 E Princess Dr, Scottsdale (85255). Phone 480/585-4848; toll-free 800/257-7544. www.fairmont.com. The Fairmont Scottsdale Princess is a cosmopolitan oasis snuggled on 450 lush acres overlooking Scottsdale and the majestic McDowell Mountains. The pink Spanish Colonial buildings are just the beginning at this comprehensive resort. Two championship golf courses, one of which hosts the PGA Tour's Phoenix Open; seven tennis courts; and an extensive fitness center please the active minded, while the Willow Stream Spa soothes the weary with its serene design and balancing principles. An aquatic recreation area features two water slides. The rooms and suites are a blend of Mediterranean design with Southwestern accents. The six restaurants and bars offer cuisine from the Italian Riviera, Mexico, and the American heartland. 650 rooms, 4 story. Check-in 4 pm, check-out noon. Six restaurants, bars. Children's activity center. Fitness room, spa. Five outdoor pools, whirlpool. Golf, 36 holes. Tennis. $$$$

LA QUINTA INN AND SUITES SCOTTSDALE—PHOENIX. ★

8888 E Shea Blvd, Scottsdale (85260). Phone 480/614-5300; toll-free 866/725-1661. www.lq.com. A great place to stay when experiencing all that Scottsdale has to offer, this location, just off the freeway, is close to the Scottsdale Fashion Square, Fort MacDowell Casino, and MLB training at Scottsdale Stadium. 140 rooms, 3 story. Pets accepted. Complimentary continental breakfast. Check-in 2 pm, check-out noon. Fitness room. Outdoor pool, whirlpool. $

HAMPTON INN SCOTTSDALE—OLDTOWN. ★

4415 Civic Center Plaza, Scottsdale (85251). Phone 480/941-9400; toll-free 800/426-7866. www.hamptoninn.com. 135 rooms. Pets accepted. Complimentary continental breakfast. Check-in 3 pm. Outdoor pool. $

LOCAL RECOMMENDATIONS

Glendale

BEST WESTERN INN PHOENIX—GLENDALE.

7116 N 59th Ave, Glendale (85301). Phone 623/939-9431; toll-free 800/333-7172. www.bestwestern.com. If you enjoy antiquing, this newly renovated hotel in historic downtown Glendale puts you within walking distance to more than 90 quality antiques shops. 80 rooms, 2 story. Pets accepted, some restrictions; fee. Complimentary continental breakfast. Check-in 2 pm, check-out 11 am. Laundry services. Children's activity center. Two outdoor pools. $

Goodyear

BEST WESTERN PHOENIX—GOODYEAR INN.

55 N Litchfield Rd, Goodyear (85338). Phone 623/932-3210; toll-free 888/449-3330. www.bestwestern.com. This full service hotel provides a quiet and serene location near the Estrella Mountains, only 8 miles from the racetrack in the southwest valley. 85 rooms, 2 story. Pets accepted, some restrictions; fee. Complimentary continental breakfast. Check-in 4 pm, check-out noon. Laundry services. Restaurant, bar. Pool. $

HAMPTON INN & SUITES, GOODYEAR.

2000 N Litchfield Rd, Goodyear (85338). Phone 623/536-1313; toll-free 800/426-7866. www.hamptoninn.com. With a basketball court on the property, the Palm Valley Golf Course next door, and the racetrack only 10 miles away, this one makes the short list. It blocks reservations around NASCAR dates, though. Romano's Macaroni Grill next door offers room service. 110 rooms, 3 story. Pets accepted. Complimentary continental breakfast. Check-in 3 pm, check-out noon. Laundry services. Fitness room, spa. Pool. $

HOLIDAY INN EXPRESS GOODYEAR.

1313 N Litchfield Rd, Goodyear (85338). Phone 623/535-1313; toll-free 800/465-4329. www.hiexpress.com. With one of the closest locations to the racetrack—8 miles—this hotel sets aside rooms for NASCAR drivers and their guests. Lucky fans may snag a canceled room. 90 rooms, 3 story. Check-in 4 pm, check-out noon. Laundry services. Fitness room, spa. Pool. $

RAMADA INN PHOENIX WEST.

1770 N Dysart Rd, Goodyear (85338). Phone 623/932-9191; toll-free 800/272-6232. www.ramada.com. This hotel is an easy 7 miles to the racetrack. 160 rooms, 2 story. Pets accepted, some restrictions. Complimentary continental breakfast. Check-in 4 pm, check-out noon. Laundry services. Restaurant, bar. Fitness room, spa. Pool. $

WINGATE INN GOODYEAR.

1188 N Dysart Rd, Goodyear (85338). Phone 623/547-1313; toll-free 800/228-1000. www.wingateinns.com. Conveniently located off Interstate 10, 7 miles from the racetrack. 100 rooms, 4 story. Pets accepted, some restrictions. Complimentary continental breakfast. Check-in 3 pm, check-out 11 am. Fitness center, spa. Pool. $

Phoenix

BEST WESTERN AIRPORT INN.

2425 S 24th St, Phoenix (85034). Phone 602/273-7251; toll-free 800/528-8199. www.bestwestern.com. Centrally located a mile south of Sky Harbor International Airport and only minutes from downtown Phoenix, Scottsdale, and Tempe. 117 rooms, 2 story. Pets accepted, some restrictions. Check-in 4 pm, check-out noon. Laundry services. Restaurant, bar. Children's activity center. Spa. Pool, whirlpool. Airport transportation available. $

BEST WESTERN BELL HOTEL.

17211 N Black Canyon Hwy, Phoenix (85023). Phone 602/993-8300; toll-free 800/937-8376. www.bestwestern.com. Located at I-17 and Bell Road, this newly renovated hotel is close to sporting events at Glendale Arena, thoroughbred racing at Turf Paradise, and shopping at the Outlets at Anthem. 100 rooms, 2 story. Pets accepted, some restrictions. Complimentary continental breakfast. Check-in 3 pm, check-out noon. Laundry services. Spa. Pool. $

BEST WESTERN CENTRAL PHOENIX INN & SUITES.

1100 N Central Ave, Phoenix (85004). Phone 602/252-2100; toll-free 888/676-2100. www.bestwestern.com. Recently renovated, this full-service hotel is the only mid-priced hotel in downtown Phoenix. It's within staggering distance to city nightlife and NASCAR promos at the Arizona Center. You'll also have quick access to cultural activities without paying to park. 106 rooms, 8 story. Complimentary continental breakfast. Check-in 3 pm, check-out 11 am. Laundry services. Restaurant, bar. Fitness room, spa. Pool. Airport transportation available. $

BEST WESTERN GRACE INN AT AHWATUKEE.

10831 S 51 St, Phoenix (85044). Phone 480/893-3000; toll-free 800/843-6010. www.bestwestern.com. This hotel sits at the gateway between downtown Phoenix Sky Harbor Airport and the east valley. You can lob tennis balls on their own courts, or take advantage of complimentary passes to Gold's Gym. Near spring training baseball games at Tempe Diablo Stadium. 160 rooms, 6 story. Check-in 3 pm, check-out noon. Restaurant, bar. Spa. Pool. Airport transportation available. $

BEST WESTERN INNSUITES HOTEL & SUITES.

1615 E Northern Ave, Phoenix (85020). Phone 602/997-6285; toll-free 800/937-8376. www.bestwestern.com. If you like to hike, this location puts you at the foot of the most popular family hiking spots in Phoenix: Squaw Peak Mountain and Camelback Mountain. You'll be within minutes of the action along the Camelback Corridor, and not far from downtown Phoenix and Scottsdale. 109 rooms, 2 story. Pets accepted, some restrictions, fee. Complimentary continental breakfast. Check-in 2 pm, check-out noon. Laundry services. Fitness room, spa. Pool. $

PIT PASS

"If you want to see your favorite racers pit, sit in the upper half of the front stretch grandstands," advises Billy Kann, racer and NASCAR Phoenix fan (and parent) himself. "You can see most of the racetrack from there, and concessions and restrooms are very accessible." Another plus? More action. "That part of the track is really narrow, so it's more exciting. When stuff happens on the front stretch, there's nowhere to go, no grass or anything. The backstretch is much easier for racers."

Scottsdale

BEST WESTERN PAPAGO INN AND RESORT.

7017 E McDowell Rd, Scottsdale (85257). Phone 480/947-7335; toll-free 866/806-4400. www.bestwestern.com. Also near Papago Park, this location is ideal for Scottsdale golf, shopping, and watching "the beautiful people" dress to the nines just to have lunch. If you prefer major league baseball, check the spring training schedule at Scottsdale Stadium. For the environmentally conscious, this hotel conserves and recycles. Reserve a "green room" and they'll not only filter and purify your air, drinking, and shower water, but will stock your room with green personal care products. 56 rooms, 2 story. Check-in 2 pm, check-out noon. Laundry services. Fitness room. Pool. $

Tempe

BEST WESTERN INN OF TEMPE.

670 N Scottsdale Rd, Tempe (85281). Phone 480/784-2233. www.bestwestern.com. This limited-service hotel is within walking distance to Arizona State University and downtown Tempe shops, bars, and eateries. There's always something going on at Tempe

Town Lake. Movie theaters and shopping malls abound, and East Valley restaurants are easy on the pocket. 103 rooms, 4 story. Pets accepted, some restrictions. Complimentary continental breakfast. Check-in 1 pm, check-out noon. Fitness room, spa. Pool. Airport transportation available. $

Sun City

BEST WESTERN INN AND SUITES OF SUN CITY.
11201 Grand Ave, Sun City (85363). Phone 623/933-8211; toll-free 800/253-2168. www.bestwestern.com. This hotel has the benefits of the quiet Sun City area, but is also just 15 miles from the noise and excitement of the speedway. 90 rooms, 2 story. Complimentary continental breakfast. Check-in 3 pm, check-out noon. Laundry services. Outdoor pool. $

RV AND CAMPING

Goodyear

COTTON LANE RV AND MOBILE HOME RESORT.
17506 W Van Buren St, Goodyear (85338). Phone 623/853-4000; toll-free 888/907-7223. www.arizonarvresorts.com. Located approximately 13 miles from the racetrack and 22 miles from downtown Phoenix, this facility features large lots, a spacious clubhouse, and decent shower facilities. 285 spaces (40 pull-through lots). Phone, Internet connections. Ramada, gas barbecue, horseshoes, bocce ball, pool table. Pool. Spa. Guest laundry. Pets accepted, some restrictions. Daily approximately $23, weekly approximately $115.

Phoenix

CRUISE AMERICA MOTORHOME CITY.
7602 S 115th Ave (at Phoenix International Raceway), Avondale (85323). Phone toll-free 800/327-7799, ext. 4. www.cruiseamerica.com. Motorhomes and spaces are available in the infield between Turns 3 and 4, with access to showers, restrooms and a general store. Phone the Phoenix International Raceway ticket office at 602/252-2227 for current information and availability.

For more lodging recommendations, go to www.mobiltravelguide.com

EAT

MOBIL STAR-RATED RESTAURANTS

Goodyear

EL PASO BAR B QUE COMPANY. ★
1408 N Litchfield Rd, Goodyear (85338). Phone 632/209-0144. Barbecue menu. Lunch, dinner. Bar. Casual attire. Outdoor seating. $$

Phoenix

BABY KAY'S CAJUN KITCHEN. ★
2119 E Camelback Rd, Phoenix (85016). Phone 602/955-0011. www.babykays.com. If you crave Creole, love Louisiana crab cakes, and can't get enough crawfish étouffée, get your fix at Baby Kay's. House specialties include gumbo and jambalaya. Come here on Wednesdays during crawfish season for crawfish boils. Otherwise, try the whole Cornish game hen with dirty rice. Located in the Town & Country Shopping Center, in the Camelback Corridor. Cajun menu. Lunch, dinner. Closed Thanksgiving, Dec 25. Bar. Casual attire. Outdoor seating. $$

FISH MARKET. ★★
1720 E Camelback Rd, Phoenix (85016). Phone 602/277-3474. www.thefishmarket.com. The Fish Market really is a fish market. Go upstairs to dine upscale, or stay downstairs and be casual—they serve the fish well-dressed either way. Sushi, seafood menu. Lunch, dinner. Closed Thanksgiving, Dec 25. Bar. Children's menu. Casual attire. Outdoor seating. $$

MONTI'S. ★★
12025 N 19th Ave, Phoenix (85029). Phone 602/997-5844. This casual restaurant is open seven days a week and specializes in seafood and steak options. Steak menu. Dinner. Closed Dec 25. Bar. Children's menu. Casual attire. Outdoor seating. $$

PRONTO RISTORANTE. ★★
3950 E Campbell, Phoenix (85018). Phone 602/956-4049. This family-friendly restaurant has a wonderful

don't miss it

ROAD FOOD

It's all about bread—world-class, high carb, high comfort bread and all that goes with bread at **Willo Bread Company and My Florist Café**, a bakery, grocery, and restaurant run by one owner. The best restaurants in town get their bread made here from scratch. Get it to go, go as you are, go late with your drinking buddies, you can't go wrong. Breakfast, lunch, dinner. Café open 6 am-midnight. Live music. *530 W McDowell Rd, Phoenix (85003). Phone 602/254-0333.*

combination of traditional Italian dishes and innovative regional cuisine. Italian menu. Dinner. Closed Sun; Thanksgiving, Dec 25. Bar. Casual attire. Dinner theater Fri-Sat. $$

RUBY BEET GOURMET. ★ ★ ★

628 E Adams St, Phoenix (85004). Phone 602/258-8700. If a day at the races has temporarily satisfied your need for speed, Ruby Beet Gourmet is the place to go for a slower pace. Located at The Silva House, a restored 100-year-old bungalow in Heritage Square, the setting couldn't be more charming or the food more textured. A popular hangout for local foodies, the menu changes often and is limited to whatever the owners find ultra-fresh and delectable that day. American menu. Dinner. Closed Sun-Mon. Casual attire. Reservations recommended. $$

RUSTLER'S ROOSTE. ★ ★

7777 S Pointe Pkwy, Phoenix (85044). Phone 602/431-6474. www.rustlersrooste.com. The meat on the menu is served a variety of ways for a cowboy's big appetite. Before you mosey on out, pickup some canned rattlesnake meat in the general store. Steak menu. Dinner. Casual attire. Valet parking. Outdoor seating. $$

Scottsdale

CHOMPIE'S. ★

9301 E Shea Blvd, Scottsdale (85260). Phone 480/860-0475. www.chompies.com. Located in the Mercado del Rancho shopping area, Chompie's serves fresh-made bagels, bialys, and stacked-high sandwiches. They say that people drive an hour to pick up what locals agree are the best bagels in town. Deli menu. Breakfast, lunch, dinner. Closed holidays. Bar. Children's menu. Casual attire. Outdoor seating. $

EVERETT'S STEAKHOUSE & BLUES BAR. ★ ★ ★

20701 N Scottsdale Rd, Scottsdale (85255). Phone 480/515-5891. A live blues band on weekends energizes this casual steakhouse located in the Grayhawk Plaza shopping center. An exhibition kitchen keeps hungry diners entertained before their cuts of prime beef arrive at the table. Steak menu. Dinner. Bar. Business casual attire. Reservations recommended. $$

PISCHKE'S PARADISE. ★

7217 East 1st St, Scottsdale (85251). Phone 480/481-0067 www.pischkesparadise.com. American menu. Dinner. Closed holidays. Bar. Casual attire. Outdoor seating. $$

THE QUILTED BEAR. ★

6316 N Scottsdale Rd, Scottsdale (85253). Phone 480/948-7760. American menu. Breakfast, lunch, dinner. Bar. Children's menu. Casual attire. Outdoor seating. $

LOCAL RECOMMENDATIONS

Avondale

RAUL & THERESA'S MEXICAN FOOD.

519 Main (Hwy 85), Avondale (85323). Phone 623/932-1120. For authentic Mexican food served graciously and prepared fresh daily from locally grown ingredients, stop in at Raul and Theresa Chayrez's restaurant, around the corner from the racetrack. Turn right onto East Main Street from Dysart Road and look for it on the left. Tell them we sent you, and go easy on the salsa. Mexican menu. Breakfast, lunch, dinner. Children's menu. Casual attire. $

TJ'S.

310 N Dysart St, Avondale (85323). Phone 623/932-0309. If you're staying anywhere near Avondale, TJ's wants to make you breakfast. The friendly staff keeps a loyal fan club coming back for second helpings of specialty omelets, biscuits and gravy, and big, beautiful Belgian waffles, all at great prices. The place is noisy in a family-friendly way (no need to shush the toddlers). American menu. Breakfast, lunch. Casual attire. $

Cave Creek

HAROLD'S CAVE CREEK CORRAL.

6895 E Cave Creek Rd, Cave Creek (85331). Phone 480/488-1906. www.haroldscorral.com. Where have all the cowboys gone? At Harold's, real dirt on the boots is *de rigueur*. The dirt on half the chap-wearing boot-scooters is probably biker grease, but it's a big corral, and everybody gets along. Live music is featured Thursday through Sunday, and Friday is all-you-can-eat fish-fry night, with Western dance lessons following. Harold's has a generous menu, great people-watching, Western gear hanging from the rafters, picnic tables, and a family-friendly crowd consisting of both locals and tourists. Pool tables, dart boards, an air hockey table, and a jukebox add to the fun. American menu. Breakfast, lunch, dinner, late-night. Children's menu. Casual attire. Reservations recommended. Outdoor seating. $$

Goodyear

BELLA LUNA RISTORANTE.

14175 W Indian School Rd, Goodyear (85338). Phone 623/535-4642. If you're looking for fresh and delicious Sicilian food, come to Bella Luna. Chef/owner Joe Billelo carefully gathered his authentic Italian recipes from Old World kitchens in Palermo. The *zuppa* and *antipasti* get the green flag, and if you like veal, you'll love the *vitello alla piccata*. With the racetrack only 11 miles away, you might see a few of the drivers quietly winding down here with their crew. Italian menu. Lunch, dinner. Children's menu. Reservations recommended. $$

Phoenix

DUCK AND DECANTER.

1651 E Camelback Rd, Phoenix (85018). Phone 602/274-5429. duckanddecanter.com. The Duck serves great sandwiches sack-lunch style. Regulars are torn between the Genoa salami with garlic cream cheese and marinated tomatoes, and the roast beef with tomatoes, avocados, jicama, and pine nuts. You might choose the smoked breast of duck sandwich with smoked turkey, cream cheese, cranberry walnut relish, and watercress on walnut-raisin country bread—it's the duckiest. Get a big hunk of carrot cake to go. American menu. Breakfast, lunch, dinner. Patio seating. Live music on weekends. Children's menu. Bar. Casual attire. Outdoor seating. $

HONEY BEAR'S BBQ.

2824 N Central Ave, Phoenix (85004). Phone 602/279-7911. Slathered in an award-winning, 50-year-old family barbecue recipe, the Tennessee-style mesquite-smoked ribs, chicken, and pulled-pork sandwiches have a hardcore local following. Napkins won't help. Barbecue menu. Lunch, dinner. Closed Thanksgiving, Dec 25. Casual attire. Outdoor seating. $

MI COCINA, MI PAIS.

4221 W Bell Rd, Phoenix (85053). Phone 602/548-7900. Lucky for us, Rosa Rosas left Ecuador for Arizona and eventually opened the colorful, six-table gem Mi Cocina, Mi Pais (My Kitchen, My Country). Ask Rosa about her *Ecuadorian sango de camarones* (shrimp stew with a mild peanut sauce), or her *sobrebarriga Bogotana* (flavorful and tender marinated slow-cooked brisket) and she'll tell you a charming story. Try the ceviches or tamales seasoned with aji chile. The food is so good—and inexpensive—you won't believe it until you eat it. South American menu. Lunch, dinner. Closed Mon. Casual attire. $

For more dining recommendations, go to www.mobiltravelguide.com

SIDETRIP

Grand Canyon National Park
Williams, AZ

The entire Grand Canyon National Park—all 1,904 square miles of it—has 277 cool miles of **Colorado River** running through it. A breathtaking 18 miles divides the north and south rims at the widest part. **The South Rim** alone runs 1,373 jagged miles between **Lake Mead** and **Lee's Ferry,** with elevations averaging 7,000 feet. While it's just too big to fully comprehend, this 6-million-year-old hole in the ground is certainly worth a glimpse.

You might begin on the west end of the South Rim, catching the shuttle bus to **Hermits Rest.** Look for the old mission bell hanging from the stone arch. Then, hike the **South Rim Trail** 2 miles back to **Grand Canyon Village.** Stop for lunch at **El Tovar Hotel,** which sits just 50 feet from the edge of the cliff. After lunch, hike a couple more miles to **Mather Point.**

Another option is to drive 26 miles east from Grand Canyon Village to the 70-foot-high **Desert View Watchtower.** Climb the tower stairs to see Hopi artist Fred Kabotie's painted murals. From the top of the tower, you can see **Comanche Point.** More adventurous hikers can blaze their own wild trail to Comanche Point, 7 miles north of Desert View and the park's east entrance.

Walk the trails, fly over by plane or helicopter, travel down by mule, or raft the river. Camp at the rim or the base and watch for raptors with 9-foot wingspans, or any of at least 287 types of birds, 76 mammals, 35 reptiles, and 6 amphibians. Even a short drive along the rim will change your perception of wide-open spaces forever.

View the Canyon from a day hike on the Grandview Trail. The pointed peak in the distance is Vishnu Temple. The Grand Canyon is located at US 93 and AZ 169, Williams (86023). Phone 928/638-7888. www.nps.gov/grca.

Spring and fall are the best seasons for hiking. Check weather information on the Grand Canyon Web site (www.nps.gov/grca/grandcanyon/weather.htm), or by phoning 928/638-7888.

For trip planning information, write: Trip Planner, Grand Canyon National Park, PO Box 129, Grand Canyon, AZ (86023).

For more Grand Canyon recommendations, go to www.mobiltravelguide.com

396

Action begins as the green flag drops to start the 2004 NASCAR Busch Series Goulds Pump/ITT Industries Salute to the Troops 250 presented by Dodge.

Pikes Peak International Raceway

Fountain, CO

24

Full-throated fans cheer their favorites during the 2004 NASCAR Busch Series Goulds Pump/ITT Industries Salute to the Troops 250 presented by Dodge.

TRACK FACTS

PIKES PEAK INTERNATIONAL RACEWAY. 16650 Midway Ranch Rd, Fountain (80817). Phone toll-free 888/306-7223. www.ppir.com.

SECURITY. Everything is subject to search. No coolers larger than 14 x 14 x 14 inches are permitted. Outside food and drink are allowed, but no alcohol or glass containers. Pets, skateboards, and bicycles prohibited, but strollers are permitted.

PARKING. Only Interstate 25 leads to and from the track, so prepare for heavy traffic. Most parking is free with shuttle service to the track. Gates open at 8 am. There are 89 trackside RV spots with great views and separate rules allowing pets and alcohol; 450 overnight RV campers can be accommodated. Call early for reservations.

FIRST AID. There is a staffed first aid station north of the box office at the main gate on the midway. For more serious injuries, find track personnel to escort you to the on-site trauma center or go to Memorial Hospital which has an emergency and trauma center (1400 E Boulder St, Colorado Springs, phone 719/365-5000).

CONCESSIONS. Services are limited. The midway offers the basics including a playground and paid amusements for kids. Food and drink run $4-$6 and are primarily cash-only. Ice is available on site.

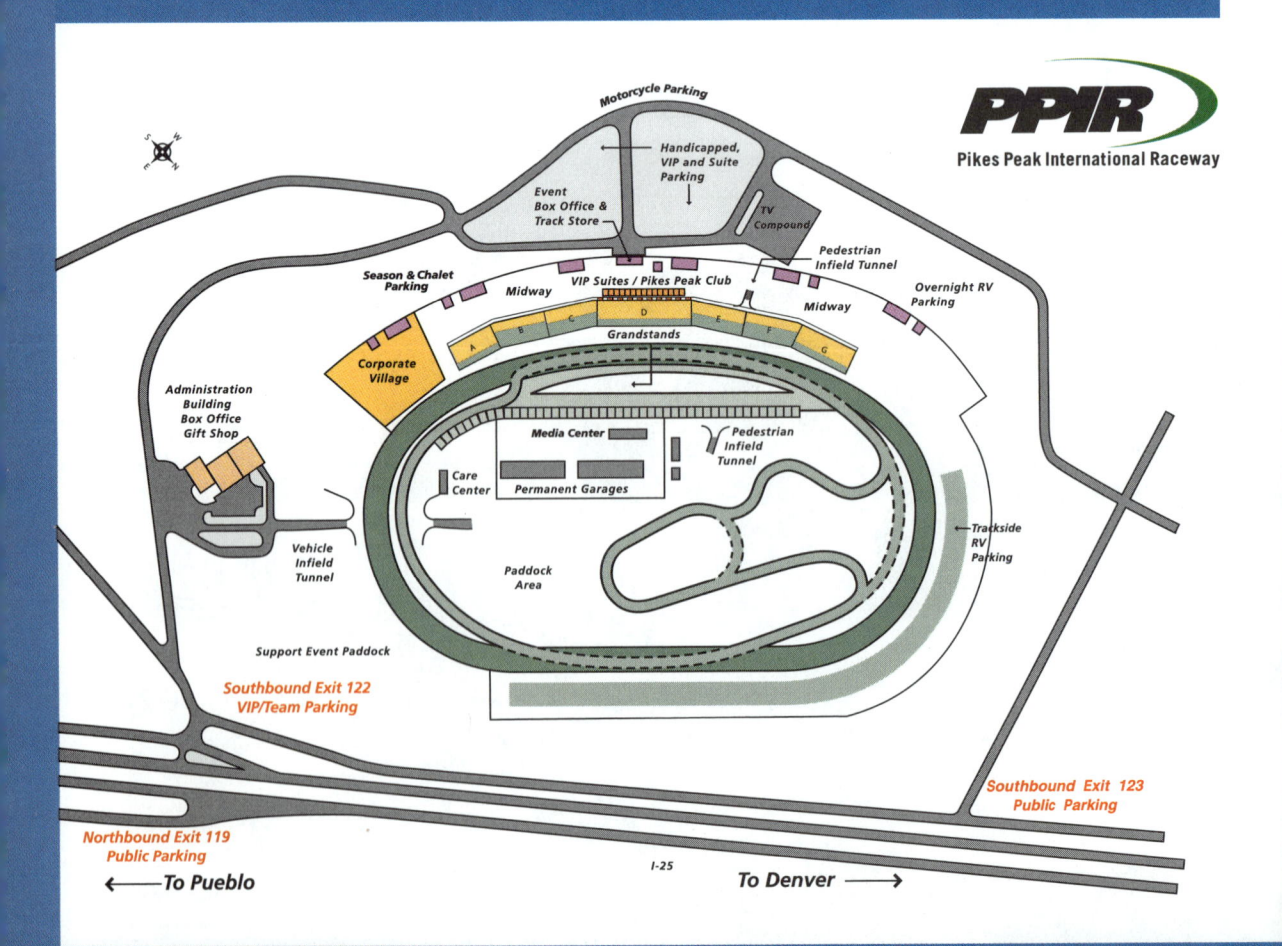

MOUNTAIN HIGHS

Pikes Peak International Raceway is located at the junction of Interstate 25 and nowhere, as if one day the track fell from the sky and landed amid the surrounding ranches. Beyond the ranches, however, lie opportunities to experience not only jaw-dropping natural beauty, but metropolitan charm. So after your raceway experience, you may only spend a short time in the area around Fountain (the track itself is 7 miles outside of town), but if you drive a few miles north and head into Colorado Springs, you will find the area's most vibrant community and scenery.

Cowboy boots are common in the Springs, but when locals talk about "going riding" they are most likely jumping on their mountain bike rather than a horse. This is the kind of place where you'll see a $3,000 machine of a bicycle perched atop a $500 jalopy of a car. Welcome to the modern Wild West, where it's all about the outdoors, outdoor gear, and athleticism.

More than a mile above sea level, Colorado Springs will take your breath away—literally. Give yourself two

If you're an extreme adventurer, get your hiking boots for a trek up Pikes Peak. You can drive it, too, or take the railway.

Test your cowboy skills and learn how the pros do it at the ProRodeo Hall of Fame.

GETTING AROUND

With everything so spread out, you'll be doing lots of driving. Set your radio to AM 950 for the Sinclair Gearhead Hour (Sat 10 am), the local motorsports show.

Traffic along I-25 around the Springs is a mystery. Backups can occur anytime, especially around the north end of town. Rush hour is always bad, afternoons more so than mornings.

Watch for speed traps on I-25 along the north end of town. Be aware that under Colorado's recently reduced blood alcohol limits, two to three drinks could get you a DUI. Also, buckle up. If you are pulled over for any reason, everybody in the car must be wearing a seatbelt, or the driver gets a ticket.

Arriving from I-25 southbound, you'll find free parking at Exit 123, VIP and handicap spots at Exit 122. From I-25 northbound, Exit 119 is your only option.

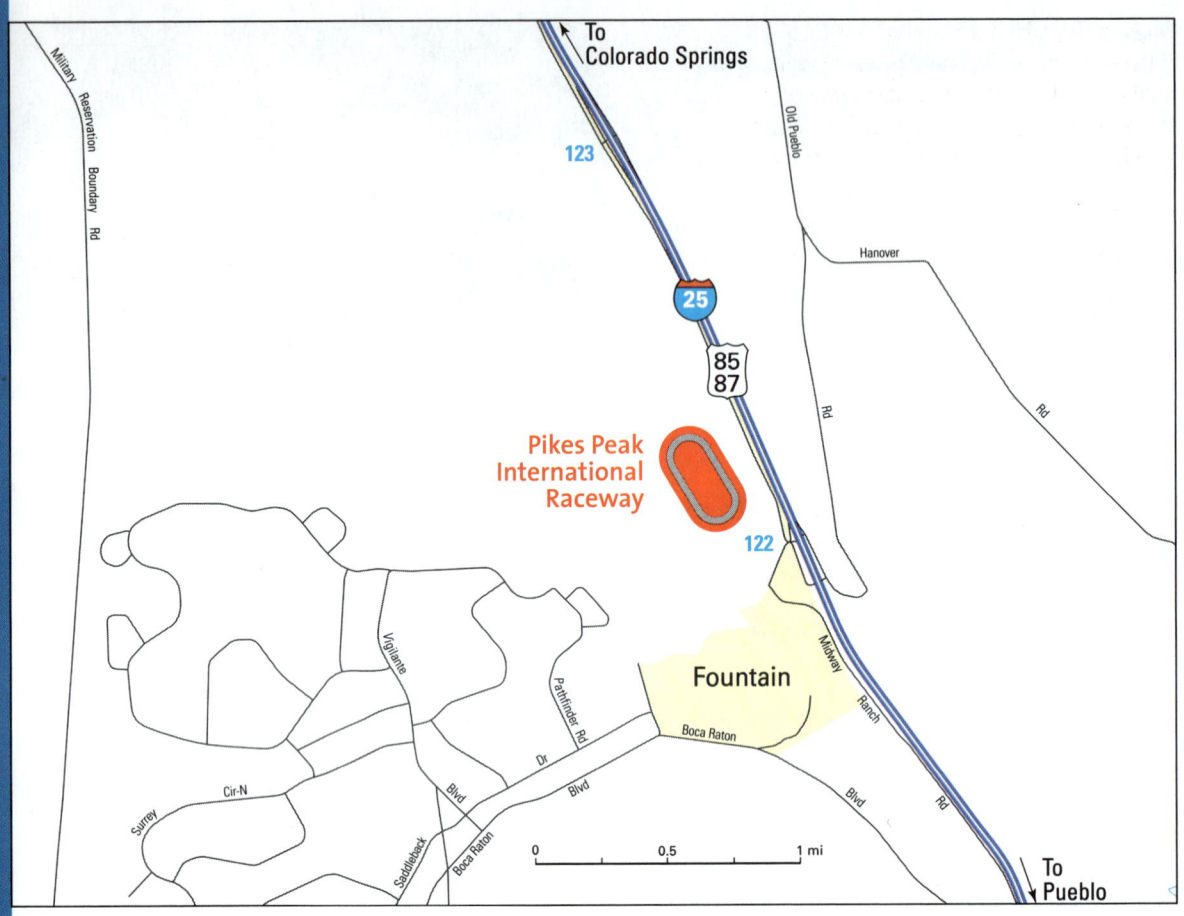

PIKES PEAK POLE POSITION:
The 10 miles surrounding Pikes Peak International Raceway.

days to acclimate, limit alcohol and tobacco consumption, don't overexert yourself, and drink plenty of water (the same is true at the raceway). This part of Colorado is a semiarid alpine desert with summer temperatures pushing 95 degrees and a bone-dry climate that will rob your body of fluids well before you feel thirsty. Slather yourself in sunscreen, use insect repellent, and add a hat and some shades, and you'll be ready to explore the stunning scenery surrounding the Springs. Start your days outdoors early to beat the crowds and the afternoon clouds. At night, bring a light jacket; temperatures can drop to the 60s.

Natural beauty abounds at **Pikes Peak** (phone toll-free 800/318-9505), the "purple mountain majesties" that inspired Katharine Lee Bates to write "America the Beautiful." The peak was explored by Zebulon Montgomery Pike in 1806 to determine the Louisiana Purchase's southwestern edge, but his attempt to scale it was interrupted by a blizzard.

In 1916, the opening of the peak's highway was commemorated with the first Pikes Peak Hill Climb race—the second-oldest auto race in the United States behind the Indianapolis 500. You can drive to the top (you don't have to race) or hitch a ride on the railway. The adventurous can hike the peak on foot. For more stunning scenery, visit the **Garden of the Gods** (phone 719/634-6666), with stunning rock formations that come alive in the light of sunrise or sunset.

After a good hike, you can soak away the resulting aches at **Sky Sox Stadium** (phone 719/597-1449, www.skysox.com) back in Colorado Springs, where you can take in a AAA baseball game from a private hot tub along the first base line. And while you're in the city, gear up for your NASCAR event at **Race Fever** (phone 719/596-7223), a NASCAR memorabilia store in the **Citadel Mall** (phone 719/591-5516, www.shopthecitadel.com).

If your preference leans to unique local stores and galleries, head to **Old Colorado City** along Colorado Avenue (phone 719/633-6767, www.shopoldcoloradocity.com) or **Manitou Springs** (www.manitousprings.org), a mountain town just 4 miles west of Colorado Springs that maintains its old-time charm without sinking into outdated cheesiness. Serious shoppers should drive 40 miles north on Interstate 25 to the **Outlets at Castle Rock** (phone toll-free 800/245-8351), or make a day of it and continue 30 miles on to Denver where the shopping in Cherry Creek, around First Avenue, is second to none.

FOUNTAIN CALENDAR

JUNE 25, 2005
Falken Tire Pikes Peak International Hill Climb. Colorado Springs (80906). Phone 719/685-4400. www.ppihc.com. Watch cars, motorcycles, and trucks travel a tricky gravel course up Pikes Peak in the second-oldest motorsports event in the United States.

JULY 22–23, 2005
NASCAR Busch Series

JULY 23–31, 2005
El Paso County Fair. Fairgrounds, 366 10th St, Calhan (80808). Phone 719/520-7880. www.elpasocountyfair.com. The festivities include a wiener dog (dachshund) costume contest, an outdoor aquarium, an antique tractor pull, petting zoo, live music, and rodeo.

JULY 30, 2005
Antiques Valuation Day. Colorado Springs Pioneers Museum, 215 South Tejon St (80903). Phone 719/385-5990. www.springsgov.com. Clean out your attic and find out if you have a treasure in your trash.

AUGUST 1–7, 2005
The International Golf Tournament. Castle Pines Golf Course, 1000 Hummingbird Dr, Greenwood Village (80108). Phone 303/660-8000; toll-free 800/755-1986. www.golfintl.com. More than 140 players will start. See who continues on to the final round.

DRIVER'S PICK

Crew chief for DEI No.1 NASCAR NEXTEL Cup Chevrolet and DEI No. 11 NASCAR Busch Series Chevrolet **Tony Gibson** has a Pikes Peak tradition. "Me and the team love **Outback Steak House.** It's a tradition with us. Thursday after inspection, we pile in the van and head for an Outback. We always get two Bloomin' Onions, and it's always either the ribs or filet for the bunch of us." *2825 Geyser Dr, Colorado Springs (80906). Phone 719/527-8745.*

PIKES PEAK OUTFIELD:
The 50 miles surrounding Pikes Peak International Raceway.

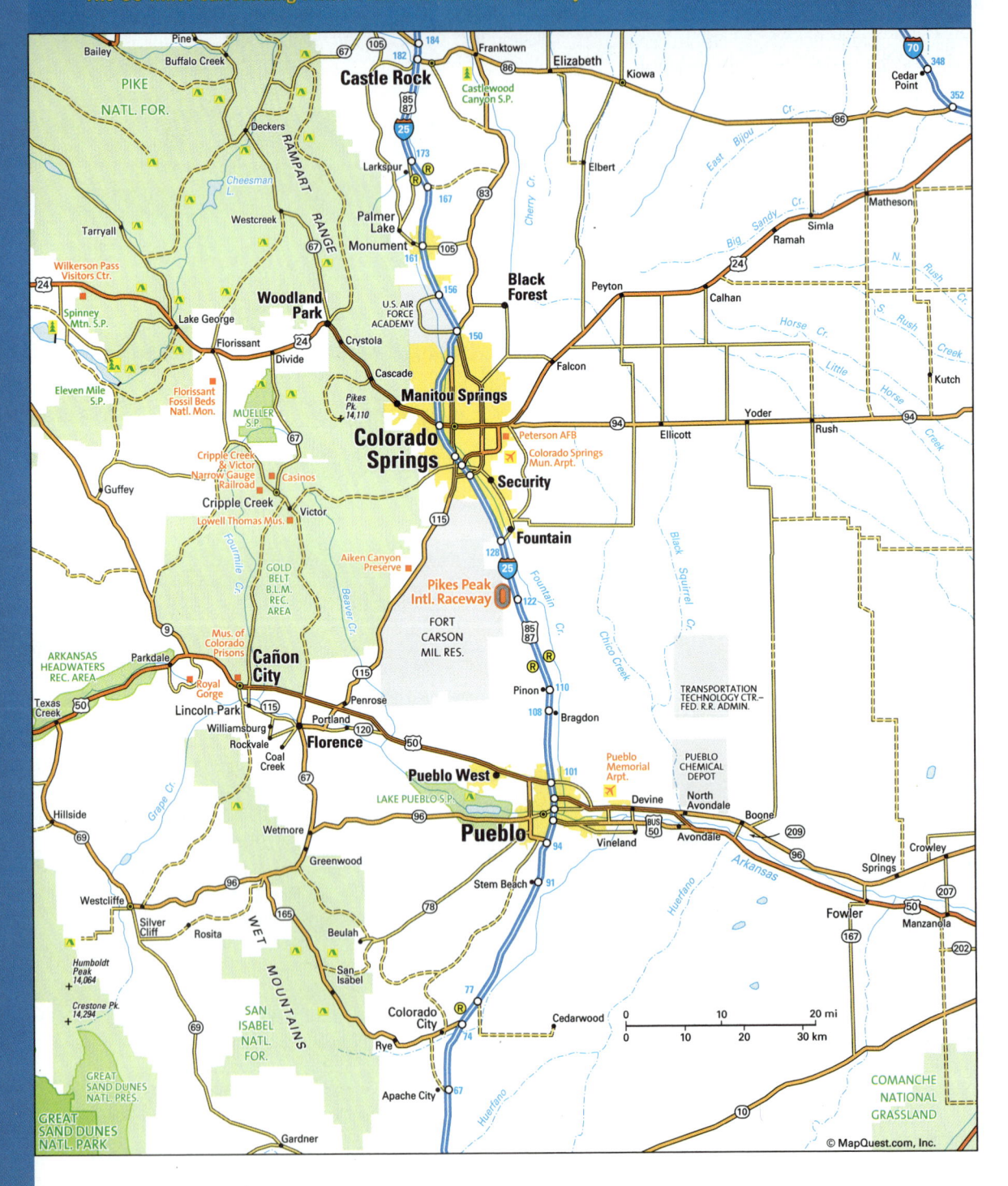

SEE

ATTRACTIONS

Colorado Springs

GARDEN OF THE GODS.
1805 N 30th St, Colorado Springs (80904). Phone 719/634-6666. www.gardenofgods.com. The sandstone formations here jut from the earth like clay-colored icebergs. Experience the garden by biking, driving, or hiking through many well-marked and relatively flat trails on your own or as part of a bus tour (fee) or free guided walking tour. Horseback trips are available through Academy Stables (phone 719/633-5667). The visitors center offers educational movies, gifts, maps, and info. Try to catch sunrise or sunset when the light plays on the rock formations. (Memorial Day-Labor Day: daily 8 am-8 pm; rest of year: daily 9 am-5 pm; closed Jan 1, Thanksgiving, Dec 25) **FREE**

PIKES PEAK MOUNTAIN BIKE TOURS.
306 S 25th St, Colorado Springs (80904). Phone toll-free 888/593-3062. www.biketours.com. Everyone from the most inexperienced rider to the expert can enjoy a bike tour through the beautiful scenery of the Rocky Mountains. Tours vary in length and endurance level, and professional guides provide all necessary equipment to make your ride safe, comfortable, and most of all, fun. (Tour schedules vary; call or visit Web site for schedule) **$$$$**

PRORODEO HALL OF FAME AND MUSEUM OF THE AMERICAN COWBOY.
101 ProRodeo Dr, Colorado Springs (80919). Phone 719/528-4761. www.prorodeo.org/hof. The Hall of Fame pays tribute to giants like nine-time world champion Casey Tibbs, while the museum will help you appreciate the life of the cowboy beyond the spotlight—especially after you try roping one of the dummy steer. (Daily 9 am-5 pm; closed holidays) **$**

US AIR FORCE ACADEMY.
2346 Academy Dr, Colorado Springs (80840). Phone 719/333-2025. www.usafa.af.mil. Located on the grounds of the academy is Cadet Chapel, the city's most famous architectural landmark, a striking combination of stained glass and 150-foot aluminum spires. Stop by the visitors center for a free self-guided tour map or to view films and informative exhibits about the Air Force. Stop in at the planetarium, which may be offering a special program, and don't miss a chance to see a T-38 and B-52 bomber up close. Call before visiting; the chapel closes for special events, and security may close the base unexpectedly. (Chapel: Mon-Sat 9 am-5 pm; Visitors Center: daily 9 am-5 pm) **FREE**

UNITED STATES OLYMPIC TRAINING CENTER.
One Olympic Plaza, Colorado Springs (80909). Phone 719/632-5551. www.usoc.org. A free hourly tour gives you an insider's view of how Olympic-level athletes train. For most of us, the closest we're getting to a medal are the replicas available in the gift shop. (Mon-Sat 9 am-5 pm; gift shop and visitor center: Sun 11 am-6 pm) **FREE**

Manitou

MANITOU AND PIKES PEAK RAILWAY.
515 Ruxton Ave, Manitou Springs (80829). Phone 719/685-5401. www.cograilway.com. Soaring 14,110 feet, Pikes Peak is the second-most-visited mountain in the world behind Mt. Fuji. To reach the peak, you can undertake an eight-hour hike or drive an hour up the 19-mile road, the last half of which is unpaved, has no guardrails, and contains steep drops (a four-by-four vehicle isn't necessary, but weather causes road closures even in summer). The surest bet to the summit is the cog railway; the trains depart usually five times daily, rain or shine, but make reservations early. Any way you go, bundle up: temperatures are 30-40 degrees cooler at the top than bottom. Water and aspirin help alleviate altitude sickness. (Apr-Dec)

PIKES PEAK.
Pikes Peak Hwy. I-25, exit 141 and follow Hwy 24 W for 10 miles, turn left at Cascade and follow signs. Phone 800/318-9505. www.pikespeakcolorado.com. Highway tolls: $10 adults, $5 child, or $35 for a full car.

For more attractions, go to
www.mobiltravelguide.com

STAY

MOBIL STAR-RATED LODGINGS

Colorado Springs

ANTLERS HILTON COLORADO SPRINGS. ★★

4 S Cascade, Colorado Springs (80903). Phone 719/473-5600; toll-free 866/299-4602. www.antlers.com. A cultural and geographic landmark for more than 100 years, the Antlers underwent a $10 million renovation, and it shows. The outside is staid, the inside urbane and smart with a grand entryway and nice touches, such as real down comforters and a pleasant staff. Ask for the fourth floor or higher and pay the small extra fee to face Pikes Peak. 292 rooms, 13 story. Check-in 3 pm, check-out noon. High-speed Internet access. Restaurant, bar. Fitness room. Indoor pool, whirlpool. Business center. $

CHEYENNE CAÑON INN. ★★★

2030 W Cheyenne Blvd, Colorado Springs (80906). Phone 719/633-0625; toll-free 800/633-0625. www.cheyennecanoninn.com. Built in 1921 for Colorado Springs' elites, this resort was originally an upscale bordello and gambling hall. This restored Mission-style mansion, with spectacular views of the mountains and Cheyenne Cañon, has warm, professional service and is an exceptional find. 10 rooms, 2 story. Complimentary full breakfast. Check-in 3 pm, check-out 11 am. Whirlpool. $

DOUBLETREE HOTEL COLORADO SPRINGS— WORLD ARENA. ★★

1775 E Cheyenne Mountain Blvd, Colorado Springs (80906). Phone 719/576-8900; toll-free 800/222-8733. www.doubletree.com. This sprawling 1970s-era hotel has a pleasant outdoor courtyard and an original disco lounge that will give you a serious case of Saturday Night Fever. The rooms are spacious—ask for one overlooking the courtyard and facing the mountains. 299 rooms, 5 story. Pets accepted; fee. Check-in 3 pm, check-out 11 am. High-speed Internet access. Restaurant, bar. Fitness room. Indoor pool, whirlpool. Airport transportation available. Business center. $

DRURY INN PIKES PEAK/COLORADO SPRINGS. ★

8155 N Academy Blvd, Colorado Springs (80920). Phone 719/598-2500; toll-free 800/325-8300. www.drury-inn.com. This family-owned hotel property wins guests over with friendly service and comfortable accommodations, and it is close to area shopping, movie theaters, and the Air Force Academy. 118 rooms, 4 story. Pets accepted, some restrictions. Complimentary continental breakfast. Check-in 3 pm, check-out noon. High-speed Internet access. Fitness room. Indoor pool, outdoor pool, whirlpool. $

FAIRFIELD INN COLORADO SPRINGS SOUTH. ★

2725 Geyser Dr, Colorado Springs (80906). Phone 719/576-1717. www.fairfieldinn.com. Just 5 miles from pretty much anything you'd want to see in Colorado Springs—Seven Falls, the Peterson Air Force Base, Fort Carson, and the World Arena—this budget-friendly hotel offers guests plenty of modern amenities at affordable rates. 85 rooms, 3 story. Pets accepted, some restrictions; fee. Complimentary continental breakfast. Check-in 3 pm, check-out noon. High-speed Internet access. Fitness room. Indoor pool, whirlpool. $

RADISSON INN COLORADO SPRINGS NORTH. ★★

8110 N Academy Blvd, Colorado Springs (80920). Phone 719/598-5770; toll-free 888/201-1718. www.radisson.com. This hotel is the closest option to the US Air Force Academy. 200 rooms, 4 story. Pets accepted, some restrictions; fee. Complimentary full breakfast. Check-in 4 pm, check-out noon. High-speed Internet access. Restaurant, bar. Fitness room. Indoor pool, whirlpool. Airport transportation available. $

SHERATON COLORADO SPRINGS HOTEL. ★★★

2886 S Circle Dr, Colorado Springs (80906). Phone 719/576-5900; toll-free 800/981-4012. www.sheraton.com. As the official hotel of Pikes Peak International Raceway, you have your best chance of seeing a driver here. Everything is on site, including a deli that's perfect for grabbing a reasonably priced bite to go. 500 rooms, 4 story. Pets accepted, some restrictions.

Check-in 3 pm, check-out 11 am. High-speed Internet access. Restaurant, bar. Fitness room. Indoor pool, children's pool, whirlpool. Tennis. Airport transportation available. Business center. $

Pueblo

MARRIOTT PUEBLO CONVENTION CENTER. ★★★

110 W First St, Pueblo (81003). Phone 719/542-3200; toll-free 888/236-2427. www.marriott.com. In the middle of downtown Pueblo, the guest rooms in this beautifully landscaped hotel feature modern furnishings, including microwaves and ergonomic desk chairs. Guests are welcome to enjoy the casual on-site restaurant or bar. 163 rooms, 7 story. Check-in 3 pm, check-out noon. Restaurant, bar. Fitness room. Indoor pool, whirlpool. Business center. $$

LOCAL RECOMMENDATIONS

Colorado Springs

BEST WESTERN AIRPORT INN.

1780 Aeroplaza Dr, Colorado Springs (80916). Phone 719/574-7707. www.bestwestern.com. For those looking to make a quick appearance at the track and then get right back on the plane, this airport property makes sense. It's just 3 miles from the airport and 5 miles from downtown Colorado Springs. 47 rooms, 2 story. Check-in noon, check-out noon. Fitness room. Indoor pool. $

BEST WESTERN EXECUTIVE INN AND SUITES.

1440 Harrison Rd, Colorado Springs (80906). Phone 719/576-2371. www.bestwestern.com. Ask for a room away from Interstate 25 and splurge for a suite if possible. The driveway entrance is tricky to find. 84 rooms, 2 story. Pets accepted, some restrictions; fee. Check-in 3 pm, check-out 11 am. Laundry services. Fitness room. Indoor pool. Complimentary continental breakfast. $

BEST WESTERN PIKES PEAK INN.

3010 N Chestnut St, Colorado Springs (80907). Phone 719/636-5201. www.bestwestern.com. This friendly property features retro 1960s-period architecture and is centrally located to attractions. 150 rooms, 2 story. Check-in 3 pm, check-out 11 am. Laundry services. Fitness room. Outdoor pool. Complimentary continental breakfast. Business center. $

CHEYENNE MOUNTAIN RESORT.

3225 Broadmoor Valley Rd, Colorado Springs (80906). Phone 719/538-4000; toll-free 800/428-8886. www.cheyennemountain.com. You'll keep busy taking advantage of everything this family-friendly resort has to offer, including golf, a private stocked lake, swimming, and tennis courts. Keep an eye out for drivers—this is the official resort of the raceway. 316 rooms, 3 story. Check-in 4 pm, check-in noon. Fitness room. High-speed Internet access. Laundry services. Restaurants. Business center. $

HEARTHSTONE INN.

506 N Cascade Ave, Colorado Springs (80903). Phone 719/473-4413; toll-free 800/521-1885. www.hearthstoneinn.com. After indulging your speed demon at the track, slow things down at the Hearthstone Inn, the oldest and largest bed-and-breakfast in Colorado Springs. You'll be so distracted by the Victorian charm and period antiques that you won't notice that your room lacks a television and, most likely, a phone (only four rooms have them). 25 rooms, 3 story. Check-in 4 pm, check-out 11 am. Restaurant. $

PIT PASS

Pre-race traffic is difficult but manageable. The real challenge is afterwards, when 42,000-plus exiting fans create a bumper-to-bumper car conga. If you're headed north, however, cut your wait in half with a simple turn: when you exit, track personnel will direct you to a bridge that crosses over I-25. If you turn left onto I-25, you've joined the road rush. Turn right, cross railroad tracks, and you're on Old Pueblo Rd. When you reach Fountain, get back onto I-25 ahead of the game.

HOLDEN HOUSE 1902 BED & BREAKFAST.
1102 W Pikes Peak Ave, Colorado Springs (80904). Phone 719/471-3980; toll-free 888/565-3980. www.holdenhouse.com. Located in a historic house and carriage house dating from 1902, this inn has modern guest rooms with Victorian charm. Two pure-bred Siamese cats stand guard. 5 rooms, 2 story. No children allowed. Complimentary full breakfast. Check-in 4-6 pm, check-out 11 am. $

OLD TOWN GUEST HOUSE.
115 S 26th St, Colorado Springs (80904). Phone 719/632-9194; toll-free 888/375-4210. www.oldtownguesthouse.com. Built in 1997, this bed-and-breakfast has all of the amenities of a modern hotel, including an elevator, but it is located in the heart of Old Colorado City. 8 rooms, 3 story. Complimentary full breakfast. Check-in 4-6 pm, check-out 11 am. Fitness room. $

RESIDENCE INN BY MARRIOTT.
2765 Geyser Dr, Colorado Springs (80906). Phone 719/576-0101; toll-free 888/236-2427. www.marriott.com. It's all about options and simplicity. Outback Steakhouse is nearby, or you can fix something in your own kitchen. There is free access to a local Bally's or World Gym nearby. The rooms are spotless, the staff genuinely friendly, and the location convenient. There is a hospitality hour with complimentary food Monday through Thursday 5-7 pm. Families can check into the two-bedroom, two-bath suite that sleeps six. 72 rooms, 3 story. Pets accepted, some restrictions; fee. Check-in 3 pm, check-out noon. High-speed Internet access. Laundry services. Outdoor pool. Business center. $

Manitou Springs

BEST WESTERN SKYWAY INN SUITES.
311 Manitou Ave, Manitou Springs (80829). Phone 719/685-5991. www.bestwestern.com. Guests intrigued by all that Manitou Springs has to offer can stop by the front desk to pick up a generous stash of discount coupons for local attractions. When booking, ask for a room facing Cheyenne Mountain. 38 rooms, 2 story. Pets accepted, some restrictions; fee. Check-in 3 pm, check-out 11 am. High-speed Internet access. Indoor pool, whirlpool. $

THE CLIFF HOUSE AT PIKES PEAK.
306 Cañon Ave, Manitou Springs (80829). Phone 719/685-3000; toll-free 888/212-7000. www.thecliffhouse.com. The Cliff House is understated chic without an over-the-top price. The dining room and wine cellar repeatedly win national awards, and yet a jacket is a suggestion, not a requirement. Built before Colorado was even a state, every charming detail of a bygone Victorian age remains as modern details are added. 55 rooms, 4 story. Check-in 3 pm, check-out 11 am. High-speed Internet access. Laundry services. Restaurant. Fitness room. $$

Pueblo

ABRIENDO INN.
300 W Abriendo Ave, Pueblo (81004). Phone 719/544-2703. Each of the ten rooms at this intimate inn, just south of downtown Pueblo, is furnished with antiques and period furniture and includes a gourmet breakfast each morning as well as late-afternoon refreshments. Guests can relax on the large front porch that overlooks the residential area in which the inn is situated, or retreat to their in-room Jacuzzi. 10 rooms, 3 story. Children over 6 years only. Complimentary full breakfast. Check-in 4 pm, check-out 11 am. High-speed Internet access. $

RV AND CAMPING

Colorado Springs

GARDEN OF THE GODS CAMPGROUND.
3704 W Colorado Ave, Colorado Springs (80904). Phone 800/248-9451. www.coloradocampground.com. No frills, nice views, and a ten-minute drive away from downtown. "Camper cabins" also available.

Fountain

KOA COLORADO SPRINGS SOUTH.
8100 Brandley Dr, Fountain (80817). Phone 719/382-7575. This campground, with 300 RV sites, is the closest to the track, offers every amenity, and is run by a top-notch staff. Ask for a spot away from Interstate 25—and ask early, as this place is popular. Organized events, organized meals. Outdoor pool, hot tub, mini-golf. Phone hook-ups, business center, wireless Internet access. Coin laundry. Convenience store.

For more lodging recommendations, go to www.mobiltravelguide.com

EAT

MOBIL STAR-RATED RESTAURANTS

Colorado Springs

EDELWEISS. ★★
34 E Ramona Ave, Colorado Springs (80906). Phone 719/633-2220. This isn't your average schnitzel joint. Some authentic German dishes—Maultaschen, Wienerschnitzel, and bratwurst—are specialties, but more contemporary selections are also available, including tomato-mozzarella salad, chicken Provencal, and angel hair pasta with shrimp. German menu. Lunch, dinner. Closed Dec 25. Bar. Casual attire. Outdoor seating. **$$**

JAKE AND TELLY'S GREEK DINING. ★★
2660 W Colorado Ave, Colorado Springs (81903). Phone 719/633-0406. Although the majority of chefs Jake and Telly Topakas's recipes come from the kitchen of their *yia-yia,* others, like lemon chicken with a feta cream sauce over linguine, come from their own imaginations. Greek menu. Lunch, dinner. Closed Thanksgiving, Dec 25. Bar. Casual attire. Reservations recommended. Outdoor seating. **$$**

LA CREPERIE. ★
204 N Tejon, Colorado Springs (80903). Phone 719/632-0984. This tiny bistro—a former streetcar horse stable—proves there's more to French crepes than fresh fruit drowning in whipped cream, although those enticing choices are available. Diners can choose from fillings such as fresh asparagus, turkey breast, ham, fresh spinach, and cheddar cheese. Topped with sauces like béchamel, hollandaise, and Mornay, the varieties are endless. French menu. Breakfast, lunch, dinner. Closed Jan 1, Dec 25. Casual attire. Reservations recommended. Outdoor seating. **$$**

LA PETITE MAISON. ★★
1015 W Colorado Ave, Colorado Springs (80904). Phone 719/632-4887. This restored Victorian cottage may look modest on the outside, but inside you'll find a charming, intimate space in which to enjoy American cuisine with a strong French influence. The restaurant has been owned and operated by Jeff Mervis for more than 25 years, and the outstanding ambience, menu, and wine list have also remained consistent. American menu. Lunch, dinner. Closed Sun-Mon; Jan 1, July 4, Dec 24-25. Reservations recommended. Outdoor seating. **$$$**

MACKENZIE'S CHOP HOUSE. ★★
128 S Tejon, Colorado Springs (80903). Phone 719/635-3536. www.mackenzieschophouse.com. Serious steak and seafood are served here with Rat Pack-esque flair. The indulgent mood is achieved with dark woods, stone masonry, and, most importantly, a marvelously decadent menu, which includes steak classics like prime rib, filet mignon, and porterhouse. Be sure to consider the day's Blue Plate Special and the tapas/martini menu. Steak, seafood menu. Lunch, dinner. Closed holidays. Outdoor seating. **$$$**

ROAD FOOD

When you visit **King's Chef,** it doesn't matter what mood you're in to order the Grump, a pile of hash browns, meat, onions, cheese, eggs, and gravy that weighs nearly 2 pounds. Open since 1956, King's Chef is one of the last remaining Valentine microdiners. Try the green chili or perfectly charred burgers; the service is like an old friend. Cash or check only. *110 E Costilla, Colorado Springs, 80903. Phone 719/634-9135. www.kingschefdiner.com.*

BRAKE HERE

If you'd rather stay at home than in a hotel, the closest you can get is renting a cabin from **Colorado Mountain Cabins and Vacation Home Rentals** (phone 719/636-5147; toll-free 866/425-4974. www.coloradomountaincabins.com). There's no maid or trash service in these fully furnished homes—just like at home—and most of the cabins are at least 30 minutes outside Colorado Springs, but they are a great alternative for families, nature lovers—or both.

Manitou Springs

MISSION BELL INN. ★★
178 Crystal Park Rd, Manitou Springs (80829). Phone 719/685-9089. www.missionbellinn.com. The first word that comes to mind when eating at this Mexican restaurant is "colorful"—the décor, margaritas, plates, and food all appear in vibrant Southwest hues. The second, unfortunately, for indecisive diners, is "combination platter." Mexican menu. Dinner. Closed Jan 1, Thanksgiving, Dec 25. Outdoor seating. **$$**

STAGE COACH. ★★
702 Manitou Ave, Manitou Springs (80829). Phone 719/685-9400. If you've never tried buffalo before, this is the place to do it, where slow-roasted buffalo dishes are the house specialty. Your decision may still be quite difficult, as you'll also be faced with old favorites like London broil, crab cakes, and chicken potpie. Steak menu. Dinner. Closed Jan 1, Dec 25. Bar. Outdoor seating. **$$**

LOCAL RECOMMENDATIONS

Colorado Springs

FAMOUS STEAKHOUSE.
31 N Tejon St, Colorado Springs (80903). Phone 719/227-7333. www.famoussteakhouse.com. "We don't serve ice cream," brags one of the owners of this eatery. The point? No freezer. Everything arrives fresh, including the corn-fed Iowa steaks that make this place, well, famous. At $37.95, the 20-ounce Prime Kansas City Bone-In Strip isn't cheap, but locals swear there is no place else they'd rather max out their credit cards or waistlines. Steak menu. Lunch, dinner. **$$$**

JOSH AND JOHN'S NATURALLY HOMEMADE ICE CREAMS.
111 E Pikes Peak Ave, Colorado Springs (80903). Phone 719/632-0299. www.joshandjohns.com. It took these two Colorado ice cream friends to give us a true American flavor like Jack Daniels. If that sounds like it might make you a wee bit wobbly, opt for Rocky Mountain Road. Here, it's all hand-churned. **$**

MASON JAR.
2925 W Colorado Ave, Colorado Springs (80904). Phone 719/632-4820. Don't let the down-home charm and comfort-food menu fool you. Besides the best budget meat and taters in town and a chicken-fried steak for the ages, the famed blackberry margarita is known to pack a flavorful wallop. The children's menu is one of the most complete around. Smokers can relax in a separate dining room. American menu. Lunch, dinner. Children's menu. **$**

PHANTOM CANYON BREWING COMPANY.
2 E Pikes Peak Ave, Colorado Springs (80903). Phone 719/635-2800. www.phantomcanyon.com. Colorado has more brewpubs than anywhere in the country, and none is better or more family-friendly than Phantom Canyon. It has won awards for its beers, and the menu is always changing, but count on some unusually tasty options including the calamari appetizer, fish and chips, pot roast, trout, buffalo burgers, and the chocolate peanut butter crunch, a dessert whose secret ingredient is Cocoa Puffs. The upstairs pool hall has 13 tables available by the hour and serves a pared-down pub menu until 1 am. American menu. Lunch, dinner, Sun brunch. **$$**

For more dining recommendations, go to www.mobiltravelguide.com

SIDETRIP
High-Altitude Adventure
Summit County, CO

If you've come to Colorado to play, don't miss a visit to Summit County. At its center is **Lake Dillon** (Dillon Marina, phone 970/468-5100, www.dillonmarina.com), where you can sail, canoe, kayak, or enjoy motorized water sports. If you want fishing, opt for one of the lake's tributaries: Blue River, Ten Mile Creek, or Snake River.

On one side of the lake is Dillon (phone 970/468-2403, www.ci.dillon.co.us), the other, Frisco (phone 970/668-5276, www.townoffrisco.com). Dillon's got the theaters and bowling alley. Frisco's got the cute main street and antiquing opportunities. Deals are plentiful at the nearby **Silverthorne Factory Stores** (phone toll-free 866/746-7686, www.silverthornefactorystores.com).

In the surrounding mountains, you'll find as much to do at a ski resort in the summer as in the winter. Your best bet is **Breckenridge** (phone 970/453-2913, www.gobreck.com), a one-time Victorian mining town that offers the most on-mountain fun and a quirky nightlife.

All the resorts allow you to ride the chairs up and hike around or bomb the descent on a mountain bike. Breck distinguishes itself with the **Peak 8 Fun Park** (phone 970/453-5000, www.breckenridge.snow.com/info/summer/ea.peak8.asp). There's a climbing wall, zip lines, high-alpine mini-golf, and the SuperSlide, an upright luge-type ride down a steep course.

The Breckenridge Golf Club (phone 970/453-9104, www.breckenridgegolfclub.com) offers 27 holes over three courses and is the only municipally owned Jack Nicklaus-designed course in the world.

Reward your athletic accomplishments with a trip to **Café Alpine** (106 E Adams Ave, phone 970/453-8218), where the menu changes nightly based on what's fresh and locally available. The converted home is an unpretentious setting for food so tasty and tastefully presented that one local said, "Eating here is like sticking your fork in a Picasso." Or take in a diverse musical lineup at the **Breckenridge Music Festival** (June-Sept; phone 970/453-9142, www.breckenridgemusicfestival.com).

Come on in, the snow is fine at Breckenridge, a perfect place to play after the race.

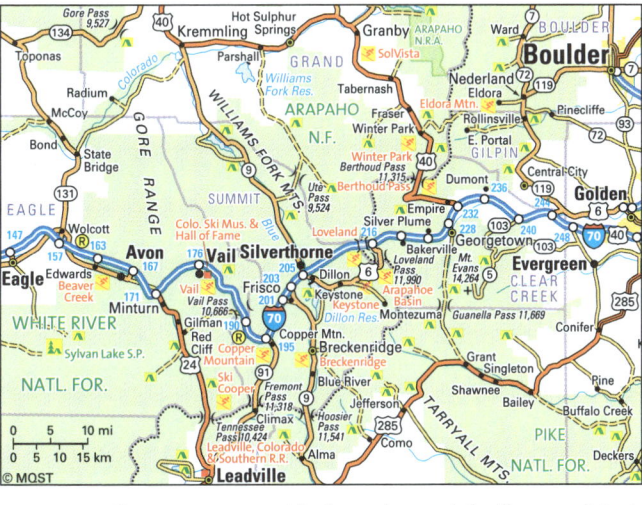

For more Summit County recommendations, go to www.mobiltravelguide.com

A huge infield crowd enjoys the Pocono 500 in the NASCAR NEXTEL Series on June 13, 2004, which was won by Jimmie Johnson.

Pocono Raceway

Long Pond, PA

25

A view from the Terrace Club during the August 1, 2004, running of the NASCAR NEXTEL Cup Pennsylvania 500.

TRACK FACTS

POCONO RACEWAY. Long Pond Rd, Long Pond (18334). Phone toll-free 800/722-3929. www.poconoraceway.com.

SECURITY. In the grandstands, coolers can be no larger than 12 x 12 x 12 inches; glass containers are prohibited. In the overnight parking areas, prohibited items include tent camping, pets, ground fires, fireworks, weapons, ATVs, motorcycles, mopeds, golf carts, and utility vehicles.

PARKING. There is free daytime parking in lots along Long Pond Road, with shuttle service to the raceway entrance. Parking is also available in the infield for campers and for fans who buy a one-day infield ticket. Handicapped parking is available next to the bus-parking area, behind the grandstands.

FIRST AID. There are three first aid centers: near the grandstands, in the paddock, and in the infield. Trauma doctors, nurses, and ambulances are on site during the day. At night, physicians' assistants, paramedics, and ambulances are available. The paddock and infield treatment centers are open 24 hours a day. Medical services are supplied by Lehigh Valley Hospital and Health Network, a level-one trauma hospital.

CONCESSIONS. Food and souvenir stands are located at each spectator viewing area and each overnight parking area.

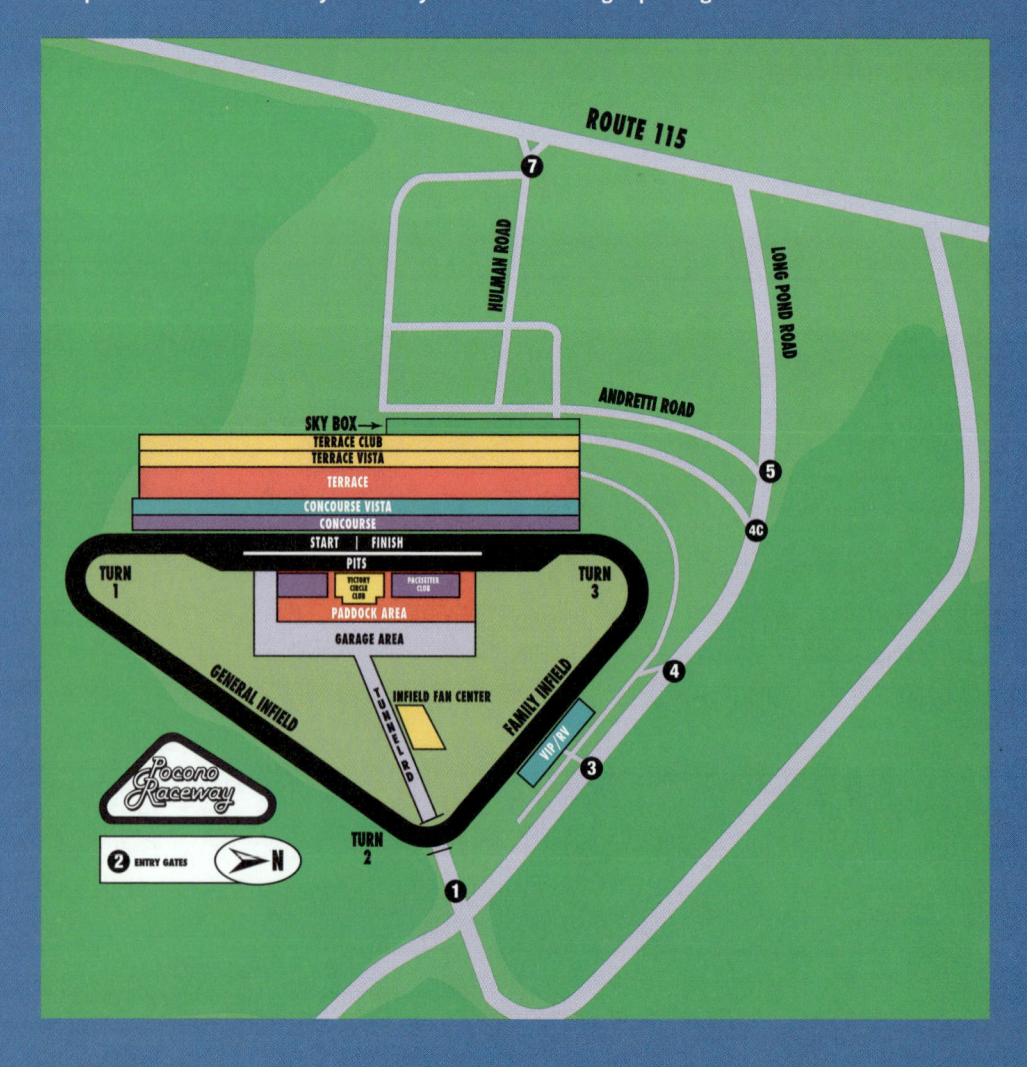

The track's unique triangular shape generates fender-to-fender action in the curves and 200-mile-per-hour blasts down the straights.

GETTING AROUND

Twice each year, Pocono Raceway becomes the third-largest city in Pennsylvania. At 6 am on race day, Hwy 115 is converted to three inbound lanes. At about lap 190 of 200 in the race, traffic switches to one-way outbound, and stays that way for up to three hours after the race ends. Other roads are also turned into one-way routes.

While there are no magical ins and outs, back roads can keep you out of the worst of the mess. The key is to avoid the 3-mile stretch along Hwy 115 between the raceway and I-80. Coming from the east on I-80, take Exit 299 and head south on Hwy 715 until you dead-end at Hwy 115. Turn right and drive 7 miles to the raceway. From the east on US 22, take Hwy 33 N just west of Easton. Exit at US 209 and drive west about 5 miles to Hwy 115. Turn right to the raceway.

Traveling from the north on I-380, get off at Exit 3 onto Hwy 940 W. At the first light, you will see a sign directing you to turn left for the raceway; don't. Instead, keep driving on Hwy 940 about 4 miles to Stony Hollow Rd. Turn left and drive under I-80 until it dead-ends, then turn right onto Long Pond Rd. From the west on I-80, the closer you are to race time, the more you should try to avoid Exit 284. If traffic is backed up at the exit, you may have better luck heading over to I-380 and following the instructions above.

Shortcuts aside, the best advice is to come early, stay late, and enjoy yourself. The parking lots are full of tailgaters grilling and socializing. After the race, by the time you've cooked dinner, eaten and relaxed, traffic will have cleared and you can head home.

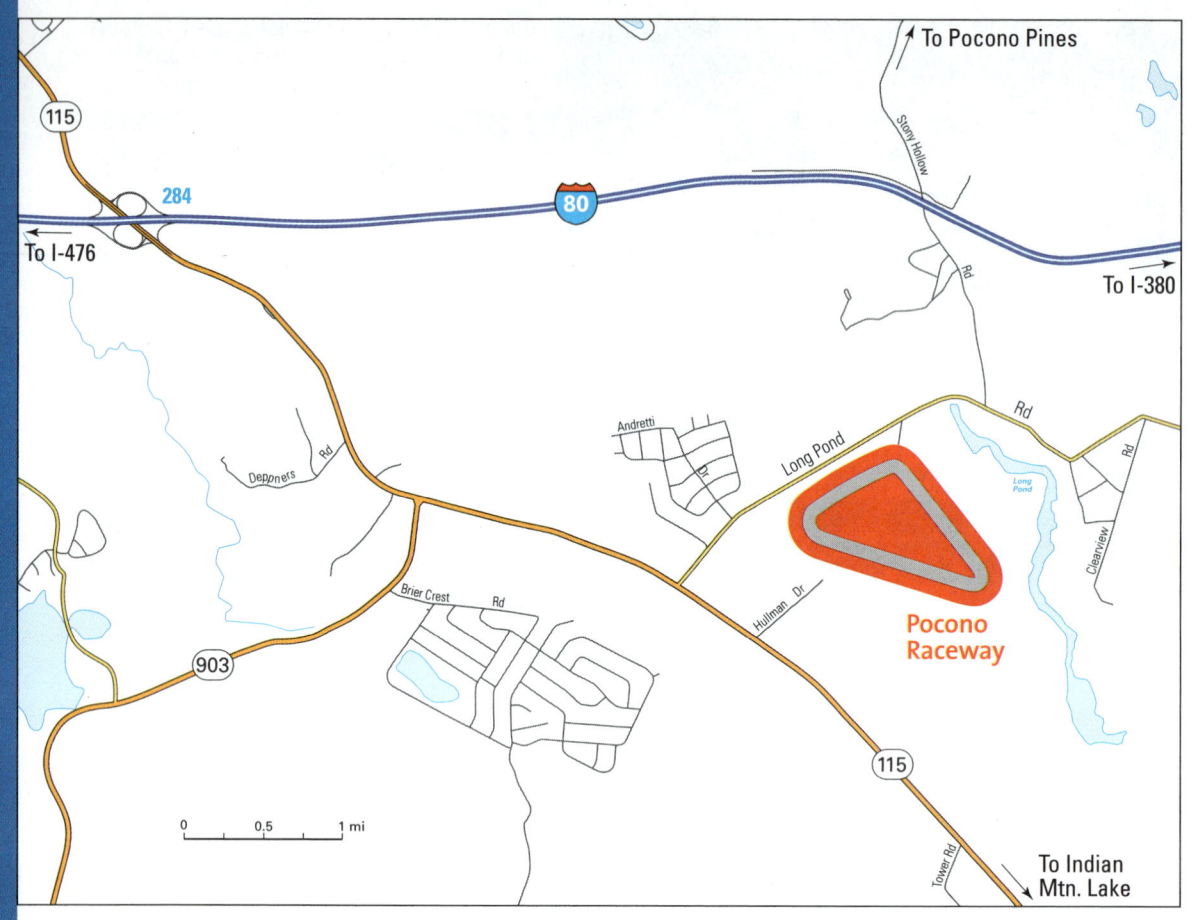

LONG POND POLE POSITION:
The 10 miles surrounding Pocono Raceway.

RETREAT TO THE MOUNTAINS

Pocono Raceway is located in a remote section of the Pocono Mountains in northeastern Pennsylvania, about 90 miles from both Philadelphia and New York City. Perhaps best known by many people as a honeymoon haven, and home to many couples-only resorts, the Poconos are still a popular family vacation destination. It is not difficult to combine a noise- and speed-filled visit to a NASCAR race with a longer, quieter stay at a nearby campground, resort, motel, or cabin.

The area covers about 2,400 square miles and includes seven state parks, 72,000 acres of state forests, the 70,000-acre **Delaware Water Gap National Recreation Area** (phone 570/588-2452, www.nps. gov/dewa), 150 lakes, and scores of rivers, streams, waterfalls, and hiking trails. It is busy year-round with vacationers and adventurers, and small towns such as Jim Thorpe and Stroudsburg attract many visitors. Get more information on the Poconos from the **Pocono Mountains Vacation Bureau** (phone 570/424-6050, toll-free 800/762-6667; www.800poconos.com).

Summer weather in the Poconos can be unpredictable—hot, dry, and sunny one week and cold, wet, and gray the next. Since it is in the mountains (well, this ain't the Rockies, but you are well above sea level), check the weather forecast at the raceway on an online weather site by entering the local ZIP code, 18334. If you are camping, bring clothing and gear for a full range of weather possibilities.

POCONO RACEWAY, PA **415**

LONG POND CALENDAR

MAY 28–29, 2005
Irish and Celtic Festival. Jack Frost Mountain, Blakeslee (18610). Phone toll-free 800/468-2442. www.jfbb.com. Music festival with Irish flair, food, and fun.

JUNE 4, 2005 (AND JULY 2, 2005)
First Saturday Downtown Stroudsburg Art Walk. Stroudsburg (18360). Phone 570/424-9131. www.stroudsburg.net. Visit galleries and shops, meet the artists, and have dinner.

JUNE 12, 2005
NASCAR NEXTEL Cup Series Laurel Blossom Festival, Jim Thorpe. Arts and crafts, entertainment, and steam-train rides.

JULY 24, 2005
NASCAR NEXTEL Cup Series

JULY 29–31, 2005
Pocono Blues Festival. Big Boulder Mountain, Blakeslee (18610). Phone toll-free 800/468-2442. www.jfbb.com. Enjoy three days of soul-lifting blues on three stages.

AUGUST, 2005
Das Awkscht Fescht (The August Festival). Macungie Memorial Park, Macungie (18062). Phone 610/967-2317. www.awkscht.com. Antique, classic, and sports cars; arts and crafts; antique toy show, entertainment, food, and fireworks. First weekend in August.

Kids will have a splashing good time at Camelbeach Waterpark.

DRIVER'S PICK

Two-time Daytona 500 winner and driver of the DEI No. 15 Chevrolet **Michael Waltrip** doesn't just like Pocono for the track. "I love a German restaurant called **The Edelweiss.** You've got to try the Steak on a Stone with a lobster tail." *Rte 940, Pocono Lake (18347). Phone 570/646-3938.*

LONG POND OUTFIELD:
The 40 miles surrounding Pocono Raceway.

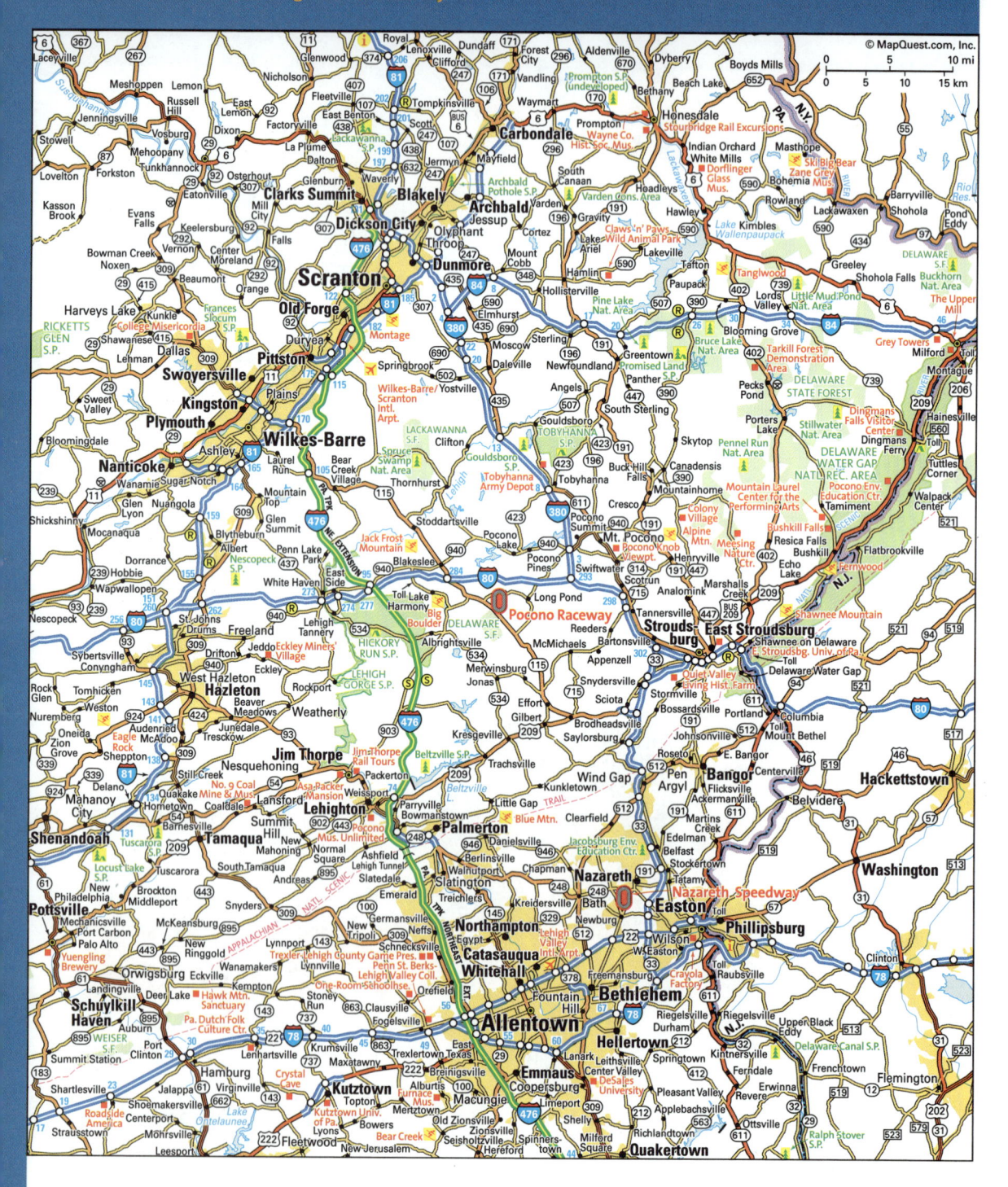

SEE

ATTRACTIONS

DELAWARE WATER GAP NATIONAL RECREATION AREA.
Phone 570/588-2452. www.nps.gov/dewa. The recreation area covers about 70,000 acres for 40 miles along the Delaware River in Pennsylvania and New Jersey. Camping, hiking, swimming, canoeing, horseback riding, and fishing are abundant. Sign up for a guided trolley tour (phone 570/476-9766) in the town of Delaware Water Gap, off Interstate 80, exit 310. Some user fees. **FREE**

Easton

CRAYOLA FACTORY.
30 Centre Sq, at Two Rivers Landing, Easton (18042). Phone 610/515-8000; toll-free 800/CRAYOLA. www.crayola.com. This isn't the main factory, which is several miles away, but it explains how crayons and markers are manufactured. There are lots of colorful interactive exhibits and plenty of opportunities to draw and color to your heart's content. (Hours vary.) **$$**

Jim Thorpe

This town of about 5,000 is named after the Native American star of the 1912 Olympic Games. The **historic district** is a treat, with antiques shops, art galleries, and museums. The well-preserved **Asa Packer Mansion Museum** (phone 570/325-3229, www.asapackermansionmuseum.homestead.com) is a remarkable Victorian home with original furnishings and woodwork. The **Old Jail Museum** (phone 570/325-5259) is full of historical significance. Local businesses such as **Jim Thorpe River Adventures** (phone 570/325-2570, www.jtraft.com) and **Blue Mountain Sports** (phone toll-free 800/599-4421, www.bikejimthorpe.com) offer whitewater rafting, kayaking, and mountain biking services.

Pocono Summit

SUMMIT LANES.
3 Park Dr E, Pocono Summit (18346). Phone 570/839-9635. www.summitlanes.com. Summit Lanes is a terrific bowling center with 36 new state-of-the-art synthetic lanes and automatic scorers with color monitors. It also has a nice billiards area, food court, pro shop, lounge, and video game room. Traveling west on Highway 940 from Highway 611, take a right at the Salvation Army onto Summit Avenue. Drive a half-mile to Park Drive East. (Daily; glow bowling Sat to 2 am.) **$**

Scranton

HOUDINI MUSEUM.
1433 N Main Ave, Scranton (18508). Phone 570/342-5555. www.houdini.org. This museum is devoted to the career and life of the great magician Harry Houdini. Tours, films featuring Houdini himself, and a magic show (with live animals) are all included. **$$$**

LACKAWANNA COAL MINE TOUR.
McDade Park (off Keyser Ave), Scranton (18503). Phone 570/963-6463; toll-free 800/238-7245. The tour of this underground coal mine provides a realistic glimpse of the working lives of anthracite miners in an earlier time. A 5-minute ride in a coal-mine car takes you into the cool and damp mine, and the ensuing hour-long tour will enlighten you about the hazards and harsh conditions faced by miners, as well as the unfortunate pit ponies, who lived permanently in the mine. Wear appropriate clothing.

Tannersville

CAMELBEACH WATERPARK.
300 Camelback Rd, Tannersville (18372). Phone 570/629-1661; toll-free 800/245-5900. www.camelbeach.com. Come wintertime, this play station is better known as Camelback Ski Area. Through the summer, however, Camelbeach has 22 water slides, including speed slides, body slides, a "Checkered Flag Challenge" ride that allows up to eight people to race, a wave pool, and a family tube slide. **$$$$**

For more attractions, go to www.mobiltravelguide.com

STAY

MOBIL STAR-RATED LODGINGS

Lake Harmony

POCONO RAMADA INN. ★★

Rte 940, Lake Harmony (18661). Phone 570/443-8471; toll-free 800/251-2610. www.poconoramada.com. Set in a wooded area, this hotel offers a variety of activities including a game room, basketball, volleyball, and miniature golf course. 138 rooms, 4 story. Pets accepted, some restrictions; fee. Check-in 4 pm, check-out noon. Two restaurants, bar. Indoor pool. Airport transportation available. $

Mount Pocono

CAESAR'S PARADISE STREAM. ★★★

Rte 940, Mount Pocono (18344). Phone 570/839-8881; toll-free 800/233-4141. www.caesarspoconoresorts.com. For that "honeymoon" experience for which the Poconos are so well known, Caesar's is the place to stay. Of the three adult-only Caesar's Pocono Resorts locations, this is the closest to Pocono Raceway. These are all-inclusive resorts, with heart-shaped tubs, round beds, and champagne-glass-shaped whirlpools that offer a romantic contrast to a day at the races. Big names often entertain. 164 rooms, 4 story. No children allowed. Check-in 3 pm, check-out 11 am. Restaurant, bar. Fitness room. Indoor pool, outdoor pool, whirlpool. Tennis. $$$

Scotrun

CAESAR'S BROOKDALE. ★★

Hwy 611 and Brookdale Rd, Scotrun (18355). Phone 570/839-8844; toll-free 800/233-4141. www.caesarspoconoresorts.com. This Caesar's Pocono Resorts location is closest to Pocono Raceway and the only one that allows children. Organized around a private lake, Caesar's Brookdale offers paddleboats, sailboats, and canoes for cruising the lake. Other activities include a playground, bicycling and in-line skating, hiking and jogging paths, miniature golf, fishing, and a game room. 119 rooms, 4 story. Check-in 3 pm, check-out 11 am. Restaurant, bar. Children's activity center. Fitness room. Indoor pool, outdoor pool, children's pool, whirlpool. Tennis. $$

Wilkes-Barre

HAMPTON INN WILKES-BARRE AT CROSS CREEK POINT. ★

1063 Hwy 315, Wilkes-Barre (18702). Phone 570/825-3838; toll-free 800/426-7866. www.hamptoninn.com. 123 rooms, 5 story. Complimentary continental breakfast. Check-in 3 pm, check-out 11 am. $

HOLIDAY INN WILKES-BARRE (ARENA). ★★

880 Kidder St, Wilkes-Barre (18702). Phone 570/824-8901; toll-free 800/465-4329. www.holiday-inn.com. 120 rooms, 2 story. Pets accepted, some restrictions. Check-in 3 pm, check-out 11 am. Restaurant, bar. Indoor pool, outdoor pool, children's pool. $

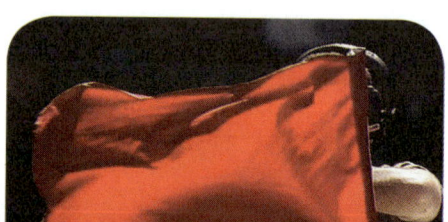

BRAKE HERE

What do stock car racers do with their free time? Some downsize at the **Lehigh Valley Quarter Midget Racing Club,** on raceway grounds near Gate 5, which holds races Saturday evenings. The track is modeled after the raceway. Drivers such as Kasey Kahne, Tony Stewart, Jeff Gordon, Dale Earnhardt Jr, and Jimmie Johnson have all been spotted at the indoor go-kart track at **S&S Speedways.** *Business Rte 209 in Snydersville. Phone 570/420-5500. www.ssspeedways.com.*

WOODLANDS INN AND RESORT. ★ ★ ★

1073 Hwy 315, Wilkes-Barre (18702). Phone 570/824-9831; toll-free 800/762-2222. www.thewoodlandsresort.com. The Woodlands Inn and Resort offers urbanites a chance to bask in nature. This wooded resort on 40 acres in the foothills of the Poconos is a perfect place to spend a family vacation. Golf and skiing are just a short distance away. The resort has five nightclubs, bars, and lounges, with live jazz and dancing. Thymes restaurant features delicious European-influenced dining with scenic views of the Laurel Run Stream. 179 rooms, 9 story. Check-out noon. Restaurant, bar. Fitness room. Indoor pool, outdoor pool, whirlpool. Tennis. Airport transportation available. $

LOCAL RECOMMENDATIONS

Blakeslee

BEST WESTERN INN AT BLAKESLEE-POCONO.

Rte 115, Blakeslee (18610). Phone 570/646-6000; toll-free 888/296-2466. www.bestwestern.com. Located just north of exit 284 off Interstate 80, this fairly new facility fills up fast, so reserve well in advance. 85 rooms, 3 story. Pets accepted, some restrictions. Complimentary continental breakfast. Check-in 3 pm, check-out noon. Laundry services. Fitness room. Indoor pool. 2 1/2 miles from Pocono Raceway. $

BLUE BERRY MOUNTAIN INN.

Thomas Rd, Blakeslee (18610). Phone 570/646-7144. www.blueberrymountaininn.com. This comfortable, smoke-free bed-and-breakfast is in a quiet, rural setting surrounded by mountains, streams, lakes, and ponds. Canoes, rowboats, fishing, picnic facilities, and a hiking trail are offered here. 6 rooms. Complimentary full breakfast. Check-in 3 pm, check-out noon. Indoor pool. $

Easton

BEST WESTERN EASTON INN.

185 S Third St, Easton (18042). Phone 610/253-9131; toll-free 800/882-0113. www.bestwestern.com. This hotel is located in downtown Easton, two blocks from Hugh Moore State Park, where the Delaware River and canal meet the Lehigh River. Pets accepted, some restrictions. Check-in 3 pm, check-out noon. Indoor pool. $

Hazleton

BEST WESTERN GENETTI LODGE.

Hwy 309, exit 262, Hazleton (18202). Phone 570/454-2494; toll-free 800/780-7234. www.bestwestern.com. Genetti Lodge is located in a commercial area surrounded by woods. 85 rooms, 2 story. Pets accepted, some restrictions. Complimentary continental breakfast. Check-in 3 pm, check-out 11 am. Laundry services. Restaurant. Outdoor pool. $

Jim Thorpe

THE INN AT JIM THORPE.

24 Broadway, Jim Thorpe (18229). Phone 570/325-2599; toll-free 800/329-2599. www.innjt.com. This historic country inn is located in the center of Jim Thorpe. The inn was built in the 1840s and has wrought-iron exterior balconies and rooms decorated in a Victorian style. The restaurant offers classic cuisine, while the Irish pub has simpler fare. 45 rooms, 4 story. Complimentary continental breakfast. Check-in 3 pm, check-out 11 am. Restaurant, bar. Fitness room. $

Pocono Lake

SULLIVAN TRAIL MOTEL.

Hwy 940, Pocono Lake (18347). Phone 570/646-3535. www.sullivantrailmotel.com. This moderately priced motel is a short drive from Pocono Raceway. Cottages are also available. 25 rooms, 1 story. Check-in 1 pm, check-out 11 am. Outdoor pool. $

Pocono Pines

MOUNTAINTOP LODGE.

Hwy 940, Pocono Pines (18350). Phone 570/646-6636. www.mountaintoplodge.com. Restored inn that offers modern conveniences in a country setting. Boat and canoe rentals are available. 12 rooms. Complimentary full breakfast. Check-in 3 pm, check-out 11 am. Beach. Outdoor pool. Tennis. $

Stroudsburg

BEST WESTERN POCONO INN.

700 Main St, Stroudsburg (18360). Phone 570/421-2200; toll-free 888/508-2378. www.bestwestern.com. Located in downtown Stroudsburg, within easy walking distance of many stores and shops, this is a nice place to stay if you plan to explore the Delaware Water Gap National Recreation Area or shop and play in the

Tannersville area. 90 rooms, 4 story. Complimentary continental breakfast. Check-in 3 pm, check-out 11 am. Laundry services. Two restaurants, bar. Indoor pool, whirlpool. $

Wilkes-Barre

BEST WESTERN EAST MOUNTAIN INN AND SUITES.

2400 East End Blvd, Wilkes-Barre (18702). Phone 570/822-1011; toll-free 800/780-7234. www.bestwestern.com. This property is located in a commercial area on a hilltop overlooking Wilkes-Barre and the Pocono Mountains. 156 rooms, 7 story. Check-in 3 pm, check-out noon. Two restaurants, bar. Fitness room. Indoor pool, whirlpool. Airport transportation available. $

BEST WESTERN GENETTI HOTEL AND CONFERENCE CENTER.

77 E Market St, Wilkes-Barre (18701). Phone 570/823-6152; toll-free 800/833-6152. www.bestwestern.com. This hotel is located in downtown Wilkes-Barre. 74 rooms, 5 story. Complimentary continental breakfast. Check-in 3 pm, check-out noon. Laundry services. Restaurant. Fitness room. Outdoor pool. $

RV AND CAMPING

Blakeslee

WT FAMILY CAMPING.

Rte 115, exit 284, Blakeslee (18610). Phone 570/646-9255. www.wtfamily.com. A clean, friendly campground a couple of miles south of Pocono Raceway with plenty of activities for the entire family. Heated pool, miniature golf, and special weekend events. Wooded sites with picnic tables and fire rings. Tent, trailer, and RV camping with full hook-ups. Convenience store. Propane, ice, and firewood available. Heated bathrooms.

Mount Pocono

MOUNT POCONO CAMPGROUND.

30 Edgewood Rd, Mount Pocono (18344). Phone 570/839-8950. www.mtpoconocampground.com. Campsites for every need on 42 wooded acres. Sunny or shaded locations. RVs, campers, tents. Full hook-ups (with cable), electric and water only, electric only, or no amenities. Heated outdoor pool, children's pool, playground, hiking trail, game room, volleyball, picnic facilities, and a grocery and camping supply store.

PIT PASS

Camping is available on raceway grounds—the best location might be in the Trackside RV section, where RVs pull up alongside the track between Turns 2 and 3. The Reserved Family Infield RV area and several other camping locations are available, some reserved and some first-come, first-served. Reserved RV camping spots sell out well in advance of the race (vehicle and per-person fees). Only self-contained RVs can enter the infield before Sunday. No dump stations, water, or electric hook-ups; restrooms and showers in the infield.

Stroudsburg

DELAWARE WATER GAP KOA.

233 Hollow Rd, East Stroudsburg (18301). Phone 570/223-8000; toll-free 800/562-0375. www.koa.com. Like many KOA facilities, this one offers supervised children's activities and has an outdoor pool, playground, game room, laundry facilities, and a store with camping supplies and groceries. Wooded and open sites, electric hook-ups, and propane.

For more lodging recommendations, go to www.mobiltravelguide.com

EAT

MOBIL STAR-RATED RESTAURANTS

Scranton

COOPER'S SEAFOOD HOUSE. ★

701 N Washington Ave, Scranton (18509). Phone 570/346-6883. www.coopers-seafood.com. The menu features fresh fish and seafood dishes, as well as steaks, chicken, and the standard children's menu fare. The restaurant enhances its nautical theme with a pirate ship replica and a newly constructed lighthouse. American menu. Lunch, dinner. Closed holidays. Bar. Children's menu. **$$**

Stroudsburg

ARLINGTON DINER. ★

834 N 9th St, Stroudsburg (18360). Phone 570/421-2329. With tons of small-town charm, this local hangout serves standard fare, and the service is usually with a smile, although, in keeping with the legend of the American diner, you might run into a grump now and again. American menu. Dinner. Children's menu. Casual attire. **$$**

BROWNIE'S IN THE BURG. ★

700 Main St, Stroudsburg (18360). Phone 570/421-2200. An ideal place to start the morning—nestle into a booth, order up some waffles or eggs Benedict, and people-watch as you sip your coffee. The café also serves lunch and dinner; try its "Almost Famous Hot Wings," apparently undiscovered by the masses, but nonetheless revered by many. American menu. Breakfast, lunch, dinner. Casual attire. **$$**

SARAH STREET GRILL. ★

550 Quaker Alley, Stroudsburg (18360). Phone 570/424-9120. www.sarahstreetgrill.com. This local grill seems like your everyday pub until you look at the menu. You'll find not only a selection of American favorites like burgers and pasta, but also a sushi menu with 19 kinds of sushi and ten types of California rolls. Whether you spring for the sushi menu or stick with the classics, the food and atmosphere guarantee a great experience. American, sushi menu. Lunch, dinner. Bar. Casual attire. Outdoor seating. **$$**

STONE BAR INN. ★ ★

Rte 209, Stroudsburg (18360). Phone 570/992-6634. This restaurant is celebrated as one of the area's best and features a comfortable, yet elegant atmosphere. Enjoy a drink at the stone bar or grab a spot on the patio for a romantic meal. Especially enticing are the wild boar rib chop with spiced apple cider sauce and the spinach and ricotta involtini. American menu. Dinner. Bar. Reservations recommended. Outdoor seating. **$$**

ROAD FOOD — don't miss it

Don't let the beer-brewing core of **Barley Creek Brewing Company** keep you from bringing the family. The menu offers burgers, steaks, fish and chips, quesadillas, fresh oysters and clams, and kid-friendly items. Kids get crayons and a game room in this establishment, built in a renovated farmhouse. A huge covered outdoor dining deck is a fine place to relax even when rain is falling. Brewery tours offered 12:30 pm weekdays. American menu. Lunch, dinner, late-night. Outdoor seating. **$$** *Sullivan Trail and Camelback Rd, Tannersville (18372). Phone 570/629-9399. www.barleycreek.com.*

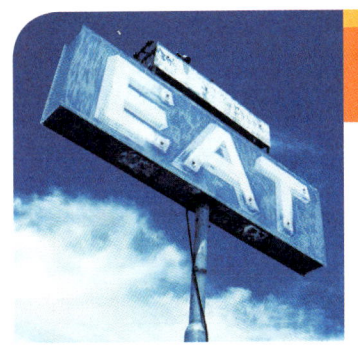

White Haven

POWERHOUSE. ★★★
Off I-80, exit 273, White Haven (18661). Phone 570/443-4480. The Powerhouse is located 11 miles west of the Pocono Raceway and is popular both for its Italian-American menu as well as the brick walls and exposed pipes and valves that serve as reminders of its earlier function as a coal-fueled power plant. American, Italian menu. Lunch, dinner. Closed Dec 24-25. Reservations recommended (weekends). $$

LOCAL RECOMMENDATIONS

Mount Pocono

BIG DADDY'S.
Hwy 611, Mount Pocono (18344). Phone 570/839-9281. Big Daddy's is a comfortable, casual family restaurant with a loyal local clientele. The varied menu offers sandwiches and ribs, stir-fries, and quesadillas. American menu. Lunch, dinner. Casual attire. Outdoor seating. $$

Pocono Pines

JUBILEE RESTAURANT.
Hwy 940, Pocono Pines (18350). Phone 570/646-2377. www.breakfastking.com. Van Gilder's Jubilee Restaurant is the self-proclaimed "Breakfast King," and it's hard to argue. The breakfast menu is enormous, offering dozens of different omelets, pancakes, and waffles, as well as creamed chipped beef, eggs Benedict, and biscuits with sausage gravy. The Jubilee also serves lunch and dinner, which can include hickory-smoked ribs and chicken, as well as steaks, meatloaf, pasta, and seafood. American menu. Breakfast, lunch, dinner. Children's menu. Casual attire. $

Pocono Summit

TOKYO TEA HOUSE.
Hwy 940, W of I-380, Pocono Summit (18346). Phone 570/839-8880. This restaurant offers some of the best sushi in the Poconos. Like many fine eateries, it's located in a shopping center. Japanese menu. Lunch, dinner. Closed Tues; also July-Aug. $$

Snydersville

SNYDERSVILLE FAMILY DINER.
Business Hwy 209, Snydersville (18360). Phone 570/992-4003. The wait at this diner is worth it. This fairly large (by diner standards) establishment has a couple of booths big enough to handle an extended family. The menu is huge, and breakfast is served all day long. The dozen or more types of homemade pies are worth the trip. American menu. Breakfast, lunch, dinner. Casual attire. No credit cards accepted. $$

Stroudsburg

PEPPE'S RISTORANTE.
Eagle Valley Mall, Business Hwys 209 and 447, East Stroudsburg (18301). Phone 570/421-4460. www.peppesonline.com. Peppe's has an extensive menu that features northern Italian cuisine. Homemade pasta, seafood, veal, and the Caesar salad are popular choices here, while steaks, chops, and poultry dishes are also offered. Italian menu. Dinner. Children's menu. Casual attire. Reservations recommended. $$$

Tannersville

SMUGGLER'S COVE.
Hwy 611, 1 mile S of Hwy 715, Tannersville (18372). Phone 570/629-2277. www.smugglerscove.net. Smuggler's Cove's big parking lot is often filled. This is a good spot to visit for lunch or dinner if you are in the mood for seafood, although steaks and burgers are also offered. Seafood, steak menu. Lunch, dinner. Bar. Casual attire. $$

For more dining recommendations, go to www.mobiltravelguide.com

SIDETRIP

A Sweet Adventure
Hershey, PA

Indulge your sweet temptations in Hershey's chocolate fantasyland, complete with Kiss-shaped street lamps and chocolate-themed amusement park.

The state of Pennsylvania has its share of unusual place names, but Hershey's is the sweetest. The town itself was founded by Milton Hershey, who began making chocolate bars there in 1903. As the business grew, so did the community, and what was once a company town is now a very popular entertainment and tourist center. Most of the primary attractions are located adjacent to one another between Highway 743 (Hershey Park Dr) and Highway 422 (Chocolate Ave). **Hersheypark** has more than 60 rides and attractions, including 11 roller coasters and six water rides. The brand-new Storm Runner is not to be missed. It rises 18 stories up and accelerates to 72 miles per hour in a mere two seconds. The park has many rides suitable for small children, as well as live entertainment, games, shops, and plenty of decent food. With your Hersheypark admission, you can also enter the **ZooAmerica** wildlife park, which houses more than 200 animals.

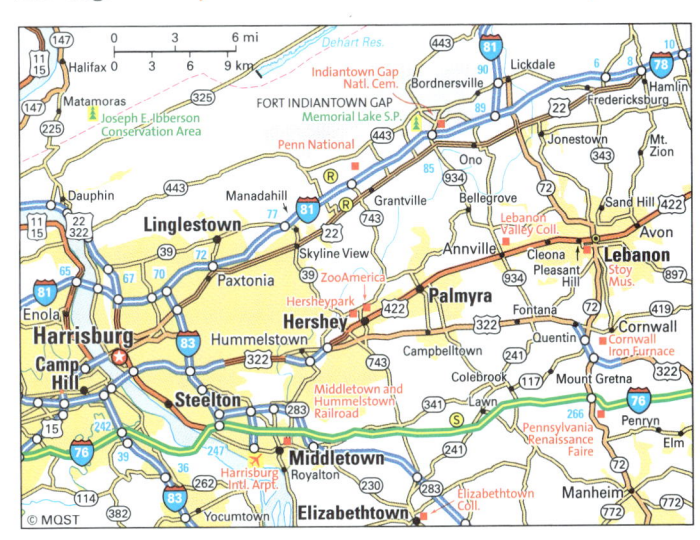

At **Hershey's Chocolate World,** you can take a simulated factory tour that highlights the chocolate-making process, from growing and harvesting cocoa beans to the finished product (a free sample awaits you at the end). It is not nearly as much fun as the real factory tours that were once offered, and it lasts less than 15 minutes, but it is educational nonetheless. The tour is free, although there is a small fee to view Hershey's Really Big 3D Show and ride the Hershey Trolley Works.

Hershey Museum, next to Hersheypark, offers a terrific glimpse of the life and work of Milton Hershey and the development of his chocolate enterprise. For more information on all that Hershey has to offer, call toll-free 800/437-7369 or visit www.HersheyPA.com or www.hersheycapitalregion.com.

Hershey is a two-hour drive southwest of Long Pond, with the bulk of the driving along Interstate 81. For more details on vacationing in Hershey, go to www.hersheypa.com.

For more Hershey recommendations, go to www.mobiltravelguide.com

424

Enthusiastic fans cheer at Richmond International Raceway.

Richmond International Raceway

Richmond, VA

26

Fans take in pre-race festivities as the sun goes down before the NASCAR NEXTEL Chevy Rock & Roll 400.

TRACK FACTS
RICHMOND INTERNATIONAL RACEWAY. 600 E Laburnum Ave, Richmond (23222). Phone toll-free 866-455-RACE (7223). www.rir.com.

PARKING. There is extensive free parking—sometimes far from the track—with tram service. The service resumes 45 minutes after the checkered flag to give fans walking to their cars a chance to clear the paths. Be patient if you want to hitch a ride. Parking overnight is prohibited except for the RV lot, which has some hook-ups. The waiting list for those spots is a couple of years long. Call the track about availability. The raceway operates shuttle buses from the Richmond Coliseum downtown beginning at 1 pm on NASCAR NEXTEL Cup Series days, but few fans take advantage of them.

FIRST AID. First aid and care centers are located outside of Turn 1 near Gate 40 and outside of Turn 4 near Gate 70.

GETTING AROUND. The earlier you leave for the track, the less traffic you'll encounter, right? Not exactly. Richmond aims to keep people entertained all day, with a midway, a fan festival, and live music prior to the race, so many fans get to the track early. Allow plenty of time. Several winding streets leading to the track will be one-way only on race days, so use the detailed city map or download the traffic map from the Web site, www.rir.com. Expect Laburnum Avenue leading to the main gate to be the most congested. Consider taking Interstate 64 to Interstate 295, Exit 177, to Meadowbridge Road, Exit 38B, which can be faster.

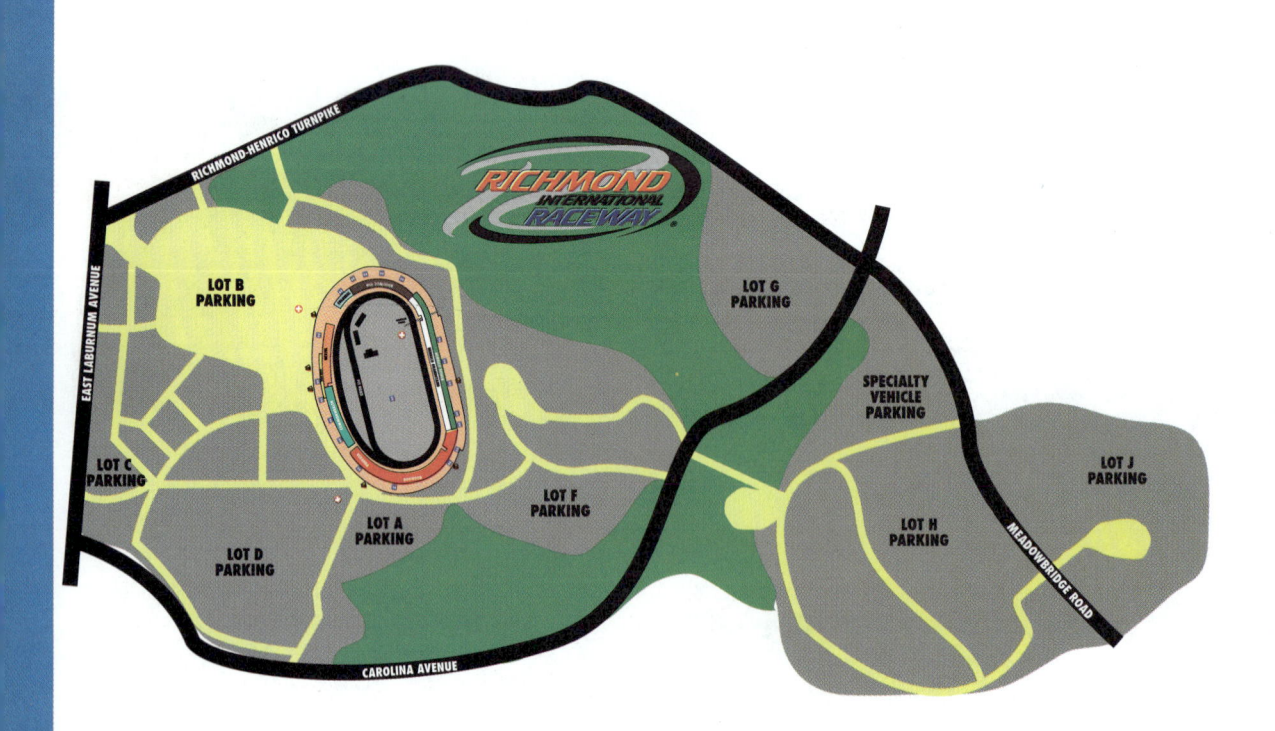

Richmond International Raceway is the only NASCAR track to hold all of its races at night under the lights.

GETTING TICKETS

Richmond, which holds 107,097 people, is one of the coveted tickets in NASCAR. The last 26 straight races have been sold out. The waiting list for season tickets is years long, but that doesn't mean you can't get seats. Each year, a couple thousand tickets, usually for seats on the lowest rows closest to the track, go on sale a few months before the May and September races. They go fast, so check with the track for the sale date and time by calling toll-free 866/455-7223, and get on the season ticket waiting list.

The raceway has local permission to expand to a capacity of 150,000. Don't expect all 43,000 new seats to be built at once, but there will be more available in coming years. Ask about the track's three alcohol-free sections, comprising about 3,300 spots.

BROKERS STEP IN

You can always get seats if you're willing to pay a premium to a broker or buy a package from a tour agency (two nights in a hotel for two, plus seats and a bus ride to the speedway runs more than $800 for the May 2005 race). If you can't get a NASCAR NEXTEL Cup Series ticket, request availability for a NASCAR Busch Series or NASCAR Craftsman Series race.

SOMETHING OLD, SOMETHING NEW

In Richmond, the genteel Old South rubs up against the exuberant New South. It's a place where Monument Avenue's statues of Confederate heroes Robert E. Lee and J. E. B. Stuart have been joined by native son Arthur Ashe.

Think of Richmond this way: if it were a driver, it would be two parts courtly veteran Mark Martin mixed with one part spirited newcomer Kasey Kahne.

These days, the former capital of the Confederacy is a city of 250,000 people in a metropolitan area encompassing almost 1 million people, but it feels more intimate and manageable, thanks to a collection of distinctive neighborhoods. Because Richmond

The center rotunda of the Virginia State Capitol Building displays portrait busts of Virginia-born presidents.

A skyline shot of Richmond, a city that blends Civil War history with present day progress.

International Raceway, in a northside neighborhood in Henrico County, is only ten minutes from downtown, you can easily explore the city while staying close to the track.

Richmond ranked tenth on the 2004 *Forbes* magazine list of the best metropolitan areas in the United States for business. So you'll see guys in starched white shirts tucking in their ties to attack a rack of ribs or firing up cigars at the bar of The Tobacco Company in Shockoe Slip. But you're also likely to sit next to a tattooed java junkie at a coffeehouse in the historic Fan District.

For history buffs, the city is a living archive. Patrick Henry uttered his defiant "give me liberty or give me death" speech at St. John's Episcopal Church. Thomas Jefferson designed the State Capitol Building on a hill downtown. But it's the Civil War that takes center stage: General Robert E. Lee and Jefferson Davis lived here during the war, and eight major battles were fought near Richmond. For a good overview, begin your adventures at the National Battlefield Civil War Visitor Center downtown along the James River.

Richmond also has plenty of less somber activities. The city has family-friendly science and children's museums, a diamond of a minor league ballpark, a riverfront suited for walking or biking, and eclectic shopping and nightlife. When it's time to chow, there are more than 400 restaurants, many of them neighborhood favorites—everything from barbecue joints to gourmet diners (yes, diners).

Paul Menard prepares to do battle in the 2004 Funai 250 NASCAR Busch Series event.

SHOP TALK

While on the road, you may need doughnuts, diapers, or just a bag of ice. Here's where to get the basics without breaking the bank.

CVS PHARMACY. *Laburnum Sq, Richmond (23231). Phone 804/222-7705. Seven miles from the raceway.*

HOME DEPOT. *7251 Bell Creek Rd, Mechanicsville (23111). Phone 804/559-7333. Five miles from the raceway.*

JIN'S GROCERY STORE. *3105 Meadowbridge Rd, Richmond (23222). Phone 804/321-3136. One mile from the Main Gate.*

ONE STOP FOOD MART. *3701 Meadowbridge Rd, Richmond (23222). Phone 804/329-7585. About 1 mile from the Main Gate.*

RITE AID. *502 E Laburnum Ave, Richmond (23222). Phone 804/329-7600. At the raceway's Main Gate.*

UKROP'S PHARMACY. *Laburnum Square Park, Richmond (23219). Phone 804/226-4933. Six miles from the Main Gate.*

WALGREENS DRUG STORE. *3715 Mechanicsville Pike, Richmond (23223). Phone 804/329-1333; pharmacy 804/329-1555. Less than 2 miles from the raceway.*

WINN-DIXIE. *3808 Mechanicsville Pike, Richmond (23223). Phone 804/321-3417. Less than 2 miles from the raceway.*

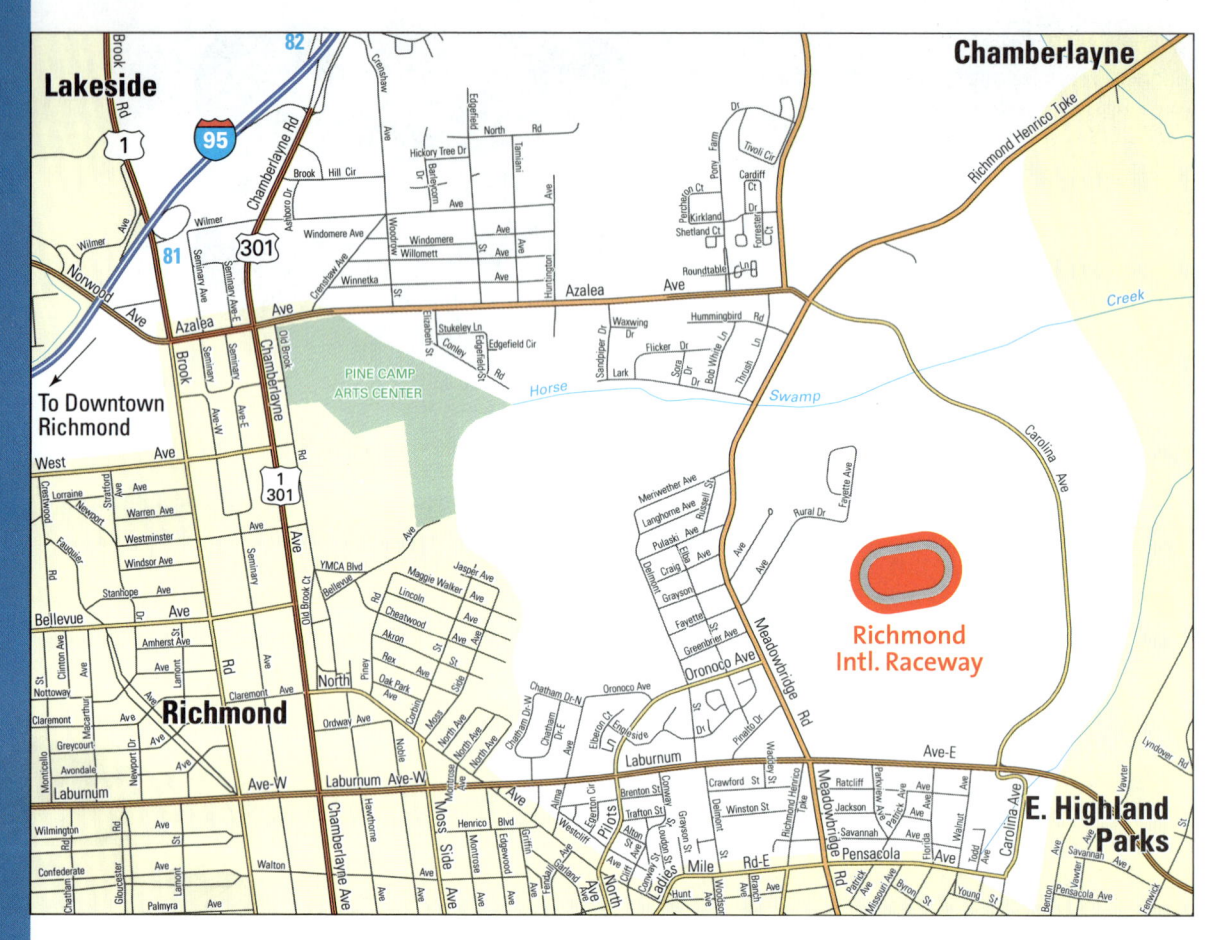

RICHMOND POLE POSITION:
The 10 miles surrounding Richmond International Raceway.

While Interstates 95 and 64 snake through the city, it's generally easier and more interesting to travel surface arteries to get from one neighborhood to another. Just remember that closest to the James River, downtown streets are one-way. Be alert for signs directing you to parking garages since on-street parking during busy weekends can be a challenge.

For nightlife, dining, and shopping, the best neighborhoods for tourists are Shockoe Slip, Shockoe Bottom, and the Fan.

If you prefer grass and trees to concrete and skyscrapers, relief is minutes away. You can fish or splash through the Class IV whitewaters of the James River, stunning views of the city's skyline visible over the shore. Twenty minutes north of the city is Paramount's Kings Dominion, featuring water rides and a dozen roller coasters. Forty-five minutes east in Williamsburg is Busch Gardens, Colonial Williamsburg, and the Williamsburg Outlet Mall, home to 40 stores, featuring brands such as Bass, Farberware, and Avon.

Summers along the James River are very humid, but the NASCAR weekends take place in late spring and fall during the city's most comfortable months, when daytime highs are in the mid-70s and nighttime temperatures drop into the high 50s and low 60s. May is one of the wetter months, so pack a light rain jacket.

RICHMOND INTERNATIONAL RACEWAY, VA **431**

OWNER'S PICK

For more than three decades, **La Petite France Restaurant** ★ ★ has been a Richmond favorite, and legendary team owner **Junie Donlavey** of Richmond agrees that it is a must-eat. "My favorite place to eat is La Petite. It's got great French food and lots of people eat there. I don't have a favorite item on the menu, everything is terrific." *2912 Maywill St, Richmond (23230). Phone 804/353-8729. www. lapetitefrance.net.*

From April through October, you can whitewater raft along the James River, with the city skyline as backdrop.

RICHMOND CALENDAR

APRIL 30–MAY 1, 2005
The Virginia Bazaar's 5th Anniversary Celebration. 8436 Ladysmith Rd, Ladysmith (22501). Phone 804/448-9488; toll-free 888/568-3532. www.vabazaar.com. Along with the loads of items for sale, from antiques to fine jewelry, this event features fire engines, clowns, antiques cars and motorcycles, and door prizes.

MAY 13, 2005
NASCAR Busch Series

MAY 14, 2005
NASCAR NEXTEL Cup Series

SEPTEMBER 3–4, 2005
Mountain Cove Labor Day Old Time Music Festival. Mountain Cove Vineyards, 1362 Fortunes Cove Ln, Lovingston (22949). Phone 434/263-5392. www.mountaincovevineyards.com. Enjoy food, music, and vineyard tours at this third annual festival on the Sunrise Side of the Blue Ridge Mountains.

SEPTEMBER 8, 2005
NASCAR Craftsman Truck Series

SEPTEMBER 9, 2005
NASCAR Busch Series

SEPTEMBER 10, 2005
NASCAR NEXTEL Cup Series

RICHMOND OUTFIELD:
The 60 miles surrounding Richmond International Raceway.

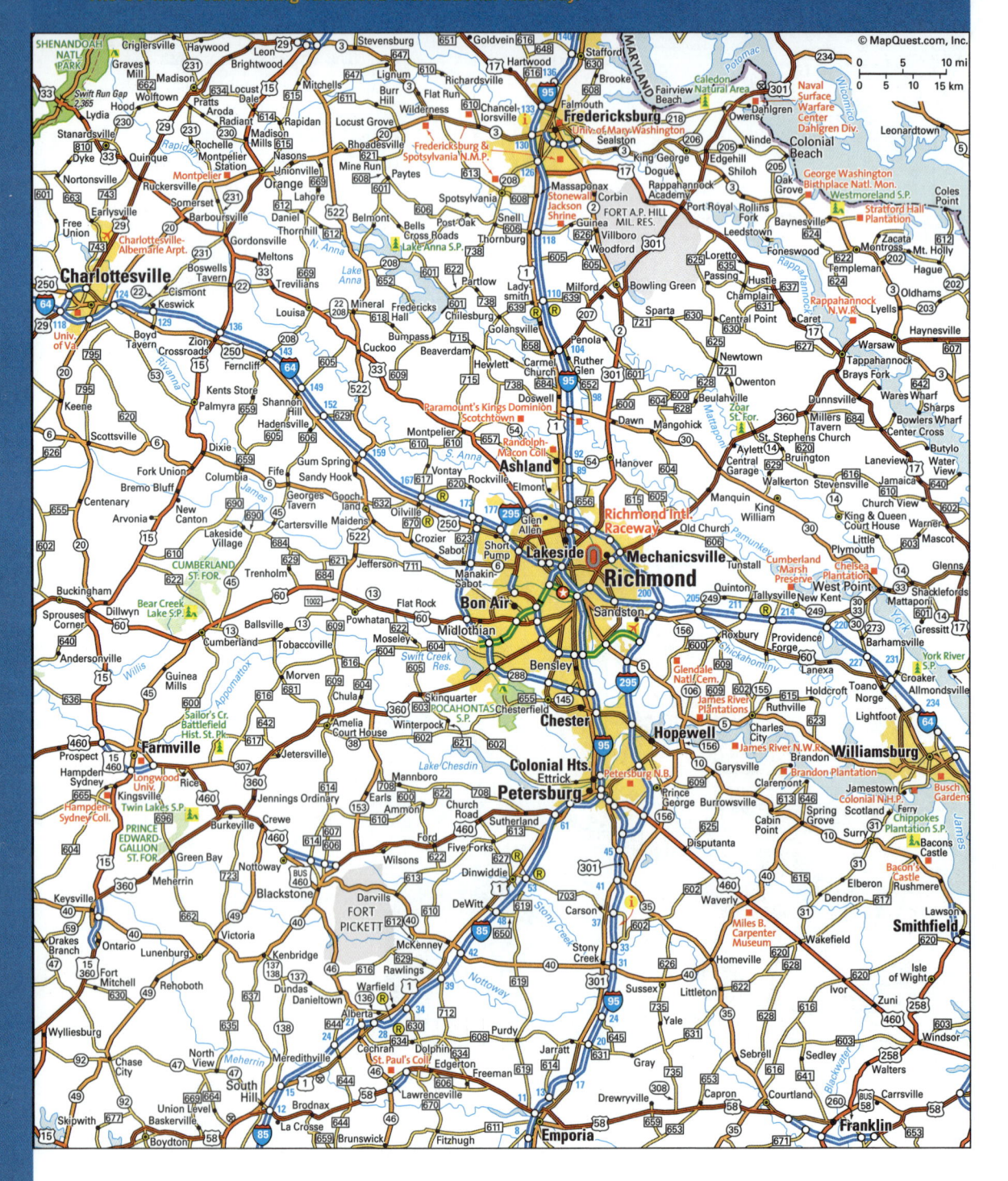

SEE

ATTRACTIONS

Doswell

PARAMOUNT'S KINGS DOMINION.
16000 Theme Park Way, Doswell (23047). I-95 N to exit 98. Phone 804/876-5000. www.kingsdominion.com. You can ride the most roller coasters on the East Coast at this park, 30 minutes north of Richmond. There's the HyperSonic XLC, Volcano, Flight of Fear, Shockwave, Anaconda, and seven more. For younger kids, try the Nickelodeon Celebration Parade, a nostalgic carousel, and Spongebob Squarepants 3-D. Admission also gets you into the adjoining water park, featuring slides, a wave pool, and a beach for the young kids. **$$**

Midlothian

SOUTHSIDE SPEEDWAY.
12800 Genito Rd, Midlothian (23112). Phone 804/744-2700. www.southside-speedway.com. If you need to see some short track action, this 1/3-mile asphalt oval is the ticket with Late Model Sportsman, Modified, and Grand Stock racing on Friday nights. Heat races begin at 7 pm with the first feature at 8 pm. Closed on NASCAR race weekends. **$**

Richmond

THE CANAL CLUB.
1545 E Cary St, Richmond (23219). Phone 804/643-2582. www.thecanalclub.com. Catch live music, especially blues and rock, or shoot a game of pool in Shockoe Bottom. A bonus: the interesting menu at The Under the Stage Cafe. (Wed-Sat)

CANAL WALK.
Enter at South 5th, 7th, 14th, 15th, or 17th sts, Richmond. The Canal Walk meanders 1 1/4 miles through downtown and features a pedestrian bridge to Brown's Island. Richmond Canal Cruises (phone 804/649-2800) depart on the hour from noon to 7 pm on Fridays and Saturdays from the Turning Basin between 14th and Virginia streets.

CHILDREN'S MUSEUM OF RICHMOND.
2626 W Broad St, Richmond (23220). Phone 804/474-2667; toll-free 877/295-2667. www.c-mor.org. A nice range of hands-on exhibits suitable for children ages 1-9, especially the interactive James River Waterplay, which explores the hydrology and history of the James River. (July-Aug: daily; Sept-June: Tues-Sun; closed holidays) **$$**

CIVIL WAR VISITOR CENTER.
470 Tredegar St, Richmond (23219). Phone 804/771-2145. www.nps.gov/rich. Begin your exploration of Richmond's Civil War heritage at the National Park Service Center at the restored Tredegar Iron Works near the James River. On the bottom floor, a continuously running film orients you to the 12 battlefields in the area. Park Service guides explain to kids how to fire the kind of cannon that Tredegar Iron Works made for the war. (Daily 9 am-5 pm) **FREE**

JAMES RIVER.
Richmond Raft Co, phone toll-free 800/540-7238, www.richmondraft.com, or Adventure Challenge, phone 804/276-7600, www.adventurechallenge.com/james.htm. The James River drops 105 feet over a 7-mile stretch that passes through downtown Richmond and produces Class IV whitewater rapids. When the river is high enough—generally April through October—you can whitewater raft practically in the shadows of the city's skyline.

THE MUSEUM OF THE CONFEDERACY.
1201 E Clay St, Richmond (23219). Phone 804/649-1861. www.moc.org. The museum features the world's largest collection of Confederate artifacts: uniforms, weapons, tattered flags, and daguerreotypes. Many of the exhibits feature artifacts from Confederate officers with descriptions of their demise. While it's comprehensive, the museum hasn't taken advantage of technology so you'll find yourself reading one typed description after another. (Mon-Sat 10 am-5 pm, Sun noon-5 pm; closed Jan 1, Thanksgiving, Dec 25) **$$**

RICHMOND BRAVES.
The Diamond, 3001 N Boulevard, Richmond (23230). Phone 804/359-4444. www.rbraves.com. The Richmond Braves are the AAA farm team of the Atlanta Braves, playing their home games in a 12,134-seat stadium just off Interstate 95. While The Diamond, built in 1985, is beginning to show its age, it remains a good place to catch a game. **$**

SEE ATTRACTIONS

SCIENCE MUSEUM OF VIRGINIA.
2500 W Broad St, Richmond (23220). N of Monument Ave. Phone 804/864-1400. www.smv.org. Located in the historic Broad Street Station (train tracks are still on the ground floor), this is an engaging museum that will appeal to children ages 5-12 with exhibits about space, flight, electricity, physics, and the atom. Be sure to check out the laboratories and animal exhibits on the second floor. (Mon-Sat 9:30 am-5 pm, Sun 11:30 am-5 pm; closed Thanksgiving, Dec 25) **$$**

VIRGINIA HISTORICAL SOCIETY.
428 N Boulevard St, Richmond (23220). Phone 804/358-4901. www.vahistorical.org. The society has a comprehensive collection of Virginia history housed in its museum with permanent and changing exhibits, and the Library of Virginia History with historical and genealogical research facilities. Well worth an afternoon to explore the city's changing place in history. (Mon-Sat, museum also Sun afternoons; closed holidays) **$$**

WHITE HOUSE OF THE CONFEDERACY.
12th and E Clay sts, Richmond (23219). N of Capitol Sq. Phone 804/649-1861. www.moc.org/exwhite.htm. Next door to the Museum of the Confederacy downtown, this Classical Revival house (1818) was used by Jefferson Davis as his official residence during the period when Richmond was the capital of the Confederacy. Abraham Lincoln met with troops here during the Union occupation of the city. (Mon-Sat 10 am-5 pm, Sun noon-5 pm; closed Jan 1, Thanksgiving, Dec 25) **$$**

For more attractions, go to www.mobiltravelguide.com

sure to ask if there is a minimum stay. Some hotels require reservations for two- or three-night stays on race weekends.

MOBIL STAR-RATED LODGINGS

Richmond

COURTYARD BY MARRIOTT RICHMOND WEST.
★★
6400 W Broad St, Richmond (23230). Phone 804/282-1881; toll-free 800/321-2211. www.courtyard.com. Set in Richmond's west end, where business and shopping locations are abundant, this appealing hotel features a courtyard with a pool and gazebo, loveseats in the comfortable guest rooms, and a restaurant with a courtyard view. 145 rooms, 3 story. Check-in 3 pm, check-out noon. High-speed Internet access. Restaurant, bar. Fitness room. Outdoor pool, whirlpool. Business center. **$**

STAY

Because Richmond International Raceway is so close to Richmond and other central Virginia locations, rooms are not hard to find, even near race day. Two weeks before the September 2004 race, for instance, there were still plenty of rooms available within 15 miles of the raceway for $89 and up. When you reserve, be

PIT PASS

FasMart operates an on-site store in the Lot D parking lot, where you can pick up essentials such as ice and snacks on race weekends. A Rite Aid Drug Store is located across the street from the Main Gate.

Fans can leave the grandstands, get a pass, and return to their cars or campers to replenish their coolers. Only soft-sided coolers, no larger than 6 x 6 x 12 inches are permitted (no glass containers). The track operates a vehicle repair service to help with flat tires, lockouts, and other minor issues (phone 804/228-7560).

CROWNE PLAZA HOTEL RICHMOND—E CANAL. ★★★

555 E Canal St, Richmond (23219). Phone 804/788-0900; toll-free 800/227-6963. www.crowneplaza.com. This hotel is situated in the heart of the historic district and minutes from area attractions such as Shockoe Slip, Sixth Street Market Place, museums, theaters, and fine dining. The higher floors have a spectacular view of the James River. 299 rooms, 16 story. Check-in 3 pm, check-out noon. High-speed Internet access. Two restaurants, bar. Fitness room. Indoor pool, whirlpool. Business center. $$

DAYS INN. ★

6910 Midlothian Tpke, Richmond (23225). Phone 804/745-7100; toll-free 800/329-7466. www.daysinn.com. 130 rooms, 3 story. Pets accepted. Complimentary continental breakfast. Check-out noon. Outdoor pool. $

EMBASSY SUITES HOTEL RICHMOND—THE COMMERCE CENTER. ★★

2925 Emerywood Pkwy, Richmond (23294). Phone 804/672-8585; toll-free 800/362-2779. www.embassysuites.com. Located in Richmond's Commerce Center on the west end of the city, this hotel offers spacious accommodations and a complimentary full cooked-to-order breakfast, advantageous for families. 226 rooms, 8 story, all suites. Complimentary full breakfast. Check-in 3 pm, check-out noon. High-speed Internet access. Restaurant, bar. Fitness room. Indoor pool, whirlpool. Airport transportation available. Business center. $

LINDEN ROW INN. ★★

100 E Franklin St, Richmond (23219). Phone 804/783-7000; toll-free 800/348-7424. www.lindenrowinn.com. With artwork from the Virginia Historical Society and many antiques throughout, guests can enjoy quiet Victorian surroundings at this elegant inn at the heart of downtown Richmond. The inn also features a secluded garden courtyard in a comfortable neighborhood setting and complimentary wine and cheese receptions in the evenings. 70 rooms, 4 story. Complimentary continental breakfast. Check-in 3 pm, check-out 11 am. High-speed Internet access. Restaurant (public by reservation). Bar. $

OMNI RICHMOND HOTEL. ★★★

100 S 12th St, Richmond (23219). Phone 804/344-7000; toll-free 800/843-6664. www.omnihotels.com. This contemporary hotel is located in the center of the financial and historic districts and features scenic river views. It's across the street from the famous Tobacco Company restaurant and a great place to stay if you intend to explore Shockoe Slip and Shockoe Bottom. 361 rooms, 19 story. Pets accepted; fee. Check-in 3 pm, check-out noon. Wireless Internet access. Restaurant, bar. Fitness room, fitness classes available. Indoor pool. Airport transportation available. Business center. $

QUALITY INN WEST. ★

8008 W Broad St, Richmond (23294). Phone 804/346-0000; toll-free 800/228-5151. www.qualityinn.com. Within walking distance to many shopping and dining locations and offering convenient access to the highway, this comfortable hotel is ideal for the business or leisure traveler on a budget. 191 rooms, 6 story. Pets accepted; fee. Complimentary continental breakfast. Check-in 3 pm, check-out 11 am. Fitness room. Outdoor pool. $

SHERATON RICHMOND WEST HOTEL. ★★

6624 W Broad St, Richmond (23230). Phone 804/285-2000; toll-free 888/625-4988. www.sheraton.com. With luxurious furnishings such as chandeliers in the lobby area and plush pillows and duvets that sit upon "Sweet Sleeper" beds, this upscale hotel is located just off the highway in a richly landscaped business park. With oversize writing desks and in-room WiFi, the hotel is geared towards the business traveler but is also a great place for leisure travelers to Richmond as well. 372 rooms, 8 story. Pets accepted. Check-in 3 pm, check-out noon. High-speed Internet access. Wireless Internet access. Two restaurants, two bars. Fitness room. Indoor pool, outdoor pool, whirlpool. Airport transportation available. Business center. $$

Sandston

DOUBLETREE HOTEL RICHMOND AIRPORT. ★★

5501 Eubank Rd, Sandston (23150). Phone 804/226-6400; toll-free 800/222-8733. www.doubletree.com. Directly across from the Richmond International

Airport. 160 rooms, 5 story. Check-out noon. High-speed Internet access. Wireless Internet access. Restaurant, bar. Fitness room. Outdoor pool, whirlpool. Airport transportation available. Business center. $

LOCAL RECOMMENDATIONS

Doswell

BEST WESTERN KINGS QUARTERS.
16102 Theme Park Way, Doswell (23047). Phone 804/876-3321; toll-free 800/780-7234. www.bestwestern.com. This hotel is located across from Paramount's Kings Dominion Theme Park. 248 rooms, 2 story. Pets accepted, some restrictions. Check-in 3 pm, check-out 11 am. Outdoor pool. $

Richmond

BEST WESTERN EXECUTIVE HOTEL.
7007 W Broad St, Richmond (23294). Phone 804/672-7007; toll-free 800/780-7234. www.bestwestern.com. 114 rooms, 4 story. Check-in 3 pm, check-out 11 am. Outdoor pool. 8 miles from raceway. $

BEST WESTERN GOVERNOR'S INN.
9826 Midlothian Tpke, Richmond (23235). Phone 804/323-0007; toll-free 800/780-7234. www.bestwestern.com. The Governor's Inn offers four rooms with Jacuzzis and features Club Razzles. 80 rooms, 3 story. Complimentary continental breakfast. Check-in 3 pm, check-out noon. Restaurant. Fitness room. Outdoor pool. 13 miles from raceway. $

HOLIDAY INN RICHMOND I-64 & WEST BROAD ST.
6531 W Broad St, Richmond (23230). Phone 804/285-9951; toll-free 800/465-4329. www.holiday-inn.com. Renovated in 2002, this hotel features the Sapphire Grill and Lounge, offering breakfast, lunch, and dinner. 282 rooms, 7 story. Check-in 3 pm, check-out noon. Laundry services. Restaurant, bar. Fitness room. Indoor pool. 6 miles from raceway. $

Sandston

BEST WESTERN AIRPORT.
5700 Williamsburg Rd, Sandston (23150). Phone 804/222-2780; toll-free 800/780-7234. www.bestwestern.com. 112 rooms, 2 story. Check-in 2 pm, check-out 11 am. Laundry services. Restaurant, bar. Outdoor pool. $

HOLIDAY INN AIRPORT.
5203 Williamsburg Rd, Sandston (23150). Phone 804/222-6450; toll-free 800/964-6886. www.holiday-inn.com. This is the largest airport hotel near Richmond featuring an outdoor pool and an exercise facility. 230 rooms, 6 story. Check-in 3 pm, check-out noon. Laundry services. Restaurant, bar. Fitness room. Outdoor pool. Business center. $

RV AND CAMPING

Amelia

AMELIA FAMILY CAMPGROUNDS.
9720 Military Rd, Amelia (23002). Phone 804/561-3011. www.ameliafamilycampgrounds.com. Water, electric, and sewer hook-ups in a wooded campground 36 miles from the raceway. Nature trail, pool, laundry, game room, camp store, fishing.

Ashland

AMERICAMPS RICHMOND NORTH.
11322 Air Park Rd, Ashland (23005). Exit 89 off I-95. Phone 804/798-5298; toll-free 800/628-2802. www.americamps.com. Located 9 miles from the raceway, Americamps is a wooded campground with 146 sites, including 116 with water and electric, 87 with sewer, and 30 for tent camping. There is a small, well-stocked camp store, pool, playground, and game room.

Bowling Green

BOWLING GREEN KOA.
17391 Richmond Tpke, Bowling Green (22514). Phone 804/633-7592; toll-free 800/562-2482. www.koa.com/where/VA/46142.htm. Water, electric, and sewer hook-ups. Swimming pool, hot tub, fishing, cabins. Bus transportation available to raceway for a fee. 37 miles from raceway.

For more lodging recommendations, go to www.mobiltravelguide.com

EAT

MOBIL STAR-RATED RESTAURANTS

Richmond

ACACIA. ★★
3325 W Cary St, Richmond (23221). Phone 804/354-6060. www.acaciarestaurant.com. Chef Dale Reitzer was named one of American's best by *Food & Wine* magazine in 1999 so this is the place for a special dinner. Located in an old church building with a front porch that overlooks the sidewalks of Carytown, Acacia has a menu that changes daily to take advantage of the freshest ingredients of the season. American menu. Lunch, dinner. Closed Sun; July 4; also early Jan. Casual attire. Reservations recommended. Outdoor seating. **$$$**

HALF WAY HOUSE. ★★
10301 Jefferson Davis Hwy, Richmond (23237). Phone 804/275-1760. This antiques-furnished manor house (1760) was a stop on the Petersburg stagecoach line until the late 19th century. It hosted Washington, Lafayette, Patrick Henry, and Jefferson, among others. It was also used as a Union headquarters during the 1864 siege of Richmond. American menu. Lunch, dinner. Business casual attire. Reservations recommended. **$$$**

SAM MILLER'S WAREHOUSE. ★★
1210 E Cary St, Richmond (23219). Phone 804/644-5465. www.sammillers.com. This seafood restaurant is located in the historic district and features antique mirrors and a lobster tank. Seafood menu. Lunch, dinner, brunch. Business casual attire. Reservations recommended. **$$$**

STRAWBERRY STREET CAFE. ★
421 Strawberry St, Richmond (23220). Phone 804/353-6860. www.strawberrystreetcafe.com. The old-fashioned bath tub that serves as the restaurant's salad bar earned its fame as a "Jeopardy!" question, but that's just part of the charm of a place filled with stained glass, rich woodwork, and a menu with a little something for every taste, from burgers to crab cakes. Located in the Fan neighborhood. American menu. Lunch, dinner, brunch. Closed Thanksgiving, Dec 25. Bar. Children's menu. Casual attire. Reservations recommended. Outdoor seating. **$$**

TOBACCO COMPANY. ★★
1201 E Cary St, Richmond (23219). Phone 804/782-9555. www.thetobaccocompany.com. The restaurant that helped pioneer the renaissance of Shockoe Slip is carved from a former tobacco warehouse. The centerpiece is a dramatic skylit atrium with an antique cage elevator servicing three floors of dining. The menu is extensive if not inventive: steaks, prime rib, lobster, veal, shrimp, scallops, salmon, rainbow trout, chicken, crab, Virginia ham, and pasta. Free buffet during happy hours, 5-7 pm, Wednesday through Friday. Cigars in the bar. American menu. Lunch, dinner, Sun brunch. Bar. Children's menu. Business casual attire. Live music. **$$$**

FAN FAVORITE

Buz and Ned's Real Barbecue is a no-frills joint where the 'cue is all that matters. And isn't it convenient for a great barbecue joint to be next to a car wash? Just what you need if you can't lick your fingers clean after going several rounds with the juicy, tender baby back ribs cooked slowly over smoldering wood. Line up, place your order, and wait for your name to be called to pick up your food in a plastic basket. And while the ribs are the stars, leave room for the jalapeño corn fries with cheese dip, the mac and three cheeses, and the cinnamon bourbon apples. Barbecue menu. Lunch, dinner. Closed Sun. Outdoor seating. **$** *1119 N Boulevard, Richmond (23230). Phone 804/355-6055. www.buzandneds.com.*

LOCAL RECOMMENDATIONS
Richmond

HAVANA '59.
16 N 17th St, Richmond (23219) Phone 804/649-2822. Itching to break out that cigar for an after-race celebration? This is the place for you. There's an after-dinner cigar menu as well as a cigar girl who roams the open-air room with a tray of offerings. The menu is seafood heavy, but also has enough variety for landlubbers. Check out the shredded pork over rice with plantains, one of the least expensive and most delicious items offered. Seafood menu. Lunch, dinner. **$$$**

JOE'S INN.
205 N Shields Ave, Richmond (23220). Phone 804/355-2282. There's a reason locals line up for a booth or a table at Joe's, where the portions of Greek-accented Italian food, notably baked spaghetti and subs, are hearty. Breakfast is served all day. Save room for the pies. Italian menu. Breakfast, lunch, dinner, Sun brunch. Children's menu. **$$**

LEGEND BREWING COMPANY.
321 W Seventh St, Richmond (23220). Phone 804/232-3446. www.legendbrewing.com. From the outside, this microbrewery across the 14th Street Bridge on the south side is just a blocky yellow building—nothing very impressive. Then you step out onto the 200-seat deck with a view of the Richmond skyline and the James River. Grab a glass of the Brown Ale, Legend's most popular, lean back in your chair, and watch the sun serenade the city. American menu. Lunch, dinner, Sun brunch. Bar. Outdoor seating. **$$**

MILLIE'S DINER.
2603 E Main St, Richmond (23223). Phone 804/643-5512. www.milliesdiner.com. Millie's is a gourmet diner. A glance at the menu, which offers items like jerk duck, veal tenderloin, and smoked pork chops, is an exercise in "name the global influences." And then there are the Seeburg 200 Wall-O-Matic tableside jukeboxes, offering everything from crooners Ray Charles and Frank Sinatra to Mel Tills and even funk from The Ohio Players. Close enough to walk to Shockoe Bottom nightlife. American menu. Lunch, dinner, Sun brunch. Closed Mon. **$$**

RIVER CITY DINER.
1712 E Main St, Richmond (23223). Phone 804/644-9418. www.rivercitydiner.com. Welcome back to the "Happy Days" of turquoise and pink. Breakfast, featuring half a dozen kinds of pancakes, is served all day and until 3 am on Fridays and Saturdays. Check out the biscuits and gravy. Locals like the late-night burgers as well. American menu. Breakfast, lunch, dinner, late-night. Children's menu. **$**

SINE.
1327 E Cary St, Richmond (23219). Phone 804/649-7767. www.sineirishpub.com/richmond. Not as cute nor as cozy as some Irish pubs, Sine is built for a Shockoe Slip crowd. However, it has one of the best decks in town, just right for hanging out and ordering another Guinness, Harp, Murphy's Stout, or one of the other dozen beers on tap. Pub menu. Lunch, dinner. Live Music. **$$**

Sandston

MEXICO.
5213 Williamsburg Rd, Sandston (23150). Phone 804/226-2388. Also 7162 Mechanicsville Tpke, Mechanicsville (23111). Phone 804/559-8126. The menu, with everything from the expected huevos rancheros to mole poblano, is so big that it may take you longer ordering than it does to get your food. And you get a lot of food for the money here. There are several locations throughout the city, but these two are less than 8 miles from the raceway. Mexican menu. Lunch, dinner. Children's menu. **$**

For more dining recommendations, go to www.mobiltravelguide.com

SIDETRIP

Navy Sees
Norfolk, Virginia

Norfolk, 90 miles southeast of Richmond, long suffered as a backwater Navy town. But in the last decade, the city has transformed its downtown into a vibrant destination with a little something for everyone—sports, history, music, theater, and dining.

The city's Elizabeth River waterfront was a littered industrial zone a couple of decades ago. Now, it features enough attractions to keep you busy for a day. Start with Nauticus, the National Maritime Center (phone 757/664-1000, toll-free 800/664-1080, www.nauticus.org), an interactive science center featuring a shark-petting lagoon, a simulated tidepool with crabs you can touch, and an interactive computer simulation that takes you aboard a Navy ship. Berthed next door is the U.S.S. *Wisconsin*, the largest and last battleship built by the US Navy.

Not far away at the Waterside Marina, the *American Rover* (phone 757/627-7245, www.americanrover.com), a three-masted tall ship, modeled after the cargo schooners that sailed the Chesapeake Bay, cruises three times a day from April through October.

Head north from the water for ten minutes and you reach The Virginia Zoological Park (phone 757/441-2374, www.virginiazoo.org), which features a number of new areas including the Africa Okavango Delta exhibit with zebras, lions, giraffes, red river hogs, and meerkats.

On the way back downtown, stop by Doumar's on Monticello Avenue for some old-fashioned curbside service at a burger and barbecue spot that claims to have invented the ice-cream cone.

For lunch or dinner, check out the more than 60 restaurants downtown, most of them on Granby Street.

If you have a free early evening, drive the 25 minutes to the Virginia Beach oceanfront and walk on what will be mostly deserted sand in May or September as the sun sets.

Sail aboard the *American Rover*, a replica of a 19th-century cargo schooner. Norfolk is less than a two-hour drive from Richmond. The most direct route takes you down Interstate 64.

For more Norfolk recommendations, go to www.mobiltravelguide.com

440

Pit crew members swarm the No. 21 Car of Ricky Rudd during the NASCAR NEXTEL Cup Aaron's 499 race.

Talladega Superspeedway®

Talladega, AL

27

One reason fans love Talladega is the close proximity of the grandstands to the racing action.

TRACK FACTS

TALLADEGA SUPERSPEEDWAY. 3366 Speedway Blvd, Talladega (35160). Phone toll-free 877/GO-2DEGA (462-3342). www.talladegasuperspeedway.com.

SECURITY. One soft-sided cooler or insulated bag, 6 x 6 x 12 inches or smaller, is allowed per ticket holder. Clear plastic bags, 18 x 18 x 4 inches, are also allowed. Food and beverages are allowed; no glass containers. Binoculars, radio scanners and cameras with neck straps and belt clips, and seat cushions are allowed. Prepare to be searched.

PARKING. Day parking is free. During race week, day parking lots open at 7 am Thursday and Friday, 5 am Saturday and Sunday. Lots must be cleared out before dark; overnight parking in North Park, West Park C, and Family Park. For information on parking packages for RVs and other vehicles, call the ticket office, 877/GO-2DEGA.

FIRST AID. There are seven first aid stations around the track area: at entrance plazas 4 and 8; two behind Allison Grandstand; one near North campground; one near West Park C, and one next to the NASCAR NEXTEL Cup Garage.

CONCESSIONS. Stands are located throughout the grandstands on the front stretch and backstretch. While you'll find souvenirs at the north end of the front stretch, Talladega old-timers will tell you to buy your heart out on Souvenir Row, where semi-trucks dedicated to individual drivers line the parking lot.

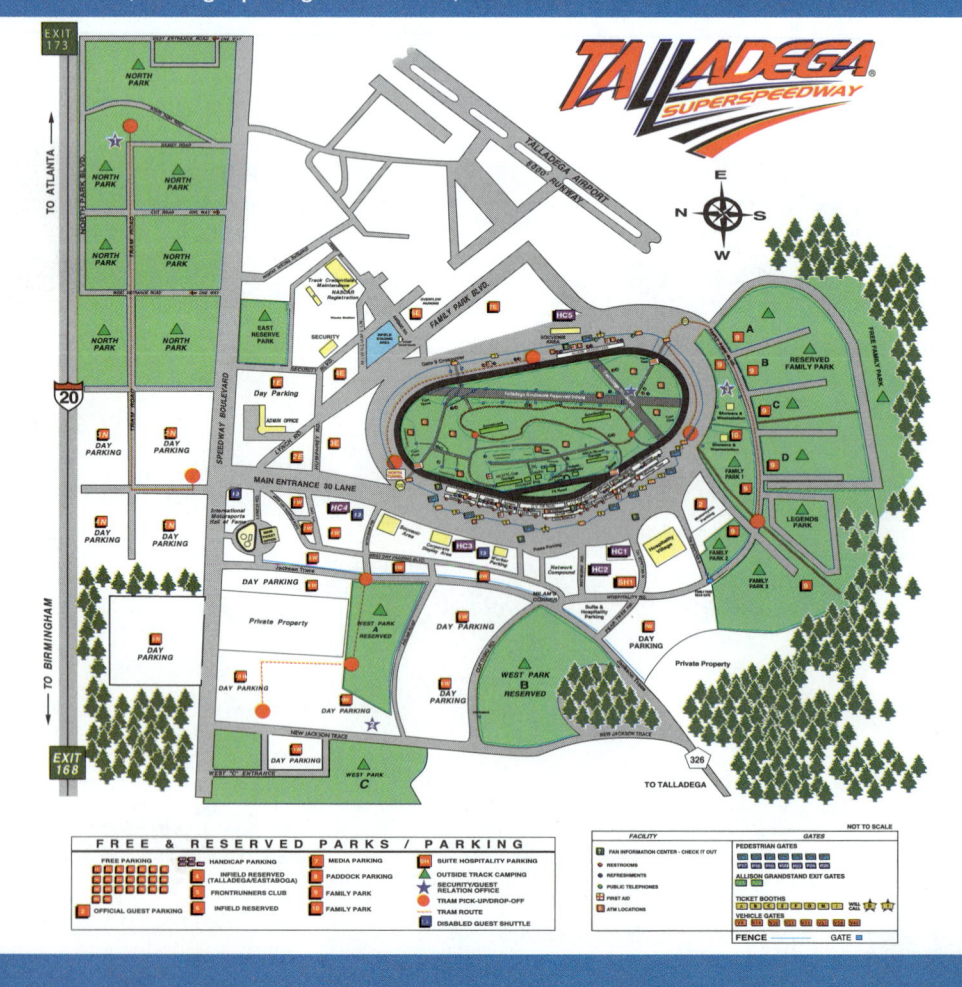

SLEEPY SOUTHERN STYLE

Talladega and the surrounding area combine two worlds: the industrial, represented by the city of Birmingham and the steel that put it on the map, and the deep natural beauty of the mountains, rolling hills, lakes, and rivers. Put the two together and you have an area unique to the NASCAR tour.

When NASCAR events aren't drawing thousands of fans, Talladega is a sleepy Southern town. Trees line the town's historic **Silk Stocking District** (phone 256/362-9075), with quaint antiques shops and antebellum and 19th-century homes, which open to the public during an annual spring pilgrimage in April.

Two local schools helped change the face of Alabama's education system: Talladega College, Alabama's first college founded by and for African-Americans in 1867, and Alabama Institute for the Deaf and Blind, founded in 1858.

In true deep Southern style, the town offers a plethora of outdoor activities—fishing, hiking, and hunting, or just plain taking it easy. Take in a round at **Robert Trent Jones Golf Trail** (phone toll-free 800/949-4444; www.rtjgolf.com), a world-class course. Or enjoy a 26-mile scenic drive through the 389,000-acre **Talladega National Forest** (phone 256/362-2909), which also offers a variety of recreational activities. Hikers will enjoy the **Pinhoti Hiking Trail** (phone 256/463-2272), Alabama's 102-mile recreational trail, winding through Talladega National Forest.

No matter where you are in the state, however, all roads lead to Birmingham. The area is the only place in the world where the elements to make iron—coal, iron ore, and limestone—are present within a 10-mile radius. A newly restored statue of Vulcan (Vulcan Park, phone 205/328-9696), the Roman god of the forge, is a fixture on the city's skyline and a reminder of the "Magic City's" quick growth during the steel industry boom of the late 1800s.

Birmingham pays homage to its past in another way. The role it played in the civil rights movement is detailed at the **Birmingham Civil Rights Institute** (520 16th St N, phone 205/328-9696, toll-free 866/328-9696). The modern city is also carving out new niches with destinations such as the **Birmingham Museum of Art** (2000 Eighth Ave N, phone 205/254-2566, www.artsbma.org), shopping at **The Summit** (phone 205/967-0111) and **Riverchase Galleria** (phone 205/985-3020), and top-rated restaurants.

Pit road is nonstop action when NASCAR NEXTEL Cup racers come in for needed adjustments to finish the race during the EA Sports 500.

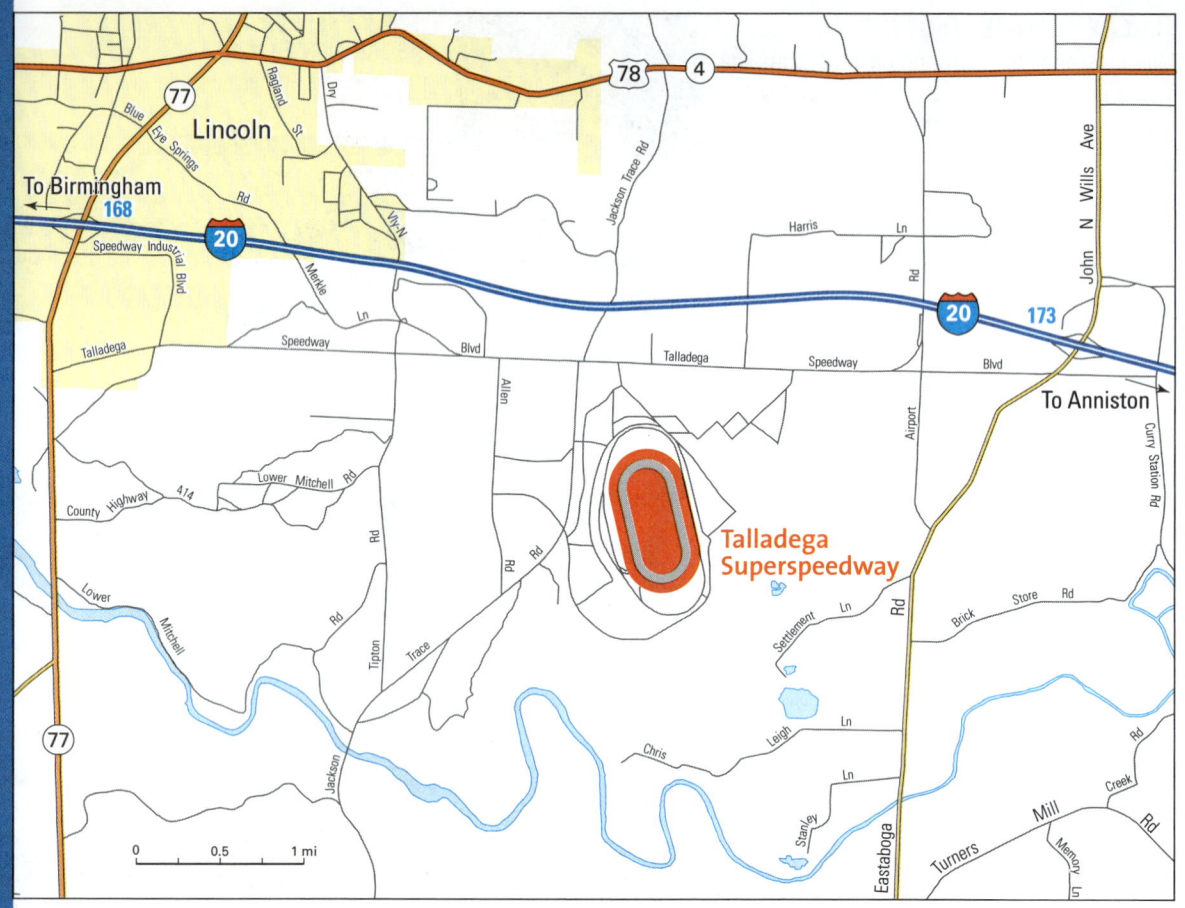

TALLADEGA POLE POSITION:
The 10 miles surrounding Talladega Superspeedway.

Northeast of Talladega are the towns of Anniston and Oxford, both rich in Alabama history and natural beauty. In Anniston, take a walking tour of the **downtown historic district** (phone 256/236-0996) and its restored shops, and the 19th-century courthouse (phone 256/237-3536). In Oxford, visit the **Coldwater Covered Bridge,** one of the oldest remaining covered bridges in the state.

Outdoors enthusiasts will want to visit the **Chief Ladiga Trail** (phone 256/447-9007), Alabama's first rails-to-trails project, taking walkers, bikers, and strollers along a 25-mile path. By the time it's completely finished, it will extend another 8 1/2 miles from Anniston to the Georgia state line.

North of Anniston is Gadsden, known for its natural beauty. **Noccalula Falls Park** (phone 256/549-4663) features a 90-foot waterfall named after the legendary Indian princess Noccalula, who leaped to her death in the waters below. From Gadsden, take a scenic drive along **Lookout Mountain Parkway** to Chattanooga, Tennessee. During the first week in August, it is filled with bargain hunters searching for a steal during the **450-mile Yard Sale** (phone 256/549-0351).

For a change from the NASCAR pace, take a hike through Talladega National Forest.

TALLADEGA CALENDAR

FEBRUARY 24–APRIL 28, 2005
Birmingham International Festival. Locations throughout Birmingham. Phone 205/252-7652. www.bifsalutes.org. This year, the city salutes Mexico with events, artists, food, and music.

APRIL 28, 2005
NASCAR Busch Series Qualifying Day

APRIL 29, 2005
Birmingham News/Birmingham Post-Herald Qualifying Day for NASCAR NEXTEL Cup Series

APRIL 30, 2005
Aaron's 312 NASCAR Busch Series

MAY 1, 2005
Aaron's 499 NASCAR NEXTEL Cup Series

SEPTEMBER 30, 2005
Discount Food Mart Qualifying Day for NASCAR NEXTEL Cup Series

OCTOBER 1–30, 2005
Pumpkin Patch Express. 1919 Ninth St, Calera (35040). Phone 205/668-3435; toll-free 800/943-4490. www.heartofdixierrmuseum.org. Find your great pumpkin. Sat-Sun in Oct.

OCTOBER 2, 2005
Talladega 500 NASCAR NEXTEL Cup Series

OCTOBER 8, 2005
10th Annual Pioneer Days. Pioneer Museum of Alabama, 248 US Hwy 231, Troy (36081). Phone 334/566-3597. www.pioneer-museum.org. Head back to pioneer days. Covers the history of Alabama.

DeSoto Caverns Park features an onyx cave larger than a football field.

DRIVER'S PICK

When the 1983 Winston Cup champion **Bobby Allison** and wife Judy head to the fastest track in the country, they slow down in nearby Bessemer. "We love a place . . . called The Bright Star. It's been in business since 1907. They serve Greek food and have the best bread pudding in the world!" **The Bright Star** ★★ *304 19th St N, Bessemer (35020). Phone 205/424-9444. www.birminghammenus.com/brightstar.*

TALLADEGA OUTFIELD:
The 60 miles surrounding Talladega Superspeedway.

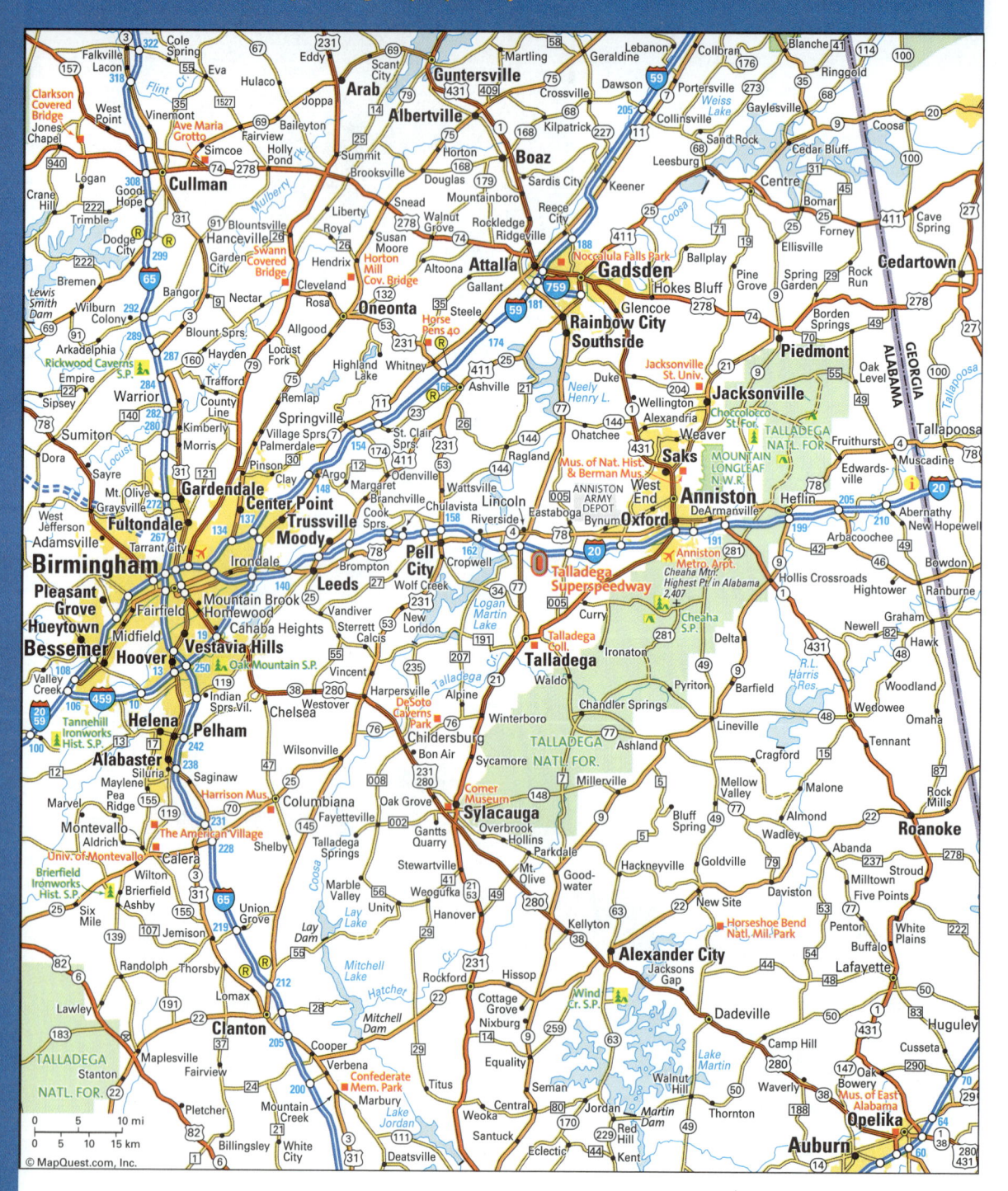

SEE

ATTRACTIONS

Anniston

ANNISTON MUSEUM OF NATURAL HISTORY.
Lagarde Park, 800 Museum Dr, Anniston (36202). Phone 256/237-6766. www.annistonmuseum.org. This museum features more than 400 mounted birds both endangered and extinct; a full-scale model of an Albertosaurus and a meteorite; Egyptian mummies; and a changing exhibition gallery. Situated in 185-acre John B. Lagarde Environmental Interpretive Park, it features nature trails and picnic facilities. (Tues-Sat 10 am-5 pm, Sun 1-5 pm; open Mon in summer; closed holidays) **$**

Birmingham

ARLINGTON ANTEBELLUM HOME AND GARDENS.
331 Cotton Ave SW, Birmingham (35211). Phone 205/780-5656. Birmingham's last remaining antebellum house, circa 1850, in the Greek Revival style features a diverse collection of 19th-century decorative art. Located on a sloping hill in Elyton, the house is surrounded by oak and magnolia trees and seasonal plantings. (Tues-Sun; closed holidays) **$$**

RUFFNER MOUNTAIN.
1214 81st St S, Birmingham (35206). Phone 205/833-8264. www.ruffnermountain.org. Contains 1,011 acres of the last undeveloped section of this area's Appalachian Mountains. Displays focus on the mountain's biology, geology, and history. Wildlife refuge with nature trails. (Tues-Sat 9 am-5 pm, Sun 1-5 pm; closed holidays) **FREE**; some special programs, **$-$$$**

SOUTHERN MUSEUM OF FLIGHT/ALABAMA AVIATION HALL OF FAME.
4343 73rd St N, Birmingham (35206). Phone 205/833-8226. www.southernmuseumofflight.org. View a full-size Wright Flyer replica, a 1912 Curtiss Pusher replica, a Fokker VII, a VariEze experimental home-built, two US Air Force fighter jet cockpit simulators, and flight-related memorabilia. (Tues-Sat 9:30 am-4:30 pm, Sun 1-4:30 pm) **$**

Childersburg

DESOTO CAVERNS PARK.
5181 DeSoto Caverns Pkwy, Childersburg (35044). 12 miles NW via Hwy 21 and County 36; on Hwy 76, 5 miles E of junction Hwy 280. Phone 256/378-7252. www.cavern.com/desoto. This scenic 80-acre wooded park features historic mammoth, onyx caverns. The caverns are the historic birthplace of the Creek Nation. The main cavern, the Great Onyx Cathedral, is larger than a football field and features a sound, laser, and water show. Picnic areas, playground, RV campground. Guided tours. (Apr-Oct: Mon-Sat 9 am-5:30 pm, Sun 1-5:30 pm; Nov-Mar: Mon-Sat 9 am-4:30 pm, Sun 1-4:30 pm; closed Thanksgiving, Dec 25) **$$$**

Pelham

OAK MOUNTAIN STATE PARK.
200 Terrace Dr, Pelham (35124). I-65, exit 246. Phone 205/620-2524. www.dcnr.state.al.us. Peavine Falls and Gorge and two lakes sit amid 9,940 acres of the state's most rugged mountains. Activities include: swimming, fishing, boating (marina, ramp, rentals); hiking, backpacking, bridle trails, golf (18 holes; fee); tennis, picnicking (shelters, barbecue pits, fireplaces), concession, camping, cabins, and a demonstration farm. **$**

For more attractions, go to www.mobiltravelguide.com

STAY

MOBIL STAR-RATED LODGINGS

Anniston

THE VICTORIA. ★★★
1604 Quintard Ave, Anniston (36202). Phone 256/236-0503. www.thevictoria.com. For a quiet and memorable getaway, this beautifully restored country inn, built in 1888, is a wonderful example of early Victorian architecture. Much thought was given to design and comfort with stylish guest rooms, fine

dining, and a piano lounge. 60 rooms, 3 story. Check-in 3 pm, check-out noon. Restaurant. Outdoor pool. $

Birmingham

BAYMONT INN. ★
513 Cahaba Park Cir, Birmingham (35242). Phone 205/995-9990; toll-free 877/229-6668. www.baymontinns.com. 102 rooms, 3 story. Pets accepted, some restrictions; fee. Complimentary continental breakfast. Check-out noon. $

CROWNE PLAZA HOTEL BIRMINGHAM—THE REDMONT. ★★
2101 5th Ave, Birmingham (35203). Phone 205/324-2101; toll-free 800/227-6963. www.crowneplaza.com. As Birmingham's oldest hotel, this downtown location has since been meticulously renovated. Guests here are in the heart of the city's business and historical district. 114 rooms, 12 story. Check-in 3 pm, check-out noon. High-speed Internet access. Restaurant, bar. Fitness room. Airport transportation available. Business center. $

HAMPTON INN BIRMINGHAM-COLONNADE. ★
3400 Colonnade Pkwy, Birmingham (35243). Phone 205/967-0002; toll-free 800/861-7168. www.hamptoninn.com. Close to area attractions such as the botanical gardens, bowling, a zoo, and shopping, and a staff that exemplifies traditional Southern hospitality, this conveniently located hotel also features mountain views. 133 rooms, 5 story. Pets accepted. Complimentary continental breakfast. Check-in 3 pm, check-out noon. High-speed Internet access. Fitness room. Outdoor pool. Business center. $

HILTON BIRMINGHAM PERIMETER PARK. ★★★
8 Perimeter Dr, Birmingham (35243). Phone 205/967-2700; toll-free 800/774-1500. www.hilton.com. Set in an up-and-coming business and entertainment area, this large hotel is close to the downtown area's cultural and corporate destinations. Among the amenities in the attractive rooms are work desks and dual-line phones. 202 rooms, 8 story. Check-out noon. Wireless Internet access. Restaurant, bar. Fitness room. Outdoor pool. Airport transportation available. Business center. $$

RADISSON HOTEL BIRMINGHAM. ★★
808 S 20th St, Birmingham (35205). Phone 205/933-9000; toll-free 800/933-9000. www.radisson.com. In the heart of downtown and two blocks from the University and UAB Medical Center, this hotel is just a short walk to the Five Points entertainment and restaurant district. 287 rooms, 14 story. Check-out noon. Restaurant, bar. Outdoor pool. Airport transportation available. $

SHERATON BIRMINGHAM. ★★★
2101 Richard Arrington Jr Blvd N, Birmingham (35203). Phone 205/324-5000; toll-free 800/325-3535. www.sheraton.com. Located in downtown Birmingham, this hotel is a short stroll on the skywalk to the convention center. Explore the zoo, art museum, and Five Points South Historical District nearby. 770 rooms, 17 story. Check-out noon. Restaurant, bar. Fitness room. Indoor pool, whirlpool. Business center. $$

THE TUTWILER—A WYNDHAM HISTORIC HOTEL. ★★★
2021 Park Pl N, Birmingham (35203). Phone 205/322-2100; toll-free 877/999-3223. www.wyndham.com. This 1914 American classic has been restored to its original

BRAKE HERE

If you are traveling to Talladega in a large group—say, more than five—an affordable alternative during race weekend is renting a house. It's a fun way to keep everyone in your party together, and keep costs to a minimum. For more information, contact the Talladega Chamber of Commerce *(phone 256/362-9075, www.talladegachamber.com),* which provides an updated list of rentals with phone numbers, or visit the Web site, which provides links to view the houses.

grandeur and now is an elegant experience with gracious service and amenities. Nearby is the McWane Center and the Birmingham Museum of Art. 147 rooms, 8 story. Check-out noon. Restaurant, bar. Airport transportation available. $

THE WYNFREY HOTEL. ★★★
1000 Riverchase Galleria, Birmingham (35244). Phone 205/987-1600; toll-free 800/996-3769. www.wynfrey.com. Located just on the edge of the city, this gracious hotel combines Southern hospitality with European panache. The rooms and suites are tastefully appointed with plentiful amenities. 329 rooms, 16 story. Check-out 11 am. Restaurant. Fitness room. Pool. Airport transportation available. Business center. $$

Oxford

COMFORT INN OF OXFORD. ★
138 Elm St, Oxford (36203). Phone 256/835-2170; toll-free 800/228-5150. www.choicehotels.com. 62 rooms, 2 story. Complimentary continental breakfast. Check-in 2 pm, check-out 11 am. Fitness room. Outdoor pool. $

DAYS INN. ★
1 Recreation Dr, Oxford (36203). Phone 256/835-0300; toll-free 800/544-8313. www.daysinn.com. 100 rooms, 2 story. Pets accepted, some restrictions; fee. Complimentary continental breakfast. Check-in 1 pm, check-out noon. Outdoor pool. $

HOWARD JOHNSON. ★
I-20, exit 185, Oxford (36203). Phone 256/835-3988; toll-free 800/446-4656. www.hojo.com. 40 rooms, 1 story. Pets accepted; fee. Complimentary continental breakfast. Check-in 2 pm, check-out noon. Outdoor pool. $

JAMESON INN. ★
161 Colonial Dr, Oxford (36203). Phone 256/835-2170; toll-free 800/526-3766. www.jamesoninns.com. 60 rooms, 3 story. Pets accepted, some restrictions; fee. Complimentary continental breakfast. Fitness room. Pool. $

TRAVELODGE. ★
1207 Hwy 21 S, Oxford (36203). Phone 256/835-0185; toll-free 800/578-7878. www.travelodge.com. 40 rooms, 2 story. Pets accepted, some restrictions; fee. Check-in 9 am, check-out 11 am. Wireless Internet access. Restaurant. $

WINGATE INN. ★
143 Colonial Dr, Oxford (36203). Phone 256/831-1921; toll-free 800/228-1000. www.wingateinns.com. 60 rooms, 3 story. Complimentary continental breakfast. Check-in 2 pm, check-out 11 am. Fitness room. Outdoor pool. Business center. $

LOCAL RECOMMENDATIONS

Childersburg

DAYS INN.
33669 Hwy 280, Childersburg (35044). Phone 256/378-6007; toll-free 800/329-7466. www.daysinn.com. Guests here can order room service from Ponderosa Steakhouse. 40 rooms, 2 story. Check-in 1 pm, check-out noon. Outdoor pool. $

KEY WEST INN.
32210 Hwy 280, Childersburg (35044). Phone 256/378-0337; toll-free 866/253-9937. www.keywestinn.net. 43 rooms, 2 story. Pets accepted, some restrictions; fee. Complimentary continental breakfast. Check-in 2 pm, check-out 11 am. $

Leeds

COMFORT INN.
1951 Village Dr, Leeds (35094). Phone 205/640-6600; toll-free 800/228-5150. www.comfortinn.com. 45 rooms, 2 story. Complimentary continental breakfast. Check-in noon, check-out 11 am. High-speed Internet access. Fitness room. Outdoor pool. $

DAYS INN.
1835 Ashville Rd, Leeds (35094). Phone 205/699-9833; toll-free 800/329-7466. www.daysinn.com. 52 rooms, 2 story. Pets accepted, some restrictions; fee. Complimentary continental breakfast. Check-in 2 pm, check-out 11 am. Pool. $

GUEST HOUSE INN.
1093 Hargrove Pkwy, Leeds (35094). Phone 205/702-2700; toll-free 800/214-8378. www.guesthouse.net. 42 rooms, 2 story. Pets accepted, some restrictions; fee. Complimentary continental breakfast. Check-in 2 pm, check-out 11 am. Business center. $

Oxford

BEST WESTERN ANNISTON.
Hwys 78 and 21 S, Oxford (36203). Phone 256/831-3410; toll-free 877/888-6654. www.bestwestern.com. 190 rooms, 2 story. Pets accepted, some restrictions; fee. Check-in 2 pm, check-out noon. Outdoor pool, whirlpool. Business center. $

Pell City

HAMPTON INN PELL CITY.
220 Vaughan Ln, Pell City (35125). Phone 205/814-3000; toll-free 800/426-7866. www.hamptoninn.com. 60 rooms, 2 story. Check-in 3 pm, check-out 11 am. Fitness center. Outdoor pool. Business center. $

TREASURE ISLAND BED AND BREAKFAST.
Treasure Island Cir, Pell City (35054). Phone 205/525-5172. www.treasureislandbedandbreakfast.com. Two-night stay includes complimentary sunset pontoon boat ride on Logan Martin Lake. 4 rooms. Complimentary full breakfast. No credit cards accepted. $$$

Riverside

BEST WESTERN RIVERSIDE INN.
11900 Hwy 78, Riverside (35135). Phone 205/338-3381; toll-free 800/780-7234. www.bestwestern.com. 70 rooms, 2 story. Pets accepted, some restrictions. Check-in 1 pm, check-out 11 am. Restaurant. Outdoor pool, children's pool. $

Talladega

BUDGET INN AND SUITES.
65600 Hwy 77, Talladega (35160). Phone 256/362-0900; toll-free 800/295-2045. www.budgetinnandsuites.com. 45 rooms, 2 story. Check-in noon, check-out 11 am. Restaurant. Outdoor pool. $

THE GOVERNOR'S HOUSE.
500 Meadowlake Ln, Talladega (35160). Phone 205/763-2186. www.governorshouse.com. Only 4 miles from both the Talladega Superspeedway and the International Motorsports Hall of Fame, this country estate provides a quiet, elegant getaway from the nearby excitement. First night deposit required at reservation. Picnic lunch/dinner with homemade dinner available for fee, guests greeted with complimentary fruits and sweets. 4 rooms. No credit cards accepted. $$

SOMERSET HOUSE.
701 North St E, Talladega (35160). Phone 256/761-9251. www.bbonline.com/al/somerset. This opulent home treats its guests to in-room fireplaces, complimentary robes and slippers, nightly turndown, and personal wake-up call service. 5 rooms. Complimentary full breakfast. High-speed Internet access. $$

SUPER 8.
220 Haynes St, Talladega (35160). Phone 256/315-9511; toll-free 800/800-8000. www.super8.com. 50 rooms, 2 story. Pets accepted, some restrictions; fee. Complimentary continental breakfast. Check-in after noon, check-out 11 am. $

Vincent

BLUESPRING MANOR BED AND BREAKFAST.
2870 Hwy 83, Vincent (35178). Phone 205/672-9955. www.bluespringmanor.com. With freshly painted rooms of bold red, deep green, and soft yellow, hardwood floors, large windows that take in the landscape of the foothills, and snug rooms, guests are sure to get a good dose of R&R. 8 rooms. Spa. Pool, whirlpool. $$

For more lodging recommendations, go to www.mobiltravelguide.com

EAT

MOBIL STAR-RATED RESTAURANTS

Alexander City

CECIL'S PUBLIC HOUSE. ★
243 Green St, Alexander City (35010). Phone 256/329-0732. Set in a restored turn-of-the-century home,

this local favorite features country standbys like chicken-fried steak and an array of sandwiches, but surprises with dishes like chicken margoux and lobster ravioli. American menu. Lunch, dinner. Closed Sun; holidays. Bar. Children's menu. $

Anniston
BETTY'S BAR-B-Q. ★
401 S Quintard Ave, Anniston (36201). Phone 256/237-1411. Barbecue menu. Lunch, dinner. Closed Sun; holidays; also the week of July 4. Children's menu. $

Birmingham
HIGHLANDS. ★★★
2011 11th Ave S, Birmingham (35205). Phone 205/939-1400. www.highlandsbarandgrill.com. One of Birmingham's premiere restaurants for many years. The menu features French food with a Southern emphasis, the chef's signature style. French menu. Dinner. Closed Sun-Mon; holidays. Bar. Valet parking. $$$

NIKI'S WEST. ★★
233 Finley Ave W, Birmingham (35204). Phone 205/252-5751. Steak and seafood are on the menu, but you are welcome to go through the busy cafeteria line as well. Niki's is known for its "meat and three" options. Come hungry. Steak, seafood menu. Lunch, dinner. Closed Sun; holidays. $$

LOCAL RECOMMENDATIONS
Birmingham
BOTTEGA.
2240 Highland Ave, Birmingham (35205). Phone 205/939-1000. www.bottegarestaurant.com. Combining the flavors of Italy with bold American flavors, the menu is just as elegant as the atmosphere. Warm wood paneling and soft lighting complement the polished, creative menu. American, Italian menu. Lunch, dinner. Closed Sun; holidays. Bar. Children's menu. Valet parking. Outdoor seating. $$$

COBB LANE.
1 Cobb Ln, Birmingham (35205). Phone 205/933-0462. People keep coming back to the cobblestoned courtyard of this place for the perfectly seasoned Southern fare as well as the atmosphere, which includes live jazz performances. While several things might entice you, like Southern-fried catfish and Ovetta's chicken salad, try the she-crab soup—once declared by Julia Child the best in the country. American menu. Lunch, dinner. Bar. Outdoor seating. $$

Gadsden
ANTONELLI'S IMPORTS.
525 Broad St, Gadsden (35901). Phone 256/543-7473. In the mood for Italian cuisine and music? On the weekends, Antonelli's features local and regional bands while you're enjoying your pizza or spaghetti. Italian menu. Dinner. Closed holidays. $

PRUETT'S BBQ.
1617 Rainbow Dr, Gadsden (35901). Phone 256/547-9817. Yes, they are known for their barbecue. But don't overlook the other menu items, such as fried catfish, that have locals coming back for more. Barbecue menu. Lunch, dinner. Closed holidays. $

don't miss it

ROAD FOOD

If you are hankering for some serious barbecue, don't leave Talladega: **The Shack BBQ** *(7744 Stemley Bridge Rd, phone 256/268-2005)* serves up some of the best ribs in the area. If you're visiting Birmingham and are looking for something outside the traditional, head to **Andrew's BBQ** *(7532 1st Ave N, phone 205/833-9123).* For more than 50 years, Andrew's has served unusual garlic-flavored ribs with a tomato sauce—and you'll still see people cleaning their plates.

Leeds

HOT RODZ DRIVE IN.
233 Parkway Dr SW, Leeds (35094). Phone 205/699-7639. How can race fans pass up a name like Hot Rodz? You'll get a true blast from the past at this retro drive-in, as well as a decent hamburger and fries. American menu. Lunch. Closed holidays. Outdoor seating. $

OLD SMOKEY BAR-B-Q.
923 Parkway Dr SW, Leeds (35094). Phone 205/699-7904. For many travelers, a trip to Alabama is all about trying as much barbecue as possible. Thirty miles from the racetrack, Old Smokey specializes in pork barbecue plates, sandwiches, ribs, and juicy hamburgers, and they get you in and out in no time. Barbecue menu. Lunch, dinner. Closed holidays. $

Oxford

FUJI JAPANESE CUISINE.
168 Davis Loop, Oxford (36203). Phone 256/835-8788. Good sushi in Alabama isn't an oxymoron at this hideaway, 14 miles from the track. In addition to the full-service sushi bar, there's a Japanese menu, for those who like their dinner cooked. Japanese menu. Lunch, dinner. Closed Sun; holidays. $$

JACK'S FAMILY RESTAURANT.
609 Snow St, Oxford (36203). Phone 256/835-0703. www.eatatjacks.com. If your family can't agree on what to eat, head to Jack's. From biscuits in the morning to hamburgers at noon and chicken at supper, there is something for every eater. Your kids can expend some energy at Jack's playground. RV parking available. Get coupons and monthly specials online. American menu. Breakfast, lunch, dinner. Closed holidays. $

SONNY'S REAL PIT BBQ.
219 Colonial Dr, Oxford (36203). Phone 256/831-7933. www.sonnysbbq.com. If you can smoke it, grill it, deep-fry it, or smother it in barbecue sauce, it's on the menu. For those who can't decide between the smoked chicken, St. Louis ribs, or pulled pork, huge combination platters are available. Barbecue menu. Lunch, dinner. Children's menu. Closed holidays. $

Pell City

CHARLIE'S COUNTRY CATFISH.
4208 Cogswell Ave, Pell City (35125). Phone 205/884-3474. Fried, baked, sautéed, nestled between two halves of a sandwich roll—you name it, they've got it here. Also popular are the fried dills. Southern menu. Lunch, dinner. Closed Sun; holidays. $

PELL CITY STEAKHOUSE.
215 Comer Ave, Pell City (35125). Phone 205/338-7714. If you want steak and your buddy wants seafood, both of you will leave Pell City Steakhouse satisfied, with its good portions of steak, chicken, seafood, and vegetables. Steak, seafood menu. Lunch, dinner. Closed holidays. $

Riverside

THE ARK RESTAURANT.
13030 Hwy 78, Riverside (35125). Phone 205/338-7420. www.thearkrestaurant.com. For more than 60 years, this old-school Southern restaurant has been an area legend, offering chicken, shrimp, and some salads. Patrons generally agree that the main reason to visit this '50s-style family eatery is the old Southern standby of catfish and hush puppies. American, Southern menu. Lunch, dinner. Closed holidays. $

Talladega

GOLDEN EAGLE RESTAURANT.
811 Battle St E, Talladega (35160). Phone 256/362-8383. Talladega's Chinese buffet restaurant serves Chinese-American favorites like sweet and sour chicken, spring rolls, and fried rice. Chinese, American menu. Lunch, dinner. Closed holidays. $

MATEHUALA MEXICAN RESTAURANT.
114 Court Sq S, Talladega (35160). Phone 256/362-5754. Named after a region in Mexico, this local favorite serves traditional Mexican food close to the NASCAR track. Mexican menu. Lunch, dinner. Closed Sun; holidays. $

OLD MILL RESTAURANT.
57900 Hwy 77, Talladega (35160). Phone 256/761-0043. Families love the down-home atmosphere at this all-American restaurant. Don't be surprised if you're the only out-of-towner—this is where the locals meet and catch up. American menu. Lunch, dinner. Closed Sun; holidays. $

For more dining recommendations, go to www.mobiltravelguide.com

SIDE TRIP

Sunny Southern Heritage
Mobile, AL

Stroll through the Bellingrath Gardens and 1935 home. Mobile is about a five-hour drive south from Talladega, with the majority of the drive along Interstate 65. The town is nestled between Mobile and Polecat bays.

Carl Carmer, author of *Stars Fell on Alabama*, said it best: "Mobile stays in the heart, loveliest of all cities." Mobile is a perfect getaway spot, proud of its 300-year-old heritage, now reflected in museums and historical homes. The 65-acre **Bellingrath Gardens and Homes** (phone 251/973-2217, www.bellingrath.org) features a garden and nature trail. **Bragg-Mitchell Mansion** (phone 251/471-6364, www.braggmitchellmansion.com), is one of Mobile's grandest restored antebellum mansions.

Fort Condé Museum (phone 251/208-7569), located in downtown Mobile, is a partial replica of the 18th-century French fort. **USS Alabama Battleship Memorial Park** (phone 251/433-2703, toll-free 800/426-4929, www.ussalabama.com), has been home to the USS *Alabama*, a World War II battleship nicknamed "Lucky A" for its ability to escape damage, since 1965. Or visit the World War II **USS** *Drum* **submarine** and other military aircraft and machinery. Nearby is the 1,327-acre **Meaher State Park** (phone 251/626-5529), with boardwalk nature trails over Mobile Delta, fishing, and camping.

New Orleans may have made Mardi Gras famous, but Mobile claims the original celebration, held 62 years before New Orleans's. Visit **William & Emily Hearin Mardis Gras Museum** (phone 251/432-3524), whose grand opening is scheduled for Mardis Gras 2005 (call ahead for exact dates). Although Mobile's party is tamer than in New Orleans, beads are still thrown, as are Moon Pies.

Speaking of food, locals will tell you not to leave without sampling some of the favorites, such as oysters any way you want them: nude, stewed, or fried. Try **Wintzell's** (phone 251/432-4605, www.wintzellsoysterhouse.com), **Original Oyster House** (phone 251/626-2188, www.originaloysterhouse.com), or **Roussos** (phone 251/433-3322, www.roussosrestaurant.com).

For more Mobile recommendations, go to www.mobiltravelguide.com

454

Cars are lined up and the stands are full before a race at Texas Motor Speedway.

Texas Motor Speedway

Fort Worth, TX

28

Jeff Gordon is surrounded by NASCAR fans as he signs autographs.

TRACK FACTS

TEXAS MOTOR SPEEDWAY. 3601 Hwy 114, Justin (76247). Phone 817/215-8500. www.texasmotorspeedway.com. (The speedway is located in a part of Fort Worth that was formerly Justin. If using an online mapping service, try entering both Justin and Fort Worth.)

SECURITY. Each ticket holder may bring in a cooler, but it must be no larger than 14 x 14 x 14 inches. Glass containers, strollers, umbrellas, and other items that might obscure views are prohibited. Backpacks and fannypacks are allowed, but subject to searches. A security trailer is located across from the South Tunnel on Allison Avenue between Lone Star and Victory circles.

PARKING. There are 60,000 unmarked free parking spots around the track, as well as an additional 20,000 paved ones. Use the numbered towers and gates on the track to mentally mark your location. Handicapped parking is on the front- and backstretches, as well as in additional free lots. Campers receive two parking passes—one for an RV and one for a personal vehicle. If your car breaks down or you lock your keys in your car, go to the security trailer and notify a security representative. Can't find your car? Security will drive you around in a golf cart to help you locate it.

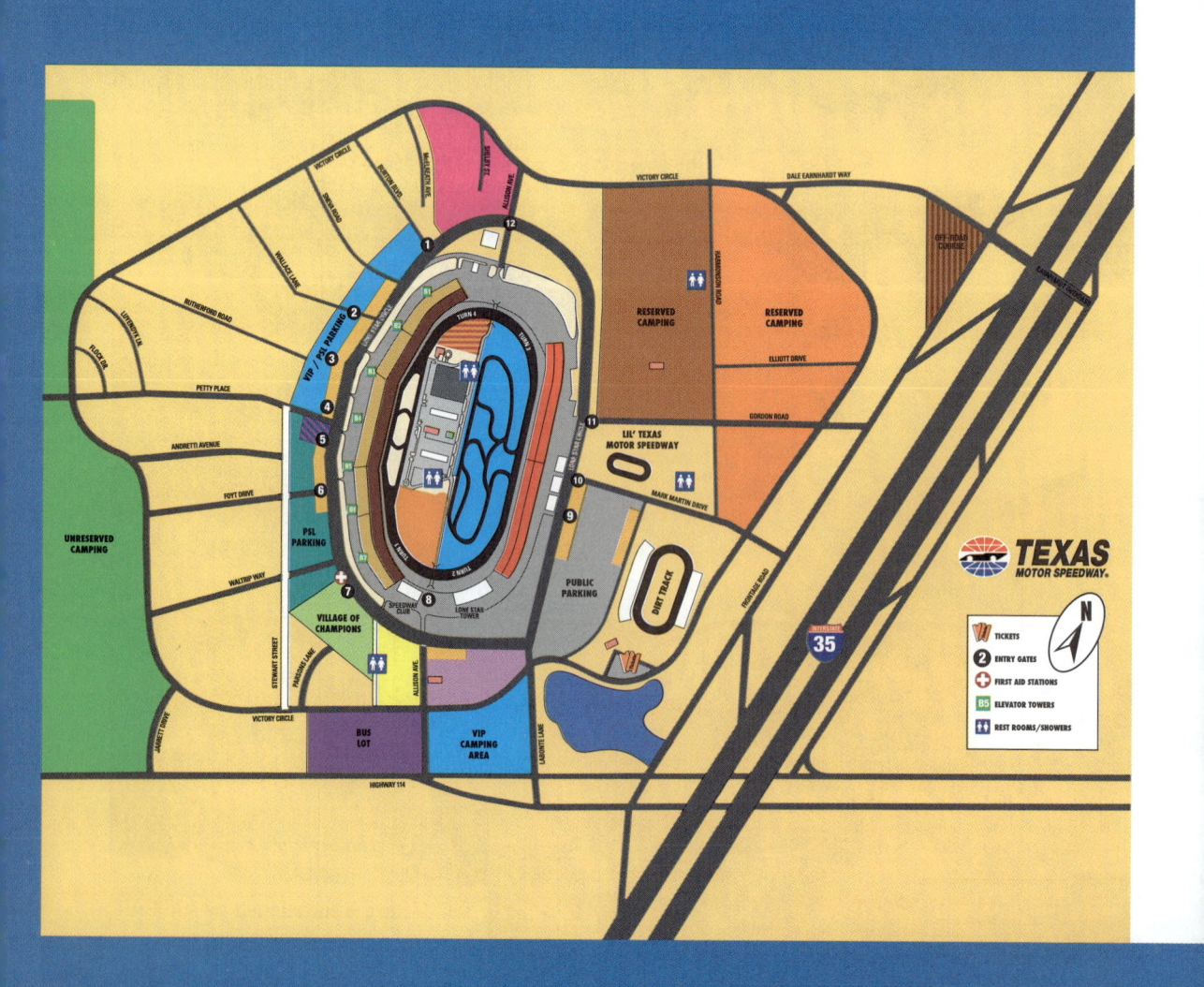

FIRST AID. Mobile medical teams roam the track before, during, and after races. If medical attention is required, give your seat number and section to a speedway representative. They will send a medical team to your seat. The nearest hospitals are Columbia North Hills Hospital in North Richland Hills (4401 Booth Calloway Rd, phone 817/255-1000), about 20 miles south of the speedway, and Denton Community Hospital (207 N Bonnie Brae, phone 940/898-7000), about 15 miles north in Denton.

CONCESSIONS. Food and drink stands are located at every gate except the two tunnel entrances at Gates 8 and 12. More than 40 vendors serve up goodies ranging from barbecue prime rib and chicken and biscuits to deep-fried pickle spears and sugared nuts. Alcoholic beverages including beer and margaritas can be purchased at beer gardens inside the speedway. A "souvenir alley" of more than 75 semitrailers selling NASCAR, driver, and track merchandise opens before the speedway gates.

RESTROOMS. The track contains 2,450 toilets with women's facilities outnumbering men's by a 2 to 1 margin. Restrooms are located near the concession stands.

Elliott Sadler celebrates the sweet taste of success as confetti rains down.

An impressive view of the speedway from high overhead on race day.

If you think NASCAR fans are wild, check out the wildlife at the Fort Worth Zoo.

Texas Motor Speedway (TMS) features a 1 1/2-mile, quad-oval track that looks similiar to the Lowe's Motor Speedway near Charlotte, North Carolina—but the two have differences. This is where Dale Earnhardt Jr. won his first NASCAR Cup race; and it's where Jeff Gordon has yet to leave his mark.

Each year, more than 200,000 enthusiastic fans converge on this speedway for the NASCAR NEXTEL Cup race, many of them approaching the track before dawn on Sunday, some as early as 4:30 am. Overall, it's well designed, with staff focused on ensuring fans a first-rate experience. Gastronomical delights range from mouthwatering Longhorn barbecue prime rib, Fletchers hand-dipped corny dogs, and Williams chicken and biscuits to the novelty deep-fried pickle spears and sugared nuts. Reata Restaurant joins the more than 40 food vendors in 2005, adding their award-winning tamales to the mix. Even "Souvenir Alley," with more than 75 tractor trailers hawking an array of driver, NASCAR, and TMS merchandise, opens before the track gates to reward the dawn owls. Fight the chill by purchasing $3 cups of coffee and $5 breakfast burritos from the outside vendors. *Tip:* to catch a glimpse of your favorite driver, don't haunt the souvenir area. Buy a ticket to the infield ($65 in advance for a wristband pass, even if you camp there), so you can press your nose against the fences surrounding the Competitor RV and Garage areas.

There are 60,000 unmarked free parking spots and 20,000 paved spots located around the speedway. Use the numbered towers and gates to mentally mark your location (or write it on your hand). Tailgating in the parking areas fires up early, so bring your gas grill—and your can-filled cooler. Bring enough coolers for tailgating, for the race (14 x 14 x 14 inches), and for the time following the race if you try to flee after the checkered flag hails the winner. Beer, margaritas, and rum-spiked smoothies are available at the gate beer gardens—but you have to imbibe there, so they're heavily congested before the race start. Avoid the mad rush to the restrooms during yellow flags. Absolutely rent or buy a scanner and headphones so you can hear the drivers talk to their pit crews. If the sun makes you cranky, nab a grandstand seat in Rows 50-66, as they're shaded by the overhanging skyboxes, and keep hydrated with the track's $4 Texas Sweet Tea and fresh-squeezed lemonade.

WHERE EAST MEETS WEST

Somewhere between Dallas and Fort Worth is an invisible line dividing the East and the West: Dallas is a slick, sophisticated town, where "new" money flows like water. Fort Worth offers a more traditional Texas atmosphere but also boasts a world-class cultural district.

You can get up close and personal with real cowboys in nearby Fort Worth, where major industries include cattle, oil, and aircraft. The city's charming downtown area is highlighted by the popular **Sundance**

Square (www.sundancesquare.com), which features trendy restaurants, shops, and theaters, including the prestigious Bass Hall. Just north of downtown is the **Fort Worth Stockyards National Historical District** (phone 817/624-4741, www.fortworthstockyards.org) with its Old West feel. It is quite safe at night, but cowboys do love to drink, so keep an eye out for bubbling brawls if you decide to do some bar-hopping. Wanna feel like a cowboy when you're in the Fort Worth Stockyards? Belly up to the bar at the **White Elephant Saloon** (106 E Exchange Ave, phone 817/624-8273, www.whiteelephantsaloon.com). This authentic Old West saloon will get you in the mood with its long wooden stand-up bar and brass foot rail. There's a lot to see, beyond the live entertainment—rumor has it that Chuck Norris makes an occasional appearance. And if you want to add some scuff to your boots, head on over to **Billy Bob's Texas** (250 Rodeo Plaza, phone 817/624-7117, www.billybobstexas.com), the world's largest honky-tonk. The place encompasses nearly 7 acres and has free line-dancing lessons every Thursday from 7 to 8 pm, so your chances of findin' a dance partner are pretty darn good.

The nationally ranked **Fort Worth Zoo** (1989 Colonial Pkwy, phone 817/759-7555, www.fortworthzoo.com) is a huge draw and a must-see. Other worthwhile attractions include the cultural district's five first-rate museums and galleries, which include the Kimbell Art Museum and the Modern Art Museum of Fort Worth.

While the summers in the Lone Star State may swelter, the average high in April is a pleasant 76 degrees. In November, conditions are still quite comfortable at 67 degrees. However, the Dallas-Fort Worth area does attract its fair share of heavy weather including tornados, particularly during April and May.

Dallas is a metropolitan city full of galleries, museums, fine cuisine—and a heavy social calendar to boot. It is also just a short drive (less than an hour) from the track.

If you live to shop, you'll adore Dallas, including the thrill of visiting the downtown headquarters of **Neiman Marcus** (One Marcus Sq, phone 214/741-6911, www.neimanmarcus.com). While whipping out that credit card, take a moment to appreciate the beautiful downtown architecture. The glass buildings are particularly gorgeous at sunset. The locals are

GETTING AROUND

When planning your travel route, it's critical to enter the track near your seating area, due to the heavy volume of vehicles converging on the speedway on NASCAR NEXTEL Cup Sunday. Most traffic snarls are on westbound Hwy 114.

If your seats are on the front stretch, and you're coming from Dallas, it's recommended you head north on I-35 E to Denton and come back south on I-35 W to the speedway, exiting on Dale Earnhardt Way (exit 72) and avoiding Hwy 114.

An alternate route to I-35 W is south on FM 156, which runs parallel to I-35 W. Coming from Fort Worth, you can branch off I-35 W onto Hwy 287, toward Decatur, and then come east on Hwy 114.

For backstretch parking, exit Dale Earnhardt Way (exit 72) from northbound I-35 W and the Hwy 114 exit (exit 70) from southbound I-35 W. Traffic will be directed to turn on Mark Martin Dr, and park in the free parking outside Gates 9 and 10. *TIP:* Remember, there is two-lane exiting at Hwy 114 and Dale Earnhardt Way from both directions off I-35 W.

You can still avoid bumper-to-bumper traffic if you arrive early—preferably by 7 am.

Remember, despite its Fort Worth location, the speedway's zip code sometimes lists it in Justin (the area was incorporated as Fort Worth in 1996). If using online services for more detailed directions, try entering both cities.

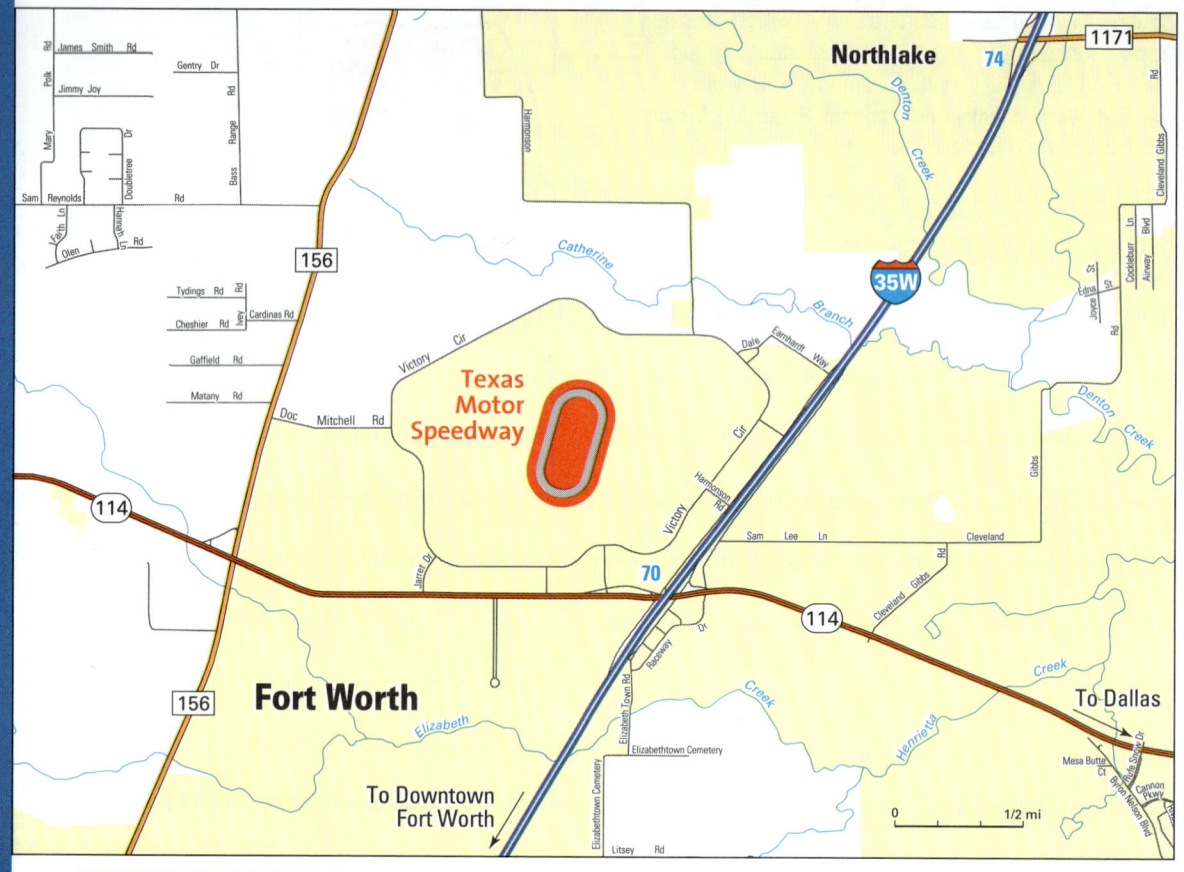

FORT WORTH POLE POSITION:
The 10 miles surrounding Texas Motor Speedway.

very friendly—although some change when they get behind the wheel.

The West End may be Dallas's true historic district, but locals know it's become a bit touristy. Sure, there are old warehouses, shops, restaurants, and a movie theater, but you may also find high prices, thick crowds, and aggressive rose vendors.

Other areas of interest include Deep Ellum (considered by many to be the "cultural heartbeat" of Dallas) or West Village. Both offer live music, bars, restaurants, and eclectic shops. **The Magnolia Theatre in West Village** (3699 McKinney Ave, phone 214/764-9106, www.landmarktheatres.com) shows cool art films.

Don't miss this: the downtown **Dallas Public Library** (1515 Young St, phone 214/670-1400, www.dallaslibrary.org) has an original copy of The Declaration of Independence on permanent display. If you decide to visit the **Southfork Ranch** (3700 Hogge Rd, phone 972/442-7800, www.southforkranch.com), the home featured in the television show *Dallas*, in nearby Murphy, you might be disappointed at how small it is—and out $8 to boot.

The highways are difficult during peak travel times (7-9 am and 4-6 pm), particularly US 75, Interstate 35, and Interstate 635, and that can bring out some bad driving: abrupt lane changes, tailgating, and speeding are common. In fact, a 2003 study found Dallas to be among the top five cities in the country for dodgy driving behavior. So, if someone lets you in, be nice and offer a friendly wave. Of particular note are the unusually short on and off ramps, so you don't have a lot of time to merge into traffic. HOV Lanes are available, but make sure you have two people in your car—or risk being ticketed.

FORT WORTH CALENDAR

APRIL 16, 2005
NASCAR Busch Series

APRIL 17, 2005
NASCAR NEXTEL Cup Series

APRIL–SEPTEMBER, 2005
Mesquite Championship Rodeo. Resistol Arena, 1818 Rodeo Dr, Mesquite (75149). Phone 972/285-8777; toll-free 800/833-9339. www.mesquiterodeo.com. What's more Texan than a rodeo? Experience the excitement of the Western Frontier. Friday and Saturday nights, April through September.

JUNE 4, 2005
Dog Days of Summer. Main St, Denton (76201). Phone 940/349-8529. www.dentonmainstreet.org. It's a dog's life at this festival complete with stupid pet tricks, a pet parade, and paw reading.

JUNE 10, 2005
NASCAR Craftsman Truck Series

NOVEMBER 4, 2005
NASCAR Craftsman Truck Series

NOVEMBER 5, 2005
NASCAR Busch Series

NOVEMBER 6, 2005
NASCAR NEXTEL Cup Series

NOVEMBER, 2005
Country at Heart Craft Show. Plano Centre, 2000 E Spring Creek Pkwy, Plano (75074). Phone toll-free 800/783-4526. A holiday shopping spree Texas-style, with traditional, country, Victorian, and Southwestern décor; clothes; toys; dolls; candles; and more. Early November.

Experience Texas life at the Fort Worth Stockyards' daily cattle drive.

INSIDER'S PICK

Everything's big in Texas...and that means even local chains attract big names. NASCAR president **Mike Helton** heads to the Alliance Center for some traditional Texas fare. "When I'm in Texas, I always go to **Sonny Bryan's Barbeque** out on Westport Parkway. They have the best barbecue I've found." $ *2421 Westport Pkwy, Fort Worth (76177). Phone 817/224-9191. www.sonnybryansbbq.com.*

FORT WORTH OUTFIELD:
The 50 miles surrounding Texas Motor Speedway.

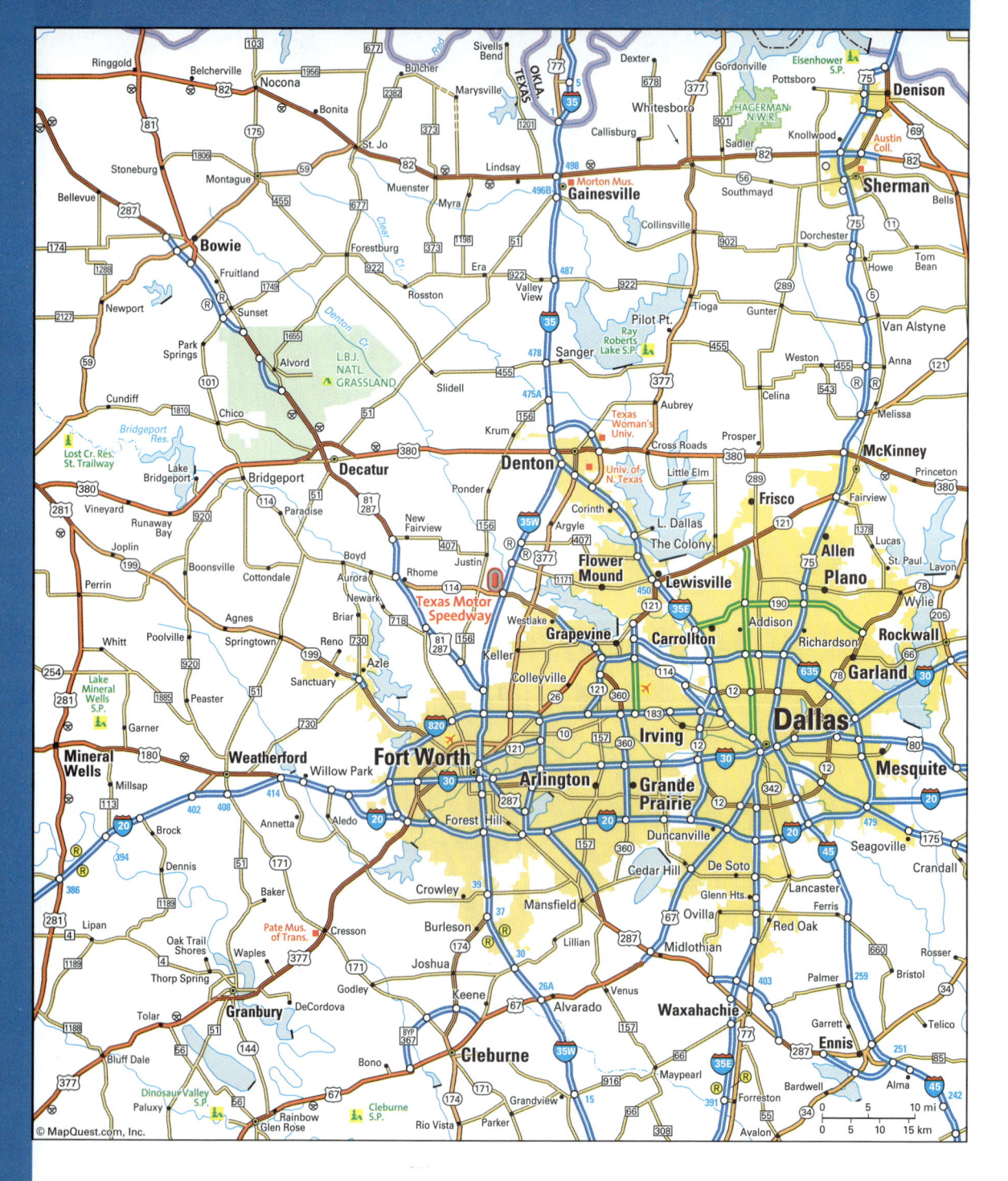

SEE

ATTRACTIONS

Arlington

LEGENDS OF THE GAME BASEBALL MUSEUM.
Ameriquest Field, 1000 Ballpark Way, Suite 400, Arlington (76011). Phone 817/273-5600. www.rangers.mlb.com/NASApp/mlb/tex/ballpark/tex_ballpark_museum.jsp. This museum is located off Interstate 30 between Dallas and Fort Worth in Ameriquest Field, home of the Texas Rangers. It showcases numerous baseball artifacts of legends such as Hank Aaron, Ty Cobb, Lou Gehrig, and Babe Ruth. The Learning Center features interactive activities for all ages. Admission includes museum and ballpark tour. (Hours vary by season; no tours on day games) **$$**

SIX FLAGS OVER TEXAS.
2201 Road to Six Flags, Arlington (76010). Phone 817/530-6000. www.sixflags.com/parks/overtexas/index.asp. The park is located just west of the junction of Highway 360 and Interstate 30. More than 100 rides, shows, and attractions including the world's top-rated wooden roller coaster, the Texas Giant, a monster that towers 14 stories and reaches 62 mph. Two new attractions: Superman Tower of Power, the tallest ride of its kind in the world, and SpongeBob SquarePants 4-D, which lets guests experience the adventures of the Nickelodeon star and his Bikini Bottom pals. *Note*: No ice chests or picnic baskets allowed. Buy tickets online and save 25 percent off the general admission price. **$$$$**

Dallas

THE SIXTH FLOOR MUSEUM AT DEALEY PLAZA.
411 Elm St, Dallas (75202). Phone 214/747-6660. www.jfk.org. In 1963, President John F. Kennedy was assassinated in Dallas while traveling in a motorcade. This downtown museum pays tribute to the president's life, death, and legacy through artifacts, historic films, interpretive displays, and photographs. The site is the former Texas School Book Depository, where a sniper's nest and rifle were found on the sixth floor after the assassination shots rang out. (Daily 9 am-6 pm) **$$**

Fort Worth

BUREAU OF ENGRAVING AND PRINTING'S WESTERN CURRENCY FACILITY TOUR AND VISITOR CENTER.
9000 Blue Mound Rd, Fort Worth (76131). Phone 817/231-4000; toll free 866/865-1194. www.moneyfactory.com. See money (bills from $1 to $50) being printed as you walk along an enclosed walkway suspended over the production floor. Two floors of interactive displays showcase the history of currency and the printing process. Theater, gift shop, vending areas. Call ahead to schedule a tour. Tours (Mon-Fri 9 am-2 pm). **FREE**

FORT WORTH MUSEUM OF SCIENCE & HISTORY.
1501 Montgomery St, Fort Worth (76107). Phone 817/255-9300; toll-free 888/255-9300. www.fortworthmuseum.org. One of the largest science and history museums in the Southwest, this outstanding facility offers exhibits on fossils, anthropology, geology, natural sciences, and history. Nine permanent exhibits include DinoDig, KIDSPACE, and Hands On Science. Visit the spectacular Omni Theater and Noble Planetarium. (Mon-Thurs 9 am-5:30 pm, Fri-Sat 9 am-8 pm, Sun 11:30 am-5:30 pm) **$$$**

FORT WORTH STOCKYARDS.
121 E Exchange Ave, Fort Worth (76106). From downtown Fort Worth, head N on N Main St to Exchange Ave and turn right. Phone 817/626-7921. www.fortworthstockyards.org. Check out the daily cattle drive as cowboys herd beefy steers down the streets at 11:30 am and 4 pm. This lively district celebrates all things Western in its ten square blocks. Down an ice-cold longneck beer in the saloon, cheer on the bull riders at the rodeo, get decked out in Western duds from one of the many stores, and go for a spin on the dance floor at Billy Bob's Texas, the "world's largest honky-tonk." Parking (fee) in lots around Stockyards Station; street parking along East Exchange Avenue is free.

FORT WORTH ZOO.
1989 Colonial Pkwy, Fort Worth (76110). Phone 817/759-7555. www.fortworthzoo.com. The zoo features more than 400 species from around the world in lush, natural-habit settings. It's one of only two US zoos with all four Great Ape species in residence: bonobos,

chimpanzees, gorillas, and orangutans. The zoo also features a train ride, carousel, and interactive displays. Visit the Parrot Paradise exhibit that features more than 600 parrots and feed the birds. The interactive exhibit features a water-filled moat and waterfall. (Apr-mid-Oct: Mon-Fri 10 am-5 pm, Sat-Sun 10 am-6 pm; mid-Oct-mid-Feb: daily 10 am-4 pm) $$

Mesquite

MESQUITE CHAMPIONSHIP RODEO.
1818 Rodeo Dr, Mesquite (75149). Phone 972/285-8777; toll-free 800/833-9339. www.mesquiterodeo.com. This world-famous bronco-bustin' fun is just 15 minutes from downtown Dallas. Ultramodern, air-conditioned facility. (Apr-Sept, weekends) $$

For more attractions, go to www.mobiltravelguide.com

STAY

MOBIL STAR-RATED LODGINGS

Dallas

HOLIDAY INN SELECT DALLAS NORTH. ★★
2645 LBJ Fwy, Dallas (75234). Phone 972/243-3563; toll-free 800/465-4329. www.holiday-inn.com. With a great location and affordable rates, this hotel is near area restaurants and shopping and offers complimentary shuttle service within 5 miles. With additional amenities for the business traveler, the comfortable accommodations here will suit every kind of guest. 377 rooms, 6 story. Check-in 3 pm, check-out noon. Restaurant, bar. Fitness room. Indoor pool, outdoor pool, whirlpool. $

SHERATON DALLAS BROOKHOLLOW HOTEL. ★★★
1241 W Mockingbird Ln, Dallas (75247). Phone 214/630-7000; toll-free 800/442-7547. www.sheraton.com. Ideally located just 10 minutes from downtown Dallas, and 30 minutes from Six Flags and Hurricane Harbor, this hotel has something for everyone. 348 rooms, 13 story. Pets accepted, some restrictions; fee. Check-in 3 pm, check-out noon. Restaurant, bar. Fitness room. Outdoor pool. Airport transportation available. $$

THE WESTIN GALLERIA DALLAS. ★★★
13340 Dallas Pkwy, Dallas (75240). Phone 972/934-9494; toll-free 800/228-3000. www.westin.com. Located within the Galleria center, this hotel provides access to more than 200 shops, several restaurants, and entertainment. 432 rooms, 17 story. Pets accepted, some restrictions. Check-in 3 pm, check-out 1 pm. High-speed Internet access. Two restaurants, three bars. Fitness room. Outdoor pool. Business center. $$$

Fort Worth

COURTYARD BY MARRIOTT DOWNTOWN. ★
601 Main St, Fort Worth (76102). Phone 817/885-8700; toll-free 800/321-2211. www.courtyard.com. This hotel's prime location within walking distance of all of Fort Worth's restaurants, attractions, and night life, makes it ideal for visitors to the city. Relax in the whirlpool or work out in the hotel's fitness room to unwind after a long day. 203 rooms, 20 story. Pets accepted, some restrictions; fee. Check-in 3 pm, check-out noon. High-speed Internet access. Fitness room. Outdoor pool, whirlpool. Business center. $

DORAL TESORO HOTEL & GOLF RESORT. ★★★
3300 Championship Pkwy, Fort Worth (76177). Phone 817/961-0800; toll-free 866/333-6725. www.doraltesoro.com. This is the official hotel of the Texas Motor Speedway and is located just across the street from the track. Set in a resort-style atmosphere, the hotel overlooks a Jay Morrish-designed 18-hole championship golf course. 286 rooms, 10 story. Pets accepted. Check-in 3 pm, check-out noon. Restaurant, bar. Fitness room. Outdoor pool, whirlpool. Golf, 18 holes. Airport transportation available. Business center. $

Irving

HOMEWOOD SUITES LAS COLINAS. ★
4300 Wingren Blvd, Irving (75039). Phone 972/556-0665. www.homewoodsuites.com. 136 rooms, all suites. Pets accepted, some restrictions; fee. Check-in 3 pm,

check-out noon. High-speed Internet access. Fitness room. Outdoor pool, whirlpool. Business center. $

LOCAL RECOMMENDATIONS

Arlington

BEST WESTERN COOPER INN & SUITES.
4024 Melear Rd, Arlington (76015). Phone 817/784-9490; toll-free 800/780-7234. www.bestwestern.com. This hotel is located 6 miles from Six Flags and 20 miles from Texas Motor Speedway. 66 rooms, 2 story. Complimentary continental breakfast. Check-in 3 pm, check-out noon. High-speed Internet access. Fitness room. Outdoor pool. $

BEST WESTERN GREAT SOUTHWEST INN.
3501 E Division St (Hwy 180), Arlington (76011). Phone 817/640-7722; toll-free 800/780-7234. www.bestwestern.com. 116 rooms, 2 story. Complimentary full breakfast. Check-in 2 pm, check-out 11 am. High-speed Internet access. Fitness room. Outdoor pool. $

Benbrook

BEST WESTERN WINSCOTT INN AND SUITES.
590 Winscott Rd, Benbrook (76126). Phone 817/249-0076; toll-free 800/780-7234. www.bestwestern.com. Located near Fort Worth Zoo, antiques shops, and several restaurants. 52 rooms, 2 story. Complimentary continental breakfast. Check-in 3 pm, check-out noon. Fitness room. Outdoor pool, whirlpool. $

Dallas

BEST WESTERN MARKET CENTER.
2023 Market Center Blvd, Dallas (75207). Phone 214/741-9000; toll-free 800/780-7234. www.bestwestern.com. 98 rooms, 2 story. Complimentary continental breakfast. Check-in 3 pm, check-out noon. High-speed Internet access. Fitness room. Outdoor pool. $

BEST WESTERN NORTHWEST INN.
2361 W Northwest Hwy, Dallas (75220). Phone 214/353-8774; toll-free 800/780-7234. www.bestwestern.com. 63 rooms, 3 story. Complimentary full breakfast. Check-in 2 pm, check-out 11 am. Fitness room. Outdoor pool. $

Fort Worth

BEST WESTERN FORT WORTH INN & SUITES.
201 W Loop 820 N, Fort Worth (76108). Phone 817/246-8777; toll-free 800/780-7234. www.bestwestern.com. This hotel is located 25 miles from Texas Motor Speedway. 50 rooms, 2 story. Check-in noon, check-out 11 am. High-speed Internet access. Fitness room. Outdoor pool, whirlpool. $

BEST WESTERN INN.
6700 Fossil Bluff Dr, Fort Worth (76137). Phone 817/847-8484; toll-free 800/780-7234. www.bestwestern.com. 66 rooms, 3 story. Complimentary continental breakfast. Check-in 2 pm, check-out noon. Fitness room. Outdoor pool, whirlpool. $

BEST WESTERN INN & SUITES.
6500 South Fwy, Fort Worth (76134). Phone 817/551-6700; toll-free 800/780-7234. www.bestwestern.com. This hotel is 21 miles from Texas Motor Speedway. 60 rooms, 2 story. Complimentary continental breakfast. Check-in 2 pm, check-out noon. High-speed Internet access. Fitness room. Outdoor pool, whirlpool. $

PIT PASS

Infield spectators in the know about where to go opt for their own lockable portable toilets. United Site Services (phone 817/819-3982 or cindie.hinojosa@unitedsiteservices.com) will rent a basic portable toilet for $72 per week. A handicapped-accessible version goes for $90 per week while a flushable version with a sink costs $125. It costs $10 to have them pumped out. Longtime fans say the porta-potties save time that might be spent standing in line. Advance orders can be charged, but if you wait until you arrive at the track, transactions are cash only.

STAY LOCAL RECOMMENDATIONS

BEST WESTERN INNSUITES HOTEL & SUITES FORT WORTH.
2000 Beach St, Fort Worth (76103). Phone 817/534-4801; toll-free 800/780-7234. www.bestwestern.com. This hotel is 20 miles from Texas Motor Speedway. 167 rooms, 2 story. Pets accepted, some restrictions; fee. Complimentary full breakfast. Check-in 3 pm, check-out noon. High-speed Internet access. Fitness room. Outdoor pool. Airport transportation available. **$**

Irving

BEST WESTERN DFW AIRPORT SUITES.
5050 W John Carpenter Hwy, Irving (75063). Phone 972/870-0530; toll-free 800/780-7234. www.bestwestern.com. This hotel is 10 miles from Texas Motor Speedway. 70 rooms, 3 story. Complimentary continental breakfast. Check-in 3 pm, check-out noon. High-speed Internet access. Fitness room. Outdoor pool. Airport transportation available. **$**

BEST WESTERN IRVING INN & SUITES AT DFW AIRPORT.
4110 W Airport Fwy, Irving (75062). Phone 972/790-2262; toll-free 800/780-7234. www.bestwestern.com. This hotel has the atmosphere of an English country inn. 140 rooms, 2 story. Complimentary continental breakfast. Check-in 3 pm, check-out 11 am. High-speed Internet access. Fitness room. Outdoor pool. Airport transportation available. **$**

Lake Worth

BEST WESTERN LAKE WORTH INN AND SUITES.
3920 Boat Club Rd, Lake Worth (76135). Phone 817/238-1199; toll-free 800/780-7234. www.bestwestern.com. This hotel is situated near shops, restaurants, museums, and the zoo. 50 rooms, 2 story. Check-in 3 pm, check-out noon. Fitness room. Outdoor pool. **$**

RV AND CAMPING

HELLMANN'S MAYONNAISE INFIELD CAMPING.
Here you can watch the race from the roof of your RV; there's no traffic to deal with once you've parked in your allotted space, and you have first dibs on the 300 Team Texas Driving School slots ($150 for three laps with an instructor). *Note:* there is a waiting list for this area known as "party central," so jump on the list.

BRAKE HERE

Featured in the TV series *Walker, Texas Ranger* and named one of the "Best 100 Bars in America" by *Esquire* magazine, the **White Elephant Saloon** is the must-stop spot for fans who need a night out. Check out the huge collection of cowboy hats on the walls and ceilings, and the extensive collection of white elephant figurines from all over the world. Live country and western music and dancing seven nights a week. From April to October, this Stockyards area beer garden offers live music outdoors on weekends. **106 E Exchange Ave, Fort Worth (76106). Phone 817/624-8273.**

TMS RESERVED CAMPING.
Some 40,000 gung-ho campers (tent and RV) transform the speedway into a small city—complete with on-site grocery—a full week before the Cup race. Many fans return yearly to the same assigned sites, where $1 million has been spent to reinforce the infield and outside camping areas with gravel. A 1 am noise curfew is enforced, but fans may continue to party quietly. *Note:* there is limited unreserved camping on the west side of the track during Cup race weeks.

WORKHORSE CUSTOM CHASSIS RESERVED CAMPING.
The 5,000 Lone Star Circle and Victory Circle sites located outside Turn 3 will put mileage on your pedometer, but a free shuttle can whisk you to the track if long treks make you puff. The shower shuttle

ferries you to two 26-stall shower facilities. Lone Star offers sloping areas and trees; Victory Circle is a flat field. While Lone Star is a better deal, as you're closer to the track, be savvy: if your choice is between the west side of Victory Circle or the east side of Lone Star (basically the same area), you'll save money by staying in Victory Circle.

WORKHORSE CUSTOM CHASSIS VIP CAMPING.
This is the only site with full hook-ups and an asphalt base; there is a waiting list to receive one of the 358 spots. VIP campers are held at least 2 1/2 hours after the race to ease traffic.

For more lodging recommendations, go to www.mobiltravelguide.com

EAT

MOBIL STAR-RATED RESTAURANTS

Arlington

CACHAREL. ★★★
2221 E Lamar Blvd, Arlington (76006). Phone 817/640-9981. www.cacharel.net. Located on the ninth floor of the Brookhollow Tower Two building and just 15 minutes from downtown Dallas or Fort Worth, this inviting country French restaurant features panoramic views of Arlington and serves new French cuisine with exquisite sauces. Pale-pink tablecloths with fresh flowers, and the unobtrusive and quietly attentive service makes this a charming oasis. French menu. Lunch, dinner. Closed Sun; holidays. Children's menu. Business casual attire. Reservations recommended. $$$

PICCOLO MONDO. ★★
829 Lamar Blvd E, Arlington (76011). Phone 817/265-9174. www.piccolomondo.com. Italian menu. Lunch, dinner. Closed Jan 1, Thanksgiving, Dec 25. Bar. Reservations recommended. $$

Dallas

DEL FRISCO'S DOUBLE EAGLE STEAK HOUSE. ★★★
5251 Spring Valley Rd, Dallas (75254). Phone 972/490-9000. This majestic steakhouse is decorated with dark mahogany, marble, mirrors, and chandeliers. Wait for a table at the beautiful hand-carved bar and listen to the lively, decked-out crowd. Prime beef stars at this beef palace, which knows exactly how to put on a deluxe dinner. Savvy servers make the evening pure pleasure, helpfully guiding diners through sensational choices like sherry-rich mock turtle soup, towers of thick-cut onion rings, silken ribeye steak, sumptuous sides of Parmesan-cream spinach, and desserts of four-layer lemon-cream cake. Fine wines and cognacs are popular, too. American, steak menu. Dinner. Valet parking. $$

MI COCINA. ★★
77 Highland Park Village, Dallas (75205). Phone 214/521-6426. Expect to find this Park Cities hangout packed to the rafters day and night with singles, couples on dates, and families. They come for the enchiladas in sunset sauce, the fajita salad, platters of grilled vegetables, and the bodacious Lucychanga. Beware of the mambo taxi; the blended margarita-sangria mixture is sweetly dangerous. Mexican menu. Lunch, dinner. $$

NICK AND SAM'S STEAK AND FISH. ★★★
3008 Maple Ave, Dallas (75201). Phone 214/871-7444. www.nick-sams.com. Steeped in a throwback spirit of elegant dinner clubs, this cavernous, sophisticated beef palace in Uptown serves exceptional prime steaks. Spectacular, bone-in ribeyes need no adornment, although the house-made steak sauce and horseradish cream are divine, and the selection of iced, fresh mollusks is always very good. There's an award-winning wine list, as well as several good wines by the glass, which diners may even taste first. Steak menu. Dinner. Bar. Reservations recommended. Valet parking. $$$

TEXADELPHIA. ★
5500 Greenville Ave, Dallas (75206). Phone 214/265-8044. This sandwich shop does justice to the Texas-sized appetite. Specialties include a Philly cheesesteak-style sandwich, which you can jazz up with jalapeños. Chips and salsa bring a Tex-Mex element to the mix. American menu. Lunch, dinner. $

Fort Worth

ANGELO'S BAR-B-QUE. ★
2533 White Settlement Rd, Fort Worth (76107). Phone 817/332-0357. www.angelobbq.com. Since 1958, the pork ribs (dry rub) and cold beer have been the specialities, and they are served until they run out of them each day. American menu. Lunch, dinner. $

EDELWEISS. ★
3801 Southwest Blvd #A, Fort Worth (76116). Phone 817/738-5934. This restaurant is a favorite with several NASCAR drivers. German, American menu. Dinner. Closed Sun-Mon; holidays. $$

JOE T. GARCIA'S. ★ ★
2201 N Commerce, Fort Worth (76106). Phone 817/626-4356. www.joets.com. Mexican menu. Lunch, dinner. Closed Thanksgiving, Dec 25. Outdoor seating. $$

Irving

VIA REÁL. ★ ★ ★
4020 N MacArthur Blvd, Irving (75038). Phone 972/650-9001. www.viareal.com. Situated adjacent to the Four Seasons Las Colinas Resort, this popular restaurant has been serving its Mexican and Southwestern cuisine for more than 11 years. The warm upscale Santa Fe décor complements the traditional Mexican dishes, as well as the seafood from Mexico's coastal regions, which were recently introduced by chef Felipe Gaytan. Southwestern, Mexican menu. Lunch, dinner, Sun brunch. Bar. $$$

LOCAL RECOMMENDATIONS

Arlington

ABUELO'S MEXICAN FOOD EMBASSY.
1041 I-20 W, Arlington (76017). Phone 817/468-2622. www.abuelos.com. Mexican menu. Lunch, dinner. $

ARLINGTON STEAK HOUSE.
1724 W Division St, Arlington (76012). Phone 817/275-7881. This restaurant serves home-style meals of chicken-fried steak. American menu. Lunch, dinner. $$

BODACIOUS BAR-B-Q.
1206 E Division St, Arlington (76013). Phone 817/860-4248. This restaurant is just down the street from Ameriquest Field. American menu. Lunch, dinner. Closed Sun. $

Dallas

RED HOT & BLUE.
9810 N Central Expy, Dallas (75231). Phone 214/368-7427. www.redhotandblue.com. This restaurant is known for their award-winning St. Louis-cut ribs that are smoked over hickory wood for hours. They offer three different types of ribs: Sweet Ribs, which are glazed with a "Suffern' Sweet BBQ sauce"; Dry Ribs, which are sprinkled with a secret blend of dry spices; or the Wet Ribs, which are slathered with a "Mojo Mild BBQ sauce." American menu. Lunch, dinner. $

Fort Worth

CATTLEMEN'S STEAK HOUSE.
2458 N Main St, Fort Worth (76106). Phone 817/624-3945. www.cattlemensteakhouse.com. Located in the Historic Stockyard District of Fort Worth, this restaurant is very popular and known internationally for its steaks. American menu. Lunch, dinner. Children's menu. $$

RAILHEAD SMOKEHOUSE.
2900 Montgomery St, Fort Worth (76107). Phone 817/738-9808. This popular barbecue spot has a ranch-house façade with wide-slung porches and rural barn wood décor. American, barbecue menu. Lunch, dinner. Outdoor seating. $

RISCKY'S BARBEQUE.
300 Main St, Fort Worth (76102). Phone 817/877-3306. www.risckys.com. This crowded, loud barbecue spot in the heart of Sundance Square attracts both locals and tourists for ribs, cold brews, and wine margaritas. It's also a great place to go for concerts. American, barbecue menu. Lunch, dinner. Casual attire. $

Fossil Creek

SALTGRASS STEAK HOUSE.
5845 Sandshell Dr, Fossil Creek (76137). Phone 817/306-7900. www.saltgrass.com. The Saltgrass Steak House (12 miles from the racetrack) recaptures the flavor of the open campfire. Steaks (certified Angus beef, topped with fresh garlic butter), chicken, and seafood, chargrilled to perfection; other specialities include Two-Fork cheesecake and Shiner Bock beer bread. American menu. Lunch, dinner. Children's menu. $$

For more dining recommendations, go to www.mobiltravelguide.com

SIDETRIP

Space Center Houston
Houston, TX

Plan a full day for an out-of-this-world experience, where you can learn to land a shuttle.

The official Visitors Center of NASA's Johnson Space Center, Space Center Houston (SCH) is all about "intelligent fun"—and the only place in the world where you can touch a real moon rock, land a shuttle, and watch astronauts train for missions. It's easy to spend an entire day there. Take the guided tram tour of NASA's Johnson Space Center. Go early, as the 90-minute tours, which leave about every 30 minutes, are popular. The tour includes the Historic Mission Control Center, Hangar X, and the Space Vehicle Mockup Facility. You can also stop at Rocket Park, home of the massive rockets used in the earliest days of the space program. Other highlights include the Kids Space Place, where your children can command a space shuttle or explore living on the space station; The Astronaut Gallery, an exhibit featuring the world's best collection of spacesuits; and the Living in Space module, which simulates what life could be like for astronauts aboard the station. A Mission Briefing Officer demonstrates how the smallest tasks, like showering and eating, are complicated by the microgravity of space. Don't miss the film shown on the five-story screen of the Mazda Theater: you'll watch what astronauts experience from the time they receive notification of their acceptance into the training program to their first mission. Gift shop. Food court. RV day parking. Open daily. Monday-Friday 10 am-5 pm, Saturday-Sunday 10 am-6 pm. Buy and print your tickets online to avoid lines. Tickets are good for one year after purchase, no refunds. Adults $17.95, seniors $16.95, kids (4-11) $13.95. Parking $4. **Space Center Houston.** 1601 NASA Rd 1, Houston (77058), approximately 25 miles south of downtown Houston in the NASA/Clear Lake area. Phone 281/244-2100. www.spacecenter.org.

For more Houston recommendations, go to www.mobiltravelguide.com

The No. 10 Car driven by Scott Riggs hits the pits during the NASCAR NEXTEL Cup Series Sirius at the Glen.

Watkins Glen International®

Watkins Glen, NY

29

Jeff Burton leads a pack of cars as they rumble along in the 2004 NASCAR NEXTEL Cup Series Sirius at the Glen.

TRACK FACTS

WATKINS GLEN INTERNATIONAL. 2790 County Route 16, Watkins Glen (14891). Phone toll-free 866/461-7223. www.theglen.com.

SECURITY. Coolers up to 6 x 6 x 12 inches are permitted; food and beverages are also permitted. Fans are allowed to carry in one clear plastic bag, which can contain cameras, binoculars, scanners, or other items. All items are subject to search.

PARKING. Free during the day. Buses run from downtown Watkins Glen as well as from Corning and Elmira. Long-distance shuttles are planned from Rochester and Syracuse. The road track means fans can buy a general admission ticket and walk around to different areas without having an assigned seat (favorite seats are at the starting line and Turn 11, a tight turn with lots of spinouts).

CONCESSIONS. Each grandstand has its own restrooms and concession stands, reducing wait times.

FIRST AID. A fully staffed medical center is located within the race course on Finger Lakes Road, between Tompkins and Richardson roads. Corning Hospital is about 18 miles southwest of Watkins Glen (176 Dennison Pkwy E, Corning, phone 607/937-7200).

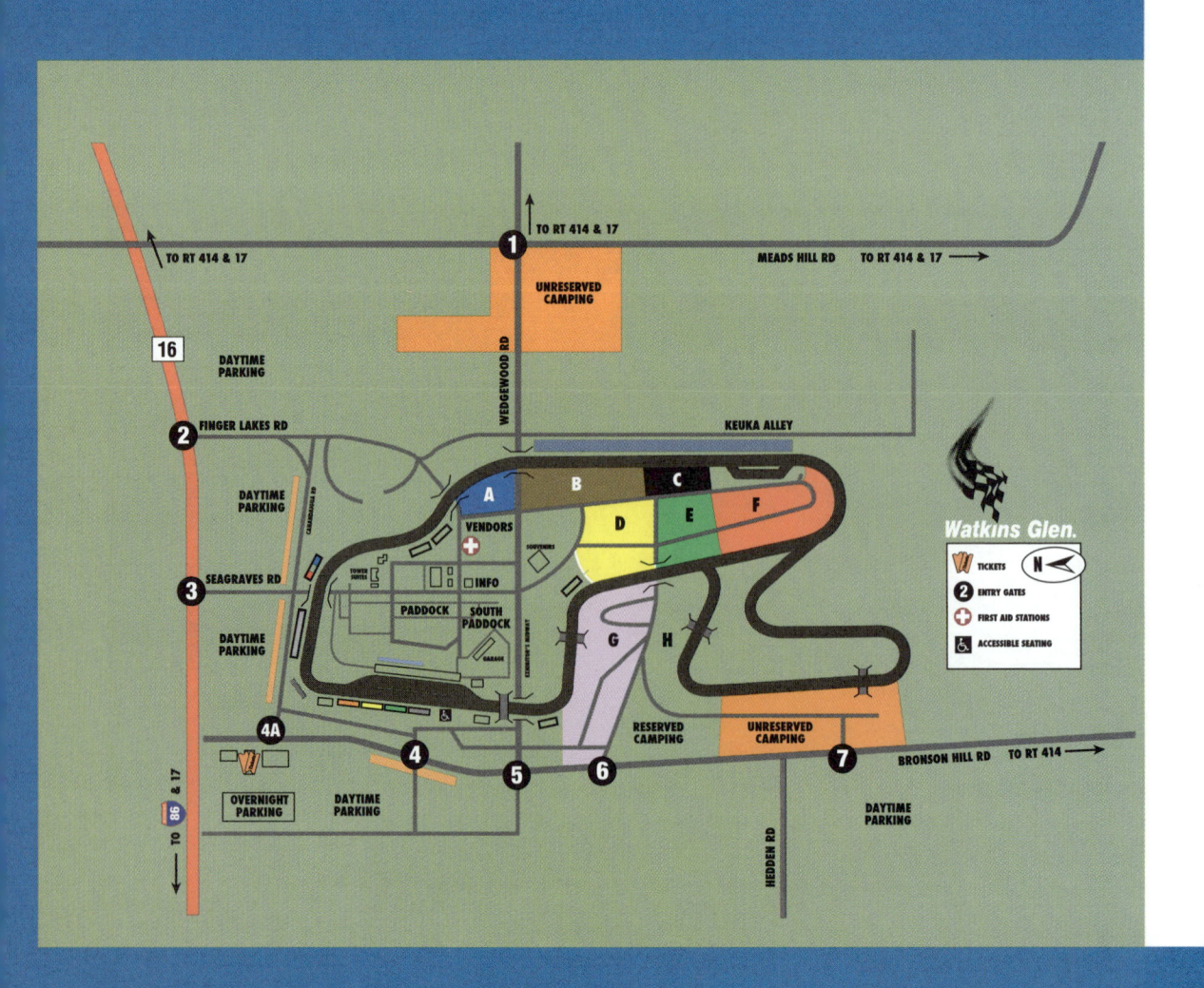

WATKINS GLEN INTERNATIONAL, NY 473

The Dodge pace truck leads the field on the first of two laps before the green flag comes down to start the NASCAR NEXTEL Cup Series Sirius at the Glen.

GETTING TICKETS

Tickets for NASCAR events can be purchased by calling the ticket office at 607/535-2481; toll-free 866/461-7223 9 am-5 pm Monday-Friday. On race weekends, the office opens at 7 am. Tickets can be purchased from the office at the track, which is located on Bronson Hill Road, just off County Road 16. Additionally, race fans can track down tickets on the Internet by visiting the Watkins Glen Web site at www.theglen.com.

FINGER LAKING GOOD

Watkins Glen is nestled at the southern end of Seneca Lake, one of New York's 11 Finger Lakes. Formed by glaciers, the Finger Lakes are long, narrow, parallel bodies of water that resemble, as the name implies, outstretched fingers, and are a haven for vacationers.

Watkins Glen is one of a number of small, delightful towns dotting the lakes' shores, perfect for strolling. Make your first stop the **Schuyler County Chamber of Commerce** (100 N Franklin St, phone 607/535-4300, www.schuylerny.com) for information on area attractions.

In addition to being known for hosting NASCAR-sanctioned events, the region is known for its wineries. The Finger Lakes area is the second-largest wine-producing region in the United States after California. More than 80 wineries call the area home, including about 40 situated around Seneca Lake. Follow the **Seneca Lake Wine Trail** to see them all and taste some samples (Seneca Lake Winery Association, 2 N Franklin St, phone toll-free 877/536-2717, www.senecalakewine.com).

Visitors have rated the historic **Great Western Winery,** also known as the **Pleasant Valley Wine Company** (8260 Pleasant Valley Rd, phone 607/569-6111), located about 18 miles west of Watkins Glen in Hammondsport, the best tour. It is likely the most expansive that any winery offers. See the old barrels and buildings, learn about winemaking history (established in 1860, Great Western is the oldest winery in the Finger Lakes region), and finish with a wine tasting.

While in Hammondsport, get a taste for New York's rich aviation history at the **Curtiss Museum** (8419 Rte 54, phone 607/569-2160). The museum is named after Glenn Hammond Curtiss, the aviation and motorcycle pioneer who called the area home. Neighboring Lake Keuka was home to the first successful seaplane flight, earning Curtiss the title of "father of naval aviation." The museum houses vintage aircraft and motor vehicles, including reproductions of the *June Bug II* (in which Curtiss made the first official 1-kilometer flight) and the V8 motorcycle that earned him the title of "fastest man in the world" in 1907.

The nearby Elmira-Corning Regional Airport is home to the **Wings of Eagles Discovery Center** (17 Aviation Dr, Horseheads, phone 607/739-8200). The facility features US fighter jets used from the 1940s through the 1970s (many still airworthy) and other military aviation memorabilia.

Toast to your favorite driver with a sample of wine from one of the 80 area wineries.

Take a tour through a natural gorge, bring a picnic, or camp out at Watkins Glen State Park.

At **Harris Hill** in Elmira, visitors can experience firsthand the history of motorless flight at the **National Soaring Museum** (51 Soaring Hill Dr, phone 607/734-3128), located in the town since 1969. Harris Hill and the surrounding geography are so well suited to motorless flight that Elmira was chosen in 1930 to be the site of the US National Soaring Championships. The world's largest collection of sailplanes and gliders—more than 120 scale models, some built as early as 1896—are on display. Weather permitting, take a glide at the **Harris Hill Soaring Center** (phone 607/734-0641); it's adjacent to the museum and offers 15-to-20-minute glider flights for a nominal fee.

Elmira is also Mark Twain country, where the author met and married his wife and lived during the summers at Quarry Farms, which is now the **Center for Mark Twain Studies at Elmira College** (One Park Place, phone 607/735-1941). The center features the Mark Twain Study, an octagonal room in which Twain wrote works such as *The Adventures of Tom Sawyer* and *A Connecticut Yankee in King Arthur's Court*. An exhibit houses photographs, memorabilia from Twain's summers in Elmira, and period furniture and clothing.

Elmira is also home to the **Christmas House** (361 Maple Ave, phone 607/734-9547, www.christmas house.com), a Victorian mansion filled with Christmas miniatures for collectors. For an excellent overview of the town, climb aboard *The Elmiran* for a narrated, hour-long tour of Elmira's points of interest, including the beautiful **Maple Avenue District,** the **Woodlawn National Cemetery** (where Twain as well as fallen Civil War soldiers are buried), and the historic **Near Westside District.** Tickets are available at the Holiday Inn Riverview (760 E Water St, phone 607/734-4211), where the tour departs. *The Elmiran* tour runs July-August.

About 20 miles southwest of Watkins Glen lies Corning, a town steeped in US industrial history, most prominently glassmaking. Corning is the birthplace of world famous CorningWare ceramic dishes. Some of that history can be seen at the **Corning Museum of Glass** (One Museum Way, phone toll-free 800/732-6845). Set aside a full day for this visit—this isn't a stodgy, static house of artifacts but a vibrant, interactive learning center with intriguing displays and hands-on educational opportunities. Watch molten glass transformed into vases and bowls, and then try your

GETTING AROUND

Watkins Glen International sits in a rural recreational area, near the south end of Seneca Lake, so expect track traffic to be heavy coming and going. From I-90 on the north, take Rte 14 south to Watkins Glen, then look for the signs for Rte 414. Continue south to Steuben Street/Country Road 16 and turn right. From I-86 on the south, exit on Rte 414 and travel north.

Be aware that on race days many of the roads leading to and from the track are turned into one-way streets for incoming and outgoing traffic.

The Finger Lakes have many opportunities for fishing and boating.

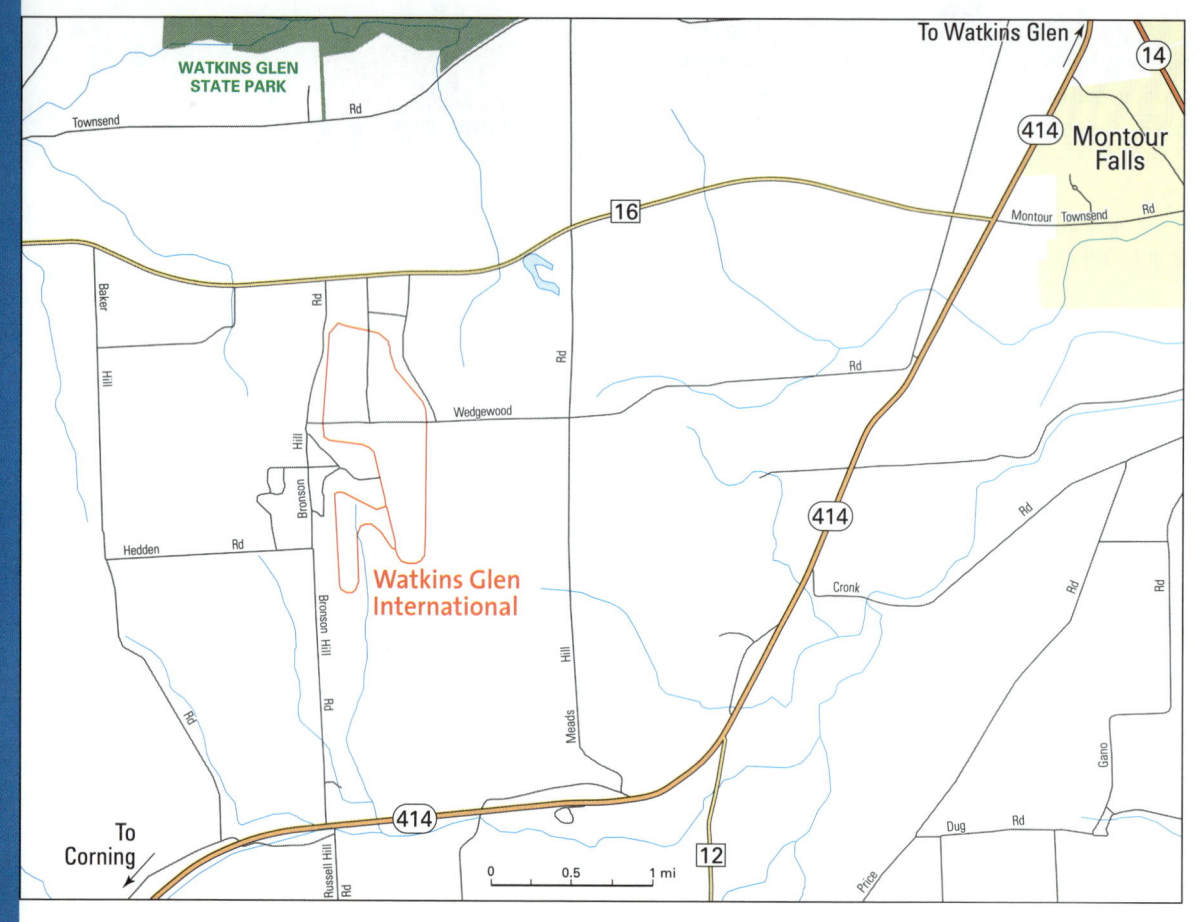

WATKINS GLEN POLE POSITION:
The 10 miles surrounding Watkins Glen International.

hand at hot glassworking at the Walk-In Workshop. Make glass beads or an original design on a drinking glass to take home as a souvenir. After a day of glassblowing, walk through the historic district of Corning and visit the **Rockwell Museum of Western Art** (111 Cedar St, phone 607/937-5386). The museum's galleries are organized by theme (for example Buffalo, Cowboy) rather than in historical order. The Remington and Russell Lodge features comfortable Western-style furniture in a big living room with art by its namesakes, antique firearms, Native American pottery, and dolls.

The scenery and nature are the real draws of the area. Beautiful sunsets over lakes, panoramic landscapes, and scenic drives abound (Route 54A west of Keuka Lake was named one of the top 15 scenic drives in the world by British Airways). Water sports, fishing, hiking, and camping are all very popular activities. **Geneva,** at the north end of Seneca Lake, is known as the "Lake Trout Capital of the World" (Geneva Area Chamber of Commerce, 35 Lakefront Dr, phone 877/543-6382, www.genevany.com).

Between the gorges, waterfalls, and rocks of **Watkins Glen State Park** (phone 607/535-4511, www.nysparks.com) and **Stony Brook State Park** (phone 585/335-8111, www.nysparks.com), and the 550-mile-plus **Finger Lakes Trail** (www.fingerlakestrail.org), there's plenty of nature to experience. Once you dip your fingers in the region, you will definitely want to come back.

WATKINS GLEN CALENDAR

AUGUST 6–7, 2005
Garlic Festival. Fox Run Vineyards, 670 Rte 14, Penn Yan (14527). Phone toll-free 800/636-9786. www.foxrunvineyards.com. Get gluttonous with garlic. Wine tasting, music, glassblowing demonstrations, vendors.

AUGUST 13, 2005
NASCAR Busch Series

AUGUST 14, 2005
NASCAR NEXTEL Cup Series

AUGUST 5–7, 2005
Italian American Festival. Clute Memorial Park, Clute Park Dr, Watkins Glen (14891). Phone 607/266-8394 x237. Games, arts and crafts, food, live entertainment, and fireworks over Seneca Lake.

AUGUST 12, 2005
Racing Thunder in The Glen Festival. Franklin St (Rte 14), Watkins Glen (14891). Phone 607/535-3003. www.watkinsglen.com. Join this rowdy street festival with vendors, arts and crafts, live entertainment, racing souvenirs, stock cars on display, and a children's area. Race held Friday.

AUGUST, 2005
Race Fever Night. Market St, Corning (14830). Phone 607/937-6292. www.gafferdistrict.com. This annual event celebrates NASCAR NEXTEL Cup racing and features driver autographs and racing displays. Night before races.

Jeff Gordon waves to fans during driver introductions before the start of a race.

SHOP TALK

Sure, race weekends are all about enjoying cold beer and hot grilled foods, but there's no reason you can't add a healthy snack to the mix. **Red Jacket Orchards Fruit Outlet** has them in abundance: apples, apricots, peaches, plums, strawberries, raspberries, and even rhubarb. Additionally, the company serves up fresh-squeezed juices and ciders, if you'd rather drink your fruit. Look for the big red building. *957 Canandaigua Rd, Geneva (14456). Phone 315/781-2749; toll-free 800/828-9410. www.redjacketorchards.com.*

WATKINS GLEN OUTFIELD:
The 50 miles surrounding Watkins Glen International.

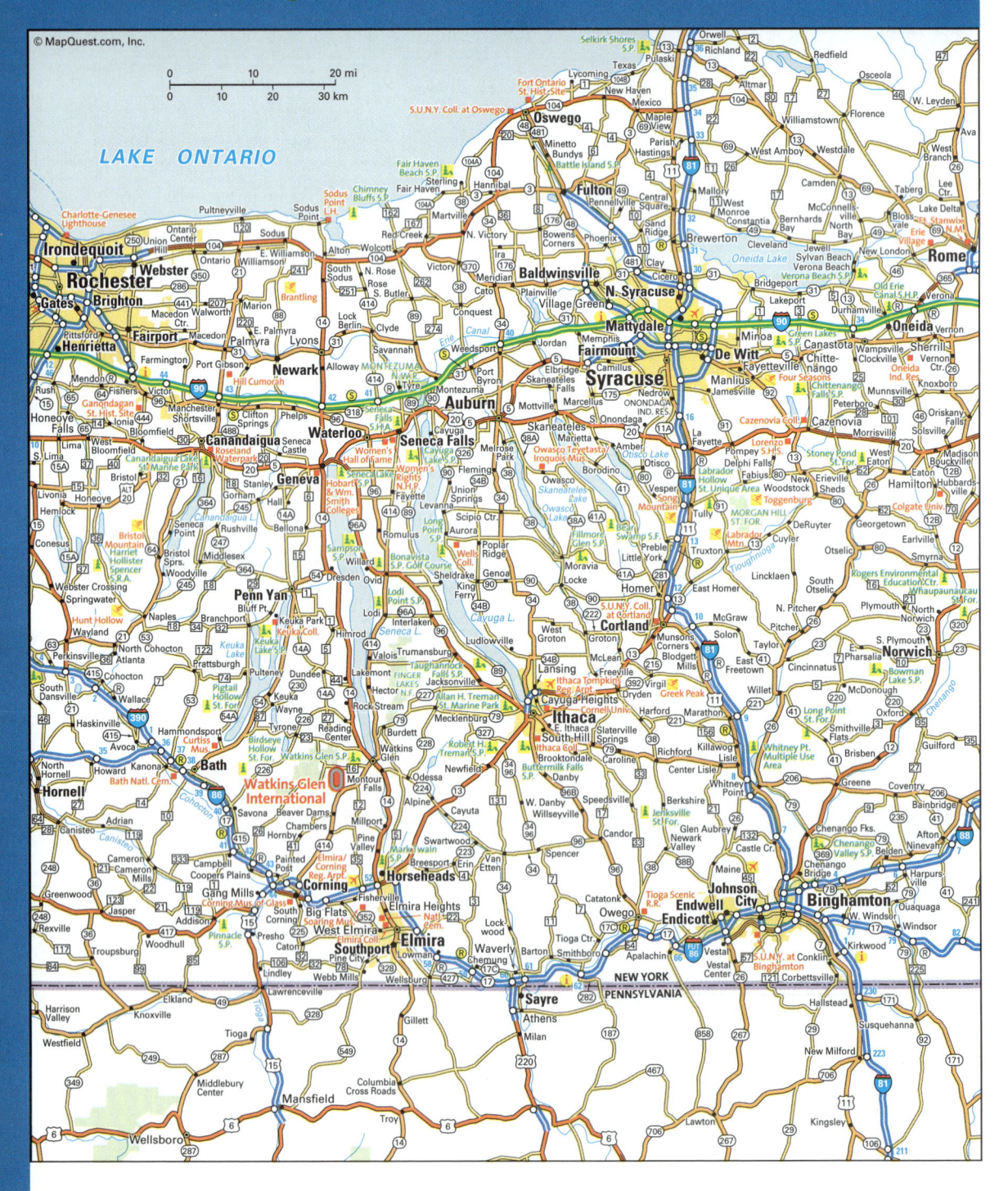

SEE

ATTRACTIONS

Corning

CORNING MUSEUM OF GLASS.
One Museum Way, Corning (14830). Phone 607/937-5371; toll-free 800/732-6845. www.cmog.org. Outstanding display of glass with live demonstrations of glassblowing. Visitors can get hands-on experience in the Walk-in Workshop and make a souvenir. (July-Labor Day: daily 9 am-8 pm; rest of year: daily 9 am-5 pm; closed Jan 1, Thanksgiving, Dec 24-25) **$$$**

ROCKWELL MUSEUM OF WESTERN ART.
111 Cedar St, Corning (14830). Phone 607/937-5386. www.rockwellmuseum.org. Learn about the history of the American West through this museum's collection of art and artifacts and special exhibits and events. (July-Labor Day: daily 9 am-8 pm; rest of year: daily 9 am-5 pm) **$$**

Elmira

HARRIS HILL PARK.
557 Harris Hill Rd, Elmira (14903). Phone 607/732-1210. High above the valley, this park offers picnicking, a playground, swimming pools, grills, and summertime amusements like batting cages, mini-golf, and go-karts.

HARRIS HILL SOARING CENTER.
PO Box 544, Elmira (14845). Phone 607/734-0641. www.harrishillsoaring.org. The birthplace of soaring offers scenic glider flights. (Early Apr-late Oct: Sat-Sun 10 am-6 pm; late June-late Aug: daily 10 am-6 pm) **$$$$**

NATIONAL SOARING MUSEUM.
51 Soaring Hill Dr, Elmira (14903). Phone 607/734-3128. www.soaringmuseum.org. Features a large collection of soaring planes that depict the history of this type of flight. The simulator is a good place to test what soaring feels like before signing up for the real thing. (Daily 10 am-5 pm) **$$**

Hammondsport

GLENN H. CURTISS MUSEUM.
8410 Rte 54, Hammondsport (14840). Phone 607/569-2160. www.linkny.com/~curtiss. Local native Curtiss, like the Wright brothers, also had a bicycle shop. His invention of the first flying boat, which took off over Lake Keuka, gave him the moniker the "father of naval aviation." The museum displays the Curtiss bicycle shop and a Dawn of Aviation Gallery. (Nov-late Apr: Mon-Sat 9 am-5 pm, Sun 11 am-5 pm; rest of year: Mon-Sat 9 am-5 pm, Sun 10 am-5 pm; closed holidays) **$$**

Horseheads

WINGS OF EAGLES.
Elmira-Corning Regional Airport, 17 Aviation Dr, Horseheads (14845). Phone 607/739-8200. www.warplane.org. Dedicated to the preservation and interpretation of military aircraft. Pretend to fly in the different planes or check out the simulator. (Mon-Fri 10 am-4 pm, Sat 9 am-5 pm, Sun 11 am-5 pm) **$$**

Watkins Glen

FAMOUS BRANDS OUTLET.
412 N Franklin St, Watkins Glen (14891). Phone 607/535-4952. www.famousbrandsoutlet.com. Popular spot for finding deals on such name brands as Carhartts, Dockers, and Woolrich. (Mon-Sat 9 am-8 pm; Sun 10 am-5 pm)

INTERNATIONAL MOTOR RACING RESEARCH CENTER AT WATKINS GLEN.
610 S Decatur St, Watkins Glen (14891). Phone 607/535-9044. www.racingarchives.org. The center features a wonderful display of all things racing. The broad collection includes cars, books, films, fine art, photographs, documents, magazines, programs, and memorabilia with a motor sports theme. (Mon-Sat 9 am-5 pm; also some Sun race days)

SENECA GRAND PRIX FAMILY FUN CENTER.
2374 State Rte 414, Watkins Glen (14891). Phone 607/535-7981. www.sgpfun.com. Located at the turn-off for the track, this park features Formula 1 cars, go-karts, bumper boats, miniature golf, and a huge balloon giraffe for the kids to jump into.

SEE ATTRACTIONS

THUNDER ROAD TOURS.
2 N Franklin St, Watkins Glen (14891). Phone 607/535-2338. See what it's like to be in the driver's seat as you follow the pace car for a few laps around the track. (Late May-late Oct: daily from noon) **$$$$**

WATKINS GLEN GORGE.
Off Rte 14, Watkins Glen (14891). Phone 607/535-4511. The gorge features 19 waterfalls along this stretch. Park in town to avoid the fee at the entrance on Franklin. **FREE**

For more attractions, go to www.mobiltravelguide.com

RADISSON HOTEL CORNING. ★★
125 Denison Pkwy E, Corning (14830). Phone 607/962-5000; toll-free 800/333-3333. www.radisson.com. The Rockwell Museum of Art is adjacent, while the Museum of Glass and area shopping and dining are also steps away. The lobby has a spacious feel, with trees and foliage, and calming sounds from an impressive waterfall fountain. 177 rooms, 3 story. High-speed Internet access. Restaurant, bar. Fitness center. Indoor pool. **$**

Elmira

HOLIDAY INN ELMIRA—RIVERVIEW. ★★
760 E Water St, Elmira (14901). Phone 607/734-4211; toll-free 800/465-4329. www.holiday-inn.com. Situated just off the highway, this well maintained, family-friendly motel is conveniently located near the town of Corning and just 30 minutes from the track. 149 rooms, 2 story. Restaurant. Fitness room. Indoor pool, outdoor pool, children's pool. **$**

STAY

MOBIL STAR-RATED LODGINGS

Corning

COMFORT INN CORNING. ★
66 W Pulteney St, Corning (14830). Phone 607/962-1515; toll-free 877/424-6423. www.comfortinn.com. A great budget-friendly option for visitors to Corning and the surrounding area, this clean, attractive motel is located near the Corning Museum of Glass and the town's historic Market Street. 62 rooms, 2 story. Complimentary continental breakfast. Check-in 2 pm, check-out 11 am. Fitness room. Indoor pool. **$**

DAYS INN CORNING. ★★
23 Riverside Dr, Corning (14830). Phone 607/936-9370; toll-free 800/329-7466. www.daysinn.com. Whether you're in Corning for a visit or just passing through, this ideally located motel—20 minutes from Watkins Glen International—has everything to make your stay comfortable. Set next to the Museum of Glass among the shops and restaurants of downtown Corning. 56 rooms, 2 story. Complimentary continental breakfast. Restaurant. Indoor pool, whirlpool. **$**

PIT PASS

You either love or hate the general-admission seating plan at Watkins Glen, but either way, officials are listening to fans and making improvements. One change, scheduled to be made in time for the 2005 season, is the removal of the wooden stands. They'll be replaced with more comfortable aluminum stands with seat backs. At 42 rows high, the new stands are also several rows higher, allowing better views.

Ithaca

HOLIDAY INN. ★★
222 S Cayuga St, Ithaca (14850). Phone 607/272-1000; toll-free 800/465-4329. www.holiday-inn.com. Set in the heart of picturesque Ithaca, this hotel is near shopping, restaurants, and the stunning Cornell University campus. Decorated with a garden theme and wrought-iron accented furnishings, the hotel has views of the surrounding hillside and is minutes from the Ithaca airport. 181 rooms, 10 story. Pets accepted; fee. Check-in 3 pm, check-out noon. Restaurant, bar. Fitness room. Indoor pool. **$**

STATLER HOTEL AT CORNELL UNIVERSITY. ★★★
11 East Ave, Ithaca (14853). Phone 607/257-2500; toll-free 800/541-2501. www.statlerhotel.cornell.edu. Because this well-appointed hotel serves as the main teaching facility for Cornell's prestigious School of Hotel Administration, no detail has been overlooked. Boasting breathtaking views of the hills and dells of the campus's picturesque Finger Lakes location, each luxurious guest room features pillow-top mattresses, complimentary coffee, and turndown service. 150 rooms, 9 story. Closed Dec 23-Jan 8. Check-in 3 pm, check-out noon. High-speed Internet access. Restaurant, bar. Fitness room. Airport transportation available. Business center. **$$**

LOCAL RECOMMENDATIONS

Corning

BEST WESTERN LODGE ON THE GREEN.
3171 Canada Rd, Corning (14870). Phone 607/962-2456; toll-free 800/780-7234. www.bestwestern.com. Located 23 miles from Watkins Glen International, the lodge is on 12 acres and features the Vintage Tavern and Blossoms Restaurant. 135 rooms, 2 story. Pets accepted; fee. Complimentary continental breakfast. Check-in 4 pm, check-out 11 am. Outdoor pool. **$**

FAIRFIELD INN RIVERSIDE—CORNING.
3 S Buffalo St, Corning (14830). Phone 607/937-9600; toll-free 800/228-2800. www.fairfieldinn.com. This inn is situated 24 miles from the track. 63 rooms, 3 story. Complimentary continental breakfast. High-speed Internet access. Indoor pool. **$**

HAMPTON INN—CORNING.
9775 Victory Hwy, Corning (14870). Phone 607/936-3344; toll-free 800/426-7866. www.hamptoninn.com. Located 20 miles from Watkins Glen International. 67 rooms, 3 story. Complimentary continental breakfast. Fitness room. Indoor pool. **$**

ROSEWOOD INN.
134 E First St, Corning (14830). Phone 607/962-3253. www.rosewoodinn.com. This elegant Victorian house sits among other period homes and is a short walk from downtown Corning. From the moment the owner greets you at the door in full Victorian attire, you'll know a stay at this inn will be memorable. 7 rooms, 2 story. Complimentary full breakfast. Check-in 3-7 pm, check-out 11 am. **$$**

STAYBRIDGE SUITES.
201 Townley Ave, Corning (14830). Phone 607/936-7800; toll-free 800/238-8000. www.staybridgesuites.com. Watkins Glen International is a 25-minute ride away from this hotel. 115 rooms, 3 story. Pets accepted. Complimentary continental breakfast. High-speed Internet access. Indoor pool. **$**

Horseheads

BEST WESTERN MARSHALL MANOR.
3527 Watkins Rd, Horseheads (14845). Phone 607/739-3891; toll-free 800/780-7234. www.bestwestern.com. A charming red brick building with white pillars, this comfortable motel is set in the rolling countryside near the racetrack, local wineries, and a large shopping mall. The rooms here are spacious with traditional furnishings and feature oversize bathrooms. 40 rooms. Pets accepted; fee. Complimentary continental breakfast. Check-in 1 pm, check-out 11 am. Outdoor pool. **$**

COUNTRY INN AND SUITES BIG FLATS.
105 E Mall Rd, Horseheads (14845). Phone 607/739-9205; toll-free 800/456-4000. This inn is located 30 minutes from the track. 70 rooms, 3 story. Complimentary continental breakfast. Wireless Internet access. Fitness center. Indoor pool, whirlpool. **$**

Ithaca

BEST WESTERN UNIVERSITY INN.
1020 Ellis Hollow Rd, Ithaca (14850). Phone 607/272-6100. Just outside the Cornell University campus, this

STAY LOCAL RECOMMENDATIONS

FAN FAVORITE — don't miss it

Each of the larger Finger Lakes has some sort of vessel—barge, paddle wheeler, or cruiser—that plies the waters for either scenic tours or dining. Enjoy lunch or dinner aboard the **Columbia** on Seneca Lake *(Captain Bill's Seneca Lake Cruises, phone 607/535-4541, www.senecaharborstation.com/cruise)* or **The Keuka Maid** on Keuka Lake *(phone 607/569-2628)*. At 200 tons and featuring three decks, the *Maid* is the largest boat of its kind on any self-contained US lake.

spacious motel has the feel of a lodge with vaulted ceilings in both the lobby and guest rooms. Located within walking distance of shopping and a short drive to the airport. 101 rooms. Pets accepted; fee. Complimentary continental breakfast. Check-in 3 pm, check-out noon. Fitness room. Outdoor pool. Airport transportation available. $

LA TOURELLE.
1150 Danby Rd, Ithaca (14850). Phone 607/273-2734; toll-free 800/765-1492. www.latourelleinn.com. Offering guests a beautiful countryside setting and panoramic views of Cayuga Lake and its surrounding hill country, this inn is adjacent to state park lands with hiking trails and fishing ponds. The location is convenient to Ithaca College and Cornell University. 35 rooms, 3 story. Pets accepted, some restrictions. Check-in 2 pm, check-out noon. High-speed Internet access. Tennis. Business center. $$

Rockstream

GOLDEN KNIGHT INN AND SUITES.
4461 Rte 14, Rockstream (14878). Phone 607/535-8012. Just a few miles north of Watkins Glen, the track is 20 minutes away. 15 rooms, 1 story. Pets accepted. Complimentary continental breakfast. $

Watkins Glen

LONGHOUSE LODGE MOTEL AND MANOR.
3625 Rte 14, Watkins Glen (14891). Phone 607/535-2565. www.longhouselodge.com. This comfortable motel has views of Seneca Lake, and Watkins Glen International is just ten minutes away. 21 rooms, 1 story. Complimentary continental breakfast. Outdoor pool. $

RV AND CAMPING

Odessa

COOL-LEA CAMPGROUND.
State Rte 228, Odessa (14869). Phone 607/594-3500. www.coolleacamp.com. 60 sites, small camp store, boat rentals, fishing. On Cayuta Lake. Supplies nearby.

Watkins Glen

SENECA LODGE.
PO Box 272, Watkins Glen (14891). Phone 607/535-2014. At the south entrance to Watkins Glen Park. Cabins, A-frames, and motel rooms available. The cabins have a private toilet and shower. The A-frames have complete housekeeping facilities and a TV. The motel offers less Spartan rooms. This place is very popular with race fans, many of whom reserve a year in advance and return year after year. On site is the historic Seneca Lodge Restaurant. The bar has NASCAR memorabilia; the mechanics hang out here.

WATKINS GLEN/CORNING KOA.
Rte 414 S, Watkins Glen (14891). Phone toll-free 800/562-7430. www.koa.com/where/ny/32161.htm. 105 campsites, 26 cabins, mini-golf, laundry, bike rentals, propane, ice, wood, swimming pool, pet friendly.

WATKINS GLEN STATE PARK.
PO Box 304, Watkins Glen (14891). Phone 607/535-4511. 305 campsites, 776 acres, hiking areas, picnic areas, trailer dumping stations. Camper recreation programs July-Aug, nature activities, gorge tours; carry in-carry out, Olympic-sized pool. Pets allowed on leashes.

For more lodging recommendations, go to www.mobiltravelguide.com

EAT

MOBIL STAR-RATED RESTAURANTS

Binghampton

NUMBER FIVE. ★ ★ ★

33 S Washington, Binghamton (13903). Phone 607/723-0555. Operating in a 100-year-old fire station, this American steak and seafood house has been open since 1978. The antiques-filled, fine-dining atmosphere is warm and romantic. American menu. Dinner. Closed Dec 25. Bar. Children's menu. **$$**

Corning

LONDON UNDERGROUND CAFÉ. ★ ★

69 E Market St, Corning (14830). Phone 607/962-2345. Features three levels of dining with a British theme. American menu. Lunch, dinner. Closed Sun, Dec. 25. Children's menu. Casual attire. Outdoor seating. **$$**

Cortland

RUSTY NAIL. ★ ★

3993 West Rd, Cortland (13045). Phone 607/753-7238. American menu. Lunch, dinner. Closed Jan 1, Thanksgiving, Dec 25. Bar. Children's menu. **$$$**

Ithaca

MOOSEWOOD. ★

215 N Cayuga, Ithaca (14850). Phone 607/273-9610. www.moosewoodrestaurant.com. This is the famous vegetarian restaurant, which has produced several cookbooks. If you're a carnivore, never fear—you may enjoy the food so much you won't realize it's meat-free. Eclectic/International menu. Lunch, dinner. Bar. Children's menu. Casual attire. Outdoor seating. **$**

LOCAL RECOMMENDATIONS

Corning

CAP'N MORGAN'S SPORTS AND SEAFOOD.

36 Bridge St, Corning (14830). Phone 607/962-1616. www.capnmorgan.com. Visit Cap'n Morgan's, a great little pub, for the only seafood in Corning. If you're not in the mood for that, try the steaks, burgers, or barbecue wings. American menu. Lunch, dinner, late-night. **$$**

MARKET STREET BREWING COMPANY.

63 W Market St, Corning (14830). Phone 607/936-2337. This microbrewery in the historic district features six locally produced beers and NASCAR specials whenever there is a race. Rooftop dining and a beer garden are available, with live music in the evenings. American menu. Bar. Lunch, dinner, late-night. Outdoor seating. **$$**

SORGE'S RESTAURANT.

66-68 W Market St, Corning (14830). Phone 607/937-5422. www.sorges.com. An Italian-American family dining tradition for over 50 years. They set the Guinness World Record for longest noodle at 418 feet. Italian, American menu. Lunch, dinner. Casual attire. **$$**

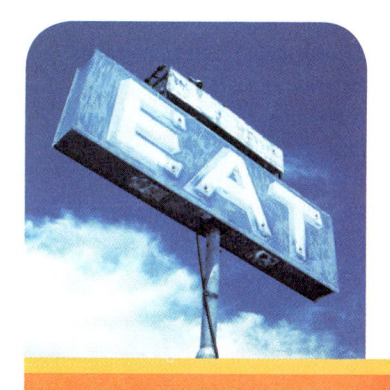

ROAD FOOD

During race weeks, there's a good chance of catching a race driver eating at the **Wildflower Café** ★★, the restaurant next door to the lively Crooked Rooster. The café offers a sedate atmosphere with American fare—including sandwiches, burgers, and other entrées—at great prices. The microbrewery on the premises serves light and dark beers. American menu. Lunch, dinner. Closed holidays. *301 N Franklin St, Watkins Glen (14891). Phone 607/535-9797.* **$$**

484 EAT LOCAL RECOMMENDATIONS

Dundee

VERAISONS.
5435 Rte 14, Dundee (14837). Phone 607/243-9500. This restaurant and winery has a great view overlooking Seneca Lake from its terrace; inside, you'll enjoy the vaulted ceiling and fireplace. The chef works with local growers to obtain farm-fresh produce. American menu. Breakfast, lunch, dinner. Outdoor seating. **$$**

Ithaca

BENCHWARMERS SPORTS BAR AND GRILL.
214 E State St (the Commons), Ithaca (14850). Phone 607/277-7539. Benchwarmers is popular with locals and the perfect sports bar for race fans—the atmosphere is lively, and the room features plenty of TVs. Dinner choices here are extensive, inexpensive, and so generous you may have to ask for a doggy bag. Bar menu. Bar. Lunch, dinner. Casual attire. **$**

VIVA TAQUERIA.
101 N Aurora St, Ithaca (14850). Phone 607/277-1752. This taqueria in downtown Ithaca is known for its tacos and burritos, but everything on the menu is inexpensive and handmade. The cantina next door has table service and whips up a great margarita. Mexican menu. Lunch, dinner. Casual attire. Outdoor seating. **$$**

Montour Falls

CHEF'S.
Rte 14, Montour Falls (14865). Phone 607/535-9975. This long-time diner from the 1940s offers reasonably priced, family-friendly fare. The menu features more than 130 items—even low-carb options, if that's your preference. American menu. Breakfast, lunch, dinner. Casual attire. **$**

Watkins Glen

BLEACHERS SPORTS BAR AND GRILL.
413 N Franklin St, Watkins Glen (14891). Phone 607/535-6705. This sports bar and grill is an unpretentious gathering spot for locals. Bar menu. Lunch, dinner. Casual attire. **$**

CROOKED ROOSTER.
223 N Franklin St, Watkins Glen (17891). Phone 607/535-9797. This Southwestern-style eatery is very popular with race fans. The front windows open up the lively atmosphere to the street. Southwestern menu. Lunch, dinner. Outdoor seating. **$$**

GLEN MOUNTAIN MARKET.
200 N Franklin St, Watkins Glen (14891). Phone 607/535-6900. The market serves food from a deli-style menu, which you can eat inside or outside. Baked goods are also offered, and a small gift shop is on site. Deli menu. Breakfast, lunch. **$**

JERLANDO'S RISTORANTE.
400 N Franklin St, Watkins Glen (14891). Phone 607/535-4254. The many Italians who have settled in the area have high standards for their cuisine, and this restaurant fits the bill—it's highly recommended and enjoyed by locals. Italian menu. Lunch, dinner. Closed Sun. **$$**

SAVARD'S FAMILY RESTAURANT.
601 N Franklin St, Watkins Glen (14891). Phone 607/535-4538. Savard's is especially popular for its great breakfast fare in a family-friendly atmosphere. American menu. Breakfast, lunch, dinner. **$**

For more dining recommendations, go to www.mobiltravelguide.com

SIDETRIP
Take the Scenic Route
Seaway Trail, NY

The Seaway Trail is a National Scenic Byway meandering more than 450 miles along the St. Lawrence River, Lake Ontario, and Lake Erie. It's easy to reach from Watkins Glen (head north on Route 14 to Sodus) and promises history and beautiful views even if you only drive part of the route.

Along the way to Sodus, you'll pass by the Erie Canal, which leads to Lake Ontario. Stop at the **Sodus Bay Lighthouse and Museum** (7606 N Ontario St, Sodus Point, phone 315/483-4936, www.peachey.com/soduslight/index.html) or enjoy some fishing. **Chimney Bluffs State Park** offers plenty of outdoor activities and breathtaking scenery.

Head west toward Rochester following the white-and-green Seaway Trail signs and stop for a water excursion on the **Sam Patch**, a boat built to resemble the packet boats that sailed the Erie Canal (12 Scheon Pl, Pittsford, phone 585/262-5661, www.sampatch.org). Once in Rochester, visit the **Strong Museum** (One Manhattan Sq, phone 585/263-2700, www.strongmuseum.org), a popular children's museum. Or visit the **George Eastman House** (900 East Ave, phone 585/271-3361, www.eastmanhouse.org), which focuses on the history of photography.

Take **The Breeze** (phone toll-free 877/825-3774, www.thebreeze.com), a new high-speed catamaran, on a quick trip to Toronto; the crossing takes about two hours and runs twice daily.

On your road trip down the Seaway Trail, Niagara Falls is a must-see natural wonder, by day or night. For more details on traveling the Seaway Trail, go to www.byways.org.

On the way to Niagara, stop at the Charlotte-Genesee, Thirty-mile point, Old Fort Niagara, Dunkirk, and Olcott lighthouses. Stop by a farm market in this fertile area or enjoy a wine tasting at a local vineyard. You'll see Old Fort Niagara and its castle on the way to **Niagara Falls** (phone 716/278-1796), one of the natural wonders of the world (if you head to the Canadian side, have proper documentation). End your drive in Buffalo to enjoy its street cafes and theater performances.

For more Seaway Trail recommendations, go to www.mobiltravelguide.com

Autodromo Hermanos Rodriguez

30 — Mexico City, Mexico

Autodromo Hermanos Rodriguez, where NASCAR-sanctioned racers will soon zoom, is part of an enormous athletic facility near Benito Juarez International Airport.

TRACK FACTS

AUTODROMO HERMANOS RODRIGUEZ. Avenida Viaducto Río Piedad and Río Churubusco S/N, Colonia Granjas Mexico, Mexico City, C.P. (08400). Phone 011 52 55 5764-8400. www.cie.com.mx.

FEATURES. The Autodromo Hermanos Rodriguez is located within the Magdalena Mixihuca sports complex, an almost 25 million square-foot facility that also houses 25 baseball diamonds, seven soccer fields, and eight field hockey fields, just to name a few of its features.

GETTING THERE. The track is in the eastern part of Mexico City, just 15 minutes from the *zócalo* and 2 miles from the Benito Juarez International Airport. Private transportation is highly recommended in Mexico City. This type of transportation will provide you with reliable, affordable, and secure transportation around the city. Private transportation can be arranged by your hotel concierge. A recommended private transportation company is Chapultepec Service (phone 011 52 55 5516-0770, www.mexicolimorent.com.mx). This company offers a bilingual staff and can coordinate transportation from the airport, shuttle service to hotels, and sightseeing tours within Mexico City.

STATISTICS. The 2.7-mile (4.35 kilometers) road course was built in 1963. The total capacity of the track is 139,772, including 25,000 general admission seats. Autodromo Hermanos Rodriguez's first NASCAR Busch Series event will start its engines on March 6, 2005. Our neighbors to the south have a history with NASCAR. NASCAR founder Bill France Sr drove in the first Mexican Road Race in 1950.

FIRST AID. There is a doctor on site. The track also has access to a medical helicopter, and two hospitals are within six minutes in the helicopter.

Fans fill the stands during race day at Autodromo Hermanos Rodriguez.

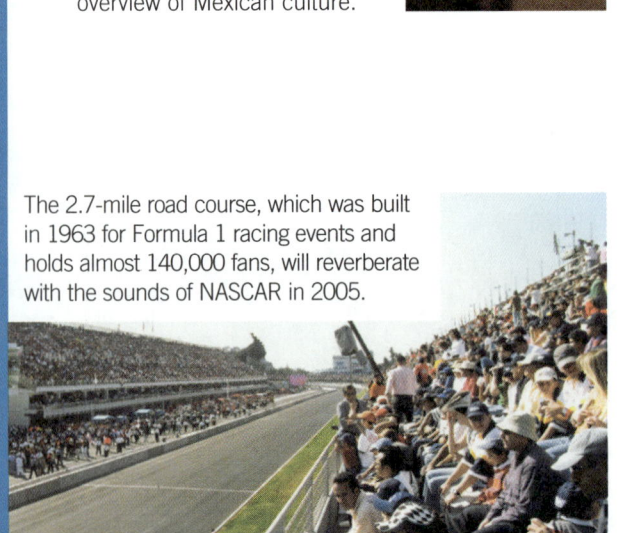

Catch the fascinating *zócalo* dancers in front of the centuries-old Metropolitan Cathedral.

In Chapultepec Park, visit the Museum of Anthropology for an overview of Mexican culture.

NASCAR GOES SOUTH OF THE BORDER

Most tourists who head to Mexico flock to the beaches and search for the tourist markets, but Mexico City, the second-largest city in the world, is a destination in its own right. A unique mixture of past and present culture and entertainment, in Mexico City you'll find the sights of New York, the food of Los Angeles, and the sounds of Chicago.

In the center of the city sits the *zócalo,* or town square. This plaza and its surrounding buildings are built on top of what was once the Aztec city Tenochtitlán. Try to catch one of the flag ceremonies held daily at 6 am and 6 pm. On the northeast corner of the *zócalo* you will find the ruins of Templo Mayor, the Aztec temple, and a museum focusing on Tenochtitlán. You can't miss the Metropolitan Cathedral on the north side of the *zócalo*. Intricate carvings adorn the exterior façade of this towering centuries-old structure, and the inside houses several small chapels and a decorated altar characteristic of those found throughout Mexico. Adjacent to the east side of the square stands Mexico's National Palace. On the second floor of the building you will find Diego Rivera's colorful murals outlining the history of Mexico.

While the *zócalo* and Chapultepec offer history and natural beauty, the more adventurous explorer might enjoy the experience of a *corrida de toros*—a bullfight.

The 2.7-mile road course, which was built in 1963 for Formula 1 racing events and holds almost 140,000 fans, will reverberate with the sounds of NASCAR in 2005.

AUTODROMO HERMANOS RODRIGUEZ, MX

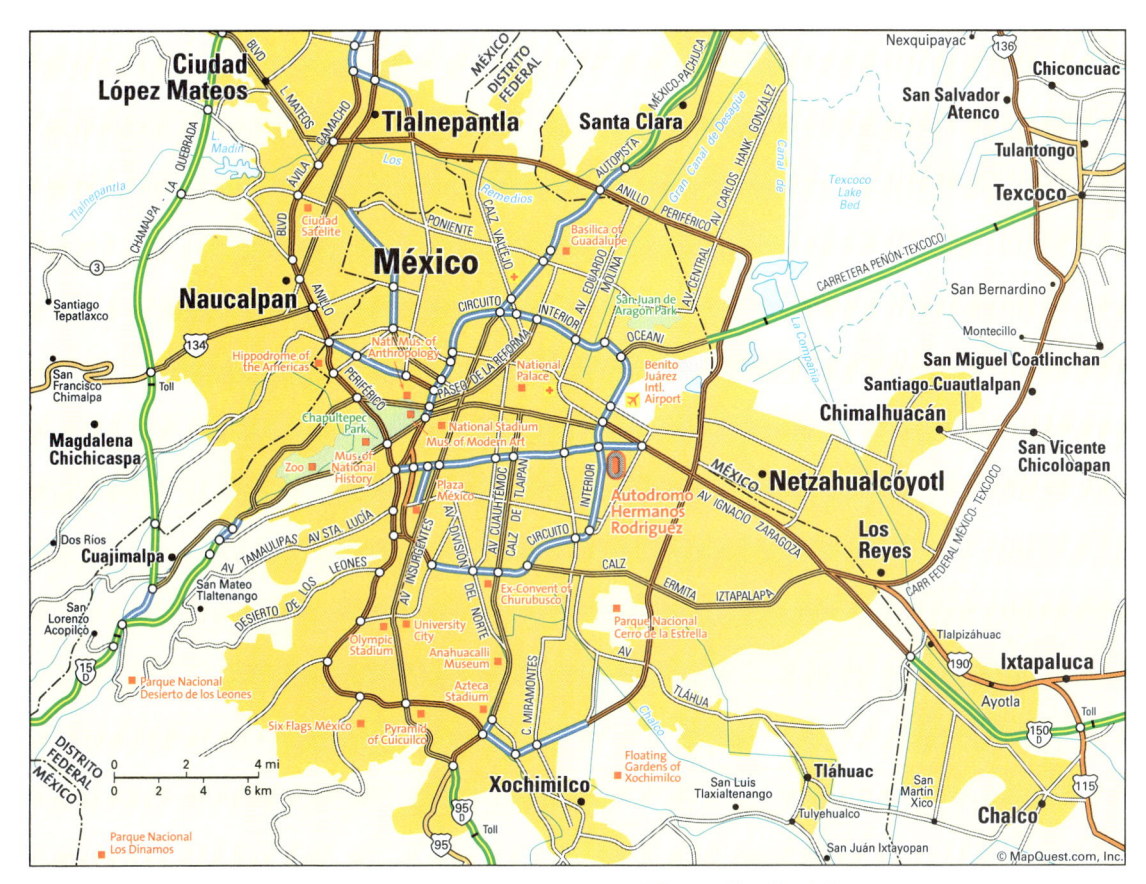

MEXICO CITY POLE POSITION:
The 12 miles (19.3 kilometers) surrounding Autodromo Hermanos Rodriguez.

The Plaza México bullring holds more than 45,000 spectators and has bullfights Sundays at 4 pm from late October to early April. A bullfight may not be the best bet for everyone, but if you think you can handle the gory sport, it is definitely worth your time to experience this aspect of Mexican culture. Tickets start cheap at $2.50, and go up to $40 for seats in the front row. Don't be surprised if you find yourself enthusiastically shouting "Olé!" along with the throngs of Mexican spectators. For more bullfight information, go to www.mytravelguide.com/city-guide/North-America/Mexico/Mexico-City/Bullfighting.

Mexico City offers a distinct and exciting blend of mouthwatering foods, friendly people, and endless entertainment—adding NASCAR to its draws only makes it all the more enticing.

GLOSSARY

You may know how to order a drink or ask, "¿Dónde está el baño?" en español, but if you are a NASCAR fan looking for track action south of the border, these are the words you really want in your vocabulary.

car – coche, carro
flag – bandera
driver – piloto
tire – llanta
fans – aficionados
gas – gasolina
cheers – aclamaciones, gritos
garage – garaje
speed – velocidad
turn – vuelta
corner – esquina

SEE

ATTRACTIONS

CHAPULTEPEC ZOO.
Paseo de la Reforma, Chapultepec Park section 1, Mexico City (11580). Phone 011 52 55 5553-6263. Before entering the zoo, which is across the street from the museum, look for the tall pole from which *voladores* (flyers) reenact an ancient ritual several times a day, spinning down head-first from the top of the pole. Once inside the zoo, be sure to check out the giant pandas and the *teporingos*. These rabbits live on the volcanoes of Central America and are now nearly extinct. Outside the zoo and at the top of the hill is Chapultepec Castle, once the home of Spanish royalty and now a museum. **FREE**

NATIONAL MUSEUM OF ANTHROPOLOGY.
Paseo de la Reforma and Calzada Ghandi, Chapultepec Park section 1, Mexico City (11580). Phone 011 52 55 5553-6266. There are several museums inside Chapultepec park, but this is the most impressive. It is a good place to visit for an overview of the development of several cultures throughout Mexico. **$**

PALACIO DE LAS BELLAS ARTES.
Avenida Hidalgo 1, Centro, C.P. 06050, Deleg. Cuauhtémoc, Mexico, D.F. Phone 011 52 55 5512-2593. The construction of the Palace of Fine Arts took more than 30 years to complete, but the decades-long wait was worth it. The building, built as an opera house, was designed by an Italian architect, and the opulent exterior is made of Italian white marble. Murals by some of Mexico's most celebrated artists, including Diego Rivera and José Clemente Orozco, grace the walls of this Art Nouveau landmark. The Ballet Folklórico performs here, as well as various classical and vocal musicians. The building also houses two museums: one devoted to art, the other to architecture.

STAY

LOCAL RECOMMENDATIONS

BEST WESTERN ESTORIL.
Luis Moya 93, Colonia Centro, Mexico City (06070). Phone 011 52 55 5518-0374; toll-free 800/780-7234. www.bestwestern.com. This recently remodeled hotel in the heart of Mexico City features an ultra-modern design with ultra-comfortable accommodations. The hotel's ideal location puts guests within walking distance to a number of historical and cultural sight-seeing opportunities, as well as Mexico City's finest shopping and dining. 125 rooms, 8 story. Complimentary full breakfast. Check-in 10 am, check-out 1 pm. High-speed Internet access. Laundry services. Restaurant, bar. Airport transportation available. **$**

BEST WESTERN HOTEL DE CORTES.
Avenida Hidalgo 85, Colonia Centro, Mexico City (06300). Phone 011 52 55 5518-2181; toll-free 800/780-7234. www.bestwestern.com. Combining a sense of history with the metropolitan energy of Mexico City, the structure of this hotel was built in 1660 and retains much of the original design and architecture. In the immediate area are activities to satisfy every kind of cultural taste—the Palace of Fine Arts and the Metropolitan Cathedral are within walking distance from the hotel, and mountain biking, dolphin swims, ecological parks, and bullfight arenas are also nearby. 29 rooms, 2 story. Check-in 3 pm, check-out 1 pm. Laundry services. Restaurant, bar. **$**

BEST WESTERN MAJESTIC.
Avenida Madero 73, Colonia Centro, Mexico City (06000). Phone 011 52 55 5521-8600; toll-free 800/780-7234. www.bestwestern.com. This historic and architecturally detailed hotel sits right on Mexico City's *zócalo* in the center of town. At the rooftop restaurant you can watch the activity on the zócalo below or enjoy the Sunday brunch buffet complete with live mariachi music. While the hotel is conveniently located near the National Palace, the Metropolitan Cathedral, as well as several shops and restaurants, guests also have easy access to the rest of the city's sights, as there is a Metro station right across the street. 85 rooms, 7 story. Check-in 3 pm, check-out 1 pm. Laundry services. Restaurant, bar. **$**

CAMINO REAL MEXICO.
Mariano Escobedo 700, Colonia Anzures, Mexico City (11590). Phone 011 52 55 5263-8888; toll-free 800/722-6466. www.caminoreal.com. The creators of this unique hotel designed it as a hotel-museum—a sanctuary from the hustle and bustle of the city that also features several notable works of art. Just as Mexico itself is a rare blend of the past and present, so is this hotel's décor a mixture of modern architecture and pre-Hispanic pyramid details. The hotel is very close to Chapultepec Park and within walking distance of the Polanco and Zona Rosa districts, two areas featuring

SIDETRIP

Teotihuacán
San Juan Teotihuacán, Mexico

The pyramids of the Sun and Moon are impressive sights in Teotihuacán.

If climbing pyramids is your idea of getting a true taste of Mexico, make a side trip to Teotihuacán. Take a taxi or the Metro to the Northern bus station (Central Camionera del Norte), where several bus companies offer trips to the pyramids about 30 miles (50 kilometers) northeast of the city. Once there, stroll down the Avenue of the Dead and climb the massive pyramids of the Sun and Moon. There are also several smaller exhibits throughout the site, and English-speaking guides are available to make sure you don't miss a thing. Just as you can do throughout Mexico, feel free to bargain with the several vendors wandering throughout the site trying to sell their homemade crafts. Make sure to bring a hat and water, as there is little refuge from the intense sun, and take extra caution while climbing the pyramids. Phone 011 52 59 4956-0052.

---

art galleries, nightclubs, and shopping boutiques. 714 rooms. Restaurants, bars. Fitness room. Two outdoor pools. Spa. Business center. **$$**

For more lodging recommendations, go to www.mobiltravelguide.com

EAT

LOCAL RECOMMENDATIONS
ARROYO.
Insurgentes Sur 4003, Colonia Tlalpan, Mexico City (14100). Phone 011 52 55 5573-4344. Arroyo is more than just a restaurant serving traditional Mexican specialties and drinks (such as pulque, a native beverage of Mesoamerica and a relative of tequila). As you dine, you'll be entertained by live mariachis and *ballet folklórico* performances. If you stop by on a Saturday between August and October, you'll also get to witness live bullfighting matches featuring an unforgettable display of *toreros* showing off their skills. Mexican menu. Breakfast, lunch, dinner. Casual attire. Live music.

BONDY.
Galileo 38 and Newton, Colonia Polanco, Mexico City (11560). Phone 011 52 55 5281-1818. This cozy restaurant located in a converted home in the trendy Polanco district just north of Chapultepec Park is a popular breakfast spot but also features delicious lunch and dinner dishes. The menu varies from traditional Mexican enchiladas to delicious European pastries and everything in between. The décor is simple and tasteful, making Bondy a comfortable and relaxing spot, perhaps for an evening glass of wine. International menu. Breakfast, lunch, dinner. **$$**

CAFE DE TACUBA.
Tacuba 28 and Bolivar, Colonia Centro, Mexico City (06010). Phone 011 52 55 5518-4950. This long-established Mexican restaurant is housed in a former convent and has been serving up delicious meals since 1912. The *enchiladas Tacuba* and *tamales* are the favorites here; for the bravest of diners, several dishes feature some of the spiciest chiles in the world. The simple and traditional décor features stained glass and talavera throughout. Mexican menu. Breakfast, lunch, dinner. Casual attire. **$**

WRITERS' CREDITS

Atlanta Motor Speedway, GA: Atlanta-based freelance writer **Karen Dean** has written for numerous national and regional publications. A NASCAR convert by marriage, she can now adeptly discuss the best value angle and cylinder head design for overhead cams and make a convincing argument regarding the use of restrictor plates. When not penning prose, she hangs out at home with her husband, dogs, cats, horses, and whatever else might stop by to eat.

Bristol Motor Speedway, TN: When business writer **Jennie Phipps** met her husband seven years ago, she thought NASCAR was Indian music. He took her to Pocono Raceway on their third date. They honeymooned at the Las Vegas Motor Speedway, where they waited for two hours to get Ken Schrader's autograph. Recently, her husband offered her a romantic getaway to Lowe's Motor Speedway, but she's holding out for Infineon, an RV with a shower, a wine country tour, and a Ryan Newman T-shirt.

California Speedway, CA: **Elizabeth Blish Hughes** drives a 1974 BMW 2002 tii. She likes taking it on the track at club events to indulge her love of speed, but has yet to match her helmet to the car—a stock yellow-green color called "golf" that turns heads and makes people smile. Having criss-crossed the United States seven times, she now wants to write about long drives. She usually writes about San Francisco and New York business and design.

Chicagoland Speedway, IL: **Paul Rogers** is a Chicago-based freelance writer whose work has appeared in the *Chicago Tribune*, *Crain's Chicago Business*, *Your Garden*, ATA Airline's *Journey*, and dozens of other publications. He also contributed to *The Dog Lover's Companion to Chicago* guidebook and *VegOut! Vegetarian Guide to Chicago*. At Chicagoland Speedway he was dismayed to learn that a surprising number of people will fake a physical handicap and risk having their license confiscated in order to get a close-in parking spot.

Darlington Raceway, SC: **Carrie Levine** is a reporter for *The Charlotte Observer* in North Carolina. She has written for *Newsday*, *Travel + Leisure*, *Yankee*, and *Fortune*, among others. She has just found out that she likes fast cars.

Daytona International Speedway, FL: In her 20-year career as a freelancer writer, **Deborah Brauser** has written her own column for the local paper while in high school, helped write and produce the University of Kansas's first video yearbook, and has written for ad agencies, corporations, and magazines. But researching the Daytona chapter from her new home of Orlando is the first time she's faced three hurricanes in the course of one assignment.

Dover International Speedway, DE: **Karen Baxter** is a freelance writer living in Maryland. She has written hundreds of articles about places and people in the Delmarva region and metropolitan Baltimore area. She also writes about parenting and consumer issues. Her work has appeared in regional publications including *The Baltimore Sun*, the *Maryland Beachcomber*, and *Harford County Kids*, as well as national publications including *The Dollar Stretcher*, iParenting.com, and Office.com.

Gateway International Raceway, IL: **John Holmes** is an editor for Turner Sports Interactive and a long-time sportswriter whose work appears in a variety of national publications ranging from *The Washington Post* to *The Economist*. He writes about golf when he's feeling the need for peace and quiet and about motorsports when he's not (which is most of the time).

Homestead-Miami Speedway, FL: **Trish Riley** is an award-winning journalist whose work on health, family, environmental issues, and travel has been published in *The Miami Herald*, *The Toronto Sun*, *Natural Home*, *Family Life*, Subaru's *Drive* magazine, and more. Author of a travel guide, *Florida's Gold Coast and the Keys* (Countryman Press), and co-author of a camping guide, she enjoys exploring and sharing the natural treasures of her Florida home. But it was growing up in Indianapolis that accelerated the pleasure of covering NASCAR racing.

Indianapolis Motor Speedway and Indianapolis Raceway Park, IN: A city with two tracks deserves two writers. **Cynthia BeMent** has written about health, fitness, and sports for ten years. She'd already lapped Indy at 145 mph in a Corvette—with shoulder belt and professional driver—pre-NASCAR. While working on her chapter, she resisted the impulse to pat Dale Jarret's trunk as he pitted during the Brickyard 400, and discovered a new home decor treasure from Gasoline Alley…a piece of Terry Labonte's radiator hose. Freelance writer and editor **Matt McClure** has written extensively for Mobil Travel Guide, covering such far-flung destinations as Hawaii, Alaska, and Idaho. He resides in Indianapolis, where he would jump at the chance to race against Jeff Gordon at the Motor Speedway—as long as the track is covered by a foot of snow and Matt's driving his all-wheel-drive Subaru wagon.

Infineon Raceway, CA: As a native of Sonoma County, **Kris Bordessa** now lives in the Sierra Foothills where she writes about family travel and activities for kids. Her work has appeared in publications such as *Parenting*, Disney's *FamilyFun*, and *Nick Jr. Family Magazine*. Her first book, a team-building activity guide, will be published in 2005. Of all her credits, though, writing about NASCAR has been the most impressive to the boys in her family.

Kansas Speedway, KS: **Jennifer Lawler** earned the nickname "NASCAR Ninja" during this assignment, possibly because she kept disappearing. Or maybe because she looks good in black. Jennifer is a martial arts instructor who writes extensively about how to kick people where it hurts, so she easily obtained no-holds-barred goods on the Kansas Speedway. Fortunately, no lawsuits have been filed yet. Jennifer took a crash course in barbecue and beefsteak from her buddies Richard Gunn Jr. and Sr. and humbly requests that they quit laughing at her ignorance.

Kentucky Speedway, KY: **Paula Andruss** is a Cincinnati-based freelance writer and editor with more than ten years of experience writing for publications such as *Parents*, *Chicago Life* magazine, *Crain's Chicago Business*, *Cincinnati Magazine*, and *Cincinnati Wedding*. She has covered a wide range of topics, including business, travel, personal finance, health care, parenting, and home building/design. In working on this book, she discovered the value of four-wheel-drive in a storm-soaked track parking area.

Las Vegas Motor Speedway, NV: **Steve Friess** is a Las Vegas-based freelance journalist whose work appears regularly in *Newsweek*, *USA Today*, *The Boston Globe*, *Wired*, and *America West*. He mentors a 14-year-old boy in the Big Brothers Big Sisters of America program whose rough life includes helping Friess grade the swimming pools and animal acts in Vegas. NASCAR is a new topic for him, but he thinks everyone should be really grateful the Vegas race is in March when it's temperate—he attended a summertime race and broiled in the hot desert sun.

Lowe's Motor Speedway, NC: Fast-car fan **Carrie Levine** also wrote the Darlington Raceway chapter.

Mansfield Motorsports Speedway, OH: **Paula Andruss,** who also wrote the Kentucky Speedway chapter, typically travels to the Columbus area for another sport—her husband is an Ohio State alum.

Martinsville Speedway, VA: **Carole Moore** writes from her home on the North Carolina coast. Her husband believes it is his duty to give advice to NASCAR drivers and their pit crews. He selflessly puts off mowing the grass or cleaning out the garage in order to donate his time and effort to the NASCAR cause. To date, no one has officially thanked him, but he doesn't mind. As for Carole, her writing credits include *Writer's Digest, The Christian Science Monitor,* and many others. She also pens several newspaper and magazine columns.

Memphis Motorsports Park, TN: Though Elvis Presley always ordered his peanut-butter-and-banana sandwiches fried, **John Hawks,** a Lexington, Kentucky-based writer specializing in business and travel, prefers them "au naturel" (white bread, no crusts, no frying). He's written six books, plus articles for more than two dozen national publications. As research for the next edition of this *Mobil Travel Guide: NASCAR Travel Planner,* he wants to take a lap around Memphis Motorsports Park in Bill Elliott's Elvis Presley "He Dared to Rock" Dodge.

Michigan International Speedway, MI: **Jennie Phipps,** who also wrote the Bristol Motor Speedway chapter, is grateful that her husband didn't know that Bristol lets people get married on the start/finish line.

The Milwaukee Mile, WI: **Melanie Radzicki McManus** has written for publications such as *Midwest Airlines Magazine, National Wildlife, National Geographic Traveler, Parents,* and *Working Mother* from her home in Sun Prairie, Wisconsin, where she lives with her husband, Ed, and three children. An avid marathoner, Melanie says she'd rather run several dozen laps around The Milwaukee Mile than drive them. Melanie won the Troutbeck Travel Writer's Contest in 1999 and 2001.

Nashville Superspeedway, TN: **John Hawks,** who also covered Memphis Motorsports Park, is the author of *Traveler's Rights* (www.mytravelrights.com). He is crossing his fingers that the Nashville Superspeedway will schedule George Jones for a future post-race concert.

New Hampshire International Speedway, NH: **Dara Chadwick** has been a freelance writer and editor for more than a decade. She writes about health, education, parenting, and food for publications like *Better Homes & Gardens, Working Mother, Parenting,* and *Woman's Day.* She's a NASCAR enthusiast by marriage, and her office overlooks a wall-mounted tire that once belonged to Darrell Waltrip. While researching this chapter, she learned that everyone in New Hampshire has a NASCAR story.

Phoenix International Raceway, AZ: Phoenix-based writer **Kathy Summers** has turned a few fast phrases for *Shape, Cooking Light, Men's Health,* and *Family Fun.* As a perk of writing this chapter, she can now say she's turned a few quick laps at PIR in her husband's Mustang, giving her a new perspective on the mysteries of men and motor sports (and the true meaning of "spin-control").

Pikes Peak International Raceway, CO: Denver-based writer **Ari Tye Radetsky** loves covering food, travel, and technology for publications like *Saveur, The Los Angeles Times Magazine,* and *Spin.* For the Pikes Peak chapter he met the ultimate fan, a Fountain, Colorado, man who erected a 500-pound black tire-shaped concrete tombstone for Dale Earnhardt in his front yard. Ari discovered he, too, could be a NASCAR fan if given the right mix of beer and earplugs. He can be reached at www.aritye.com.

Pocono Raceway, PA: **Jeff Beneke's** promising career in racing ended abruptly many years ago when the wheels came off his Soap Box Derby racer. He turned to writing and has written over a dozen books, most covering home improvement and renovation. His *The Fence Bible* (Storey Books) will be published in 2005. He lives near Ithaca, New York, where he wonders if anyone plans to challenge Pocono Raceway's claim of having "the biggest toilet facility in the world."

Richmond International Raceway, VA: **Jim Morrison** has done barrel rolls with the Navy's Blue Angels (he didn't barf), climbed and slept overnight in the top of a 243-foot-tall redwood (he didn't fall), and gone one-on-one with Muhammad Ali (he didn't flinch). His award-winning stories have appeared in *Smithsonian, The New York Times, The Wall Street Journal, Reader's Digest,* and numerous other magazines. While researching his chapter, he wheeled around "The Action Track"—at the speed limit and in the passenger seat. Next time, he plans to hijack the 8 Car.

Talladega Superspeedway, AL: **Apryl Chapman Thomas** is a resident of Georgia but grew up in Southern Alabama. A graduate of the University of Alabama and a lifelong Crimson Tide football fan, her work has appeared in *AAA Home & Away, AAA Going Places, USA Weekend,* and consumer magazines. No matter how many times she drives past Talladega Superspeedway, she is still stunned by its sheer size. On race weekends, she rolls down her car window to hear the crowd noise.

Texas Motor Speedway, TX: **Sheri Bell-Rehwoldt** is an award-winning freelance writer who loves to highlight the unique and fantastic. She has penned numerous articles for publications including *American Profile, Family Circle, Ladies' Home Journal, Lucent Books,* and *Ripley's Believe It or Not.* Born in Bryan, Texas, Sheri has two-stepped in more than ten Lone Star cities. She imagines only the Texas Motor Speedway could be more dizzying, due to its testosterone levels and gastronomical delights.

Watkins Glen International, NY: As the author of *Bed, Breakfast & Bike Midwest* (Anacus Press), **Theresa Russell** typically writes about races on two-wheels, not four. Her favorite quote from a security guard at Watkins Glen: "If the terrorists bombed this track it would be a tragedy for NASCAR because half the drivers could be killed."

Autodromo Hermanos Rodriguez, Mexico City: **Jane Optie** loves learning about possible vacation destinations, which is enhanced with her work at Mobil Travel Guide. She lived in Mexico for a period of time and, until now, thought the fastest cars in Mexico were the taxis flying down the *autopistas*. She aspires to be a Mexican soap opera star.

Illustrator: Nashville-based illustrator **DG Strong** spent decades preparing for this assignment, practicing oval-drawing everywhere from the sandbox to the margarita salt. His work has appeared in *The Readerville Journal,* as well as glove compartments throughout the Southeast. He drives with two lead feet. His 18 track diagrams appear on pages 76, 94, 108, 154, 172, 174, 210, 254, 272, 286, 300, 332, 348, 364, 412, 426, 456, and 472. He can be reached at www.dgstrong.com.

PHOTOGRAPHY CREDITS

Front cover (top) Rhonda Greer

Front cover (middle) Corbis

Front cover (bottom) Digital Vision

Page 3, 15, 330, 331, 333 Russ Lake

Page 4, 11, 16, 63, 113 (top), 159 (bottom), 179 (bottom), 275, 305, 337 (bottom), 415 (bottom), 461 (bottom) NASCAR

Page 5 Roark Johnson

Page 13, 346, 353 (left) Dover Motorsports Inc.

Pages 20, 23, 24, 25, 27, 31, 56, 59, 63, 81 (top), 92, 93, 95, 106, 107, 109, 113, 129 (top), 152, 153, 155, 159, 170, 171, 173, 179, 197 (bottom) 236, 237, 239, 252, 255, 259, 284, 285, 287, 314, 315, 317, 321, 337, 362, 424, 429, 431, 440, 441, 454, 455, 457, 461, 470, 473, 477, BRAKE HERE, FAN FAVORITE, back cover Sherryl Creekmore/NASCAR

Pages 28, 29 Henry County CVB

Page 31, 243, 431 International Motorsports Hall of Fame

Page 41 Savannah Convention and Visitors Bureau

Pages 42, 45 (right) Tom Whitemore/VPS

Pages 43, 45 (left), 347, 349 Worth Canoy/VPS

Pages 47 (top), 55 Tennessee Tourism

Pages 47 (bottom), 57, 97, 259, 385, 425, 443, 445, 471 Motorsports Images and Archives

Page 60 (top left, top right), 61 Arnesen Photography/LACVB

Page 60 (bottom right) Michele and Tom Grimm/LACVB

Page 73 San Diego Convention and Visitors Bureau

Pages 74, 75, 77, 81 Chicagoland Speedway

Page 78 (top right, bottom left) Joliet Tourism Center

Page 78 (bottom right) Courtesy of the Chicago Office of Tourism

Page 79 Courtesy of the Chicago Office of Tourism/Willy Schmidt

Page 91 Springfield Convention and Visitors Bureau

Page 97 (middle) South Carolina Convention and Visitors Bureau

Page 97 (bottom) Greater Florence Chamber of Commerce

Page 105 Myrtle Beach Area Chamber of Commerce

Pages 110, 111 Daytona Beach Convention and Visitors Bureau

Page 123 SJCVCB

Page 124 Dan Gill

Pages 125, Worth Canoy

Page 127 Carla Varisco

Page 129 (bottom) Mike Baker, Action Images

Page 129 (middle) Delaware Tourism Office

Page 135 Randy Dickerson

Page 137 Baltimore Area Convention and Visitors Association

Pages 138, 139, 141 Jim Compton

Page 143 St. Louis Convention and Visitors Bureau

Page 151 Hannibal Convention and Visitors Bureau

Pages 156, 157 Greater Miami Convention and Visitors Bureau

Page 169 The Florida Keys and Key West Monroe County Tourist Development Council

Page 175 Dave Gansert, IRP Photographer

Page 176 (top) Indianapolis Convention and Visitors Association

Pages 176 (bottom), 177, 179 Michael Vaughn Photography

Page 178 Shawn Spence Photography

Page 189 Brown County Convention and Visitors Bureau

Page 190 Chucke Walkden

Page 191 Bob Campbell

Page 193 Nate Jacobson

Page 195 Joe Jacobson

Pages 194, 197 Sonoma Valley Visitors Bureau

Page 207 El Dorado Lake Tahoe Film and Media Office

Pages 208, 209, 211 Kansas Speedway

Page 213 Kansas City Convention and Visitors Bureau

Page 221 Branson/Lakes Area Chamber of Commerce and Convention and Visitors Bureau

Pages 222, 223, 225 High Sierra Photography

Page 227 Kentucky Department of Tourism

Page 235 National Park Service

Pages 240, 241 Las Vegas Convention and Visitors Bureau

Page 243 NASCAR Cafe

Page 251 Zion National Park Service

Page 253 Harold Hinson

Page 256 (top) North Carolina Department of Commerce

Page 256 (bottom) NC Division of Tourism, Film, and Sports Development

Page 257 NC Division of Tourism, Film, and Sports Development

Page 269 Asheville Convention and Visitors Bureau

Pages 270, 271, 273 High Sierra Photography

Page 275 Ohio Division of Travel and Tourism www.DiscoverOhio.com

Page 283 Cedar Point Amusement Park/Resort

Page 289 Danville Division of Tourism

Page 297 NC Division of Tourism, Film, and Sports Development

Pages 298, 299, 301 Phil Bowden/Memphis Motorsports Park

Pages 302, 303, 305 Tennessee Tourism

Page 313 Little Rock Convention and Visitors Bureau

Pages 318, 319 Travel Michigan

Page 329 Mark Arpin

Page 334 (top) R.J. and Linda Miller-Wisconsin Department of Tourism

Page 334 (bottom) Donald S. Abrams-Wisconsin Department of Tourism

Page 335 Wisconsin Department of Tourism

Page 337 Discovery World Museum-Wisconsin Department of Tourism

Page 345 Philip G. Olson-Wisconsin Department of Tourism

Pages 347, 349 Worth Canoy/NASCAR

Page 350 Country Music Hall of Fame® and Museum/Timothy Hursley

Page 351 Barry M. Winiker

Page 353 (top right) Terry Clements

Page 361 Chattanooga Convention and Visitors Bureau

Pages 363, 365 NHIS

Page 366 NHDTTD/Canterbury Shaker Village

Page 367 NHDTTD/Craig Alness

Page 369 NHDTTD/Bob Grant

Page 377 NHDTTD

Pages 378, 379, 381, 385 Phoenix International Raceway

Pages 382, 383 Greater Phoenix Convention and Visitors Bureau

Pages 394, 395, 396, 397 Gary Caskey

Page 395 Grand Canyon National Park

Page 399 (top) Eric Wunrow, (bottom) J.C. Leacock CTO

Page 409 Carl Scofield/Breckenridge Resort Chamber

Pages 410, 411, 413 PIR-Photo

Page 415 Camelbeach Waterpark

Page 423 Hershey-Capital Region Visitors Bureau

Page 427 John Harrelson

Page 428 (top) Richmond Metropolitan Convention and Visitors Bureau

Page 428 (bottom) Buddy Mays, courtesy of Richmond Metropolitan Convention and Visitors Bureau

Page 431 Richmond Raft Co., courtesy Richmond Metropolitan Convention and Visitors Bureau

Page 439 Norfolk Convention and Visitors Bureau

Pages 444, 445 Karim Shamsi-Basha, courtesy Alabama Bureau of Tourism and Travel

Page 453 Mobile Bay Convention and Visitors Bureau

Pages 458, 461 Fort Worth Convention and Visitors Bureau

Page 469 Johnson Space Center

Pages 474 (top), 475 Finger Lakes Visitors Connection

Page 474 (bottom) Schuyler County Chamber of Commerce

Page 485 Buffalo Niagara CVB and Angel Art Ltd.

Pages 486, 487, 488 (bottom) Autodromo Hermanos Rodriguez

Pages 488 (top right, left), 491 Mexico Tourism Board

ROAD FOOD, SHOP TALK, Getty Images

KIDS' PICK, Myrtle Beach Area Chamber of Commerce

TOLL-FREE NUMBERS
Useful Toll-Free Numbers and Web sites

LODGING

Best Western International
The Official Hotel of NASCAR
800/937-8376
www.bestwestern.com

America's Best Inns & Suites
800/237-8466
www.americasbestinns.com

AmericInn
800/634-3444
www.americinn.com

AmeriHost Inn
800/434-5800
www.amerihostinn.com

Amerisuites
877/774-6467
www.amerisuites.com

Baymont Inns
877/229-6668
www.baymontinns.com

Best Value Inns
888/315-2378
www.bestvalueinn.com

Budget Host Inn
800/283-4678
www.budgethost.com

Cal-Am RV Resorts
888/940-8989
www.cal-am.com

Clarion Hotels
800/252-7466
www.choicehotels.com

Comfort Inns and Suites
800/252-7466
www.choicehotels.com

Country Inns & Suites
800/456-4000
www.countryinns.com

Cruise America
800/327-7799
www.cruiseamerica.com

Days Inn
800/544-8313
www.daysinn.com

Delta Hotels
800/268-1133
www.deltahotels.com

Doubletree Hotels
800/222-8733
www.doubletree.com

Drury Inn
800/378-7946
www.druryinn.com

Econolodge
800/553-2666
www.econolodge.com

Encore and Sunburst RV Parks of America
877/267-8737
www.rvonthego.com

ExelInns of America
800/367-3935
www.exelinns.com

Fairfield Inn by Marriott
888/236-2427
www.fairfieldinn.com

Hampton Inn
800/426-7866
www.hamptoninn.com

Hilton Hotels and Resorts (US)
800/774-1500
www.hilton.com

Holiday Inn Express
800/465-4329
www.hiexpress.com

Holiday Inn Hotels and Resorts
800/465-4329
www.holiday-inn.com

Homestead Studio Suites
888/782-9473
www.homesteadhotels.com

Homewood Suites
800/225-5466
www.homewoodsuites.com

Howard Johnson
800/406-1411
www.hojo.com

Hyatt
800/633-7313
www.hyatt.com

Inns of America
800/826-0778
www.innsofamerica.com

Knights Inn
800/843-5644
www.knightsinn.com

KOA Kampgrounds
www.koakampgrounds.com

La Quinta
800/531-5900
www.laquinta.com

MainStay Suites
800/660-6246
www.choicehotels.com

Marriott Hotels, Resorts, and Suites
888/236-2427
www.marriott.com

Microtel Inns & Suites
800/771-7171
www.microtelinn.com

Motel 6
800/466-8356
www.motel6.com

Park Inn & Park Plaza
888/201-1801
www.parkhtls.com

Quality Inn
800/228-5151
www.qualityinn.com

Radisson Hotels
800/333-3333
www.radisson.com

Ramada Plazas, Limiteds, and Inns
800/272-6232
www.ramada.com

Red Lion Inns
800/733-5466
www.redlion.com

Red Roof Inns
800/733-7663
www.redroof.com

Residence Inns
888/236-2427
www.residenceinn.com

Rodeway Inns
800/228-2000
www.rodeway.com

Select Inn
800/641-1000
www.selectinn.com

Sheraton
888/625-5144
www.sheraton.com

Shilo Inns
800/222-2244
www.shiloinns.com

Shoney's Inns
800/552-4667
www.shoneysinn.com

Signature/Jameson Inns
800/526-3766
www.jamesoninns.com

Sleep Inns
800/453-3746
www.sleepinn.com

Summit International
800/457-4000
www.summithotels.com

Super 8 Motels
800/800-8000
www.super8.com

TownePlace Suites
888/236-2427
www.towneplace.com

Travelodge
800/578-7878
www.travelodge.com

Vagabond Inns
800/522-1555
www.vagabondinns.com

Wellesley Inn and Suites
800/444-8888
www.wellesleyinnandsuites.com

Westin Hotels & Resorts
800/937-8461
www.westin.com

Woodfin Suite Hotels
800/966-3346
www.woodfinsuitehotels.com

AIRLINES

Air Canada
888/247-2262
www.aircanada.ca

AirTran
800/247-8726
www.airtran.com

Alaska Airlines
800/252-7522
www.alaskaair.com

American Airlines
800/433-7300
www.aa.com

America West
800/235-9292
www.americawest.com

ATA
800/435-9282
www.ata.com

Continental Airlines
800/523-3273
www.continental.com

Delta Air Lines
800/221-1212
www.delta.com

Frontier Airlines
800/432-1359
www.frontierairlines.com

Jet Blue Airways
800/538-2583
www.jetblue.com

Midwest Airlines
800/452-2022
www.midwestairlines.com

Northwest Airlines
800/225-2525
www.nwa.com

Southwest Airlines
800/435-9792
www.southwest.com

Spirit Airlines
800/772-7117
www.spiritair.com

United Airlines
800/241-6522
www.ual.com

US Airways
800/428-4322
www.usairways.com

Vanguard Airlines
800/826-4827
www.flyvanguard.com

CAR RENTALS

Advantage
800/777-5500
www.arac.com

Alamo
800/327-9633
www.alamo.com

Avis
800/831-2847
www.avis.com

Budget
800/527-0700
www.budget.com

Dollar
800/800-4000
www.dollar.com

Enterprise
800/325-8007
www.enterprise.com

Hertz
800/654-3131
www.hertz.com

National
800/227-7368
www.nationalcar.com

Payless
800/729-5377
www.paylesscarrental.com

Rent-A-Wreck.com
800/535-1391
www.rent-a-wreck.com

Thrifty
800/847-4389
www.thrifty.com

INDEX

3 Seasons Camping Resort (Rehoboth Beach, DE), *134–135*
10th Annual Pioneer Days (Troy, AL), *445*
450-Mile Yard Sale (Chattanooga, TN), *444*

A

Abingdon, VA
   attractions, *49*
   lodgings, *50, 51*
   restaurants, *53*
   RV and camping, *52*
Abingdon Manor (Latta, SC), *101*
Abraham Lincoln Presidential Library and Museum (Springfield, IL), *91*
Abriendo Inn (Pueblo, CO), *406*
Abuelo's Mexican Food Embassy (Arlington, TX), *468*
Acapulco Hotel and Resort (Daytona Beach Shores, FL), *118*
Action Duckpin Bowl (Indianapolis, IN), *181*
Admiralty of Plantation Oaks, The (Millington, TN), *310*
Adrian, MI
   lodgings, *325*
Air Mobility Command Museum (Dover, DE), *128, 129, 131*
Akron, OH
   lodgings, *278–279*
   restaurants, *281*
Alexander City, AL
   restaurants, *450*
Alfred's (Memphis, TN), *311*
Alison's Restaurant (Abingdon, VA), *53*
All American Campground (Bluff City, TN), *52*
Allen, Johnny, *259*
Allerton Crowne Plaza Hotel (Chicago, IL), *85*
Alliance Center (Fort Worth, TX), *461*
Alligator Adventure (Myrtle Beach, SC), *105*
Alligator Farm and Zoological Park (St. Augustine, FL), *123*
Allison, Bobby, *445*
Alton, IL, *146, 150*
   lodgings, *146*
   restaurants, *150*
Alum Creek State Park (Delaware, OH), *277*
Amalfi's (Charlotte, NC), *267*
Amelia, VA
   RV and camping, *436*
Amelia Earhart Festival (Atchison, KS), *213*
Amelia Family Campgrounds (Amelia, VA), *436*
America West Arena (Phoenix, AZ), *383*
Americamps Richmond North (Ashland, VA), *436*
American Jazz Museum (Kansas City, KS), *212*
American Rover (Norfolk, VA), *439*
American Serb Memorial Hall (Milwaukee, WI), *340*
American Star (Branson, MO), *221*
Americana on the River (Hannibal, MO), *151*
America's Best Campground (Branson, MO), *221*
Amerihost Inn (Ashland, OH), *279*
Amerisuites Indianapolis Keystone (Indianapolis, IN), *185*
Amherst, OH
   attractions, *277*
Amish Country Market and Preview Party and Sale (Noblesville, IN), *179*
Anaheim, CA
   attractions, *65*
   lodgings, *67–68*
   restaurants, *70–71*
Andew's BBQ (Talladega, AL), *451*
Andrew Jackson Statute (Nashville, TN), *353*
Andria's (O'Fallon, IL), *150*
Angelina's Ristorante Italiano (Concord, NH), *375–376*
Angelo's Bar-B-Que (Fort Worth, TX), *468*
Anheuser-Busch Brewery (St. Louis, MO), *145*
Anheuser-Busch Michelob Ultra Weekend Bicycle Race (Carondelet Park, MO), *143*
Ann Arbor, MI
   lodgings, *324–325, 325*
   restaurants, *327*
Ann Arbor Art Fairs (Ann Arbor, MI), *321*
Anniston, AL
   attractions, *447*
   lodgings, *447–448*
   restaurants, *450*
Anniston Museum of Natural History (Anniston, AL), *447*
Ann's Italian Restaurant (Hales Corners, WI), *344*
Annual Harvest Jubilee and Wine Festival (Altavista, VA), *289*
Antioch, TN, *358*
   lodgings, *358*
Antiques (Brooklyn, MI), *323*
Antiques Valuation Day (Colorado Days, CO), *401*
Antiquing on State Street and Commonwealth Avenue (Bristol, TN/VA), *49*
Antlers Hilton Colorado Springs (Colorado Springs, CO), *404*
Antonelli's Imports (Gadsden, AL), *451*
Apollo Mobile Home and Travel Park (Concord, NC), *265–266*
Appalachian Caverns (Blountville, TN), *49*
Appalachian Trial (Asheville, NC), *269*
Apple Cake Tea Room (Knoxville, TN), *53*
Arcelia's (St. Louis, MO), *150*
Aristocrat Pub (Indianapolis, IN), *186*
Arizona Center (Phoenix, AZ), *381, 382, 387*
Ark Restaurant, the (Riverside, AL), *452*
Arkansas Governor's Mansion (Little Rock, AK), *313*
Arlington, TX
   attractions, *463*
   lodgings, *465*
   restaurants, *467, 468*
Arlington Antebellum Home and Gardens (Birmingham, AL), *447*
Arlington Diner (Stroudsburg, PA), *421*
Arlington Steak House (Arlington, TX), *468*
Armani (Chicago, IL), *80*
Arnie's Place (Concord, NH), *376*
Arroyo (Mexico City, MX), *491*
Art Deco District (Miami, FL), *158*
Artesian Wells (Cement City, MI), *328*
Arthur Bryant's (Kansas City, KS), *220*
Asheville, NC, *269*
Ashland, NH
   RV and camping, *374*
Ashland, OH
   attractions, *277*
   lodgings, *279*
   restaurants, *281*
Ashland, VA
   RV and camping, *436*
Ashley Quarters (Florence, KY), *230*
Athens, GA
   restaurants, *37*
Atlanta, GA
   area maps, *28, 32*
   attractions, *33*
   lodgings, *34–35, 36*
   restaurants, *37–40*
Atlantic Avenue (Daytona Beach, FL), *115*
Atlanta Marriott Marquis (Atlanta, GA), *34*
Atlanta Motor Speedway (Hampton, GA), *25–41*
   concessions, *26*
   first aid, *26*
   getting around, *29*
   getting tickets, *29*
   parking, *26*
   RV and camping, *37*
   security, *26*
Atlanta Motor Speedway Track Tours (Hampton, GA), *34*
Atlantic Coast Inn (Fenwick Island, DE), *132*
Atwood, Casey, *92*
Atwoods (Dover, DE), *135*
Augusta, GA
   lodgings, *35–36*
Augusta Towers Hotel and Convention Center (Augusta, GA), *36*
Aunt Catfish's on the River (Daytona Beach, FL), *121*
Austell, GA
   attractions, *34*
Autodromo Hermanos Rodriguez (Mexico City, MX), *486–491*
   first aid, *487*
   getting around, *487*
Automatic Slim's Tonga Club (Memphis, TN), *311*
Auton, Wayne, *275*
Avenue of the Dead (San Juan Teotihuacán, MX), *491*
Avondale, AZ. *See also* Phoenix International Raceway (Avondale, AZ)
   area maps, *384, 386*
   calendar, *385*
   restaurants, *393–394*
Axton, VA
   RV and camping, *294*
Azalea Inn (Augusta, GA), *35–36*

B

B. B. King's Blues Club (Memphis, TN), *312*
B Mae's Resort Inn and Suites (Gilford, NH), *373*
Baby Kay's Cajun Kitchen (Phoenix, AZ), *392*
Badgerland RV Rental LLC (West Allis, WI), *343*
Bahama Breeze (Orlando, FL), *122*
Balistreri's Blue Mound Inn (Milwaukee, WI), *343*
Baltimore, MD, *137*
Banana Boat Resort and Marina (Florida Keys, FL), *169*
Bank One Ballpark (Phoenix, AZ), *383–384*
Barefoot Landing (Myrtle Beach, SC), *105*
Barton on Park Place (Covington, KY), *233*
Barton's Motel (Laconia, NH), *372*
"Baseball As America" (Forest Park, MO), *143*
Bass Pro Shop MBNA 500 NASCAR NEXTEL Cup Series (Atlanta Motor Speedway Hampton, GA), *31*
Bass Pro Shops Sportsmans Warehouse (St. Charles, MO), *146*
Bastille Days (Milwaukee, WI), *337*
Bates, Katharine Lee, *400*
Bay View (Bodega Bay, CA), *204*
Baylink Ferry (San Francisco, CA), *196*
Baymont Inn and Suites (Cutler Ridge/Miami, FL), *163*
Baymont Inn & Suites (Mansfield, OH), *280*
Baymont Inn (Birmingham, AL), *448*
Bayside Marketplace (Miami, FL), *161*
Bazaar del Mundo (San Diego, CA), *73*
BB Riverboat (KY), *227*
Beach, The (Daytona Beach, FL), *115*
Beach and Flagler Avenue Shops, The (New Smyrna Beach, FL), *116*
Beach Bar (Clark Lake, MI), *328*
Beachcomber Daytona Beach Resort (Daytona Beach, FL), *117*
Beale Street Entertainment District (Memphis, TN), *307*
Beale Street Fourth of July (Memphis, TN), *305*
Beale Street (Memphis, TN), *302*
Beanstalk (Loudon, NH), *373*
Bear, DE
   RV and camping, *134*
Bear Flag Monument (Sonoma, CA), *197*
Bear Republic Brewing Company (Healdsburg, CA), *206*
Behle Street Café (Covington, KY), *233*
Bell Tower Hotel (Ann Arbor, MI), *324*
Bella Luna Ristorante (Goodyear, AZ), *394*
Bellagio Conservatory (Las Vegas, NV), *241*
Belle Aire Biplane Rides (Millington, TN), *308*
Belle Meade Plantation (Nashville, TN), *355*
Belleville, IL, *149, 150*
   restaurants, *149, 150*
Bellevue, OH
   attractions, *277*
   restaurants, *281*
Bellingrath Gardens and Homes (Mobile, AL), *453*
Bellville, OH
   lodgings, *279–280*
   restaurants, *281*
Belmont, NH
   restaurants, *375*
Benbrook, TX
   lodgings, *465*
Benicia, CA
   lodgings, *201*
Benito Juarez International Airport (Mexico City, MX), *486*
Berghoff, The (Chicago, IL), *88*
Berliner Bear (Kansas City, MO), *218*
Best Holiday Trav-L-Park Memphis (Marion, AR), *310*
Best Value Inn & Suites—Williamstown (Williamstown, KY), *231*
Best Value Inn (Darlington, SC), *102*
Best Western 55 South Inn (St. Louis, MO), *148*
Best Western Airport Inn (Charlotte, NC), *264*
Best Western Airport Inn (Colorado Springs, CO), *405*
Best Western Airport Inn (Nashville, TN), *358*
Best Western Airport Inn (Phoenix, AZ), *390*
Best Western Airport Inn (St. Louis, MO), *148*
Best Western Airport (Sandston, VA), *436*
Best Western Airport Suites (Indianapolis, IN), *184*
Best Western Aku Tiki Inn (Daytona Beach, FL), *119*
Best Western Anniston (Oxford, AL), *450*
Best Western Atlanta Airport East (Hapeville, GA), *37*
Best Western Atlanta South (Stockbridge, GA), *37*

Best Western Beach Resort (Miami Beach, FL), 164
Best Western Bell Hotel (Phoenix, AZ), 391
Best Western Benchmark Hotel (Memphis, TN), 309
Best Western Blue Ridge Plaza (Boone, NC), 51
Best Western Camelot Inn of Fairview Heights (Fairview Heights, IL), 147
Best Western Camelot Inn (Pontoon Beach, IL), 147–148
Best Western Carowinds (Fort Mill, SC), 265
Best Western Castleton Inn (Indianapolis, IN), 184
Best Western Central Phoenix Inn & Suites (Phoenix, AZ), 391
Best Western Chateableau Hotel (Coral Gables, FL), 163
Best Western City Centre Hotel & Suites (Indianapolis, IN), 185
Best Western Concord Inn and Suites (Concord, NH), 373
Best Western Cooper Inn & Suites (Arlington, TX), 465
Best Western Cordelia Inn (Fairfield, CA), 201
Best Western Country Inn Airport (Kansas City, MO), 217
Best Western Country Inn Near Worlds of Fun (Kansas City, MO), 217–218
Best Western Country Inn North (Kansas City, MO), 218
Best Western Country Inn (Ontario, CA), 69
Best Western Country Suites (Indianapolis, IN), 185
Best Western Crown Suites (Pineville, NC), 265
Best Western Deep River (Greensboro, NC), 292
Best Western Denton Inn (Denton, DE), 134
Best Western DFW Airport Suites (Irving, TX), 466
Best Western Downtown/Convention Center (Nashville, TN), 358
Best Western East Mountain Inn and Suites (Wilkes-Barre, PA), 420
Best Western Easton Inn (Easton, PA), 419
Best Western Elm House Inn (Napa, CA), 202
Best Western Empire Inn (Rialto, CA), 70
Best Western Estoril (Mexico City, MX), 490
Best Western Executive Court Inn and Conference Center (Manchester, NH), 374
Best Western Executive Hotel (Richmond, VA), 436
Best Western Executive Inn and Suites (Colorado Springs, CO), 405
Best Western Executive Inn (Carrollton, KY), 231
Best Western Executive Inn (Gastonia, NC), 265
Best Western Executive Inn (Lebanon, TN), 358
Best Western Executive Inn (Memphis, TN), 309
Best Western Executive Inn (Mount Gilead, OH), 280
Best Western Executive Plaza (Ann Arbor, MI), 325
Best Western Fairwinds Inn (Goodlettsville, TN), 358
Best Western Floridian Hotel (Cutler Ridge/Miami, FL), 163
Best Western Fort Mitchell Inn (Fort Mitchell, KY), 231
Best Western Fort Worth Inn & Suites (Fort Worth, TX), 465
Best Western Galaxy Inn (Dover, DE), 134

Best Western Garden Inn (Santa Rosa, CA), 202
Best Western Genetti Hotel and Conference Center (Wilkes-Barre, PA), 420
Best Western Genetti Lodge (Hazleton, PA), 419
Best Western Governor's Inn (Richmond, VA), 436
Best Western Grace Inn at Ahwatukee (Phoenix, AZ), 391
Best Western Granada Suite Hotel Downtown (Atlanta, GA), 36
Best Western Grandview Inn (Sturtevant, WI), 342
Best Western Grant Park Hotel (Chicago, IL), 87
Best Western Great Southwest Inn (Arlington, TX), 465
Best Western Hazelwood Inn (Hazelwood, MO), 147
Best Western Heritage Inn (Benicia, CA), 201
Best Western Heritage Inn (Rancho Cucamonga, CA), 70
Best Western Homestead/Florida City's Gateway to the Keys (Florida City, FL), 163
Best Western Hospitality Lane (San Bernardino, CA), 70
Best Western Hotel De Cortes (Mexico City, MX), 490
Best Western Image Inn & Suites (Moreno Valley, CA), 69
Best Western Indianapolis South (Indianapolis, IN), 185
Best Western Inn and Conference Center (Kansas City, KS), 217
Best Western Inn & Suites—Monroe (Monroe, NC), 265
Best Western Inn & Suites (Fort Worth, TX), 465
Best Western Inn and Suites of Sun City (Sun City, AZ), 392
Best Western Inn & Suites—Midway Airport (Burbank, IL), 86
Best Western Inn at Blakeslee-Pocono (Blakeslee, PA), 419
Best Western Inn at Marine World (Vallejo, CA), 201
Best Western Inn at the Park (St. Louis, MO), 148
Best Western Inn at the Peachtree (Atlanta, GA), 36
Best Western Inn at the Vines (Napa, CA), 202
Best Western Inn at Valley View (Roanoke, VA), 294
Best Western Inn (Florence, SC), 102
Best Western Inn (Fort Worth, TX), 465
Best Western Inn (Millington, TN), 310
Best Western Inn of Chicago (Chicago, IL), 87
Best Western Inn of Tempe (Tempe, AZ), 391–392
Best Western Inn Phoenix—Glendale (Glendale, AZ), 390
Best Western Inn (Rock Hill, SC), 265
Best Western Inn (Rohnert Park, CA), 202
Best Western Inn Towne Hotel (Milwaukee, WI), 342
Best Western Innsuites Hotel & Suites Fort Worth (Fort Worth, TX), 466
Best Western InnSuites Hotel & Suites (Phoenix, AZ), 391
Best Western Irving Inn & Suites at DFW Airport (Irving, TX), 466
Best Western Johnson City Hotel & Conference Center (Johnson City, TN), 51
Best Western Joliet Inn & Suites (Joliet, IL), 87
Best Western Kannapolis (Kannapolis, NC), 265

Best Western Kearney Inn (Kearney, MO), 218
Best Western Kings Quarters (Doswell, VA), 436
Best Western Kirkwood Inn (St. Louis, MO), 148
Best Western La Playa Resort (Daytona Beach, FL), 119
Best Western Lake Norman (Cornelius, NC), 265
Best Western Lake Worth Inn and Suites (Lake Worth, TX), 466
Best Western Lodge on the Green (Corning, NY), 481
Best Western Main St Inn (Off-Strip/Downtown Las Vegas, NV), 248
Best Western Mainsail Inn & Suites (Ormond Beach, FL), 120
Best Western Majestic (Mexico City, MX), 490
Best Western Mardi Gras Hotel & Casino (Las Vegas Strip and Vicinity, NV), 247
Best Western Market Center (Dallas, TX), 465
Best Western Marshall Manor (Horseheads, NY), 481
Best Western Martinsville Inn (Martinsville, VA), 294
Best Western Mayan Inn Beachfront (Daytona Beach, FL), 119
Best Western McCarran Inn (Las Vegas Strip and Vicinity, NV), 247
Best Western McDonough Inn and Suites (McDonough, GA), 37
Best Western Miami Airport West Inn and Suites (Miami, FL), 164
Best Western Midway Hotel (Brookfield, WI), 341
Best Western Milwaukee Airport Hotel & Conference Center (Milwaukee, WI), 342
Best Western Monee Inn (Monee, IL), 87
Best Western Mountain View Inn & Suites (Upland, CA), 70
Best Western Music City Inn (Antioch, TN), 358
Best Western Music Row Inn (Nashville, TN), 358
Best Western Naperville Inn (Naperville, IL), 87
Best Western Nellis Motor Inn (Off-Strip/Downtown Las Vegas, NV), 248
Best Western North Plaza Inn (Griffin, GA), 36
Best Western Northwest Inn (Dallas, TX), 465
Best Western Novato Oaks Inn (Novato, CA), 201
Best Western Oceanfront Resort (Miami Beach, FL), 164
Best Western of Riverside (Riverside, CA), 70
Best Western On the Bay Inn and Marina (Miami Beach, FL), 164
Best Western Ontario Airport (Ontario, CA), 69
Best Western Papago Inn and Resort (Scottsdale, AZ), 391
Best Western Parkview Inn (Off-Strip/Downtown Las Vegas, NV), 248
Best Western Peachtree City Inn/Suites (Peachtree City, GA), 37
Best Western Pear Tree Inn (Collinsville, IL), 147
Best Western Petaluma Inn (Petaluma, CA), 202
Best Western Phoenix—Goodyear Inn (Goodyear, AZ), 390
Best Western Pikes Peak Inn (Colorado Springs, CO), 405
Best Western Pine Tree Motel (Chino, CA), 69
Best Western Pocono Inn (Stroudsburg, PA), 419–420

Best Western Prairie View Inn & Suites (Platte City, MO), 218
Best Western Quiet House & Suites (Mequon, WI), 342
Best Western Regency Motor Inn (Marion, AR), 309
Best Western Riverside Inn (Riverside, AL), 450
Best Western Romeoville Inn (Romeoville, IL), 87
Best Western Royal Inn and Suites (Pilot Mountain, NC), 292–293
Best Western Sandman Motel (Redlands, CA), 70
Best Western Seville Plaza Hotel (Kansas City, MO), 218
Best Western Skyway Inn Suites (Manitou Springs, CO), 406
Best Western Sonoma Valley Inn (Sonoma Valley, CA), 202
Best Western South Beach (Miami Beach, FL), 165
Best Western South Miami (Miami, FL), 164
Best Western Southhaven (Southhaven, MS), 310
Best Western Southlake Inn (Morrow, GA), 37
Best Western St. Charles Inn (St. Charles, MO), 148
Best Western Sterling Hotel & Suites (Charlotte, NC), 264
Best Western Stevenson Manor Inn (Calistoga, CA), 202
Best Western Suites at Key Largo (Key Largo, FL), 164
Best Western Suites (Memphis, TN), 309
Best Western Suites Near Opryland (Nashville, TN), 358
Best Western Sumter Inn (Sumter, SC), 102
Best Western Thunderbird Beach Resort (Miami Beach, FL), 165
Best Western Travelers Inn (Memphis, TN), 309
Best Western Truman Inn (Independence, MO), 217
Best Western University Inn (Ithaca, NY), 481–482
Best Western Waukesha Grand (Pewaukee, WI), 342
Best Western Wendover Plaza (Greensboro, NC), 292
Best Western West Memphis Inn (Memphis, TN), 309–310
Best Western Westfield Inn (Westfield, IN), 185
Best Western Westport Park Hotel (Maryland Heights, MO), 147
Best Western Windsor Suites (Danville, VA), 293
Best Western Winscott Inn and Suites (Benbrook, TX), 465
Best Western Woods View Inn (Milwaukee, WI), 342
Best Western Kings Inn (Corona, CA), 69
Bethany Beach, DE
 restaurants, 135
Betty Brinn Children's Museum (Milwaukee, WI), 339
Betty's Bar-B-Q (Anniston, AL), 451
Bicycle Program (Tempe, AZ), 384
Big Bone Lick State Park (Union, KY), 230
Big Chalk Weekend (Phoenix, AZ), 385
Big Daddy's (Mount Pocono, PA), 422
Big Pink (Miami Beach, FL), 160
Big T Bar-B-Que (Columbia, SC), 104
Bigfoot 4X4 Inc. (Hazelwood, MO), 145
Bike Week, Daytona Beach, FL), 113
Bill Spoon's Barbecue (Charlotte, NC) 267
Billy Bob's Texas (Fort Worth, TX), 459

Billy's Ritz (Roanoke, VA), *295*
Biltmore Estate (Asheville, NC), *269*
Biltmore Hotel Coral Gables (Coral Gables, FL), *162*
Binghamton, NY
　restaurants, *483*
Birmingham, AL
　attractions, *447*
　lodgings, *448–449*
　restaurants, *445, 450–451*
Birmingham Civil Rights Institute (Talladega, AL) *443*
Birmingham International Festival, AL, *445*
Birmingham Museum of Art (Talladega, AL), *443*
Birmingham News/Business Post-Herald Qualifying Day for NASCAR NEXTEL Cup Series (Talladega Superspeedway, Talladega, AL), *445*
Birthplace of Country Music Alliance Museum, The (Bristol, VA), *49*
Biscayne National Park (Homestead, FL), *156, 161*
Bishopville, SC
　RV and camping, *103*
Blacksmith Shop (Abingdon, VA), *49*
Blakeslee, PA, *419, 420*
　lodgings, *419*
　RV and camping, *420*
Bleachers Sports Bar and Grill (Watkins Glen, NY), *484*
Blessing of the Inlet Sound (Myrtle Beach, SC), *97*
Block Party (Fontana, CA), *63*
Blountville, TN
　attractions, *49*
Blue Berry Mountain Inn (Blakeslee, PA), *419*
Blue Moon (Rehoboth Beach, DE), *135*
Blue Ox Campground at Bristol Dragway (Bristol, TN), *52*
Blue Ridge Parkway, VA/NC/TN, *287, 297*
Blue Room (Kansas City, KS), *212*
Bluegrass Festival (Carrollton, KY), *227*
Bluespring Manor Bed and Breakfast (Childersburg, AL), *450*
Bluff City, TN
　restaurants, *52*
　RV and camping, *52*
Boardwalk Mobile Home and RV Park (Homestead, FL), *165*
Boardwalk Plaza Hotel (Rehoboth Beach, DE), *133*
Boar's Tavern (Loudon, NH), *376*
Bodacious Bar-B-Q (Arlington, TX), *468*
Bodega Bay, CA
　restaurants, *203–204, 205*
　RV and camping, *202*
Bombay Hook National Wildlife Refuge (Smyrna, DE), *131*
Bombay Restaurant (Ontario, CA), *72*
Bondy (Mexico City, MX), *491*
Bones (Atlanta, GA), *40*
Boo at the Zoo (Kansas City, MO), *213*
Boone, NC
　lodgings, *51*
Bootlegger Bistro (Las Vegas Strip and Vicinity, NV), *250*
Boston Lobster Feast (Orlando, FL), *122*
Bothe-Napa Valley State Park (Napa, CA), *202*
Bottega (Birmingham, AL), *451*
Bougainvillea's Old Florida Tavern (South Miami, FL), *168*
Boulder Creek Dining Company (Brownsburg, IN), *187*
Bourbon Street Blues and Boogie Bar (Nashville, TN), *360*
Bowling Green, VA
　RV and camping, *436*

Bowling Green KOA (Bowling Green, VA), *436*
Bowman Gray Stadium (Winston-Salem, NC), *262*
Boykin, SC
　restaurants, *104*
Boykin's at the Mill Pond (Boykin, SC), *104*
Bradford, NH
　lodgings, *373*
Bragg-Mitchell Mansion (Mobile, AL), *453*
Branding Iron (Delaware, OH), *281*
Brandywine Suites Hotel (Wilmington, DE), *133*
Branson, MO, *221*
Branson Café (Branson, MO), *221*
Branson Stagecoach RV Park (Branson, MO), *221*
Brasington, Buddy, *101*
Bravo Cucina Italiano (Kansas City, MO), *220*
Breckenridge Golf Club (Summit County, CO), *409*
Breckenridge Music Festival (Summit County, CO), *409*
Breckenridge (Summit County, CO), *409*
Brew City Queen (Milwaukee, WI), *339*
Brick Walter Tavern Antiques (Brooklyn, MI), *323*
Brickyard 400 (Indianapolis Motor Speedway Indianapolis Raceway Park, Indianapolis, IN), *171*
Brickyard Crossing Golf Course (Indianapolis, IN), *181*
Brickyard Crossing Golf Resort Inn (Indianapolis, IN), *185*
Bridgeview Inn New Castle Wilmington (New Castle, DE), *134*
Bright Star (Birmingham, AL), *445*
Brighton Suites Hotel (Rehoboth Beach, DE), *133*
Bristol, TN. *See also* Bristol Motor Speedway (Bristol, TN)
　area maps, *46, 48*
　attractions, *49*
　calendar, *47*
　lodgings, *51*
　restaurants, *54*
　RV and camping, *52*
Bristol, VA
　attractions, *49*
　lodgings, *50, 51*
　restaurants, *54*
Bristol Caverns (Bristol, TN), *49*
Bristol Motor Speedway (Bristol, TN), *42–55*
　concessions, *44*
　fan experience, *45*
　first aid, *44*
　getting around, *45*
　getting tickets, *45*
　parking, *44*
　RV and camping, *52*
　security, *44*
　temporary housing, *45*
Bristol Renaissance Faire (Kenosha, WI), *339*
Bristol White Sox (Bristol, VA), *49*
Broad Ripple Brew Pub (Indianapolis, IN), *187*
Broadway at the Beach (Myrtle Beach, SC), *105*
Brookfest (Tipton, MI), *326*
Brookfield, IL
　attractions, *83*
Brookfield, WI
　lodgings, *341–342*
　restaurants, *344*
Brookfield Zoo (Brookfield, IL), *83*
Brooklyn, MI. *See also* Michigan International Speedway (Brooklyn, MI)
　area maps, *320, 322*
　attractions, *323*
　calendar, *321*

　lodgings, *324–327*
　restaurants, *327–328*
Brooklyn Highway Campground (Tipton, MI), *326*
Brown County (Nashville, TN), *189*
Brown County State Park (Nashville, TN), *189*
Brown Derby Roadhouse, The (Ontario, OH), *282*
Brownie's in the Burg (Stroudsburg, PA), *421*
Brownsburg, IN
　lodgings, *184*
　restaurants, *187*
Brunches Café (Mansfield, OH), *282*
Bryan, Sonny, *461*
Buckley's Fine Filet Grill (Memphis, TN), *312*
Buck's Bar & Grill (Lexington, OH), *282*
Bucyrus, OH
　restaurants, *282*
Budget Inn and Suites (Talladega, AL), *450*
Buena Vista Winery (Sonoma, CA), *194, 196*
Buffalo Billiards and Havana Lounge (Nashville, TN), *360*
Buffalo Inn (Brooklyn, MI), *325*
Buffet at the Bellagio, The (Las Vegas Strip and Vicinity, NV), *248–249*
Bun's of Delaware (Delaware, OH), *281*
Burbank, IL
　lodgings, *86*
Burberry (Chicago, IL), *80*
Bureau of Engraving and Printing's Western Currency Facility Tour and Visitor Center (Fort Worth, TX), *463*
Burger Bar (Bristol, VA), *54*
Busch, Kurt, *45*
Busch, Kyle, *223, 305*
Butler, OH
　RV and camping, *280*
Butler Mohican Koa (Butler, OH), *280*

C

Cabela'a Campground (Tipton, MI), *326*
Cabela's (Kansas City, KS), *213*
Cabin, The (Ashland, OH), *281*
Cabin, The (Atlanta, GA), *37–38*
Cable Car Museum (San Francisco, CA), *200*
Cabrillo Park (San Diego, CA), *73*
Cacharel (Arlington, TX), *467*
Cacti (Novato, CA), *204*
Cades Cove (Pigeon Forge, TN), *55*
Cadet Karting Course (Infineon Raceway, Sonoma, CA), *203*
Caesar's Brookdale (Scotrun, PA), *418*
Caesars Palace's Forum Shops (Las Vegas, NV), *241–242*
Caesar's Paradise Stream (Mount Pocono, PA), *418*
Café Alpine (Summit County, CO), *409*
Cafe De Tacuba (Mexico City, MX), *491*
Café Lahaye (Sonoma, CA), *204*
Cafe Patachou (Indianapolis, IN), *186*
Cahokia, IL, *148*
　RV and campground, *148*
Cahokia RV Parque (Cahokia, IL), *148*
Cajun Queen (Charlotte, NC), *267*
Calaveras Big Trees State Park (Placerville, CA), *207*
Calendonia, WI
　RV and camping, *342*
Calhouns (Knoxville, TN), *53*
California Speedway (Fontana, CA), *56–73, 60*
　concessions
　　first aid, *58*
　first aid, *58*
　getting around, *61*

　getting tickets, *61*
　RV rentals, *66*
　security, *58*
Californos (Kansas City, MO), *218*
Calistoga, CA
　attractions, *199*
　lodgings, *202*
　restaurants, *204*
　RV and camping, *203*
Cambridge Junction Historic State Park/ Walker Tavern Historic Complex (Brooklyn, MI), *323*
Camby, IN
　attractions, *181*
Camden, SC
　attractions, *99*
　lodgings, *101*
　restaurants, *103–104*
Camelbeach Waterpark (Tannersville, PA), *415, 417*
Camino Real Mexico (Mexico City, MX), *490*
Canal Club, The (Richmond, VA), *433*
Canal Walk (Richmond, VA), *433*
Cancun Lagoon Bar & Grill (Daytona Beach, FL), *121*
Cannery Casino and Hotel (North Las Vegas, NV), *247*
Cannery Row Buffet (North Las Vegas, NV), *250*
Canobie Lake Park (Salem, NH), *371*
Canterbury, NH
　attractions, *371*
Canterbury Hotel (Indianapolis, IN), *183*
Canterbury Shaker Village (Canterbury, NH), *367, 371*
Cap'N Morgan's Sports and Seafood (Corning, NY), *483*
Capri (Florida City, FL), *160*
Capriotti's (Las Vegas, NV), *249*
Captain Pip's Marina and Hideaway (Florida Keys, FL), *169*
Captain's Galley (Huntersville, NC), *267*
Cardinals Stadium (Phoenix, AZ), *384*
Caribbean Jack's Restaurant & Marina (Daytona Beach, FL), *121*
Carmel, IN
　lodgings, *182*
Carolina Renaissance Festival (Huntersville, NC), *259*
Carrollton, GA
　restaurants, *40*
Carrollton, KY
　attractions, *229*
　lodgings, *230, 231*
　restaurants, *232–233*
Carson Pirie Scott (Chicago, IL), *80*
Carter Fold, The (Hiltons, VA), *50*
Cartier (Chicago, IL), *80*
Casa Juancho (Miami, FL), *160*
Casa Sanchez (Ontario, CA), *72*
Cascone's Italian Restaurant (Kansas City, MO), *219*
Cash, Johnny, *303*
Casino Queen RV Park (East St. Louis, IL), *148*
Cask 'N' Cleaver (Rancho Cucamonga, CA), *72*
Castillo de San Marcos (St. Augustine, FL), *123*
Cathay Kitchen (Florence, KY), *233*
Cattlemens Restaurant (Santa Rosa, CA), *206*
Cattlemen's Steakhouse (Fort Worth, TX), *468*
Cave Creek, AZ
　restaurants, *394*
CBS Television City Research Center (Las Vegas, NV), *242*
Cecil's Public House (Alexander City, AL), *450*

Cedar Point Amusement Park/Resort (Sandusky, OH), 283
Cedar Point Beach (Sandusky, OH), 283
Cedarburg Strawberry Festival (Cedarburg, WI), 337
Cement City, MI
  restaurants, 328
Center for Mark Twain Studies at Elmira College (Elmira, NY), 475
Central Camionera del Norte (San Juan Teotihuacán, MX), 491
Challenge Park Xtreme (Joliet, IL), 84
Champs Fine Food and Spirits (Laurinburg, NC), 104
Chandler, AZ
  lodgings, 388
Chanteclair (Indianapolis, IN), 186
Chapell's (Kansas City, MO), 219
Chapultepec Park (Mexico City, MX), 488
Chapultepec Zoo (Mexico City, MX), 490
Charles Mill Lake Park (Mansfield, OH), 280–281
Charlie Vergos Rendezvous (Memphis, TN), 311
Charlie's Country Catfish (Pell City, AL), 452
Charlotte, NC
  attractions, 261, 264
  lodgings, 262–263
  restaurants, 264, 266–268
Charlotte Shout! Festival (Charlotte, NC), 259
Chart House (Daytona Beach, FL), 120
Charter Communications Pole Day (Bristol Motor Speedway, Bristol, TN), 47
Chateau Avalon (Kansas City, MO), 218
Chatham, VA
  lodgings, 293
Chattanooga, TN, 361
Chattanooga Choo Choo (Chattanooga, TN), 361
Chebacco Dude Ranch (Effingham, NH), 367–368
Cheekwood Botanical Garden and Museum of Art (Nashville, TN), 350
Chef's (Montour Falls, NY), 484
Chelsea, MI
  restaurants, 328
Cheraw, SC
  attractions, 99
  RV and camping, 103
Cheraw Historical District (Cheraw, SC), 99
Cheraw State Park (Cheraw, SC), 99, 103
Chesapeake's (Knoxville, TN), 53
Cheyenne Cañon Inn (Colorado Springs, CO), 404
Cheyenne Mountain Resort (Colorado Springs, CO), 405
Chicago, IL
  area maps, 80, 82
  attractions, 83–84
  lodgings, 85–86, 87
  restaurants, 81, 88–89
Chicagoland Speedway (Joliet, IL), 74–91
  concessions, 76
  first aid, 76
  getting around, 79
  getting tickets, 77
  security, 76
Chicago Street Bar & Grill (Joliet, IL), 90
Chief Ladiga Trail (Anniston, AL), 444
Childersburg, AL
  attractions, 447
  lodgings, 449
Children's Museum of Indianapolis (Indianapolis, IN), 176, 177, 181
Children's Museum of Richmond (Richmond, VA), 433

Chimney Bluffs State Park (Seaway Trail, NY), 485
Chino, CA
  lodgings, 69
Chompie's (Scottsdale, AZ), 393
Chops (Atlanta, GA), 38
Christa McAuliffe Planetarium (Concord, NH), 367, 371
Christmas House (Elmira, NY), 475
Christmas Island Resort (Weirs Beach, NH), 374
Chula Vista Theme Resort (Wisconsin Dells, WI), 345
Churchill Manor (Carrollton, KY), 232
Chuy Arzola's (St. Louis, MO), 149
Ciao Bella (Riverside, CA), 72
Cinco de Mayo Fiesta (Mesa, AZ), 385
Circle Centre Mall (Indianapolis, IN), 178, 181
Circus Circus Hotel & Las Vegas KOA RV Park (Las Vegas, NV), 247
Citadell Mall (Colorado Springs, CO), 401
City Coffee House and Creperie (St. Louis, MO), 149
City of Dover Arts on the Green (Dover, DE), 129
Civil Rights Museum (Memphis, TN), 305
Civil War Show (Mansfield, OH), 275
Civil War Visitor Center (Richmond, VA), 433
Claddagh Irish Pub (Newport, KY), 234
Clarence's Steak & Seafood House (Greensboro, NC), 295
Clarion Hotel Roanoke Airport (Roanoke, Va), 292
Clark Lake, MI
  restaurants, 328
Clark's Trading Post (White Mountains, NH), 377
Classic Cup Café (Kansas City, MO), 219
Clevelander (Miami, FL), 158
Cliff House at Pikes Peak (Manitou Springs, CO), 406
Clifty Falls State Park (Madison, IN), 229, 231
Clinton Presidential Center (Little Rock, AK), 313
Club Deep (Miami, FL), 158
CMA Music Festival (Nashville, TN), 351
CNN Center (Atlanta, GA), 27, 33
Cobb Lane (Birmingham, AL), 451
Coconut Cay Resort and Marina (Florida Keys, FL), 169
Coconut Grove, FL
  lodgings, 162
  restaurants, 167
Coco's Bakery Restaurant (Ontario, CA), 72
Coffee Catz (Sebastopol, CA), 206
Coffee Pub (Off-Strip/Downtown Las Vegas, NV), 250
Colby Hill Inn (Manchester, NH), 375
Cold Spring, KY
  restaurants, 233
Cold Spring Roadhouse (Cold Spring, KY), 233
Coldwater Covered Bridge (Oxford, AL), 444
Collinsville, IL, 147
  lodgings, 147
Collinsville, VA
  lodgings, 293
  restaurants, 295–296
Colorado Mountain Cabins and Vacation Home Rentals (Colorado Springs, CO), 408
Colorado River (Williams, AZ), 395
Colorado Springs, CO
  area maps, 400, 402
  attractions, 403
  lodgings, 404–406, 408
  restaurants, 407, 408
  RV and camping, 406
Columbia, SC
  restaurants, 104

Columbia State Historic Park (Placerville, CA), 207
Comanche Point (Williams, AZ), 395
Comfort Inn Abingdon (Abingdon, VA), 50
Comfort Inn & Suites (Bellville, OH), 279
Comfort Inn & Suites (Cornelius, NC), 264
Comfort Inn Bristol (Bristol, VA), 50
Comfort Inn Concord (Concord, NH), 372
Comfort Inn Corning (Corning, TX), 480
Comfort Inn (Dover, DE), 132
Comfort Inn Florida City (Florida City, FL), 164
Comfort Inn (Laurinburg, NC), 101
Comfort Inn (Leeds, AL), 449
Comfort Inn (Marion, OH), 279
Comfort Inn (Milan, OH), 279
Comfort Inn North—Mansfield (Mansfield, OH), 279
Comfort Inn of Oxford (Oxford, AL), 449
Comfort Inn (Rehoboth Beach, DE), 133
Comfort Inn (Riverside, CA), 68
Comfort Inn (Stockbridge, GA), 37
Comfort Suites (Brownsburg, IN), 184
Comfort Suites (Lebanon, TN), 358
Comfort Suites Sumter (Sumter, SC), 102–103
Common Grill (Chelsea, MI), 328
Concord, NC. See also Lowe's Motor Speedway (Concord, NC)
  area maps, 258, 260
  attractions, 261
  calendar, 259
  lodgings, 264–265, 372, 373
  restaurants, 259, 268
  RV and camping, 265–266
Concord, NH
  attractions, 371
  restaurants, 375–376
Concord Mills (Concord, NC), 261
Concord Motorsport Park (Concord, NC), 261
Coney Island Diner (Mansfield, OH), 282
Congaree National Park (Hopkins, SC), 100
Conner Prairie (Fishers, IN), 177, 181
Conway, NH, 377
Conway Scenic Railroad (White Mountains, NH), 377
Cook, Jerry, 47
Cool-Lea Campground (Odessa, NY), 482
Cooper's Seafood House (Scranton, PA), 421
Cootie Brown's (Johnson City, TN), 54
Copper Cellar (Knoxville, TN), 53
Coral Beach Motel (Ormond Beach, FL), 120
Coral Gables, FL
  attractions, 161
  lodgings, 162, 163
  restaurants, 165–166
Corky's Ribs & BBQ (Memphis, TN), 305
Cornelius, NC
  lodgings, 264, 265
Corner Café (Joliet, IL), 90
Corning, NY
  attractions, 479
  lodgings, 480, 481
  restaurants, 483
Corning Museum of Glass (Corning, NY), 475, 479
Cornwell's Turkeyville (Marshall, MI), 327
Corona, CA
  lodgings, 69
  restaurants, 72
Cortland, NY
  restaurants, 483
Cotton Lane RV and Mobile Home Resort (Goodyear, AZ), 392
Country at Heart Craft Show (Plano, TX), 461
Country Bumpkin Café (Lovejoy, GA), 40
Country Cookin' (Collinsville, VA), 295–296
Country Grill (Dry Ridge, KY), 232

Country Hearth Inn Jackson (Jackson, MI), 325
Country Inn and Suites Big Flats (Horseheads, NY), 481
Country Inn & Suites by Carlson (Brookfield, WI), 341
Country Inn and Suites (Florence, SC), 102
Country Inn and Suites (Lebanon, TN), 358
Country Inn & Suites (Mansfield, OH), 280
Country Music Association Music Festival (Lebanon, TN), 353
Country Music Hall of Fame and Museum (Nashville, TN), 350, 355
Country View Campground (Mukwonago, WI), 342
Countryside RV Resort (Lebanon, TN), 358
Courtyard by Marriott Augusta (Augusta, GA), 36
Courtyard by Marriott Charlotte University (Charlotte, NC), 262
Courtyard by Marriott Downtown (Fort Worth, TX), 464
Courtyard by Marriott Downtown (Indianapolis, IN), 183
Courtyard by Marriott Florence (Florence, SC), 102
Courtyard by Marriott Gastonia (Gastonia, NC), 265
Courtyard by Marriott Memphis Park Avenue East (Memphis, TN), 308
Courtyard by Marriott (Miami, FL), 163
Courtyard by Marriott (Nashville, TN), 356
Courtyard by Marriott Richmond West (Richmond, VA), 434
Courtyard by Marriott (Riverside, CA), 69
Courtyard by Marriott San Francisco Downtown (San Francisco, CA), 200–201
Courtyard by Marriott St. Louis Downtown (St. Louis, MO), 146
Courtyard by Marriott (Wilmington, DE), 133
Courtyard by Marriott—Downtown (Milwaukee, WI), 340
Covington, KY
  attractions, 229
  restaurants, 232, 233
Cowtippers (Atlanta, GA), 38
Coyote Café (Las Vegas Strip and Vicinity, NV), 249
Cozumel's Grill (Lebanon, TN), 360
Crabby Joe's Deck & Grill (Daytona Beach, FL), 121
Crane Point Museum of Natural History of the Florida Keys (Florida Keys, FL), 169
Crawford Notch State Park (White Mountains, NH), 377
Crayola Factory (Easton, PA), 417
Crest Hill, IL
  restaurants, 89
Crocodile Café (Anaheim, CA), 71
Crooked Rooster (Watkins Glen, NY), 484
Crown Candy Kitchen (St. Louis, MO), 149
Crowne Plaza Hotel Akron Quaker-Square (Akron, OH), 278–279
Crowne Plaza Hotel Birmingham—The Redmont (Birmingham, AL), 448
Crowne Plaza Hotel Richmond—E Canal (Richmond, VA), 435
Crowne Plaza Hotel San Francisco—Union Square (San Francisco, CA), 201
Crowne Plaza Hotel Union Station (Indianapolis, IN), 183
Cruise America Motorhome City (Phoenix, AZ), 392
Cruise Night at Scottsdale Pavilions (Scottsdale, AZ), 387–388
Cunetto House of Pasta (St. Louis, MO), 149
Cupboard, The (Memphis, TN), 311
Curtiss Museum (Hammondsport, NY), 473–474

Cutler Ridge/Miami, FL
    lodgings, 163
CVS Pharmacy (Richmond, VA), 429

D

Da Awkscht Fescht (Macungie, PA), 415
Daddy Jack's (Indianapolis, IN), 186
Dahlmann Campus Inn Ann Arbor (Ann Arbor, MI), 324
Daily Grind (Camden, SC), 104
Dale Earnhardt, Inc. (Mooresville, NC), 266
Dale Earnhardt Tribute (Kannapolis, NC), 262
Dallas, TX
    attractions, 463
    lodgings, 464, 465
    restaurants, 467, 468
Dallas Public Library (Dallas, TX), 460
Dan Marino's Town Tavern (Orlando, FL), 122
Dan River Factory Outlet Store (Martinsville, VA), 288
Dan's River Grill (Manchester, MI), 328
Dante's Down the Hatch (Atlanta, GA), 38
Danville, VA
    attractions, 291
    lodgings, 292, 293
    restaurants, 296
Danville Historic District (Danville, VA), 291
Danville Museum of Fine Arts and History (Danville, VA), 287–288, 291
Danville Pittsylvania County Fair (Ringgold, VA), 289
Danville Riverview Rotary Christmas Parade (Danville, VA), 289
Darfons Restaurant and Lounge (Nashville, TN), 359
Darlington, SC. See also Darlington Raceway (Darlington, SC)
    area maps, 96, 98
    attractions, 99, 101
    calendar, 97
    lodgings, 102
    restaurants, 103, 104
Darlington Raceway (Darlington, SC), 92–105
    concessions, 94
    first aid, 94
    getting around, 95
    getting tickets, 95
    RV and camping, 95
    security, 94
Darlington Raceway Stock Car Museum and National Motorsports Press Association Hall of Fame (Darlington, SC), 99
Darrell Waltrip's "Racing Experience" (Pigeon Forge, TN), 55
David and Julia's RV Park (Axton, VA), 294
Dawsonville Pool Hall (Dawsonville, GA), 31
Days Inn (Abingdon, VA), 50
Days Inn Adrian (Adrian, MI), 325
Days Inn Ashland (Ashland, OH), 279
Days Inn (Carrollton, KY), 231
Days Inn (Childersburg, AL), 449
Days Inn Corning (Corning, TX), 480
Days Inn (Leeds, AL), 449
Days Inn North (Florence, SC), 102
Days Inn of Martinsville (Martinsville, VA), 294
Days Inn (Oxford, AL), 449
Days Inn (Richmond, VA), 435
Days Inn (Williamstown, KY), 230
Daytona Beach, FL. See also Daytona International Speedway (Daytona, FL)
    area maps, 112, 114
    attractions, 115–116
    calendar, 113
    lodgings, 117–118
    restaurants, 120, 121–122
    RV and camping, 120
Daytona Beach Shores, FL
    lodgings, 118–119
Daytona Fun Park (Laconia, NH), 371
Daytona International Speedway (Daytona Beach, FL), 106–123
    child safety, 108
    concessions, 109
    first aid, 109
    getting around, 111
    getting tickets, 109
    security, 108
Daytona Lagoon (Daytona Beach, FL), 116
Daytona USA (Daytona Beach, FL), 115
De Schmire (Petaluma, CA), 204
Deal, J. J., 320
Deal Buggy Factory (Brooklyn, MI), 320
Deanna Rose Children's Farmstead (Overland Park, KS), 215
Dee Felice Cafe (Covington, KY), 232
Deering Estate at Cutler (Miami, FL), 161
Del Frisco's Double Eagle Steak House (Dallas, TX), 467
Delaware, OH
    attractions, 277
    restaurants, 281
Delaware Art Museum (Wilmington, DE), 131
Delaware State Museums (DE), 127
Delaware State Park (Delaware, OH), 277
Delaware Water Gap National Recreation Area (Long Pond, PA), 414
Dells Boat Tour (Wisconsin Dells, WI), 345
Denton, DE
    lodgings, 134
Desert Botanical Garden (Phoenix, AZ), 383, 387
Desert View Watchtower (Williams, AZ), 395
DeSoto Caverns Park (Childersburg, AL), 445, 447
Detroit, MI, 329
Detroit APBA Gold Cup (Belle Isle, MI), 321
Deuce (Sonoma, CA), 205
Diamond State Drive-In Theater (Felton, DE), 132
Dick Clark's American Bandstand Grill (Overland Park, KS), 219
Dierdorf and Hart's Steak House (St. Louis, MO), 149
Dillon, SC
    attractions, 99
    RV and camping, 103
Discount Food Mart Qualifying Day for NASCAR NEXTEL Cup Series (Talladega Superspeedway, Talladega, AL), 445
Discovery Place (Charlotte, NC), 264
Discovery World: The James Lovell Museum of Science, Economics and Technology (Milwaukee, WI), 337, 339
Disneyland (Anaheim, CA), 60, 65
Disneyland Hotel (Anaheim, CA), 67
Disney's Paradise Pier Hotel (Anaheim, CA), 67
Dixie Barbecue Co. (Johnson City, TN), 54
Dixie Café (Memphis, TN), 312
Dog Days Summer (Denton, TX), 461
Dog Head Brewings and Eats (Rehoboth Beach, DE), 136
Dolly Parton's Dixie Stampede (Orlando, FL), 116
Dollywood (Pigeon Forge, TN), 55
Dominic's Waterside Grill (Danville, VA), 296
Don Shula's Hotel (Miami Lakes, FL), 163
Donlavey, Junie, 431
Doral Golf Resort and Spa (Miami, FL), 163
Doral Tesoro Hotel & Golf Resort (Fort Worth, TX), 464

Doran Regional Park (Bodega Bay, CA), 202
Doswell, VA
    attractions, 433
    lodgings, 436
Doubletree Guest Suites (Carmel, IN), 182
Doubletree Guest Suites Phoenix Gateway Center (Phoenix, AZ), 389
Doubletree Hotel (Charlotte, NC), 262
Doubletree Hotel (Coconut Grove, FL), 162
Doubletree Hotel Colorado Springs—World Arena (Colorado Springs, CO), 404
Doubletree Hotel Johnson City (Johnson City, TN), 50–51
Doubletree Hotel (Nashville, TN), 356
Doubletree Hotel Ontario Airport (Ontario, CA), 68
Doubletree Hotel Richmond Airport (Sandston, VA), 435–436
Doubletree Hotel (Wilmington, DE), 133
Doubletree Murfreesboro (Murfreesboro, TN), 356
Doumar's (Norfolk, VA), 439
Dover, DE. See also Dover International Speedway (Dover, DE)
    area maps, 128, 130
    attractions, 131
    calendar, 129
    lodgings, 132, 134
    restaurants, 135, 136
    RV and camping, 134
Dover Air Force Base (Dover, DE), 128
Dover International Speedway (Dover, DE), 124–137
    concessions, 126
    first aid, 126
    parking, 126
    security, 126
Downtown Historic District (Anniston, AL), 444
Dragon Inn (Rancho Cucamonga, CA), 72
Drawbridge Inn (Fort Mitchell, KY), 230
Drunken Fish (Nashville, TN), 359
Drury Inn Pikes Peak/Colorado Springs (Colorado Springs, CO), 404
Dry Ridge, KY
    restaurants, 232, 233
Duck and Decanter (Phoenix, AZ), 394
Dundee, NY
    restaurants, 484
Dusty's Barbecue (Atlanta, GA), 38
Dutch Heritage Restaurant (Bellville, OH), 281
Dutch Inn Restaurant (Collinsville, VA), 296
Dutch Inn/Quality Inn (Collinsville, VA), 293
Dynasty Suites Riverside (Riverside, CA), 69

E

Earhart, Amelia, Festival (Atchison, KS), 213
Earhart Station (Bristol, TN), 52
Earnhardt, Dale, 266
Earnhardt, Dale, Inc. (Mooresville, NC), 266
Earnhardt, Dale, Jr, 195, 236, 284
Earnhardt, Dale, Tribute (Kannapolis, NC), 262
East St. Louis, IL
    RV and campground, 148
East End Grill (Memphis, TN), 312
Eastman, George, House (Seaway Trail, NY), 485
Easton, PA, 419
    attractions, 417
    lodgings, 419
EasyCare Vehicle Service Contracts 200
NASCAR Craftsman Truck Series (Atlanta Motor Speedway, Hampton, GA), 24, 31

Eckert's Country Restaurant (Belleville, IL), 150
Ed Debevic's (Chicago, IL), 88
Edelweiss, The (Pocono Lake, PA), 415
Edelweiss (Colorado Springs, CO), 407
Edelweiss (Fort Worth, TX), 468
Edge of Speedway Campground (Sparta, KY), 232
Edison Birthplace Museum, The (Milan, OH), 278
Edwards, Carl, 271
Eiteljorg Museum of American Indian and Western Art (Indianapolis, IN), 182
El Campesino (Mansfield, OH), 282
El Coyote Southwestern Grille (Covington, KY), 233
El Dorado County Historical Museum (Placerville, CA), 207
El Paso Bar B Que Company (Goodyear, AZ), 392
El Paso County Fair (Calhan, CO), 401
El Ranchito (Collinsville, VA), 296
El Toro Taco (Homestead, FL), 167
El Tovar Hotel (Williams, AZ), 395
Eldridge Hotel (Lawrence, KS), 217
Elliott, Bill, 299
Elliston Place Soda Shop (Nashville, TN), 360
Elmira, NY
    attractions, 479
    lodgings, 480
Elvis Festival (Dewey Beach, DE), 129
Elvis Presley's Heartbreak Hotel (Memphis, TN), 310
Elvis Week (Memphis, TN), 305
Elwood, IL
    restaurants, 90
    RV and camping, 88
Embassy Suites Hotel Atlanta at Centennial Olympic Park (Atlanta, GA), 34–35
Embassy Suites Hotel Kansas City—Overland Park (Overland Park, KS), 217
Embassy Suites Hotel Las Vegas (Las Vegas Strip and Vicinity, NV), 246
Embassy Suites Hotel Phoenix—Biltmore (Phoenix, AZ), 389
Embassy Suites Hotel Richmond—The Commerce Center (Richmond, VA), 435
Embassy Suites Hotel (St. Louis, MO), 148
Embassy Suites (Memphis, TN), 308
Embassy Suites (Nashville, TN), 357
Emeril's (Orlando, FL), 122
Epping, NH
    attractions, 371
Erling Jensen (Memphis, TN), 311
Ernest Tubb Record Shop (Nashville, TN), 353
Erwin, TN
    attractions, 49
ESPN Russell Racing School (Sonoma, CA), 203
Estrella Mountain Ranch Golf Club (Goodyear, AZ), 387
Eureka, MO, 145
    attractions, 145
Everett's Steakhouse & Blues Bar (Scottsdale, AZ), 393
Everglades Alligator Farm (Florida City, FL), 157
Everglades International Hostel (Homestead, FL), 164
Everglades National Park (Homestead, FL), 156, 161
Expo Village Events (Chicagoland Speedway, Joliet, IL), 81
Extreme World (Wisconsin Dells, WI), 345

F

Fairchild Tropical Botanic Garden (Homestead, FL), *156, 161*
Fairfield, CA
　attractions, *199*
　lodgings, *200, 201*
Fairfield Inn and Suites Atlanta Midtown (Atlanta, GA), *35*
Fairfield Inn & Suites (Chicago, IL), *85*
Fairfield Inn at Marriott Anaheim Disneyland (Anaheim, CA), *68*
Fairfield Inn by Marriott Joliet North (Joliet, IL), *87*
Fairfield Inn by Marriott Joliet South (Joliet, IL), *87*
Fairfield Inn by Marriott (Kannapolis, NC), *265*
Fairfield Inn by Marriott Manchester (Manchester, NH), *372*
Fairfield Inn by Marriott (Mooresville, NC), *265*
Fairfield Inn by Marriott Nashville Opryland (Nashville, TN), *357*
Fairfield Inn (Chandler, AZ), *388*
Fairfield Inn Colorado Springs South (Colorado Springs, CO), *404*
Fairfield Inn (Dover, DE), *134*
Fairfield Inn (Las Vegas Strip and Vicinity, NV), *246*
Fairfield Inn Ontario Mansfield (Mansfield, OH), *280*
Fairfield Inn Riverside—Corning (Corning, NY), *481*
Fairfield Inn (Sumter, SC), *101*
Fairmont Kansas City at the Plaza (Kansas City, MO), *216*
Fairmont Scottsdale Princess (Scottsdale, AZ), *389*
Fairview Heights, IL, *146, 147, 149*
　lodgings, *146, 147*
　restaurants, *149*
Fairy Stone State Park (Stuart, VA), *287, 291, 294*
Falken Tire Pikes Peak International Hill Climb (Colorado Springs, CO), *401*
Famous Brands Outlet (Watkins Glen, NY), *479*
Famous Dave's Bar-B-Que (Florence, KY), *234*
Famous Steakhouse (Colorado Springs, CO), *408*
Farmer Bob's Campground (Bluff City, TN), *52*
Farmer's Market Restaurant (Florida City, FL), *167*
Fast Eddie's Bon—Air (Alton, IL), *150*
Fedewa, Tim, *353*
FedExForum (Memphis, TN), *303*
Felton, DE
　attractions, *131, 132*
　RV and camping, *134*
Fenwick Island, DE
　attractions, *131*
　lodgings, *132*
Fenwick Island Lighthouse (Fenwick Island, DE), *131*
Fernbank Museum of Natural History (Atlanta, GA), *27, 33*
Fernbank Science Center (Atlanta, GA), *27, 33*
Field Museum of Natural History, The (Chicago, IL), *83*
Fifth Annual Triad Area Spring Pottery Festival (Greensboro, NC), *289*
Finger Lakes (Elmira, NY), *475*
Finger Lakes Trail (Elmira, NY), *476*
Fiorella's Jack Stack Bar-B-Q (Kansas City, MO), *219*

Fiori di Como chandelier (Las Vegas, NV), *241*
Fire of Brazil Churrascaria (Atlanta, GA), *38*
Firehouse (Johnson City, TN), *53*
First Saturday Downtown Stroudsburg Art Walk (Stroudsburg, PA), *415*
Fischer's (Belleville, IL), *149*
Fish Market (Phoenix, AZ), *392*
Fisherman's Wharf (San Francisco, CA), *196*
Fishers, IN
　attractions, *181*
Fishing (Brooklyn, MI), *323*
Fishtales & Pigtales (Bristol, VA), *54*
Flamingo Las Vegas (Las Vegas Strip and Vicinity, NV), *246*
Fleetwood RV Racing Resort at Charlotte, Lowe's Motor Speedway (Concord, NC), *266*
Florence, KY
　attractions, *229*
　lodgings, *230, 231*
　restaurants, *233–234*
Florence, SC
　attractions, *99–100*
　lodgings, *102*
　restaurants, *104*
Florence Cinemas (Florence, KY), *229*
Florence Museum of Art, Science and History (Florence, SC), *99*
Florence National Cemetery (Florence, SC), *99–100*
Florence Stockade (Florence, SC), *100*
Florida City, FL
　lodgings, *163–164*
　restaurants, *166, 167*
　RV and camping, *165*
Florida International Festival, Daytona Beach, FL), *113*
Florida Keys, FL, *155, 169*
Flying Biscuit Café (Atlanta, GA), *40*
Flying Saucer Draft Emporium (Charlotte, NC), *268*
Flying Turtle Café Mansfield (Mansfield, OH), *282*
Fogo De Chao (Chicago, IL), *88*
Fontana, CA. *See also* California Speedway (Fontana, CA)
　area maps, *62, 64*
　attractions, *65*
　calendar, *63*
　restaurants, *71*
Fontana Skate Park (Fontana, CA), *65*
Food City 500 (Bristol Motor Speedway, Bristol, TN), *45*
Food City Family Race Night (Bristol Motor Speedway, Bristol, TN), *47*
Food Lion Speed Street Festival (Charlotte, NC), *259*
Fork & Fingers Restaurant (Mansfield, OH), *282*
Fort Condé Museum (Mobile, AL), *453*
Fort Mill, SC
　lodgings, *265*
Fort Mitchell, KY
　attractions, *229*
　lodgings, *230, 231*
　restaurants, *232, 234*
Fort Worth, TX. *See also* Texas Motor Speedway (Fort Worth, TX)
　area maps, *460, 462*
　attractions, *463–464*
　calendar, *461*
　lodgings, *464, 465–466*
　restaurants, *468*
Fort Worth Museum of Science & History (Fort Worth, TX), *463*
Fort Worth Stockyards National Historical District (Fort Worth, TX), *459, 461*
Fort Worth Stockyards (Fort Worth, TX), *463*

Fort Worth Zoo (Fort Worth, TX), *458, 459, 463–464*
Fort Wright, KY
　restaurants, *234*
Fossil Creek, TX
　restaurants, *468*
Fountain, CO, *396–409. See also* Pikes Peak International Raceway (Fountain, CO)
　area maps, *400, 402*
　calendar, *401*
　RV and camping, *406*
Fountains of Bellagio (Las Vegas, NV), *241*
Four Points by Sheraton Ann Arbor (Ann Arbor, MI), *324*
Four Points by Sheraton Fairview Heights (Fairview Heights, IL), *147*
Four Points by Sheraton Manchester (Manchester, NH), *372*
Fox, Ray, *31*
Fox Theatre, The (Atlanta, GA), *27, 33*
Francis, Brian, *159*
Franciscan (San Francisco, CA), *203*
Franconia Notch State Park (White Mountains, NH), *377*
Fratelli Di Napoli (Atlanta, GA), *40*
Fremont Street Experience (Off-Strip/Downtown Las Vegas, NV), *242*
French Quarter Suites Inn (Memphis, TN), *308*
Froggy's (Dover, DE), *136*
Frontier Army Museum (Leavenworth, KS), *215*
Fruit and Spice Park (Homestead, FL), *167*
Fuji Japanese Cuisine (Oxford, AL), *452*
Funspot (Weirs Beach, NH), *367, 371–372*
Fuse Box (Charlotte, NC), *266*

G

G & R Campground (Houston, DE), *134*
Gadsden, AL
　restaurants, *451*
Gage Park (Topeka, KS), *215*
Galpin Wildlife and Bird Sanctuary (Milan, OH), *278*
Gammage Auditorium (Phoenix, AZ), *383*
Garcia's, Joe T. (Fort Worth, TX), *468*
Garden of the Gods Campground (Colorado Springs, CO), *406*
Garden of the Gods (Colorado Springs, CO), *400, 403*
Garlic Festival (Penn Yan, NY), *477*
Garlic's, Johnny, California Pasta Grill (Petaluma, CA), *206*
Gaslamp Quarter (San Diego, CA), *73*
Gastonia, NC
　attractions, *261–262*
　lodgings, *264, 265*
Gate City Chop House (Greensboro, NC), *295*
Gatehouse Tavern (Fort Mitchell, KY), *234*
Gates B-B-Q (Kansas City, KS), *220*
Gateway Arch (St. Louis, MO), *141, 143, 145*
Gateway Classic Cars (Fairmont City, IL), *143*
Gateway International Raceway (Madison, IL), *138–151*
　concessions, *140*
　first aid, *140*
　security, *140*
Gator Park (Little Rock, AK), *313*
Gatorland (Orlando, FL), *116–117*
Gaughan, Brendan, *141*
Gaylord Opryland Resort and Conference Center (Nashville, TN), *351, 357*
General Butler State Resort Park (Carrollton, KY), *229, 230*
General Jackson Showboat (Nashville, TN), *355*

Geneva (Seneca Lake, NY), *476*
Gentry's Parking & Camping (Bristol, TN), *52*
George Eastman House (Seaway Trail, NY), *485*
George Washington Bookstore & Tavern (Concord, NC), *268*
Georgia, *25–41*
Georgia Grille (Atlanta, GA), *38*
Georgia Mountain Fall Festival (Hiawassee, GA), *31*
Georgia Power Qualifying Night and NASCAR Craftsman Truck Series (Atlanta Motor Speedway, Hampton, GA), *31*
Georgia—Pacific Qualifying Night (Atlanta Motor Speedway, Hampton, GA), *31*
Giant Garage Sale (Henderson, NV), *243*
Gibson, Tony, *401*
Gilford, NH
　lodgings, *373*
　RV and camping, *374*
Gilford Rotary Club (Loudon, NH), *375*
Gilles Frozen Custard (Milwaukee, WI), *344*
Glen Ellen, CA
　attractions, *200*
　RV and camping, *203*
Glen Mountain Market (Watkins Glen, NY), *484*
Glendale, AZ
　attractions, *387*
　lodgings, *390*
Glendale Arena (Glendale, AZ), *384, 387*
Glenn H. Curtiss Museum (Hammondsport, NY), *479*
Gloria Ferrer Champagne Caves (Sonoma, CA), *196*
GoJo Japanese Steak House (Kansas City, MO), *220*
Gold Coaster Manufactured Home and RV Resort (Homestead, FL), *165*
Golden Corral 500 (Atlanta Motor Speedway (Hampton, GA), *27*
Golden Dragon (Bristol, VA), *54*
Golden Eagle Restaurant (Talledega, AL), *452*
Golden Gate Bridge (San Francisco, CA), *196*
Golden Knight Inn and Suites (Rockstream, NY), *482*
Golden Nugget Hotel and Casino (Off-Strip/Downtown Las Vegas, NV), *247*
Golden Nugget Restaurant (Onsted, MI), *328*
Golden Ox (Kansas City, MO), *219*
Golfing (Brooklyn, MI), *323*
Golfing (Daytona Beach, FL), *115*
Goodlettsville, TN, *358*
　lodgings, *358*
Goodyear, AZ
　attractions, *387*
　lodgings, *390*
　restaurants, *392, 394*
　RV and camping, *392*
Gordon, Jeff, *96, 170, 455*
Gospel Music Week (Lebanon, TN), *353*
Governor's House, The (Talladega, AL), *450*
Graceland (Memphis, TN), *302–303, 307*
Grafton, IL, *145*
　attractions, *145*
Grand Canyon National Park (Williams, AZ), *395*
Grand Canyon Village (Williams, AZ), *395*
Grand Ole Opry (Nashville, TN), *350, 355*
Granite City, IL, *148*
　RV and campground, *148*
Granite State Candy Shoppe (Concord, NH), *369*
Graton, CA
　restaurants, *205*
Grazianos (Petaluma, CA), *204*
Great Mall of the Great Plains (Olathe, KS), *215*

Great Smoky Mountains National Park (Pigeon Forge, TN), 55
Great Wall Restaurant (Memphis, TN), 312
Great Western Winery (Watkins Glen, NY), 473
Greek Isles (Charlotte, NC), 268
Green Fields Campground Inc. (Elwood, IL), 88
Green Valley Ranch Resort & Spa (Henderson, NV), 245–246
Greenbriar Campground (Tipton, MI), 326
Greenfield, IN
   lodgings, 182–183
Greenleaf Inn (Camden, SC), 101
Greenleaf Inn of Camden (Camden, SC), 104
Greensboro, NC
   attractions, 291
   lodgings, 292
   restaurants, 268, 295
Greensboro Historical Museum (Greensboro, NC), 288, 291
Greyhound Tavern (Fort Mitchell, KY), 234
Griffin, GA
   lodgings, 36
Griffith Observatory (Hollywood Hills, CA), 60
Grill Fish (Miami, FL), 159
Grinding Rock State Historic Park (Placerville, CA), 207
Grove Arcade Public Market (Asheville, NC), 269
Grove Isle Resort (Coconut Grove, FL), 162
Guest House Inn (Leeds, AL), 450
Gunstock Campground (Gilford, NH), 374
Guntown Mountain (Mammoth Cave, KY), 235
Gurtis, Andrew, 97
Gusto's Grill and Bar (Florida City, FL), 167

H

H. H. Bennett Studio & History Center (Wisconsin Dells, WI), 345
Hales Corners, WI
   restaurants, 344
Half Moon Amusement Arcades (Weirs Beach, NH), 372
Half Way House (Richmond, VA), 437
Halifax Historical Museum (Daytona Beach, FL), 115
Halifax Museum (Daytona International Speedway, Daytona Beach, FL), 111
Halloween on the Square (Collierville, TN), 305
Hamilton, Bobby, 92, 301, 353
Hammondsport, NY
   attractions, 479
Hampton, GA. See also Atlanta Motor Speedway (Hampton, GA)
   attractions, 34
   calendar, 31
   restaurants, 40
Hampton, TN
   attractions, 49–50
Hampton Inn—Sycamore View (Memphis, TN), 310
Hampton Inn & Suites, Goodyear (Goodyear, AZ), 390
Hampton Inn and Suites—Charlotte at Concord Mills (Concord, NC), 264
Hampton Inn & Suites (Chicago, IL), 85
Hampton Inn and Suites Florence—Civic Center (Florence, SC), 102
Hampton Inn Birmingham—Colonnade (Birmingham, AL), 448
Hampton Inn Bristol (Bristol, TN), 51
Hampton Inn (Carrollton, KY), 231
Hampton Inn (Concord, NC), 264
Hampton Inn (Danville, VA), 293

Hampton Inn Daytona Speedway/Airport (Daytona Beach, FL), 117
Hampton Inn (Dover, DE), 134
Hampton Inn Fairfield/Napa Valley (Fairfield, CA), 200
Hampton Inn Gastonia (Gastonia, NC), 264
Hampton Inn Gateway Arch (St. Louis, MO), 148
Hampton Inn Indianapolis—Downtown Circle Centre (Indianapolis, IN), 183
Hampton Inn Joliet/I-55 (Joliet, IL), 87
Hampton Inn Joliet/I-80 (Joliet, IL), 87
Hampton Inn (Kansas City, MO), 218
Hampton Inn Lake Norman (Cornelius, NC), 264
Hampton Inn (Lebanon, TN), 356
Hampton Inn Miami/Florida City (Florida City, FL), 164
Hampton Inn Milwaukee/Brookfield (Brookfield, WI), 341–342
Hampton Inn Murfreesboro (Murfreesboro, TN), 356
Hampton Inn Pell City (Pell City, AL), 450
Hampton Inn Scottsdale—Oldtown (Scottsdale, AZ), 390
Hampton Inn St. Louis Union Station (St. Louis, MO), 147
Hampton Inn St. Louis/Fairview Heights (Fairview Heights, IL), 146
Hampton Inn Sumter (Sumter, SC), 103
Hampton Inn Wilkes-Barre at Cross Creek Point (Wilkes-Barre, PA), 418
Hampton Inn—Corning (Corning, NY), 481
Hannibal, MO, 151
Hapeville, GA
   lodgings, 37
Hard Rock Hotel Chicago (Chicago, IL), 86
Harley-Davidson Café (Las Vegas Strip and Vicinity, NV), 250
Harley-Davidson Tour (Wauwatosa, WI), 335, 340
Harold's Cave Creek Corral (Cave Creek, AZ), 394
Harold's Place (Brooklyn, MI), 328
Harris Hill Park (Elmira, NY), 475, 479
Harris Hill Soaring Center (Elmira, NY), 475, 479
Harry Bissett's New Orleans Café (Athens, GA), 37
Harry Caray's (Chicago, IL), 89
Hart's Turkey Farm (Meredith, NH), 375
Hartsville, SC
   attractions, 100
Hartsville Museum (Hartsville, SC), 100
Hastert, Bob, Jr., 89
Hastert, Doris, 89
Haunted Trails Amusement Park & Entertainment Center (Joliet, IL), 84
Havana '59 (Richmond, VA), 438
Hayes, WJ State Park (Tipton, MI), 327
Hazelwood, MO, 145, 147
   attractions, 145
   lodgings, 147
Hazleton, PA, 419
   lodgings, 419
Healdsburg, CA
   restaurants, 205
Heard Museum (Phoenix, AZ), 382, 387
Hearthstone Inn (Colorado Springs, CO), 405
Heartland Crossing Golf Links (Camby, IN), 181
Hellmann's Mayonnaise Infield Camping (Lake Worth, TX), 466
Helton, Mike, 461
Henderson, NV
   lodgings, 245–246
Henry, Patrick, 429
Henry Ford Museum (Detroit, MI), 329

Henry Maier Festival Grounds (Milwaukee, WI), 337
Herberger Theater Center (Phoenix, AZ), 382
Hereford Barn Steak House (Charlotte, NC), 266
Hereford House (Kansas City, MO), 220
Heritage Square (Phoenix, AZ), 383
Hermitage Hotel (Nashville, TN), 357
Hermits Rest, 395
Heroes & Legends Sports Bar & Grill (Joliet, IL), 90
Hershey, PA, 423
Hershey Museum (Hershey, PA), 423
Hersheypark (Hershey, PA), 423
Hershey's Chocolate World (Hershey, PA), 423
H. H. Bennett Studio & History Center (Wisconsin Dells, WI) 345
Hickory Stick Farm (Belmont, NH), 375
Hidden Lake Gardens (Brooklyn, MI), 323
Hideaway Country Inn (Bucyrus, OH), 282
Highlander Inn (Manchester, NH), 374
Highlands (Birmingham, AL), 451
Hillsborough Balloon Festival and Fair (Hillsborough, NH), 369
Hilltop Café (Napa, CA), 205
Hilton Atlanta and Towers (Atlanta, GA), 35
Hilton Birmingham Perimeter Park (Birmingham, AL), 448
Hilton Charlotte Center City (Charlotte, NC), 263
Hilton Daytona Beach at Ocean Walk Village (Daytona Beach, FL), 119
Hilton Garden Inn Daytona Beach (Daytona Beach, FL), 117
Hilton Greater Cincinnati Airport (Florence, KY), 230
Hilton Memphis (Memphis, TN), 308
Hilton Miami Airport and Towers (Miami, FL), 163
Hilton Milwaukee City Center (Milwaukee, WI), 341
Hilton Pasadena (Pasadena, CA), 68
Hilton Sonoma County Santa Rosa (Santa Rosa, CA), 201
Hilton University Place Charlotte (Charlotte, NC), 263
Hilton Wilmington/Christiana (Newark, DE), 133
Hiltons, VA
   attractions, 50
Historic Camden (Camden, SC), 99
Historic Curtis Inn on the Square (Mount Vernon, OH), 279
Historic Lyme Village (Bellevue, OH), 277
Historic Savannah Foundation (Savannah, GA), 41
Historical Carrousel District (Mansfield, OH), 274
Hofbrauhaus (Newport, KY), 234
Hog Heaven (Nashville, TN), 360
Holden House 1902 Bed & Breakfast (Colorado Springs, CO), 406
Holderness, NH
   attractions, 371
Holiday Inn—Sycamore View (Memphis, TN), 310
Holiday Inn Airport (Sandston, VA), 436
Holiday Inn Alton (Alton, IL), 146
Holiday Inn & Suites Bristol Conference Center (Bristol, VA), 51
Holiday Inn and Suites Hotel (Florence, SC), 102
Holiday Inn Charlotte—Lake Norman (Cornelius, NC), 264
Holiday Inn Collinsville (Collinsville, IL), 147
Holiday Inn Elmira—Riverview (Elmira, NY), 480

Holiday Inn Express and Suites (Dover, DE), 134
Holiday Inn Express (Carrollton, KY), 230
Holiday Inn Express (Concord, NC), 264
Holiday Inn Express (Danville, Va), 292
Holiday Inn Express Daytona Speedway and I-95 (Daytona Beach, FL), 118
Holiday Inn Express Goodyear (Goodyear, AZ), 390
Holiday Inn Express Hotel and Suites Florence (Florence, SC), 102
Holiday Inn Express Indianapolis—Brownsburg (Brownsburg, IN), 184
Holiday Inn Express Joliet (Joliet, IL), 87
Holiday Inn Express (Lebanon, TN), 358
Holiday Inn Express Milwaukee—West Medical Center (Wauwatosa, WI), 341
Holiday Inn Express (North Las Vegas, NV), 247–248
Holiday Inn Hotel & Suites—Manfield Conference Center (Mansfield, OH), 279
Holiday Inn (Ithaca, NY), 481
Holiday Inn (Key Largo, FL), 162
Holiday Inn Manchester (Manchester, NH), 372
Holiday Inn Milwaukee—Downtown (Milwaukee, WI), 341
Holiday Inn (Morris, IL), 86
Holiday Inn Murfreesboro (Murfreesboro, TN), 356
Holiday Inn (Newark, DE), 133
Holiday Inn Overland Park—West (Overland Park, KS), 217
Holiday Inn Richmond I-64 & West Broad St. (Richmond, VA), 436
Holiday Inn Roanoke—Tanglewood (Roanoke, VA), 292
Holiday Inn Select Dallas North (Dallas, TX), 464
Holiday Inn Select Memphis—Downtown (Beale Street) (Memphis, TN), 308
Holiday Inn Select Memphis Airport (Memphis, TN), 310
Holiday Inn Vallejo—Napa Valley Gateway (Vallejo, CA), 201–202
Holiday Inn Wilkes-Barre (Arena) (Wilkes-Barre, PA), 418
Holiday Living Craft Show (South Boston, VA), 289
Holiday-Nashville Travel Park (Nashville, TN), 358–359
Hollyhock Hill (Indianapolis, IN), 186
Hollywood, CA
   attractions, 60, 65–66
Hollywood Walk of Fame (Hollywood, CA), 65
Hollywood Wax Museum (Branson, MO), 221
Home & Garden Show (Las Vegas, NV), 243
Home Depot (Jackson, MS), 321
Home Depot (Richmond, VA), 429
Homegrown Tomato Challenge (St. Louis, MO), 143
Homestead, FL. See also Homestead-Miami Speedway (Homestead, FL)
   attractions, 155–156, 161
   calendar, 159
   lodgings, 164
   restaurants, 167–168
   RV and camping, 165
Homestead Inn (Milan, OH), 281
Homestead-Miami Speedway (Homestead, FL)
   area maps, 158, 160
   concessions, 154
   first aid, 154
   getting around, 157
   getting tickets, 157
   security, 154
Homewood Suites Las Colinas (Irving, TX), 464–465

Honey Bear's BBQ (Phoenix, AZ), *394*
Hoover Dam, NV, *245*
Hopkins, SC
 attractions, *100*
Horizons (Sausalito, CA), *204*
Horseheads, NY
 attractions, *479*
 lodgings, *481*
Horseradish Grill (Atlanta, GA), *39*
Hot Rodz Drive Inn (Leeds, AL), *452*
Hotel Du Pont (Wilmington, DE), *133–134*
Hotel Phillips (Kansas City, MO), *216*
Hotel Roanoke and Conference Center (Roanoke, VA), *292*
Hotel Savoy (Kansas City, MO), *216*
Houdini Museum (Scranton, PA), *417*
House of Blues, A Loews Hotel (Chicago, IL), *86*
House of Blues (Orlando, FL), *122*
Houston, DE
 RV and camping, *134*
Houston, TX
Howard Johnson (Oxford, AL), *449*
Huntersville, NC
 attractions, *262*
 restaurants, *267*
Hyatt at Fisherman's Wharf (San Francisco, CA), *201*
Hyatt Regency (Atlanta, GA), *35*
Hyatt Regency Crown Center (Kansas City, MO), *216–217*
Hyatt Regency Milwaukee (Milwaukee, WI), *341*
Hyatt Vineyard Creek Hotel—Sonoma County (Santa Rosa, CA), *201*

I

Iguana Grill (Rehoboth Beach, DE), *136*
IMAX Theater (Indianapolis, IN), *182*
Imperial Fez (Atlanta, GA), *38*
Independence, MO
 lodgings, *217*
 restaurants, *218*
Indiana Historical Society's History Market (Indianapolis, IN), *183*
Indiana State Fair (Indianapolis, IN), *179*
Indianapolis, IN. *See also*
 Indianapolis Motor Speedway
 Indianapolis Raceway Park (Indianapolis, IN)
 area maps, *178, 180*
 attractions, *181–182, 183*
 calendar, *179*
 lodgings, *183–185*
 restaurants, *186–188*
Indianapolis Motor Speedway Hall of Fame Museum (Indianapolis, IN), *181*
Indianapolis Motor Speedway (Indianapolis, IN), *170–189*
Indianapolis Raceway Park (Indianapolis, IN), *170–189*
 concessions, *172, 174*
 first aid, *172, 174*
 getting around, *177*
 getting tickets, *173, 175*
 security, *172, 174*
Indianapolis Zoo (Indianapolis, IN), *182*
Indigo Coastal Grill (Atlanta, GA), *38*
Infield, The (Lexington, OH), *277*
Infineon Raceway (Sonoma, CA), *190–207*
 concessions, *192*
 first aid, *192*
 getting around, *195*
 getting tickets, *192*
 parking, *192*
 restrooms, *192*
 security, *192*
Inlet Harbor Marina and Restaurant (Ponce Inlet, FL), *122*
Inn at Canal Square (Lewes, DE), *132*
Inn at Honey Run (Millersburg, OH), *280*
Inn at Jim Thorpe (Jim Thorpe, PA), *419*
In-n-Out (Fontana, CA), *71*
International Billiard & Home Recreation Expo at Las Vegas Conference Center (Las Vegas, NV), *243*
International Bowling Museum and Hall of Fame (St. Louis, MO), *145*
International Golf Tournament (Greenwood Village, CO), *401*
International Motor Racing Research Center at Watkins Glen (Watkins Glen, NY), *479*
International RV Park and Campground (Daytona Beach, FL), *120*
Irish and Celtic Festival (Blakeslee, PA), *415*
Irish Hills Antiques and Outdoor Market (Brooklyn, MI), *323*
Irish Hills Fun Center (Brooklyn, MI), *323*
Irish Hills Resort Kampground (Tipton, MI), *327*
Irving, TX
 lodgings, *464–465, 466*
 restaurants, *468*
Irwindale, CA
 attractions, *66*
Irwindale Speedway (Irwindale, CA), *66*
Islamorada (Florida Keys, FL), *169*
Italian American Festival (Watkins Glen, NY), *477*
Ithaca, NY
 lodgings, *481–482*
 restaurants, *483*

J

J. B.'s Fish Camp & Restaurant (New Smyrna Beach, FL), *122*
Jack London State Historic Park (Glen Ellen, CA), *200*
Jack's Family Restaurant (Oxford, AL), *452*
Jackson, Andrew, Statute (Nashville, TN), *353*
Jackson, MI
 lodgings, *325*
 restaurants, *327*
Jake and Telly's Greek Dining (Colorado Springs, CO), *407*
James River (Richmond, VA), *433*
Jameson Inn (Oxford, AL), *449*
Jarrett, Dale, *121, 471*
Jefferson County Train Station Museum (Madison, IN), *229*
Jelly Belly Factory Tours (Fairfield, CA), *199*
Jerlando's Ristorante (Watkins Glen, NY), *484*
Jerry's Pub and Restaurant (Brooklyn, MI), *328*
Jess & Jim's Steakhouse (Kansas City, MO), *219*
Jewel's Deluxe Restaurant (Darlington, SC), *104*
Jillian's (Covington, KY), *229*
Jim Thorpe, PA, *419*
 attractions, *417*
 lodgings, *419*
Jimmy Buffett's Margaritaville (Orlando, FL), *122*
Jin's Grocery Store (Richmond, VA), *429*
Joe T. Garcia's (Fort Worth, TX), *468*
Joe's Inn (Richmond, VA), *438*
Joe's Stone Crab (Miami Beach, FL), *168*
John Hancock Center (Chicago, IL), *80*
John Martin's (Coral Gables, FL), *165*
Johnny Appleseed Outdoor Historical Drama (Ashland, OH), *274, 277*
Johnny Garlic's California Pasta Grill (Petaluma, CA), *206*
Johnson, Jimmie, *252, 259, 378, 410*
Johnson, Tom, Camping Center Campground (Martinsville, VA), *294*
Johnson City, TN
 lodgings, *50 51*
 restaurants, *53, 54*
Johnson Victoria Museum (DE), *127*
Joliet, IL. *See also* Chicagoland Speedway (Joliet, IL)
 area maps, *80, 82*
 attractions, *84–85*
 calendar, *81*
 lodgings, *87*
 restaurants, *89–90*
 RV and camping, *88*
Joliet FanFest (Joliet, IL), *78*
Joliet Jackhammers (Joliet, IL), *84*
Josh and John's Naturally Homemade Ice Creams (Colorado Springs, CO), *408*
Jubilee Restaurant (Pocono Pines, PA), *422*
June Jam (Houston, DE), *129*
Jungle Jim's (Rehoboth Beach, DE), *131*
Juneau, Solomon, *334*
Juniper Hills, Inc. (Tipton, MI), *326*

K

K. C. Masterpiece (Overland Park, KS), *219*
K. C. Masterpiece (St. Louis, MO), *150*
Kabob House (Charlotte, NC), *266*
Kabuki Japanese Steak House (Roanoke, VA), *295*
Kahne, Kasey, *59*
Kalmia Gardens of Coker College (Hartsville, SC), *100*
Kannapolis, NC
 attractions, *262*
 lodgings, *265*
Kansas City, KS. *See also* Kansas Speedway (Kansas City, KS)
 area maps, *212, 214*
 attractions, *215*
 calendar, *213*
 lodgings, *217*
 restaurants, *220*
Kansas City, MO
 attractions, *215*
 lodgings, *216–217, 217–218*
 restaurants, *218–219, 224*
Kansas City Zoo (Kansas City, MO), *215*
Kansas Speedway (Kansas City, KS), *208–221*
 concessions, *210*
 first aid, *210*
 getting around, *211*
 getting tickets, *211*
 parking, *210*
 security, *210*
Karl Ratzch's (Milwaukee, WI), *343*
Karlo's Bistro Itallia (Florence, KY), *234*
Kearney, MO
 lodgings, *218*
Kelly's Bleachers (Milwaukee, WI), *344*
Kenosha, WI
 attractions, *339*
Kensington Court Hotel Ann Arbor, The (Ann Arbor, MI), *324*
Kentucky Action Park (Mammoth Cave, KY), *235*
Kentucky Down Under (Mammoth Cave, KY), *235*
Kentucky Speedway (Sparta, KY), *222–235*
 concessions, *224*
 first aid, *224*
 getting around, *225*
 getting tickets, *225*
 RV and camping, *225*
 security, *224*
Kenwood Fourth of July Celebrations and World Pillow Fighting Championships (Kenwood, CA), *197*
Keslowski, Brad, *273*
Key Largo, FL
 lodgings, *162–163, 164*
Key West Inn (Childersburg, AL), *449*
Key West Shrimp House (Madison, IN), *232*
Key's Seafood House (Florida City, FL), *167*
Kid Shelleens (Wilmington, DE), *136*
Kidspace Children's Museum (Pasadena, CA), *66*
Killens Pond State Park (Felton, DE), *131, 134*
Killens Pond Water Park (Felton, DE), *131*
Kilwin's (St. Augustine, FL), *123*
Kimball-Jenkins Estate (Concord, NH), *367*
King, B. B., *303*
King Taco (Fontana, CA), *71*
King's Chef (Colorado Springs, CO), *407*
Kingwood Center (Mansfield, OH), *278*
Klondike Kate's (Newark, DE), *135*
Knife & Fork (Charlotte, NC), *268*
Knights of Columbus (Joliet, IL), *90*
Knight's Steakhouse and Grill (Jackson, MI), *327*
Knoxville, TN
 restaurants, *53*
KOA Colorado Springs South (Fountain, CO), *406*
Kolob Arch (Springdale, UT), *251*
Kroger Speed Fest (Indianapolis, IN), *179*
Kulwicki, Alan, *331*
Kyma (Atlanta, GA), *38*

L

La Creperie (Colorado Springs, CO), *407*
La Petite France Restaurant (Richmond, VA), *431*
La Petite Maison (Colorado Springs, CO), *407*
La Querbradita Taqueria (Homestead, FL), *168*
La Quinta Inn & Suites Daytona Beach (Daytona Beach, FL), *119*
La Quinta Inn and Suites Scottsdale—Phoenix (Scottsdale, AZ), *390*
La Quinta Inn Bristol (Bristol, VA), *50*
La Quinta Inn Las Vegas Convention Center (Las Vegas Strip and Vicinity, NV), *246*
La Tolteca (Dover, DE), *136*
La Tourelle (Ithaca, NY), *482*
Labonte, Bobby, *74*
Lackawanna Coal Mine Tour (Scranton, PA), *417*
Laconia, NH
 attractions, *371*
 lodgings, *372, 373–374*
 restaurants, *376*
Lake Dillon (Summit County, CO), *409*
Lake Dow (Atlanta, GA), *28*
Lake Harmony, PA, *418*
 lodgings, *418*
Lake Mead (Williams, AZ), *395*
Lake Shawnee Recreational Area (Topeka, KS), *216*
Lake Worth, TX
 lodgings, *466*
Lakeside Speedway (Kansas City, KS), *215*
Lanning's (Akron, OH), *281*
Laquinta Nellis (Off-Strip/Downtown Las Vegas, NV), *248*

Las Vegas, NV. *See also* Las Vegas Motor Speedway (Las Vegas, NV)
    area maps, 242, 244
    attractions, 245
    calendar, 243
    lodgings, 246–247
    restaurants, 243, 248–250
    RV and camping, 248
Las Vegas Motor Speedway (Las Vegas, NV), 236–251
    concessions, 239
    first aid, 238
    getting around, 241
    security, 238
    tickets and seating, 238
Latta, SC
    lodgings, 101
Latta Plantation Nature Center and Preserve (Huntersville, NC), 262
Laurel Blossom Festival (Pocono Raceway, Long Pond, PA), 415
Laurinburg, NC
    lodgings, 101
    restaurants, 104
Lavecchia's Seafood Grille (Charlotte, NC), 266
Lawrence, KS
    lodgings, 217
Leavenworth, KS
    attractions, 215
Leawood, KS
    restaurants, 220
Lebanon, TN, 356, 358, 360. *See also* Nashville Superspeedway (Lebanon, TN)
    area maps, 352, 354
    calendar, 353
    lodgings, 356, 358
    restaurants, 360
    RV and camping, 358
Lee, Robert E., 428, 429
Lee State Natural Area (Bishopville, SC), 103
Leeds, AL
    lodgings, 449
    restaurants, 451
Lee's Ferry (Williams, AZ), 395
Lees Inn Greenfield (Greenfield, IN), 182–183
Legend Brewing Company (Richmond, VA), 438
Legends at the Castle Restaurant (Loudonville, OH), 282
Legends of NASCAR Benefit Golf Tournament (Sierra Lakes, CA), 63
Legends of the Game Baseball Museum (Arlington, TX), 463
Lehman's Hardware (Kidron, OH), 280
Leipsic, DE
    restaurants, 136
Lemont, IL
    restaurants, 89
Leonardo's Little Italy (St. Louis, MO), 150
Levine Museum of the New South (Charlotte, NC), 261
Lewes, DE
    lodgings, 132–133
    restaurants, 135
Lewis, Jerry Lee, 303
Lewis and Clark State Historic Site (Hartford, IL), 141
Lexington, OH
    attractions, 277
    restaurants, 282
Liberace Museum (Las Vegas, NV), 245
Liberty Lane Walk of Fame (Darlington, SC), 99
Libertyland (Memphis, TN), 307
Lighthouse (Lewes, DE), 135
Lilifred's of Camden (Rembert, SC), 104
Lincoln Depot (Springfield, IL), 91

Lincoln Home National Historic Site (Springfield, IL), 91
Lincoln Park Zoo (Chicago, IL), 83
Lincoln Tomb State Historic Site (Springfield, IL), 91
Lincoln-Herndon Law Office Building (Springfield, IL), 91
Linden Row Inn (Richmond, VA), 435
Lindo Michaocan (Off-Strip/Downtown Las Vegas, NV), 250
Litchfield Park, AZ
    lodgings, 389
Little Haiti (Florida City, FL), 157
Little Havana (Florida City, FL), 157, 161
Little Pee Dee State Park (Dillon, SC), 99, 103
Little River Blue Crab Festival (Little River, SC), 407
Little Rock, AK, 313
Little Rock Central High School (Little Rock, AK), 313
Little Rock Zoo, The (Little Rock, AK), 313
Little Shrimp Restaurant (Dry Ridge, KY), 233
Living Legends of Auto Racing Museum (Daytona Beach, FL), 115
Lockport, IL
    restaurants, 90
Lodge, The (Carrollton, KY), 233
London, Jack, State Historic Park (Glen Ellen, CA), 200
London Underground Café (Corning, NY), 483
Long Pond, PA. *See also* Pocono Raceway (Long Pond, PA)
    area maps, 414, 416
    calendar, 415
Longhorn Steakhouse (Concord, NH), 376
Longhouse Lodge Motel and Manor (Watkins Glen, NY), 482
Lookingglass Theatre Company (Chicago, IL), 80
Lookout Mountain Caverns (Chattanooga, TN), 361
Lookout Mountain (Chattanooga, TN), 361
Lookout Mountain Incline Railway (Chattanooga, TN), 361
Lookout Mountain Parkway (Gadsden, AL), 444
Lorain Speedway (Amherst, OH), 277
Lori's Diner (San Francisco, CA), 205
Los Angeles, CA
    attractions, 66
Los Angeles County Fair (Pomona, CA), 63
Lost Lands RV Park (Dover, DE), 134
Lotawata Creek (Fairview Heights, IL), 149
Loudon, NH. *See also* New Hampshire International Speedway (Loudon, NH)
    area maps, 368, 370
    lodgings, 374
    restaurants, 373, 375, 376
Loudonville, OH
    restaurants, 282
    RV and camping, 280
Lovejoy, GA
    restaurants, 40
Loveless Café (Nashville, TN), 359
Lowe's Motor Speedway (Concord, NC), 252–269
    concessions, 254
    first aid, 254
    getting around, 257
    getting tickets, 255
    parking, 254
    security, 254
Luberty Lane Walk of Fame (Darlington, SC), 96
Lucas, OH
    attractions, 278
Lucas Wharf (Bodega Bay, CA), 204

Lucy's (Camden, SC), 103–104
Lums Pond State Park (Bear, DE), 134
Lupie's Café (Charlotte, NC), 268
Luxor Hotel and Casino (Las Vegas Strip and Vicinity, NV), 246

M

M & M Biscuits, Inc. (Hampton, GA), 40
Macarena's Restaurant (Martinsville, VA), 296
MacArthur Park Historic District (Little Rock, AK), 313
Mackenzie's Chop House (Colorado Springs, CO), 407
Macon Georgia's International Cherry Blossom Festival (Macon, GA), 31
Mac's Acadian Seafood Shack (Saline, MI), 328
Mad Greek Restaurant (Bristol, TN), 54
Mad River and NKP Railroad Society Museum (Bellevue, OH), 277
Madison, IL. *See also* Gateway International Raceway (Madison, IL)
    area maps, 142, 144
    calendar, 143
Madison, IN
    attractions, 229
    restaurants, 232
    RV and camping, 231
Maggiano's Little Italy (Chicago, IL), 89
Magnificent Mile (Chicago, IL), 80
Magnolia House Bed and Breakfast (Sumter, SC), 101
Magnolia Inn (Millington, TN), 310
Magnolia Theatre in West Village (Dallas, TX), 460
Main St. Café (Homestead, FL), 168
Main Street Brewery (Corona, CA), 72
Main Street Steakhouse (Daytona Beach, FL), 120
MainStrasse Village Classic Car Show (Covington, KY), 227
MainStrasse Village (Covington, KY), 229
Majerle's Sports Grill (Phoenix, AZ), 388
Makris Lobster and Steak House (Concord, NH), 376
Malabar Farm State Park (Lucas, OH), 278
Malabar Inn, The (Perrysville, OH), 282
Mama Fu's Asian House (Charlotte, NC), 268
Mama Mia's (Brookfield, WI), 344
Mama's Touch of Italy (Mansfield, OH), 275
Mambo Café (Miami, FL), 160
Mammoth Cave Hotel (Mammoth Cave, KY), 235
Mammoth Cave National Park (Mammoth Cave, KY), 235
Manchester, MI
    restaurants, 328
Manchester, NH
    lodgings, 372, 374
    restaurants, 375
Mango's (Bethany Beach, DE), 135
Manhattan, IL
    RV and camping, 88
Manitou, CO
    attractions, 403
Manitou and Pikes Peak Railway (Manitou, CO), 401, 403
Manitou Springs, CO
    lodgings, 406
    restaurants, 408
Manny's (Kansas City, MO), 220
Mansfield, OH. *See also* Mansfield Motorsports Speedway (Mansfield, OH)
    area maps, 274, 276

attractions, 278
calendar, 275
lodgings, 279, 280
restaurants, 275, 282
RV and camping, 280–281
Mansfield Motorsports Speedway (Mansfield, OH), 270–283
    concessions, 272
    first aid, 272
    getting around, 273
    getting tickets, 273
    security, 272
Maple Avenue District (Elmira, NY), 475
Maple Street Mansion (Carrollton, GA), 40
Marathon (Florida Keys, FL), 169
March Field Air Museum (Riverside, CA), 67
Margate on Winnipesaukee (Laconia, NH), 373
Maria Bonita (Daytona Beach, FL), 120
Marine Science Center (Daytona Beach, FL), 115–116
Marino's, Dan, Town Tavern (Orlando, FL), 122
Marion, AR
    lodgings, 309
    RV and camping, 310
Marion, OH
    lodgings, 279
Marion County Fair (Marion, OH), 275
Mario's Ristorante (Nashville, TN), 359
Maritime Museum (San Francisco, CA), 199
Mark Twain Boyhood Home and Museum (Hannibal, MO), 151
Mark Twain Cave (Hannibal, MO), 151
Mark Twain Memorial Lighthouse (Hannibal, MO), 151
Market Broiler (Riverside, CA), 72
Market Days and Summer Music Festival (Concord, NH), 369
Market Street Brewing Company (Corning, NY), 483
Marriott Charlotte City Center (Charlotte, NC), 263
Marriott Downtown (Indianapolis, IN), 184
Marriott Kansas City Downtown (Kansas City, MO), 217
Marriott Key Largo Bay Beach (Key Largo, FL), 162
Marriott Memphis Downtown (Memphis, TN), 308–309
Marriott Ontario Airport (Ontario, CA), 68
Marriott Pueblo Convention Center (Pueblo, CO), 405
Marriott Riverside (Riverside, CA), 69
Marshall, James, 207
Marshall, MI
    restaurants, 327
Marshall Field's (Chicago, IL), 80
Marshall Gold Discovery State Historic Park (Placerville, CA), 207
Martha Washington Inn, The (Abingdon, VA), 50
Martin, Abe, 189
Martin, Mark, 113, 129
Martinsville, VA. *See also* Martinsville Speedway (Martinsville, VA)
    area maps, 288, 290
    attractions, 291
    calendar, 289
    lodgings, 294
    restaurants, 296
    RV and camping, 294
Martinsville Speedway (Martinsville, VA), 284–297, 293
    concessions, 286
    first aid, 286
    parking, 286
    security, 286
Mary Mac's Tea Room (Atlanta, GA), 38–39

Maryland Heights, MO, *147*
  lodgings, *147*
Maryland Science Center (Baltimore, MD), *137*
Mason Jar (Colorado Springs, CO), *408*
Matehuala Mexican Restaurant (Talladega, AL), *452*
Mather Point (Williams, AZ), *395*
Mayor's Cup Soccer Tournament (Chicago, IL), *81*
MAZO's Fine Foods (Milwaukee, WI), *344*
McClain's (Bellevue, OH), *281*
McCormick–Stillman Railroad Park (Scottsdale, AZ), *388*
McDonough, GA
  lodgings, *37*
  restaurants, *40*
McFarland, Mark, *273*
McKinnon's Louisiane (Atlanta, GA), *39*
McLaughlin, Mike, *129*
McMurray, Jamie, *190*
Meaher State Park (Mobile, AL), *453*
Melody Inn (Coral Gables, FL), *165*
Memory Lane Motorsports & Historic Automotive Museum (Mooresville, NC), *262*
Memphis, TN. *See also* Memphis Motorsports Park (Memphis, TN)
  area maps, *304, 306*
  attractions, *307*
  calendar, *305*
  lodgings, *308–310*
  restaurants, *311–312*
  RV and camping, *310*
Memphis Motorsports Park (Memphis, TN), *298–313*
  concessions, *300*
  first aid, *300*
  getting around, *303*
  getting tickets, *301*
  parking, *300*
  security, *300*
Memphis Queen Line Riverboats (Memphis, TN), *308*
Memphis Rock 'N' Soul Museum (Memphis, TN), *307*
Memphis Zoo (Memphis, TN), *307*
Memphis-Graceland RV Park & Campground (Memphis, TN), *310*
Menard, Paul, *429*
Mequon, WI
  lodgings, *342*
Meredith, NH
  restaurants, *375*
Merichka's Restaurant (Crest Hill, IL), *89*
Mert's Heart and Soul (Charlotte, NC), *267*
Mesquite, TX
  attractions, *464*
Mesquite Championship Rodeo (Mesquite, TX), *461, 464*
Mesquite Charlie's Steakhouse (Branson, MO), *221*
Metropolitan Atlanta Rapid Transit Authority (MARTA) (Atlanta, GA), *29*
Metropolitan Cathedral (Mexico City, MX), *488*
MetroZoo (Miami, FL), *156*
Mexico City, MX. *See also* Autodromo Hermanos Rodriguez (Mexico City, MX)
  area map, *489*
  attractions, *490*
  lodgings, *490*
  restaurants, *491*
Mexico (Sandston, VA), *438*
Mexico's National Palace (Mexico City, MX), *488*
Mi Cocina, Mi Pais (Phoenix, AZ), *394*
Mi Cocina (Dallas, TX), *467*
Miami, FL
  attractions, *161*
  lodgings, *163, 164*
  restaurants, *166, 168*
Miami Beach, FL
  lodgings, *164–165*
  restaurants, *166–167, 168*
Miami Everglades Campground (Homestead, FL), *165*
Miami Lakes, FL
  lodgings, *163*
Miami Metrozoo (Miami, FL), *161*
Michael Oliver's (Delaware, OH), *281*
Michele's Gourmet Restaurant (Dover, DE), *136*
Michigan International Speedway (Brooklyn, MI), *314–329*
  concessions, *316*
  first aid, *316*
  getting around, *319*
  getting tickets, *317*
  security, *316*
Microtel Inn (Gastonia, NC), *265*
Mid City Grill (Johnson City, TN), *54*
Midlothian, VA
  attractions, *433*
Midway Speedway (Rehoboth, DE), *131*
Mike Fink (Covington, KY), *232*
Mike Kelley's Westsider (Kansas City, MO), *220*
Mike Shannon's (St. Louis, MO), *150*
Milan, OH
  attractions, *278*
  lodgings, *279*
  restaurants, *281*
Millennium Maxwell House Nashville (Nashville, TN), *357*
Millennium Park (Chicago, IL), *78, 79, 80*
Miller, A. B., *59*
Miller Brewery Tour (Milwaukee, WI), *339*
Miller Park Tour (Milwaukee, WI), *339–340*
Millersburg, OH
  lodgings, *280*
Millie's Diner (Richmond, VA), *438*
Millington, TN
  attractions, *308*
  lodgings, *310*
  restaurants, *311*
Milwaukee, WI
  area maps, *336, 338*
  attractions, *339–340*
  lodgings, *340–341, 342*
  restaurants, *343–344*
  RV and camping, *342*
Milwaukee County Zoo (Milwaukee, WI), *339*
Milwaukee Mile, The (West Allis, WI), *330–345*
  concessions, *333*
  first aid, *332*
  getting around, *335*
  getting tickets, *333*
  pit/paddock passes, *333*
  restrooms, *333*
  security, *332*
Mint Museum of Art (Charlotte, NC), *261*
Mirage, The (Las Vegas, NV), *241*
Miss Martha's Ice Cream Crankin' (Lebanon, TN), *353*
Miss Ohio Festival (Mansfield, OH), *275*
Miss Sipps Catfish Saloon (Millington, TN), *311*
Mission Bell Inn (Manitou Springs, CO), *408*
Mission Inn (Riverside, CA), *69*
Mister Mark's Fun Park (Florence, SC), *100*
Mi Place (Anaheim, CA), *71*
Mobile, AL, *453*
Mohican Campground and Cabins (Loudonville, OH), *280*
Molly Gonzales' La Casita (Memphis, TN), *312*
Monee, IL

lodgings, *87*
Monell's (Nashville, TN), *359–360*
Monroe, NC
  lodgings, *265*
Monster Mile® (Dover International Speedway, Dover, DE), *124*
Monster Racing Ride Day (Dover International Speedway, Dover, DE), *129*
Monti's (Phoenix, AZ), *392*
Montour Falls, NY
  restaurants, *484*
Monty's Stone Crab (Miami Beach, FL), *167*
Monument Circle (Indianapolis, IN), *178–179*
Mooresville, NC
  attractions, *262*
  lodgings, *265*
  restaurants, *268*
Moosewood (Ithaca, NY), *483*
Moreno Valley, CA
  lodgings, *69*
Morris, IL
  lodgings, *86*
  restaurants, *90*
Morrow, GA
  lodgings, *37*
Mo's Gourmet Hamburgers (San Francisco, CA), *203*
Motor Muster (Michigan International Speedway, Brooklyn, MI), *321*
Motor Sports Hall of Fame of America (Detroit, MI), *329*
Mt. Kearsarge Indian Museum (Concord, NH), *367*
Mt. Washington Auto Road (White Mountains, NH), *368*
Mount Gilead, OH
  attractions, *278*
  lodgings, *280*
Mount Gilead State Park (Mount Gilead, OH), *278*
Mount Pocono, PA, *418, 420, 422*
  lodgings, *418*
  restaurants, *422*
  RV and camping, *420*
Mount Vernon, OH
  lodgings, *279*
Mount Washington Cog Railway (White Mountain, NH), *368*
Mount Washington Cruises (Weirs Beach, NH), *367, 372*
Mountain Cove Labor Day Old Time Music Festival (Lovingston, VA), *431*
Mountain Lake Inn (Bradford, NH), *373*
Mountaintop Lodge (Pocono Pines, PA), *419*
Mr. B's Bar & Grill (Elwood, IL), *90*
Mr. Goodcents Subs & Pastas (Daytona Beach, FL), *121*
Mr. Stox (Anaheim, CA), *70*
MRC Group Research Institute (Las Vegas, NV), *242*
Mt. Pocono Campground (Mount Pocono, PA), *420*
Mug 'N Bun Drive-In (Indianapolis, IN), *187*
Mukwonago, WI
  RV and camping, *342*
Murfreesboro, TN, *356*
  lodgings, *356*
Museum of Anthropology (Mexico City, MX), *488*
Museum of Contemporary Art (Chicago, IL), *80*
Museum of New Hampshire History (Concord, NH), *366*
Museum of Science and Industry (Chicago, IL), *83*
Museum of Small Town Life (Dover, DE), *127*
Museum of the Confederacy (Richmond, VA), *433*

Music Valley Wax Museum (Nashville, TN), *351*
Mutineer (Florida City), *160*
My Florist Café (Phoenix, AZ), *393*
Myrtle Beach, SC, *105*
  attractions, *100*
  restaurants, *104*
Myrtle Beach Pavilion Amusement Park (Myrtle Beach, SC), *105*

N

Napa, CA
  lodgings, *202*
  restaurants, *204, 206*
  RV and camping, *203*
Napa County Fair (Calistoga, CA), *197*
Naperville, IL
  lodgings, *87*
NASCAR Busch and NEXTEL Cup Series (Texas Motor Speedway, Fort Worth, TX), *461*
NASCAR Busch North Series (Dover International Speedway, Dover, DE), *129*
NASCAR Busch Series, Charlotte 300 (Lowe's Motor Speedway, Concord, NC), *259*
NASCAR Busch Series, Sam's Town 250 (Memphis Motorsports Park, Memphis, TN), *305*
NASCAR Busch Series 300 (Chicagoland Speedway, Joliet, IL), *81*
NASCAR Busch Series 300-mile race (Kansas Speedway, Kansas City, KS), *213*
NASCAR Busch Series 2004 Alan Kulwicki 250 (Milwaukee Mile, West Allis, WI), *331*
NASCAR Busch Series Aaron's 312 (Atlanta Motor Speedway, Hampton, GA), *31*
NASCAR Busch Series (Bristol Motor Speedway, Bristol, TN), *47*
NASCAR Busch Series CARQUEST Auto Parts 300 (Lowe's Motor Speedway, Concord, NC), *259*
NASCAR Busch Series (Darlington Raceway, Darlington, SC), *97*
NASCAR Busch Series Diamond Hill Plywood Co. 200 (Darlington Raceway, Darlington, SC), *92*
NASCAR Busch Series (Dover International Speedway, Dover, DE), *129*
NASCAR Busch Series (Gateway International Raceway, Madison, IL), *143*
NASCAR Busch Series (Daytona International Speedway, Daytona Beach, FL), *113*
NASCAR Busch Series (Homestead-Miami Speedway, Homestead, FL), *152, 153, 154*
NASCAR Busch Series (Kentucky Speedway (Sparta, KY), *227*
NASCAR Busch Series (Las Vegas Motor Speedway, Las Vegas, NV), *243*
NASCAR Busch Series (Milwaukee Mile, West Allis, WI), *330, 337*
NASCAR Busch Series (Nashville Superspeedway, Lebanon, TN), *353*
NASCAR Busch Series (New Hampshire International Speedway, Loudon, NH), *369*
NASCAR Busch Series (Phoenix International Raceway, Avondale, AZ), *385*
NASCAR Busch Series (Pikes Peak International Raceway, Fountain, CO), *401*
NASCAR Busch Series Qualifying Day (Talladega Superspeedway, Talladega, AL), *445*
NASCAR Busch Series Slater Bros. 300 (California Speedway, Fontana, CA), *63*
NASCAR Busch Series Target House 300 (California Speedway, Fontana, CA), *63*

NASCAR Busch Series (Watkins Glen International, Watkins Glen, NY), 477
NASCAR Cafe (Greensboro, NC), 268
NASCAR Cafe (Johnson City, TN), 54
NASCAR Cafe (Las Vegas Strip and Vicinity, NV), 243, 249–250
NASCAR Cafe (Myrtle Beach, SC), 104, 105
NASCAR Cafe (Orlando, FL), 122
NASCAR Cafe (Sevierville, TN), 54
NASCAR Craftsman Truck Series (Bristol Motor Speedway, Bristol, TN), 47
NASCAR Craftsman Truck Series American Racing Wheels 200 (California Speedway, Fontana, CA), 63
NASCAR Craftsman Truck Series, O'Reilly 200 (Memphis Motorsports Park, Memphis, TN), 305
NASCAR Craftsman Truck Series, Tailgate 200 (Lowe's Motor Speedway, Concord, NC), 259
NASCAR Craftsman Truck Series (Dover International Speedway, Dover, DE), 129
NASCAR Craftsman Truck Series (Daytona International Speedway, Daytona Beach, FL), 113
NASCAR Craftsman Truck Series (Gateway International Raceway, Madison, IL), 143
NASCAR Craftsman Truck Series (Kansas Speedway, Kansas City, KS), 213
NASCAR Craftsman Truck Series (Kentucky Speedway (Sparta, KY), 227
NASCAR Craftsman Truck Series (Las Vegas Motor Speedway, Las Vegas, NV), 243
NASCAR Craftsman Truck Series (Mansfield Motorsports Speedway, Mansfield, OH), 275
NASCAR Craftsman Truck Series (Martinsville Speedway, Martinsville, VA), 289
NASCAR Craftsman Truck Series (Michigan International Speedway, Brooklyn, MI), 321
NASCAR Craftsman Truck Series (Milwaukee Mile, West Allis, WI), 337
NASCAR Craftsman Truck Series (Nashville Superspeedway, Lebanon, TN), 353
NASCAR Craftsman Truck Series (New Hampshire International Speedway, Loudon, NH), 369
NASCAR Craftsman Truck Series (Phoenix International Raceway, Avondale, AZ), 385
NASCAR Craftsman Truck Series (Richmond International Raceway, Richmond, VA), 431
NASCAR Craftsman Truck Series (Texas Motor Speedway, Fort Worth, TX), 461
NASCAR Elite Midwest Touring Series for MMS (Mansfield Motorsports Speedway, Mansfield, OH), 275
NASCAR NEXTEL All-Star Challenge (Lowe's Motor Speedway, Concord, NC), 259
NASCAR NEXTEL Cup (California Speedway, Fontana, CA), 57
NASCAR NEXTEL Cup DHL 400 (Michigan International Speedway, Brooklyn, MI), 315
NASCAR NEXTEL Cup Pennsylvania 500 (Pocono Raceway, Long Pond, PA), 411
NASCAR NEXTEL Cup Phoenix (Phoenix International Raceway, Avondale, AZ), 378
NASCAR NEXTEL Cup Series, Carolina Dodge Dealers 500 (Darlington Raceway, Darlington, SC), 97
NASCAR NEXTEL Cup Series, Coca-Cola 600 (Lowe's Motor Speedway, Concord, NC), 259
NASCAR NEXTEL Cup Series, (Daytona International Speedway, Daytona Beach, FL), 113
NASCAR NEXTEL Cup Series, UAW-GM Quality 500 (Lowe's Motor Speedway, Concord, NC), 259
NASCAR NEXTEL Cup Series 400 (Chicagoland Speedway, Joliet, IL), 81

NASCAR NEXTEL Cup Series 2004 Advance Auto Parts 500 (Martinsville Speedway, Ridgeway, VA), 287
NASCAR NEXTEL Cup Series Auto Club 500 (California Speedway, Fontana, CA), 63
NASCAR NEXTEL Cup Series (Bristol Motor Speedway, Bristol, TN), 47
NASCAR NEXTEL Cup Series Checker Auto Parts 500 (Phoenix International Raceway, Avondale, AZ), 385
NASCAR NEXTEL Cup Series (Dover International Speedway, Dover, DE), 129
NASCAR NEXTEL Cup Series GFF Marketplace 400 (Michigan International Speedway, Brooklyn, MI), 321
NASCAR NEXTEL Cup Series Golden Corral 500 (Atlanta Motor Speedway, Hampton, GA), 31
NASCAR NEXTEL Cup Series (Infineon Raceway, Sonoma, CA), 197
NASCAR NEXTEL Cup Series (Kansas Speedway, Kansas City, KS), 213
NASCAR NEXTEL Cup Series (Martinsville Speedway, Martinsville, VA), 289
NASCAR NEXTEL Cup Series (Dover International Speedway, Dover, DE), 129
NASCAR NEXTEL Cup Series (Michigan International Speedway, Brooklyn, MI), 321
NASCAR NEXTEL Cup Series New England 300 (New Hampshire International Speedway, Loudon, NH), 363
NASCAR NEXTEL Cup Series (New Hampshire International Speedway, Loudon, NH), 369
NASCAR NEXTEL Cup Series (Phoenix International Raceway, Avondale, AZ), 385
NASCAR NEXTEL Cup Series (Pocono Raceway, Long Pond, PA), 415
NASCAR NEXTEL Cup Series Pop Secret 500 (California Speedway, Fontana, CA), 63
NASCAR NEXTEL Cup Series (Richmond International Raceway, Richmond, VA), 431
NASCAR NEXTEL Cup Series (Talladega Superspeedway, Talladega, AL), 445
NASCAR NEXTEL Cup Series (Texas Motor Speedway, Fort Worth, TX), 461
NASCAR NEXTEL Cup Series (Watkins Glen International, Watkins Glen, NY), 477
NASCAR NEXTEL Series (Las Vegas Motor Speedway, Las Vegas, NV), 243
NASCAR NEXTEL Series (Pocono Raceway, Long Pond, PA), 410
NASCAR Silicon Motor Speedway (Universal City, CA), 67
NASCAR Speedpark, Concord Mills (Concord, NC), 261
NASCAR Speedpark (Hazelwood, MO), 145
NASCAR Speedpark (Myrtle Beach, SC), 100, 105
NASCAR SpeedPark (Sevierville, TN), 51
Nashville, TN, 355, 356–360
  area maps, 352, 354
  attractions, 355
  lodgings, 356–358
  restaurants, 359–360
  RV and camping, 358–359
Nashville Koa Kampground (Nashville, TN), 359
Nashville Palace Restaurant and Dinner Theater (Nashville, TN), 360
Nashville Superspeedway (Lebanon, TN), 346–361
  concessions, 348
  first aid, 348
  getting around, 351
  getting tickets, 349
  security, 348
Nashville Zoo (Nashville, TN), 355

Nassau Valley Vineyards (Dover, DE), 128
Naswa Beach Bar and Grill (Laconia, NH), 376
Naswa Resort (Laconia, NH), 373–374
National Aquarium (Baltimore, MD), 137
National Battlefield Civil War Visitor Center (Richmond, VA), 429
National Civil Rights Museum (Memphis, TN), 302, 307
National Historic Landmark District (Savannah, GA), 41
National Maritime Center (Norfolk, VA), 439
National Museum of Anthropology (Mexico City, MX), 490
National Soaring Museum (Elmira, NY), 475, 479
National Tom Sawyer Days (Hannibal, MO), 151
Natural Science Center of Greensboro (Greensboro, NC), 288, 291
Nauticus (Norfolk, VA), 439
Navy Pier (Chicago, IL), 83–84
NBA City (Orlando, FL), 122
NCAA Hall of Champions (Indianapolis, IN), 182
NCAA Men's Basketball Final Four (St. Louis. MO), 143
Near Westside District (Elmira, NY), 475
Nebraska Furniture Mart (Kansas City, KS), 213
Neely's Bar-B-Que (Memphis, TN), 312
Neewollah Festival (Independence, KS), 213
Neiman Marcus (Dallas, TX), 459
Nemechek, Joe, 113
Neptune's Hideaway (Key Largo, FL), 164
New Castle, DE
  lodgings, 134
New Hampshire International Speedway (Loudon, NH), 362–377
  concessions, 364
  first aid, 364
  getting around, 367
  getting tickets, 365
  security, 364
New Hampshire State House (Concord, NH), 366–367
New Smyrna Beach, FL
  attractions, 116
  restaurants, 120, 122
Newark, DE
  lodgings, 133
  restaurants, 135
Newman, Ryan, 209, 315
Newport, KY
  attractions, 230
  restaurants, 234
Newport on the Levee Entertainment Center (Newport, KY), 225, 230
Niagara Falls (Seaway Trail, NY), 485
Nick and Sam's Steak and Fish (Dallas, TX), 467
Niki's West (Birmingham, AL), 451
Nikko Japanese Restaurant (Homestead, FL), 168
Noah's Ark (Wisconsin Dells, WI), 345
Noccalula Falls Park (Gadsden, AL), 444
Nolichucky River (Erwin, TN), 49'
Norcross, GA
  restaurants, 40
Norfolk, VA, 439
Norman Couser's Country Cooking (Nashville, TN), 360
North Carolina Auto Racing Hall of Fame (Mooresville, NC), 262
North Las Vegas, NV
  lodgings, 247–248
  restaurants, 250

Norwood's Restaurant & Wine Shop (New Smyrna Beach, FL), 120
Novato, CA
  lodgings, 201
  restaurants, 204
Number Five (Binghamton, NY), 483

O

Oak Creek Campground (Walton, KY), 232
Oak Hill Cottage (Mansfield, OH), 278
Oak Mountain State Park (Pelham, AL), 447
Obrycki's (Baltimore, MD), 137
Ob's BBQ (McDonough, GA), 40
Occidental, CA
  restaurants, 206
Ocean Deck Restaurant & Beach Club (Daytona Beach, FL), 121–122
Ocean Walk Resort at the Village (Daytona Beach, FL), 119
Ocean Walk Shoppes @ The Village (Daytona Beach, FL), 116
Odessa, NY
  RV and camping, 482
O'Dowd's Little Dublin (Kansas City, MO), 219
O'Fallon, IL, 150
  restaurants, 150
Off-Strip/Downtown Las Vegas, NV
  lodgings, 247, 248
  restaurants, 250
Ohio State Reformatory (Mansfield, OH), 278
Oktoberfest (Helen, GA), 31
Olathe, KS
  attractions, 215
Old Chain of Rocks Bridge (St. Louis, MO), 141
Old Colorado City (Colorado City, CO), 401
Old Faithful Geyser of California (Calistoga, CA), 199
Old Fashioned Pancake House (Joliet, IL), 90
Old Heidelberg (Nashville, TN), 360
Old Jail (St. Augustine, FL), 123
Old Mill (Little Rock, AK), 313
Old Mill Restaurant (Talladega, AL), 452
Old Smokey Bar-B-Q (Leeds, AL), 452
Old South Restaurant (Camden, SC), 104
Old State Capitol State Historic Site (Springfield, IL), 91
Old State House (Dover, DE), 127, 131
Old Town Guest House (Colorado Springs, CO), 406
Old Town San Diego (San Diego, CA), 73
Old Town Trolley Tour (St. Augustine, FL), 123
Oldest House (St. Augustine, FL), 123
Olema, CA
  RV and camping, 203
Olema Ranch Campground (Olema, CA), 203
Olentangy Indian Caverns and Ohio Frontierland (Delaware, OH), 277
Omni Charlotte Hotel (Charlotte, NC), 263
Omni Hotel at CNN Center (Atlanta, GA), 35
Omni Richmond Hotel (Richmond, VA), 435
On Speedway Grounds (Tipton, MI), 326
One Stop Food Mart (Richmond, VA), 429
Onsted, MI
  restaurants, 328
Ontario, CA
  attractions, 66
  lodgings, 68, 69
  restaurants, 63, 72
Ontario, OH
  restaurants, 282
Ontario Mills Mall (Ontario, CA), 60, 66
Opry Mills (Nashville, TN), 355
Oriental Wok (Fort Mitchell, KY), 232

Original Oyster House (Mobile, AL), 453
Original Wisconsin Duck(r) (Wisconsin Dells, WI), 345
Orlando, FL
    attractions, 116–117
    restaurants, 122
Orleans Hotel and Casino (Las Vegas Strip and Vicinity, NV), 246
Ormond Beach, FL
    lodgings, 120
    RV and camping, 120
Ortanique (Las Vegas Strip and Vicinity, NV), 249
Ortanique on the Mile (Coral Gables, FL), 160
Outback Steak House (Colorado Springs, CO), 401
Outlets at Castle Rock (Castle Rock, CO), 401
Overland Park, KS
    attractions, 215
    lodgings, 217
    restaurants, 219
Oxford, AL
    lodgings, 449, 450
    restaurants, 452

P

Pacifico (Calistoga, CA), 203
Paesano's (Ann Arbor, MI), 327
Palacio De Las Bellas Artes (Mexico City, MX), 490
Palm Drive RV Parking (Homestead, FL), 165
Palomino (Indianapolis, IN), 186
Panch, Bettie, 243
Panch, Marvin, 243
Papa's Gondola (Mansfield, OH), 282
Paradise Garden Buffet (Las Vegas Strip and Vicinity, NV), 250
Paramount's Carowinds (Charlotte, NC), 261
Paramount's Kings Dominion (Doswell, VA), 430, 433
Park Hotel (Charlotte, NC), 263
Parker, Hank, Jr., 271
Parson, Benny, 63
Party Zone (California Speedway, CA), 68
Pasadena, CA
    attractions, 66
    lodgings, 68
Patrick Amiot's Art (Sebastopol, CA), 200
Paul & Mary's Raceway Camping LLC (Manhattan, IL), 88
Paymon's Mediterranean Café and Hookah Lounge (Off-Strip/Downtown Las Vegas, NV), 250
Peabody Memphis, The (Memphis, TN), 304, 309
Peachtree City, GA
    lodgings, 37
Peak 8 Fun Park (Summit County, CO), 409
Pee Dee Golfing (Florence, SC), 100
Pee Dee Pride Minor League Hockey Team (Florence, SC), 100
Pee Dee State Farmer's Market (Darlington, SC), 103
Peerless (Johnson City, TN), 53
Peggy Notebaert Nature Museum (Chicago, IL), 84
Pelham, AL
    attractions, 447
Pell City, AL
    lodgings, 450
    restaurants, 452
Pell City Steakhouse (Pell City, AL), 452
Penske, Roger, 319
Peppe's Ristorante (Stroudsburg, PA), 422

Pepsi 300 NASCAR Busch Series (Nashville Superspeedway, Lebanon, TN), 347, 353
Perimeter, The (Atlanta, GA), 28
Perkins, Carl, 303
Permanent Tribute to Heroes, A (Las Vegas, NV), 242
Perrysville, OH
    restaurants, 282
Petaluma, CA
    lodgings, 203
    restaurants, 204, 206
    RV and camping, 203
Petaluma KOA (Petaluma, CA), 203
Petco Park (San Diego, CA), 73
Petersen Automotive Museum (Los Angeles, CA), 66
Petrified Forest, The (Calistoga, CA), 199
Petty, Kyle, 179
Petty, Richard, 121
Petty Driving Experience (Concord, NC), 261
Pewaukee, WI
    lodgings, 342
Pfister Hotel (Milwaukee, WI), 341
Phantom Canyon Brewing Company (Colorado Springs, CO), 408
Pharaoh's Pheast (Las Vegas Strip and Vicinity, NV), 249
Philippe's Bistro (Atlanta, GA), 39
Phillips Harborplace (Baltimore, MD), 137
Philpott Lake (Stuart, VA), 291
Phoenix, AZ
    area maps, 384, 386
    attractions, 387
    lodgings, 389, 390–391
    restaurants, 385, 388, 392–393, 394
    RV and camping, 392
Phoenix Art Museum (Phoenix, AZ), 382
Phoenix Greyhound Park (Phoenix, AZ), 384
Phoenix International Raceway (Avondale, AZ), 378–395
    concessions, 381
    first aid, 380
    getting around, 381
    getting tickets, 381
    parking, 380
    security, 380
Phoenix Zoo (Phoenix, AZ), 383, 387
Picasso Sculpture (Chicago, IL), 80
Piccolino's Italian Café (Napa, CA), 205
Piccolo Mondo (Arlington, TX), 467
Piedmont Mall (Martinsville, VA), 288
Pigeon Forge, TN, 55
Pikes Peak International Raceway (Fountain, CO), 396–409
    concessions, 398
    first aid, 398
    getting around, 399
    parking, 398
    security, 398
Pikes Peak (Manitou, CO), 403
Pikes Peak Mountain Bike Tours (Colorado Springs, CO), 403
Pikes Peak (Pikes Peak, CO), 399, 400
Pilot Mountain, NC
    lodgings, 292–293
Pineville, NC
    lodgings, 265
Pinhoti Hiking Trail (Talladega, AL), 443
Pirkle, Gordon, 31
Pischke's Paradise (Scottsdale, AZ), 393
Pit Stop Grille (Sparta, KY), 234
Pit Stop Pub (Kansas City, KS), 216
Placerville, CA, 207
Placerville Hardware (Placerville, CA), 207
Plainfield, IN
    restaurants, 187
Plainfield Diner (Plainfield, IN), 187
Planet Hollywood (Orlando, FL), 122

Platte City, MO
    lodgings, 218
Plaza III—The Steakhouse (Kansas City, MO), 219
Plaza México (Mexico City, MX), 489
Plaza Resort and Spa (Daytona Beach, FL), 118
Pleasant Peasant (Atlanta, GA), 39
Pocono Blues Festival (Blakeslee, PA), 415
Pocono Lake, PA, 419
    lodgings, 419
    restaurants, 415
Pocono Mountains Vacation Bureau (Pocono Raceway, Long Pond, PA), 414
Pocono Pines, PA, 419, 422
    lodgings, 419
    restaurants, 422
Pocono Raceway (Long Pond, PA), 410–423
    concessions, 412
    first aid, 412
    getting around, 413
    security, 412
Pocono Ramada Inn (Lake Harmony, PA), 418
Pocono Summit, PA, 422
    attractions, 417
    restaurants, 422
Pointe South Mountain Resort (Phoenix, AZ), 389
Pomona, CA
    lodgings, 69–70
Ponak's Mexican Kitchen (Kansas City, MO), 220
Ponce de Leon Lighthouse (Daytona Beach, FL), 110, 116
Ponce de Leon's Fountain of Youth (St. Augustine, FL), 123
Ponce Inlet, FL
    restaurants, 118, 122
Pontoon Beach, IL
    lodgings, 147–148
Poppa's Place (Brooklyn, MI), 328
Port Discovery Children's Museum (Baltimore, MD), 137
Powell's Sweet Shoppe (Windsor, CA), 206
Powerhouse, PA, 422
Prairie View RV Park LLC (Elwood, IL), 88
Presley, Elvis, 299, 303
Presto Bar and Grill (Charlotte, NC), 268
Prickly Pear (Mooresville, NC), 268
Prime Hotel & Suites Phoenix/Chandler (Chandler, AZ), 388
Pronto Ristorante (Phoenix, AZ), 392–393
ProRodeo Hall of Fame and Museum of the American Cowboy (Colorado Springs, CO), 399, 403
Prosser RV/Cruise America (Milwaukee, WI), 342, 343
Pruett's BBQ (Gadsden, AL), 451
Pub, The (Kansas City, KS), 216
Public Landing (Lockport, IL), 90
Pueblo, CO
    lodgings, 405, 406
Pumpkin Patch Express (Calera, AL), 445
Puritan Backroom (Manchester, NH), 375

Q

Quality Inn & Suites (Abingdon, VA), 51
Quality Inn & Suites (Bellville, OH), 279–280
Quality Inn Ocean Palms (Daytona Beach Shores, FL), 118
Quality Inn West (Richmond, VA), 435
Quilted Bear (Scottsdale, AZ), 393

R

Race Express Bus (Newark, DE), 135
Race Fever (Colorado Springs, CO), 401
Race Fever Night (Watkins Glen International, Watkins Glen, NY), 477
Race-On Driving Experience (Memphis Motorsports Park, Memphis, TN), 312
Racetrack RV Park (Daytona Beach, FL), 120
Racin' and Tastin' (Danville, VA), 289
Racin' the Bases Celebrity Softball Challenge, The (Joliet, IL), 78–79, 81
Racing Thunder in the Glen Festival (Watkins Glen, NY), 477
Racing's North Turn Beach Bar & Grille (Ponce Inlet, FL), 118
Radisson Hotel Birmingham (Birmingham, AL), 448
Radisson Hotel Corning (Corning, TX), 480
Radisson Hotel (Memphis, TN), 309
Radisson Hotel Milwaukee West (Milwaukee, WI), 342
Radisson Inn Colorado Springs North (Colorado Springs, CO), 404
Rafferty's (Florence, KY), 233
Ragged Edge Resort (Florida Keys, FL), 169
Raging Rivers Waterpark (Grafton, IL), 145
Railhead Smokehouse (Fort Worth, TX), 468
Railroad Museum (Florence, SC), 97
Railtown 1897 State Historic Park (Placerville, CA), 207
Rainbow Bend Resort (Florida Keys, FL), 169
Rainbow Café (Charlotte, NC), 267
Rainforest Café (Orlando, FL), 122
RainTree Resort & Conference Center (Wisconsin Dells, WI), 345
Ramada Inn Bristol (Bristol, VA), 50
Ramada Inn Fairview Heights (Fairview Heights, IL), 146
Ramada Inn Phoenix West (Goodyear, AZ), 390
Ramada Inn Speedway (Daytona Beach, FL), 119
Ramada Limited & Suites (Sparta, KY), 231
Ramada Limited Cincinnati Airport/Florence (Florence, KY), 230
Ramsey's Pond (Darlington, SC), 101
Ranch House (Charlotte, NC), 267
Rancho Cucamonga, CA
    lodgings, 70
    restaurants, 72
Raphael Hotel (Kansas City, MO), 217
Rathskeller (Indianapolis, IN), 188
Raul & Theresa's Mexican Food (Avondale, AZ), 393–394
Ray's on the River (Atlanta, GA), 39
Recreational Vehicle Park (West Allis, WI), 343
Red Blazer Restaurant and Pub (Concord, NH), 376
Red Hot & Blue (Dallas, TX), 468
Red Jacket Orchards Fruit Outlet (Geneva, NY), 477
Red Lobster (Concord, NC), 259
Red Roof Inn (Loudon, NH), 374
Red Star Tavern (Charlotte, NC), 268
Redland Hotel (Homestead, FL), 155, 164
Redlands, CA
    lodgings, 70
Redwood Empire Ice Arena (Santa Rosa, CA), 199
Reed Gold Mine State Historic Site (Midland, NC), 263
Regatta and Governor's Cup Race (Madison, IN), 227
Regency Inn (Bristol, TN), 51
Rehoboth, DE
    attractions, 131
Rehoboth Beach, DE

attractions, *131*
lodgings, *133*
restaurants, *135–136, 136*
RV and camping, *134–135*
Reiffen's (Carrollton, KY), *233*
Rembert, SC
restaurants, *104*
Renaissance Concourse Hotel (Atlanta, GA), *36*
Renaissance Festival (Bonner Springs, KS), *213*
Renaissance St. Louis Hotel (St. Louis, MO), *147*
Residence Inn by Marriott Ann Arbor (Ann Arbor, MI), *324*
Residence Inn by Marriott (Colorado Springs, CO), *406*
Restaurant at the Canterbury (Indianapolis, IN), *186*
Reuben's (Danville, VA), *296*
Reutimann, David, *271*
Rheinland Haus (Charlotte, NC), *267*
Rhythm & Roots Reunion (Bristol, TN), *47*
Rialto, CA
lodgings, *70*
Rialto Square Theatre (Joliet, IL), *78*
Richland Carrousel Park (Mansfield, OH), *274, 278*
Richmond, VA. *See also* Richmond International Raceway (Richmond, VA)
area maps, *430, 432*
attractions, *433–434*
calendar, *431*
lodgings, *434–435, 436*
restaurants, *431, 437–438*
Richmond Braves (Richmond, VA), *433*
Richmond International Raceway (Richmond, VA), *424–439*
first aid, *426*
getting around, *426*
getting tickets, *427*
parking, *426*
Rick's Cafe Boatyard (Indianapolis, IN), *187*
calendar, *289*
Ridgewood Barbecue (Bluff City, TN), *53*
Riggs, Scott, *470*
Ripley's Believe It or Not (St. Augustine, FL), *123*
Ripley's (Branson, MO), *221*
Riscky's Barebque (Fort Worth, TX), *468*
Rite Aid (Richmond, VA), *429*
River City Diner (Richmond, VA), *438*
Rivera, Diego, *488*
Riverboat Cruises (Covington, KY), *229*
Riverchase Galleria (Talladega, AL), *443*
Riverfest (Columbia, SC), *97*
Riverside, AL
lodgings, *450*
restaurants, *452*
Riverside, CA
attractions, *67*
lodgings, *68–69, 70*
restaurants, *72*
Riverside Campground (Abingdon, VA), *52*
RiverSplash (Marquette Park, WI), *337*
Riverview (Covington, KY), *232*
Roanoke, VA
lodgings, *292, 294*
restaurants, *295*
Robert is Here (Homestead, FL), *167*
Robert Trent Jones Golf Trail (Talladega, AL), *443*
Roberts, Edward Glenn "Fireball," *96*
Rock City Gardens (Chattanooga, TN), *361*
Rock Hill, SC
lodgings, *265*
Rockstream, NY
lodgings, *482*

Rockwell Inn (Morris, IL), *90*
Rockwell Museum of Western Art (Corning, NY), *476, 479*
Rocky's Pub (Mansfield, OH), *282*
Roger's Bar-B-Cue Restaurant (Florence, SC), *104*
Rohnert Park, CA
lodgings, *202*
Romeoville, IL, *87*
Ronaldo Grisanti and Sons (Memphis, TN), *311*
Ron's Southern Skillet (Stockbridge, GA), *40*
Rosa's (Ontario, CA), *63*
Rosewood Inn (Corning, NY), *481*
Rosita's Restaurant (Florida City, FL), *167*
Roush, Jack, *197*
Roussos (Mobile, AL), *453*
Roy Rogers-Dale Evans Museum (Branson, MO), *221*
R-Place Family Eatery (Morris, IL), *90*
Ruby Beet Gourmet (Phoenix, AZ), *393*
Ruffino's (Napa, CA), *204*
Ruffner Mountain (Birmingham, AL), *447*
Ruggles Mine (Canterbury, NH), *367*
Rustler's Rooste (Phoenix, AZ), *393*
Rusty Nail (Cortland, NY), *483*
Ruth's Chris Steak House (Chicago, IL), *81*
RV Park at the Napa County Fairgrounds (Calistoga, CA), *202*
Ryman Auditorium (Nashville, TN), *355*

S

Saddles Steakhouse (Sonoma, CA), *205*
Sadler, Elliott, *457*
Safari West Wildlife Preserve (Santa Rosa, CA), *199*
Safe House (Milwaukee, WI), *344*
Sahara Hotel and Casino (Las Vegas Strip and Vicinity, NV), *246–247*
St. Augustine, FL, *123*
St. Charles, MO, *148*
attractions, *146*
lodgings, *148*
St. Elmo Steak House (Indianapolis, IN), *179*
St. George Street (St. Augustine, FL), *123*
St. Jude Children's Research Hospital (Memphis, TN), *303*
St. Louis, MO
attractions, *145–146*
lodgings, *146–147, 148*
restaurants, *149–150*
St. Louis Cardinals Museum (St. Louis, MO), *145*
St. Louis Cardinals (St. Louis, MO), *141*
St. Louis NE/Granite City KOA Campground (Granite City, IL), *148*
St. Louis Rams (St. Louis, MO), *141*
Saint Louis University (St. Louis, MO), *141*
St. Louis Zoo (St. Louis, MO), *146*
Salem, NH
attractions, *371*
Saline, MI
restaurants, *328*
Saltgrass Steak House (Fossil Creek, TX), *468*
Sam Bass Gallery (Concord, NC), *261*
Sam Miller's Warehouse (Richmond, VA), *437*
Sam Patch (Seaway Trail, NY), *485*
Sam Woo BBQ (Las Vegas Strip and Vicinity, NV), *249*
Sambo's Tavern (Leipsic, DE), *136*
Sam's Club (Jackson, MI), *321*
Sam's Town RV Park (Las Vegas, NV), *248*
San Bernardino, CA
lodgings, *70*

San Diego, CA, *73*
San Diego Zoo (San Diego, CA), *73*
San Francisco, CA
attractions, *199*
lodgings, *200–201*
restaurants, *203, 205*
San Juan Teotihuacán, Mexico, *491*
San Sebastian Winery (St. Augustine, FL), *123*
Sandpiper Dockside Café & Restaurant (Bodega Bay, CA), *206*
Sandston, VA
lodgings, *435–436, 436*
restaurants, *438*
Sandusky, OH, *283*
Santa Monica, CA
attractions, *67*
Santa Monica Pier Aquarium (Santa Monica, CA), *67*
Santa Monica Pier (Santa Monica, CA), *67*
Santa Rosa, CA
attractions, *199*
lodgings, *201, 202*
restaurants, *206*
Sarah Street Grill (Stroudsburg, PA), *421*
Sausalito, CA
restaurants, *197, 204*
Savannah, GA, *41*
Savannah Tour of Homes & Gardens (Savannah, GA), *31*
Savard's Family Restaurant (Watkins Glen, NY), *484*
Saz's State House (Milwaukee, WI), *344*
Schiele Museum of Natural History & Planetarium (Gastonia, NC), *261–262*
Schnitzelfest (Hillsborough, NH), *369*
Schofield House (Madison, IN), *229*
Schuler's of Marshall (Marshall, MI), *328*
Schuyler County Chamber of Commerce (Watkins Glen, NY), *473*
Science Museum of Virginia (Richmond, VA), *434*
Scoma's of Sausalito (Sausalito, CA), *197*
Scotrun, PA, *418*
lodgings, *418*
Scottsdale, AZ
attractions, *387–388*
lodgings, *389–390, 391*
restaurants, *393*
Scottsdale Center for the Arts (Scottsdale, AZ), *383*
Scottsdale Culinary Festival (Scottsdale, AZ), *385*
Scotty's Landing (Coconut Grove, FL), *167*
Scranton, PA, *421*
attractions, *417*
restaurants, *421*
Seaport Village (San Diego, CA), *73*
Seaway Trail, NY, *485*
SeaWorld (San Diego, CA), *73*
Sebastiani Sonoma Clark Cellars (Sonoma, CA), *196*
Sebastopol, CA
attractions, *200*
restaurants, *206*
Seminole Theater (Homestead, FL), *155*
Seneca Caverns (Bellevue, OH), *277*
Seneca Grand Prix Family Fun Center (Watkins Glen, NY), *479*
Seneca Lake Wine Trail (Seneca Lake, NY), *473*
Seneca Lodge (Watkins Glen, NY), *482*
Sevierville, TN
restaurants, *54*
Shack, The (Branson, MO), *221*
Shack BBQ, The (Talladega, AL), *451*
Shadrack Campground (Bristol, TN), *52*
Shapiro's Delicatessen (Indianapolis, IN), *188*

Shark Reef, Mandalay Bay Resort & Casino (Las Vegas, NV), *245*
Shedd Aquarium (Chicago, IL), *84*
Sheraton Atlanta Hotel (Atlanta, GA), *35*
Sheraton Beach Resort Key Largo (Key Largo, FL), *163*
Sheraton Birmingham (Birmingham, AL), *448*
Sheraton Colorado Springs Hotel (Colorado Springs, CO), *404–405*
Sheraton Dallas Brookhollow Hotel (Dallas, TX), *464*
Sheraton Dover Hotel (Dover, DE), *132*
Sheraton Music City Hotel (Nashville, TN), *357*
Sheraton Pasadena Hotel (Pasadena, CA), *68*
Sheraton Richmond West Hotel (Richmond, VA), *435*
Sheraton Suites Fairplex (Pomona, CA), *69*
Shilo Inn Hotel Pomona (Pomona, CA), *70*
Shiro (Anaheim, CA), *71*
Shiver's Bar-B-Q (Homestead, FL), *168*
Short Sugar's (Danville, VA), *296*
Show-Me's on the Landing (St. Louis, MO), *150*
Shepherd of the Hills Homestead (Branson, MO), *221*
Silk Stocking District (Talladega, AL), *443*
Silver Dollar City (Branson, MO), *221*
Silverado Concours d'Elegance (Mare Island, CA), *197*
Silverthorne Factory Stores (Summit County, CO), *409*
Silverton Hotel Casino RV Park (Las Vegas, NV), *248*
Simply Delicious Market Place (Bristol, TN), *54*
Sims-Mitchell House B&B (Chatham, VA), *293*
Sine (Richmond, VA), *438*
SIRIUS at the Glen NASCAR NEXTEL Cup Race (Watkins Glen International, Watkins Glen, NY), *470, 471*
Six Flags Marine World (Vallejo, CA), *199*
Six Flags Over Georgia (Austell, GA), *34*
Six Flags Over Texas (Arlington, TX), *463*
Six Flags St. Louis (Eureka, MO), *145*
Sixth Floor Museum at Dealey Plaza (Dallas, TX), *463*
Skinner, Mike, *337*
Sky Sox Stadium (Colorado Springs, CO), *401*
Skyway East (Mansfield, OH), *282*
Slippery Noodle Inn (Indianapolis, IN), *188*
Smith, O. Bruton, *46*
Smoky's Grill (Charlotte, NC), *267*
Smuggler's Cove (Tannersville, PA), *422*
Smyrna, DE
attractions, *131*
restaurants, *136*
Snappers (Miami, FL), *160*
Snydersville, PA, *422*
restaurants, *422*
Snydersville Family Diner (Snydersville, PA), *422*
Sodus Bay Lighthouse and Museum (Seaway Trail, NY), *485*
Sofitel Chicago Water Tower (Chicago, IL), *86*
Somerset House (Talladega, AL), *450*
Sonny Bryan's Barbeque (Fort Worth, TX), *461*
Sonny's Real Pit BBQ (Oxford, AL), *452*
Sonoma, CA. *See also* Infineon Raceway (Sonoma, CA)
area maps, *196, 198*
attractions, *199–200*
calendar, *197*
lodgings, *202*
restaurants, *204–205, 206*
Sonoma Cheese Factory (Sonoma, CA), *206*
Sonoma County Hot Air Balloon Classic (Windsor, CA), *197*
Sonoma Train Town (Sonoma, CA), *200*

Sophisticated Otter Restaurant & Brewery (Johnson City, TN), 54
Sorge's Restaurant (Corning, NY), 483
South Beach (Miami, FL), 158
South Boston, VA
    attractions, 291
South Boston Speedway (South Boston, VA), 291
South City Kitchen (Atlanta, GA), 39
South Miami, FL
    restaurants, 168
South Rim (Williams, AZ), 395
Southern Comfort RV Resort (Florida City, FL), 165
Southern Museum of Flight/Alabama Aviation Hall of Fame (Birmingham, AL), 447
Southfork Ranch (Dallas, TX), 460
Southhaven, MS
    lodgings, 310
Southside Speedway (Midlothian, VA), 433
Space Center Houston (Houston, TX), 469
Spanish Quarter Village (St. Augustine, FL), 123
Sparta, KY. *See also* Kentucky Speedway (Sparta, KY)
    area maps, 224, 228
    calendar, 227
    lodgings, 231
    restaurants, 234
    RV and camping, 232
Speedway Club at Lowe's Motor Speedway (Concord, NC), 268
Speedweeks (Daytona International Speedway, Daytona Beach, FL), 113
Sperber, Bryan, 385
Splash Playground (Tempe, AZ), 388
Splash Station Waterpark (Joliet, IL), 84–85
Sprague, Jack, 270
Spring Plowing Days (Lucas, OH), 275
Springdale, UT, 251
Springfield, IL, 91
Springhill Suites by Marriott Florence (Florence, SC), 102
Springhill Suites Charlotte Concord Mills/Speedway (Concord, NC), 265
Spruce Hill Inn & Cottages (Mansfield, OH), 280
Squam Lakes National Science Center (Holderness, NH), 371
Stage Coach (Manitou Springs, CO), 408
Star Speedway (Epping, NH), 371
Stargazer Amphitheatre (Madison, IN), 227
Starwood Amphitheatre (Nashville, TN), 350
State Line Bar and Grille (Bristol, TN), 54
State of Illinois Building (Chicago, IL), 80
State Street (Chicago, IL), 80
Statler Hotel at Cornell University (Ithaca, NY), 481
Stax Museum of American Soul Music, The (Memphis, TN), 307
Staybridge Suites (Corning, NY), 481
Steak House at Circus Circus (Las Vegas, NV), 243
Steak 'n Shake (Chicago, IL), 81
Stefano's Italian Restaurant (Florence, SC), 104
Steve's Dakota Grill—Ontario (Ontario, OH), 282
Stewart, Tony, 153
Stockbridge, GA
    lodgings, 37
    restaurants, 40
Stone Bar Inn (Stroudsburg, PA), 421
Stone Mountain, GA
    attractions, 34
Stone Mountain Park (Stone Mountain, GA), 34

Stony Brook State Park (Watkins Glen, NY), 476
Story, IN, 189
Story Inn (Story, IN), 189
Story Land (White Mountains, NH), 377
Stratford Inn (Danville, VA), 292
Strawberry Street Cafe (Richmond, VA), 437
Stremme, David, 92
Strong Museum (Seaway Trail, NY), 485
Stroudsburg, PA, 419–420, 421, 422
    lodgings, 419–420
    restaurants, 421, 422
    RV and camping, 420
Stuart, J. E. B., 428
Stuart, VA
    attractions, 291
    RV and camping, 294
Sturtevant, WI
    lodgings, 342
Sugarloaf Ridge State Park (Glen Ellen, CA), 203
Sullivan Trail Motel (Pocono Lake, PA), 419
Summerfest (Milwaukee, WI), 337
Summerfield Suites by Wyndham—Charlotte (Charlotte, NC), 263
Summit, The (Birmingham, AL), 443
Summit County, CO, 409
Summit Lanes (Pocono Summit, PA), 417
Sumter, SC
    attractions, 100–101
    lodgings, 101, 102–103
Sumter Opera House (Sumter, SC), 100–101
Sun and Moon Pyramids (San Juan Teotihuacán, MX), 491
Sun City, AZ
    lodgings, 392
Sun Devil Stadium (Phoenix, AZ), 384
Sun Studio (Memphis, TN), 299, 302, 303, 307
Sun Viking Lodge (Daytona Beach, FL), 118
Sundance Square (Fort Worth, TX), 459
Sunny Southern Heritage (Mobile, AL), 453
Sunset Restaurant (Lebanon, TN), 88
Sun Studio (Memphis, TN), 302, 303, 307
Super 8 Motel Tilton/Lake Winnipesaukee (Tilton, NH), 372–373
Super 8 (Talladega, AL), 450
Sweeney's Too (Mansfield, OH), 282
Sweetie Pies (Placerville, CA), 207
Syl's Restaurant (Rockdale, IL), 90
Symphony Hall (Phoenix, AZ), 382–383

T

T J's (Avondale, AZ), 394
Tage Inn Manchester Airport (Manchester, NH), 374
Talladega, AL. *See also* Talladega Superspeedway (Talladega, AL)
    area maps, 444, 446
    calendar, 445
    lodgings, 450
    restaurants, 452
Talladega Chamber of Commerce (Talladega, AL), 448
Talladega National Forest (Talladega, AL), 443, 444
Talladega Superspeedway (Talladega, AL), 440–453
    concessions, 442
    first aid, 442
    security, 442
Tanger Factory Outlet Center (Tilton, NH), 371
Tanger Outler Center (Dover, DE), 127

Tangier (Akron, OH), 281
Tango's Bistro (Dover, DE), 136
Tanner's Bar and Grill (Kansas City, MO), 220
Tannersville, PA, 422
    attractions, 417
    restaurants, 422
Tarbell's (Phoenix, AZ), 385
Taste of Chicago (Chicago, IL), 80
Taste of Darlington (Darlington, SC), 97
Taste of Polonia (Joliet, IL), 86
Tavern Restaurant, The (Abingdon, VA), 47
Tecumseh, MI
    lodgings, 325
Tecumseh Inn Motel (Tecumseh, MI), 325
Ted Ranch Campground (Tipton, MI), 327
Tempe, AZ
    attractions, 388
    lodgings, 391–392
Tempe Town Lake (Tempe, AZ), 383, 388
Templo Mayor (Mexico City, MX), 488
Tennessee Aquarium (Chattanooga, TN), 361
Tennessee Valley Railroad (Chattanooga, TN), 361
Teotihuacán (San Juan Teotihuacán, MX), 491
Terrace Club (Pocono Raceway, Long Pond, PA), 411
Texadelphia (Dallas, TX), 467
Texas Motor Speedway (Fort Worth, TX), 454–469
    concessions, 457
    first aid, 457
    getting around, 459
    restrooms, 457
    security, 456
Texas Steakhouse (Martinsville, VA), 296
Texas Troubadour Theatre (Nashville, TN), 353
Thai House (Indianapolis, IN), 188
Theater District (Chicago, IL), 80
Third Annual Wolfeboro Scarecrow Festival (Wolfeboro, NH), 369
Third Street Promenade (Santa Monica, CA), 67
Thomas, James, 46
Thomas England House (Smyrna, DE), 136
Thomas Wolfe Home (Asheville, NC), 269
Three-1-Three (Belleville, IL), 150
Thrill Rides Atop the Stratosphere Hotel (Las Vegas, NV), 245
Thunder Road Tours (Watkins Glen, NY), 480
Tilt'n Diner (Tilton, NH), 376
Tilton, NH
    attractions, 371
    lodgings, 372–373
    restaurants, 376
Tin Angel (Nashville, TN), 360
Tipton, MI
    lodgings, 325
    restaurants, 328
TJ's (Wooster, OH), 281
TMS Reserved Camping (Lake Worth, TX), 466
Tobacco Company (Richmond, VA), 437
Tobacco Road (Miami, FL), 168
Tokyo Tea House (Pocono Summit, PA), 422
Tokyo Tokyo (Ontario, CA), 72
Tom Johnson Camping Center Campground (Martinsville, VA), 294
Tom Raper RVS/Chicagoland Speedway Campground (Joliet, IL), 88
Tom Sawyer's Mississippi River RV Park (Marion, AR), 310
Tomoka State Park (Ormond Beach, FL), 120
Top O' the Hill Truck Stop and Family Restaurant (Tipton, MI), 328
Topeka, KS
    attractions, 215–216
Town House Tea Room and Restaurant (Nashville, TN), 360
Tradewinds RV Park (Vallejo, CA), 202

Travelodge (Oxford, AL), 449
Treasure Island Bed and Breakfast (Pell City, AL), 450
Treasure Island Inn (Daytona Beach Shores, FL), 119
Trolleyboat Tours (Daytona Beach, FL), 116
Tropical Manor Motel (Daytona Beach Shores, FL), 119
Troutdale Dining Room (Bristol, TN), 54
Truth (Joliet, IL), 89–90
Tubb, Ernest, 353
Turf Paradise (Phoenix, AZ), 384
Turn 2 Dale Earnhardt Terraces (Infineon Raceway, Sonoma, CA), 195
Turn 3 All Nite Parking and Camping (Tipton, MI), 327
Turn of the Century Lighting Co. (Clinton, MI), 323
Tuscany Trattoria (Miami, FL), 160
Tutwiler—A Wyndham Historic Hotel (Birmingham, AL), 448
Twin Anchors Restaurant and Tavern (Chicago, IL), 89
Twin Gables Motel (Brooklyn, MI), 325
Twin Palms (Anaheim, CA), 71
Twist, Tony, 138
Two Rivers Campground (Nashville, TN), 359

U

Ukrop's Pharmacy (Richmond, VA), 429
Underground Atlanta (Atlanta, GA), 30, 33
Union, KY
    attractions, 230
Union Hotel (Occidental, CA), 206
Union Jack Pub (Indianapolis, IN), 187
Union Station (Kansas City, MO), 215
United States Olympic Training Center (Colorado Springs, CO), 403
US Air Force Academy (Colorado Springs, CO), 403
US Cowboy Tour Professional Rodeo (Daytona Beach), FL, 113
US Mint (Charlotte, NC), 257
USS *Wisconsin* (Norfolk, VA), 439
Universal City, CA
    attractions, 67
Upland, CA
    lodgings, 70
Urban Trail (Asheville, NC), 269
USS Alabama Battleship Memorial Park (Mobile, AL), 453
USS *Constellation* (Baltimore, MD), 137
USS *Drum* submarine (Mobile, AL), 453

V

Vallejo, CA
    attractions, 199
    lodgings, 201–202
    RV and camping, 202
Valley of Fire State Park (Las Vegas, NV), 245
Varsity, The (Atlanta, GA), 39
Venetian Pool (Coral Gables, FL), 161
Vent Haven Museum (Fort Mitchell, KY), 229
Venus Pancake House (Florence, SC), 104
Veraisons (Dundee, NY), 484
Versaille's (Miami, FL), 160
Veterans Memorial Museum (Pigeon Forge, TN), 55
Via Reál (Irving, TX), 468
Victoria, The (Anniston, AL), 447–448

Victory Family Campground (Word of Life Fellowship) (Tipton, MI), *327*
Villa Jidiot (Chatham, VA), *293*
Villa Marre (Little Rock, AK), *313*
Village West (Kansas City, KS), *213*
Vinings Inn, The (Atlanta, GA), *39*
Vinnie's Sardine Grill and Raw Bar (Mooresville, NC), *268*
Virginia Bazaar's 5th Anniversary Celebration, The (Ladysmith, VA), *431*
Virginia Creeper National Recreation Trail (Abington, VA), *49*
Virginia Highlands Festival (Abingdon, VA), *47*
Virginia Historical Society (Richmond, VA), *434*
Virginia Museum of Natural History (Martinsville, VA), *291*
Virginia State Capitol Building (Richmond, VA), *428*
Virginia Zoological Park (Norfolk, VA), *439*
Visitor's Center of NASA's Johnson Space Center Houston (Houston, TX), *469*
Viva Taqueria (Dundee, NY), *484*
Vroomz, *34*
V's Italiano (Independence, MO), *218*

W

Walgreens Drug Store (Richmond, VA), *429*
Wallace, Rusty, *46*
Wally's Bar-B-Que (Smyrna, DE), *136*
Wal-Mart Supercenter (Martinsville, VA), *289*
Walt Michael's RV Super Store Turn 2 Campground (Tipton, MI), *326*
Walter P. Chrysler Museum (Detroit, MI), *329*
Walton, KY
 RV and camping, *232*
Waltrip, Michael, *106, 347, 349, 415*
Walt's Hitching Post (Fort Wright, KY), *234*
War Between the States Museum (Florence, SC), *100*
Warriors' Path State Park (Kingsport, TN), *52*
Watauga Lake (Hampton, TN), *50*
Water Tower Place (Chicago, IL), *80*
Waterfront (Covington, KY), *232*
Watkins Glen, NY. *See also* Watkins Glen International (Watkins Glen, NY)
 area maps, *476, 478*
 attractions, *479–480*
 calendar, *477*
 lodgings, *482*
 restaurants, *484*
 RV and camping, *482*
Watkins Glen Gorge (Watkins Glen, NY), *480*
Watkins Glen International (Watkins Glen, NY), *470–485*
 concessions, *472*
 first aid, *472*
 getting around, *475*
 getting tickets, *473*
 security, *472*
Watkins Glen State Park (Watkins Glen, NY), *474, 476, 482*
Watkins Glen/Corning KOA (Watkins Glen, NY), *482*
Wauponsee Glacial Trail (Joliet, IL), *78*
Wauwatosa, WI
 attractions, *340*
 lodgings, *341*
Weber's Inn (Ann Arbor, MI), *324–325*
Weirs Beach, NH
 attractions, *371–372*
 lodgings, *374*
 restaurants, *376*
 RV and camping, *374*

Weirs Beach Tent and Trailer Park (Weirs Beach, NH), *374–375*
Wertheim's (Covington, KY), *233*
West Allis, WI. *See also* Milwaukee Mile (West Allis, WI)
 area maps, *336, 338*
 calendar, *337*
 RV and camping, *343*
Western Currency Facility Tour and Visitor Center, Bureau of Engraving and Printing (Fort Worth, TX), *463*
Westfield, IN
 lodgings, *185*
Westfield Shoppingtown Louis Joliet (Joliet, IL), *85*
Westin Galleria Dallas (Dallas, TX), *464*
Westin Peachtree Plaza (Atlanta, GA), *35*
WEVL FM 90 Blues on the Bluff (Memphis, TN), *305*
Where Pigs Fly (Dover, DE), *136*
Whispering Lake's Resort (Tipton, MI), *325*
White Elephant Saloon (Fort Worth, TX), *459*
White Fence Farm (Lemont, IL), *89*
White Haven, PA, *422*
 restaurants, *422*
White House of the Confederacy (Richmond, VA), *434*
White Mountain National Forest (White Mountains, NH), *377*
White Mountains, NH, *377*
White River Gardens (Indianapolis, IN), *182*
White River State Park (Indianapolis, IN), *178, 182*
White Water Park (Branson, MO), *221*
White's Mill (Abingdon, VA), *49*
Wigwam Resort and Golf Club (Litchfield Park, AZ), *389*
Wild River Country (Little Rock, AK), *313*
Wildhorse Saloon (Nashville, TN), *350, 355*
Wildwood Inn (Florence, KY), *231*
Wilkes-Barre, PA, *418–419, 420*
 lodgings, *418, 420*
William & Emily Hearin Mardis Gras Museum (Mobile, AL), *453*
Williamstown, KY
 lodgings, *230, 231*
Willie's Sport Café (Covington, KY), *233*
Willo Bread Company (Phoenix, AZ), *393*
Willow Springs (Little Rock, AK), *313*
Willow Wood Market Café (Graton, CA), *206*
Willow's Steak and Spirits (Weirs Beach, NH), *376*
Wilmington, DE
 attractions, *131*
 lodgings, *133–134*
 restaurants, *136*
Wimmer, Scott, *314*
Windsor, CA
 restaurants, *206*
Wingate Inn (Florence, SC), *102*
Wingate Inn (Goodyear, AZ), *390*
Wingate Inn (Joliet, IL), *87*
Wingate Inn (Oxford, AL), *449*
Wings of Eagles Discovery Center (Horseheads, NY), *474*
Wings of Eagles (Horseheads, NY), *479*
Winn-Dixie (Richmond, VA), *429*
Winston-Salem, NC
 attractions, *262*
Winterthur, DE
 attractions, *132*
Wintherthur Museum, Garden, and Library (Winterthur, DE), *132*
Wintzell's (Mobile, AL), *453*
Wisconsin Dells, WI, *345*
Wisconsin Lake Schooner (Milwaukee, WI), *340*
Wishbone (Chicago, IL), *89*

WJ Hayes State Park (Tipton, MI), *327*
Wolf Lair Village & Campground (Abingdon, VA), *52*
Wolfe Memorial's Visitor Center (Asheville, NC), *269*
Wood, Len, *81*
Wood Brothers Racing Museum (Stuart, VA), *287, 291*
Wooden Schoolhouse and Drugstore (St. Augustine, FL), *123*
Woodlands, The (Kansas City, KS), *215*
Woodlands Inn and Resort (Wilkes-Barre, PA), *419*
Woodlawn National Cemetery (Elmira, NY), *475*
Woodward Dream Cruise (Detroit, MI), *321, 329*
Woody's Bar-B-Que (Rancho Cucamonga, CA), *72*
Wooster, OH
 restaurants, *279, 281*
Wooster Inn (Wooster, OH), *279, 281*
Workhorse Custom Chassis Reserved Camping (Lake Worth, TX), *467*
Workhorse Custom Chassis VIP Camping (Lake Worth, TX), *466*
World of Coca-Cola (Atlanta, GA), *33*
World of Sports (Florence, KY), *229*
Worlds of Fun/Oceans of Fun (Kansas City, MO), *215*
Wreck Riverfront Bar & Grill, The (Daytona Beach, FL), *122*
WT Family Camping (Blakeslee, PA), *420*
Wyndham Atlanta Downtown Hotel (Atlanta, GA), *35*
Wyndham Garden (Memphis, TN), *310*
Wyndham Milwaukee Center (Milwaukee, WI), *341*
Wyndham Union Station Hotel (Nashville, TN), *358*
Wyndham Wilmington Hotel (Wilmington, DE), *134*
Wynfrey Hotel (Birmingham, AL), *449*

X

Xiomara (Anaheim, CA), *71*

Y

Yahooz (Leawood, KS), *220*
Yamabuki (Anaheim, CA), *70*
Yamato's Japanese Restaurant (Martinsville, VA), *296*
Yats (Brownsburg, IN), *187*
Yeley, J. J., *59*
Yogi Bear's Jellystone Park (Ashland, NH), *374*
Yogi Bear's Jellystone Park (Calendonia, WI), *342*

Z

Z Pie (Placerville, CA), *207*
Zapata (Norcross, GA), *40*
Zion Canyon Scenic Drive (Springdale, UT), *251*
Zion Human History Museum (Springdale, UT), *251*
Zion Lodge (Springdale, UT), *251*
Zion National Park (Springdale, UT), *251*
Zocalo (Atlanta, GA), *40*
Zoo Atlanta (Atlanta, GA), *29, 33*
ZooAmerica (Hershey, PA), *423*
Zuzu (Napa, CA), *205*
Zwaanendael Inn (Lewes, DE), *132*